Contents

Preface

Even before my co-author's sudden death in 1996 during a lecture visit to Moscow, a start had been made on assembling many important improvements to our book. These have largely proceeded from experience in using *The Student's Grammar* and its splendid accompanying *Wookbook* by Sylvia Chalker (Longman 1992), and it is a pleasurable duty to thank colleagues throughout the world for their valuable help in sending their comments and suggestions to the Survey of English Usage at University College London. Well over two hundred revisions, clarifications, and expansions have now been incorporated, and I hope that in consequence this revised version of the *Grammar* will be of enhanced value to teachers and their students.

RANDOLPH QUIRK

London
October 1997

1 The English language

The use of English

1.1 English is the world's most widely used language. A distinction is often made that depends on how the language is learned: as a *native* language (or *mother tongue*), acquired when the speaker is a young child (generally in the home), or as a *foreign* language, acquired at some subsequent period. Overlapping with this distinction is that between its use as a *first* language, the primary language of the speaker, and as an *additional* language. In some countries (particularly of course where it is the dominant native language), English is used principally for internal purposes as an *intranational* language, for speakers to communicate with other speakers of the same country; in other countries such as Germany and Japan, it serves chiefly as an *international* language, the medium of communication with speakers from other countries.

But in numerous countries such as India, the Philippines, and Nigeria, where English is for the most part a foreign language too, it nonetheless has prominent internal functions within these countries in addition to its international role. Such domestic use of 'English as a foreign language' is often called 'English as a second language'.

The meanings of 'grammar'

Syntax and inflections

1.2 We shall be using 'grammar' in this book to include both SYNTAX and that aspect of MORPHOLOGY (the internal structure of words) that deals with INFLECTIONS (or ACCIDENCE). The fact that the past tense of *buy* is *bought* [inflection] and the fact that the interrogative form of *He bought it* is *Did he buy it?* [syntax] are therefore both equally within grammar. Our usage corresponds to one of the common lay uses of the word in the English-speaking world. A teacher may comment:

John uses good grammar but his spelling is awful.

The comment shows that spelling is excluded from grammar; and if John wrote *interloper* where the context demanded *interpreter*, the te cher would say that he had used the wrong word, not that he had made a mistake in grammar. But in the education systems of the English-speaking countries, it is possible also to use the term 'grammar' loosely so as to include both spelling and lexicology.

There is a further use of 'grammar' that derives from a period in which the teaching of Latin and Greek was widespread. Since the aspect of Latin grammar on which teaching has traditionally concentrated is the paradigms (or model sets) of inflections, it made sense for the learner to say:

> Latin has a good deal of grammar, but English has hardly any.

This meaning of 'grammar' has continued to be used by lay native speakers. In effect, grammar is identified with inflections.

Rules and the native speaker

1.3 Yet another sense appears in the remark:

> French has a well-defined grammar, but in English we're free to speak as we like.

Here 'grammar' is used as a virtual synonym of 'syntax'.

Such a comment by a native speaker probably owes a good deal to the fact that he does not feel the rules of his own language – rules that he has acquired unconsciously – to be at all constraining; and if ever he happens to be called on to explain one such rule to a foreigner he has very great difficulty. By contrast, the grammatical rules he learns for a foreign language seem much more rigid and they also seem clearer because they have been actually spelled out to him in the learning process.

But another important point is revealed in this sentence. The distinction refers to 'grammar' not as the observed patterns in the use of French but as a codification of rules compiled by the French (especially by the Académie Française) to show the French themselves how their language should be used. This is grammar as codified by grammarians: the Academy Grammar. There is no such Academy for the English language and so (our naive native speaker imagines) the English speaker has more 'freedom' in his usage.

The codification of rules

1.4 The 'codification' sense of grammar is readily identified with the specific compilation of a specific grammarian:

> Jespersen wrote a good grammar, and so did Kruisinga.

And this sense naturally leads to the concrete use as in:

> Did you bring your grammars?

Naturally, too, the codification may refer to grammar in any of the senses already mentioned. It will also vary, however, according to the linguistic theory embraced by the authors, their idea of the nature of grammar rather than their statement of the grammar of a particular language:

> Chomsky developed a transformational grammar that differed considerably from earlier grammars.

Thus, in the framework of formal linguistics, some grammarians speak of 'the grammar' as embracing rules not only for syntax but for phonological, lexical, and semantic specification as well.

Prescriptive grammar

1.5 Finally we come to the use of 'grammar' in statements such as:

> It's bad grammar to end a sentence with a preposition.

Here the term refers to a way of speaking or writing that is to be either preferred or avoided. Such statements pertain to PRESCRIPTIVE GRAMMAR, a set of regulations that are based on what is evaluated as correct or incorrect in the standard language. Since we do not have an Academy of the English Language, there is no one set of regulations that could be considered 'authoritative'. Instead, evaluations are made by self-appointed authorities who, reflecting varying judgments of acceptability and appropriateness, often disagree (though on usually very minor matters).

Authorities on USAGE, in this restricted sense, primarily deal with DISPUTED usage, a relatively small number of syntactic and lexical items that are controversial within the standard language. Their objections may persuade some to avoid certain usages, at least in their formal writing. Over the last two centuries prescriptive rules have accumulated into a general prescriptive tradition for formal writing that is embodied (with some variation) in school textbooks and student reference handbooks, and in usage guides for the general public.

As an occasional consequence of prescriptive pressures, some speakers have mistakenly extended particular prescriptive rules in an attempt to avoid mistakes. A classic instance of such HYPERCORRECTION is the use of *whom* as subject, as in *the students whom I hope will join us*. Others are the pseudo-subjunctive *were* as in *I wonder if he were here* and the use of the subjective pronoun *I* in the phrase *between you and I*.

Our primary concern in this book is to describe the grammar of English. But we occasionally refer to the prescriptive tradition not only because it may lead to hypercorrection but also because it may affect attitudes towards particular uses that may in turn influence the preferences of some native speakers, at least in formal or more considered styles. It may lead some, for example, to replace their usual *was* by subjunctive *were* in *If I was strong enough, I would help you*, or to replace *who* by *whom* in *the teacher who I most admired*.

Varieties of English

Types of variation

1.6 There are numerous varieties of English, but we shall recognize in this book five major types of variation. Any use of the language necessarily involves variation within all five types, although for purposes of analysis we may abstract individual varieties:

(a) region
(b) social group
(c) field of discourse
(d) medium
(e) attitude

The first two types of variation relate primarily to the language *user*. People use a regional variety because they live in a region or have once lived in that region. Similarly, people use a social variety because of their affiliation with a social group. These varieties are relatively permanent for the language user. At the same time, we should be aware that many people can communicate in more than one regional or social variety and can therefore (consciously or unconsciously) switch varieties according to the situation. And of course people move to other regions or change their social affiliations, and may then adopt a new regional or social variety.

The last three types of variation relate to language *use*. People select the varieties according to the situation and the purpose of the communication. The field of discourse relates to the activity in which they are engaged; the medium may be spoken or written, generally depending on the proximity of the participants in the communication; and the attitude expressed through language is conditioned by the relationship of the participants in the particular situation. A COMMON CORE is present in all the varieties so that, however esoteric a variety may be, it has running through it a set of grammatical and other characteristics that are present in all the others. It is this fact that justifies the application of the name 'English' to all the varieties.

Regional variation

1.7 Varieties according to region have a well-established label both in popular and technical use: DIALECTS. Geographical dispersion is in fact the classic basis for linguistic variation, and in the course of time, with poor communications and relative remoteness, such dispersion results in dialects becoming so distinct that we regard them as different languages. This latter stage was long ago reached with the Germanic dialects that are now Dutch, English, German, Swedish, etc, but it has not been reached (and may not necessarily ever be reached, given the modern ease and range of communication) with the dialects of English that have resulted from the regional separation of communities within the British Isles and (since the voyages of exploration and settlement in Shakespeare's time) elsewhere in the world.

It is pointless to ask how many dialects of English there are: there are indefinitely many, depending on how detailed we wish to be in our observations. But they are of course more obviously numerous in long-settled Britain than in areas more recently settled by English speakers, such as North America or, still more recently, Australia and New Zealand. The degree of generality in our observation depends crucially upon our standpoint as well as upon our experience. An Englishman will hear an American Southerner primarily as an American, and only as a Southerner in addition if further subclassification is called for and if his experience of American English dialects enables him to make it. To an American the same speaker will be heard first as a Southerner and then (subject to similar conditions) as, say, a Virginian, and then perhaps as a Piedmont Virginian.

Social variation

1.8 Within each of the dialects there is considerable variation in speech according to education, socioeconomic group, and ethnic group. Some differences correlate with age and sex. Much (if not most) of the variation does not involve categorical distinctions; rather it is a matter of the frequency with which certain linguistic features are found in the groups.

There is an important polarity between uneducated and educated speech in which the former can be identified with the nonstandard regional dialect most completely and the latter moves away from regional usage to a form of English that cuts across regional boundaries. An outsider (who was not a skilled dialectologist) might not readily find a New Englander who said *see* for *saw*, a Pennsylvanian who said *seen*, and a Virginian who said *seed*. These are forms that tend to be replaced by *saw* with schooling, and in speaking to a stranger a dialect speaker would tend to use 'school' forms. On the other hand, there is no simple equation of regional and uneducated English. Just as educated English *I saw* cuts across regional boundaries, so do many features of uneducated use: a prominent example is the double negative as in *I don't want no cake*, which has been outlawed from all educated English by the prescriptive grammar tradition for over two hundred years but which continues to thrive as an emphatic form in uneducated speech wherever English is spoken.

Educated English naturally tends to be given the additional prestige of government agencies, the professions, the political parties, the press, the law court, and the pulpit – any institution which must attempt to address itself to a public beyond the smallest dialectal community. It is codified in dictionaries, grammars, and guides to usage, and it is taught in the school system at all levels. It is almost exclusively the language of printed matter. Because educated English is thus accorded implicit social and political sanction, it comes to be referred to as STANDARD ENGLISH, and provided we remember that this does not mean an English that has been formally standardized by official action, as weights and measures are standardized, the term is useful and appropriate. In contrast with standard English, forms that are especially associated with uneducated (rather than dialectal) use are generally called NONSTANDARD.

Standard English

1.9 The degree of acceptance of a single standard of English throughout the world, across a multiplicity of political and social systems, is a truly remarkable phenomenon: the more so since the extent of the uniformity involved has, if anything, increased in the present century. Uniformity is greatest in orthography, which is from most viewpoints the least important type of linguistic organization. Although printing houses in all English-speaking countries retain a tiny element of individual decision (*eg: realize/realise, judgment/judgement*), there is basically a single spelling and punctuation system throughout: with two minor subsystems. The one is the subsystem with British orientation (used in most English-speaking countries other than the United States), with distinctive forms in only a small class of words, *colour*, *centre*, *levelled*, etc. The other is the American subsystem, with *color*, *center*, *leveled*, etc.

In grammar and vocabulary, standard English presents somewhat less of a monolithic character, but even so the world-wide agreement is extraordinary and – as has been suggested earlier – seems actually to be increasing under the impact of closer world communication and the spread of identical material and nonmaterial culture. The uniformity is especially close in neutral or formal styles of written English on subject matter not of obviously localized interest: in such circumstances one can frequently go on for page after page without encountering a feature which would identify the English as belonging to one of the national standards.

National standards of English

British and American English

1.10 What we are calling national standards should be seen as distinct from the standard English which we have been discussing and which we should think of as being supranational, embracing what is common to all. Again, as with orthography, there are two national standards that are overwhelmingly predominant both in the number of distinctive usages and in the degree to which these distinctions are institutionalized: American English ⟨AmE⟩ and British English ⟨BrE⟩. Grammatical differences are few and the most conspicuous are known to many users of both national standards: the fact that AmE has two past participles for *get* and BrE only one, for example, and that in BrE either a singular or a plural verb may be used with a singular collective noun:

The government $\begin{Bmatrix} \text{is} \\ \text{are} \end{Bmatrix}$ in favour of economic sanctions.

whereas in AmE a singular verb is required here.

Lexical differences are far more numerous, but many of these are familiar to users of both standards. Recent innovations tend to spread rapidly from one standard to the other. Thus while radio sets have had *valves* in BrE but *tubes* in AmE, television sets have *tubes* in both, and *transistors* and computer *software* are likewise used in both standards. Mass communication neutralizes differences; the pop music culture, in particular, uses a 'mid-Atlantic' dialect that levels differences even in pronunciation.

The United States and Britain have been separate political entities for two centuries; for generations, thousands of books have been appearing annually; there is a long tradition of publishing descriptions of both AmE and BrE. These are important factors in establishing and institutionalizing the two national standards, and in the relative absence of such conditions other national standards are both less distinct (being more open to the influence of either AmE or BrE) and less institutionalized.

One attitudinal phenomenon in the United States is of sociolinguistic interest. In affirming the students' right to their own varieties of language, many American educationalists have declared that Standard American English is a myth, some asserting the independent status (for example) of Black English. At the same time they have acknowledged the existence of a written standard dialect, sometimes termed 'Edited American English'.

Other national standards

1.11 Scots, with ancient national and educational institutions, is perhaps nearest to the self-confident independence of BrE and AmE, though the differences in grammar and vocabulary are rather few. On the other hand, the 'Lallans' Scots, which has some currency for literary purposes, has a highly independent set of lexical, grammatical, phonological, and orthographical conventions, all of which make it seem more like a separate language than a regional dialect.

Hiberno-English, or Irish English, may also be considered a national standard, since it is explicitly regarded as independent of BrE by educational and broadcasting services. The proximity to Britain and the pervasive influence of AmE, and similar factors mean, however, that there is little room for the assertion and development of a separate grammar and vocabulary.

Canadian English is in a similar position in relation to AmE. Close economic, social, and intellectual links along a 4,000-mile frontier have naturally caused the larger community to have an enormous influence on the smaller, not least in language. Though in many respects Canadian English follows British rather than United States practice and has a modest area of independent lexical use, in many other respects it has approximated to AmE, and in the absence of strong institutionalizing forces it would continue in this direction. However, counteracting this tendency in language as in other matters is the tendency for Canadians to resist the influence of their powerful neighbour in their assertion of an independent national identity.

South Africa, Australia, and New Zealand are in a very different position, remote from the direct day-to-day impact of either BrE or AmE. While in orthography and grammar the South African English in educated use is virtually identical with BrE, rather considerable differences in vocabulary have developed, largely under the influence of Afrikaans, one of the country's other official languages.

New Zealand English is more like BrE than any other non-European variety, though it has adopted quite a number of words from the indigenous Maoris and over the past half-century has come under the powerful influence of Australia and to a considerable extent of the United States.

Australian English is undoubtedly the dominant form of English in the Antipodes and by reason of Australia's increased wealth, population, and influence in world affairs, this national standard (though still by no means fully institutionalized) is exerting an influence in the northern hemisphere, particularly in Britain. Much of what is distinctive in Australian English is confined to familiar use. This is especially so of grammatical features.

There are other regional or national variants that approximate to the status of a standard. Beside the widespread Creole in the Caribbean, for example, it is the view of many that the language of government and other agencies observes an indigenous standard that can be referred to as Caribbean English. In addition, some believe there are emerging standards in countries where English is a 'second' language, such as India and Nigeria.

Pronunciation and standard English

1.12 All the variants of standard English are remarkable primarily in the tiny extent to which even the most firmly established, BrE and AmE, differ from each other in vocabulary, grammar, and orthography. Pronunciation, however, is a special case in that it distinguishes one national standard from another most immediately and completely and it links in a most obvious way the national standards to the regional varieties. In BrE, one type of pronunciation is often seen as having the status of 'standard': it is the accent associated with the older schools and universities of England, 'Received Pronunciation' or 'RP'. It is nonregional and enjoys prestige from the social importance of its speakers. Although RP no longer has the unique authority it had in the first half of the twentieth century, it remains prominent in teaching the British variety of English as a foreign language, as can be easily seen from dictionaries and textbooks intended for countries that teach BrE.

Varieties according to field of discourse

1.13 The field of discourse is the type of activity engaged in through language. A speaker has a repertoire of varieties according to field and switches to the appropriate one as occasion demands. Typically, the switch involves nothing more than turning to the particular set of lexical items habitually used for handling the field in question: law, cookery, engineering, football. As with dialects, there are indefinitely many fields, depending on how detailed we wish our analysis to be.

Varieties according to medium

1.14 The differences between spoken and written English derive from two sources. One is situational: since the use of a written medium normally presupposes the absence of the person(s) addressed, writers must be far more explicit to ensure that they are understood. The second source of difference is that many of the devices we use to transmit language by speech (stress, rhythm, intonation, tempo, for example) are impossible to represent with the relatively limited repertoire of conventional orthography. In consequence, writers often have to reformulate their sentences to convey fully and successfully what they want to express within the orthographic system.

Varieties according to attitude

1.15 Varieties according to attitude are often called 'stylistic', but 'style' is a term which is used with several different meanings. We are concerned here with choice that depends on our attitude to the hearer (or reader), to the topic, and to the purpose of our communication. We recognize a gradient in attitude between formal (relatively stiff, cold, polite, impersonal) and informal (relatively relaxed, warm, casual, friendly). We also acknowledge that there is a neutral English bearing no obvious attitudinal colouring and it belongs to the common core of English (*cf* 1.6). We shall for the most part confine ourselves to this three-term distinction, leaving the neutral variety unmarked.

Acceptability and frequency

1.16 Our approach in this book is to focus on the common core that is shared by standard BrE and standard AmE. We leave unmarked any features that the two standard varieties have in common, marking as ⟨BrE⟩ or ⟨AmE⟩ only the points at which they differ. But usually we find it necessary to say ⟨esp(ecially) BrE⟩ or ⟨esp(ecially) AmE⟩, for it is rare for a feature to be found exclusively in one variety. Similarly, we do not mark features that are neutral with respect to medium and attitude. We distinguish where necessary spoken and written language, generally using 'speaker' and 'hearer' as unmarked forms for the participants in an act of communication, but drawing on the combinations 'speaker/writer' and 'hearer/reader' when we wish to emphasize that what is said applies across the media. We also frequently need to label features according to variation in attitude, drawing attention to those that are formal or informal.

The metaphor of the common core points to a distinction that applies to two other aspects of our description of English grammar. We distinguish between the central and the marginal also for acceptability and frequency.

Acceptability is a concept that does not apply exclusively to grammar. Native speakers may find a particular sentence unacceptable because (for example) they consider it logically absurd or because they cannot find a plausible context for its use or because it sounds clumsy or impolite. However, we are concerned only with the acceptability of forms or constructions on the grounds of their morphology or syntax.

In general, our examples are fully acceptable if they are left unmarked. But we sometimes contrast acceptable and unacceptable examples, marking the latter by placing an asterisk '*' before them. If they are tending to unacceptability but are not fully unacceptable, we put a query '?' before the asterisk. A query alone signifies that native speakers are unsure about the particular language feature. If native speakers differ in their reactions, we put the asterisk or query in parentheses.

Assessments by native speakers of relative acceptability largely correlate with their assessments of relative frequency. We leave unmarked those features of the language that occur frequently, drawing attention just to those that occur extremely frequently or only rarely.

In this book we offer a descriptive presentation of English grammar. We make a direct connection between forms and their meaning, conducting excursions into lexicology, semantics, and pragmatics where these impinge closely on our grammatical description.

NOTE The diamond bracket convention applies to stylistic and other variants. Phonetic symbols used in the book are those of the International Phonetic Alphabet (IPA); prosodic symbols are explained in 2.13–15, and abbreviations in the Index. Among other conventions: parentheses indicate optional items, curved braces free alternatives, square braces contingent alternatives (*eg* selection of the top alternative in one pair requires selection of the top one in the other).

Bibliographical note

On varieties of English, see Bailey and Görlach (1982); Biber (1988); Hughes and Trudgill (1979); Kachru (1988); McDavid (1963); Quirk (1988, 1989).

On acceptability and language attitudes, see Bolinger (1980); Greenbaum (1977, 1985, 1988); Quirk and Stein (1990).

2 A general framework

The plan of this book

2.1 Grammar is a complex system, the parts of which cannot be properly explained in abstraction from the whole. In this sense, all parts of a grammar are mutually defining, and there is no simple linear path we can take in explaining one part in terms of another. The method of presentation adopted in this book will be to order the description of English grammar so that features which are simpler (in the sense that their explanation presupposes less) come before those which are more complex (in the sense that their explanation presupposes more).

Our mode of progression will therefore be cyclic, rather than linear. In this first cycle we present a general framework, along with some major concepts and categories that are essential for the understanding of grammar.

The second cycle, Chapters 3–11, is concerned with the basic constituents which make up the simple sentence. Thus Chapters 3 and 4 present the grammar and semantics of the verb phrase, and Chapters 5 and 6 the basic constituents of the noun phrase, in particular determiners, nouns, and pronouns. Chapter 7 deals with adjectives and adverbs, Chapter 8 with adverbials, and Chapter 9 with prepositions and prepositional phrases. In the light of these detailed studies, Chapters 10 and 11 then explore the simple sentence in all its structural variety.

The third cycle treats matters which involve still more complexity of syntactic structure. Chapters 12 and 13 move beyond the simple sentence, dealing with substitution, ellipsis, and coordination: three operations which may be carried out on simple sentences in order to produce structures of greater complexity. Chapters 14 and 15 introduce a further factor of complexity, the subordination of one clause to another, and we proceed to a more general study of the complex sentence. Chapter 16 follows up Chapters 3 and 4 in giving further attention to the verb phrase, with special reference to verb classification, together with issues relating to phrasal and prepositional verbs, and to verb and adjective complementation. Similarly, Chapter 17 resumes the topic of Chapters 5 and 6, exploring the full complexity of the noun phrase in terms of structures separately examined in earlier chapters. Chapter 18 also involves a knowledge of the whole grammar as described in preceding chapters, but this time with a view to showing the various ways in which individual parts of a sentence can be arranged for focus, emphasis, and the effective presentation of information. Finally, Chapter 19 considers the ways in which sentence grammar relates to the formation of texts, including those comprising extended discourse in speech or writing.

NOTE At the end of each chapter, there is a bibliographical note giving guidance on further reading, especially recent monographs and articles. We assume that the reader will have access to the major grammarians of the past whose works are not mentioned in these notes though they are of course listed in the general Bibliography at the end of the book. These include the compendious works of Jespersen, Kruisinga and others, as well as bibliographies by Scheurweghs and Vorlat. To the work of such scholars all subsequent studies are heavily indebted, not least our own *Comprehensive Grammar* of 1985 to which the present book is directly related.

Sentences and clauses

2.2 Let us begin by looking at some examples of *sentences*, those language units which we must regard as primary, in comprising a minimum sense of completeness and unity:

She's selling her car. [1]
He sounded a bit doubtful. [2]
You should always clean your teeth after meals. [3]

Of course, these cannot mean much to us unless we know who 'she' is in [1] and who 'he' is in [2]; we would also want to know in [2] what he seemed doubtful about. For the place of such sentences in a wider *textual* context, we must wait till Chapter 19, but the sense of grammatical completeness in [1], [2], and [3] is none the less valid.

There are several ways of looking at the constituents of a sentence in establishing what needs to be present to make a stretch of language a sentence. The constituents most widely familiar are the *subject* and the *predicate*. If we heard someone say

went off without paying [4]

we would at once wish to ask '*Who* (went off without paying)?' In [4] we have a possible predicate but no subject. But equally if we heard someone say

that elderly man [5]

we would want to ask '*What about* that elderly man?' sensing that we had in [5] a possible subject but no predicate. By contrast with [4] and [5], we have a complete sentence in [6]:

That elderly man went off without paying. [6]

Let us now compare the subject of [1], [2], [3], and [6] (*She*, *He*, *You*, *That elderly man*) with the predicates. The latter are not merely longer but rather obviously more heterogeneous:

's selling her car
sounded a bit doubtful
should always clean your teeth after meals
went off without paying

As well as seeing that a sentence comprises a subject and a predicate, therefore, we need to look at the constituents of the predicate itself.

Elements

2.3 One of the indications that the subject is a clearly identifiable constituent of a sentence is, as we have seen, a specific question:

Who went off without paying? [1]
That elderly man (went off without paying). [1a]

Parts of the predicate can similarly be identified with questions. For example, *the object*:

What is she selling? [2]
(She's selling) *her car*. [2a]

So too, some *adverbials*:

When should you always clean your teeth? [3]
(You should always clean your teeth) *after meals*. [3a]

Subjects, objects, and adverbials will be referred to as *elements* of sentence structure. Other elements that we shall distinguish include the *complement* as in '(He sounded) *a bit doubtful*' and of course the *verb* as in '(He) *sounded* (a bit doubtful)', '(She)'*s selling* (her car)', '(You) *should* (always) *clean* (your teeth after meals)'.

As we shall see, especially in Chapter 10, sentences differ widely as to *which* elements and *how many* elements they include. This is related primarily to the type of verb element. If the V is *intransitive*, there need be no other elements beside S and V:

My watch [S] has disappeared. [V] [4]

If the V is *transitive*, on the other hand, it is accompanied by an object:

Someone [S] must have taken [V] *my watch*. [O] [5]
A policeman [S] witnessed [V] *the accident*. [O] [6]

Transitive verbs can be turned into the passive voice (3.25), with the result that corresponding to [6] there is a sentence of basically the same meaning [6′] in which the O of [6] becomes the S:

The accident was witnessed by a policeman. [6′]

For the present, we need mention only one other type of V, the *copular* verbs, which require a complement:

He [S] sounded [V] *a bit doubtful*. [C] [7]
One of my sisters [S] has become [V] *a computer expert*. [C] [8]

Adverbial elements may be added irrespective of the verb type:

My watch has disappeared *from this desk*. [A] [4a]
Someone must *apparently* [A] have taken my watch *from this desk*. [A] [5a]
By chance [A] a policeman witnessed the accident. [6a]
He sounded a bit doubtful *that night*. [A] [7a]
To everyone's delight [A] one of my sisters has *quite rapidly* [A] become a computer expert. [8a]

But with some verbs, adverbials are obligatory; for example:

Did you put the watch *in this drawer*? [9]

2.4 The sentence elements illustrated in 2.3 draw attention to a major issue in the study of grammar: the distinction between *function* and *form*. The same formal unit *my watch* has one function in [4] and quite another in [5]. Equally, the same function can obviously be performed by units that are very different in form. Thus as V we have *witnessed* in [6], *sounded* in [7], *has disappeared* in [4], and *must have taken* in [5]. But at least these all involve verbs (2.10) and we capture what they thus have formally in common by referring to them as *verb phrases* whether they comprise one word such as *sounded* or several words, as in *must have taken*.

The realizations of S are still more various: *he* in [7], *someone* in [5], *my watch* in [4], and *one of my sisters* in [8]. But all these involve either pronouns or nouns (2.6) and to capture their formal properties we refer to them as *noun phrases*, whether they comprise one word as with *he* or several words such as *one of my sisters*. The function O is again fulfilled by noun phrases: *my watch* in [5], *the accident* in [6].

On the other hand, C is realized by a noun phrase in [8], *a computer expert*, but by a different formal structure in [7], *a bit doubtful*. Forms like this (*a bit doubtful, quite happy, more successful*) we shall call *adjective phrases*, since they are either adjectives (2.6) or expansions of adjectives.

Most various of all in its formal realizations is the function A. We have a noun phrase *that night* in [7a]; *adverb phrases, ie* adverbs (2.6) or expansions of adverbs, *apparently* in [5a] and *quite rapidly* in [8a]; and we also have A realized by *prepositional phrases*, that is, a structure comprising a preposition (2.6) and a noun phrase: *from this desk* in [4a], *by chance* in [6a], and *to everyone's delight* in [8a].

Clauses

2.5 Let us now consider a somewhat longer sentence than those examined in 2.2*f*:

My sister [S] is [V] normally [A] a cheerful person, [C] but she [S] seemed [V] rather unhappy [C] that day. [A] [1]

Here we have two units each with the internal structure that we have been attributing to sentences. We call these units *clauses* and we can now see that the elements discussed in 2.3*f* should be considered as constituents of clauses rather than of sentences. In other words, a sentence comprises one or more clauses, each of which in turn comprises elements.

In [1] the two clauses are as it were on an equal footing and are said to be *coordinated* to form the sentence. But a clause may equally be *subordinated* within another clause as one of its elements: clearly, the noun phrase as A in [2] performs the same function as the clause as A in [2a]:

She seemed rather unhappy *that day.* [2]
She seemed rather unhappy *when I was with her.* [2a]

We must therefore revise our list of formal realizations of elements as given in 2.3 since the function A can be performed by clauses as in [2a], and the functions of O and S can also be performed by clauses as we see by comparing [3] and [3a], [4] and [4a] respectively:

I suddenly remembered *something.* [3]
I suddenly remembered *that I had an appointment.* [3a]
Your failure is most regrettable. [4]
That you failed the exam is most regrettable. [4a]

But as well as constituting whole elements as in [2a], [3a] and [4a], clauses may constitute only a *part* of an element, especially as relative clauses in noun-phrase structure (17.5*ff*). Compare the noun phrases functioning as O in [5] and [5a]:

The police questioned *every local resident.* [5]
The police questioned *every person who lived in the neighbourhood.* [5a]

In [5a], the noun phrase as O includes the postmodifying clause:

who [S] lived [V] in the neighbourhood [A]

Words and word classes

2.6 Every constituent of a sentence ultimately consists of *words*. We have already (for example in 2.4) referred to these units in terms of the traditional 'parts of speech' and it is time now to look at a classification of words in some detail.

It is useful to consider words as falling into two broad categories, *closed* and *open*. The former comprises, as the term suggests, classes that are finite (and often small) with a membership that is relatively stable and unchanging in the language: words like *this*, *in*, *shall*. These words play a major part in English grammar, often corresponding to inflections in some other languages, and they are sometimes referred to as 'grammatical words', 'function words', or 'structure words'.

By contrast, the *open* classes of words are constantly changing their membership as old words drop out of the language and new ones are coined or adopted to reflect cultural changes in society. These are words like *forest*, *computer*, *decorative*, and *signify*; their numbers are vast and are the subject matter of dictionaries. Appropriately, they are often called 'lexical words'.

Closed classes:

pronoun, such as *she*, *they*, *anybody*
determiner, such as *the*, *a*, *that*, *some*
primary verb, such as *be*
modal verb, such as *can*, *might*
preposition, such as *in*, *during*, *round*
conjunction, such as *and*, *or*, *while*, *yet*

Open classes:

noun, such as *hospital*, *play*, *orchestra*, *Millicent*
adjective, such as *sufficient*, *happy*, *changeable*, *round*
full verbs, such as *grow*, *befriend*, *interrogate*, *play*
adverb, such as *sufficiently*, *really*, *afterwards*, *yet*

NOTE **[a]** Other categories of words include *numerals*, such as *three*, *seventy-six*; and *interjections*, such as *oh*, *aha*.

[b] Even from the few examples given, we see that a word may belong to more than one class. Thus *round* is given as both a preposition (as in *Drive round the corner*) and an adjective (as in *She has a round face*); we could have gone further and listed it as, for example, a full verb: *The car rounded the bend*. Moreover, relations across classes can be seen in the verb *befriend* (*cf* the noun *friend*), the adjective *changeable* (*cf* the verb *change*), and above all in adverbs in *-ly* which are systematically related to adjectives: *sufficient* ~ *sufficiently*.

2.7 We assign words to their various classes on grammatical grounds: that is, according to their properties in entering phrasal and clausal structure. For example, determiners (5.3*ff*) link up with nouns to form noun phrases as in *a soldier*; pronouns can replace noun phrases as in 'I saw *a soldier* and I asked *him* the time'. But this is not to deny the general validity of traditional definitions based on meaning: 'naming things' is indeed a semantic property of nouns and many verbs are indeed concerned with 'doing things'.

In fact it is neither possible nor desirable to separate grammatical from semantic factors, whether we are considering the status of a word or the structure of a whole sentence. Let us examine the following examples:

The tiger lives in China, India, and Malaysia. [1]
These tigers are living in a very cramped cage. [2]
A keeper is coming to feed the tiger. [3]

In [1], *the tiger* can hardly refer to any particular tiger; the phrase is *generic* and illustrates a particular use of the determiner *the* with a singular noun; the plural noun phrase *the tigers* could not be generic. By contrast, *these tigers* in [2] and *the tiger* in [3] must refer to particular *tigers* and the noun phrase is *specific*. But as well as introducing the important distinction between generic and specific, [1] and [2] illustrate a related distinction that recurs in the study of grammar. The singular form *tiger* is *unmarked* as compared with the plural form *tigers* which is *marked* for plural by the inflectional ending *-s*. But in being literally 'unmarked' inflectionally, the singular in [1] is correspondingly 'unmarked' semantically: it refers to all tigers at all times and embraces both male tigers and female tigresses (*tigress* being thus a 'marked' form).

Moreover the distinction between generic and specific, unmarked and marked, extends beyond the noun phrase as S. The use in [1] of the unmarked present tense *lives* as V (embracing reference to future and past as well as the literal present) appropriately matches the generic S. Equally the specific reference of the S in [2] is matched by the verb phrase *are living* as V, the progressive aspect (4.7*ff*) marking the verb in respect of something specifically in progress at the present time.

Stative and dynamic

2.8 A further and related contrast is illustrated by [1] and [2] in 2.7; this is the distinction between *stative* and *dynamic*. Most verbs in most contexts relate to action, activity, and to temporary or changeable conditions:

> The car *struck* a lamppost as I *was parking* it.
> What aria *did* she *sing* last night?

Verbs whose meaning denotes lack of motion can be equally dynamic in their grammar:

> I *was* quietly *resting* after a busy day.
> *Are* you *sitting* comfortably?

But it is not uncommon to find verbs which may be used either dynamically or statively. If we say that some specific tigers *are living* in a cramped cage, we imply that this is (or ought to be) a temporary condition and the verb phrase is dynamic in its use. On the other hand, when we say that the species of animal known as the tiger *lives* or *is found* in China, the generic statement entails that this is not a temporary circumstance and the verb phrase is stative.

Stative use is not, however, confined to generic statements:

> Mrs Frost *knew* a great deal about economics.
> *Did* you *hear* the thunder last night?

(Note that it is actually ungrammatical to say '*Mrs Frost *was knowing* a great deal . . .'.) Nor is the category stative confined to a minority of verb usages. In contrast to verbs (which are normally dynamic), most nouns and adjectives are stative in that they denote phenomena or qualities that are regarded for linguistic purposes as stable and indeed for all practical purposes permanent:

Jack is {*an engineer.* / *very tall.*}

(We may note that it would be very odd indeed to add here an adverbial like *this afternoon* which would suggest that Jack's profession or height applied only to the moment of speaking.) On the other hand, just as some verbs such as *live* can be used statively as well as dynamically, so also can some nouns and adjectives be used dynamically as well as statively:

> My little boy seems to like being *a nuisance* when we have friends to supper.
> Do you really like my poem or are you just being *kind*?

Pro-forms and ellipsis

2.9 One fundamental feature of grammar is providing the means of referring back to an expression without repeating it. This is achieved by means of *pro-forms*:

> *Their beautiful new car* was badly damaged when *it* was struck by a falling tree. [1]
> Jack was born in a British *industrial town* and Gillian grew up in an American *one*. [2]
> My parents live *in the north of the country* and my husband's people live *there* too. [3]
> I raised the proposal *in the early months of 1988*, but no one was *then* particularly interested. [4]
> She hoped they would *play a Mozart quartet* and they will *do so*. [5]

In [1] we have the pronoun *it* referring back to the whole noun phrase *their beautiful new car*. In [2], the pronoun *one* refers back to the head part *industrial town* of the noun phrase *a British (industrial town)*. In [3] *there* is a pro-form for the adverbial of place *in the north of the country*, while *then* in [4] refers comparably to the time adverbial *in the early months of 1988*. In [5], the pro-form *do so* refers to a unit not so far discussed, the *predication* (2.10), and thus corresponds to the whole of *play a Mozart quartet*.

In some constructions, repetition can be avoided by ellipsis (12.14). Thus instead of [5], we might have:

> She hoped they would *play a Mozart quartet* and they will.

Again instead of [3], we might have ellipsis of the V and an A in the second part:

My parents *live in the north of the country* and my husband's people too.

Note also the ellipted V in

Her daughter is studying physics and her son history.

Some pro-forms can refer forward to what has not been stated rather than, as in [1]–[5], back to what has been stated. There are, for example, the *wh*-items, as in

What was badly damaged? (*Their beautiful new car*) [1a]
Jack was born in a British *what*? (*Industrial town*) [2a]
Where do your parents live? (*In the north of the country*) [3a]
When did you raise the proposal? (*In the early months of 1988*) [4a]
What did she hope they would *do*? (*Play a Mozart quartet*) [5a]

Cf also '*Which* is their car?' (*That beautiful new one*).

NOTE But *wh*-items have a further role in subordinate clauses (14.1) when their reference may be backward as in [6] or forward as in [7]:

I met her *in 1985*, *when* she was still a student. [6]
Please tell me *what* is worrying you. [7]

Operator and predication

2.10 In 2.2*f*, we looked at the traditional division of a sentence into subject and predicate, noting the heterogeneous character of the latter. Bearing in mind what was said in 2.3 about sentence constituents being identified by specific questions, it should be noted that no question elicits the predicate as such. If, however, we see the English sentence as comprising a *subject*, an *operator*, and a *predication*, we have in this last a constituent that can indeed be elicited by a question. *Cf* [5a] in 2.9. But the analysis of predicate as operator plus predication has a much wider relevance than this.

We shall consider the operator in more detail in 3.11, but for the present we may define it as the first or only auxiliary in the verb phrase realizing the sentence element V. Note first of all the way in which the operator permits the coordination (13.17) of two predications:

You should *telephone your mother* and *find out if she's recovered from her cold*.
He is either *cleaning the car* or *working in the garden*.

Secondly, instead of representing a predication by the *do so* pro-form (as in 2.9, [5]), an operator can be used alone, with total ellipsis of the predication that is to be understood:

She hoped that they would *play a Mozart quartet* {and they *will*. / but they *won't*.}

The second variant in this example draws attention to a further characteristic of the operator: it can be followed by the informal contraction *n't* (as well as by the full form *not*).

The position immediately after the operator is in fact crucial in forming a negation or a question:

(a) *Negation* is expressed by inserting *not* (informally *n't*) after the operator:

They *should* have bought a new house.
They *should not* have bought a new house.

(b) *Questions* are formed by placing the subject of the sentence after the operator:

They should have bought a new house.
Should they have bought a new house?

Where the V element in a positive declarative sentence has no operator, a form of *do* is introduced as operator in the negative or interrogative version:

They *bought* a new house.
They *didn't buy* a new house.
Did they *buy* a new house?

Where the V element is realized by a form of *be*, this functions as itself an operator:

The sea *is* very rough.
The sea *is not* very rough.
Is the sea very rough?

NOTE The verb *have* can function like *be*, especially in BrE:

She *has* the time to spare.
She *hasn't* the time to spare.
Has she the time to spare?

But see further 3.14 Notes **[a]** and **[b]**.

Assertive and nonassertive

2.11 If we consider the following examples, we see that more can be involved than what occupies the position after the operator, when we move from a positive statement as in [1] and [3] to negation or question:

She has finished her thesis already. [1]
She has*n't* finished her thesis *yet*. [2]
The priest gave some money to some of the beggars. [3]
Did *the priest* give *any* money to *any* of the beggars? [4]

In [2], *yet* corresponds to the occurrence of *already* in [1], and in [4], *any* twice corresponds to the use of *some* in [3]. We express these differences by saying that the predication in positive statements is 'assertive territory' and that the predication in negative sentences and in questions is 'nonassertive territory'. While most words can be used equally in assertive and nonassertive predications, some determiners, pronouns, and adverbs have specifically assertive or nonassertive use. See further, 10.37.

NOTE [a] As well as assertive and nonassertive forms, there are also some negative forms. Compare

I saw *somebody*.	[assertive pronoun]
I didn't see *anybody*.	[nonassertive pronoun]
I saw *nobody*.	[negative pronoun]

[b] Nonassertive territory is not confined to negation and question predications, as we shall see in 10.37 Note [b]; for example

If you *ever* want *anything*, please ask.
She is more intelligent than *anyone* I know.

The primacy of speech

2.12 All the material in this book is necessarily expressed in the silence of the printed word. But in 2.1 we referred to 'discourse in speech or writing', and at no point must we forget that language is normally *spoken* and *heard*. Even what we write and read needs to be accompanied by an imagined realization in terms of pronunciation and such prosodic features as stress and intonation. The familiar graphic devices of spaces between words and punctuation marks such as comma, colon, semi-colon, and period help us to recover from writing how sentences would sound if spoken, but the correspondence between punctuation and prosody is only partial. From time to time, we shall need in this book to express examples with the help of a 'prosodic transcription', and we now explain the transcription system and the phenomena it represents.

Stress, rhythm and intonation

Stress

2.13 The relative prominence of a syllable within a word, or of a word within a phrase, is indicated by relative stress. In transcription, we mark the stressed segment by putting in front of it a short raised vertical stroke:

in'dignant
in the 'middle

An exceptionally heavy stress can be shown by a double vertical, and a lower level of stress ('secondary stress') can be marked by a lowered vertical stroke. For example:

It's ˌabso'lutely in"credible.

The ability to indicate stress is particularly valuable where it is unusual, as for example in a contrast:

Well, 'you may think she's 'happy, but in 'fact she's 'very "unhappy.

Pronouns are normally unstressed and the speaker here emphasizes *you* to indicate the addressee's isolation in so thinking; likewise, although prefixes like *un-* are normally unstressed, here it is emphasized in contrast with the previous mention of *happy*.

Rhythm

2.14 English connected speech is characterized by stressed syllables interspersed by unstressed ones such that, when the speaker is unaffected by hesitation on the one hand or excitement on the other, the stressed syllables occur at fairly regular intervals of time. Absolute regularity of rhythm is avoided for the most part, as oppressively mechanical, but is often used in children's verse:

'Hickory 'dickory 'dock
The 'mouse ran 'up the 'clock.

It is also heard when a speaker is speaking severely or stating a rule:

You should 'always 'clean your 'teeth 'after 'meals.

But absolute regularity is quite normal as an aid to keeping track of numbers when we are counting things:

'one 'two 'three 'four . . . 'sevenˌteen 'eighˌteen 'nineˌteen 'twenty ˌtwenty-'one ˌtwenty-'two . . .

NOTE When not part of a counting series, *-teen* numbers have the main stress on this element: *She is nine'teen.*

Intonation

2.15 Like stress, intonation is a mode of indicating relative prominence, but with intonation the variable is *pitch*, the aspect of sound which we perceive in terms of 'high' and 'low'. Intonation is normally realized in *tone units* comprising a sequence of stressed and unstressed syllables, with at least one of the stressed syllables made prominent by pitch. We call such a syllable the *nucleus* of the tone unit and we mark it by printing it in small capitals. The first prominent syllable in a tone unit is called the *onset* and where necessary it is marked with a slender long vertical and the end of the tone unit can be indicated with a thicker vertical:

She's |selling her CAR **|**

Pitch prominence at the nucleus is usually associated with pitch change and the direction of this can be indicated by the use of accents. The commonest form of pitch change is a *fall*, as in:

She's |selling her CÀR|

But if the speaker were using these words not to make a statement but to ask a question, the next commonest pitch change would be used, a *rise*:

She's |selling her CÁR|

Other nuclear tones to be especially noted are the *fall-rise* and the *fall-plus-rise*:

He |sounded a bit DǑUBTful|
It's |THÌs type that I LÍKE|

Conclusion

2.16 The material presented in this chapter constitutes a modest but essential foundation for studying English grammar as a whole. We have introduced features and concepts which cut across the individual topics that will now occupy our attention, chapter by chapter. Thus we have illustrated a system by which intonation and other prosodic features of speech can be related to grammar; we have outlined major concepts such as the distinctions between generic and specific, stative and dynamic, assertive and nonassertive.

But we have also provided a framework of sentence analysis, within which the detailed material of individual chapters may be fitted, much as these must in turn modify and clarify this framework. Thus we have examined the 'parts of speech'; the sentence elements such as object and complement; the segmentation of sentences into subject, operator, and predication; and some of the chief grammatical processes such as those relating positive to negative, statement to question.

Bibliographical note

For a fuller treatment of the material here and elsewhere in this book, see Quirk et al. (1985); *cf* also Attal (1987).

On the theory of English grammar, see Huddleston (1984); Langacker (1987); Radford (1988).

On intonation and related features of speech, see Bolinger (1972b); Crystal (1969).

On syntactic and semantic relations, see Li (1976); Lyons (1977); Matthews (1981).

3 Verbs and auxiliaries

Major verb classes

3.1 The term VERB is used in two senses:

1 The verb is one of the elements in clause structure, like the subject and the object.

2 A verb is a member of a word class, like a noun and an adjective.

The two senses are related in this way: A VERB PHRASE consists of one or more verbs (sense 2), *eg linked, is making, can believe, might be leaving* in the sentences below; the verb phrase operates as the verb (sense 1) in the clause, *eg*:

They *linked* hands.	He *is making* a noise.
I *can believe* you.	She *might be leaving* soon.

As a word class, verbs can be divided into three major categories, according to their function within the verb phrase: the open class of FULL VERBS (or lexical verbs, 3.2*ff*) and the very small closed classes of PRIMARY VERBS (3.13*ff*) and MODAL AUXILIARY VERBS (3.16*ff*). Since the primary verbs and the modal auxiliary verbs are closed classes, we can list them in full.

FULL VERBS	*believe, follow, like, see, . . .*
PRIMARY VERBS	*be, have, do*
MODAL AUXILIARIES	*can, may, shall, will, must, could, might, should, would*

If there is only one verb in the verb phrase, it is the MAIN VERB. If there is more than one verb, the final one is the main verb, and the one or more verbs that come before it are auxiliaries. For example, *leaving* is the main verb in this sentence, and *might* and *be* are auxiliaries:

She *might be leaving* soon.

Of the three classes of verbs, the full verbs can act only as main verbs, the modal auxiliaries can act only as auxiliary verbs, and the primary verbs can act either as main verbs or as auxiliary verbs.

NOTE [**a**] Some verbs have a status intermediate between that of main verbs and that of auxiliary verbs, *cf* 3.18.

[**b**] Notice that in *Did they believe you?* the verb phrase *Did . . . believe* is discontinuous. The verb phrase is similarly discontinuous in sentences such as *They **do not believe** me* and *I **can** perhaps **help** you.*

[c] Sometimes the main verb (and perhaps other words too) is understood from the context, so that only auxiliaries are present in the verb phrase:

> I can't tell them, but you *can*. [*ie* 'can tell them']
> Your parents may not have suspected anything, but your sister *may have*. [*ie* 'may have suspected something']

[d] There are also multi-word verbs, which consist of a verb and one or more other words, *eg*: *turn on, look at, put up with, take place, take advantage of*. *Cf* 16.2*ff*.

Full verbs

Verb forms

3.2 Regular full verbs, *eg*: CALL, have four morphological forms: (1) base form, (2) *-s* form, (3) *-ing* participle, (4) *-ed* form. Irregular full verbs vary in this respect; for example, the verb SPEAK has five forms, whereas CUT has only three. Since most verbs have the *-ed* inflection for both the simple past (*They called*) and the past participle or passive participle (*They have called*; *They were called*), we extend the term '*-ed* form' to cover these two sets of functions for all verbs.

In some irregular verbs, *eg*: SPEAK, there are two *-ed* forms with distinct syntactic functions: the past *-ed* form and the *-ed* participle. In other irregular verbs, *eg*: CUT, and in all regular verbs, *eg*: CALL, the two *-ed* syntactic forms are identical.

They *spoke* to me.	They have *spoken* to me.
She *cut* herself.	She has *cut* herself.
I *called* him.	I have *called* him.

NOTE **[a]** Regular verbs are called such because if we know their base form (*ie* the dictionary entry form) we can predict their three other forms (*-s*, *-ing*, and *-ed*) by rule. The vast majority of English verbs are regular, and new words that are coined or borrowed from other languages adopt the regular pattern.
[b] The primary verb BE (*cf* 3.13) has eight forms.

The functions of verb forms

3.3 The verb forms have different functions in finite and nonfinite verb phrases (*cf* 3.19*f*). The *-s* form and the past form are always FINITE, whereas the *-ing* participle and the *-ed* participle are always NONFINITE. The BASE form (the form which has no inflection) is sometimes finite, and sometimes nonfinite (see below). In a finite verb phrase (the kind of verb phrase which normally occurs in simple sentences), only the first verb word (in bold face below) is finite:

> She ***calls*** him every day. She ***has*** *called* twice today.

and the subsequent verbs, if any, are nonfinite. In a nonfinite verb phrase, on the other hand, all verbs are nonfinite; *eg*:

> *Calling* early, she found him at home.
> *Called* early, he ate a quick breakfast.
> *Having been called* early, he felt sleepy all day.

Here are the verb forms with their syntactic functions:

1 The BASE FORM (*call*) is a FINITE verb in:
   (i) the present tense in all persons and numbers except 3rd person singular (which has the *-s* form): *I/you/we/they call regularly.*
   (ii) the imperative: *Call at once!*
   (iii) the present subjunctive: *They demanded that she call and see them.*
   It is a NONFINITE verb in:
   (i) the bare infinitive: *He may call tonight.*
   (ii) the *to*-infinitive: *We want her to call.*
2 The *-S* FORM (*calls*) is a FINITE verb in the 3rd person singular present tense: *He/She calls every day.*
3 The *-ING* PARTICIPLE (*calling*) is a NONFINITE verb in:
   (i) the progressive aspect following BE: *He's calling her now.*
   (ii) *-ing* participle clauses: *Calling early, I found her at home.*
4 The PAST FORM (*called*) is a FINITE verb in the past tense: *Someone called yesterday.*
5 The *-ED* PARTICIPLE (*called*) is a NONFINITE verb in:
   (i) the perfect aspect following HAVE: *He has called twice today.*
   (ii) the passive voice following BE: *Her brother is called John.*
   (iii) *-ed* participle clauses: *Called early, he ate a quick breakfast.*

The *-ing* and *-s* forms of all verbs

3.4 The *-ing* and *-s* forms are almost invariably predictable from the base of both regular and irregular verbs. The *-ing* inflection is merely added to the base (but *cf* 3.6):

> *walk ~ walking*   *push ~ pushing*

The *-s* inflection has three pronunciations:

1 /ɪz/ after bases ending in voiced or voiceless sibilants, *eg*:

pass ~ passes	*budge ~ budges*
buzz ~ buzzes	*push ~ pushes*
catch ~ catches	*camouflage ~ camouflages*

In these cases, the *-s* form always ends in *-es*.

2 /z/ after bases ending in other voiced sounds, *eg*:

> *call ~ calls*   *flee ~ flees*   *try ~ tries*

3 /s/ after bases ending in other voiceless sounds, *eg*:

> *cut ~ cuts*   *hop ~ hops*   *lock ~ locks*

The spelling rules for the *-ing* and *-s* forms are detailed in 3.6*ff*. The rules for the *-s* forms are the same as for the regular plural of nouns (*cf* 5.36).

NOTE [a] Notice the irregular *-s* forms of *say* /seɪ/ ~ *says* /sez/, *have* ~ *has*, *do* /duː/ ~ *does* /dʌz/ and derivatives of DO, *eg*: *outdo* /-duː/ ~ *outdoes* /-dʌz/. The *-s* form of BE is highly irregular: *is*.
[b] Syllabic /l/ usually ceases to be syllabic before the *-ing* inflection, *eg*: *wriggle* ~ *wriggling*.

The *-ed* forms of regular verbs

3.5 The *-ed* forms of regular verbs have three pronunciations:
(a) /ɪd/ after bases ending in /d/ and /t/, *eg*:

pad ~ *padded* /-dɪd/   *pat* ~ *patted* /-tɪd/

(b) /d/ after bases ending in voiced sounds other than /d/, including vowels, *eg*:

buzz ~ *buzzed* /-zd/   *budge* ~ *budged* /-dʒd/
call ~ *called* /-ld/   *tow* ~ *towed* /-əʊd/

(c) /t/ after bases ending in voiceless sounds other than /t/, *eg*:

pass ~ *passed* /-st/   *pack* ~ *packed* /-kt/

The spelling of regular verb inflections

Doubling of consonant before *-ing* and *-ed*

3.6 A single consonant letter at the end of the base is doubled before *-ing* and *-ed* when the preceding vowel is stressed and spelled with a single letter:

bar ~ *'barring* ~ *barred*   *oc'cur* ~ *oc'curring* ~ *oc'curred*

There is normally no doubling when the preceding vowel is unstressed (*'enter* ~ *'entering* ~ *'entered*, *'visit* ~ *'visiting* ~ *'visited*) or is written with two letters (*dread* ~ *dreading* ~ *dreaded*).

For some exceptions, see the Notes below.

NOTE [a] BrE breaks the rule by doubling after unstressed syllables ending in *-l*, *-m*, and *-p*; doubling is less usual in AmE.

travel	~ *travelling*, *travelled* (BrE and AmE)
	~ *traveling*, *traveled* (AmE only)
program(me)	~ *programming*, *programmed* (BrE and AmE)
	~ *programing*, *programed* (AmE only)
worship	~ *worshipping*, *worshipped* (BrE and AmE)
	~ *worshiping*, *worshiped* (AmE only)

The verbs *handicap* and *kidnap* follow the pattern of *worship*, but most other verbs ending in *-p* follow the regular rule in both AmE and BrE, *eg*: *develop*, *envelop*, *gallop*, *gossip*.

[b] In both BrE and AmE the general rule is broken by the doubling of *-g* in *humbug* ~ *humbugging* ~ *humbugged* and of words ending in *c* (spelled *-ck-*), *eg*: *panic* ~ *panicking* ~ *panicked*.

[c] In certain verbs whose base ends in a vowel followed by *-s*, there is variation between *-s-* and *-ss-* when the inflection is added:

'bias	*'biasing/'biassing*	*'biased/'biassed*
bus	*'busing/'bussing*	*bused/bussed*
'focus	*'focusing/'focussing*	*'focused/'focussed*

Deletion of and addition of *-e*

3.7 If the base ends in an unpronounced *-e*, this *-e* is regularly dropped before the *-ing* and *-ed* inflections:

create ~ *creating* ~ *created*	*shave* ~ *shaving* ~ *shaved*
bake ~ *baking* ~ *baked*	*type* ~ *typing* ~ *typed*

Verbs with monosyllabic bases in *-ye*, *-oe*, and *-nge*, pronounced /ndʒ/, are exceptions to this rule: they do not lose the *-e* before *-ing*, but they do lose it before *-ed*:

dye ~ *dyeing* ~ *dyed*	*singe* ~ *singeing* ~ *singed*
hoe ~ *hoeing* ~ *hoed*	*tinge* ~ *tingeing* ~ *tinged*

The final *-e* is also lost before *-ed* by verbs ending in *-ie* or *-ee*: *tie* ~ *tied*, *die* ~ *died*, *agree* ~ *agreed*.

Before the *-s* ending, on the other hand, an *-e* is added after the following letters, representing sibilant consonants:

-s	*pass* ~ *passes*	*-ch*	*watch* ~ *watches*	*-x*	*coax* ~ *coaxes*
-z	*buzz* ~ *buzzes*	*-sh*	*wash* ~ *washes*		

NOTE **[a]** An *-e* is added after *-o* in GO (~*goes*), DO (~*does* /dʌz/), ECHO (~*echoes*), VETO (~*vetoes*).

[b] The *-e* is regularly dropped in *impinging* and *infringing*.

Treatment of *-y*

3.8 In bases ending in a consonant followed by *-y*, the following changes take place:

(a) *-y* changes to *-ie-* before *-s*: *carry* ~ *carries*, *try* ~ *tries*

(b) *-y* changes to *-i-* before *-ed*: *carry* ~ *carried*, *try* ~ *tried*

The *-y* remains, however, where it follows a vowel letter: *stay* ~ *stayed*, *alloy* ~ *alloys*, etc; or where it precedes *-ing*: *carry* ~ *carrying*, *stay* ~ *staying*.

A different spelling change occurs in verbs whose bases end in *-ie*: DIE, LIE, TIE, VIE. In these cases, the *-ie* changes to *-y-* before *-ing* is added: *die* ~ *dying*, *lie* ~ *lying*, *tie* ~ *tying*, *vie* ~ *vying*.

NOTE Exceptions to these rules are certain verbs where the *y* changes to *i* after *-a-*: PAY (~*paid*) and LAY (~*laid*) and their derivatives, *eg*: REPAY (~*repaid*), MISLAY (~*mislaid*). The irregular verb SAY follows the same pattern (~*said*).

The morphology of irregular full verbs

3.9 Irregular full verbs differ from regular verbs in that either the past inflection, or the *-ed* participle inflection, or both of these, are irregular. More precisely the major differences are:

(a) Irregular verbs either do not have the regular *-ed* inflection, or else have a variant of that inflection in which the /d/ is devoiced to /t/ (*eg*: *burn* ~ *burnt*, which occurs alongside the regular *burned*).

(b) Irregular verbs typically, but not invariably, have variation in their base vowel: *choose* ~ *chose* ~ *chosen*, *write* ~ *wrote* ~ *written*.

(c) Irregular verbs have a varying number of distinct forms. Since the *-s* form and the *-ing* form are predictable for regular and irregular verbs alike, the only forms that need be listed for irregular verbs are the base form (V), the past (V-ed_1), and the *-ed* participle (V-ed_2). These are traditionally known as the PRINCIPAL PARTS of the verb. Most irregular verbs have, like regular verbs, only one common form for the past and the *-ed* participle; but there is considerable variation in this respect, as the table shows:

	V	V-ed_1	V-ed_2
all three forms alike:	*cut*	*cut*	*cut*
V-ed_1 = V-ed_2:	*meet*	*met*	*met*
V = V-ed_1:	*beat*	*beat*	*beaten*
V = V-ed_2:	*come*	*came*	*come*
all three forms different:	*speak*	*spoke*	*spoken*

Irregular verbs in alphabetical order

3.10 Irregular verbs can be classified on the basis of criteria derived from the variation discussed in 3.9. However, we shall merely list alphabetically the principal parts (including common variants) of the most common irregular verbs. The list omits most verbs with a prefix such as *out-*, *over-*, *re-*, and *un-* that have otherwise the same parts as the corresponding unprefixed verbs.

BASE (V)	PAST TENSE (V-ed_1)	*-ed* PARTICIPLE (V-ed_2)
arise	arose	arisen
awake	awoke, awaked	awoken, awaked
be	was, were	been
bear	bore	borne
beat	beat	beaten
become	became	become
begin	began	begun
bend	bent	bent
bereave	bereft, bereaved	bereft, bereaved
beseech	besought, beseeched	besought, beseeched
beset	beset	beset

BASE (V)	PAST TENSE (V-ed_1)	*-ed* PARTICIPLE (V-ed_2)
bet	bet, betted	bet, betted
bid	bad(e), bid	bade, bid, bidden
bind	bound	bound
bite	bit	bitten
bleed	bled	bled
blow	blew	blown
break	broke	broken
breed	bred	bred
bring	brought	brought
broadcast	broadcast	broadcast
build	built	built
burn	burnt, burned	burnt, burned
burst	burst	burst
buy	bought	bought
cast	cast	cast
catch	caught	caught
choose	chose	chosen
cling	clung	clung
come	came	come
cost	cost	cost
creep	crept	crept
cut	cut	cut
deal	dealt	dealt
deepfreeze	deepfroze, -freezed	deepfrozen, -freezed
dig	dug	dug
dive	dived, ⟨AmE⟩ dove	dived
do	did	done
draw	drew	drawn
dream	dreamt, dreamed	dreamt, dreamed
drink	drank	drunk
drive	drove	driven
eat	ate	eaten
fall	fell	fallen
feed	fed	fed
feel	felt	felt
fight	fought	fought
find	found	found
flee	fled	fled
fling	flung	flung
fly	flew	flown

BASE (V)	PAST TENSE (V-ed_1)	-*ed* PARTICIPLE (V-ed_2)
forbid	forbade, forbad	forbidden
forecast	forecast	forecast
forget	forgot	forgotten
forgive	forgave	forgiven
forgo	forwent	forgone
forsake	forsook	forsaken
freeze	froze	frozen
get	got	{got / gotten ⟨AmE⟩}
give	gave	given
go	went	gone
grind	ground	ground
grow	grew	grown
hamstring	hamstrung	hamstrung
hang	hung (see Note)	hung
have	had	had
hear	heard	heard
heave	heaved, hove	heaved, hove
hide	hid	hidden
hit	hit	hit
hold	held	held
hurt	hurt	hurt
keep	kept	kept
kneel	knelt, kneeled	knelt, kneeled
knit	knitted, knit	knitted, knit
know	knew	known
lead	led	led
lean	leant, leaned	leant, leaned
leap	leapt, leaped	leapt, leaped
learn	learnt, learned	learnt, learned
leave	left	left
lend	lent	lent
let	let	let
lie	lay	lain
light	lit, lighted	lit, lighted
lose	lost	lost
make	made	made
mean	meant	meant
meet	met	met
miscast	miscast	miscast

BASE (V)	PAST TENSE (V-ed_1)	*-ed* PARTICIPLE (V-ed_2)
mislead	misled	misled
misspell	misspelt, misspelled	misspelt, misspelled
mistake	mistook	mistaken
misunderstand	misunderstood	misunderstood
mow	mowed	mown, mowed
offset	offset	offset
put	put	put
quit	quit, quitted	quit, quitted
read	read	read
rend	rent	rent
rid	rid, ridded	rid, ridded
ride	rode	ridden
ring	rang	rung
rise	rose	risen
run	ran	run
saw	sawed	sawn, sawed
say	said	said
see	saw	seen
seek	sought	sought
sell	sold	sold
send	sent	sent
set	set	set
sew	sewed	sewn, sewed
shake	shook	shaken
shear	sheared	shorn, sheared
shed	shed	shed
shine	shone, shined	shone, shined
shoot	shot	shot
show	showed	shown
shrink	shrank	shrunk
shut	shut	shut
sing	sang	sung
sink	sank	sunk
sit	sat	sat
sleep	slept	slept
slide	slid	slid
sling	slung	slung
slit	slit	slit
smell	smelt, smelled	smelt, smelled

BASE (V)	PAST TENSE (V-ed_1)	*-ed* PARTICIPLE (V-ed_2)
sow	sowed	sown, sowed
speak	spoke	spoken
speed	sped, speeded	sped, speeded
spell	spelt, spelled	spelt, spelled
spend	spent	spent
spill	spilt, spilled	spilt, spilled
spin	spun, span	spun
spit	spat, spit	spat, spit
split	split	split
spoil	spoilt, spoiled	spoilt, spoiled
spread	spread	spread
spring	sprang	sprung
stand	stood	stood
steal	stole	stolen
stick	stuck	stuck
sting	stung	stung
stink	stank	stunk
stride	strode	stridden, strid, strode
strike	struck	struck
string	strung	strung
strive	strove, strived	striven, strived
swear	swore	sworn
sweat	sweat, sweated	sweat, sweated
sweep	swept	swept
swell	swelled	swollen, swelled
swim	swam	swum
swing	swung	swung
take	took	taken
teach	taught	taught
tear	tore	torn
telecast	telecast	telecast
tell	told	told
think	thought	thought
thrive	thrived	thrived
throw	threw	thrown
thrust	thrust	thrust
tread	trod	trodden
underbid	underbid	underbid
undergo	underwent	undergone
understand	understood	understood
undertake	undertook	undertaken
underwrite	underwrote	underwritten

BASE (V)	PAST TENSE (V-ed_1)	*-ed* PARTICIPLE (V-ed_2)
uphold	upheld	upheld
upset	upset	upset
wake	woke, waked	woken, waked
wear	wore	worn
weave	wove	woven
wed	wedded, wed	wedded, wed
weep	wept	wept
wet	wetted, wet	wetted, wet
win	won	won
wind	wound	wound
withdraw	withdrew	withdrawn
withhold	withheld	withheld
withstand	withstood	withstood
wring	wrung	wrung
write	wrote	written

NOTE In BrE the verb *fit* is regular, but in AmE *fit* is an alternative to *fitted* in the past and the *-ed* participle. *Hang* has also the regular form *hanged* for the past and the *-ed* participle in the sense 'put to death by hanging'.

Primary verbs and modal auxiliaries

Verbs as operators

3.11 Auxiliaries have one important syntactic function in common: they become the OPERATOR when they occur as the first verb of a finite verb phrase (*cf* 3.19). The main verb BE and (sometimes, especially in BrE) the main verb HAVE are also operators when they are the only verb in the verb phrase. On the other hand, only the auxiliary DO is an operator (as in 'She *does* not know me'), not the main verb DO (as in 'She *does* a lot of work').

Operators share the following main characteristics:

(a) To negate a finite clause, we put *not* immediately after the operator. Contrast:

She *may* do it. ~ She *may not* do it.
She *saw* the play. ~ *She *saw not* the play.

(b) To form an interrogative clause, we put the operator in front of the subject (subject–operator inversion). Contrast:

He will speak first. ~ *Will* he speak first?
He plans to speak first. ~ **Plans* he to speak first?

Subject–operator inversion occurs also in sentences with introductory negatives or semi-negatives (*cf* 10.35*f*):

At no time *was* the entrance left unguarded.

(c) The operator can carry nuclear stress to mark a finite clause as positive rather than negative:

Won't you try again? ~ Yes, I WÌLL try again.
You must speak to the teacher. ~ I HÀVE spoken to him.

The function of this emphatic positive is to deny a negative which has been stated or implied.

(d) The operator functions in a range of elliptical clauses where the rest of the predication is omitted (*cf* 12.20). The clause is understood to repeat the omitted part.

Won't you try again? ~ Yes, I WÌLL.
~ No, I CÀN'T.

If there is no operator in a corresponding positive declarative sentence, the dummy (or 'empty') operator DO is introduced under the above conditions:

(a) She saw the play. ~ She *did not* (or: *didn't*) see the play.
(b) He plans to speak first. ~ *Does* he plan to speak first?
(c) You never listen to your mother. ~ But I DÒ listen to her.
(d) Do you drive a car? ~ Yes, I DÒ.
No, I DÒN'T.

The use of the operator DO is termed DO-SUPPORT.

The main verbs BE and HAVE are operators in these sentences:

I *haven't* a car. ⟨esp BrE⟩ *Is* she your sister?

NOTE **[a]** The enclitic particle *n't* can be attached to most operators as a contraction of the negative word *not*, *eg*: *isn't*, *didn't*, *won't* (*cf* 3.13*ff*). In addition, many operators have contracted forms:

BE: *am* ~ *'m*; *is* ~ *'s*; *are* ~ *'re*
HAVE: *have* ~ *'ve*; *has* ~ *'s*; *had* ~ *'d*
modals: *will* ~ *'ll*; *would* ~ *'d*

The final /t/ in the negative contraction is commonly not sounded. Notice that the contraction *'s* may represent either *is* or *has*, and that the contraction *'d* may represent either *had* or *would*.

[b] The contractions mentioned in **[a]** are simplified forms that are institutionalized in both speech and writing. They are to be distinguished from cases of phonological reduction only, *eg* /kən/ in the pronunciation of *can*.

Characteristics of modal auxiliaries

3.12 Certain characteristics additional to those listed in 3.11 apply specifically to modal auxiliaries:

(a) They are followed by the bare infinitive (*ie* the base form of the verb alone without a preceding *to*):

You *will ask* the questions. They *might have* stolen it.

(b) They cannot occur in nonfinite functions, *ie* as infinitives or participles: *may* ~ **to may*, **maying*, **mayed*. In consequence they can occur only as the first verb in the verb phrase.

(c) They have no *-s* form for the 3rd person singular of the present tense. Contrast:

You *must* write. ~ She *must* write.
You *like* to write. ~ She *likes* to write.

(d) Their past forms can be used to refer to present and future time (often with a tentative meaning):

I think he *may*/*might* be outside.
Will/*Would* you phone him tomorrow?

NOTE The dummy auxiliary DO, like the modal auxiliaries, is followed by the bare infinitive and cannot occur in nonfinite functions. The primary auxiliaries BE, HAVE, and DO have an *-s* form, but it is irregular (*cf* 3.13*ff*). For the marginal modal auxiliaries, see 3.17.

The primary verbs BE, HAVE, and DO

Be

3.13 The verb *be* is a main verb (with a copular function: *cf* 10.3) in:

Ann *is* a happy girl.   *Is* that building a hotel?

But *be* also has two auxiliary functions: as an aspect auxiliary for the progressive (4.10*ff*):

Ann *is* learning Spanish.
The weather has *been* improving.

and as a passive auxiliary (3.25*f*):

Ann *was* awarded a prize.
Our team has never *been* beaten.

Be is unique in having a full set of both finite and nonfinite forms in auxiliary function; it is also unique among English verbs in having as many as eight different forms. In the nonnegative column of Table 3.13 the unstressed pronunciations (with vowel reduction) are given after the stressed pronunciation, where they differ.

Table 3.13 Forms of *Be*

	NONNEGATIVE	UNCONTRACTED NEGATIVE	CONTRACTED NEGATIVE
base	*be* /biː/, /bɪ/		
present			
1st person singular present	*am* /æm/, /əm/ *'m* /m/	*am not*, *'m not*	(*aren't*)
3rd person singular present	*is* /ɪz/ *'s* /z/, /s/	*is not*, *'s not*	*isn't* /ˈɪznt/
2nd person present, 1st and 3rd person plural present	*are* /ɑːʳ/ *'re* /əʳ/	*are not* *'re not*	*aren't* /ɑːʳnt/
past			
1st and 3rd person singular past	*was* /wɒz/, /w(ə)z/	*was not*	*wasn't* /ˈwɒznt/
2nd person past 1st and 3rd person plural past	*were* /wɜːʳ/, /wəʳ/	*were not*	*weren't* /wɜːʳnt/
-ing form	*being* /ˈbiːɪŋ/	*not being*	
-ed participle	*been* /biːn/, /bɪn/	*not been*	

NOTE [a] *Ain't* is a nonstandard contraction used commonly (especially in AmE) in place of *am not*, *is not*, *are not*, *has not*, and *have not*. *Aren't* is the standard contraction for *am not* in questions (especially in BrE): *Aren't I tall?*
[b] There is a rare use of *be* as a perfect auxiliary with the verb *go*: *The guests are* [also *have*] *gone*.

Have

3.14 *Have* functions both as an auxiliary and as a main verb. As an auxiliary for perfect aspect (*cf* 4.8*f*), *have* combines with an *-ed* participle to form complex verb phrases:

I *have* finished. It must *have* been eaten.

As a main verb, it normally takes a direct object: *I have no money*. The *-ed* participle is not used as an auxiliary.

Table **3.14 Forms of *Have***

	NONNEGATIVE	UNCONTRACTED NEGATIVE	CONTRACTED NEGATIVE
base	*have* /hæv/, /(h)əv/ *'ve* /v/, /f/	*have not* *'ve not*	 *haven't* /'hævn̩t/
-s form	*has* /hæz/, /(h)əz/ *'s* /z/, /s/	*has not* *'s not*	 *hasn't* /'hæzn̩t/
past	*had* /hæd/, /(h)əd/ *'d* /d/	*had not* *'d not*	 *hadn't* /'hædn̩t/
-ing form	*having* /'hævɪŋ/	*not having*	
-ed participle	*had* /hæd/, /(h)əd/		

NOTE **[a]** In stative senses (*cf* 4.10*f*), *have* is used (generally in rather formal style) as an operator, especially in BrE. There is also the informal *have got* construction, which is frequently preferred (especially in BrE) as an alternative to stative *have*. In some stative senses, we can therefore have three alternatives:

(a) We *haven't* any butter. ~ We *have* some.
(b) We *haven't got* any butter. ~ We *have got* (We'*ve got*) some.
(c) We *don't have* any butter. ~ We *do have* some.

Of these, (a) is especially BrE ⟨more formal⟩; (b) is especially BrE ⟨informal⟩; (c) is AmE, and also common now in BrE.

[b] In dynamic senses (*cf* 4.10*f*), *have* normally has DO-support, and *have got* is not possible:

A: *Does* she *have* coffee with her breakfast?
B: Yes, she *does*.

Do

3.15 *Do*, like *be* and *have* can be both an auxiliary and a main verb. As an auxiliary, *do* has no nonfinite forms, but only present and past forms.

Table **3.15 Forms of *Do***

	NONNEGATIVE	UNCONTRACTED NEGATIVE	CONTRACTED NEGATIVE
base	*do* /du:/, /dʊ/, /də/	*do not*	*don't* /dəunt/
-s form	*does* /dʌz/, /dəz/ /z/, /s/	*does not*	*doesn't* /'dʌzn̩t/
past	*did* /dɪd/	*did not*	*didn't* /'dɪdnt/
-ing form (main verb only)	*doing* /'du:ɪŋ/		
-ed participle (main verb only)	*done* /dʌn/		

NOTE [a] As a main verb, *do* can function as a pro-predicate or pro-predication (*cf* 12.6*ff*) referring to some unspecified action or actions, alone or in combination with *so*, *it*, *this*, *that*, interrogative *what*, or an indefinite pronoun:

She didn't earn as much as she might have *done*. ⟨esp BrE⟩
I don't know what to *do*, so I *did* nothing.
A: I'm throwing these books away.
B: Why are you *doing* THÀT?
A: What have they been *doing* to the road?
B: Widening it.

[b] The main verb *do* has a wide range of uses as a general-purpose transitive verb, especially in informal speech:

Let's *do* the dishes. Who *does* your car?

[c] As shown in Table 3.15, *does* can be informally pronounced /z/ (*When does the show begin?*) or /s/ (*What does he want?*).

Modal auxiliaries

3.16 The central modal auxiliaries are in Table 3.16. Rare forms are in parentheses.

***Table* 3.16 Forms of the modal auxiliary verbs**

NONNEGATIVE	UNCONTRACTED NEGATIVE	CONTRACTED NEGATIVE
can /kæn, kən/	*cannot, can not*	*can't* /kɑːnt/ ⟨BrE⟩, /kænt/ ⟨AmE⟩
could /kʊd, kəd/	*could not*	*couldn't* /ˈkʊdn̩t/
may /meɪ/	*may not*	(*mayn't* /meɪnt/)
might /maɪt/	*might not*	*mightn't* /ˈmaɪtn̩t/
shall /ʃæl, ʃ(ə)l/	*shall not*	(*shan't* /ʃɑːnt/ ⟨BrE⟩)
should /ʃʊd, ʃ(ə)d/	*should not*	*shouldn't* /ˈʃʊdn̩t/, /ˈʃədn̩t/
will /wɪl/	*will not*	*won't* /wəʊnt/
'll /(ə)l/	*'ll not*	
would /wʊd/	*would not*	*wouldn't* /ˈwʊdn̩t/
'd /(ə)d/	*'d not*	
must /mʌst, məst/	*must not*	*mustn't* /ˈmʌsn̩t/

NOTE *Mayn't* and *shan't* are virtually nonexistent in AmE, while in BrE *shan't* is becoming rare and *mayn't* even more so.

Marginal modal auxiliaries

3.17 The marginal modal auxiliaries are *used to*, *ought to*, *dare*, and *need*.

Used to always takes the *to*-infinitive and occurs only in the past tense:

She *used to* attend regularly.

It is used both as an auxiliary and as a main verb with DO-support:

He *usedn't* (or: *used not*) *to* smoke. ⟨BrE⟩
He *didn't use(d) to* smoke. ⟨BrE and informal AmE⟩

The normal interrogative construction is with DO-support, even in BrE:

Did he *use to* drink? He used to drink, *didn't* he?

Ought to normally has the *to*-infinitive, but the *to* is optional following *ought* in ellipsis:

You *oughtn't to* smoke so much.
A: *Ought* I *to* stop smoking?
B: Yes, I think you *ought (to)*.

Dare and *need* can be used either as modal auxiliaries (with bare infinitive and without the inflected forms) or as main verbs (with *to*-infinitive and with inflected *-s*, *-ing*, and past forms). The modal construction is restricted to nonassertive contexts, *ie* mainly negative and interrogative sentences, whereas the main verb construction can always be used, and is in fact more common.

NOTE Blends of the two constructions (modal auxiliary and main verb) are widely acceptable for *dare*:

They *do* not *dare* ask for me. *Do* they *dare* ask for more?

Modal idioms and semi-auxiliaries

3.18 Two other categories of verbs are intermediate between auxiliaries and main verbs. They express modal or aspectual meaning.

(a) The MODAL IDIOMS are a combination of auxiliary and infinitive or adverb. None of them have nonfinite forms and they are therefore always the first verb in the verb phrase. The most common modal idioms are *had better*, *would rather*, *have got to*, and *be to*.

(b) The SEMI-AUXILIARIES are a set of verb idioms which are introduced by one of the primary verbs HAVE and BE. They have nonfinite forms and can therefore occur in combination with preceding auxiliaries. Indeed, two or more semi-auxiliaries can occur in sequence. Common semi-auxiliaries include:

be able to	*be bound to*	*be going to*	*be supposed to*
be about to	*be due to*	*be likely to*	*have to*

NOTE Like auxiliaries – in having meanings similar to those for the aspectual and modal auxiliaries (*cf* 4.7, 4.21) – are the catenatives, such as *appear to*, *happen to*, *seem to*. Some catenatives are followed by *-ing* or *-ed* participles rather than by infinitives: *start* (working), *go on* (talking), *keep (on)* (smoking), *get* (trapped).

The structure of verb phrases

Finite verb phrases

3.19 A finite verb phrase is a verb phrase in which the first or only word is a finite verb (*cf* 3.3), the rest of the verb phrase (if any) consisting of nonfinite verbs. Finite verb phrases can be distinguished as follows:

(a) Finite verb phrases can occur as the verb phrase of independent clauses.

(b) Finite verb phrases have tense contrast, *ie* the distinction between present and past tenses:

He *is* a journalist now.
He *worked* as a travel agent last summer.

(c) There is person concord and number concord between the subject of a clause and the finite verb phrase. Concord is particularly clear with the present tense of *be*:

I *am* / You *are* } here. He/She/It *is* / We/They *are* } here.

But with most full verbs overt concord is restricted to a contrast between the 3rd person singular present and other persons or plural number:

He/She/Jim *reads* / I/We/You/They *read* } the paper every morning.

With modal auxiliaries there is no overt concord at all (*cf* 3.12):

I/You/She/We/They *can* play the cello.

(d) Finite verb phrases have mood, which indicates the factual, nonfactual, or counterfactual status of the predication. In contrast to the 'unmarked' INDICATIVE mood, we distinguish the 'marked' moods IMPERATIVE (used to express commands and other directive speech acts; *cf* 11.15 *ff*), and SUBJUNCTIVE (used to express a wish, recommendation, etc; *cf* 3.23*f*).

A clause with a finite verb phrase as its V element is called a 'finite verb clause' or, more tersely, a 'finite clause'. Similarly, a clause with a nonfinite verb phrase as its V element is called a 'nonfinite (verb) clause' (*cf* 14.3*f*).

Nonfinite verb phrases

3.20 The infinitive ((*to*) *call*), the *-ing* participle (*calling*), and the *-ed* participle (*called*) are the nonfinite forms of the verb. Hence any phrase in which one of these verb forms is the first or only word (disregarding the infinitive marker *to*) is a nonfinite verb phrase. Such phrases do not normally occur as the verb phrase of an independent clause. Compare:

FINITE VERB PHRASES	NONFINITE VERB PHRASES
He *smokes*.	*To smoke* like that must be dangerous.
Mary *is having* a smoke.	I regret having started *to smoke*.
He *must smoke* 40 a day.	The cigars *smoked* here tend to be expensive.
You *have been smoking* all day.	That was the last cigarette *to have been smoked* by me.

Simple and complex verb phrases

3.21 The finite verb phrase is SIMPLE when (without ellipsis) it consists of only one word. It is complex when it consists of two or more words.

The auxiliaries follow a strict order in the complex verb phrase:

(a) MODAL, followed by an infinitive:
must go

(b) PERFECT (the auxiliary *have*) followed by an *-ed* participle:
has examined; must *have* examined

(c) PROGRESSIVE (the auxiliary *be*), followed by an *-ing* participle:
was talking; must have *been* talking

(d) PASSIVE (the auxiliary *be*), followed by an *-ed* participle:
was visited; must have been *being* visited

While the above order is strictly followed, gaps are perfectly normal:

(a) + (c): must be going (modal + progressive)
(b) + (d): has been examined (perfect + passive)
(a) + (d): may be visited (modal + passive)

Contrasts expressed in the verb phrase

3.22 It may be convenient to list here the contrasts in which the verb phrase plays an important part.

(a) *Tense* requires a choice between present and past in the first or only verb in a finite verb phrase (*cf* 4.3*ff*):

She *works* hard. She *worked* hard.

(b) *Aspect* requires a choice between the nonperfect and the perfect and between the nonprogressive and the progressive (*cf* 4.7*ff*):

He *writes* poems. (simple: nonperfect, nonprogressive)
He *has written* poems. (perfect, nonprogressive)
He *is writing* poems. (progressive, nonperfect)
He *has been writing* poems. (perfect, progressive)

(c) *Mood* requires a choice between the indicative, imperative, and subjunctive (*cf* 11.15*ff*, 3.23*f*):

He {*listens* / *is listening* to me.} (indicative)

Listen to me. (imperative)
I demand that he *listen* to me. (subjunctive)

(d) *Finiteness* requires a choice between the finite and nonfinite (3.19*f*):

She *plays* tennis.
Playing tennis is good for your health.

The verb element of a finite clause (as in the first sentence) is a finite verb phrase; the verb element of a nonfinite clause is a nonfinite verb phrase (*eg*: *Playing* in *Playing tennis*).

(e) *Voice* involves a contrast between active and passive (*cf* 3.25*f*):

A doctor *will examine* the applicants. (active)
The applicants *will be examined* by a doctor. (passive)

(f) *Questions* generally require subject–operator inversion (*cf* 11.3*ff*; for an exception, *cf* 11.10):

I *should* pay for you. ~ *Should* I pay for you?
The students *objected*. ~ *Did* the students object?

(g) *Negation* makes use of operators (*cf* 10.33, but *cf* 3.23 Note [b]):

I *should* pay for you. ~ I *shouldn't* pay for you.
The students *objected*. ~ The students *didn't* object.

(h) *Emphasis* is frequently carried by an operator (*cf* 3.11):

I SHOULD pay.
The students DID object.

The subjunctive mood

Forms of the subjunctive

3.23 There are two forms of the subjunctive. They are traditionally called the present and past subjunctive, although the distinction relates more to mood than to tense.

The present subjunctive is expressed by the base form of the verb. For the verb *be*, the subjunctive form *be* is distinct from the indicative forms *am*, *is*, and *are*. For other verbs, the subjunctive is distinctive only in the 3rd person singular:

I insist that we *reconsider* the Council's decisions. [indicative or subjunctive] [1]
I insist that the Council *reconsider* its decisions. [subjunctive] [2]
I insist that the Council's decision(s) *be* reconsidered. [subjunctive] [3]

The past subjunctive (or *were*-subjunctive) survives only in *were* as a past form of BE. It is distinguishable from the past indicative of BE only in the 1st and 3rd persons singular:

> If she *was* leaving, you would have heard about it. [indicative]
> If she *were* leaving, you would have heard about it. [subjunctive]

The indicative *was* is more common in less formal style.

NOTE [a] Only *were* is acceptable in *as it were* ('so to speak'); *were* is usual in *if I were you*.
[b] Negation of the present subjunctive does not require an operator. Hence, *reconsider* in [1a] is unambiguously subjunctive:

> I insist that we not reconsider the Council's decision. [1a]

Uses of the subjunctive

3.24 We distinguish two main uses of the present subjunctive:

(a) The MANDATIVE SUBJUNCTIVE is used in a *that*-clause after an expression of such notions as demand, recommendation, proposal, intention (*eg*: *We insist*, *prefer*, *request*; *It is necessary*, *desirable*, *imperative*; *the decision*, *requirement*, *resolution*). This use is more characteristic of AmE than BrE, but seems to be increasing in BrE. In BrE the alternatives are putative *should* (14.14) and the indicative.

> The employees demanded that he { *resign*. ⟨esp AmE⟩ / *should resign*. ⟨esp BrE⟩ / *resigns*. }

(b) The FORMULAIC (or 'optative') SUBJUNCTIVE is used in certain set expressions:

> God *save* the Queen. — Heaven *forbid* that . . .
> Long *live* the King. — *Be* that as it may, . . .
> *Come* what may, . . . — *Suffice* it to say that . . .

The past subjunctive is hypothetical in meaning. It is used in conditional and concessive clauses and in subordinate clauses after *wish* and *suppose*:

> If I *were* a rich man, I would . . .
> I wish the journey *were* over.
> Just suppose everyone *were* to act like you.

Subjunctive *were* is often replaced in nonformal style by indicative *was*.

Voice

Active and passive

3.25 The distinction between active and passive applies only to sentences where the verb is transitive. The difference between the active voice and the passive voice involves both the verb phrase and the clause as a whole. In the verb phrase, the passive adds a form of the auxiliary *be* followed by the *-ed* participle of the main verb. For example:

kisses	*is kissed*
has kissed	*has been kissed*
may be kissing	*may be being kissed*

At the clause level, changing from active to passive has the following results:

(a) The active subject, if retained, becomes the passive AGENT.
(b) The active object becomes the passive subject.
(c) The preposition *by* is inserted before the agent.

The butler murdered the detective. [ACTIVE]
The detective was murdered (by the butler). [PASSIVE]
The explanation was followed by an example.

The prepositional phrase (AGENT *BY*-PHRASE) of passive sentences is in most cases an optional element and is commonly omitted.

NOTE **[a]** *Get* is frequently used with the passive in informal English: *get caught, get dressed, get run over*. It often conveys the connotation that the referent of the subject has some responsibility for the action. Compare the construction with a reflexive pronoun: 'She got herself caught.'

[b] The change to passive is highly restricted if the active object is a clause. It becomes acceptable when the clause is extraposed and replaced by anticipatory *it*:

They thought *that she was attractive*.
It was thought *that she was attractive*.

[c] Some stative transitive verbs, called 'middle verbs', normally occur only in the active (*cf* 16.15), *eg*:

They *have* a nice house.	The auditorium *holds* 500 people.
He *lacks* confidence.	Will this *suit* you?

[d] In the 'statal passive' the *-ed* form refers to a state resulting from an action, and the construction contains a copular verb and a subject complement:

The building is *demolished*.
Her arm was already *broken* when I saw her.

A sentence such as *Her arm was broken* is ambiguous between a dynamic passive reading ('Someone broke her arm') and a statal reading ('Her arm was in a state of fracture').

Uses of the passive

3.26 In sentences where there is a choice between active and passive, the active is the norm.

Speakers or writers use the passive for the following reasons. In considering the examples, bear in mind that more than one reason may apply. Reasons 1–4 illustrate the uses of the passive without the agent *by*-phrase, which is commonly omitted:

1 They do not know the identity of the agent of the action.

Many lifeboats *were launched* from the Titanic only partly filled.

2 They want to avoid identifying the agent because they do not want to assign or accept responsibility.

My letter *has* not yet *been answered.*

A mistake *has been made* in calculating your change.

3 They feel that there is no reason for mention of the agent because the identification is unimportant or obvious from the context.

The small thin pieces of metal at the sides are to protect the appliance during handling and *may be discarded.*

Nowadays sleeping sickness *can* usually *be cured* if it *is detected* early enough.

4 In scientific and technical writing, writers often use the passive to avoid the constant repetition of the subject *I* or *we* and to put the emphasis on processes and experimental procedures. This use of the passive helps to give the writing the objective tone that the writers wish to convey.

The subject *was blindfolded* and a pencil *was placed* in the left hand.

5 To put emphasis on the agent of the action;
6 To avoid what would otherwise be a long active subject;
7 To retain the same subject throughout a long sentence.

The following sentence exemplifies a combination of these last three reasons for using the passive (*cf* 18.22):

As a cat moves, it *is kept informed* of its movements not only by its eyes, but also by messages from its pads and elsewhere in its skin, its organs of balance, and its sense organs of joints and muscles.

Bibliographical note

For general treatments of the English verb, see Palmer (1988); Allen (1966); Joos (1964); Huddleston (1976).

On the passive see Granger (1983); Stein (1979); Svartvik (1966). For studies relating more particularly to meaning in the verb phrase, consult the Bibliographical note to Chapter 4.

4 The semantics of the verb phrase

Time, tense, and the verb

4.1 In abstraction from any given language, we can think of time as a line on which is located, as a continuously moving point, the present moment. Anything ahead of the present moment is in the future, and anything behind it is in the past (see Fig 4.1a):

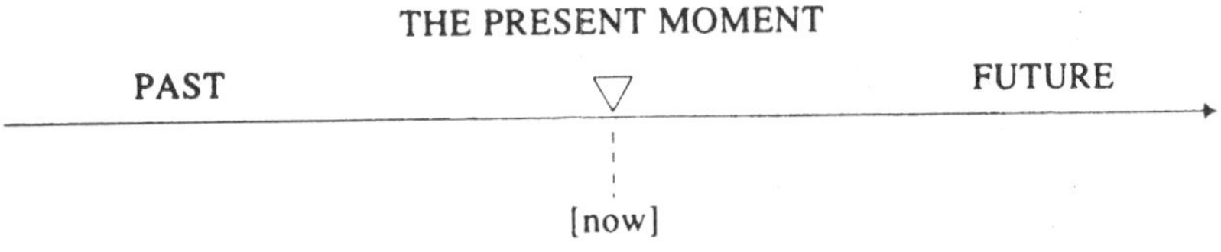

Fig 4.1a

In relating this REFERENTIAL view of time to the meaning of verbs, it is useful to reformulate it so that on the SEMANTIC level of interpretation something is defined as 'present' if it exists at the present moment and may also exist in the past and in the future. Hence *Paris stands on the River Seine* may be correctly said to describe a 'present' situation, even though this situation has existed for many centuries in the past and may well exist for an indefinitely long period in the future. The same is true for sentences of more limited time span: *John boasts a lot* applies to past and present, and carries the implication that it will apply to an indefinite period in the future (see Fig 4.1b):

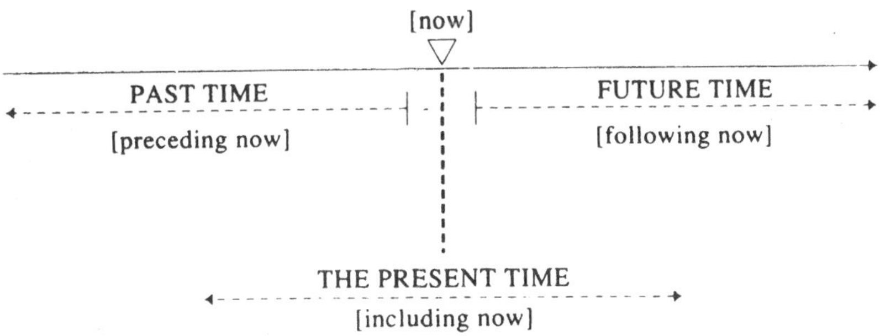

Fig 4.1b

TENSE is a grammatical category that is realized by verb inflection. Since English has no future inflected form of the verb, the threefold semantic opposition is reduced to two tenses: the PRESENT TENSE and the PAST TENSE, which typically refer to present and past time respectively.

NOTE Future meaning is conveyed by various means, including the present tense: *Tomorrow is Tuesday*. *Cf* 4.13*ff*.

Stative and dynamic senses of verbs

4.2 We draw a broad distinction between the STATIVE and DYNAMIC senses in which verbs are used to refer to situations (*cf* 4.11). Verbs like *be*, *have*, and *know* have stative senses when they refer to a single unbroken state of affairs:

I *have known* the Penfolds all my life.

Verbs like *drive*, *speak*, and *attack* have dynamic senses, as can be seen when they are used with the present perfect to refer to a sequence of separate events:

I *have driven* sports cars for years.

NOTE [a] A verb may shift in sense from one category to another. *Have*, for example, is usually stative: *She has two sisters*. But it has a dynamic sense in *We have dinner at Maxim's quite frequently*.
[b] Dynamic verb senses can regularly occur with the imperative and progressive, but stative verb senses cannot:

Learn how to swim.	**Know* how to swim.
I *am learning* to swim.	*I *am knowing* how to swim.

In general, only dynamic senses follow *do* in a pseudo-cleft sentence (*cf* 18.20):

What she did was (to) *learn* Spanish.
*What she did was (to) *know* Spanish.

Tense

Simple present tense for present time

4.3 (a) The STATE PRESENT is used with stative verb senses to refer to a single unbroken state of affairs that has existed in the past, exists now, and is likely to continue to exist in the future. It includes the 'timeless present', which refers to 'eternal truths' such as *Two and three make five* or to less extreme instances of timelessness, such as *The British Isles have a temperate climate*. It also includes more restricted time spans:

Margaret *is* tall.	He *does not believe* in hard work.
We *live* near Toronto.	This soup *tastes* delicious.

(b) The HABITUAL PRESENT is used with dynamic verb senses to refer to events that repeatedly occur without limitation on their extension into the past or future. Like the state present, it includes the 'timeless present', such as *Water boils at 100 °C* and *The earth moves round the sun*, and more restricted time spans:

We *go* to Brussels every year.	She *doesn't smoke.*
She *makes* her own dresses.	Bill *drinks* heavily.

Whereas the state present always refers to something that applies at the time of speaking or writing, this is very often not so for the habitual present: We can say *Bill drinks heavily* when Bill is not actually drinking.

(c) The INSTANTANEOUS PRESENT is used with dynamic verb senses to refer to a single event with little or no duration that occurs at the time of speaking or writing. It is used only in certain restricted situations; for example, in commentaries and self-commentaries (*Black passes the ball to Fernandez; I enclose a form of application*) and with performative verbs that refer to the speech acts performed by uttering the sentences (*I apologize for my behaviour; We thank you for your recent enquiry*).

NOTE It is a sign of the habitual present that one can easily add a frequency adverbial (*eg*: *often, once a day, every year*) to specify the frequency of the event.

Simple present tense for past and future

4.4 There are three additional kinds of uses of the simple present that are best seen as extended interpretations of the basic meanings of 4.3.

(a) The HISTORIC PRESENT refers to past time, and is characteristic of popular narrative style. It conveys the dramatic immediacy of an event happening at the time of narration:

Just as we arrived, up *comes* Ben and *slaps* me on the back as if we'*re* life-long friends.

It is used as a stylistically marked device in fictional narrative for imaginary events in the past:

The crowd *swarms* around the gateway, and *seethes* with delighted anticipation; excitement *grows*, as suddenly their hero *makes* his entrance . . .

(b) The simple present is optionally used to refer to the past with verbs of communication or reception of communication to suggest that the information communicated is still valid:

Jack *tells* me that the position is still vacant.
The Bible *prohibits* the committing of adultery.
I *hear* that you need an assistant.
I *understand* that the game has been postponed.

(c) In main clauses, the simple present typically occurs with time-position adverbials to suggest that a future event is certain to take place:

The plane *leaves* for Ankara at eight o'clock tonight.

The use of the simple present for future time is much more common in subordinate clauses, particularly in conditional and temporal clauses (*cf* 14.11):

He'll do it if you *pay* him.
I'll let you know as soon as I *hear* from her.

NOTE Somewhat akin to the other optional uses of the simple present for past time is its use in reference to writers, composers, etc, and their works (*cf* 19.13):

Dickens *draws* his characters from the London underworld of his time.
Beethoven's Ninth *is* his best composition.

Simple past tense for past time

4.5 The simple past is used to refer to a situation set at a definite time in the past.

(a) The EVENT PAST is used with dynamic verb senses to refer to a single definite event in the past. The event may take place over an extended period (*The Normans invaded England in 1066*) or at a point of time (*The plane left at 9 a.m.*).
(b) The HABITUAL PAST is used with dynamic verb senses to refer to past events that repeatedly occur: *We spent our holidays in Spain when we were children.*
(c) The STATE PAST is used with stative verb senses to refer to a single unbroken state of affairs in the past: *I once liked reading novels.*

NOTE [a] The habitual and state meanings of the past can be paraphrased by *used to*.
[b] The definite time may be conveyed by a previous or subsequent time expression in the linguistic context, for example by a time adverbial such as *in 1066*. It may also be presupposed on the basis of knowledge shared by speaker and hearer. For example, *Your brother was at school with me* presupposes as common knowledge that a specific period of time is spent at school.

Special uses of the simple past tense

4.6 There are three special uses of the simple past (*cf* 4.9 Note):

(a) In INDIRECT SPEECH OR INDIRECT THOUGHT (*cf* 14.17*f*), the simple past in the reporting verb may cause the verb in the subordinate reported clause to be backshifted into the simple past: *She said that she knew you*; *I thought you were in Paris.*
(b) The ATTITUDINAL PAST is optionally used to refer more tentatively (and therefore more politely) to a present state of mind: *Did you want to see me now?*; *I wondered whether you are / were free tomorrow* (*cf* 14.18).
(c) The HYPOTHETICAL PAST is used in certain subordinate clauses, especially *if*-clauses, to convey what is contrary to the belief or expectation of the speaker (*cf* 14.12):

If you *knew* him, you wouldn't say that. [1]
If she *asked* me, I would help her. [2]
I wish I *had* a memory like yours. [3]

The implication of [1] is that you do not know him, of [2] that she will not ask me, and of [3] that I do not have such a memory.

Aspect

4.7 ASPECT is a grammatical category that reflects the way in which the action of a verb is viewed with respect to time. We recognize two aspects in English, the perfect and the progressive, which may combine in a complex verb phrase, and are marked for present or past tense:

present perfect	*has examined*
past perfect	*had examined*
present progressive	*is examining*
past progressive	*was examining*
present perfect progressive	*has been examining*
past perfect progressive	*had been examining*

The present perfect

4.8 The present perfect is used to refer to a situation set at some indefinite time within a period beginning in the past and leading up to the present.

(a) The STATE PRESENT PERFECT is used with stative verb senses to refer to a state that began in the past and extends to the present, and will perhaps continue in the future:

They *have been* unhappy for a long time.
We *have lived* in Amsterdam for five years.
She *has owned* the house since her father died.
I'*ve* always *liked* her.

(b) The EVENT PRESENT PERFECT is used with dynamic verb senses to refer to one or more events that have occurred at some time within a period leading up to the present. We distinguish two subtypes:

1 The event or events are reported as news; usually they have occurred shortly before the present time:

The Republicans *have won* the election.
I'*ve* just *got* a new job.
There'*s been* a serious accident.

2 The event or events occurred at some more remote time in the past. but the implicit time period that frames the event or events leads up to the present:

She *has given* an interview only once in her life (but she may yet give another interview).
Have you *seen* the new production of *King Lear* at the National Theatre? (You still can do so.)
All our children *have had* measles (and they are not likely to have it again).

(c) The HABITUAL PRESENT PERFECT is used with dynamic verb senses to refer to past events that repeatedly occur up to and including the present.

The magazine *has been* published every month (since 1975).
I'*ve been* reading only science fiction (till now).
Socrates *has influenced* many philosophers (till now).

Unlike the simple past, the present perfect does not normally cooccur with adverbials that indicate a specific point or period of time in the past. Contrast:

I *saw* her a week ago.	[simple past]
*I *have seen* her a week ago.	[present perfect]

NOTE [a] The use of the present perfect for recent events may imply that the result of the event still applies: *He's broken his arm* ('His arm is broken'); *I've emptied the basket* ('The basket is empty'); *The train has arrived on Platform 4* ('The train is now on Platform 4').

[b] The simple past is often used in place of the present perfect for recent events, especially in AmE: *I just got a new job.*

[c] Some adverbials cooccur with the present perfect and not with the simple past. They include the adverb *since* (*I haven't seen him since*); prepositional phrases and clauses introduced by *since* (*since Monday*; *since I met you*); the phrases *till/up to now* and *so far*. *Cf* 8.22 Note [a].

[d] The simple past must be used if the implicit time period does not reach up to the present moment:

She *gave* an interview only once in her life. (She can give no more interviews, since she is dead.)
Did you *see* the new production of *King Lear* at the National Theatre? (You can no longer do so, because the production has closed.)

[e] If *will* (or *shall*) is combined with the perfect, the resulting future perfect conveys the meaning 'past in future':

By next week, they *will have completed* their contract.

A similar meaning may be conveyed with other modals:

By next week, they *may have completed* their contract. ['It is possible that they will have completed . . .']

But the combination with the modal may represent a simple past or a present perfect:

I *may have left* the keys at the office. ['It is possible that I left/have left . . .']

The past perfect

4.9 The past perfect (or 'pluperfect') refers to a time earlier than another past time. It may represent the past of the simple past, a time earlier than that indicated by the simple past:

They *had moved* into the house before the baby was born. [1]

The simple past can often replace the past perfect in such cases, if the time-relationship between the two situations is clear:

They *moved* into the house before the baby was born. [1a]

The past perfect may also represent the past of the present perfect:

She *had owned* the house since her parents died. [2]

Contrast:

She *has owned* the house since her parents died. [2a]

Whereas [2a] entails that she still owns the house, [2] implies that she does not own it now.

NOTE The past perfect has special uses analogous to those for the simple past (*cf* 4.6): **[a]** In indirect speech constructions it indicates a backshift into the more remote past: *I told her the parcel had not arrived.*
[b] The ATTITUDINAL PAST PERFECT refers more politely than the simple past to a present state of mind: *I had wondered whether you are / were free now* (*cf.* 14.18).
[c] The HYPOTHETICAL PAST PERFECT is used in certain subordinate clauses, especially *if*-clauses, to imply that the situation did not occur (*cf* 14.12): *If I had been there, it would not have happened.*

Progressive aspect

4.10 The progressive (or 'continuous') focuses on the situation as being in progress at a particular time. In consequence, it may imply that the situation has limited duration, and that it is not necessarily complete.

(a) Generally, verbs with stative senses do not occur in the progressive, since there is no conception of progression in states of affairs:

*I *am liking* your sister.
*He *was knowing* English.

When verbs that are ordinarily stative occur in the progressive, they adopt dynamic meanings. They may indicate a type of behaviour with limited duration:

You *are being* obstinate.
He *was being* silly.

Verbs expressing emotion or attitude, which are ordinarily stative, indicate tentativeness when they occur in the progressive:

I'*m hoping* to take my exam soon.
I *was wondering* whether you could help me.

(b) The EVENT PROGRESSIVE is used with dynamic verb senses to refer to an event that has duration and is not completed:

I *was reading* an economics book last night. [1]
One of the boys *was drowning*, but I dived in and saved him. [2]

The past progressive in [1] suggests that the book was perhaps not finished. In contrast, the simple past in [1a] indicates that I had finished reading the book:

I *read* an economics book last night. [1a]

The simple past *drowned* could not replace the past progressive *was drowning* in [2], because it would not be compatible with the report that the boy was saved.

The present progressive is more commonly used than the simple present for events in present time, because present events are usually regarded as having some duration:

What *are* you *doing*? I'*m writing* a letter.

(c) The HABITUAL PROGRESSIVE is used with dynamic verb senses to refer to events that repeatedly occur, with the implication that they take place over a limited period of time:

She'*s writing* some short stories. [3]
He'*s teaching* in a comprehensive school. [4]

Contrast the nonprogressive in [3a] and [4a]:

She *writes* short stories. [3a]
He *teaches* in a comprehensive school. [3b]

The progressive implies temporariness, whereas the nonprogressive implies permanence ('She's a short-story writer'; 'He's a teacher in a comprehensive school'). The normally stative verb *have* in [5] carries the implication of temporariness, and the initial time adverbial reinforces that notion:

At the time she *was having* singing lessons. [5]

NOTE [a] The progressive also has some special uses:

1 To refer to events anticipated in the future, or to events anticipated in the past (future in the past): *The train is leaving at nine (tomorrow)*; *They were getting married the following spring.*
2 After *will* (or *shall*) to imply that the situation will take place 'as a matter of course' in the future: *I'll be seeing you next week.*

[b] Verbs denoting states of bodily sensation may be used more or less interchangeably in the progressive and the nonprogressive when referring to a temporary state: *My foot hurts/is hurting, My back aches/is aching; I feel/am feeling cold.*
[c] The habitual progressive is not used to refer to sporadic events, (**She's sometimes walking to the office*); the nonprogressive is required for this purpose (*She sometimes walks to the office*). In combination with indefinite frequency adverbs such as *always* and *continually*, the habitual progressive loses its temporary meaning; it often conveys disapproval: *Bill is always working late at the office.* The pejorative sense may also be expressed with the simple present or past in combination with these adverbs.
[d] The relationship between two simple forms is normally one of TIME-SEQUENCE: *When we arrived, Jan made some fresh coffee* (The arrival came before the coffee-making). The relationship between progressive and a simple form is normally one of TIME-INCLUSION: *When we arrived, Jan was making some coffee* (The arrival took place during the coffee-making).

Verb senses and the progressive

4.11 We have pointed out that verbs with stative senses generally do not occur in the progressive (*cf* 4.10). Below we list classes of verbs that typically occur with stative and dynamic senses, and we give a few examples of each class. Stance verbs are intermediate between stative and dynamic verbs.

(a) STATIVE
1 States of 'being' and 'having': *be, contain, depend, have, resemble.*
2 Intellectual states: *believe, know, realize, think, understand.*
3 States of emotion or attitude: *disagree, dislike, like, want, wish.*
4 States of perception: *feel, hear, see, smell, taste.*
5 States of bodily sensation: *ache, feel sick, hurt, itch, tickle.*

(b) STANCE: *lie, live, sit, stand.*

(c) DYNAMIC DURATIVE (taking place over a period of time)
1 Activities performed by inanimate forces: (wind) *blow*, (engine) *run*, *rain*, (watch) *work.*
2 Activities performed by animate agents: *dance, eat, play, sing, work.*
3 Processes (denoting change of state taking place over a period): *change, deteriorate, grow, ripen, widen.*
4 Accomplishments (activities having a goal or endpoint): *finish* (the book), *knit* (a sweater), *read* (the paper), *write* (an essay).

(d) DYNAMIC PUNCTUAL (with little or no duration)
1 Momentary events and acts: *bang, jump, knock, nod, tap.* In the progressive, they indicate the repetition of the event, *eg*: *He was knocking on the door.*

2 Transitional events and acts: *arrive, die, drown, land, leave, stop.* In the progressive, they refer to a period leading up to the change of state, *eg*: *the train is (now) arriving at Platform 4.*

NOTE Stance verbs may be used with either the progressive or the nonprogressive, often with little to choose between the variants. But sometimes they seem to be used with the nonprogressive to express a permanent state and with the progressive to express a temporary state:

> James *lives* in Copenhagen. [permanent residence]
> James *is living* in Copenhagen. [temporary residence]

The perfect progressive

4.12 When the perfect and progressive aspects are combined in the same verb phrase (*eg*: *has been working*), the features of meaning associated with each aspect are also combined to refer to a TEMPORARY SITUATION LEADING UP TO THE PRESENT when the perfect auxiliary is present tense *has* or *have*.

The combination conveys the sense of a situation in progress with limited duration: *I've been writing a letter to my nephew*; *It's been snowing again*. We may contrast these with the nonprogressive sense in *I've written a letter to my nephew*; *It's snowed again*.

If the perfect progressive sense is combined with accomplishment predications or process predications (*cf* 4.11), then the verb phrase conveys the possibility of incompleteness:

> *I've been cleaning* the windows. [The job may not be finished; contrast: *I've cleaned the windows*.]
> The weather *has been getting* warmer. [It may get warmer still.]

The present perfect progressive may be used with dynamic verb senses to refer to a TEMPORARY HABIT UP TO THE PRESENT. The events occur repeatedly up to the present and possibly into the future:

> Martin *has been scoring* plenty of goals (this season).
> *I've been working* on the night shift for several weeks.

The perfect progressive may combine with the past tense and with modals:

> The fire *had been raging* for over a week. [1]
> By Friday, we *will have been living* here for ten years. [2]

In [1] the temporary event leads up to some point in the past. In [2] the temporary state is earlier than the time in the future indicated by *Friday*. The combination with the past tense or a modal need not presuppose an earlier time, and it can therefore be accompanied by an adverbial of time position (*cf* 4.8 Note [e]):

> I *had been talking* with him only last Monday.
> I *must have been talking* with him last Monday.

Some means of expressing future time

4.13 In the absence of an inflectional tense, there are several possibilities for expressing future time in English. Future time is expressed by means of modal auxiliaries, modal idioms, and semi-auxiliaries (*cf* 3.18), or by the simple present and progressive forms.

Will/shall + infinitive

4.14 The most common way of expressing futurity is the construction of *will* or *'ll* with the infinitive:

> He *will be* here in half an hour.
> *Will* you *need* any help?
> No doubt I'*ll see* you next week.

Shall is also sometimes used with the infinitive (especially in Southern BrE) to indicate futurity with a 1st person subject:

> No doubt *I shall see* you next week.

Although these constructions are the closest approximations to a colourless, neutral future, they also cover a range of modal meanings (*cf* 4.27*f*).

Be going to + infinitive

4.15 The general meaning of the construction of *be going to* with the infinitive is 'future fulfilment of the present'. We can further distinguish two specific meanings. The first, 'future fulfilment of a present intention', is chiefly associated with personal subjects and agentive verbs:

> When *are* you *going to* get married?
> Martha *is going to lend* us her camera.
> I'*m going to complain* if things don't improve.

The other meaning, 'future result of a present cause', is found with both personal and nonpersonal subjects:

> It'*s going to rain.*
> There'*s going to be* trouble.
> She'*s going to have* a baby.
> You'*re going to get* soaked.

Present progressive

4.16 The general meaning of the present progressive is 'future arising from present arrangement, plan, or programme':

The orchestra *is playing* a Mozart symphony after this.
The match *is starting* at 2.30 (tomorrow).
I'*m taking* the children to the zoo (next week).

Simple present

4.17 The future use of the simple present is frequent only in subordinate clauses:

What will you say if I *marry* the boss?
At this rate, the guests will be drunk before they *leave*.

In main clauses, the future use represents a marked future of unusual certainty, attributing to the future the degree of certainty one normally associates with the present and the past. For example, it is used for statements about the calendar:

Tomorrow *is* Thursday. School *finishes* on 21st March.

Also to describe immutable events:

When *is* high tide? What time *does* the match begin?

Like the present progressive, it is used with certain dynamic, transitional verbs (*eg*: *arrive*, *come*, *leave*; *cf* 4.11) to convey the meaning of plan or programme:

I *go*/*am going* on vacation next week.
The plane *takes* off/*is taking* off at 20:30 tonight.

It is also used with stative verbs to convey the same meaning, but the progressive is then not possible:

I'*m* on vacation next week.

Will/*shall*+ progressive

4.18 The construction of *will*/*shall* with the progressive may indicate a future period of time within which another situation occurs:

When you reach the end of the bridge, I'*ll be waiting* there to show you the way.

Another use denotes 'future as a matter of course'. (It avoids the interpretation of volition, intention, promise, etc, to which *will*, *shall*, and *be going to* are liable.)

We'*ll be flying* at 30,000 feet.

Spoken by the pilot of an aircraft to the passengers, the statement implies that 30,000 feet is the normal and expected altitude for the flight. This implication accounts for the use of the construction to convey greater tact than the nonprogressive with *will/shall*:

> When *will* you *be paying* back the money?

Be (about) to

4.19 *Be to* + infinitive is used to refer to a future arrangement or plan, a future requirement, and intention:

> Their daughter *is to be* married soon.
> There'*s to be* an official enquiry
> You *are to be* back by 10 o'clock. ['You are required to be . . .']
> If he'*s to succeed* in his new profession, he must try harder. ['If he intends to succeed . . .']

Be about to + infinitive simply expresses near future:

> The train *is about to leave.*
> I'*m about to read* your essay.

The negative *be not about to* 〈esp informal〉 may be paraphrased 'have no intention of' (*She's not about to complain*).

NOTE Futurity is often indicated by modals other than *will/shall*: *The weather may improve (tomorrow)*; *You must have dinner with us (soon)*. It is also indicated by semi-auxiliaries such as *be sure to, be bound to, be likely to*, and by full verbs such as *hope, intend, plan.*

Future time in the past

4.20 Most of the future constructions just discussed can be used in the past tense to describe something which is in the future when seen from a viewpoint in the past.

(a) MODAL VERB CONSTRUCTION with *would* 〈rare; literary narrative style〉

> The time was not far off when he *would* regret this decision.

(b) *BE GOING TO* + INFINITIVE (often with the sense of 'unfulfilled intention')

> You *were going to* give me your address. ['. . . but you didn't . . .']
> The police *were going to* charge her, but at last she persuaded them she was innocent.

(c) PAST PROGRESSIVE (arrangement predetermined in the past)

> I *was meeting* him in Bordeaux the next day.

(d) *BE TO* + INFINITIVE 〈formal〉; (i) = 'was destined to'; (ii) = 'arrangement'

(i) He *was* eventually *to* end up in the bankruptcy court.
(ii) The meeting *was to* be held the following week.

(e) BE ABOUT TO + INFINITIVE ('on the point of'; often with the sense of 'unfulfilled intention')

He *was about to* hit me.

Meanings of the modals

4.21 We distinguish two main kinds of meanings for modal auxiliaries:
(a) INTRINSIC modality (which includes 'permission', 'obligation', and 'volition') involves some intrinsic human control over events;
(b) EXTRINSIC modality (which includes 'possibility', 'necessity', and 'prediction') involves human judgment of what is or is not likely to happen.

Each of the modals has both intrinsic and extrinsic uses. In some instances there is an overlap of the two uses; for example, the *will* in sentences such as *I'll see you tomorrow then* can be said to combine the meanings of volition and prediction.

Most of the modals can be paired into present and past forms (*can/could, may/might, shall/should, will/would*). From the point of view of meaning, the past forms are often merely more tentative or more polite variants of the present forms (*cf* 4.32).

NOTE Various terms are used for these contrasts in modal meanings. Approximate synonyms for *intrinsic* are *deontic* and *root*; for *extrinsic* the common variant is *epistemic*.

Can/could

4.22 (a) POSSIBILITY

Even expert drivers *can* make mistakes. ['It is possible for even . . .']
Her performance was the best that *could* be hoped for.
If it's raining tomorrow, the sports *can* take place indoors. ['It will be possible for the sports to . . .']

(b) ABILITY

Can you remember where they live? ['Are you able to remember . . .']
Magda *could* speak three languages by the age of six.
They say Bill *can* cook better than his wife.

(c) PERMISSION

Can we borrow these books from the library? ['Are we allowed to . . .']

In those days only men *could* vote in elections.

In this sense, *can/could* is less formal than *may*, which has been favoured by prescriptive tradition.

May/might

4.23 (a) POSSIBILITY

We *may* never succeed. ['It is possible that we'll never succeed.']
You *may* be right. ['It is possible that you are right.']
There *might* be some complaints.

Here *may* denotes the possibility of a given proposition's being or becoming true.

(b) PERMISSION

You *may* borrow my bicycle if you wish. ['I permit you to borrow . . .']
Visitors *may* reclaim necessary travel expenses up to a limit of £50.
Might I ask whether you are using the typewriter?

As a permission auxiliary, *may* is more formal and less common than *can*, which (except in fixed phrases such as *if I may*) can be substituted for it.

NOTE In formal English, *may/might* is sometimes used in the same possibility sense as *can/could*:

During the autumn, many rare birds *may* be observed on the rocky northern coasts of the island.

May here is a more formal substitute for *can*, and the whole sentence could be paraphrased *It is possible to observe . . .*

Must

4.24 (a) (LOGICAL) NECESSITY

There *must* be some mistake.
You *must* be feeling tired.
The Smiths *must* have a lot of money.

The 'logical necessity' meaning of *must* is parallel to the possibility meaning of *may* since it implies that the speaker judges the proposition expressed by the clause to be necessarily true, or at least to have a high likelihood of being true. *Must* in this sense means that the speaker has drawn a conclusion from things already known or observed. *Must* [= logical necessity] cannot normally be used in interrogative or negative clauses. *Can* is generally used in place of *must* in questions, so that corresponding to *She must be the one you mean* is the question *Can she be the one you mean?* The negative of *can* [= possibility] fills the negative gap, so that *You must be joking* ['It is necessarily the case that you are joking'] is synonymous with *You can't be serious* ['It is impossible that you are serious']. Similarly:

She *must* be asleep = She *can't* be awake.

There is another necessity meaning of *must* in examples like:

To be healthy, a plant *must* receive a good supply of both sunshine and moisture. ['It is necessary for a plant to . . .']

(b) OBLIGATION *or* COMPULSION

You *must* be back by ten o'clock. ['You are obliged to be back . . .'; 'I require you to be back . . .']
We *must* all share our skills and knowledge.
Productivity *must* be improved, if the nation is to be prosperous.

In these examples, there is the implication, to a greater or lesser extent, that the speaker is advocating a certain form of behaviour. Thus *must*, unlike *have* (*got*) *to*, typically suggests that the speaker is exercising his authority.

Need, have (got) to

4.25 *Need* (constructed as an auxiliary *cf* 3.17) is used (esp in BrE) as the negative and question form of *must* in the sense 'necessary for':

Need they make all that noise? [= '*Do* they *need*/*have to* make all that noise?'] ⟨esp BrE⟩
You *needn't* worry about the test. [= 'You *don't need*/*have to* worry about that test'.] ⟨esp BrE⟩

As the above glosses show, however, it is possible, and indeed, more common even in BrE, to replace auxiliary *need* by *need to* or *have to* accompanied by *do*-support.

Have (*got*) *to* can also be substituted for *must* with little or no difference of meaning. Compare the following with the parallel sentences in 4.24:

(a) (LOGICAL) NECESSITY

There *has* (*got*) *to* be some mistake. ⟨esp AmE⟩
To be healthy, a plant *has* (*got*) *to* receive a good supply of both sunshine and moisture.

(b) OBLIGATION *or* COMPULSION

You *have* (*got*) *to* be back by ten o'clock.
We *have* all *got to* share our skills and knowledge.
Productivity will *have to* be improved, if the nation is to be prosperous.

Since *must* has no past tense form and no nonfinite forms, *have to* is used in many contexts where *must* is impossible, *eg* following a modal verb: *We'll have to be patient*.

Ought to, should

4.26 (a) TENTATIVE INFERENCE

The mountains $\left\{\begin{array}{l}\textit{should}\\ \textit{ought to}\end{array}\right\}$ be visible from here.

These plants $\left\{\begin{array}{l}\textit{should}\\ \textit{ought to}\end{array}\right\}$ reach maturity after five years.

The speaker does not know if his statement is true, but tentatively concludes that it is true, on the basis of whatever he knows.

(b) OBLIGATION

You $\left\{\begin{array}{l}\textit{should}\\ \textit{ought to}\end{array}\right\}$ do as he says.

The floor $\left\{\begin{array}{l}\textit{should}\\ \textit{ought to}\end{array}\right\}$ be washed at least once a week.

With the perfect aspect, *should* and *ought to* typically have the implication that the recommendation has *not* been carried out:

They $\left\{\begin{array}{l}\textit{should}\\ \textit{ought to}\end{array}\right\}$ have met her at the station.

The likely implication is '. . . but they didn't'. In both senses (a) and (b), *should* is more frequent than *ought to*.

NOTE *Ought to* and synonymous uses of *should* express the same basic modalities of 'necessity' and 'obligation' as do *must* and *have (got) to*. They contrast with *must* and *have (got) to* in not expressing the speaker's confidence in the occurrence of the event or state described. Hence [1] is nonsensical, but [2] is not:

*Sarah $\left\{\begin{array}{l}\textit{must}\\ \textit{has to}\end{array}\right\}$ be home by now, but she isn't. [1]

Sarah $\left\{\begin{array}{l}\textit{should}\\ \textit{ought to}\end{array}\right\}$ be home by now, but she isn't. [2]

Will / would ('ll / 'd)

4.27 (a) PREDICTION

1 The common FUTURE predictive sense of *will* in *You will* (or *You'll*) *feel better after this medicine* has been discussed in 4.14 and 4.18. The corresponding 'prediction in the past' sense of *would* is illustrated by:

I was told I *would* feel better after this medicine.

2 The PRESENT predictive sense of *will*, which is comparatively rare, is similar in meaning to *must* in the 'logical necessity' sense:

She *will* have had her dinner by now.
That'*ll* be the postman. [on hearing the doorbell ring]

3 The HABITUAL predictive meaning often occurs in conditional sentences:

> If litmus paper is dipped in acid, it *will* turn red.

or in timeless statements of 'predictability':

> Oil *will* float on water.

In addition, it occurs in descriptions of personal habits or characteristic behaviour:

> He'*ll* talk for hours, if you let him. [said of a chatterbox]
> She'*ll* sit on the floor quietly all day. She'*ll* just play with her toys, and you *won't* hear a murmur from her. [of a good baby]
> Every morning he *would* go for a long walk. [*ie* 'it was his custom to go . . .']

(b) VOLITION

1 INTENTION (often in combination with a sense of prediction)

> I'*ll* write as soon as I can.
> We *won't* stay longer than two hours.
> The manager said he *would* phone me after lunch.

2 WILLINGNESS

> *Will*/*Would* you help me to address these letters?
> I'*ll* do it, if you like.

This meaning is common in requests and offers. On the greater politeness of *would*, *cf* 4.32.

3 INSISTENCE

> If you '*will* go out without your overcoat, what can you expect?
> She '*would* keep interrupting me.

This somewhat rare use implies wilfulness on the part of the subject referent. The auxiliary is always stressed, and cannot be contracted to '*ll* or '*d*. In this case, the past form *would* expresses past time, rather than tentativeness or politeness.

Shall

4.28 *Shall* is in present-day English (especially in AmE) a rather rare auxiliary and only two uses, both with a 1st person subject, are generally current:

(a) PREDICTION (with 1st person subjects)

Shall is a substitute for the future use of *will* in formal style:

> According to the opinion polls, I $\left\{\begin{matrix} \textit{will} \\ \textit{shall} \end{matrix}\right\}$ win quite easily.

> When $\left\{\begin{matrix} \textit{will} \\ \textit{shall} \end{matrix}\right\}$ we know the results of the election?

Especially in BrE, prescriptive tradition forbids *will* as a future auxiliary with *I* or *we*, but this prescription is old-fashioned and is nowadays widely ignored.

(b) VOLITION (with 1st person subjects)

In the intentional sense, *shall* is again a formal (and traditionally prescribed) alternative to *will* after *I* or *we*:

> We {*will* / *shall*} uphold the wishes of the people.

In questions containing *Shall I/we*, *shall* consults the wishes of the addressee, and thus moves from a volitional towards an obligational meaning. It is suitable for making offers:

> *Shall* I/we deliver the goods to your home address? [= Do you want me/us to . . .?] [1]

and for making suggestions about shared activities:

> What *shall* we do this evening? *Shall* we go to the theatre? [2]

It is only in such questions that *shall* cannot regularly be replaced by *will*.

The past tense forms of the modals

'Past time' in indirect speech

4.29 The past tense modals *could*, *might*, *would*, and *should* are used quite regularly as past tense equivalents of *can*, *may*, *will*, and *shall* in indirect speech constructions (*cf* 14.21):

> You *can/may* do as you wish. [= permission]
> ~ She said we *could/might* do as we wished.
> It *may* rain later. [= possibility]
> ~ We were afraid that it *might* rain later.
> The plan *will* succeed. [= prediction]
> ~ I felt sure that the plan *would* succeed.

Must, together with *need* (as auxiliary), *ought to*, and *had better*, has no present/past distinction. These verbs are therefore unchanged in indirect speech constructions, even where they refer to past time.

'Past time' in other constructions

4.30 Outside indirect speech contexts, the behaviour of the past tense modal forms is less predictable. *Could* and *would* act as the 'past time' equivalents of *can* and *will*; but on the whole, *might* and *should* do not act as the 'past time' equivalents of *may* and *shall*.

(a) *CAN ~ COULD*

> There were no rules: we *could* do just what we wanted. [= permission]
> In those days, a transatlantic voyage *could* be dangerous. [= possibility]
> Few of the tourists *could* speak English. [= ability]

(b) *WILL ~ WOULD*

Later, he *would* learn his error. [= prediction]
The old lady *would* sit in front of the television continuously.
[= habitual prediction]
We tried to borrow a boat, but no one *would* lend us one.
[= willingness]
He '*would* leave the house in a muddle. [= insistence]

NOTE Outside indirect speech *would* is not used in the sense of intention; hence a sentence such as *He would meet me the next day* is almost inevitably interpreted as free indirect speech (*cf* 14.22).

Hypothetical meaning

4.31 The past tense modals can be used in the hypothetical sense of the past tense (*cf* 4.6) in both main and subordinate clauses. Compare:

If United *can* win this game, they *may* become league champions. [1]
If United *could* win this game, they *might* become league champions. [2]

Sentence [2], unlike [1], expresses a hypothetical condition; *ie* it conveys the speaker's expectation that United *will not* win the game, and therefore will *not* become league champions. For past hypothetical meaning (which normally has a contrary-to-fact interpretation), we have to add the perfect aspect:

If United *could have won* that game, they *might have become* league champions. [3]

The usual implication of this is that United did *not* win the game.

Tentativeness or politeness: *could, might, would*

4.32 (a) TENTATIVE PERMISSION (in polite requests):

Could I see your driving licence?
I wonder if I *might* borrow some coffee?

(b) TENTATIVE VOLITION (in polite requests):

Would you lend me a dollar? [more polite than *will*]
I'd be grateful if someone *would* hold the door open.

(c) TENTATIVE POSSIBILITY

1 in expressing a tentative opinion:

There *could* be something wrong with the light switch.
Of course, I *might* be wrong.

2 in polite directives and requests:

Could you (please) open the door?
You *could* answer these letters for me.

'Mood markers': *would* and *should*

4.33 (a) *WOULD/SHOULD* AS A MARKER OF HYPOTHETICAL MEANING

Would (and sometimes, with a 1st person subject, *should*) may express hypothetical meaning in main clauses (*cf* 14.12):

If you pressed that button, the engine *would* stop. [1]
If there were an accident, we *would/should* have to report it. [2]

Although the conditional sentence, as in [1] and [2], is the most typical context in which hypothetical *would/should* occurs, there are many other contexts in which hypothetical *would/should* is appropriately used:

I'*d* hate to lose this pen. [3]
It *would* be impossible to estimate how many crimes went undetected last year. [4]
Don't bother to read all these papers. It *would* take too long. [5]

In such sentences, there is often an implicit *if*...; for example, [5] could be expanded: *It would take too long if you did (try to read them all).*

(b) *SHOULD* AS A MARKER OF 'PUTATIVE' MEANING

In this use *should*+infinitive is often equivalent to the mandative subjunctive (*cf* 3.24). In using *should*, the speaker entertains, as it were, some 'putative' world, recognizing that it may well exist or come into existence (*cf* 4.14):

She insisted that we *should* stay.
It's unfair that so many people *should* lose their jobs.
Let me know if you *should* hear some more news.
Why *should* anyone object to her enjoying herself?
I can't think why he *should* have been so angry.

Putative *should* is more common in BrE than in AmE.

The modals with the perfect and progressive aspects

4.34 The perfect and progressive aspects are normally excluded when the modals express 'ability' or 'permission', and also when *shall* or *will* expresses 'volition'. These aspects are freely used, however, with extrinsic modal meanings other than ability; *eg*:

'possibility'	He *may/might have* miss*ed* the train.
	She *can't/couldn't be* swimm*ing* all day.
'necessity'	He *must have* lef*t* his umbrella on the bus.
	You *must be* dream*ing*.
'prediction' etc	The guests *will/would have* arriv*ed* by that time.
	Hussein *will/would* still *be* read*ing* his paper.

(On the meaning of the perfect aspect after a modal, and in particular the possibility of paraphrasing it by means of the simple past tense, *cf* 14.8 Note [e]).

'Obligation' can only be expressed with the perfect or progressive when combined with *should* or *ought to*:

'obligation' I *ought to be* work*ing* now. ['. . . but I'm not']
You *should have* finish*ed* it. ['. . . but you haven't']
She *shouldn't have* left him. ['. . . but she did']

The combination of both perfect and progressive constructions with the modals is also possible, subject to the conditions already mentioned:

You *must have been* dream*ing*.
She *could*n't *have been* swimm*ing* all day.
The guests *would have been* arriv*ing* by now.

Meaning in the nonfinite verb phrase

4.35 Nonfinite verb phrases do not accept modal auxiliaries, but the meanings of the modals can be expressed through the use of semi-auxiliaries, such as *have to*, *be (un)able to*, *be allowed to*, *be about to*:

I am sorry to *have to* repeat this warning.
Being unable to free himself, he lay beneath the debris until rescued.
The suspects admitted *being about to* commit a crime.
Many inmates hate not *being allowed to* leave the premises.

We have seen that the distinction between present and past tense does not apply to nonfinite verb phrases (*cf* 3.19). Although there are nonfinite perfect constructions, the meaning conveyed by the perfect in such constructions is simply time preceding some other time.

The full range of perfect and progressive aspect forms is only possible within an infinitive phrase:

Sir Topaz appears {
to be winning his race. [simple progressive]
to have won his race. [simple perfect]
to have been winning his race. [perfect progressive]

In an *-ing* participle phrase in adverbial clauses, the perfect/nonperfect contrast is sometimes available:

Eating a hearty breakfast, } we prepared for our long journey. [1]
Having eaten a hearty breakfast, } [2]

From [1], we understand that the eating and the preparation took place together, while from [2], we understand that the breakfast preceded the preparation.

But the progressive/nonprogressive contrast is not normally applicable here, since *-ing* participle phrases are incapable of expressing this distinction formally. Moreover, the *-ing* participle itself is not, in spite of its appearance, necessarily associated with the progressive:

> { *Being* an enemy of the Duke's,
> { *Realizing* he was in danger,
> { *Having* no news of his wife, } he left the court immediately. [3]

The participles in [3] are stative verbs, normally incompatible with the progressive.

Nevertheless, there are constructions in which the *-ing* participle construction has aspect contrast with the infinitive, and is progressive in meaning (*cf* 16.28*f*):

> I { saw / heard } them { *shoot* at him. / *shooting* at him. }

Whereas the infinitive *shoot* suggests a single shot, the *-ing* participle suggests a repetitive action lasting over a period of time, in accordance with the interpretation of the progressive aspect in finite verb phrases referring to momentary events. In:

> I watched them { *climb* the tower. [4]
> I watched them { *climbing* the tower. [5]

the infinitive *climb* suggests that they reached the top of the tower, whereas the participle *climbing* leaves open the possibility that the action was not completed.

The *-ed* participle phrase has no formal contrasts of aspect, and is therefore the most restricted type of phrase in terms of semantic contrasts. Here again, however, there is a potential contrast with the passive *-ing* participle phrase:

> I saw the tower { *climbed* by a student. [6]
> I saw the tower { *being climbed* by a student. [7]

The participle *climbed* in [6] is the passive counterpart of the infinitive *climb* in [4]; it describes the climb as a completed event, whereas *being climbed* in [7] describes it as in progress, and as possibly incomplete. Compare also the perfect passive *-ing* participle phrase in *Having been reprimanded, I . . .*

Bibliographical note

General treatments of the meaning and use of verb constructions: Leech (1987); Palmer (1988).

On tense and aspect in general, see Lyons (1977, vol. 2); Schopf (1987, 1989).

On the perfective aspect, see McCoard (1978).

On stative, agentive, and other classes of verb meaning, see Bache (1982); Cruse (1973); Jacobson (1980); Vendler (1957).

On expression of future time, see Wekker (1976).

On modal meanings in general, see Coates (1983); Hermerén (1978); Johannesson (1976); Leech and Coates (1980); Lyons (1977, vol. 2); Palmer (1979).

5 Nouns and determiners

5.1 **Nouns fall into different classes as shown in Fig 5.1.**

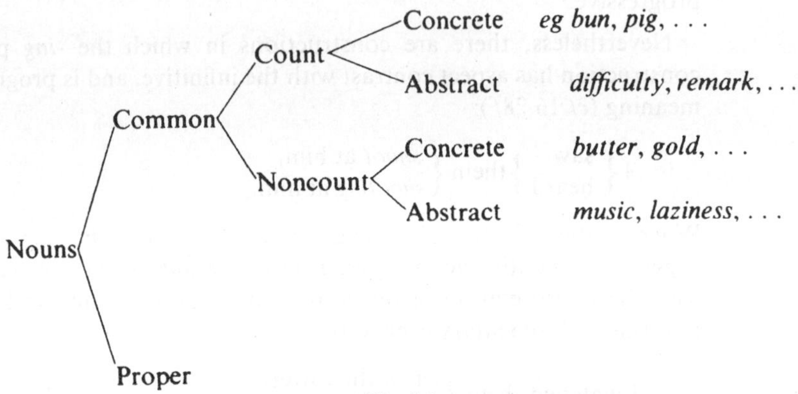

Fig 5.1

The distinction between *concrete* (accessible to the senses, observable, measurable, etc) and *abstract* (typically nonobservable and nonmeasurable) is important semantically. Of more relevance to *grammar*, however, is the distinction between *proper* and *common* nouns. Since the former have unique reference (*cf* 5.25*ff*), determiner and number contrast cannot occur: **the Indonesia*, **some Chicagos*. Contrast with common nouns *the butter, some difficulties*. But among nouns, we have the further distinction between *count* (also called 'countable') and *noncount* (also called 'mass') nouns. Like the distinction between proper and common, we have here a difference that has both semantic and grammatical significance, since count and noncount nouns permit a different range of determiners. In Table 5.1, we display the various determiner constraints as they affect the

***Table* 5.1**

	PROPER	COMMON		
		COUNT	NONCOUNT	COUNT or NONCOUNT
(a)	Freda	*book	music	brick
(b)	*the Freda	the book	the music	the brick
(c)	*a Freda	a book	*a music	a brick
(d)	*some Freda	*some book	some music	some brick
(e)	*Fredas	books	*musics	bricks

classes of nouns, the fourth column showing that some common nouns can be used as both count and noncount. Thus nouns like *cake* or *brick* can refer either to the substance (noncount) or to units made of the substance (count). The lines (a)–(e) represent different determiner constraints: Can the singular noun occur (a) without a determiner? (b) with the definite article? (c) with the indefinite article? (d) with the partitive *some*, /səm/? Can the plural noun occur (e) without a determiner?

NOTE [a] On apparent exceptions like '*The Chicago* of my youth', see 5.26*f*.
[b] The absence of article in *I like Freda* and *I like music* makes the two nouns only superficially similar; in the former there is *no article* where in the latter there is *zero article* which can contrast with *the*. Compare

*I like *Freda*, but *the Freda* this evening is boring.
I like *music*, but *the music* this evening is boring.

But *cf* 5.22*f*.

Partitive constructions

5.2 Both count and noncount nouns can enter constructions denoting part of a whole. Such partitive expressions may relate to (a) quantity or (b) quality, and in either case the partition may be singular or plural. It thus affords a means of imposing number on noncount nouns, since the partition is generally expressed by a count noun of partitive meaning (such as *piece* or *sort*, which can be singular or plural), followed by an *of*-phrase.

(a) QUANTITY PARTITION

(i) Of noncount nouns; *eg*:

a *piece of* cake	two *pieces of* cake
an *item of* clothing	several *items of* clothing

These partitives (as also the informal *bit*) can be used very generally, but with some nouns specific partitives occur; *eg*:

a *blade of* grass
some *specks of* dust
two *slices of* meat/bread/cake

(ii) Of plural count nouns; here we tend to have partitives relating to specific sets of nouns; *eg*:

a *flock of* sheep/pigeons	a *series of* concerts/lectures
two *flocks of* sheep/pigeons	two *series of* concerts/lectures

(iii) Of singular count nouns; *eg*:

a *piece of* a leather belt	two *pieces of* a broken cup
a *page of* a book	two *acts of* a play

(b) QUALITY PARTITION is expressed most commonly with *kind* and *sort*; *eg*:

count	a new *kind of* computer	several new *kinds of* computer(s)
	one *sort of* silk tie	two *sorts of* silk tie(s)
noncount	a delicious *kind of* bread	some delicious *kinds of* bread
	a fashionable *sort of* wallpaper	fashionable *sorts of* wallpaper

Other quality partitives include *type*, *variety*, and (especially with such materials as coffee or tobacco) *blend*.

NOTE [a] Both quantity and quality partition may be expressed by treating the noun itself as though it expressed a quantity or quality. Thus a noncount noun can be given count characteristics and *two coffees* may in appropriate contexts mean either 'two *cups of* coffee' or 'two *types of* coffee'.

[b] Quantity partitives may be expressions of precise measure; *eg* a *yard of* cloth, two *kilos of* potatoes. There can also be fractional partition and this may cooccur with normal quantity partition, as in 'He ate a *quarter of* that (*joint of*) beef'.

[c] Since there is no necessary connection between countability and referential meaning, many English nouns can simulate the plural only by partitive constructions where their translation equivalents in some other languages are count nouns with singular and plural forms. *Eg*:

some information ~ some *pieces of* information
his anger ~ his *bursts of* anger

Determiners

5.3 In actual usage, nouns appear in *noun phrases* (Chapter 17), and the kind of reference such a noun phrase has depends on the accompanying DETERMINER. We distinguish three classes of determiners, set up on the basis of their position in the noun phrase in relation to each other:

Central determiners (*eg*: *the*, *a*, *this*)
Predeterminers (*eg*: *half*, *all*, *double*; as in *all the people*)
Postdeterminers (*eg*: *seven*, *many*, *few*; as in *the many passengers*)

Central determiners

the, *a*, and zero

5.4 The definite and indefinite articles are the commonest central determiners and, as we saw in 5.1, their distribution is dependent upon the class of the accompanying noun. Relating definiteness to number, we have the following system for count and noncount nouns:

		COUNT	NONCOUNT
SINGULAR	definite	the book	the music
	indefinite	a book	music
PLURAL	definite	the books	
	indefinite	books	

Beside the sole definite article *the*, we thus have two indefinite articles *a* and zero, the former occurring with singular count nouns, its zero analogue with noncount and plural count nouns. Both *the* and *a* have a different form when the following word begins with a vowel, though *the* does not display this difference in writing:

> *the bird* [ðə] ~ *the owl* [ði]
> *a bird* [ə] ~ *an owl* [ən]

The use of the articles is examined in 5.11*ff*.

NOTE [a] The indefinite article *a/an* can be regarded as an unstressed numeral *one*; *cf one or two pounds* ~ *a pound or two*.

[b] With nouns beginning with *h*, the prevocalic forms are used if this is not pronounced:

> [ði] *honour* *an hour*

Thus for those who do not pronounce *h* before unstressed syllables a difference is observed between such pairs as '*history* and *hi'storical*:

> *a history book* ~ *an historical novel*

[c] When the articles are stressed for any reason (as for example in slow speech and especially in AmE), they are pronounced [ði], [ei], [æn].

5.5 Like the definite article, there are several other determiners that can cooccur equally with singular count, plural count, and noncount nouns.

(a) The DEMONSTRATIVES *this* and *that* (with noncount and singular count nouns), *these* and *those* (with plural count nouns):

> I prefer *this* picture/music to *that* (picture/music).
> *These* desks are imported but *those* tables are made locally.

(b) The POSSESSIVES *my*, *our*, *your*, *his*, *her*, *its*, *their*:

> I admire *her* house/*her* books/*her* taste.

(c) The *wh*-determiners *which*, *whose*, *whichever*, *whatever*, *whosever*, whether as relatives, indefinite relatives, or interrogatives:

Please come at noon, by *which* time I shall be back in my office.
The woman *whose* book you reviewed is on TV tonight.
They will disapprove of *whatever* music is played.
Which house do you prefer?
What time is it?

(d) The NEGATIVE DETERMINER *no*:

He has *no* car/*no* children/*no* concentration.

All these determiners (sometimes with a modification of form as in *theirs*, *none*) have a pronominal role as well, and they will be treated in more detail below (6.16*ff*).

Like the indefinite article, there are determiners that cooccur only with singular count nouns.

(a) The UNIVERSAL DETERMINERS *every* and *each*.

We need to interview *every/each* student separately.

(b) The NONASSERTIVE DUAL DETERMINER *either*:

There is no parking permitted on *either* side of the street.

(c) The NEGATIVE DUAL DETERMINER *neither*:

Parking is permitted on *neither* side of the street.

5.6 Like the zero article, there are determiners that cooccur only with noncount nouns and plural count nouns:

(a) The GENERAL ASSERTIVE DETERMINER *some* [səm]:

I would like *some* bread/*some* rolls, please.

(b) The GENERAL NONASSERTIVE DETERMINER *any*:

We haven't *any* bread/*any* rolls left.

(c) The QUANTITATIVE DETERMINER *enough*:

We have *enough* equipment/*enough* tools for the job.

These determiners will be discussed in more detail when we come to their pronominal functions (6.25*f*).

NOTE **[a]** When stressed in some circumstances, *any* can occur with singular count nouns, as in 'She will consider "*any* offer – however small'.

[b] A stressed form of *some* [sʌm] is used with the meaning of strong indefiniteness ('one unidentified, a certain') and this has the same distribution potential as items in 5.4:

You will win *some* day; *some* days she feels better; I found *some* stranger waiting for me; they are playing *some* peculiar music that no one has heard before.

Predeterminers

5.7 Predeterminers form a class in generally being mutually exclusive, preceding those central determiners with which they can cooccur, and in having to do with quantification. It is useful to distinguish two subsets:

(a) *all, both, half*

(b) the multipliers

NOTE The items *such* and *what* are exceptional in referring to quality rather than quantity ('*what* a day we had; I can't remember *such* a time') and this accounts for combinations like *all such*.

All, both, half

5.8 These have in common the positive characteristic of being able to occur before the articles, the demonstratives, and the possessives:

$$\left\{\begin{matrix} \textit{all} \\ \textit{both} \\ \textit{half} \end{matrix}\right\} \left\{\begin{matrix} \textit{the} \\ \textit{these} \\ \textit{our} \end{matrix}\right\} \textit{students}$$

They also have the negative characteristic of not occurring before determiners that themselves entail quantification: *every, each, (n)either, some, any, no, enough*. Beyond these generalizations, their occurrence needs to be described on an individual basis:

ALL occurs with plural count nouns and with noncount nouns, as in

all the books	all the music
all books	all music

BOTH occurs with plural count nouns, as in

both the books both books

HALF occurs with singular and plural count nouns and with noncount nouns, as in

half the book(s)	half the music
half a book	(*but* *half music)

NOTE [a] As well as being predeterminers, *all, both* and *half* can, like demonstratives, be used pronominally:

$$\left\{\begin{matrix} \textit{All} \\ \textit{Both} \\ \textit{Half} \end{matrix}\right\} \text{the students sat for their exam} \left\{\begin{matrix} \text{and} \left\{\begin{matrix} \textit{all} \\ \textit{both} \end{matrix}\right\} \text{passed.} \\ \text{but} \quad \textit{half} \quad \text{failed.} \end{matrix}\right.$$

They can also be followed by an *of*-phrase:

All/Both/Half of the students . . .

Moreover, *all* and *both* may appear at the adverbial *M* position (after the operator: 8.11), as in:

The students {*all* / *both*} sat for the exam.

The students were {*all* / *both*} sitting for the exam.

[b] Since *half* may modify a following noun as an *ad hoc* or institutionalized compound, we can have pairs such as *half an hour* and *a half hour* (where there is little difference of meaning) or *half a bottle of wine* (half of the contents) and *a half bottle of wine* (a small bottle holding half the contents of an ordinary bottle).
[c] Fractions other than *half* are usually followed by an *of*-phrase and must normally be preceded by a numeral or the indefinite article. Compare:

> She read *half* the book.
>
> She read {*a quarter* / *three quarters*} of the book.

But, especially with *time*, *distance*, *height*, we sometimes find fractions used as predeterminers:

> He was given six months for the work but he finished in *two-thirds* the time.

5.9 The MULTIPLIERS have two uses as predeterminers. When the following determiner is the definite article, demonstrative or possessive, the multiplier applies to the noun so determined:

> *twice/double* the length ('a length twice as great')
> *three times* her salary ('a salary three times as large')

When the following determiner is the indefinite article or *each* or *every*, the multiplier applies to a measure (such as frequency) set against the unit specified by the following noun:

> *once* a day
> *twice* each game
> *four times* every year

NOTE We can compare expressions of costing:

> Oil then cost only *fifteen dollars* a barrel.
> Her salary is *ten thousand yen* a/per month.

Postdeterminers

5.10 Postdeterminers take their place immediately after determiners just as predeterminers take their place immediately before determiners. Compare:

> Predeterminer: *Both* the young women were successful.
> Postdeterminer: The *two* young women were successful.

With zero determiner, of course, the distinction is neutralized:

Both young women were successful.
Two young women were successful.

Postdeterminers fall into two classes:
(a) ordinals, such as *first*, *fourth*, *last*, *other*;
(b) quantifiers, such as *seven*, *ninety*, *many*, *few*, *plenty of*, *a lot of*.
Where they can cooccur, items from (a) usually precede items from (b); for example:

the *first two* poems
my *last few* possessions
her *other many* accomplishments

Among the (b) items, there are two important distinctions involving *few* and *little*. First, *few* occurs only with plural count nouns, *little* only with noncount nouns. Second, when preceded by *a*, each has a positive meaning; without *a*, each has a negative meaning. Thus:

I play *a few* games (*ie* 'several').
I play *few* games (*ie* 'hardly any').
She ate *a little* bread (*ie* 'some').
She ate *little* bread (*ie* 'hardly any').

We should note also a contrast involving assertive and nonassertive usage (2.11). Some items are predominantly *assertive* (such as *plenty of*, *a few*, *a little*, *a good many*), while others are predominantly *nonassertive* (such as *much*, *many*):

We need *plenty of* time.
~We don't need *much* time.
She has written *a good many* poems.
~She hasn't written *many* poems.

The articles in specific reference

The definite article

5.11 The article *the* marks a noun phrase as *definite*: that is, as referring to something which can be identified uniquely in the contextual or general knowledge shared by speaker and hearer. Such shared knowledge is partly a knowledge of the world and partly a knowledge of English grammar, as we shall see in 5.12–14.

5.12 Where the use of *the* depends on shared knowledge of the world, we may speak of SITUATIONAL REFERENCE, and this is of two kinds. We first distinguish *the* used in connection with the IMMEDIATE situation:

Do you see *the* bird sitting on *the* lower branch?
Oh dear! *The* stain hasn't come out of *the* carpet.

In such cases, the identity of the particular bird, branch, stain, and carpet is obvious because they are physically present and visible. But the reference might be obvious because the situational reference was in the minds of speaker and listener:

When *the* policeman had gone, I remembered that I hadn't told him about *the* damaged window-pane.

Secondly, we have the LARGER situation, where identification of the reference depends on assumptions about general knowledge more than on the specific experience of the particular speaker and listener:

I do most of my travelling by overnight train, and of course in *the* dark one has no idea of what *the* countryside looks like.

So also with reference to *the Pope*, *the President*, *the government*, *the Equator*, *the stars*; and as we see in these examples, the shared assumption of *uniqueness* in reference is often matched by use of an initial capital in writing. *Cf* 5.25*ff*.

NOTE The same phrase may involve *the* with immediate or larger situational reference:

Would *the* children like to go out and play?
When we design schools, do we ask ourselves what *the* children would like?

As with the latter example, larger situational reference often overlaps with generic use: *cf* 5.22*ff*.

5.13 Special cases of the larger situation occur with the use of *the* for SPORADIC reference and for reference to the BODY. In *sporadic* reference, we promote to institutional status a phenomenon of common experience. Thus in contrast to the particular newspaper that a particular individual buys, or the particular theatre that stands in a particular street, we may use *the paper* or *the theatre* more broadly:

You'll probably see it in *the paper* tomorrow.
I like to go to *the theatre* about once a month.

Cf also:

She's not on *the* telephone yet, though she may have one installed soon.
I won't come by car; I'll take *the* train.
Everyone would sleep better with *the* windows open.

With reference to parts of the body, *the* is often used in prepositional phrases instead of a possessive such as *my* or *her*:

I grabbed him by *the* arm.
She banged herself on *the* forehead.

He has a fracture of *the* collarbone.
The child has a pain in *the* chest.

In medical usage, *the* can replace a possessive without the body part or function being in a prepositional phrase; thus (doctor to patient):

How is the chest now? Has the breathing been affected?

5.14 The use of *the* may be determined by *logical* and *grammatical* factors. The uniqueness of a referent may be recognized not by general knowledge of the world but be logically imposed by meaning. Nouns premodified by superlatives, ordinals and similar restrictive items such as *sole* will thus be made logically unique:

When is *the* next flight?
She was *the* sole survivor.
They judged him to be *the* most original painter.

Grammatical determination is of two kinds:

(a) *Anaphoric* reference, where *the* indicates identity of reference with that established earlier in the discourse:

Fred bought a radio and a video-recorder, but he returned *the* radio.

Here the anaphora is 'direct'; but anaphoric reference may be 'indirect', requiring some support from general knowledge:

When she tried to open her front door, she couldn't get *the* key into *the* lock.

Here the two definite articles are correctly interpreted as grammatically anaphoric only because we know that a front door has a lock, and opening one involves using a key.

(b) *Cataphoric* reference, where *the* indicates that the identity of the reference will be established by what follows:

I am trying to find *the* book that I wanted to show you.

Here, *the* is only justified by the addressee knowing that the speaker had planned to show him or her a book. Similarly, in

How did you get *the* (= 'that') mud on your coat?

there is the presumption that the addressee knows there is mud on the coat. Contrast:

Do you know that you have { **the* mud / mud } on your coat?

The indefinite article

5.15 In contrast to *the*, an indefinite article is used when a reference cannot be regarded as uniquely identifiable from the shared knowledge of speaker and addressee:

I am just about to move into *an* apartment quite near where you live.

Contrast the uniquely identifiable apartment which justifies the cataphoric *the* in:

I am just about to move into *the* apartment directly above yours.

The indefinite article is commonly associated with 'first mention' of an item with which anaphoric *the* would be used in subsequent mention:

Her house was burgled and she lost *a* camera, *a* radio, and *a* purse – though fortunately *the* purse contained very little money and *the* camera was insured.

NOTE [a] Body parts which are multiple can be individually referred to with the indefinite article:

Jack has broken *a* finger/*a* rib.

but

Jack has bumped *his* head.

[b] While identical noun phrases with *the* are taken to be coreferential, this is not the case when the article is indefinite:

Mary bought *the* camera from her sister and she has now sold *the* camera to me. [1]
Mary bought *a* camera last week and sold *a* camera this week. [2]

In [1], only one camera is involved; in [2], the presumption is that reference is made to two different cameras.
[c] Note also the use of zero with complements of some verbs:

She turned linguist. ~ She became a linguist.
They made him chairman.

The indefinite article and the numeral *one*

5.16 We often use the indefinite article in ways that reflect its origin as an unstressed variant of the numeral. In such cases, *one* could replace *a*/*an* with only a slight implication of greater emphasis:

Our neighbours have two daughters and $\left\{\begin{array}{l} \textit{a} \\ \textit{one} \end{array}\right\}$ son.

This cost $\left\{\begin{array}{l} \textit{a} \\ \textit{one} \end{array}\right\}$ pound/ $\left\{\begin{array}{l} \textit{a} \\ \textit{one} \end{array}\right\}$ hundred/thousand/million pounds.

Compare also variant phrases in which *one* is used when a conjunction follows:

We walked for $\left\{\begin{array}{l} \textit{a} \text{ mile or two.} \\ \textit{one} \text{ or two miles.} \end{array}\right.$

The water is only $\left\{\begin{array}{l} \textit{a} \text{ foot and a half deep.} \\ \textit{one} \text{ and a half feet deep.} \end{array}\right.$

NOTE In phrases of measure like 'half *an* hour', 'ten dollars *a* day', the numerical function cannot be fulfilled by *one* without expansion and recasting: 'ten dollars for *one* day'.

The zero article

Zero article and *some/any*

5.17 With noncount and plural count nouns, the role of indefinite article is fulfilled by either zero or (where quantification is to be expressed) *some* or its nonassertive (2.11) analogue *any*.

> Do you know what {*a* boysenberry looks like? / boysenberries look like?}
>
> She bought her son {*an* apple. / *some* apples.}
>
> I like milk with my coffee.
>
> I would like *some* milk with my coffee, please.
>
> He hasn't bought *any* books for years, whereas she spends half her salary on books.
>
> She has men as well as women on her staff.

If we inserted *some* before both *men* and *women* in this last sentence, there would be little difference in meaning. But if we inserted *some* before one and not before the other, it would give the impression that this indicated the minority:

> She has men as well as *some* women on her staff.

But the greater generality of zero as compared with *some* must not lead us to confound this general use of zero with the *generic* use which we shall consider in 5.22. Compare:

> Quantitative: *Some* coffee will calm this nervousness of yours.
> General: Coffee can be bought almost anywhere.
> Generic: Coffee is a common stimulant.

Zero article with definite meaning

5.18 Despite its widespread correspondence to the indefinite article, the zero article can, conversely, be used in ways that closely resemble the definite article. This is notably so where a phrase specifies a unique role or task. In the following examples, the parenthesized *the* could be present or absent with very little difference of meaning:

> Maureen is (*the*) *captain of netball* this year.
>
> As (*the*) *chairman*, I must rule you out of order.
>
> The speaker will be Mr Watanabe, (*the*) *author of a recent book on international affairs* and of course (*the*) *presenter of several TV talk shows*.
>
> Although she declined the position of *director*, she accepted the role of *unofficial adviser*.

NOTE **[a]** We should note also the contrast between restrictive and nonrestrictive apposition (17.27):

> Prime Minister Gandhi ~ *the* Prime Minister, Mr Rajiv Gandhi

[b] In institutional usage, zero replaces *the* in a way that implies proper-name status for an item:

> Council will consider this in due course ~ *The* Council will . . .

[c] Articles are usually omitted in headlines ('Crew deserts ship in harbour') and on official forms ('Please state reason for application and give names of two supporters').

5.19 Analogous to the use of *the* with sporadic reference (5.13), we have zero with implication of definite rather than indefinite meaning. This is especially so with idiomatically institutionalized expressions relating to common experience.

(a) *Quasi-locatives* (where a particular activity or role in connection with the location is implied):

be in / go to	town	beside	*The* town is very old.
	bed		It's on *the* bed.
	church		How far is *the* church?
	prison		Don't stop near *the* prison.
be at, go	home		This was *the* home of a financier.
go to	sea		*The* sea looks calm.
	college		She drove to *the* college.

Frequently there is a distinction in meaning between zero and *the*; thus *on stage* will usually refer to a play or participant in current theatrical production, while *on the stage* refers to literal physical location or is an idiom denoting the acting profession: 'She was a teacher but now she's on the stage.' Again, there are distinctions in meaning between AmE and BrE; thus *in school* would be used in AmE for the state of being a school pupil (BrE *at school*) but in BrE it would refer merely to being inside the building; *in the hospital* in AmE is used of a patient (BrE *in hospital*) but in BrE denotes physical location.

(b) *Transport and communication*: when *by* precedes the mode in question, zero occurs:

travel / come / go	by	bicycle	beside	*The* bicycle was damaged.
		bus		She was on *the* bus.
		train		Should we take *the* train?
		car		etc
		plane		
send it by		telex		
		post ⟨esp BrE⟩		*The* post/mail is late today.
		mail ⟨esp AmE⟩		*The* satellite is a new one.
		satellite		

Cf also: 'The message came *by hand/by special delivery*'.

(c) *Time expressions*: zero is common, especially after the prepositions *at*, *by*, *after*, *before*:

at dawn/daybreak/sunset/night
by morning/evening ('when morning/evening came')
by day/night ('during')
after dark/nightfall
before dawn/dusk

Cf also '(They worked) day and night', 'It's almost dawn', 'I'll be travelling all night/week/month'.

In less stereotyped expressions, *the* is used, as in '*The* sunrise was beautiful', 'I'll rest during *the* evening', 'Can you stay for *the* night?'

With *in*, seasons may also have zero, unless a particular one is meant:

In winter/spring/autumn (*but AmE* in *the* fall), I like to have a break in Switzerland.
This year I am going to Switzerland in *the* winter/spring/autumn.

(d) *Meals*: as with seasons, zero is usual unless reference is being made to a particular one:

What time do you normally have breakfast/lunch/supper?
(The) breakfast/lunch/dinner was served late that day.

(e) *Illness*: zero is normal, especially where the illness bears a technical medical name:

She has anaemia/cancer/diabetes/influenza/pneumonia/toothache.

But *the* is also used for afflictions less technically designated:

She had (*the*) flu/hiccups/measles/mumps.

Some conditions call for the indefinite article:

a cold (*but* catch cold), *a* fever, *a* headache, *a* temperature

Fixed phrases

5.20 We noted of several expressions in 5.19 that zero corresponded to a certain idiomatic fixity as compared with analogous expressions using *the*. Fixity is particularly notable with some common prepositional phrases and complex prepositions (9.3):

on foot, in step, out of step, in turn, by heart, in case of, by reason of, with intent to

Zero is characteristic of binomial expressions used adverbially:

They walked arm in arm/hand in hand/mile after mile/day in, day out.

We stood face to face/side by side/back to back.

Cf also *inch by inch, eye to eye, turn and turn about, man to man, from beginning to end, from father to son.*

NOTE Not all binomials with zero are adverbials, but when they are not, articles are usually optional:

I am glad to say that (the) mother and (the) child are both doing well.
The crash resulted in the death of (both) (a) father and (a) son.

Article usage with abstract nouns

5.21 Abstract nouns tend to be *count* when they refer to unitary phenomena such as events and *noncount* when they refer to activities, states, and qualities.

Typically count: *meeting, arrival, discovery*
Genuine *discoveries* are rarer than gradual *improvements.*
Typically noncount: *employment, happiness, sleep, swimming*
Sleep is necessary for good *health.*

But as we saw in 5.1, some nouns can be both noncount and count; compare:

Every child needs to be treated with *kindness.*

He did me { *a (great) kindness* that day. / *many kindnesses* over the years. }

They hoped that { *revolution* / *a revolution* } would improve their conditions.

She is studying *European history.*
The country has *a troubled history.*

It will be seen from these examples that the effect of the indefinite article is partitive and that this can be qualitative (*a troubled history*) or quantitative (*a great kindness*). *Cf* 5.2. The partitive effect is often accompanied by modification of the noun:

This ten-year-old plays the oboe with { *sensitivity.* / *a striking sensitivity.* / **a sensitivity.* }

NOTE Names of languages usually have zero article:

She speaks *Japanese* quite fluently.
How do you say this in *Italian*?

But in some expressions, *the* can be used:

Beckett's works in *English* have often been translated from *(the) French.*

And the indefinite article can be used for qualitative partition:

She speaks *a tolerable French.*

The articles in generic reference

5.22 Consider the following sentences:

> My neighbour apparently has *dogs*; I hear them barking at night.
> *Dogs* make admirable companions for children and adults alike.

In the former the reference is *specific* to particular dogs. In the latter the reference is *generic*: the sentence speaks not of particular dogs but of the whole class of dogs. All three types of article can be used to make a generic reference: *the* usually, and *a/an* always, with singular count nouns; zero with plural count nouns and with noncount nouns. For example:

> *The car* }
> *A car* } became an increasing necessity of life in the twentieth century.
> *Cars* }
>
> *Velvet* is an excellent material for curtains.

In fact, however, the three article modes are on a very different footing, with zero by far the most natural way of expressing the generic, irrespective of the function or position of the noun phrase in sentence structure:

> *Research* is vital for *human progress*.
> Many professors prefer *research* to *teaching*.
> *Crime* is often attributable to *drugs*.
> *Horses* are still *wild animals* in some parts of the world.

Exceptionally, some count nouns function as noncount generics in this way:

> Mary is studying *dance* as well as *film*.
> When *man* meets *woman*, a certain tension seems natural.

But more usually when *man* occurs with zero it is generic for *humanity* (a usage resisted on grounds of sexism):

> Nuclear warfare would jeopardize the survival of *man*.

5.23 By contrast, the indefinite article has a distinctly limited role in conveying generic meaning, since it tends in non-referring use to carry a general partitive implication (such that *a* means 'any') which may in certain contexts be merely *tantamount* to a generic. The limitations on generic implication can be seen in comparing the following examples:

> *Tigers* run }
> *A tiger* runs } more gracefully than most animals.
>
> *Tigers* are }
> **A tiger* is } becoming extinct.

NOTE The foregoing reflects the strong association of the indefinite article (and zero) with a descriptive and hence non-referring role in such functions as grammatical complement:

Paganini was *a* great violinist.
My daughter is training as *a* radiologist.
When were you appointed (as) (*a*) professor?
My book will be on Jung as (*a*) thinker.

5.24 The DEFINITE ARTICLE with *singular* nouns conveys a rather formal tone in generic use:

No one can say with certainty when *the wheel* was invented.
My work on anatomy is focused on *the lung*.

But in more general use we find *the* used with musical instruments and dances:

Marianne plays *the* harp, frequently accompanied by her brother on *the* piano.
Do you remember when everyone was keen on *the* rumba?

When the noun is meant, however, to represent a class of human beings by such a typical specimen, *the* often sounds inappropriate and artificial:

? As *the* child grows, there is always a rapid extension of vocabulary.
? *The* Welshman is a good singer.

With *plural* nouns, *the* is used to express generic meaning:
(a) where the referent is a national or ethnic group, as in *the Chinese*, *the Russians*;
(b) in phrases comprising an adjective head with human reference: *the blind*, *the affluent*, *the unemployed*.

It could be argued, however, that in neither case are the noun phrases so much generic as collective phrases with unique and specific denotation.

NOTE Nationality names that have distinct singular and plural forms (such as *Frenchman*, *Frenchmen*; *German*, *Germans*) are treated differently in respect of generic and collective statements from those which do not (such as *British*, *Swiss*, *Chinese*):

The Welsh are fond of singing.	[generic]
Welshmen are fond of singing.	[generic]
The Welshman is fond of singing.	[generic or specific]
The Welshmen are fond of singing.	[specific]
*Welsh is are fond of singing.	

On nationality names, see further 5.33*f*.

Proper nouns

5.25 Proper nouns are basically *names*, by which we understand the designation of specific people (*Gorbachev*), places (*Tokyo*, *Park Lane*) and institutions (*The South China Morning Post*, *Thames Polytechnic*). But as can be seen from these examples, names embrace both single-word nouns (*Tokyo*) and quite lengthy phrases, often incorporating a definite article as part of the name with or without premodifying items (*The Hague*, *The (New York) Times*). Moreover, the concept of name extends to some markers of time and to seasons that are also festivals (*Monday*, *March*, *Easter*, *Passover*, *Ramadan*).

NOTE Names reflect their uniqueness of reference in writing by our use of initial capitals. This device enables us, if we so wish, to raise to the uniqueness of proper-noun status such concepts as *Fate* and *Heaven*, including generics such as *Nature*, *Truth*, *Man*.

Grammatical features

5.26 As we saw in 5.1, proper nouns of their nature exclude such features as determiner and number contrast. Likewise, the transparent elements of phrasal names are treated as parts of a unique whole and are grammatically invariant:

> *The New*er* York Times
> *The *thoroughly* Asian Wall Street Journal

But there are many apparent exceptions to these restrictions. Since it is only the *referent* that is unique, and different referents may share the same name, the nouns or phrases conveying the name can be used as though they were common nouns. Thus if we can say

> There are several places called *Richmond*.

we can equally say

> There is *a Richmond* in the south of England and *a Richmond* in the north, not to mention a dozen *Richmonds* outside the British Isles.

So too:

> I'm trying to find *Philip Johnson* in the phone book but unless he's one of the several *P. Johnsons* he's not in.

The situation is very different with the admission of number and determination with the names of days, months, and festivals. These derive their proximity to uniqueness largely in respect of specific instances. Thus in

> She'll be here on *Monday*/in *October*/at *Christmas*.

the reference in each case is to a particular time of a particular year; *Monday* is as uniquely contrasted with *Tuesday* as *Tokyo* is with *Kyoto*. But we know that there is a Monday every week and a Christmas every year, that the former is characterized by being (for example) the first working day of each week and that every Christmas has even more sharply defined characteristics. In other words, *Mondays* necessarily have something in common, whereas the various *Richmonds* do not. So when we say

She's always here on (*a*) *Monday*/in *October*/at *Christmas*.

the items no longer have specific reference, and the sentence can be paralleled with

She always spends her *Mondays*/*Octobers*/*Christmases* here.

There are of course no analogies with names of persons, places and institutions:

* *Richmonds* are always splendid for a vacation.

5.27 On the other hand, it is not only the fact that several places or people may bear the same name that permits determination, number contrast or modification. We have the informal convention that a married couple, Mr and Mrs Johnson, can be referred to as *the Johnsons* (a designation that could also embrace their whole household). Again, we can use a famous name to mean the type that made it famous; the sentence

There were *no Shakespeares* in the nineteenth century.

does not mean there were no people called 'Shakespeare' but no writers who towered over contemporaries as William Shakespeare did over his. Similarly:

Lu Xun is revered as *the Chinese Gorki*.
Every large city should have *a Hyde Park*.

Somewhat akin is partitive restrictive modification:

The young Joyce already showed signs of the genius that was to be fulfilled in *Ulysses*. ('Even while he was young, James Joyce . . .')
The Dublin of Joyce is still there for everyone to experience. ('The features of Dublin reflected in Joyce's writing are still there.')

But there is also nonrestrictive modification, on the one hand colloquial and stereotyped (as in *poor old Mrs Fletcher*), on the other formal and often stylized (as in *the fondly remembered John F. Kennedy*, *VISIT HISTORIC YORK*).

Names with the definite article

5.28 It is not difficult to see why *the* finds a place in phrases institutionalized as names. We can imagine a group of musicians deciding to set up *a school* where music will be taught: *a school of music*. They decide to enhance its attractiveness by locating it in a *central* position of the city, and they hope that it will not be merely *a central school of music* but the only school meriting this description: *the central school of music*. It is a short step from this to the further decision that this should be not just a description but the name: *The Central School of Music.* So too a building in the form of a pentagon can come to be called *the Pentagon*, a canal built through the Panama Isthmus becomes *the Panama Canal.* When a president or a prime minister is elected or an earl created, the result is *the President (of France), the Prime Minister (of India), the Earl (of Gwynedd).*

NOTE Even where *the* is always present in continuous text (spoken or written), it has variable status as part of the name: *The Hague* at one extreme (and always with initial capital) to *the University of London* at the other (where *the* is never capitalized and is absent from the university's letter-head). *Cf* also (the) *Asian Wall Street Journal.* Where a name embodies premodification as distinct from postmodification (17.2), as in *(The) Lord Williams, the* is largely confined to formal and official style.

5.29 It may be convenient to group names with *the* in classes:

(a) Some titular names of persons and deities:

The Marquis of Salisbury, the King of Sweden, the President of General Motors, the Reverend John Fox, the Cardinal Archbishop of Westminster, the Queen, (the) Prince Edward, (the) Archduke Ferdinand, the God of Israel, the Lord of Hosts, the Buddha.

(b) Geographical names of plural form, notably:
 (i) groups of islands, as in *the Hebrides, the Bahamas*;
 (ii) mountain ranges, as in *the Himalayas, the Pyrenees.*
 Note also *the Netherlands, the Midlands, the Dardanelles.*

(c) Names of rivers, canals, expanses of water, areas of territory:

the (River) Thames, the Rhine, the Potomac (River); the Suez Canal, the Erie Canal; the Atlantic (Ocean), the Baltic (Sea), the Bosphorus; the Crimea, the Ruhr, the Sahara (Desert).

Note the absence of *the* in lake names:

Lake Huron, Derwentwater.

(d) Geographical names of the form *the* N_1 *of* N_2, as in *the Isle of Man, the Gulf of Mexico, the Cape of Good Hope, the Bay of Naples.* (Contrast: *Long Island, Hudson Bay.*)

(e) Names of theatres, galleries and major buildings, etc, as in *the Aldwych (Theatre), the Huntington (Library), the Ashmolean (Museum), the Middlesex (Hospital), the Taj Mahal, the Tate (Gallery), the Hilton (Hotel).*

(f) Names of ships and (less commonly) aircraft, as in *the Queen Mary, the Mayflower, the Spirit of St Louis.*

(g) Names of journals, as in *The Economist, The Times, The New York Review of Books.* (Contrast: *Punch, Time, New Scientist.*) If in discourse the title requires premodification, the article is discarded, as in 'Malcolm lent me today's *Times*/a recent *New York Review of Books*'.

Names without article

5.30 Whether names have articles (as in 5.28*f*) or not, they operate without a determiner contrast, and while it is normal for names to reflect the uniqueness of their referents by having no article, it must be clearly understood that 'No article' does not mean 'Zero article' (*cf* 5.1 Note). There are two major classes of names to consider: names of *persons* and names of *places*. On smaller classes, such as the names of months, see 5.25.

Personal names

5.31 These comprise:

(a) *Forenames* (also called first, given, or Christian names), used alone to or of family or friends:

> It's good to see you, *Frank*; how are you?
> Unfortunately, *Jacqueline* was unable to be present.

(b) *Family* names (surnames), used alone without discourtesy in address only in certain male circles (for example, in military use) and in 3rd person discourse for rather formal and distant (for example, historical) reference:

> What time do you have to report, *Watkinson*?
> The theories of *Keynes* continue to be influential.

(c) *Combinations of forenames and family names*, occasionally found in epistolary address ('Dear Mildred Carter') but chiefly used where 'full name' is required in self-introduction or in 3rd person reference:

> I am *Roger Middleton*; the manager is expecting me.
> *Freda Johnson* is writing a book on *Wilfred Owen*.

(d) *Combinations involving a title* are bipartite in address but can be tripartite in 3rd person reference:

> You are very welcome, *Mrs Johnson/Mrs Green/Mr Parker/Dr Lowe/Major Fielding/Sir John*.
> The committee decided to co-opt *Mrs (Freda) Johnson/Ms (Jacqueline) Green/Mr (D R) Parker/Dr (James F) Lowe/Major (William) Fielding/Sir John (Needham)*.

NOTE [a] Favourite animals (especially household pets) are given names, which in the case of pedigree animals are bestowed and registered with special care. Names of ships, often connotatively female, are also usually without article; but *cf* 5.29.

[b] Some terms of close kinship are treated as names in family discourse:

> Where's *Grandma/Dad*?

Some others are used as titles, as in 'Where's *Uncle Harry*?'

Locational names

5.32 These are used without article and comprise a wide range of designations:
(a) extraterrestrial: *Jupiter*, *Mars* (but *the moon*, *the sun*);
(b) continents: *Asia*, *(South) America*;
(c) countries, provinces, etc: *(Great) Britain*, *Canada*, *Ontario*, *(County) Kerry* (but *the United Kingdom*, *(the) Sudan*);
(d) lakes: *Lake Michigan*, *Loch Ness*, *Ullswater*;
(e) mountains: *(Mount) Everest*, *Snowdon*;
(f) cities, etc: *New York*, *Stratford-upon-Avon* (but *The Hague*, *the Bronx*);
(g) streets, buildings, etc: *Fifth Avenue*, *Park Lane*, *Brooklyn Bridge*, *Canterbury Cathedral*, *Scotland Yard*, *Waterloo Station*, *Oxford Street* (but *the Old Kent Road*).

On examples with *the*, *cf* 5.28*f*.

Nouns relating to region and nationality

5.33 Many names of regions and countries yield corresponding adjectives and noun forms of the following pattern, all reflecting their 'proper' affinity by being written with an initial capital. Thus, related to *Russia*, we have:

I General adjective:

A new *Russian* spacecraft has just been launched.
Both the men are *Russian*.

II Language name:

She reads *Russian* but she doesn't speak it very well.

III Singular noun with specific reference:

He is *a Russian*, I think.

IV Plural noun with specific reference:

There are several *Russians* among my students.

V Plural nouns used generically:

The Russians are a deeply patriotic people.

Normally, the form of II–V is predictable from I; for example *Greece*: I *Greek*, II *Greek*, III *a Greek*, IV *Greeks*, V *the Greeks*. In many instances, of course, there is no language corresponding to form II ('*She doesn't speak *European*'), but leaving this aside, the following sets are regularly predictable and behave as illustrated above:

Africa ~ African	America ~ American
Asia ~ Asian	Australia ~ Australian

and all other names in *-(i)a*. So too:

Belgium ~ Belgian	Brazil ~ Brazilian
Europe ~ European	Germany ~ German
Hungary ~ Hungarian	Italy ~ Italian
Norway ~ Norwegian	Iraq ~ Iraqi
Israel ~ Israeli	Pakistan ~ Pakistani

5.34 But there are name sets in which we encounter irregularities of form or restrictions in use. Thus where forms I and II (which are always identical) end in *-ese* or *-ish* (*-sh*, *-ch*), the same form is used for V (*cf* 7.12) but not usually for III and IV. Instead we use either form I plus a suitable noun (*a Chinese lady*), indicated in Table 5.34 by '(N)', '(Ns)', or a distinctive noun form (*a Spaniard*). With many items where form I ends in *-ish*, forms III and IV are traditionally *-ishman*, *-ishmen*, but the resistance to *man* as a human generic causes widespread hesitation to use these forms except of males. The chief irregular sets are listed in Table 5.34.

***Table* 5.34**

	I (and II where relevant)	III	IV	V
China	Chinese	a Chinese (citizen)	Chinese (people)	the Chinese
Japan	Japanese	a Japanese (N)	Japanese (Ns)	the Japanese
Portugal	Portuguese	a Portuguese (N)	Portuguese (Ns)	the Portuguese
Vietnam	Vietnamese	a Vietnamese (N)	Vietnamese (Ns)	the Vietnamese
Switzerland	Swiss	a Swiss (N)	Swiss (Ns)	the Swiss
Britain	British	a British (N)	British (Ns)	the British
England	English	an Englishman	Englishmen	the English
Ireland	Irish	an Irishman	Irishmen	the Irish
Wales	Welsh	a Welshman	Welshmen	the Welsh
France	French	a Frenchman	Frenchmen	the French
Holland the Netherlands	Dutch	a Dutchman	Dutchmen	the Dutch
Scotland	Scots	a Scotsman	Scotsmen	the Scots
Denmark	Danish	a Dane	Danes	the Danish
Sweden	Swedish	a Swede	Swedes	the Swedish
Finland	Finnish	a Finn	Finns	the Finnish
Poland	Polish	a Pole	Poles	the Polish
Spain	Spanish	a Spaniard	Spaniards	the Spanish

NOTE [a] For *Britain*, there is limited currency of *Briton(s)* as forms III and IV (informally also *Britisher(s)*, with *Brit(s)* more informal still).

[b] For Scotland, there are alternatives as follows: form I *Scottish*, *Scotch*; form III *a Scot*, *a Scotchman*; form IV *Scots*, *Scotchmen*; form V *the Scotch*. But the use of *Scotch(-)* is controversial; *Scotch* tends to be limited to designating such things as *whisky*.

[c] *Arabic* is form II, *Arab(s)* forms III–V, but the actual locational noun *Arabia* is now only rarely used to denote the large area of the Middle East concerned.

Number

5.35 The grammatical category of number, operating for example through subject–verb concord and pronominal reference, requires that every noun form be understood grammatically as either *singular* or *plural*. Singular relates to the quantity 'one' for count nouns, to the unique referent for most proper nouns (*eg*: *Tokyo*), and to undifferentiated mass for noncount nouns. Plural relates to the quantity 'two or more' for count nouns, to the unique referent for some proper nouns (*eg*: *the Azores*), and to individual operational units that are seen as reflecting plural composition (*eg*: *binoculars*, *goods*). For example:

Singular: This *suit fits* me and I'll buy *it*.
Nara was full of tourists when I visited *it*.
The *milk is* sour and I bought *it* only yesterday.

Plural: Two/three/several *students are* hoping you will see *them*.
The *Azores are* administered by Portugal but *they* are nearly a thousand miles away.
I thought my *binoculars were* in this drawer but I can't find *them*.

NOTE [a] The distinction between singular and plural is not always clear-cut; for different reasons, there is vacillation over such words as *politics*, *mumps*, *data*, *criteria*.
[b] Within 'plural', there is evidence in the language for some special provision for dual number; *cf* such words as *both*.

Plural formation

5.36 The vast majority of English nouns are count, with separate singular and plural forms. The singular is the unmarked form (*cf* 2.7) and as such is the citation form of the word (for example, in dictionaries). For the most part, plurals are formed in a regular and predictable way:

(a) in SOUND:

– add /ɪz/ if the singular ends with a sibilant, namely:

/s/ as in *horse*	/z/ as in *prize*
/ʃ/ as in *blush*	/ʒ/ as in *mirage*
/tʃ/ as in *church*	/dʒ/ as in *language*

for example: /praɪz/ ~ /praɪzɪz/

– add /z/ if the singular ends with a vowel or with a voiced consonant other than a sibilant for example: /deɪ/ ~ /deɪz/   /bed/ ~ /bedz/

– add /s/ if the singular ends with a voiceless consonant other than a sibilant

for example: /kat/ ~ /kats/

(b) In SPELLING:

With the vast majority of nouns, we simply add *-s* to the singular; for example:

horse ~ horses, prize ~ prizes

But, quite apart from the nouns that are fundamentally irregular in respect of number (5.37*ff*), the *-s* rule requires amplification and modification for many nouns:

(i) If the singular ends with a sibilant (see (a) above) that is not already followed by *-e*, the plural ending is *-es*; for example: *box ~ boxes, bush ~ bushes, switch ~ switches*; *cf language ~ languages*.

(ii) If the singular ends with *-y*, this is replaced by *i* and the plural ending is then *-ies*; for example: *spy ~ spies, poppy ~ poppies, soliloquy ~ soliloquies*. But *-y* remains, and the plural ending is *-ys*, if the singular ends with a letter having vowel-value as in *-ay, -ey, -oy* (thus *days, ospreys, boys*), or if the item is a proper noun (*the two Germanys*; *cf* 5.26).

(iii) If the singular ends with *-o*, the plural is usually regular (as with *studios, kangaroos, pianos*), but with some nouns the plural ending is *-es* (as with *echoes, embargoes, heroes, potatoes, tomatoes, torpedoes, vetoes*), and in a few cases there is variation, as with *buffalo(e)s, cargo(e)s, halo(e)s, motto(e)s, volcano(e)s*.

NOTE [a] Some further spelling points: In a few words requiring *-es* there is doubling as with *quiz ~ quizzes*. With unusual plurals such as numerals or initials, an apostrophe is sometimes introduced (thus *in the 1990's, some PhD's*). In formal writing, some abbreviations can show plural by doubling: *p ~ pp* ('pages'), *c ~ cc* ('copies'); with *f ~ ff*, the abbreviations are to be understood as 'the following numbered unit(s)', where the unit may be a section, page, chapter, or even volume.

[b] Compound nouns are usually regular in adding *-(e)s* to the final element (as in *babysitters, grown-ups*). But in some cases where the compound has an obvious head noun, it is to this element that the plural ending is affixed (as in *passers-by, grants-in-aid*), and with a few there is variation (as in *mouthfuls ~ mouthsful, court martials ~ courts martial*). With some appositional compounds (of the form *XY*, where 'The *X* is a *Y*') both elements have the plural inflection (*woman doctor ~ women doctors*).

[c] Where a title applies to more than one succeeding name, it can sometimes be pluralized, as in *Professors Wagner and Watson, Drs Brown, Smith, and Weindling*; but the commonest cannot (*Mrs Kramer, Mrs Pugh, and Mrs Hunter*), though *Mr* can have a plural *Messrs* /ˈmesəz/, especially in BrE commercial use ('the firm of *Messrs Gray and Witherspoon*'). Members of the same sex sharing a name can have the name in the plural: 'The two *Miss Smiths* as well as their parents were present at the ceremony.'

Irregular plural formation

Voicing

5.37 While in spelling the pair *house* ~ *houses* is regular, in pronunciation it is not, the final voiceless fricative consonant of the singular becoming voiced in the plural: /haus/ ~ /hauziz/. Several singulars ending in /f/ and /θ/ undergo voicing in this way, the former reflected in spelling, the latter not:

knife ~ knives /naɪf/ ~ /naɪvz/
mouth ~ mouths /mauθ/ ~ /mauðz/

Like *knife* are *calf, half, leaf, life, loaf, self, shelf, thief, wife, wolf*, and a few others. With some nouns, such as *handkerchief, hoof*, and *scarf*, the plural may involve voicing or be regular (-/fs/); with others, such as *belief, cliff, proof*, the plural is always regular.

Like *mouth* are *bath, oath, path, sheath, truth, wreath, youth*, though in most cases the plural can equally be regular (-/θs/). In other cases, only the regular plural is found, as with *cloth, death, faith, moth*, and where there is a consonant preceding the fricative this is always so (as with *birth, length*, etc).

Vowel change

5.38 In a small number of nouns, there is a change of vowel sound and spelling ('mutation plurals') without an ending:

foot ~ feet	goose ~ geese
louse ~ lice	man ~ men
mouse ~ mice	tooth ~ teeth
woman /'wumən/ ~ women /'wɪmɪn/	

NOTE [a] Compounds in unstressed *-man* such as *fireman, Frenchman* have plurals that are often identical in sound since both the *-man* and *-men* have schwa.
[b] The plural of *child* involves both vowel change and an irregular ending, *children* /tʃɪldrən/. The noun *brother*, when used in the sense 'fellow member', sometimes has a similar plural formation, *brethren* /breðrən/. *Cf* also, without vowel change, *ox* ~ *oxen*.

Zero plural

Words for some animals

5.39 The nouns *sheep, deer, cod*, while being unquestionably count, have no difference in form between singular and plural:

This *sheep* has just had a lamb.
These *sheep* have just had lambs.

Nouns referring to some other animals, birds, and fishes can have zero plurals, especially when viewed as prey:

They shot two *reindeer*, though this is strictly forbidden.
The *woodcock/pheasant/herring/trout/salmon/fish* are not very plentiful this year.

Compare:

Aren't those *pheasants* beautiful?

NOTE Some of the nouns considered in 5.42*f* as resistant to number contrast could also be regarded as having zero plural.

Nouns of quantity

5.40 There is a strong tendency for units of number, of length, of value, and of weight to have zero plural when premodified by another quantitative word. For example:

(a) How many people live there? About three *dozen*/Several *hundred*/ More than five *thousand*/Almost four *million*.

(b) My son is nearly six *foot* tall.
The tickets cost four *pound* fifty each.
Three *pound*/*stone* of potatoes, please.

But in set (b), zero is much less common than the use of inflected plurals and in some cases zero is largely dialectal ('She lives five *mile* from me'). Moreover, items in set (a) have normal plural forms when not preceded by numerals:

Dozens (and *dozens*) (of people) crowded into the room.
I have no precise idea how many people live there: *thousands* certainly, perhaps *millions*.

Foreign plurals

5.41 Numerous nouns adopted from foreign languages, especially Latin and Greek, retain the foreign inflection for plural. In some cases there are two plurals, an English regular form (5.36) being used in non-technical discourse.

(a) Nouns in *-us* /əs/ with plural *-i* /aɪ/:

stimulus focus alumnus bacillus

(b) Nouns in *-us* /əs/ with plural *-a* /ə/ (only in technical use):

corpus ~ corpora genus ~ genera

(c) Nouns in *-a* /ə/ with plural *-ae* /iː/ or /aɪ/:

antenna formula nebula

The plural ending in *vertebrae* is also pronounced /ei/.

(d) Nouns in *-um* /əm/ with plural *-a* /ə/:

addendum curriculum erratum
ovum stratum

(e) Nouns in *-ex*, *-ix* with plural *-ices* /ɪsiːz/:

appendix index matrix

(f) Nouns in *-is* /ɪs/ with plural *-es* /iːz/

analysis	basis	crisis
hypothesis	synopsis	thesis

(g) Nouns in *-on* /ən/ with plural *-a* /ə/:

automaton criterion phenomenon

(h) Nouns in *-o* /əʊ/ with plural *-i* /ɪ/; a few words in the field of music retain their Italian plural, especially in specialized discourse:

libretto tempo virtuoso

(i) Nouns from French sometimes retain a French plural in writing, with the French (*ie* zero) ending in speech or – more usually – a regular English one:

bureau ~ bureaux *or* bureaus /-əʊ/ or /-əʊz/

So also *plateau, tableau.* Some other nouns with no change of spelling in the plural, have regular English plurals in speech: for example, *chassis* /ʃasɪ/, pl /ʃasɪːz/

NOTE [a] The plural *-im* is sometimes found in the English use of Hebrew words, as in *kibbutzim.*

[b] Most originally foreign nouns take only regular plural endings (*museum ~ museums*, etc), and in several cases the historically plural ending is reinterpreted as a singular (*agenda, insignia*, etc):

This *agenda* is rather lengthy as I'm afraid most Senate *agendas* tend to be.

Nouns resistant to number contrast

5.42 Whether or not with inflectional regularity, number essentially involves the distinction between one and more than one:

This school is . . .	These schools are . . .
This woman is . . .	Those women are . . .
This sheep is . . .	These sheep are . . .

But as we noted in 5.35, there are singular nouns that cannot ordinarily be plural (*eg*: *meat*) and plural nouns that cannot ordinarily be singular (*eg*: *binoculars*). We shall look at such nouns under these two broad heads.

Ordinarily singular

5.43 (a) Proper nouns such as *London* or *Navratilova* are plural only in such circumstances as are described in 5.26*f*.

(b) Noncount nouns such as *cheese* or *solidarity* can be plural when used to indicate partition by quantity or quality (5.2). Abstract nouns in the plural indicate instances of the phenomenon concerned (as in 'many *injustices*') or intensification of the phenomenon (as in 'I must express my *regrets*'). Intensification accounts also for the plural of some concrete noncount nouns; for example, *wood* in the sense of 'forest':

This is a beautiful little *wood.*
Their house is in the middle of those extensive *woods.*

(c) The noun *news* and certain other items ending in *-s*:
(i) nouns in *-ics* such as *acoustics, physics*
(ii) names of diseases such as *mumps, shingles*
(iii) words for some games such as *billiards, dominoes, fives*
But when *politics* refers to an individual's views, it is treated as plural ('Her politics *are* becoming more extreme') and for some speakers such disease words as *mumps* can also be plural. Again, when *statistics* is used loosely to mean 'figures' it can be plural and have a corresponding singular: 'There is one surprising *statistic* in your report.'

(d) Collective nouns such as *committee, council, government, team* (though in BrE these are often treated as plural aggregate nouns: 'The *committee* were unanimous'; *cf* 5.44).

NOTE Unlike aggregate nouns, collective nouns retain singular determiners even where plural concord is used: *'This committee were unanimous.'

Ordinarily plural

5.44 (a) *Binary* nouns are those that refer to entities which comprise or are perceived as comprising two parts: tools and instruments such as *binoculars, forceps, scissors*; articles of dress such as *jeans, pants, trousers*:

These *scissors* are too blunt.
Those *trousers* don't match your shirt.

Number contrast is usually achieved through quantity partition (5.2) with *a pair of, several pairs of.* With binary nouns like *gloves* or *socks*, where the two pairs are more obviously separate, the unit is readily divisible into two singulars.

He was wearing a green *sock* and a brown *sock.*

Contrast:

There is a stain on {the left leg of your *trousers.* / (?) your left *trouser.*}

(b) *Aggregate* nouns are those that refer to entities which comprise or may be perceived as comprising an indefinite number of parts. These may be *plural in form*, as for instance *arms* ('weapons'), *communications* ('means of communication'), *data, goods, media, outskirts, remains, troops, works* ('factory'). With some items there is vacillation between singular and plural; for example

This *barracks* is } heavily defended.
These *barracks* are }

The *data* is/are insufficient.

But many aggregate nouns are *not plural in form*; thus *cattle*, *clergy*, *offspring*, *people*, *police*, *poultry*, *vermin*. Here again there is vacillation between singular and plural with some items:

The *clergy* is/are strongly opposed to divorce.

Cf 5.43(d).

NOTE Some nouns could be regarded either as 'ordinarily plural' or as having zero plural (5.39). Thus

She has one *offspring*/several *offspring*.
Did he leave *offspring*?

We are organizing {a new *series* / three further *series*} of lectures.

Others have a singular with some shift of meaning. Thus beside 'She used her *brains* in defeating her opponent', we can have 'She has a good *brain*', meaning approximately '*brains* of good quality'; beside 'He didn't receive his *wages* last week', we can have 'He has a living *wage*', meaning 'a level of *wages* that can support him'.

Gender

5.45 In English, gender is not a feature of nouns themselves (as in such languages as German or Russian). Rather, it relates directly to the *meanings* of nouns, with particular reference to biological sex. Gender then enters the province of grammar by determining the selection of reference pronouns: *wh*-, personal, and reflexive (6.2*ff*, 6.13, 6.17). The *wh*- items *who* and *which* oblige us to distinguish two broad gender classes, personal and nonpersonal, the former largely human in reference, the latter largely nonhuman and including inanimates:

This is the *pedestrian who* witnessed the accident.
That is the *cow which* has just had a calf.

Then within the personal gender class, the personal and reflexive pronouns relate to male and female sex:

Please help my {*husband*; *he* has hurt *himself*. / *wife*; *she* has hurt *herself*.}

But the sex-related pronouns can be used of items marked as nonpersonal by the *wh*- pronouns, as in

> *She* is the *cow which* has just had a calf.
> *She* is the *ship which* was launched last month.

In consequence, we have a rather complex pattern of gender classes, with some overlapping, as summarized in Fig. 5.2.

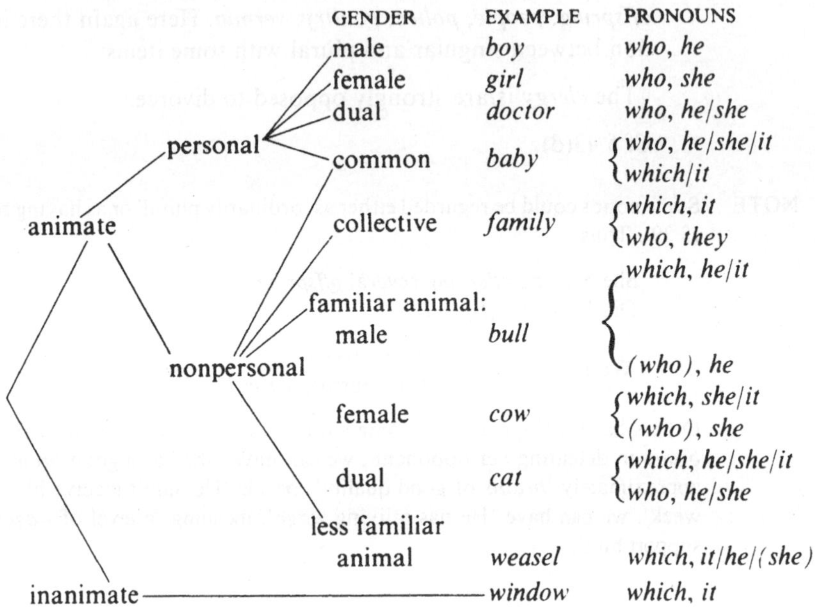

Fig. **5.2**

Nouns with personal reference

5.46 These commonly occur in *male* and *female* pairs such as *father* ~ *mother*, *boy* ~ *girl*, *king* ~ *queen*. In some cases, the female member is morphologically marked: *god* ~ *goddess*, *hero* ~ *heroine*, *usher* ~ *usherette*, *man* ~ *woman*. With *widower* ~ *widow*, it is the male that is marked.

But many personal nouns can be regarded as having *dual* gender, since they can be male or female in reference as required; for example, *friend*, *guest*, *parent*, and *person*. Most of these are nouns of agency such as *artist*, *cook*, *doctor*, *inhabitant*, *librarian*, *novelist*, *professor*, *singer*, *speaker*, *student*, *teacher*, *writer*. By contrast, *common* gender applies to those nouns like *baby*, *infant*, *child*, which though referring undoubtedly to male or female human beings make gender so irrelevant that we can use the neuter pronoun *it(s)*:

> The *baby* lost *its* parents when *it* was three weeks old.

The remaining class of person-referring nouns is *collective* where, like the common gender nouns, the sex of the persons concerned is irrelevant, as is shown by our use of *it* and *which*:

> The *committee*, *which* met soon after *it* was appointed, had difficulty in agreeing *its* method of procedure.

But, especially in BrE, such collectives can take piural concord with the personal *wh*-pronoun:

> The *audience*, *who* were largely students, were soon on *their* feet as *they* cheered the performers.

Further collectives: *army*, *association*, *class*, *club*, *community*, *company*, *council*, *crew*, *crowd*, *family*, *firm*, *government*, *jury*, *party*, *team*, *university*. Some occur with the definite article, for example: *the clergy*, *the intelligentsia*, *the public*. Some are proper names, for example: *the Vatican*, *Longman*, *General Motors*, *British Gas*, *Everton* (football team).

NOTE [a] Nouns morphologically marked for gender often tend to be avoided, especially where the sex of the referent is irrelevant; in consequence, nouns with dual gender such as *author*, *chair(person)*, *poet*, *supervisor*, may be preferred to *authoress*, *chairman*, *poetess*, *foreman*.

[b] Although unmarked forms have traditionally been expressed as male while subsuming female ('*Man* is mortal', 'If any *person* is caught stealing from this store, *he* will be prosecuted': *cf* 6.4), reaction against sexual bias has resulted in evasions such as:

A	*doctor* *parent* *singer*	may appeal if	*he or she* wishes. *they* wish.

[c] Countries and ships (especially by name) are often treated as female: '*France* is increasing *her* exports', '*The Lotus* sank when *she* struck a reef'.

Nouns referring to animals and inanimates

5.47 Among animals, we must distinguish between what we may call the FAMILIAR and the LESS FAMILIAR. The former embrace the range of animals, birds, etc, in which human society takes a special interest, and which significantly impinge on familiar experience (for example, in farming or as domestic pets). Many of the nouns for these occur in MALE and FEMALE pairs, as with personal nouns, often with *he* ~ *she* as the reference pronoun though usually with *which* as the relative:

> This is the *bull which* has a brand mark on *his*/(*its*) back.
>
> This is the *cow which* had *her*/(*its*) first calf when *she*/(*it*) was already seven years old.

Other such pairs include *ram* ~ *ewe*, *stallion* ~ *mare*, *hen* ~ *cock(erel)*, and there are some with morphological marking, as in *lion* ~ *lioness*, *tiger* ~ *tigress*. But frequently, despite such pairs as *dog* ~ *bitch*, one of the two is used with *dual* gender, or an item outside the pairing (such as *sheep*, beside *ram* ~ *ewe*) so operates:

> This *horse* is two years old; isn't *she* beautiful?
>
> This *horse* has sired *his* first foal.

But LESS FAMILIAR animals constitute by far the majority of creatures in the animate world. Squirrels, ants, starlings, and moths may be fancifully referred to as *he* or *she*, but for the most part they are treated grammatically as though they were inanimate:

> Do you see that *spider*? *It's* hanging from the beam.
> Do you see that *balloon*? *It's* hanging from the beam.

Case

5.48 As distinct from pronouns (6.6*f*), English nouns have only two cases, the unmarked COMMON case and the marked GENITIVE. The latter is sometimes called the 'possessive', by reason of one of the main functions of the case (as in *The child's coat*, 'The coat belonging to the child').

The genitive inflection is phonologically identical with the regular plural inflection (5.36) with a consequent neutralization of the case distinction in the plural:

The /kau/ was grazing.	The /kauz/ were grazing.
One /kauz/ tail was waving.	All the /kauz/ tails were waving.

With irregular nouns where no such neutralization can occur, a fourfold distinction is observed:

The /man/ was watching.	The /men/ were watching.
The /manz/ car was locked.	The /menz/ cars were locked.

Orthographically a fourfold distinction always obtains, since the genitive ending is always spelled with an apostrophe: before the ending for the singular, after it for the plural:

> One *cow's* tail   All the *cows'* tails

NOTE [a] Where noun phrases with postmodification do not have the plural inflection at the end (5.36 Note [b]) there is a distinction between genitive and plural; compare:

> The chief of staff ~ The chiefs of staff
> The chief of staff's role ~ The chiefs of staff's role

But where postmodification is less institutionalized, such a 'group genitive' – though common informally – is often avoided in favour of the *of*-construction (5.49): 'The name *of the man in the dark suit*.'

[b] In being phonologically identical with the plural, the regular genitive plural is sometimes called the 'zero genitive'. Such a zero genitive is common with names that end in /z/, especially if they are foreign names:

> Socrates' /-tiːz/ doctrines
> Moses' /-zɪz/ laws

But Dickens' novels /dɪkɪnz/ *or* /dɪkɪnzɪz/

Note the zero genitive also in some expressions such as *for goodness' sake*.

The genitive and the *of*-construction

5.49 We frequently find a choice between using a premodifying genitive and a postmodifying prepositional phrase with *of*; the similarity in meaning and function has caused the latter to be called by some the '*of*-genitive'. For example:

There were strong objections from { *the island's* inhabitants. / the inhabitants *of the island*. }

But although both versions in this instance are equally acceptable, with a choice determined largely by preferred focus (*cf* 18.5*ff*), for the most part we must select either the genitive or the *of*-construction. For example:

These are *father's* trousers.	*These are the trousers *of father*.
Let's go to the front *of the house*.	*Let's go to *the house's* front.

Genitive meanings

5.50 The meanings expressed by the genitive can conveniently be shown through paraphrase; at the same time, we can compare the analogous use of the *of*-construction (*cf* 5.50*f*).

(a) Possessive genitive:

Mrs Johnson's coat. — Mrs Johnson owns this coat.
The ship's funnel. — The ship has a funnel.

Cf The funnel *of the ship*.

(b) Genitive of attribute:

The victim's outstanding courage. — The victim was very courageous.

Cf The outstanding courage *of the victim*.

(c) Partitive genitive:

The heart's two ventricles. — The heart contains two ventricles.

Cf The two ventricles *of the heart*.

(d) Subjective genitive:

The parents' consent. — The parents consented.

Cf The consent *of the parents*.

(e) Objective genitive:

The prisoner's release. — (. . .) released the prisoner.

Cf The release *of the prisoner*.

(f) Genitive of origin:

Mother's letter.	The letter is from Mother.
England's cheeses.	The cheeses were produced in England.

Cf The cheeses of *England.*

(g) Descriptive genitive:

Children's shoes.	The shoes are designed for children.
A *doctor's* degree.	The degree is a doctorate.

NOTE The distinction between (a), (b), and (c) is far from clear-cut and much depends on gender (*cf* 5.51) and on contextual viewpoint. In general, the closer the relation can be seen to literal possession, the more suitable is the genitive; by contrast, attribution and partition are usually more appropriately expressed by the *of*-construction. Where both genitive and *of*-construction are grammatically possible, the decision often turns on the principle of end-focus or end-weight (18.5 and Note [a]):

My father's DEATH ~ The death of my FATHER
John's age ~ The age of my oldest and dearest friend

Gender and the genitive

5.51 The genitive is not used with all nouns equally but tends to be associated with those of animate gender, especially with those having personal reference (5.45*f*). For example:

The dog's name.
Segovia's most famous pupil.
The student's precious possessions.
The committee's decision.

Geographical names take the genitive inflection, especially when they are used to imply human collectivity; thus *China's policy* more plausibly than *China's mountains.* So too with other strictly inanimate nouns when used with special relevance to human activity or concern: *The hotel's occupants* rather than *The hotel's furniture*, *The book's true importance* rather than *The book's colour.*

NOTE [**a**] The part played by personal gender in admitting the genitive is well illustrated by the indefinite pronouns:

I think I can see down there {the shadow *of somebody*. / *somebody's* shadow. / the shadow *of something*. / **something's* shadow.}

[**b**] In some expressions, the genitive depends less on the noun so inflected than on the noun following. The items *edge* and *sake* are especially notable in this connection:

He stood at the water's edge.	(*Cf also* . . . the edge of the water)
She did it for her country's sake.	(*Cf also* . . . the sake of her country)

With *worth*, no *of-* variant is possible:

We must try to get our money's worth.

The grammatical status of the genitive

As determiner

5.52 For the most part, genitives function exactly like central definite determiners and thus preclude the cooccurrence of other determiners.

A new briefcase.
The new briefcase. (*A the new briefcase.)
This new briefcase. (*The this new briefcase.)
Joan's new briefcase. (*The Joan's new briefcase.)

This equally applies when the genitive is a phrase incorporating its own determiner.

My cousin's new briefcase. (≠ *My* new briefcase.)
My handsome cousin's new briefcase.

In other words, items preceding the genitive relate to the inflected noun, such that a phrase like

That old gentleman's son

must be understood as 'The son of that old gentleman', and not as 'That son of the old gentleman.'

But an exception must be made where the preceding item is a predeterminer, since this may relate either to the genitive noun as in [1] or to the noun that follows as in [2].

We attributed *both the girls'* success to their hard work. [1]
(*ie* the success of *both the girls*)
Both *the girl's* parents were present. [2]
(*ie* both the parents *of the girl*)

As modifier

5.53 Where the genitive is used descriptively (5.50(g)), however, it functions not as a determiner but as a modifier with a classifying role. Determiners in such noun phrases usually relate not to the genitive but to the noun following it, as can be plainly seen from the following, where the singular *a* could obviously not cooccur with the plural *women*:

They attend a *women's* university in Kyoto.

So also, other modifying items in the noun phrase are less likely to relate to the genitive noun than to the noun that follows it; thus in

She lives in a quaint old *shepherd's* cottage.

it is probably the cottage that is quaint and old, not the shepherd. Grammatically, some phrases can be ambiguous, though it would be rare for the context not to make the meaning clear:

Where did you find these children's clothes?

(*Either* '*These children* had lost their clothes'; genitive as determiner. *Or* '*These clothes* were obviously made for children'; genitive as modifier.)

The independent genitive

5.54 It is common to ellipt the noun following the genitive if the reference is contextually clear. For example:

Jennifer's is the only face I recognize here.
(*ie* Jennifer's face)
He has a devotion to work like *his father's*.
(*ie* his father's *devotion to work*)

By contrast, with the *of*-construction, *that* or *those* usually replaces the corresponding item:

The wines *of France* are more expensive than *those of California*.
(*ie the wines* of California)

A special case of the independent genitive occurs when the unexpressed item refers to homes or businesses:

When I arrived at *Fred's*, I found I'd come on the wrong day.
My butcher's stays open late on Fridays.
She wouldn't miss *St Martin's* on Easter morning.

In most such instances of the 'local genitive', one could not specify uniquely the unexpressed item, and in many cases it would sound artificial if one attempted a fuller phrase, often because what is meant is more abstract and general than any specific noun would convey:

I hate going to *the dentist's* (? surgery, ? place, ? establishment).

NOTE With the names of major firms, what begins as a local genitive develops into a plural, often so spelled and observing plural concord:

Harrod's is a vast store.
Harrods are having a sale.

A further development is to drop the ending and to treat the item as a collective (*cf* 5.46).

The 'post-genitive'

5.55 Since in its determiner role, the genitive must be definite (5.52), we can be in some difficulty with a sentence like

George's sister is coming to stay with us.

If it needs to be understood that George has more than one sister, this can be expressed in one of two ways, each involving a partitive *of*-construction:

One of George's sisters is coming to stay with us.
A sister of George's is coming to stay with us.

It is the latter that is called the 'post-genitive' (or 'double-genitive').

Bibliographical note

On noun classes, see Algeo (1973); Allerton (1987); Seppänen (1974).

On reference and determiners, see Auwera (1980); Burton-Roberts (1977); Declerck (1986); Hawkins (1978); Hewson (1972); Kaluza (1981); Kramsky (1972); Perlmutter (1970); Takami (1985).

On number, see Hirtle (1982); Juul (1975); Lehrer (1986); Sørensen (1985). On gender and case, see Dahl (1971); Jahr Sørheim (1980).

6 Pronouns

6.1 As we noted in 2.9, pro-forms play a vital role in grammar (see especially 12.1*ff*). One category of pro-forms is particularly associated with noun phrases and this is the PRONOUN. How wide-ranging and heterogeneous this category is becomes apparent from considering the italicized items in the following:

> As *it* turned out, *somebody* offered Elaine a bicycle at a price *which* *she* and *her* friends knew was well below *that* of a new *one*.

But as with pro-forms in general, all these pronouns have one thing in common: their referential meaning is determined purely by the grammar of English and the linguistic or situational context in which they occur. Beyond this, it is necessary to see pronouns as falling into the following classes and subclasses:

CENTRAL
- personal – *eg*: *I, me, they, them*
- reflexive – *eg*: *myself, themselves*
- possessive – *eg*: *my/mine, their/theirs*

RELATIVE – *eg*: *which, that*
INTERROGATIVE – *eg*: *who, what*
DEMONSTRATIVE – *eg*: *this, those*

INDEFINITE
- positive
  - universal – *eg*: *both, each*
  - assertive – *eg*: *some, several*
  - nonassertive – *eg*: *any, either*
- negative – *eg*: *nobody, neither*

Central pronouns

Personal pronouns

6.2 Like all the central pronouns, the personal pronouns display a *person* contrast; that is, they have separate 1st, 2nd, and 3rd person forms. In the 3rd person, there is a three-way *gender* contrast: masculine, feminine, and nonpersonal. There are also *number* contrasts (singular, plural) and in the personal subclass a 1st and 3rd person contrast in *case* also (subjective, objective). The system of central pronouns is presented as a whole in Table 6.2.

NOTE We follow the tradition of applying the term 'personal pronoun' only to a subclass of the central pronouns. What are here termed 'possessive pronouns' are often treated as a third case (genitive) of the primary pronouns; on the paired forms of possessives (*eg*: *my/mine*), see 6.16.

Table 6.2 Central pronouns

PERSON	NUMBER AND GENDER	PRIMARY: SUBJECTIVE CASE	PRIMARY: OBJECTIVE CASE	REFLEXIVE	POSSESSIVE: DETERMINER FUNCTION	POSSESSIVE: INDEPENDENT FUNCTION
1st	singular	I	me	myself	my	mine
	plural	we	us	ourselves	our	ours
2nd	singular	you	you	yourself	your	yours
	plural	you	you	yourselves	your	yours
3rd	singular masculine	he	him	himself	his	his
	singular feminine	she	her	herself	her	hers
	singular nonpersonal	it	it	itself	its	(its)
	plural	they	them	themselves	their	theirs

6.3 PERSON distinguishes the speaker or writer (1st person) from the addressee (2nd person) and from those persons or things which are neither (3rd person):

I hope that *you* will express an opinion on *them*.

If pronouns of different persons are coordinated, the sequence is treated as 1st person if it includes *I* or *we*, 2nd person if it includes *you* but not *I* or *we*. Thus:

You and *I* can go together, can't *we*?

You and {*Gillian* / *she*} agree with that, don't *you*?

If neither 1st nor 2nd person pronouns occur in the coordination, the sequence is of course 3rd person:

{*Fred* / *He*} and {*Mona* / *she*} met in Tunis, didn't *they*?

The ordering of pronouns in coordination is important from the viewpoint of style and courtesy: the 1st person comes last (especially if it is the singular) and the 2nd person usually comes first:

You, {*Jack*, / *he*,} and *I* will still be at work.

Why didn't they invite *you* and {*John*? / *me*? / *her*?}

3rd person coordinates usually have the masculine before the feminine, the pronoun before the noun phrase:

{*He* and *she* / *She* and *another student*} were both elected.

6.4 GENDER enforces a three-way distinction on the 3rd person singular, with masculine, feminine, and nonpersonal forms (5.45*ff*):

He has hurt *his* hand.
She asked *herself* why *she* had bought *it* when *its* lens was so obviously scratched.

This causes problems, especially when there is no basis for deciding between masculine and feminine, either because the gender is unknown or because it must be inclusive:

Someone is knocking so I'd better go and let *h . . ?* in.
An ambitious player must discipline *h . . ?self*.

Traditionally, the masculine can be used as the unmarked form (2.7) covering male and female reference in such cases, but sensitivity to sexual bias makes many people prefer a cumbersome coordination:

An ambitious player must discipline *himself or herself*.

More generally, where an informal disregard for strict number concord is felt tolerable, the gender-neutral plural is used:

Someone has parked *their* car right under the 'No Parking' sign.

NOTE The graphic device *s/he* to embrace *he* and *she* is of limited value since there is no equally convenient objective, possessive, or reflexive form (though full forms are often used, such as *him/her*).

6.5 NUMBER has to be treated separately for each of the three persons of pronouns. With the 3rd person, number is closest in value to that with nouns:

A male *officer* and a woman *officer* interrogated the prisoner but the *officers* disagreed over procedure.
He and *she* interrogated the prisoner but *they* disagreed over procedure.

With the 2nd person, there is a number contrast only in the reflexive pronoun. Compare:

> Look at *your* hand, Jack; *you*'ve cut *yourself.*
> Keep *your* voices down, children; *you* must behave *yourselves.*

But, while *you . . . yourselves* is straightforwardly the plural of more than one addressee, each of which might be addressed as *you . . . yourself*, the plural with the 1st person is on quite a different basis. *We* is not the plural of *I* (*'We, that is, I and I and I are glad to see you') but a pronoun meaning *I* and one or more other people ('We, that is, Jill and I', 'We the undersigned'). See below, 6.10.

NOTE In archaic style, there is a set of singular 2nd person pronouns *thou* (objective *thee*), *thy(self)*, *thine*, and a special subjective plural form *ye*.

6.6 CASE in personal pronouns involves a distinction absent from nouns, marking broadly the grammatical roles of subject and object. Compare:

> *The policeman* detained *this young woman.*
> *He* detained *her.*
> *The woman* resisted *the policeman.*
> *She* resisted *him.*

Corresponding to the genitive case in nouns (5.48*ff*), we have in pronouns the subclass of possessives, treated below in 6.16:

> *The girl's* dog bit *an old man's* ankle.
> *Her* dog bit *his* ankle.

6.7 The choice of subjective and objective forms does not depend solely upon the strict grammatical distinction between subject and object. Rather, usage shows that we are concerned more with subject 'territory' (the pre-verbal part of a clause) in contrast to object 'territory' (the post-verbal part of a clause). In consequence of the latter consideration, it is usual in informal style to find objective forms selected in such instances as the following:

> His sister is taller than *him.*
> Whoever left the door unlocked, it certainly wasn't *me.*

Many people are uncomfortable about such forms, however, especially in writing, though the subject variants are almost equally objectionable in seeming unnatural. Where an operator can be added, of course, the problem of choice satisfactorily disappears:

> His sister is taller than *he* is.

See also 6.11.

NOTE [a] In contrast with *except* which is always treated as a preposition and therefore followed by the objective case ('Nobody except *her* objected'), there is vacillation over prepositional *but*, many people preferring the subjective form if it is in subject 'territory'. Thus:

Nobody but *she* objected.

Even in object territory, *but* can be followed by either form, as with *as* and *than*:

Nobody objected but *she/her*.

[b] The frequency of the coordination *you and I* seems to have resulted in a tendency to make it case-invariant, though such examples as the following are felt to be uneasily hypercorrect:

Let's *you and I* go together then.
Between *you and I*, there was some cheating.

Specific reference

6.8 Central pronouns resemble noun phrases with *the* in normally having definite meaning, and they also usually have specific reference. In the case of 3rd person pronouns, the identity of the reference is typically supplied by the linguistic context, anaphorically as in [1] or cataphorically as in [2] (*cf* 5.14):

There is *an excellent museum* here and everyone should visit *it*. [1]
When *she* had examined the patient, *the doctor* picked up the telephone. [2]

In [1], *it* is understood as 'the museum'; in [2], *she* is understood as 'the doctor'. Cataphoric reference is conditional upon grammatical subordination; thus [2] could not be restated as:

**She* examined the patient and then *the doctor* picked up the telephone.

Anaphoric reference has no such constraint, and [2] could be replaced by:

When *the doctor* had examined the patient, *she* picked up the telephone.

On the other hand, the relative freedom of anaphoric reference can result in indeterminacy as to identification:

Ms Fairweather asked Janice if *she*^{1} could come into *her* room; *she*^{2} seemed to be more upset than *she* had ever seen *her*.

English grammar determines only that the italicized items have singular feminine reference; it does not determine the specific identities. In such a case, the speaker/writer would have to make sure that the larger context or the situation left it clear whether, for example, *she*^{1} referred to Ms Fairweather or to Janice and whether *she*^{2} had the same reference as *she*^{1}. Did Ms Fairweather ask for the interview because Janice seemed upset or is Janice reflecting that the interview is sought because Ms Fairweather seemed upset?

The pronoun *it*

6.9 Any singular noun phrase that does not determine reference by *he* or *she* is referred to by *it*; thus collectives, noncount concretes, and abstractions:

> *The committee* met soon after *it* had been appointed.
> He bought *some salmon* because *it* was her favourite food.
> When you are ready to report *it*, I would like to know *your assessment of the problem*.

Since this last noun phrase is a nominalization (17.23) of a clause ('You are assessing the problem'), it is easy to see that *it* can refer to the content of whole sentences and sequences of sentences:

> I don't like to say *it* but I must. *You have lost your job because you didn't work hard enough. You have only yourself to blame.*

Such a cataphoric use of *it* with sentential reference is analogous to the extrapositional *it* (18.23*ff*):

> *It* has to be said *that you have lost your job because . . .*

Analogous too is the anticipatory *it* in cleft sentences (18.18*f*):

> *It* was only last week that the death was announced.

In many cases where *it* seems to be superficially anaphoric, it is to be explained in terms of this anticipatory use with subsequent ellipsis. Compare:

> I asked where she lived and *it* turned out to be in my street.
> The phone rang and *it* was the police.

On the other hand, *it* as a prop ('dummy') subject frequently occurs where no plausible sentential reference can be claimed:

> If *it* stops raining, we can go out for a walk; but we must be home before *it* gets dark.

NOTE A prop *it* is not confined to subject function:

> I take *it* that she has declined the invitation.
> He had a hard time of *it* in the army.

The 1st person plural forms

6.10 The pronoun for the 1st person plural is a device for referring to 'I' and one or more other people. The latter may be INCLUSIVE of the addressee(s):

> I'm glad to see you, Marie, and I hope *we* (*ie* 'you and I') can have a long talk.
> Ladies and gentlemen, I hope *we* (*ie* 'you and I') can agree this evening on a policy for the future.

The latter is akin to the persuasive *we* associated with sermons and political speeches as well as with scholarly writing; for example:

We must increase our vigilance if *we* are not to fall victim to temptation.
As *we* saw in Chapter Three, *we* can trace the origins of human conflict to . . .

The artificial nature of the inclusiveness in this last example (which really means 'As I hope *you* saw in Chapter Three . . .') is accentuated in the rhetorical use of *we*, where the reference is to a general human collectivity – possibly in the remote past – and where paraphrase by 'you and I' may be unthinkable:

In the eighteenth century, *we* had little idea of the effect that industrial inventions would have.

Artificial inclusiveness of a different kind is found in the informal *we* used by doctor to patient:

And how are *we* (*ie* 'you') feeling today?

The obverse of this occurs in the *exclusive* use of the 1st person plural where 'you' the addressee is not included:

Ms Rogers and I have finished the report, Minister; shall *we* (*ie* 'she and I') leave it on your desk?

Related to this is the traditional 'editorial' *we*:

We can now reveal that the visit was cancelled because of threatened terrorist activity.

NOTE The royal *we*, now restricted to highly formal material such as charters, can be regarded as an extreme form of exclusive *we*.

Modification of pronouns

6.11 There is very limited scope for modification and it largely concerns the personal pronouns with the objective case (*cf* 6.7):

(a) Adjectives, chiefly in informal exclamations:

Poor me! *Clever you*! *Good old him*!

(b) Appositive nouns, with plural 1st and 2nd person:

Will *you others* please wait here?
You nurses have earned the respect of the entire country, and *we politicians* must see that you get a proper reward.
Us locals are going to protest. ⟨familiar⟩

(c) *Here* and *there*, with 1st person plural and 2nd person respectively (the latter tending to sound rude):

Whatever you others do, *we here* would be willing to leave now.
Could *you there* collect your passports at the desk?

(d) Prepositional phrases, with 1st person (usually plural) and 2nd person:

It is very much the concern of $\left\{\begin{matrix}\textit{you}\\ \textit{us}\end{matrix}\right\}$ *in the learned professions.*

(e) Emphatic reflexives:

I myself, she herself, they themselves

(f) Universal pronouns, with plurals:

We all accept responsibility.

$\left.\begin{matrix}\textit{You both}\\ \textit{They each}\end{matrix}\right\}$ need help.

(g) Relative clauses, chiefly in formal style:

We who fought for this principle will not lightly abandon it.
He or she who left a case in my office should claim it as soon as possible.

They that (**They who*) is rare, *those who* being preferred.

Generic reference

6.12 In the type of modification illustrated in 6.11(g), most instances have generic rather than specific reference, as in the proverbial

He (*ie* 'Anyone') *who hesitates* is lost.

For ordinary purposes, the pronouns *we*, *you*, and *they* have widespread use as generics; for example:

We live in an age of moral dilemmas. [1]
You can always tell if someone is lying. ⟨informal⟩ [2]
They'll soon find a cure for cancer. ⟨informal⟩ [3]

In each case, the subject could be replaced by the generic *one* but with major stylistic and semantic differences. Stylistically, *one* would be more formal in each case, but especially so in [3]. Semantically, *we* retains the inclusionary warmth of implied 1st person involvement (6.10), *you* comparably implies special interest in the addressee, while *they* detaches the general observation equally from both the speaker and the addressee. In consequence, it is especially convenient in relation to regret or disapproval:

I wonder why *they* don't repair the roads more often.

The reflexives

6.13 The reflexive pronouns are always coreferential with a noun or another pronoun, agreeing with it in gender, number, and person:

Veronica *herself* saw the accident. [1]
The dog was scratching *itself*. [2]
He and his wife poured *themselves* a drink. [3]

The reflexives here are coreferential with *Veronica* (as appositive subject), *The dog* (as object), and *He and his wife* (as indirect object). By contrast, in

He and his wife poured *them* a drink. [4]

the indirect object *them* refers to people other than the subject.

The coreference must be within the clause; thus we have a contrast between

Penelope begged Jane to look after *her*. (= Penelope)
Penelope begged Jane to look after *herself*. (= Jane)

But the item determining the reflexive may be absent from the clause in question; for example, imperative clauses are understood to involve 2nd person, and nonfinite clauses may reveal the subject in a neighbouring main clause:

Look at *yourself* in the mirror!
Freeing *itself* from the trap, the rat limped away.

NOTE [a] Where a pronoun object is only partially coreferential with the subject, the reflexive is not used. Thus beside '*I* could make *myself* an omelette', '*We* could make *ourselves* an omelette', we have '*I* could make *us* an omelette'.
[b] Appositive use of reflexives is associated with the need for emphasis.

6.14 A few transitive verbs require that subject and object are coreferential:

They pride *themselves* on their well-kept garden.
The witness was suspected of having perjured *himself*.

So also *absent oneself*, *ingratiate oneself*, *behave oneself*, though with this last the reflexive can be omitted. With some other verbs, there is a threefold choice:

She dressed *herself* with care. [1]
She dressed with care. [2] = [1]
She dressed *him* with care. [3]

So also *wash*, *shave*, *hide*, *prepare* etc.

6.15 Prepositional complements coreferential with an item in the same clause take reflexive form where the preposition has a close relationship with the verb (as in the prepositional verbs *look at*, *look after*, *listen to*: *cf* 16.5*ff*). The same holds in sequences concerned with representation:

Janet {took a photo of / told a story about} {*herself* (= Janet) / *her* (≠ Janet)}

But where the prepositional phrase is adverbial (especially relating to space: *cf* 8.2, 8.16*ff*), coreference can be expressed without the reflexive:

> Fred closed the door behind *him*.
> Fred draped a blanket about *him*.

In such cases, context alone would show whether *him* referred to *Fred* or to someone else; replacement of *him* by *himself* would of course remove any doubt but this would be unusual unless emphasis were required.

NOTE With some common existential expressions (18.30*ff*), the reflexive is rare or impossible in the prepositional complement:

> She hadn't any money on *her*.
> I have my wife with *me*.

On the other hand, there are idiomatic phrases in which the prepositional complement must be reflexive:

> They were beside *themselves* with rage.
> I was sitting by *myself*.

Contrast:

> They were beside *me*. ('near')
> I was sitting by *her*. ('near')

The possessives

6.16 As shown in Table 6.2, most of the possessive pronouns differ in form according as they function as determiners or as independent items. Compare:

> These are {Miriam's / *her*} books. ~ These books are {Miriam's. / *hers*.}
> That is *my* bicycle. ~ That bicycle is *mine*.
> Which are *their* clothes? ~ Which clothes are *theirs*?
> Is this *his* car? ~ Is this car *his*?
> BUT Those are *its* paw-marks. ~ *?Those paw-marks are *its*.

When the emphatic (*very*) *own* follows a possessive (the only form of modification admitted), there is no difference between determiner and independent function:

> That is *my own* bicycle. ~ That bicycle is *my own*.

With this modification, even *its* can now sometimes assume enough weight for independent status:

> The cat knows that this is *its (very) own* dish. ~ The cat knows that this dish is *its (very) own*.

NOTE Possessives are used with items such as parts of the body without any feeling of tautology:

> She shook *her* head:
> I tried to keep *my* balance.

Pronouns without a person contrast

Relative pronouns

6.17 Relative pronouns comprise two series:

> (1) *wh-* items: *who, whom, whose, which*
> (2) *that* and zero, the latter indicated below as ( )

Compare:

> I'd like to come and see the house {*which* / *that* / ( )} you have for sale.

In neither series are there distinctions of person or number, but in (1) we have some distinctions of *gender* and *case*. With *who* and *whom* the antecedent must have personal gender (5.45); with *which* it must have nonpersonal gender; with *whose* the antecedent is usually personal but can also be nonpersonal. Thus:

> Are you the doctor *who* looked after my daughter?
> That is the hospital *which* is to be expanded.
> That is the {doctor / hospital} *whose* phone number I gave you.

While *who* and *whom* share gender reference, their difference in form reflects the case distinction, subjective and objective respectively, within the relative clause:

> The man {*who* greeted me / *whom* I greeted / *to whom* I spoke} is a neighbour.

But see 17.8*ff*.

In series (2), *that* can be used without reference to the gender of the antecedent or the function within the relative clause, except that it cannot be preceded by a preposition:

> {The actor / The play} {*that* pleased me / *that* I admired / *that* I was attracted to} is new to London.

Zero has a similar range, lacking only the subject function:

> The actor } { ( ) I admired } is new to London.
> The play } { ( ) I was attracted to }

A major difference between the two series is that items in (2) can operate only in restrictive clauses. See 17.8.

Interrogative pronouns

6.18 There are five interrogative pronouns:

> who whom whose which what

The first four are identical with series (1) of the relative pronouns (6.17), but there are notable differences both in their reference and in their grammar within the clause. *Whose* as well as *who* and *whom* can be used only with reference to items of personal gender; nor is *whose* restricted to determiner function. While *whom* can function only as the objective case, *who* can be both subjective and (especially in speech) objective except after a preposition. To illustrate these points:

> *Who* owns this house?
> *Who(m)* does this house belong to?
> *To whom* does this house belong? ⟨formal⟩
> *Whose* is this house?

With *which*, reference can be both personal and nonpersonal:

> Of these {cars, / students,} *which* {is best? / do you like most?}

When *what* is used as a pronoun, the questioner assumes that the reference is nonpersonal:

> *What* {is in that box? / were you wearing that day?}

But *what* and *which* can also be determiners (5.3), and in this function the noun phrase can be personal or nonpersonal, the difference then being that *which* assumes a limited choice of known answers:

> *What* doctor(s) would refuse to see a patient?
> *Which* doctor (s) [of those we are discussing] gave an opinion on this problem?

As determiner, *whose* retains its personal reference:

> *Whose* house is this?

NOTE The distinction between *who*, *what*, and *which* is brought out in a set like the following:

Who is his wife? The novelist Felicity Smith. (*cf* 5.11)
What is his wife? A novelist. (*cf* 5.15, 23)
Which is his wife? The woman nearest the door.

Demonstrative pronouns

6.19 The demonstratives have the same formal range and semantic contrast both as pronouns and as determiners (5.5), *this/these* suggesting relative proximity to the speaker, *that/those* relative remoteness:

We shall compare	*this* (picture) *these* (pictures)	here with	*that* (picture) *those* (pictures)	over there.

But while all can be used as determiners irrespective of the gender of the noun head, as pronouns the reference must be to nouns of nonpersonal (and usually inanimate) gender:

In the garden, I noticed { *this* plastic bag. ~ *this*
this kitten. ~ ?*this*
this woman. ~ **this* }

An exception is where the demonstrative pronoun is subject of a *be*-clause with a noun phrase of specific reference as complement:

That is my kitten.
These are the children I told you about.

Cf also 'Who is *that*?' 'Who is *it*?' beside 'Who are *you*?' 'Who is *she*?' Occasionally too the demonstratives may be used as pronouns with animate reference where there is ellipsis:

I attended to *that* patient but not *this* (one).

As in the example, however, it would be usual to add the pronoun *one*.
A further partial exception is that *those* with postmodification (17.2) can readily have personal reference:

Will *those seated in rows 20 to 30* now please board the aircraft.
Success comes to *those who have determination*.

NOTE Whether as determiners or pronouns, the demonstratives can be modified by predeterminers (5.7*ff*):

She painted *all (of) those* (pictures) last year.
His fee was twenty dollars but now it's *twice that* (amount).

6.20 The deictic or 'pointing' contrast between *this/these* and *that/those* is not confined to spatial perception. While *this morning* usually refers to 'today', *that morning* refers to a more distant morning, past or future. More generally, *this/these* have more immediate or impending relevance than *that/those*:

These figures have just been compiled; *those* of yours are out of date.

In consequence, *this/these* tend to be associated with cataphoric reference (5.14), *that/those* with anaphoric reference:

> Watch carefully and I'll show you: *this* is how it's done.
> So now you know: *that*'s how it's done.
> *This* is an announcement: will Mrs Peterson please go to the enquiry desk.
> And *that* was the six o'clock news.

NOTE Especially in informal usage, a further extension of the polarity tends to equate *this/these* with the speaker's approval, and especially *that/those* with disapproval:

> How can *this* intelligent girl think of marrying *that* awful bore?

Indefinite pronouns

6.21 Indefinite pronouns are heterogeneous in form and they embrace also a wide range both of meanings and of grammatical properties. They are characterized as a whole, however, by having a general and nonspecific reference which the term 'indefinite' seeks to capture. Equally, they are characterized by having functions directly involved in expressing *quantity*, from totality ('all') to its converse ('nothing'). Reference in some cases invokes gender, such that items in *-body* are personal, items in *-thing* nonpersonal. Quantification in some cases invokes countability and number, such that *each* is singular count, *both* dual count, while *some* may be noncount or plural count.

Several of the indefinites can function both as determiners and as pronouns, as we shall see in what follows.

The universal items

6.22 We may first consider the compound indefinites (*everyone*, *everybody*, *everything*; *no one*, *nobody*, *nothing*), noting that all except *no one* are written as single words. These function only as pronouns, and despite their entailment of plural meaning they take singular verbs:

> The room was full of youngsters and *everyone/everybody* was listening intently to the speeches.
> I appealed to the whole crowd, but *no one/nobody* was willing to get up and speak.
>
> Father was very particular about how his tools were arranged in the workshop; he knew where *everything* was supposed to be and he insisted that *nothing* was ever to be misplaced.

These and the other universal indefinites are shown together in Table 6.22.

***Table* 6.22: Universal indefinites**

NUMBER	FUNCTION	COUNT: PERSONAL	COUNT: NONPERSONAL	NONCOUNT
Positive singular	pronoun	everyone everybody	everything	all
		each		
	determiner	every each		
plural	pronoun	all/both		
	determiner	all/both		
Negative singular	pronoun	no one nobody	nothing	none
		none		
	pronoun and determiner	neither		
plural	pronoun	none		
singular or plural	determiner	no		

NOTE [**a**] The forms in *-one* are commoner in written usage than those in *-body*, but in speech it is the latter that are more frequent.

[**b**] The pronouns in *-one* and *-body* have a genitive:

> Safety is *everyone's* responsibility, but in this case the accident seems to have been *nobody's* fault.

[**c**] Pronunciation obscures the origin of the compound *nothing*: /nʌθɪŋ/.

[**d**] Though *everywhere* and *nowhere* chiefly function as indefinite adverbials, they can also be pronouns.

> *Everywhere* is draughty and *nowhere* is comfortable.

6.23 Two further indefinites are *each* and *none*, both able to operate irrespective of gender with singular reference:

> Many members hesitated but although *each* was pressed to act, *none* was in the end willing.
>
> There were several knives in the drawer, but although *each* was tried in turn, *none* was sharp enough to cut through the rope.

Each (but not *none*) can also function as a determiner, in which role it is closely paralleled by *every*:

Each / *Every* } candidate will be individually interviewed.

Where they differ is that *each* is more targeted on the individual among the totality, *every* on the totality itself. In consequence, *every* is subject to quantitative modification as in

Almost every candidate was over the age of twenty-five.

By contrast with *each*, *none* is not restricted to singular reference, though plurals like the following are objectionable to some users:

Hundreds were examined but *none were* acceptable.

With the determiner *no* which corresponds to *none*, however, plural is as universally used as the singular:

No photography is permitted during the ceremony.
There were *no* passengers on the train.

NOTE The individualizing role of *each* can be preserved in otherwise plural environments:

The knives were *each* tried in turn.

6.24 With *all* and *both*, we make plural and dual universal reference:

The factory produces luxury cars and *all* are for export.
Police interviewed the (two) suspects and *both* were arrested.

These two items also have a predeterminer function:

All these cars are for export.
Both (the) suspects were arrested.

The converse of *all* is *no(ne)* (6.23); that of *both* is *neither*, usually with singular verb concord:

Police interviewed the (two) suspects but *neither* was arrested.

It has a parallel determiner function:

Neither suspect was arrested.

NOTE As with *each* (6.23 Note), *all* and *both* can appear medially.

The cars were *all* for export.
The (two) suspects were *both* arrested.

In this function *all* is used freely with a noncount reference otherwise largely confined to its predeterminer function:

The money had *all* been spent.
All the money had been spent.

Partitive indefinites

6.25 In dealing with the partitives (see Table 6.25), we must make a primary distinction between (a) those in *assertive* use, and (b) those in *non-assertive* use (2.11):

(a) I can see {*someone* / *somebody*} climbing that tree.
There's *something* I want to tell you.
There are nuts here; please have *some*.
There is wine here; please have *some*.
All the students speak French and *some* speak Italian as well.

(b) Did you see {*anyone* / *anybody*} in the vicinity?
I couldn't find *anything* to read.
I'd like nuts, if you have *any*.
I'd like wine, if you have *any*.
All the students work hard and I don't think *any* will fail.

When used pronominally, *some* and *any* usually have clear contextual reference to a noun phrase. Both occur more freely as determiners:

(a) I would love *some* nuts and *some* wine, please.
(b) If you haven't *any* nuts, I'll not have *any* wine, thank you.

The examples above illustrate the use of these items with personal, nonpersonal, count, and noncount reference. But it should be further noted that with *any* the number distinction is typically blurred:

The woman said she'd seen *an animal* running for cover, but her companion said that he hadn't seen *any animal(s)* at all.

NOTE [a] On *-one* and *-body*, see 6.22 Notes [a] and [b].
[b] Corresponding fairly closely to the negative *neither* (6.24), there is the nonassertive *either*:

The police did not arrest *either* (suspect).

[c] Beside the partitive *some* [səm] as determiner, a stressed form [sʌm] can be used with singular count nouns in the sense 'a certain' (5.6 Note [b]):

'Some man stopped me to ask the way.

[d] Like *everywhere*, *nowhere* (6.22 Note [d]), we have *somewhere*, *anywhere*; in AmE also *-place*.
[e] Assertive forms can be used in nonassertive 'territory' when the presupposition is positive:

Can you see *someone* in the garden (= There is someone in the garden; can you see him/her?)
Would you like *some* wine (= I invite you to have some wine).

***Table* 6.25: Partitive indefinites**

NUMBER	FUNCTION	COUNT		NONCOUNT
		PERSONAL	NONPERSONAL	
Assertive singular	pronoun	someone somebody	something	
	determiner	a (an)		some
plural	pronoun and determiner	some		
Nonassertive singular	pronoun	anyone anybody	anything	
	determiner	either any		any
plural	pronoun and determiner	any		

6.26 The partitives include quantifiers, which may (a) increase or (b) decrease the implications of *some*; thus beside 'There are *some* who would disagree', we have:

(a) There are *many* who would disagree.
(b) There are *a few* who would disagree.

Analogously with noncount reference:

The bread looked delicious and I ate { *some.* / *a great deal.* / *a little.* }

This use of quantifiers is not paralleled exactly in nonassertive contexts, where the contrast is rather between total and partial exclusion:

There aren't *any* who would disagree. (= No one)
There aren't *many* who would disagree. (= A few)
The wine was inferior and I didn't drink *any*. (= None)
The wine was inferior and I didn't drink *much*. (= A little)

As well as being pronouns, *many*, *a few*, *a little*, and *much* can be determiners.

The *of*-partitives

6.27 It is typical of the indefinites which have both a pronoun and a determiner role to fuse these roles in *of*-expressions where the final part is a personal pronoun or a noun preceded by a definite determiner; for example:

Some are doing well.
Some students are doing well.

Some of { *the students* / *these students* / *them* } are doing well.

Thus, with singular count partition:

each of
one of
any of
either of
none of
neither of
} (*the students*)

With plural count partition:

all of
both of
some of
many of
more of
most of
(a) few of
fewer, -est of
} (*our supporters*)

With noncount partition:

all of
some of
a great deal of
much of
more of
most of
(a) little of
less of
least of
any of
none of
} (*Beethoven's music*)

NOTE Comparative forms can be preceded by items of absolute meaning:

There were *a few more of our supporters* than I had expected.
She played *much less of Beethoven's music* than we had hoped.

6.28 As well as *one*, the other cardinal numerals are readily used in *of*-partitives:

Three of my friends are coming to dinner.

So too the ordinals, and these can be used with both count and noncount expressions:

A/one quarter of his books were destroyed in the fire.
She regulates her life carefully, devoting at least *five-sixths of her free time* to practising at the piano.

With *half*, there is considerable freedom in usage; as a predeterminer, it must itself be without a preceding determiner:

I saw half the {performance. / players.}

In *of*-partitives or otherwise pronominally, it may be determined:

I saw {half / a half / one half} of the {performance. / players.}

Outside *of*-partitives, *another* has only limited use as a pronoun:

There was *another of those unexplained fires* in the city yesterday.

But *cf*:

There have been many fires in the city recently;
{*another* was / *several* were} reported yesterday.

By contrast, *other* does not enter into *of*-partitives, but in its plural form is otherwise common in pronoun usage:

You should treat *others* as you would like to be treated yourself.

NOTE **[a]** In association with *each* and *one*, *other* and *another* function as reciprocal pronouns. For example:

One student will often help *another*.
Each of us must support *the other*.
The children were very fond of {*each other*. / *one another*.}

[b] The pattern (in figures and words) of the cardinal and ordinal numerals is as set out below. As ordinals, items are usually preceded by *the*, as fractions by *a* or *one*: '*the fourth* of July', '*a third* of a litre'.

0 nought, zero	
1 one	1st first
2 two	2nd second (*as fraction*, a half)
3 three	3rd third
4 four	4th fourth
5 five	5th fifth
6 six	6th sixth
7 seven	7th seventh

8 eight	8th eighth
9 nine	9th ninth
10 ten	10th tenth
11 eleven	11th eleventh
12 twelve	12th twelfth
13 thirteen	13th thirteenth
14 fourteen	14th fourteenth
15 fifteen	15th fifteenth
16 sixteen	16th sixteenth
17 seventeen	17th seventeenth
18 eighteen	18th eighteenth
19 nineteen	19th nineteenth
20 twenty	20th twentieth
21 twenty-one	21st twenty-first
22 twenty-two	22nd twenty-second
23 twenty-three	23rd twenty-third
24 twenty-four (etc)	24th twenty-fourth (etc)
30 thirty	30th thirtieth
40 forty	40th fortieth
50 fifty	50th fiftieth
60 sixty	60th sixtieth
70 seventy	70th seventieth
80 eighty	80th eightieth
90 ninety	90th ninetieth
100 a/one hundred	100th hundredth
120 a/one hundred and twenty	120th hundred and twentieth
1,000 a/one thousand	1,000th thousandth
1,500 a/one thousand five hundred	1,500th thousand five hundredth
2,000 two thousand (etc)	2,000th two thousandth (etc)
100,000 a/one hundred thousand	100,000th hundred thousandth
1,000,000 a/one million	1,000,000th millionth
1,000,000,000 a/one billion	1,000,000,000th billionth

Bibliographical note

On pronouns in general, see Bolinger (1979); Jackendoff (1968); Stevenson and Vitkovitch (1986).

On central pronouns, see Helke (1979); Jacobsson (1968); Saha (1987); Seppänen (1980); Thavenius (1983); on reciprocal pronouns, see Kjellmer (1982); on indefinite pronouns, see Sahlin (1979); on numerals, see Hurford (1975).

7 Adjectives and adverbs

Adjectives

Characteristics of the adjective

7.1 Four features are commonly considered to be characteristic of adjectives:

(a) They can freely occur in ATTRIBUTIVE function, *ie* they can premodify a noun, appearing between the determiner (including zero article) and the head of a noun phrase:

an *ugly* painting, the *round* table, *dirty* linen

(b) They can freely occur in PREDICATIVE function, *ie* they can function as subject complement, as in [1], or as object complement, as in [2], *eg*:

The painting is *ugly*. [1]
He thought the painting *ugly*. [2]

(c) They can be premodified by the intensifier *very*, *eg*:

The children are very *happy*.

(d) They can take COMPARATIVE and SUPERLATIVE forms. The comparison may be by means of inflections (*-er* and *-est*), as in [3–4], or by the addition of the premodifiers *more* and *most* ('periphrastic comparison'), as in [5–6]:

The children are *happier* now. [3]
They are the *happiest* people I know. [4]
These students are *more intelligent*. [5]
They are the *most beautiful* paintings I have ever seen. [6]

Not all words that are traditionally regarded as adjectives possess all these four features. The last two features generally coincide for a particular word and depend on a semantic feature, gradability. The adjective *atomic* in *atomic scientist*, for example, is not gradable and we therefore do not find **very atomic* or **more atomic*. Gradability cuts across word classes. Many adverbs are gradable, and since they also take premodification by *very* and comparison, these two features do not distinguish adjectives from adverbs.

The ability to function attributively and the ability to function predicatively are central features of adjectives. Adjectives like *happy* and *infinite*, which have both these features, are therefore CENTRAL adjectives. Those like *utter* that can be only attributive and those like *afraid* that can be only predicative are PERIPHERAL adjectives.

NOTE Some suffixes are found only, or typically, with adjectives, *eg*:

-able: comfortable	*-al*: seasonal
-ful: playful	*-ic*: scientific
-ish: greyish	*-less*: useless
-ous: dangerous	*-y*: dirty

However, many common adjectives have no identifying form, *eg*: *good, hot, little, young, fat*.

The adjective and other word classes

Adjective and adverb homomorphs

7.2 Normally there is a regular difference of form between an adjective and a corresponding adverb in that the adverb is distinguished by its *-ly* suffix. In *a rapid car*, *rapid* is an adjective; in *He drove rapidly*, *rapidly* is an adverb.

However, there are some words that have the same form, without the *-ly* suffix, in adjective and adverb functions, *eg*:

Bill has a *fast* car. [adjective]
Bill drove *fast*. [adverb]
Norma arrived in the *late* afternoon. [adjective]
Norma arrived *late* in the afternoon. [adverb]

Sometimes there is also an *-ly* adverb form but with a different meaning:

Have you seen her *lately*? ['recently']

And sometimes there are two forms: one may be used as either adjective or adverb and the other is an adverb with an *-ly* suffix:

Take a *deep* breath. [adjective]

Breathe { *deep*. ⟨esp informal⟩ / *deeply*. } [adverb]

Finally, there are some words in *-ly* that can function both as adjectives and as adverbs, *eg*:

I caught an *early* train. [adjective]
We finished *early* today. [adverb]
That was a *kindly* gesture. [adjective]
Will you *kindly* refrain from smoking? [adverb]

They include a set of words denoting time, *eg*: *daily*, *hourly*, *monthly*, *weekly*.

NOTE [a] Where there is variation, some people prefer the *-ly* form for the adverb function, particularly in formal style. The adjective form cannot precede the verb:

Ted will pay { *dear* / *dearly* } for his mistake.

Ted will { **dear* / *dearly* } pay for his mistake.

[**b**] When we require adverbs corresponding to *-ly* adjectives such as *friendly*, *lively*, and *masterly*, we normally use an adjective construction, thereby avoiding the double suffix *-lily*:

She received us *in a friendly way* [NOT: *She received us *friendlily*.]

Adjectives and adverbs beginning with *a-*

7.3 Some words beginning with *a-* are adjectives and can be used predicatively with both *be* and other copular verbs, but the *a*-adverbs can be used only with *be*. The distinction differentiates adjectives from adverbs.

The patient was { *asleep.* / *hungry.* } [adjectives]
The patient was { *abroad.* / *there.* } [adverbs]

The patient seemed { *asleep.* / *hungry.* } [adjectives]
The patient seemed { **abroad.* / **there.* } [adverbs]

Another difference is that *a*-adjectives refer to temporary states and cannot be part of the predication after verbs of motion; *a*-adverbs, on the other hand, denote direction after such verbs.

Jean went { **asleep*/**alert*. [adjectives] / *abroad*/*away*. [adverbs] }

Common *a*-adjectives include *ablaze*, *afloat*, *afraid*, *alert*, *alone*, *ashamed*, *asleep*, *aware*, *awake*.

NOTE [**a**] *Alert* and *aloof* are freely used attributively. Most other *a*-adjectives can occur attributively only when they are modified: *a somewhat afraid soldier*, *the fast-asleep children*, *a really alive student* ('lively').
[**b**] Some *a*-adjectives freely take premodification by *very* and comparison, *eg*: *very afraid*, *more alert*. Others do so marginally, *eg*: *asleep* and *awake*.

Adjectives and nouns

7.4 Nouns commonly function as premodifiers of other nouns (*cf* 17.35):

the *bus* station, a *business* friend, *student* grants

However, they do not share other characteristics of most adjectives:
(a) There is no corresponding predicative function:

the *bus* station *The station is *bus*.

(b) They cannot be modified by *very*:

*a very *bus* station

(c) They cannot take comparison:

*a *busser* station

Furthermore, nouns have other features which distinguish them from adjectives; for example article contrast (*the bus/a bus*), number contrast (*one bus/two buses*), genitive inflection (*the student's essays*), premodification by an adjective (*the young student*).

The basically nominal character of a premodifying noun, such as *garden* in *garden tools*, is shown by its correspondence to a prepositional phrase with the noun as complement: *tools for the garden*. Compare also:

the *city* council ~ the council *for the city*
a *stone* wall ~ a wall (made) *of stone*
August weather ~ weather (usual) *in August*

Such a correspondence is not available for attributive adjectives:

a *long* poem	a *thick* wall
the *urban* council	*hot* weather

Some items can be both adjectives and nouns. For example, *criminal* is an adjective in that it can be used both attributively (*a criminal attack*) and predicatively (*The attack seemed criminal to us*). On the other hand, *criminal* has been converted into a noun in *The criminal pleaded guilty* and *They are violent criminals*. Here are other examples of conversion from adjective to noun:

ADJECTIVES	NOUNS
an *annual* custom	She is hoping to publish an *annual* for children.
a *black* student	There was only one *black* in my class.
a *classic* book	You won't find many *classics* in our library.
intellectual interests	She considers herself an *intellectual*.
a *noble* family	The king greeted his *nobles*.
a *natural* skier	He's a *natural* for the job.
a *six-year-old* boy	Our *six-year-old* is at school.

NOTE [a] Like adjectives, nouns can function as subject complement after copular verbs, in particular after *be*:

That man is *a fool*.
The noise you heard was *thunder*.
She became *a nurse*.

Some nouns can also be used within the subject complement after *seem* ⟨esp BrE⟩:

He seems *a fool*. [=*foolish*]
Your remark seems (complete) *nonsense* to me. [=*nonsensical*]
My stay there seemed *sheer bliss*. [=*blissful*]
His friend seems very much *an Englishman*. [=very *English*]

Note however the change of premodifier in: *very much an Englishman* ~ *very English*; and the use of the indefinite article (a sure sign of noun status) in *a fool* and *an Englishman*.

[**b**] Some noun forms can function both attributively and predicatively, in which case we can perhaps regard them as adjectives. They denote style or material from which things are made:

that *concrete* floor ~ That floor is *concrete*.
Worcester porcelain ~ This porcelain is *Worcester*.
those *apple* pies ~ Those pies are *apple*. ⟨informal⟩

Adjectives and participles

7.5 There are many adjectives that have the same suffixes as participles in *-ing* or *-ed* (including other forms corresponding to *-ed*, *cf* 3.2, 3.9*f*). These are PARTICIPIAL ADJECTIVES:

PREDICATIVE USE	ATTRIBUTIVE USE
His views were very *surprising*.	~ his *surprising* views
The man seemed very *offended*.	~ the *offended* man

They include forms in *-ed* that have no corresponding verbs:

The results were *unexpected*.	~ the *unexpected* results
Her children must be *downhearted*.	~ her *downhearted* children
All his friends are *talented*.	~ his *talented* friends
His lung is *diseased*.	~ his *diseased* lung

When there are no corresponding verbs (**to unexpect*, **to downheart*, **to talent*, **to disease*), the forms are obviously not participles.

When there is a corresponding verb, attributively used *-ed* forms usually have a passive meaning, *eg*:

lost property ~ property that *has been lost*

NOTE [**a**] In some cases the *-ed* participle is not interpreted as passive. The passive interpretation is excluded if the corresponding verb can be used only intransitively:

the *escaped* prisoner ['the prisoner who has escaped']
the *departed* guests ['the guests who have departed']

But even in other instances, the participle relates to the intransitive use of the verb; thus the passive interpretation is impossible in:

a *grown* person ['a person who has grown (to maturity)']

It is unlikely in:

the *faded* curtains ['the curtains which have faded'.]
the *retired* manager ['the manager who has retired']

Predicative use occurs only with some of these participial adjectives:

The curtains are *faded* ['The curtains have faded']
Her father is now *retired*.

Her son is *grown*. [dubious in BrE, but *full-grown* or *grown-up* is fully acceptable]
The guests are *departed*. ⟨archaic⟩

[b] Sometimes there is a corresponding verb, but it has a different meaning. We can therefore have ambiguous sentences where the ambiguity depends on whether the word is a participle or a participial adjective:

{ADJECTIVE: She is (very) *calculating* (but her husband is frank).
{PARTICIPLE: She is *calculating* (our salaries). ['. . . so don't disturb her while she is doing the arithmetic'.]

{ADJECTIVE: They were (very) *relieved* (to find her at home).
{PARTICIPLE: They were *relieved* (by the next group of sentries).

7.6 Often the difference between the adjective and the participle is not clear-cut (*cf* 17.30*ff*). The verbal force of the participle is explicit for the *-ing* form when a direct object is present. Hence, the following *-ing* forms are participles that constitute a verb phrase with the preceding auxiliary:

Her views were *alarming* her audience.
You are *frightening* the children.
They are *insulting* us.

Similarly, the verbal force is explicit for the *-ed* form when a *by*-agent phrase with a personal agent is present, indicating the correspondence to the active form of the sentence:

The man was *offended* by the policeman.
He is *appreciated* by his students.
She was *misunderstood* by her parents.

For both participle forms, premodification by the intensifier *very* is an explicit indication that the forms have achieved adjective status:

Her views were very *alarming*.
You are very *frightening*.
The man was very *offended*.

We might therefore expect that the presence of *very* together with an explicit indicator of verbal force would produce an unacceptable sentence. This is certainly so for the *-ing* participle form:

*His views were very *alarming* his audience.

However, with the *-ed* participle, there appears to be divided usage, with increasing acceptance of the cooccurence of *very* with a *by*-agent phrase containing a personal agent:

?The man was very *offended* by the policeman.

In the absence of any explicit indicator, the status of the participle form is indeterminate:

The man was *offended*.

For the *-ed* form in this example, the participle interpretation focuses on the process, while the adjective interpretation focuses on the state resulting from the process. For the *-ing* form the difference is perhaps clearer. In the sentence *John is insulting*, with no object present, the participle interpretation is implausible because the verb is normally transitive.

NOTE [**a**] Generally, *-ed* participle forms accepting *very* can retain *very* when they cooccur with a *by*-phrase containing a nonpersonal noun phrase that expresses the notion of cause or reason:

> I'm *very disturbed* by your attitude.
> We were *very pleased* by his behaviour.

[**b**] The participle sometimes reaches full adjective status when it is compounded with another element:

> It is *breaking* my heart. ~ It is (very) *heart-breaking*.

[**c**] Like participial adjectives, *-ing* and *-ed* participles can be attributive, as the following examples show:

her *crying* children	a *married* couple
a *winning* team	his *published* work
boiling water	the *captured* prisoner

Some verbs have different participle forms for verbal and adjectival use:

You have *drunk too much*.	~ *drunk(en)* driving/driver
Have you *shaved*?	~ a *clean-shaven* young man
The shirt has *shrunk*.	~ a *shrunken* shirt

Note the pronunciation /ɪd/ of the ending *-ed* in some adjectives, *eg*: *beloved* /bɪˈlʌvɪd/. Other examples:

crooked	*dogged*	*jagged*	*learned*
naked	*ragged*	*wicked*	*wretched*

The suffix of *aged* is pronounced as a separate syllable /ɪd/ when the word is predicative or is attributive of a personal noun (*The man is aged*; *an aged man* 'old'), but not, for example, in *an aged wine* or *a man aged fifty*.

Syntactic functions of adjectives

Attributive and predicative

7.7 Adjectives are attributive when they premodify the head of a noun phrase (17.29):

> a *small* garden   *popular* ballads

They are predicative when they function as subject complement or object complement (*cf* 10.5):

> He seems *careless*. (C_s)
> I find him *careless*. (C_o)

Adjectives are subject complement not only to noun phrases, but also to finite clauses and nonfinite clauses:

> That you need a car is *obvious*.
> Whether she will resign is *uncertain*.
> To complain may be *dangerous*.
> Playing chess can be *enjoyable*.

Adjectives can also be object complement to clauses:

> I consider {what he did / taking such risks} *foolish*.

NOTE The adjective functioning as object complement often expresses the result of the process denoted by the verb:

> He pulled his belt *tight*. [1]
> He pushed the window *open*. [2]
> He writes his letters *large*. [3]

The result can be stated for each sentence by using the verb *be*:

> His belt is *tight*. [1a]
> The window is *open*. [2a]
> His letters are *large*. [3a]

Postpositive

7.8 Adjectives can sometimes be postpositive, *ie* they can immediately follow the noun or pronoun they modify. We may thus have three positions of adjectives:

> PREDICATIVE: This information is *useful*. [1]
> ATTRIBUTIVE: *useful* information [2]
> POSTPOSITIVE: something *useful* [3]

A postpositive adjective can usually be regarded as a reduced relative clause:

> something *that is useful* [3a]

Compound indefinite pronouns and adverbs ending in *-body*, *-one*, *-thing*, *-where* can be modified only postpositively:

> *Anyone* (who is) *intelligent* can do it.
> I want to try on *something* (that is) *larger*.
> We're not going *anywhere very exciting*.

Of course, adjectives that can occur only attributively (*cf* 7.17*ff*) are excluded:

> *something (which is) *main*   *somebody (who is) *mere*

NOTE [a] Postposition is obligatory for *proper* in the meaning 'as strictly defined', *eg*: *the City of London proper*.

[b] In several institutionalized expressions (mostly in official designations), the adjective is postpositive, *eg*: *the president elect, heir apparent, attorney general, notary public, body politic, proof positive*.
[c] Adjectives ending in *-able* and *-ible* can be postpositive, as well as attributive, when they are modified by another adjective in the superlative degree or by certain other modifiers: *the best use possible, the greatest insult imaginable, the only actor suitable*; the adjective phrase is then discontinuous (*cf the best possible use* and 7.9). Some can be postpositive without this constraint, *eg*: *the stars visible, rivers navigable*. These convey the implication that what they are denoting has only a temporary application. Thus, *the stars visible* refers to stars that are visible at a time specified or implied, while *the visible stars* more aptly refers to a category of stars that can (at appropriate times) be seen.

Postposition is usual for *absent, present, concerned,* and *involved* when they designate temporary as opposed to permanent attributes:

> The soldiers *present* were his supporters.

[d] *Appointed, desired, required, followed, past,* and *preceding* can also be postpositive as well as attributive, *eg*: *at the time appointed, in years past*.

Adjectives with complementation

7.9 Adjectives with complementation normally cannot have attributive position but require postposition. Compare:

> a *suitable* actor   BUT NOT: *a *suitable for the part* actor

The complementation can be a prepositional phrase or a *to*-infinitive clause:

> I know an actor *suitable for the part*. [1]
> They have a house *larger than yours*. [2]
> The boys *easiest to teach* were in my class. [3]
> Students *brave enough to attempt the course* deserve to succeed. [4]

If the adjective is alone or merely premodified by an intensifier, postposition is not normally allowed:

> *They have a house *(much) larger*.
> *The soldiers *(rather) timid* approached their officer.

However, if the noun phrase is generic and indefinite, we can postpone coordinated adjectives, or adjectives with some clause element added, though such constructions are formal and rather infrequent:

> Soldiers *timid or cowardly* don't fight well. [5]
> A man *usually honest* will sometimes cheat. [6]

The more usual constructions are premodification or a relative clause:

> *Timid or cowardly* soldiers . . . [5a]
> A man *who is usually honest* . . . [6a]

The adjective phrase can be discontinuous (*cf* 7.8 Note [c]): the adjective is attributive and its complementation is in postposition. Thus, equivalent to sentences [2] and [3]:

They have a *larger* house *than yours*. [2a]
The *easiest* boys *to teach* were in my class. [3a]

NOTE [a] An adjective modified by *enough*, *too*, or *so* can be separated from its complementation if the modified adjective is placed before the indefinite (or zero) article of the noun phrase:

She is *brave enough* a student *to attempt the course*. [7]
It was *too boring* a book *to read*. [8]
They are *so difficult* people *to please*. [9]

But with *enough* and *too*, this construction seems to be possible only if the adjective phrase is part of the subject complement or object complement:

**Brave enough* a student *to attempt the course* deserves to succeed. [7b]

With *so*, the construction is also possible if the adjective phrase is part of the subject:

A man *so difficult* } *to please* must be hard to work with.
So difficult a man }

[b] Exceptionally, certain short prepositional phrases may also premodify an adjective in attributive position:

a *by no means* irresponsible action
~an action (which is) by no means irresponsible

Adjectives as heads of noun phrases

7.10 Adjectives can function as heads of noun phrases, which (like all noun phrases) can be subject of the sentence, complement, object, and prepositional complement. Adjectives as noun-phrase heads, unlike nouns, do not inflect for number or for the genitive case and they usually require a definite determiner.

Adjectives are typically used as heads of noun phrases to refer to certain fairly well-established classes of persons: *eg*: *the brave*, *the weak*, *the maladjusted*, *the elderly*, *the underprivileged*.

There are three types of adjectives functioning as noun-phrase heads, and these are exemplified in the following sentences:

(a) *The innocent* are often deceived by *the unscrupulous*. (7.11)
(b) *The industrious Dutch* are admired by their neighbours. (7.12)
(c) She admires *the mystical*. (7.13)

Type (a): *the innocent*

7.11 Adjectives which can premodify personal nouns (*the young people*) can be noun-phrase heads (*the young*) with plural and generic reference denoting classes, categories, or types of people. The adjective can itself be premodified [3–5] or postmodified [6–7]:

The poor are causing the nation's leaders great concern. [1]
There is a lack of communication between *the young* and *the old*. [2]
The extremely old need a great deal of attention. [3]

The emotionally disturbed and *the physically and mentally handicapped* need the aid of society. [4]
The very wise avoid such temptations. [5]
The young in spirit enjoy life. [6]
The old who resist change are brushed aside. [7]

NOTE [**a**] Modification of the adjective is usually restrictive, *eg* [5]: *the very wise*. Inflected comparison forms of the adjective are also possible (*the wiser*). Comparative inflection and adverb modification are indications of the adjective status of these noun-phrase heads, while modification by adjectives (as in *the hungry poor*) is more typical of nouns, and modification by relative clauses is normally an indication of noun status.

[**b**] The definite determiner is normally the generic definite article *the*. Note, however, the use of the possessive determiner in:

We will nurse *your sick*, clothe *your naked*, and feed *your hungry*.
It is the duty of the Government to care for *our poor, our unemployed*.

The adjectives can function without a determiner if they are conjoined (*cf* 5.20):

He is acceptable to *both (the) old and (the) young*.

Also in some *of*-constructions:

The number of *jobless* is rising.

Type (b): *the Dutch*

7.12 Some adjectives denoting nationalities (*cf* 5.33*f*) can be noun-phrase heads:

The industrious Dutch are admired by their neighbours.
You French and we British ought to be allies.

As with type (a) in 7.11, these noun phrases normally have generic reference and take plural concord. The adjectives in question are restricted to words ending in *-(i)sh* (*eg*: *British, Spanish, Welsh*), *-ch* (*eg*: *Dutch, French*), *-ese* (*eg*: *Chinese, Japanese*), and the adjective *Swiss*.

NOTE These adjectives can in turn be modified by adjectives, which are normally nonrestrictive:

the industrious Dutch ['the Dutch, who are industrious']

Postmodifying prepositional phrases and relative clauses can be either restrictive or nonrestrictive (*cf* 17.3):

The Irish (who live) in America retain sentimental links with Ireland.
The Dutch, for many of whom speaking English is second nature, have produced many of the greatest grammarians of the English language.

Type (c): *the mystical*

7.13 Some adjectives can function as noun-phrase heads with abstract reference. They include, in particular, superlatives, in which case we can sometimes insert a general noun like *thing* in its abstract sense:

The latest (thing/news) is that he is going to run for re-election.

Unlike types (a) and (b), type (c) adjectives functioning as noun-phrase heads take singular concord:

They ventured into *the unknown*, which was . . .
The best is yet to come.

Type (c) is restricted chiefly to certain fixed expressions. Thus, for example, *the supernatural, the exotic, the unreal* are more likely to occur than *the lovely, the foreign, the exciting*, with abstract, generic reference.

NOTE [a] Some of these adjectives can be modified by adverbs:

The very best is yet to come.
He went from *the extremely sublime* to *the extremely ridiculous.*

[b] There are some set expressions in which an adjective with abstract reference is the complement of a preposition:

He left *for good.*	He enjoyed it *to the full.*
in public/private/secret	*from bad to worse*
in short	*out of the ordinary*
on the sly	*in common*

Verbless clauses

7.14 Adjectives can function as the sole realization of a verbless clause (*cf* 14.6, 15.34*f*) or as the head of an adjective phrase realizing the clause:

The man, *quietly assertive*, spoke to the assembled workers.
Unhappy with the result, she returned to work.
Glad to accept, the boy nodded his agreement.
Anxious for a quick decision, the chairman called for a vote.
Long and untidy, his hair played in the breeze.

The clause is mobile:

The chairman called for a vote, *anxious for a quick decision.*

Its implied subject is usually the subject of the sentence ('The chairman is anxious for a vote'). However, if the clause contains additional clause constituents, it can be related to a noun phrase other than the subject:

She glanced with disgust at the cat, *now quiet in her daughter's lap.*

Sometimes the adjective phrase can be replaced by an adverb phrase with little change of meaning:

Rather nervous, the man opened the letter.
Rather nervously, the man opened the letter.

In this function, the adverb phrase is like the adjective phrase in referring to an attribute of the subject ('The man, who was rather nervous, opened the letter'), but it normally does so specifically in relation to the performance of an action.

NOTE The implied subject of the clause can be the whole of the superordinate clause:

> *Strange*, it was she who initiated divorce proceedings.
> *Most important*, his report offered prospects of a great profit.
> *More remarkable still*, he is in charge of the project.

Here too it is possible to substitute an adverb for the adjective with little or no difference in meaning (*cf* content disjuncts in 8.42):

> *Strangely*, it was she who initiated divorce proceedings.

Contingent verbless clauses

7.15 One type of verbless clause, which is often introduced by a subordinator, expresses the circumstance or condition under which what is said in the superordinate clause applies:

> *(Whether) right or wrong*, he always comes off worst in an argument because of his inability to speak cogently.
> *When fit*, the Labrador is an excellent retriever.
> *If wet*, these shoes should never be placed too close to the heat.

The contingent clause can also refer to the object of the superordinate clause, in which case it usually appears in final position:

> You must eat it *when fresh*.

NOTE The clause can also refer to the whole of the superordinate clause (which would be realized in the subordinate clause by the pro-form *it*). In such cases the subordinator cannot be omitted:

> *When* (it is) *necessary*, he can be taken to the doctor.
> You must come *as soon as* (it is) *possible*.

Exclamatory adjective clauses

7.16 Adjectives can be exclamations, with or without an initial *wh*-element:

> *Excellent!* (How) *wonderful!* (How) *good of you!*

Such clauses need not be dependent on any previous linguistic context, but may be a comment on some object or activity in the situational context.

Syntactic subclassification of adjectives

Attributive only

7.17 In general, adjectives that are restricted to attributive position, or that occur predominantly in attributive position, do not characterize the referent of the noun directly. For example, *old* can be either a central adjective or an adjective restricted to attributive position. In *that old man* (the opposite of *that young man*), *old* is a central adjective, and can thus also be predicative: *That man is old.* On the other hand, in the usual sense of *an old friend of mine* ['a friend of old, a long-standing friend'], *old* is restricted to attributive position and cannot be related to *My friend is old.* In this case, *old* is the opposite of *new* ['recently acquired']. The person referred to is not being identified as old; it is his friendship that is old.

When adjectives characterize the referent of the noun directly (*that old man, My friend is old*) they are termed INHERENT, when they do not (*an old friend of mine*) they are termed NONINHERENT (*cf* 7.25).

NOTE A few adjectives with strongly emotive value are restricted to attributive position, though the scope of the adjective clearly extends to the person referred to by the noun, *eg*: *you poor man, my dear lady, that wretched woman.*

Intensifying adjectives

7.18 Some adjectives have a heightening effect on the noun they modify, or the reverse, a lowering effect. At least three semantic subclasses of intensifying adjectives can be distinguished:

(a) emphasizers
(b) amplifiers
(c) downtoners

(a) EMPHASIZERS have a general heightening effect and are generally attributive only, *eg*:

a *true* scholar	*plain* nonsense
a *clear* failure	the *simple* truth
pure ['sheer'] fabrication	an *outright* lie
a *real* ['undoubted'] hero	*sheer* arrogance
a *certain* winner	a *sure* sign

(b) AMPLIFIERS scale upwards from an assumed norm, and are central adjectives if they are inherent and denote a high or extreme degree:

a *complete* victory ~ The victory was *complete.*
great destruction ~ The destruction was *great.*

On the other hand, when they are noninherent, amplifiers are attributive only:

a *complete* fool ≁ *The fool is *complete.*
a *firm* friend ≁ *The friend is *firm.*

Complete refers to the completeness of the folly, and *firm* to the firmness of the friendship (in which sense it is asterisked here).

In addition, amplifiers are only attributive when they are used as emphasizers, conveying principally emphasis rather than degree. For example, *total* in *total nonsense* is an emphasizer, while in *total destruction* it is an amplifier and has a literal application ('the destruction of everything'). Hence the contrast:

total nonsense ≁ *The nonsense was *total.*
total destruction ~ The destruction was *total.*

Further examples of adjectives as amplifiers that are attributive only:

utter folly	the *absolute* limit
a *close* friend	a *complete* stranger
an *extreme* enemy	his *entire* salary
a *great* supporter	a *perfect* stranger
a *strong* opponent	*total* irresponsibility

(c) DOWNTONERS have a lowering effect, usually scaling downwards from an assumed norm. They are relatively few (*eg*: *slight* in *a slight effort*, *feeble* in *a feeble joke*) and can be ignored for our present purpose, since they are generally central adjectives.

Restrictive adjectives

7.19 Restrictive adjectives restrict the reference of the noun exclusively, particularly, or chiefly. Examples, within noun phrases, include:

a *certain* person	his *chief* excuse
the *principal* objection	the *exact* answer
the *same* student	the *sole* argument
the *only* occasion	the *specific* point
a *particular* child	the *very* man

Again, some of these have homonyms. For example, *certain* in *a certain person* is a restrictive (equivalent to 'a particular person'), while in *a certain winner* it is an intensifier (equivalent to 'a sure winner').

NOTE Notice the use of *very* as a restrictive adjective:

You are *the very man* I want.

Adjectives related to adverbs

7.20 Some noninherent adjectives that are only attributive can be related to adverbs, even though they are not intensifying or restrictive. They include:

my *former* friend	['formerly my friend']
an *old* friend	['a friend of old']
past students	['students in the past']
a *possible* friend	['possibly a friend']
the *present* king	['the king at present']
an *occasional* visitor	['occasionally a visitor']

Some adjectives require implications additional to the adverbial:

the *late* president ['the person who was formerly the president (but is now dead)']

If the adjectives premodify agentive nouns, the latter also suggest a relationship to an associated verb:

a *big* eater ['someone who eats a lot']
a *clever* liar ['someone who lies cleverly']
a *hard* worker ['someone who works hard']
a *heavy* smoker ['someone who smokes heavily']
a *sound* sleeper ['someone who sleeps soundly']

NOTE The noun can be inanimate:

rapid calculations ['calculations made rapidly']
occasional showers ['showers occurring occasionally']
a *fast* car ['a car that can go fast']
a *fast* road ['a road on which one can drive fast']

Adjectives related to nouns

7.21 Denominal adjectives (*ie* adjectives derived from nouns) tend to be restricted to attributive position:

an *atomic* scientist ['a scientist specializing in the theory of atoms']
a *criminal* court ['a court dealing with crime']
a *criminal* lawyer ['a lawyer specializing in cases of crime']
a *polar* bear ['a bear living near the pole']
a *medical* school ['a school for students of medicine']
musical comedy ['a comedy accompanied by music']
a *tidal* wave ['a wave produced by the tide']

Predicative only

7.22 Adjectives that are restricted, or virtually restricted, to predicative position are most like verbs and adverbs. They tend to refer to a (possibly temporary) condition rather than to a characteristic. Perhaps the most common are those referring to the health (or lack of health) of an animate being:

He felt *ill/poorly* <both esp BrE>/*well/faint/unwell.*

However, many people use such adjectives as attributives too; for example:

A *well* person need see a doctor only for a periodic checkup.

A large group of adjectives that are restricted to predicative position comprises adjectives which can take complementation (*cf* 16.38*ff*):

able (*to* + infinitive)	*fond* (*of*)
afraid (*that, of, about*)	*glad* (*that, to*)
answerable (*to*)	*happy* (*that, to, with, about*)
averse (*to, from*)	*loath* (*to*)
aware (*of*)	*subject* (*to*)
conscious (*that, of*)	*tantamount* (*to*)

Some of these adjectives must take complementation (*eg*: *subject to* and *tantamount to*), and many normally do.

Many of these adjectives closely resemble verbs semantically:

He *is afraid to* do it. ['He *fears to* do it.']
They *are fond of* her. ['They *like* her.']
That *is tantamount to* an ultimatum. ['That *amounts to* an ultimatum.']

NOTE [a] *Sick* is the exception among the 'health' adjectives in that its attributive use is very common:

the *sick* woman ['The woman is sick.']

[b] Some of the adjectives that are restricted to predicative position have homonyms that can occur both predicatively and attributively, *eg*:

the *conscious* patient ~ The patient is *conscious*. [= 'awake']
Cf: He is *conscious* of his faults. [= 'aware']

Semantic subclassification of adjectives

Stative/dynamic

7.23 Adjectives are characteristically stative. Many adjectives, however, can be seen as dynamic. In particular, most adjectives that are susceptible to subjective measurement are capable of being dynamic. Stative and dynamic adjectives differ syntactically in a number of ways. For example, a stative adjective such as *tall* cannot be used with the progressive aspect or with the imperative:

*He's being *tall*. *Be *tall*.

On the other hand, we can use *funny* as a dynamic adjective:

I didn't realize he was being *funny*. Her story was very *funny*.

Adjectives that can be used dynamically include *brave*, *calm*, *cheerful*, *conceited*, *cruel*, *foolish*, *friendly*, *funny*, *good*, *greedy*, *helpful*, *jealous*, *naughty*, *noisy*, *tidy*.

Gradable/nongradable

7.24 Most adjectives are gradable. Gradability is manifested through comparison:

tall	~ tall*er*	~ tall*est*
beautiful	~ *more* beautiful	~ *most* beautiful

It is also manifested through modification by intensifiers:

very tall *so* beautiful *extremely* useful

Gradability applies to adverbs as well as adjectives (*cf* 7.39*ff*).

All dynamic and most stative adjectives (*eg*: *tall*, *old*) are gradable; some stative adjectives are not, principally denominal adjectives like *atomic* (*scientist*) and *hydrochloric* (*acid*), and adjectives denoting provenance, *eg*: *British*.

Inherent/noninherent

7.25 Most adjectives are inherent. For example, the inherent adjective in *a wooden cross* applies to the referent of the object directly: a wooden cross is also a wooden object. On the other hand, in *a wooden actor* the adjective is noninherent: a wooden actor is not (presumably) a wooden man. Some other examples:

INHERENT	NONINHERENT
a *firm* handshake	a *firm* friend
a *perfect* alibi	a *perfect* stranger
a *certain* result	a *certain winner*
a true report	a *true* scholar

NOTE Modification of a noun by means of a noninherent adjective can be seen as an extension of the basic sense of the noun. Thus *a firm friend* is 'a friend whose friendship is firm', and *a perfect stranger* is 'a stranger who is perfectly strange'.

Ordering of adjectives in premodification

7.26 When two or more adjectives cooccur in attributive position, the order of the adjectives is to a large extent determined by their semantic properties. The principles for the order of items in premodification are discussed in 17.41. Here we will only mention the major positional ranges of adjectives in premodifying position.

In the premodification structure of the noun phrase, adjectives are placed between the determiners and the head of the noun phrase (*cf* 17.2). We distinguish four zones:

(I) PRECENTRAL

Here, after the determiners, is where peripheral, nongradable adjectives are placed, in particular the intensifying adjectives (*cf* 7.18); *eg*: *certain, definite, sheer, complete, slight.*

(II) CENTRAL

This zone is the place of the central adjectives (*cf* 7.1); *eg*: *hungry, ugly, funny, stupid, silent, rich, empty.*

(III) POSTCENTRAL

This zone includes participles, *eg*: *retired, sleeping*, and colour adjectives, *eg*: *red, pink*.

(IV) PREHEAD

This zone includes the 'least adjectival and the most nominal' items, such as denominal adjectives (*cf* 7.21) denoting nationality, ethnic background, *eg*: *Austrian, Midwestern*, and denominal adjectives with the meaning 'consisting of', 'involving', 'relating to', *eg*: *experimental, statistical, political, statutory*. In the prehead zone we also find nouns in attributive position (*cf* further 17.35).

On the basis of this classification, we can expect the following order:

I + II	*certain important* people
I + III	the *same restricted* income

I + IV	your *present annual* turnover
II + III	a *funny red* hat
II + IV	an *enormous tidal* wave
I + II + IV	*certain rich American* producers

Adverbs

Characteristics of the adverb

7.27 There are two types of syntactic functions that characterize the traditional adverbs, but an adverb need have only one of these:

(a) clause element adverbial (*cf* 7.31):

He *quite* forgot about it.

(b) premodifier of adjective and adverb (7.32*f*):

They are *quite* {happy. / happily married.}

The most conspicuous example of an adverb that functions only as a modifier of adjectives and adverbs, and not as a clause element, is *very*. (For *very* as an adjective, *cf* 7.19 Note.)

Morphologically, we can distinguish three types of adverb, of which two are closed classes (simple and compound), and one is an open class (derivational):

(a) SIMPLE adverbs, *eg*: *just*, *only*, *well*. Many simple adverbs denote position and direction, *eg*: *back*, *down*, *near*, *out*, *under*.
(b) COMPOUND adverbs, *eg*: *somehow*, *somewhere*, *therefore*.
(c) DERIVATIONAL adverbs. The majority of derivational adverbs have the suffix *-ly*, by means of which new adverbs are created from adjectives (including participial adjectives): *odd* ~ *oddly*; *interesting* ~ *interestingly*. Other, less common, derivational suffixes are:

-wise:	clockwise	*-ways*:	sideways
-ward (s):	northward(s)	*-style*:	cowboy-style
-fashion:	schoolboy-fashion		

The adverb and other word classes

Conjunct adverb and conjunction

7.28 A few adverbs functioning as conjuncts (*cf* 8.43*ff*), such as *so* and *yet*, resemble coordinators both in being connectives and in having certain syntactic features. In particular, these adverbs cannot be transposed with their clause in front of the preceding clause. Thus, the order of the following two clauses (with the conjunct adverb *so* in the second clause) is fixed:

We paid him a very large sum. *So* he kept quiet about what he saw. [1]

If we reverse the order of the clauses, the relationship between the two clauses is changed, and *so* must now refer to some preceding clause:

So he kept quiet about what he saw. We paid him a very large sum. [2]

However, the conjunct adverbs differ from coordinators in that they can be preceded by a coordinator:

We paid him a very large sum, ***and so*** he kept quiet about what he saw. [1a]

Reaction signal and initiator

7.29 Certain other items must be positioned initially. They are important because of their high frequency in spoken English. Some are restricted to the spoken language. These can be assigned to two small classes:

(i) 'reaction signals', *eg*: *no, yes, yeah, yep, m, hm, mhm*
(ii) 'initiators', *eg*: *well, oh, ah*; *oh well, well then, why* ⟨esp AmE⟩

Adverb and preposition

7.30 There are various combinations of verbs plus particles (*cf* 16.3*ff*). Since a preposition is normally followed by its complement, the particle is an adverb if the verb is intransitive:

The plane has taken *off*.

When a noun phrase follows the particle, the latter may still be an adverb. The particle in the phrasal verb in [1] is an adverb because it can be transposed to follow the verb, as in [1a]:

They turned *on* the light. [1]
They turned the light *on*. [1a]

In contrast, *to* in [2] is a preposition, part of the prepositional verb *take to*, because its position is fixed, as we see from [2a]:

They took *to* us. [2]
*They took us *to*. [2a]

Syntactic functions of adverbs

Adverb as adverbial

7.31 ADJUNCTS and SUBJUNCTS are relatively integrated within the structure of the clause (*cf* 8.13, 8.32). Examples of adjuncts:

Slowly they walked back home.
He spoke to me about it *briefly*.

Examples of subjuncts:

> We haven't *yet* finished.
> Would you *kindly* wait for me.

By contrast, disjuncts and conjuncts have a more peripheral relation in the sentence. Semantically, DISJUNCTS (*cf* 8.40) express an evaluation of what is being said either with respect to the form of the communication or to its meaning. We identify disjuncts with the speaker's authority for, or comment on, the accompanying clause:

> *Frankly*, I'm tired.
> *Fortunately*, no one complained.
> They are *probably* at home.
> She *wisely* didn't attempt to apologize.

CONJUNCTS (*cf* 8.43) express the speaker's assessment of the relation between two linguistic units, *eg*:

> She has bought a big house, *so* she must have a lot of money.
> We have complained several times about the noise, and *yet* he does nothing about it.
> All our friends are going to Paris this summer. We, *however*, are going to London.
> If they open all the windows, *then* I'm leaving.
> I didn't invite her. She wouldn't have come, *anyway*.

Adverb as modifier

Modifier of adjective

7.32 An adverb may premodify an adjective. Most commonly the adverb is an intensifier or emphasizer (*cf* 8.36*f*):

extremely dangerous	*really* beautiful
deeply concerned	*very* good
perfectly reasonable	*just* impossible

Some premodifiers are related to adverbs that express such notions as manner and means but also have some intensifying effect:

easily debatable	*quietly* assertive
openly hostile	*readily* available

Some premodifiers express 'viewpoint' (*cf* 8.33):

> *politically* expedient ('expedient from a political point of view')
> *theoretically* sound   *technically* possible

NOTE *Enough* may postmodify an adjective: *old enough*. Like *indeed*, it may also postmodify an adverb, though *indeed* tends to go with a premodifying *very*: *carefully enough*, *very easily indeed*.

Modifier of adverb and preposition

7.33 An adverb may premodify another adverb:

very heavily　　*surprisingly* well
extremely quickly　　*so* clearly

Adverbs modifying other adverbs can only be intensifiers. On postmodifying *enough* and *indeed*, see 7.32 Note.

A few intensifying adverbs, particularly *right* and *well*, premodify prepositions:

The nail went *right* through the wall.
He made his application *well* within the time.
Her parents are *dead* against the trip. ⟨informal⟩

Modifier of pronoun, predeterminer, and numeral

7.34 Intensifying adverbs can premodify:

(a) indefinite pronouns (*cf* 6.21*ff*):

Nearly ⟨everybody⟩ came to our party.

(b) predeterminers (*cf* 5.7*ff*):

They recovered *roughly* ⟨half⟩ their equipment.

(c) cardinal numerals (*cf* 6.28 Note [b]):

Over/under ⟨two hundred⟩ deaths were reported.

(d) ordinals and superlatives (*cf* 7.39) in which case a definite determiner is obligatory:

We counted *approximately* ⟨the first⟩ thousand votes.
She gave me *almost* ⟨the largest⟩ piece of cake.

Modifier of noun phrase

7.35 A few intensifiers may premodify noun phrases and precede the determiner when they do so. The most common among adverbs are *quite* and *rather* ⟨esp BrE⟩:

We had *quite* a party.
They were *quite* some players.
It was *rather* a mess. ⟨esp BrE⟩

The predeterminers *such* and *what* have a similar function:

He is *such* a fool.　　*What* a mess they made!

A few intensifiers precede the indefinite article when it is equivalent to the numeral *one*:

They will stay for *about* a week.
Nearly a thousand demonstrators attended the meeting.

NOTE **[a]** *Kind of* and *sort of* (both informal) usually follow the determiner:

This must be a *sort of* joke.

Other *of*-phrases precede the determiner:

I had *a bit of* a shock.

[b] *Ever* can be an intensifier with interrogative *wh*-words:

Why *ever* should she apply for such a post?

7.36 Some time and place adverbs postmodify nouns:

the meeting *yesterday*	her trip *abroad*
the meal *afterwards*	the way *ahead*

Others may either premodify or postmodify:

the *downstairs* hall	the hall *downstairs*
the *above* quotation	the quotation *above*

A very few may only premodify:

an *away* game   *inside* information

NOTE *Else* can postmodify:
[a] compound indefinite pronouns and compound adverbs in *-body*, *-one*, *-where*, etc:

somebody else, *someone else's*, *nowhere else*, *something else*

[b] interrogative *wh*-pronouns and *wh*-adverbs:

who else, *what else*, *how else*, *when else*

[c] singular *all*, *much*, *a great/good deal*, *a lot*, *little*:

all else, *much else*, *little else*.

Adverb as complement of preposition

7.37 Some place and time adverbs function as complement of a preposition:

over *here*	since *recently*
near *there*	till *then*
from *abroad*	from *now*
from *behind*	for *ever*

Correspondence between adjective and adverb

7.38 We have earlier observed (7.27) that open-class adverbs are regularly, though not invariably, derived from adjectives by suffixation. There is another sense in which adjectives and adverbs are related. A correspondence often exists between constructions containing adjectives and constructions containing the corresponding adverbs. The simplest illustration is with adverbs equivalent to prepositional phrases containing a noun phrase with the corresponding adjective as premodifier:

He liked Mary *considerably*.
~ He liked Mary *to a considerable extent*.
She explained the process *brilliantly*.
~ She explained the process *in a brilliant manner*.
He wrote *frequently*.
~ He wrote *on frequent occasions*.
Politically, it is a bad decision.
~ *From the political point of view*, it is a bad decision.

Here are some other examples of adjective–adverb correspondences:

a *heavy* sleeper	somebody who sleeps *heavily*
a *former* student	somebody who was *formerly* a student
a *faithful* friend	a friend who acts *faithfully*
a *neat* typewriter	a typewriter that types *neatly*
his *legible* writing	He writes *legibly*
a *true* scholar	She is *truly* a scholar
the *main* reason	It was *mainly* the reason

Comparison of adjectives and adverbs

7.39 With gradable adjectives and adverbs there are three types of COMPARISON:
(a) to a higher degree
(b) to the same degree
(c) to a lower degree
The three types of comparison are expressed by these means:

(a) Comparison to a higher degree is expressed by the inflected forms in *-er* and *-est* or their periphrastic equivalents with *more* and *most*:

Anna is {*cleverer* / *more clever*} than Susan.

Anna is the {*cleverest* / *most clever*} student in the class.

(b) Comparison to the same degree is expressed by *as* (or sometimes *so*) . . . *as*:

Anna is *as tall as* Bill.

Anna is not {*as* / *so*} *tall as* John.

(c) Comparison to a lower degree is expressed by *less* and *least*:

> This problem is *less difficult* than the previous one.
> This is the *least difficult* problem of all.

For higher degree comparisons, English has a three-term inflectional contrast between ABSOLUTE, COMPARATIVE, and SUPERLATIVE forms for many adjectives and for a few adverbs. In Table 7.39 the three inflectional forms are displayed with their periphrastic equivalents.

***Table* 7.39 Comparison of adjectives and adverbs**

	ABSOLUTE	COMPARATIVE	SUPERLATIVE
INFLECTION			
adjective	*high*	*higher*	*highest*
adverb	*soon*	*sooner*	*soonest*
PERIPHRASIS			
adjective	*complex*	*more complex*	*most complex*
adverb	*comfortably*	*more comfortably*	*most comfortably*

NOTE Comparatives of adjectives and adverbs, whether inflectional or periphrastic, can be modified by intensifiers:

much easier	somewhat shorter
much more difficult	a lot more inconvenient
very much better	a good deal sooner
very much more carefully	a great deal more easily

Similarly, superlatives can be modified by intensifiers:

> the youngest candidate ever
> the most remarkable result ever
> by far the best solution
> the most absurd answer by far

Inflected superlatives can be premodified by *very*, if a definite determiner is present: *at the very last moment, the very youngest*. But neither periphrastic superlatives nor comparatives can be premodified by *very*.

7.40 The comparative is generally used to express a comparison between two persons, two items, or two sets:

> Jane is *cleverer* than her sister.
> Jane is *cleverer* than all the other students in the class.

The superlative is generally used when more than two are involved:

> Jane is the *cleverest* of the three sisters.
> Jane is the *cleverest* of all the students in the class.

With the superlative, Jane is included in the group and compared with the others.

NOTE *More* and *most* have other uses in which they are not equivalent to the comparison inflections. Notice the paraphrases in the following two uses of *more*:

He is *more than happy* about it. ['He is happy about it to a degree that is not adequately expressed by the word *happy*.']
He is *more good than bad*. ['It is more accurate to say that he is good than that he is bad.']

She is *more keen than wise*. ['She is keen rather than wise.']

Most may have an intensifying meaning, as in *Della is a most efficient publisher*.

Comparison of adjectives

Irregular forms of comparison

7.41 A small group of highly frequent adjectives have comparative and superlative forms with stems which are different from the base:

good	~*better*	~*best*
bad	~*worse*	~*worst*
far	~*further*	~*furthest*
	~*farther*	~*farthest*

NOTE **[a]** *Old* is regularly inflected as *older*~*oldest*. In attributive position, particularly when referring to the order of birth of members of a family, the irregular forms *elder*~*eldest* are normally substituted (especially in BrE):

My *elder/older* sister is an artist.
His *eldest/oldest* son is still at school.

However, *elder* is not a true comparative in that it cannot be followed by *than*:

My sister is three years {*older* / **elder*} than me.

[b] *Well* ['in good health'] and *ill* ['in bad health' <esp BrE>] are inflected like *good* and *bad*, respectively, for the comparative: *He feels better/worse*. *He is better* can mean either (a) 'He is well again' or (b) 'He is less ill'.

Regular forms of comparison

7.42 With adjectives taking the regular inflections, certain changes in spelling or pronunciation may be introduced in the base of the adjective when the suffixes are added.

(a) A single consonant at the end of the base is doubled before *-er* and *-est* when the preceding vowel is stressed and spelled with a single letter (*cf* the spelling of verb forms, 3.6):

big	~*bigger*	~*biggest*

But contrast:

neat	~*neater*	~*neatest*
thick	~*thicker*	~*thickest*

(b) In bases ending in a consonant followed by *-y*, *y* changes to *-i* before *-er* and *-est*:

angry ~*angrier* ~*angriest*

(c) If the base ends in a mute (unpronounced) *-e*, this *e* is dropped before the inflection:

pure ~*purer* ~*purest*

The same applies if the base ends in *-ee*:

free ~*freer* ~*freest* /'friːɪst/

(d) Syllabic /*l*/, as in *simple*, ceases to be syllabic when inflections are added.

(e) Even for speakers who do not pronounce final *r*, the *r* is pronounced before the inflection, as in *poorer*.

NOTE There is a variant spelling in:

cruel { ~*crueller* ~*cruellest*
~*crueler* ~*cruelest* ⟨esp AmE⟩ }

Choice between inflectional and periphrastic comparison

7.43 (a) Monosyllabic adjectives normally form their comparison by inflection:

low ~*lower* ~*lowest*

(b) Many disyllabic adjectives can also take inflections, though they have the alternative of the periphrastic forms:

Her children are { *politer/more polite.*
(the) politest/(the) most polite. }

Disyllabic adjectives that can most readily take inflected forms are those ending in an unstressed vowel, syllabic /*l*/, or *r*, *eg*:

-y: early, easy, funny, happy, noisy, wealthy, pretty
-ow: mellow, narrow, shallow
-le: able, feeble, gentle, noble, simple

(c) Trisyllabic or longer adjectives can only take periphrastic forms:

beautiful
~*more beautiful* [BUT NOT: **beautifuller*]
~*the most beautiful* [BUT NOT: **beautifullest*]

Adjectives with the negative *un*-prefix, such as *unhappy* and *untidy*, are exceptions:

~*unhappier* ~*unhappiest* ~*untidier* ~*untidiest*

NOTE [a] Participle forms which are used as adjectives regularly take only periphrastic forms:

interesting	~*more interesting*	~*most interesting*
wounded	~*more wounded*	~*most wounded*
worn	~*more worn*	~*most worn*

[b] Most adjectives that are inflected for comparison can also take the periphrastic forms with *more* and *most*. With *more*, they seem to do so more easily when they are predicative and are followed by a *than*-clause:

He is *more wealthy* than I thought.

Comparison of adverbs

7.44 For a small number of adverbs, the inflected forms used for comparison are the same as those for adjectives. As with adjectives, there is a small group with comparatives and superlatives formed from different stems. The comparative and superlative inflections are identical with those for the corresponding adjectives *good*, *bad*, and *far*, and the quantifiers *much* and *little*:

badly	~*worse*	~*worst*
well	~*better*	~*best*
little	~*less* (*lesser*)	~*least*
far	{~*further*	~*furthest*
	~*farther*	~*farthest*
much	~*more*	~*most*

Adverbs that are identical in form with adjectives take inflections if the adjectives do so: *fast*, *hard*, *late*, *long*, *quick*. They follow the same spelling and phonological rules as for adjectives, *eg*: *early*~*earlier*~*earliest*:

The unmarked term in measure expressions

7.45 We use the adjective *old* in measure expressions (*x years old*) when we refer to a person's age, regardless of the age:

Mr Jespersen is 75 years *old*.
His granddaughter is two years *old*.

In the scale of measurement, *old* indicates the upper range (*He is old*) but it is also the unmarked term for the whole range, so that *She is two years old* is equivalent to *Her age is two years*. The measure adjectives used in this way are the following, with the marked term in parentheses:

deep (*shallow*) *high* (*low*) *long* (*short*) *old* (*young*) *tall* (*short*) *thick* (*thin*) *wide* (*narrow*)

These unmarked terms are also used in *how*-questions and, again, they do not assume the upper range. *How old is she?* is equivalent to *What is her age?* Other adjectives are also used in the same way in *how*-questions, *eg*:

big (*small*), *bright* (*dim*), *fat* (*thin*), *heavy* (*light*), *large* (*little*), *strong* (*weak*).

> *How heavy* is your computer?
> *How accurate* is that clock?

Some adverbs are also used as an unmarked term in *how*-questions, *eg*:

> *How much* does it cost?
> *How far* did you drive today?

NOTE If we use the marked term, as in *How young is John?*, we are asking a question that presupposes that the relevant norm is towards the lower end of the scale, *ie* that John is young, whereas the unmarked term in *How old is John?* does not presuppose that John is old. Notice that neither term is neutral in exclamations:

> *How young* he is! ['He is extremely young!']
> *How old* he is! ['He is extremely old!']

Bibliographical note

On adjectives and adverbs, see Bolinger (1967a); Vendler (1968); Warren (1984). On adverbs, see bibliographical note in Chapter 8.

On comparison and intensification, see Bolinger (1967b, 1972a); Bresnan (1973); Gnutzman et al. (1973); Rusiecki (1985).

8 The semantics and grammar of adverbials

8.1 The adverbial element (A) in clause structure has a wider range of roles than the other four elements, subject (S), verb (V), object (O), and complement (C). This is reflected in its having a wider range of meanings, of forms, of positions, and of grammatical functions; not least, it is reflected in our ability to include several adverbial elements within a single sentence. The following example illustrates not only multiple occurrence but also a variety of meanings, forms, positions, and grammatical relations:

> *Next Tuesday* [A1], I shall *probably* [A2] visit her mother *in London* [A3] *for an hour or so* [A4] *to see if she's feeling better* [A5], *unless she telephones me before that* [A6].

Semantic roles

Space

8.2 Adverbials can express five different types of spatial meaning:

(a) *Position*, as in:

> The dog was asleep *on the grass*.

(b) *Direction*, as in:

> They walked *down the hill*.

(c) *Goal*, as in:

> She hurried *to the station*.

(d) *Source*, as in:

> This book cannot be taken *from the library*.

(e) *Distance*, as in:

> We mustn't go *very much further*.

Time

8.3 Adverbials distinguish five types of temporal meaning and there are analogies both semantic and formal with the spatial meanings of 8.2:

(a) *Position*, as in:

She was born *in 1980*.

(b) *Duration of forward span*, as in:

I shall be in Chicago *until Thursday*.

(c) *Duration of backward span*, as in:

We have been at the airport *since midday*.

(d) *Frequency*, as in:

They *very seldom* went to see their parents.

(e) *Relationship between one time and another*, as in:

She must *still* be in her office.

NOTE Duration may indicate a span that does not distinguish between 'forward' and 'backward'; for example:

I forget exactly when I arrived but I am staying here *for six months altogether*.

Process

8.4 Here we have four types of meaning:

(a) *Manner*, as in:

The minister explained his policy *very clearly*.

(b) *Means*, as in:

By her insight, she grasped the patient's real problem.

(c) *Instrument*, as in:

I have difficulty eating *with chopsticks*.

(d) *Agency*, as in:

Penicillin was discovered *by Sir Alexander Fleming*.

Respect

8.5 An adverbial can be used to provide a point of reference with respect to which the clause in question derives its truth value. For example:

She helped him *with his research*.

In the following, if *legally* meant 'lawfully, not illegally', the adverbial would be the manner subclass of process (8.4(a)); normally, however, it would mean 'on points of law, with respect to law':

They are advising me *legally*.

Contingency

8.6 Here we have six types of meaning expressed adverbially:

(a) *Cause*, as in:

She died *of cancer*.

(b) *Reason*, as in:

He bought the book *through an interest in metaphysics*.

(c) *Purpose*, as in:

He bought the book *to study metaphysics*.

(d) *Result*, as in:

He read the book carefully, *so he acquired a good knowledge of metaphysics*.

(e) *Condition*, as in:

If he reads the book carefully, he will acquire a good knowledge of metaphysics.

(f) *Concession*, as in:

Though he read the book carefully, he didn't achieve much knowledge of metaphysics.

Modality

8.7 The truth value of a sentence can be changed (*eg* enhanced or diminished) by the use of adverbials. We distinguish three ways:

(a) *Emphasis*, as in:

She *certainly* helped him with his research.

(b) *Approximation*, as in:

They are *probably* going to emigrate.

(c) *Restriction*, as in:

I shall be in Chicago *only* until Thursday.

Degree

8.8 Like adverbials of modality in changing the truth value of a sentence, adverbials of degree add a special semantic component, gradability. There are two types:

(a) *Amplification*, as in:

He *badly* needed consolation.

(b) *Diminution*, as in:

She helped him *a little* with his research.

Formal realization

8.9 The A-element can be realized by a wide range of linguistic structures:

An adverb phrase (2.4) with a closed-class (2.6) adverb as head:

(Just) then, the telephone rang.

An adverb phrase with an open-class (2.6) adverb as head:

You should have opened it *((a bit) more) carefully*.

A noun phrase (17.1*ff*):

They had travelled *a very long way*.

A prepositional phrase (9.1):

Rowena hurried *across the field*.

A verbless clause (14.3):

When in doubt the answer is 'no'.

A nonfinite clause (14.3):

She realized, *lying there*, what she must do.

A finite clause (14.3):

We sent for you *because you were absent yesterday*.

8.10 Some of these realization types occur more frequently than others: prepositional phrases are very common and nonfinite clauses relatively rare, for example. Some are particularly associated with specific meanings, grammatical functions, and adverbial positions: noun phrases with time adjuncts, for example, and finite clauses with end position.

Position

8.11 As compared with other sentence elements (2.3), the A-element can be placed with relative freedom in several positions in a sentence:

I	*By then* the book should have been returned to the library.
iM	The book *by then* should have been returned to the library.
M	The book should *by then* have been returned to the library.
mM	The book should have *by then* been returned to the library.
eM	The book should have been *by then* returned to the library.
iE	The book should have been returned *by then* to the library.
E	The book should have been returned to the library *by then*.

As the notation implies, there are three main positions: *I(nitial)*, *M(edial)*, and *E(nd)*, but there are three subordinate variants of *M* (initial, medial, and end) and one of *E* (initial). *I* and *E* are self-explanatory, but the primary *M* position may need clarification. It is the position immediately following the operator (2.10) or the copula *be*:

Timothy has *at last* finished his thesis.
Timothy is *at last* a doctor of philosophy.

Where no operator is present, there can be no variants such as *eM*, and *M* is simply the position between the *S* and the *V*; it is similarly the position before *V* when the *S* is ellipted:

The play *daringly* explores a hitherto forbidden subject.
Sharon spoke at this point and *strongly* supported the motion.

The choice of position for an adverbial is determined by semantic and grammatical factors as we shall see in the course of this chapter, but also by the demands of information processing and the principle of end-weight (18.5 and Note [a]). If no special factors determine otherwise, the adverbial is placed at *E*, the position in fact taken in the majority of cases.

NOTE Since the majority of verb phrases combine either the main verb alone or the main verb preceded by only one auxiliary (the operator), it is natural that the *M* position is normally felt to be immediately before the main verb form. This helps to account for the tendency (despite long-standing disapproval) to place an adverbial between *to* and an infinitive ('the split infinitive'). Compare the similarity between the following:

Martha *always* finishes first.
Martha had *always* finished first.
Martha tried to *always* finish first.

Grammatical functions

8.12 In terms of their grammatical functions, adverbials fall into four main categories:

Adjunct
Subjunct
Disjunct
Conjunct

We shall deal with these in turn, along with their respective subcategories.

Adjuncts

8.13 More than other adverbials, adjuncts have grammatical properties resembling the sentence elements S, C, and O. Like them, adjuncts can be the focus of a cleft sentence (18.18*f*):

Hilda [S] helped Tony [O] because of his injury [A].
It was *Hilda* that helped Tony because of his injury.
It was *Tony* that Hilda helped because of his injury.
It was *because of his injury* that Hilda helped Tony.

The parallels extend to the potentiality for being the focus of subjuncts (8.32*ff*):

Only Hilda helped Tony . . . [S]
Hilda helped Tony *only* because of his injury. [A]

to elicitation by question forms:

Who helped Tony? [S]
Who(m) did Hilda help? [O]
Why did Hilda help Tony? [A]

and to alternative interrogation and negation:

Did Hilda help *Tony* or did *Marjorie* (help him)? [S]
Did she help him *because of his injury* or (did she help him) *because she was bored*? [A]
Hilda didn't help *Tony* but (she helped) *Bill.* [O]
Hilda didn't help Tony *because of his injury* but (she helped him) *because she was bored.* [A]

Finally, irrespective of their position (8.11), adjuncts function like other post-operator elements in coming within the scope of predication ellipsis or pro-forms (12.20, 12.6*ff*). In consequence, the following sentences are synonymous:

Grace became *a teacher* [C] *in 1981* [A] and Hamish also became *a teacher* [C] *in 1981* [A].
In 1981, Grace became *a teacher* and so also did Hamish.

But while these characteristics hold generally for all adjuncts, there are three subcategories ranging in 'centrality' from the obligatory predication adjunct (which resembles an object in being both relatively indispensable and fixed in position) to the sentence adjunct whose position is more variable and whose presence is always optional:

Adjunct
- predication
  - obligatory
  - optional
- sentence

Predication adjuncts

8.14 As their name implies, the relations of predication adjuncts are not so much with a whole sentence as with its predication, the post-operator section (2.10). This is true for both of the following:

She put the letter *on the kitchen table*. [1]
She found the letter *on the kitchen table*. [2]

But whereas in [2] the adverbial is *optional* and its omission leaves an acceptable sentence ('She found the letter'), omission is impossible with [1] (*'She put the letter') where the adverbial is thus an *obligatory* component of the sentence.

Predication adjuncts are normally placed at *E* but may be at *iE* if another post-verb element is lengthy and complex:

She put *on the table* a letter she had just received from her lawyer.

In striving for rhetorical effect, such adjuncts can even appear at *I*; for example in highlighting a balance or contrast, as in:

From Australia he came and *to Australia* he has returned.

Sentence adjuncts

8.15 Since we can utter 'Ralph kissed his mother' without needing to add an adjunct, it follows that in each of the following the adjunct is optional:

Ralph kissed his mother *on the cheek*. [1]
Ralph kissed his mother *on the platform*. [2]

But only in the second can the adjunct seem equally natural at *I*:

On the platform, Ralph kissed his mother.

This is a characteristic of the sentence adjunct, demonstrating its relatively 'peripheral' relationship to the rest of the sentence as compared with the relatively 'central' relationship of the predication adjunct in [1].

But the difference does not necessarily lie, as in [1] and [2], in the adjuncts themselves. The same phrase can be used as either predication or sentence adjunct, according as it pinpoints new information (18.4) in the predication or provides general background information for the sentence as a whole:

(I looked everywhere for it and eventually) I found the letter *in the kitchen*. [3]
(I had totally forgotten about the matter, but then, almost by chance,) I found the letter(,) *in the kitchen*. [4]

The contexts supplied show that the adjunct in [3] is predicational while that in [4] is sentential. The parenthesized comma further suggests the relatively peripheral relation of the adjunct, which might occupy a separate tone unit in speech (18.3), as it certainly would if moved from *E*:

. . . but then, *in the kitchen*, almost by chance, I found the letter.

NOTE In many cases, it is convenient to see predication adjuncts as 'object-related' and sentence adjuncts as 'subject-related'. Thus in the following the adjunct would normally be interpreted as relating to the date of the disaster:

We foresaw a disaster *in June.*

By contrast, the adjunct in the following seems naturally to relate to the subject and therefore to the time of the foreseeing:

In June, we foresaw a disaster.

The semantic roles of adjuncts

Adjuncts of space

8.16 Spatial adjuncts realize the roles set out in 8.2 chiefly by means of prepositional phrases since these roles can be clearly and conveniently specified through the respective prepositional meanings (9.4*ff*). But noun phrases can be used as predication adjuncts of distance:

They travelled {a very long way. / several miles.}

So too adjuncts of direction with the determiners *this*, *that*, and *which*:

He came *this way* but *which direction* did he go then?

Clausal realization is common and is convenient in enabling one to transcend the specifics of location or even semantic role:

She still lives *where she was born.*
They want to know *where we are sending them.*

These examples reflect the fact that space adjuncts are elicited (again often neutralizing semantic role) by the question *where*:

Where did you stay?	(position)
Where are they going?	(direction)
Where is the train coming *from*?	(source)

But *cf how far* as in:

How far did you drive yesterday? (distance)

NOTE [a] The spatial pro-forms *here* and *there* have 'near' and 'far' orientation as with *this* and *that* (6.19).
[b] The position role with respect to persons is often expressed by a *with*-phrase:

Where is Mildred? She is (staying) *with her brother.*

8.17 Direction adjuncts (whether goal or source) can normally be used only with verbs of motion or with verbs used dynamically so as to allow a literal or metaphorical motional meaning:

The boy kicked the ball *through the open window.*
She was speaking *into a tiny microphone.*

By contrast, position and distance adjuncts can be used freely with verbs in stative or dynamic use:

They live {*in London.* / *20 kilometres from here.*}

He's travelling {*in Yorkshire* at present. / *a long way.*}

With *be*, we can have position adjuncts:

Charles is *on the top floor.*

Given that the verb is appropriate, more than one space adjunct can be used in the same sentence; distance and position as in [1], direction and position as in [2], distance and direction as in [3]:

They swam *a mile* [A1] *in the open sea* [A2]. [1]
He fell *into the water* [A1] *near that rock* [A2]. [2]
She walked *a few steps* [A1] *towards him* [A2]. [3]

Since space adjuncts (especially of position) can enter a hierarchical relationship, we can also have two adjuncts even of the same semantic role:

Many people eat *in restaurants* [A1] *in London* [A2].

The order here is essential in order to match the logical relationship, but since the larger location is relatively peripheral, this referring adjunct (but not the other) may be at *I*:

In London, many people eat *in restaurants.*

Direction adjuncts of goal and source may also be paired, with a choice of order dependent largely on information processing (18.4*ff*):

We flew {*from Cairo* [A1] *to Istanbul* [A2]. / *to Istanbul* [A1] *from Cairo* [A2].}

When adjuncts are coordinated, they must have the same semantic role:

We can meet you *in the theatre* or *at the station.*
I drove *down Gower Street* and *into University College.*

8.18 Irrespective of semantic role, space adjuncts are normally at *E*, but where two or more adjuncts are clustered at *E*, they are ordered as follows:

distance–direction (source, goal) – position

For example:

She walked *a few steps* [A1] *towards him* [A2] *in the darkened room* [A3].

Adjuncts of position can be more easily moved to *I*:

On the top of the building, two men were gesticulating wildly.

Some adjuncts, especially if short, can also be at *M*:

You could *there* catch a train to Manchester.

With *be*, it is very common for *there* and *here* to be at *I*, with subject–verb inversion (18.16) unless the subject is a pronoun:

There he was, waiting in the cold.
Here is the book.

In a similar way, predication adjuncts of position and direction can occur at *I*:

Down {swooped the hawk. / it swooped.}

In a neighbouring street lived my mother.

In negative sentences, predication adjuncts must be at *E*:

My mother did not live *in a neighbouring street.*

But sentence adjuncts can be at *I* and remain within the scope of negation:

In Delhi, it sometimes did not rain for months on end.

Adjuncts of time

8.19 We tend to use the language of spatial dimensions figuratively when we refer to time. In consequence, adjuncts of time are predominantly realized by prepositional phrases, with figurative adaptation of the prepositional meanings (*cf* 9.9*ff*). For example:

The music stopped *at midnight.*
On the following day, we decided to go out for a picnic.
I completed the painting *in two days.*

But in addition, a wider range of structures is available for time than for any other type of adjunct. Noun phrases, as in:

They visit her *every month.*

Finite verb clauses, as in:

Stay in bed *until your temperature comes down.*

Nonfinite clauses, as in:

Travelling on the Continent, I miss the English pub.

Verbless clauses, as in:

I go to the theatre *as often as possible.*

Closed-class adverb phrases, as in:

She *(almost) always* leaves home before 8 a.m.

Open-class adverb phrases, as in:

He spoke to me about it *quite recently*.

Time-position adjuncts

8.20 Time-position adjuncts can be elicited by the question word *when* and the time specified may be narrowly stated or left rather vague:

When did she arrive? { *At 10.15.* / *Some hours ago.* }

Moreover, the time position itself may be narrow as in [1] or broad as in [2], irrespective of the specification:

Mozart was born { *in 1756.* / *in the eighteenth century.* } [1]

Mozart lived { *in the eighteenth century.* / *in a period of great musical creativity.* } [2]

The general anaphoric pro-form for time-position reference is *then* and it is normally associated with the past, especially in contrast to *now*:

I worked in publishing *then*, but *now* I work for an advertising firm.

But *then* can refer equally to a time in the future:

She will telephone you *tomorrow afternoon* and hopes that you will be able to speak to her *then*.

Nor is *now* necessarily confined to present-time reference; in the following example, *now* means 'by that time', 'then':

They had been courting for two years and he *now* felt that she knew his worst faults.

Like spatial adjuncts of position, time-position adjuncts can be in a hierarchical relation, usually with the one denoting the longer or superordinate period coming second:

I'll see you *at nine* [A1] on *Monday* [A2].
The doctor wants to see you *again* [A1] *afterwards* [A2].

But this sequence can be readily reversed if end-weight (18.5 Note [a]) or other communicative requirement is to be served:

I lived there *in the fifties* [A1] *when my first child was born* [A2].

NOTE Out of context, a *when*-clause may be ambiguous:

Tell me *when you're ready*.

This may be a noun clause as object ('Let me know *the time at which you'll be ready*') or a time-position adjunct ('*When you're ready*, let me know').

Adjuncts of duration and span

8.21 Adjuncts may express duration of specific ('for ten minutes') or indefinite ('for a short time') length, the durations in question being in the past, the present, or the future:

She worked in China *for several years.* [1]
At present his grandchildren are staying with him *for a few days.* [2]
I intend to go skiing *for three weeks.* [3]

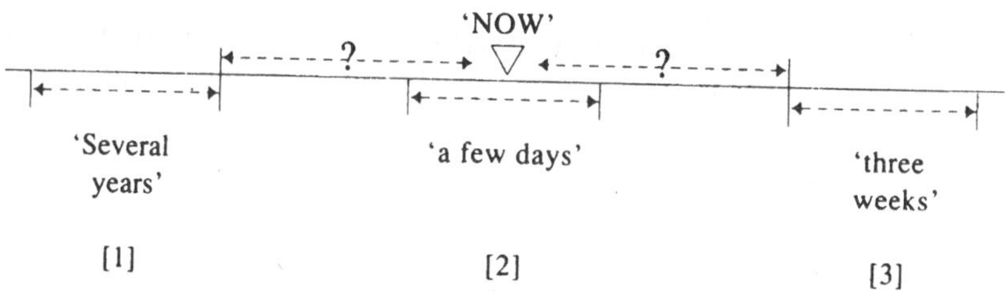

Although in [3], we know the precise duration, in none of the sentences [1], [2], or [3] can we relate the beginning or end of the periods mentioned to the speaker's 'NOW'. By contrast, adjuncts of forward and backward span specifically relate duration to such a 'NOW' (or other fixed point of orientation), though again without necessarily being definite about the length of the duration itself.

Forward span is particularly associated with *till* and *until*:

I shall be in my office *until five o'clock.*

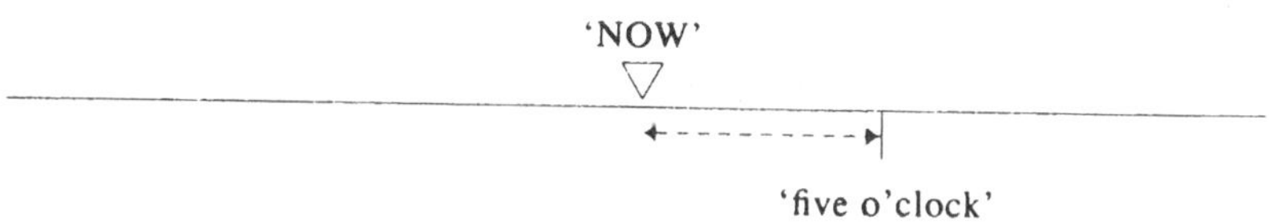

The beginning of the time span is fixed in relation to the speaker's orientation point, but its terminus is as indicated by the adjunct only if the clause is positive:

He waited *until she returned.*

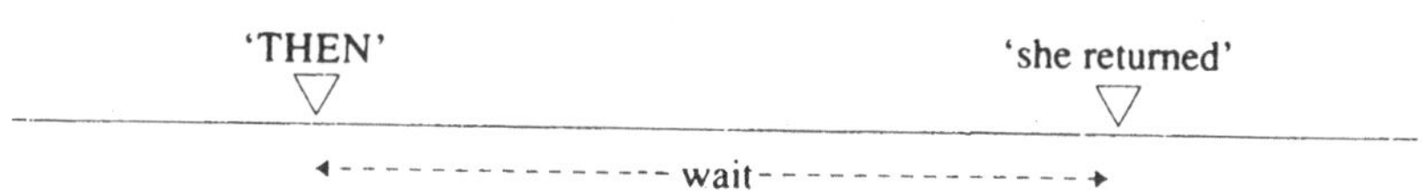

By contrast:

He didn't wait *until she returned.*

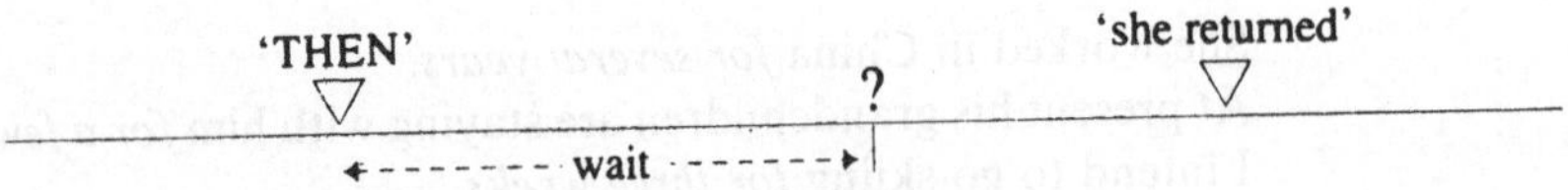

With negative clauses and verbs of momentary meaning, on the other hand, the span indicated by the adjunct marks the extent of the nonoccurrence of the momentary action:

He didn't arrive *until she returned.*

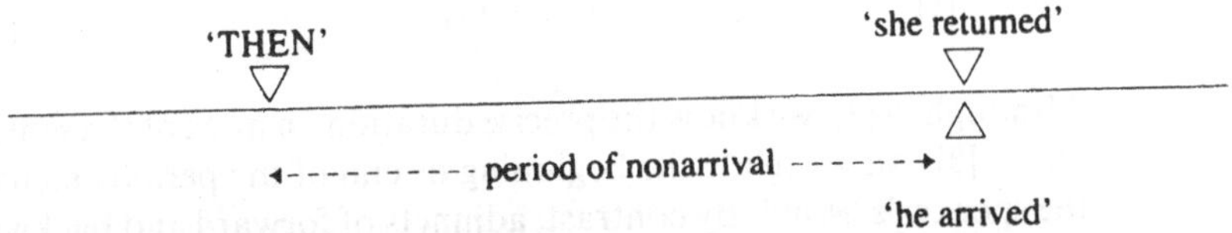

Compare also:

I slept *till nine o'clock.*

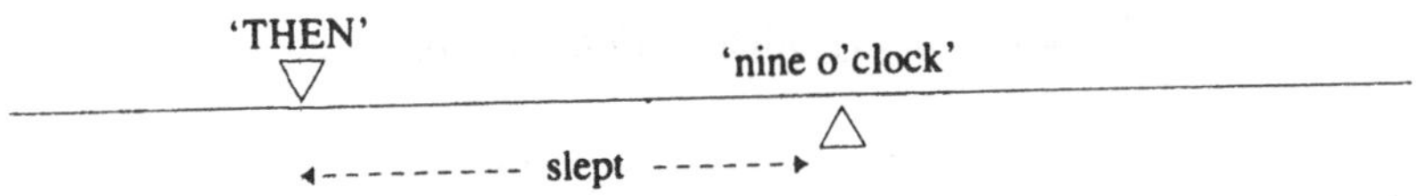

I didn't sleep *till nine o'clock.*

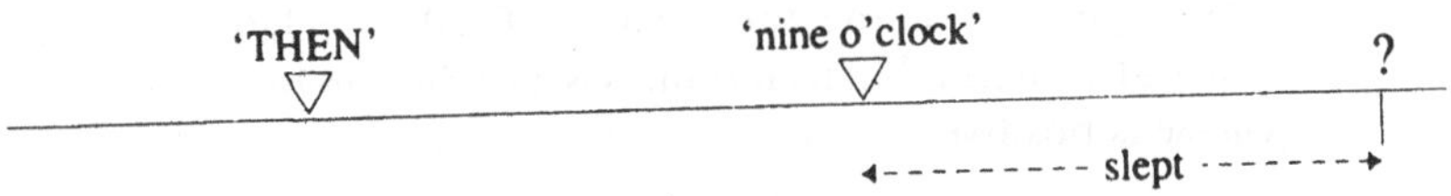

8.22 *Backward span* is particularly associated with *since* and the perfect aspect:

I have been in my office *since nine o'clock.*

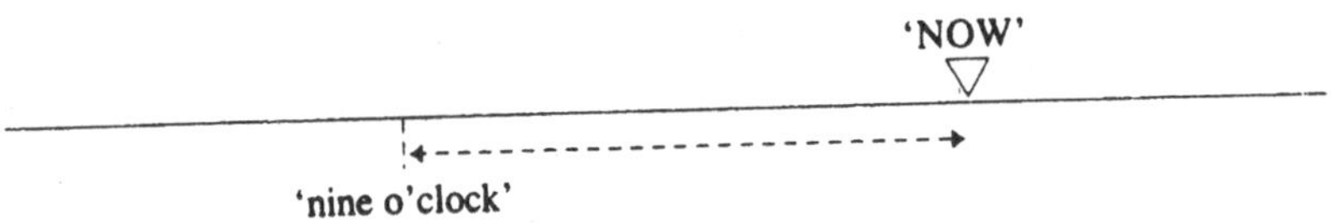

But adjuncts with *since* must specify a definite starting point; if the span is more general, *for* can be used or a noun phrase without *for*:

> I have been in my office *(for) several hours.*

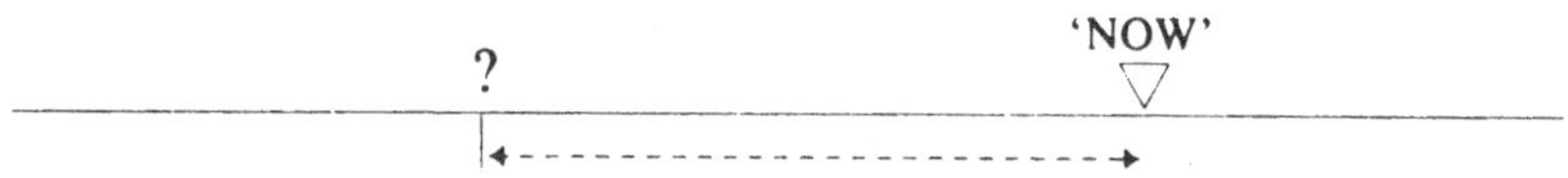

If the backward span is not to be related to the speaker's orientation point, the verb phrase is not in the perfect, and we are now dealing simply with duration which may be definite or indefinite. For example:

> She was running her own business { *for three years.*
> { *(for) quite a long time.*

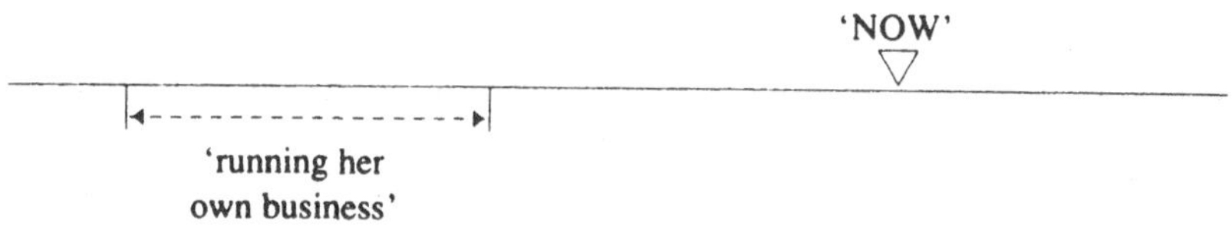

Finally, we may note *since*-clauses according as these clauses do or do not have verbs in the perfect:

> She has become much better off *since she has worked with us.* [1]
> She has become much better off *since she worked with us.* [2]

In both cases, the period of improvement extends to the present, but whereas [1] entails that she still works 'with us', [2] implies that she does not. If the verb in the *since*-clause does not itself involve duration, on the other hand, the contrast is less absolute:

> He's been getting bad headaches { *since he has joined the army.* [3]
> { *since he joined the army.* [4]

While [3] certainly entails that he is still in the army, [4] leaves it open as to whether or not he is still in the army.

NOTE [a] Span may be specified also by *from*, *up to*, *over*, *by*, *before*, and by noun phrases like *this past (month)*, *these last (few days)*, *this next year*:

> We'll be here *up to midday.*
> She has worked here *only this last week.*

The beginning and end of a span can be indicated by the correlatives *from . . . to* ⟨esp BrE⟩, *from . . . through* ⟨esp AmE⟩, *between . . . and*:

> The office is closed *between one and two o'clock.*

[b] Especially informally, especially in AmE, and especially where the main clause refers to the present, backward span can be expressed without the perfect:

> Things *are* much worse *since you left*.
> I never *saw* you here *before*.

[c] Adjuncts of duration and span usually answer questions of the form *How long . . .*? or more specifically *Till when . . .*? *Since when . . .*?

Time-frequency adjuncts

Definite frequency

8.23 It is necessary to distinguish frequency of *occasion* ('How many times?') from frequency of *period* within which occasions took place ('How often?'). The former are normally predication adjuncts, the latter sentence adjuncts, and when in a hierarchical relation these are placed in the more peripheral position:

> Veronica came to see me *twice*. [occasion]
> Veronica came to see me *daily*. [period]
> Veronica came to see me *twice* [o] *daily* [p].
> *Each year* [p] I have to make a presidential address *three times* [o].

Indefinite frequency

8.24 Here we must, on both semantic and grammatical grounds, distinguish four subsets:

(a) Denoting usual occurrence (*normally*, *generally*, *ordinarily*, etc), as in

> Jenny *usually* goes to bed before midnight.

Since one can speak of something normally *not* occurring, it is a characteristic of these adjuncts to be sentential and to be capable of preceding a clausal negative:

> *Usually*, Jenny doesn't go to bed before midnight.

(b) Denoting universal frequency (*always*, *continually*, *permanently*, etc), as in

> He has been asking for you *incessantly*.

(c) Denoting high frequency (*often*, *time and again*, *repeatedly*, etc), as in

> She has had plays broadcast *frequently*.

(d) Denoting low frequency (*occasionally*, *rarely*, *seldom*, *never*, etc), as in

> I *very seldom* play golf these days.

If placed at *I*, some items in (d) can oblige us to invert subject and operator:

> *Never* have I experienced such rudeness.

Unlike the adjuncts in (a) and (b), some of those in (c) and (d) can be used in antithetic sentence sequences:

> *Often* he takes his medicine, but *often* he doesn't.
> She *occasionally* greets me but *occasionally* she doesn't.

Items from (a) and other subsets as sentence adjuncts can readily cooccur with predication adjuncts from (b), (c), or (d):

> *Generally* (a), they are *continually* (b) complaining.
> He (*almost*) *never* (d) goes out at night, *normally* (a).
> *Sometimes* (d), the dog barks *repeatedly* (c).

Time-relationship adjuncts

8.25 The time adjuncts which express a relationship between two time positions are of three types:

(a) Typically denoting a temporal sequence, as in

> When did you *previously* go to the dentist?

(b) Typically implying a concessive relation, as in

> I don't understand (*even*) NÒW.

(c) Typically contrasting one time with another, as in

> Maureen should complain about it *again*.

NOTE But time relationship is often expressed by subjuncts (*cf* 8.35) such as *already*, *still*, *yet*.

Positions of time adjuncts

8.26 Although like other adjuncts, time adjuncts are most frequently at *E*, all types can readily take the 'scene-setting' *I* position:

> *In 1982*, the economy started to recover.
> *For many years*, no one seemed interested in buying the house.
> *Normally*, late nights have a bad effect on me.
> *Even after that*, he refused to cooperate.

But *M* is also common for time adjuncts, especially those realized by adverbs:

> She has *recently* completed a new play.
> We may not *often* get such an opportunity.

Where time adjuncts cooccur in the same sentence, time duration tends to be most 'central', time position most 'peripheral', so that if the three main types all occurred at *E* they would most likely be ordered as in:

> I was there *for a short while* [dur] *every day or so* [freq] *last year*. [pos]

NOTE Placing of a time adjunct is acutely affected if there is a decided orientation towards either the subject or the object; *cf* 8.15 Note.

Process adjuncts

Manner adjuncts

8.27 Manner adjuncts are chiefly realized by adverb phrases, by *like*-phrases, *as*-clauses, and by prepositional or noun phrases involving such nouns as *way* and *manner*; for example:

> She looked at him *coldly*.
> He walks *like his father*.
> Please don't speak *in that rude way*.
> They cook *((in) the) French style*.
> I wish I could write *as you do*.

Manner adjuncts are almost always at *E*, but although thus associated with the greatest rhetorical weight in a clause, there is no simple interrogative device for eliciting them.

Adjuncts of means, instrument, and agency

8.28 There are close semantic similarities between means, instrument, and agent, and there is considerable overlap in realization. The means and the agent are often expressed with *by*-phrases, but the latter is grammatically distinct in correlating with the passive (and hence corresponding to a transitive clause); for example:

> He was killed *by a terrorist*. (~A terrorist killed him.)

A means adjunct, on the other hand, can easily occur in a transitive clause:

> She influenced me *by her example*.

Instrument adjuncts differ from both means and agent adjuncts in generally being realized by *with*-phrases:

> He was killed *with a hunting knife*.

But means and instrument adjuncts can share realization with adverbs; thus means in:

> They decided to treat the patient *surgically*. (='by means of surgery')

Similarly, instrument in:

> She examined the specimen *microscopically*. (where the adverb is here intended to mean 'with a microscope')

NOTE [a] If in the last example, *microscopically* meant 'in microscopic detail', the adjunct would be one of manner (8.27) and could be gradable, '(quite) microscopically'.
[b] Means and instrument adjuncts can be elicited by *how*-questions: '*How* are you travelling to Hamburg?' '*By air*/*By Lufthansa*'.

[c] All process adjuncts are normally placed at *E*, though manner adjuncts can be at *M*. Cooccurrence of process adjuncts is by no means unusual; for example:

> She was *accidentally* [manner] struck *with a racket* [instrument] *by her partner* [agent].

Adjuncts of respect

8.29 A wide range of realization is available for adjuncts that express the respect in which the truth value of a sentence is being claimed. For example:

> A neighbour is advising me { *legally.* / *on legal issues.* / *so far as legal matters are concerned.* / *in respect to law.* / *from a legal standpoint.* }

Respect is a relationship often expressed by subjuncts or disjuncts (8.33, 8.41), but when adjuncts are involved they are usually predicational and are placed at *E*.

Adjuncts of contingency

8.30 Contingency relations are commonly expressed by disjuncts (8.41), but adjuncts are often used for *reason* and its correlate *purpose*, both of which can be elicited by the same question forms, *Why . . . ? What . . . for?* as in:

> He did it { *because he was angry.* [reason] / *to relieve his anger.* [purpose] }

As well as by finite clauses, reason adjuncts are realized by prepositional phrases and nonfinite clauses; for example:

> She made the sacrifice *for her son.*
> There were many deaths *from malnutrition.*
> *With him being so angry*, I didn't tell him the worst part.

Purpose adjuncts are realized by nonfinite (infinitive) clauses:

> The driver slowed down { *(in order)* / *(so as)* } *to avoid an accident.*

In formal style, finite clauses can occur:

> Inoculation must be carried out *lest the disease spread.*
> He died *(in order) that others might live.*

But some forms of finite clause are used more generally:

> Turn the gas off *in case there's an explosion.*
> We'd better leave now *so we can get home before dark.*

When the *concessive* relation is expressed by an adjunct, this takes the form of a prepositional phrase:

> She gave the lecture *despite her illness.*

Contingency adjuncts are usually sentential and although normally at *E* they are commonly (especially those of purpose and concession) placed at *I*.

Relative positions of adjuncts

8.31 Looking now at the whole range of adjunct types (8.16–8.30), we can consider some general principles of their relative ordering in cooccurence:

(a) the order, especially of sentence adjuncts, can be dictated by such considerations as what can be taken for granted and what needs to have most impact (*cf* 18.4*ff* on information processing);

(b) shorter adjuncts tend to precede longer ones.

But subject to (a) and (b), where adjuncts cluster at *E*, they will tend to occur in the following sequence:

respect – process – space – time – contingency

It is less usual to find more than one adjunct at *I*, but any such cluster would tend to follow a converse order; *eg*: space (or process) – time.

Subjuncts

8.32 Subjuncts have a subordinate and parenthetic role in comparison with adjuncts; they lack the grammatical parity with other sentence elements that we saw as criterial in 8.13. There are two main types, each with subtypes (Fig 8.32). Those with *narrow orientation* are chiefly related to the predication or to a particular part of the predication. Those with *wide orientation* relate more to the sentence as a whole, but show their subjunct character in tending to achieve this through a particular relationship with one of the clause elements, especially the subject.

SUBJUNCT
- wide orientation
  - viewpoint
  - courtesy
- narrow orientation
  - item
    - subject
    - predication
  - emphasizer
  - intensifier
  - focusing

Fig 8.32

Wide orientation

Viewpoint subjuncts

8.33 The subjuncts which express a viewpoint are largely concerned with the semantic concept of respect, are predominantly expressed by nongradable (7.1) adverb phrases, and are characteristically placed at *I*. For example:

Architecturally, the plans represent a magnificent conception.

But there can be other forms of realization:

From a personal viewpoint, he is likely to do well in this post.
Looked at politically, the proposal seems dangerous.

Especially in AmE, we find adverbs in *-wise*:

Weatherwise, the outlook is dismal.

Courtesy subjuncts

8.34 A small number of adverbs in *-ly*, along with *please*, serve to convey a formulaic tone of politeness to a sentence. They normally occur at *M*:

You are *cordially* invited to take your places.
He asked if I would *please* read his manuscript.

Courtesy subjuncts obviously involve the semantic category manner but are quite distinct from manner adjuncts. Contrast:

She *kindly* [subjunct] offered me her seat.
('She was kind enough to offer . . .')
She offered me her seat *kindly* [adjunct].
('She offered me her seat *in a kind manner*.')

NOTE Though *thanks* (or *thank you*) communicatively matches *please* as a response form, there are few grammatical similarities except that both can occur in isolation:

'Would you like a drink?' '*Please*'.
'Here is your drink.' '*Thanks*'.

While *please* usually occurs at *M* (= *I* with the imperative), *thanks* is at *E*:

'(Will you) *please* have another helping.'
'I really have had enough, *thanks*.'

Narrow orientation

Item subjuncts

8.35 The commonest item to be associated with subjuncts is the *subject* of a clause, with the subjunct operating in the semantic area of *manner* but distinguished from the corresponding manner adjunct by being placed at *I* or *M*:

She has *consistently* opposed the lawyers's arguments.

This does not mean that her own arguments have been conducted consistently but that she has been consistent in always opposing the lawyer's.

Many such subjuncts express volition, as in:

Intentionally, they said nothing to him about the fire.
With great reluctance, he rose to speak.

Since many *predication* subjuncts are idiomatically linked with particular verbs, they are best treated under phrasal verbs in 16.2*ff*. Here, however, we should mention the subjuncts associated with the expression of time. The uses of *already*, *still*, and *yet* as time-relation subjuncts can be summarized as follows:

Declarative positive:

I {*already* / *still*} admire him. (*but*: *I *yet* admire him.)

Declarative negative, with subjunct *preceding* the negative:

I *still* haven't spoken to him. (*but*: *I *already*/*yet* haven't . . .)

Declarative negative, with subjunct *following* the negative:

He can't {*yet* drive. / drive *yet*.}

?He can't *still* drive/drive *still*. (*He can't *already* drive.)

Interrogative positive:

Is he *already*/*still*/*yet* here? (all three – esp *yet* – also at *E*)

Interrogative negative:

Isn't he *already*/*still*/*yet* here? (all three – esp *yet* – also at *E*)

NOTE [a] *Any more* and *any longer* function as nonassertive, and *no more* and *no longer* as negative time-relation subjuncts:

He doesn't work for us *any more*/*longer*.
He *no longer* works for us.
She said she would see me *no more*.

[b] Other common time subjuncts are *just*, *(n)ever*, the first cooccurring mainly with the perfect or progressive:

I've *just* finished my supper.
She was *just* talking to him a moment ago.
They {don't *ever* / *never*} seem to read books.

Emphasizers

8.36 Emphasizers are subjuncts expressing (largely at *iM* or *M*) the semantic role of *modality* with a reinforcing effect on the meaning of a sentence. For example:

I {*just* / *really* / *simply*} can't believe a word he says!

Some emphasizers are characteristic of very informal speech; for example:

I wish I could *darned well* find that book.
They told him to get *the hell* off their land.

Others occur only in certain grammatical environments, notably *always* and *well* with modalized verb phrases:

Even if you didn't know where I was, you could *always* have telephoned to ask.
She said that she had no money and that may *well* be true.

NOTE Emphasizer subjuncts can frequently occur as responses; thus to the question 'Are you willing to help?' we might have

(Yes) *certainly*.
Sure(ly). ⟨esp AmE⟩
(Yes) *indeed*.
Certainly not.

Intensifiers

8.37 The intensifier subjuncts are broadly concerned with the semantic category of *degree*, indicating an increase or decrease of the intensity with which a predication (usually containing an attitudinal verb) is expressed. They characteristically appear at *M*.

(a) Increased intensification to various degrees is realized by *amplifiers*, as in:

They *fully* appreciate the problem.
He has *completely* ignored my question.
She was *badly* in need of help.
How (very much) they must have suffered!

(b) Decreased intensification to various degrees is realized by *downtoners*, as in:

They have *practically* forced him to resign.
In spite of his manners, I *rather* like him.
She *sort of* laughed at the idea. ⟨informal⟩
I was *only* joking.
He didn't *in the least* enjoy the party.

Especially at the extremes of intensity, subjuncts of (a) and (b) can be given emphasis by appearing at *E*:

I understand your attitude *totally*.
She won't mind *in the slightest*.

NOTE [a] Some intensifiers occur only in specific environments; for example, *possibly* with *can('t)* in nonassertive clauses:

She can't *possibly* expect you to wait so long.

[b] As well as relating to attitude, intensifiers are used in respect of quantity and time:

> I paid him *a great deal* for his advice.
> She slept *a little* in the afternoon.

Focusing subjuncts

8.38 Special attention may be called to a part of a sentence as broad as predication or as narrow as a constituent within a phrase. There are two types of focusing subjunct that can so operate; one is *restrictive*, as in:

> I *merely* wanted to know his name. (*ie* I didn't want to know anything else)
> *Only* her sister visited her in hospital. (*ie* No one else did so)

The other is *additive*, as in:

> Fred had *also* invited his mother-in-law. (*ie* in addition to others)
> *Even* on Sundays, my doctor is willing to come and see me. (*ie* in addition to ordinary working days)

With most focusing subjuncts, the usual position is immediately before the part to be focused, and if that is the whole or part of the predication, the position is *M*. As with negation, therefore, there is the possibility of ambiguity:

> She had {*not* / *only* / *also*} questioned her patients the previous week.

Since it is normal to give the prosodic emphasis to the final phrase of a sentence, this would usually be spoken, read, and understood with the focus on the time adjunct. But of course in speech, the focus could be clearly placed on any of the three post-operator constituents.

> . . . QUÈSTIONED her patients . . . (*ie* as opposed to examining them)
> . . . questioned her PÀTIENTS . . . (*ie* as opposed to her colleagues)
> . . . questioned her patients the PRÈVIOUS week . . . (*ie* as opposed to the current week)

In writing, care can be taken to place a focusing subjunct in close proximity to the part required (and prescriptive tradition urges this particularly with *only*). Usually this is before the item ('*only* her patients') but may be after it ('the previous week *only*'), and this is obligatory with *alone* and *too* ('her patients *too*') but is disallowed with *just* and generally with *even* (*?'the previous week *even*').

NOTE In focusing *wh*-items, *exactly* and *just* are common:

> I know *exactly* where to find him.
> *Just* when did you send in your application?

8.39 Focusing can involve correlative constructions. For example:

> I saw her *neither* that day *nor* the day after.
> They had *neither* met the author *nor (even)* read any of his novels.

With either of these items at *I*, there is subject–operator inversion:

> They had *neither* met the author, *nor* had they (*even*) read any of his novels.

Cf also:

> She had *both* written poems *and (also)* had some published.
> We must ignore *not only* his manners *but (also)* the way he is dressed.

Such correlation is frequently achieved through a construction resembling a cleft sentence (18.18):

> It was *not just* that she ignored me; it was *particularly* that she was so pointedly nice to my wife.

More formally, *not only* and *not merely* can be in *I*-position with consequent subject–operator inversion:

> *Not merely* have I lent you money; I have (*also*) helped you get jobs.

Disjuncts

8.40 Where adjuncts are seen as on a par with such sentence elements as S and O, while subjuncts are seen as having a lesser role, disjuncts have by contrast a superior role to sentence elements, being somewhat detached from and superordinate to the rest of the sentence. There are two broad types, each with subtypes (see Fig 8.40). First we have the relatively small class of STYLE disjuncts, conveying the speaker's comment on the style and form of what is being said and defining in some way the conditions under which 'authority' is being assumed for the statement. Thus where [1] is stated as an unsupported fact, [2] is conditioned by a style disjunct:

> Mr Forster neglects his children. [1]
> *From my personal observation*, Mr Forster neglects his children. [2]

The second type is the much larger class of CONTENT disjuncts, making an observation on the actual content of an utterance and on its truth conditions:

> *To the disgust of his neighbours*, Mr Forster neglects his children. [3]

- DISJUNCT
  - style
    - modality and manner
    - respect
  - content
    - relating to certainty
    - relating to evaluation

***Fig* 8.40**

Although not restricted as to position (and while some, as we shall see, are often at *M*), most disjuncts appear at *I*.

Style disjuncts

8.41 Many style disjuncts can be seen as abbreviated clauses in which the adverbial would have the role of manner adjunct:

> *Frankly*, I am tired.
> (*cf*: 'I tell you *frankly* that I am tired'.)

Sometimes the disjunct has full clausal form:

> *If I may say so without giving you offence*, I think your writing is rather immature.

More often, a clausal disjunct is nonfinite, as in *to be frank*, *putting it bluntly*, *considered candidly*.

The semantic roles of disjuncts fall under two main heads:

(a) Manner and modality, thus involving items such as *crudely*, *frankly*, *honestly*, *truthfully*; *eg*:

> *(To put it) briefly*, there is nothing I can do to help.
> You can, *in all honesty*, expect no further payments.

(b) Respect, thus involving items such as *generally*, *literally*, *personally*, *strictly*; *eg*:

> *Strictly (in terms of the rules)*, she should have conceded the point to her opponent.
> I would not, *(speaking) personally*, have taken offence at the remark.
> *From what he said*, the other driver was in the wrong.

It will be seen that disjuncts in (b) often constitute ways of guardedly 'hedging' the accompanying statement. A particular case of this arises in *metalinguistic* comment in which the disjunct draws attention to a point of terminology:

> *In a word*, he is a traitor, though I would not say that he had *literally* betrayed anyone.

NOTE [a] When used in questions, disjuncts in (a) may relate to the speaker or to the addressee:

> *Privately*, was Henry ever in prison?

This can mean either 'I ask you privately to tell me' or 'I ask you to tell me privately'.
[b] Disjuncts in (b) can be expressed by *if-*, *since-* and *because*-clauses, but the latter must be at *E*:

> He was drunk, *because he couldn't stand.*

Content disjuncts

8.42 Comment on the content of an utterance may be of two kinds:
(a) relating to *certainty*;
(b) relating to *evaluation*.
Both can be expressed by a wide range of adverb phrases, by prepositional phrases and – especially those in (a) – by clauses.

(a) *Certainty*. These disjuncts comment on the truth value of what is said, firmly endorsing it, expressing doubt, or posing contingencies such as conditions or reasons. For example, beside the statement 'The play was written by Francis Beaumont', we may have:

$$\text{The play was} \begin{Bmatrix} \textit{undoubtedly} \\ \textit{apparently} \\ \textit{perhaps} \end{Bmatrix} \text{written by Francis Beaumont.}$$

Compare also:

> *In essence*, the judge called her evidence in question.
> *Since she had no time to have the car fixed*, Rachel telephoned for a taxi.
> The proposal would have been accepted *if the chairman had put it more forcibly*.

(b) *Evaluation*. These disjuncts express an attitude to an utterance by way of evaluation. Some express a judgment on the utterance as a whole, including its subject:

> *Wisely*, Mrs Jensen consulted her lawyer.
> ('Mrs Jensen was wise in consulting her lawyer.')

So also *correctly*, *cunningly*, *foolishly*, *justly*, *rightly*, *stupidly*, etc. Other evaluation disjuncts carry no implication of comment on the subject:

> *Naturally*, my husband expected me home by then.
> ('It was natural for my husband to expect me back by then' – *not* 'My husband was natural . . .')

So also *curiously*, *funnily (enough)*, *strangely*, *unexpectedly*, *predictably*, *understandably*, *disturbingly*, *pleasingly*, *regrettably*, *fortunately*, *happily*, *luckily*, *sadly*, *amusingly*, *hopefully* <esp AmE>, *significantly*. Prepositional phrases and relative clauses (sentential and nominal) involving such lexical bases are also used:

> *To my regret*, she did not seek nomination.
> *What is especially fortunate*, the child was unhurt.
> We were not, *which is surprising*, invited to meet the new members of staff.

NOTE [**a**] The semantic difference between the relationships in (a) and (b) is underlined by the fact that sentence paraphrases for (a) cannot involve putative *should* (14.14), whereas those for (b) always can:

(a) *Obviously*, the child is recovering.
~ 'It is obvious that the child is recovering.'

(b) *Fortunately*, the child is recovering.
~ 'It is fortunate that the child {is / should be} recovering.'

[**b**] Just as in *to my regret* (in contrast to *regrettably*) it is made explicit as to who feels the regret, so with some adverbs we may add such a specification with a *for*-phrase. For example:

> *Luckily (for Peter)*, the doctor arrived speedily.

Conjuncts

8.43 As their name implies, conjuncts serve to conjoin two utterances or parts of an utterance, and they do so by expressing at the same time the semantic relationship (*eg* of time or contingency) obtaining between them. For example:

> The candidate is a fine teacher, a broadcaster of some experience, and a respected drama critic. *All the same*, there is a feeling on the committee that someone younger should be appointed.

The conjunct *all the same* here connects two separate sentences, indicating a concessive relation between them: *despite* the candidate's high qualifications, some members of the committee were not satisfied.

As in this example, conjuncts are usually at *I*, but their connective role is often achieved more smoothly when they are placed at *M*:

> The cinema has lost none of its attractions in India and the film industry has *in consequence* continued to flourish.

Although some conjuncts (such as the informal *though*) commonly appear at *E*, this position can somewhat obscure the connective role.

NOTE [**a**] Conjuncts often correspond to adverbials in an otherwise unexpressed clause:

> My wife is very busy this evening, and [I tell you something] *in addition*, she is not feeling very well.

[b] As well as *connecting* utterances, some of the commonest conjuncts such as *now* and *so* have a major role as discourse *initiators*. Consider the following as the first words of a street encounter:

> *So* you're better again, Bill!

Here an *extralinguistic* situation seems to be conjoined as it were, with an appropriate *linguistic* reaction to it: 'I see you up and about, *so* I conclude you've recovered from your illness.'

The commonest discourse initiator of all (*well*) is less easy to account for plausibly. When used connectively it has a *transitional* function ('Given that my previous point is *well* founded, my next point is . . .'), as in:

> I hear you've bought a new house; *well*, when are you moving?

Note the following exchange in Matt Cohen's novel *Flowers of Darkness* (1981):

> 'Well,' said Donna.
> 'Well,' Annabelle replied. *Well* was always Donna's opening remark, delivered in a way to make clear that she knew Annabelle was in the midst of some inadmissible train of thought.

[c] Conjuncts can semantically endorse a connection already expressed by grammatical subordination; for example:

> I see her regularly because she is, *by the way*, a friend of my brother's.

The semantics of conjuncts

8.44 We now group some of the commoner conjuncts according to their semantic roles:

A: LISTING

(i) *Enumerative*, as in:

> *In the first place*, the economy is recovering, and *secondly* unemployment is beginning to decline.

Cf also *for one thing* (. . . *for another thing*), *next*, *then (again)*, *finally*; especially in formal and technical use, we find *a* . . . *b* . . . *c* . . ., *one* . . . *two* . . . *three* . . .

(ii) *Additive*, as in:

> She has the ability, the experience, and *above all* the courage to tackle the problem.

Cf also *furthermore*, *moreover*, *what is more*, *similarly*, *in addition*, *on top of that*.

B: SUMMATIVE, as in:

> He was late for work, he quarrelled with a colleague, and he lost his wallet; *all in all*, it was a bad day.

Cf also *altogether*, *overall*, *therefore*, *in sum*, *to sum up*.

C: APPOSITIVE, as in:

There was one snag; *namely*, the weather.

Cf also *that is (to say), ie, for example, eg, in other words, specifically.*

D: RESULTIVE, as in:

I got there very late, *so* I missed most of the fun.

Cf also *therefore, as a result, accordingly, in consequence, of course.*

E: INFERENTIAL, as in:

You haven't answered my question; *in other words*, you disapprove of the proposal.

Cf also *in that case, so, then, otherwise, else.*

F: CONTRASTIVE

(i) *Reformulatory* and *replacive*, as in:

She's asked some of her friends – some of her husband's friends, *rather*.

Cf also *(or) better, more accurately, in other words, alias, worse.*

(ii) *Antithetic*, as in:

They had expected to enjoy being in Manila but *instead* they both fell ill.

Cf also *on the contrary, by contrast, on the other hand, then.*

(iii) *Concessive*, as in:

My age is against me: *still*, it's worth a try.

Cf also, *however, nevertheless, yet, all the same, of course, that said,* and several informal expressions such as *anyhow, anyways* ⟨esp AmE⟩, *still and all* ⟨esp AmE⟩, *only, though.*

G: TRANSITIONAL

(i) *Discoursal*, as in:

Let me introduce you to my sister, and *by the way*, did I tell you that I'm moving?

Cf also *incidentally, now.*

(ii) *Temporal*, as in:

The ambulance got stuck in rush-hour traffic and *in the meantime* the child became delirious.

Cf also *meanwhile, originally, subsequently, eventually.*

Cooccurrence and correlation

8.45 Conjuncts from different sets can appear in the same sentence:

> *So* [resultive] I did reasonably well, *all in all* [summative].
> *Then* [inferential] she'll get the job *nevertheless* [concessive]?

Conjuncts from the same set are sometimes used in reinforcement; for example, the additive items in:

> *Moreover*, he had *in addition* a qualification in accountancy.

More usually, such reinforcement occurs through conjuncts appearing along with compatible conjunctions. These may involve coordination (as with *and so*, *but yet*, *or rather*) or subordination (as with *if . . . then*, *although . . . still*):

> *Even if* you're taking the car only a short distance, you should *nevertheless* have your driving licence with you.

NOTE Correlation often seems excessively heavy and formal, especially perhaps in causal relationships (*because . . . therefore*). By contrast, reinforcement where no subordination is involved often seems over-informal (as in '*But still*, she got the job, *though*') and in some cases it is regarded as objectionably tautologous (as in the sequence *but however*).

Bibliographical note

For general studies of adverbials, see Buysschaert (1982); Greenbaum (1969); Guimier (1988); Huang (1975); Nilsen (1972); with a theoretical emphasis, Bartsch (1976), Emons (1974); Schreiber (1972); Ungerer (1988).

On particular subsets of English adverbials, see Aarts (1989b); Bolinger (1972); Dudman (1984); Hartvigson (1969); Heny (1973); Jacobson (1978, 1981); Lee (1987); Schiffrin (1985); Svartvik (1980).

On adverbial collocations, see Bäcklund (1970); Crystal (1966); Greenbaum (1970).

On adverbial positions, see Jacobson (1964, 1975).

On intonational aspects of adverbial usage, see Halliday (1967); Taglicht (1983).

Other relevant studies include: Anderson (1976); Greenbaum (1973); Halliday and Hasan (1976); Lakoff (1975); Larson (1985).

9 Prepositions and prepositional phrases

9.1 Prepositions are a closed class of items (2.6, but *cf* 9.3) connecting two units in a sentence and specifying a relationship between them. For example:

(I don't like to) drink *out of* a cracked cup. [1]
(He was) very grateful *for* her help. [2]
The elderly man *in* the raincoat (looks ill.) [3]

In all three, the second unit is the *prepositional complement*, but in [1] the link is to a verb phrase, in [2] an adjective phrase, and in [3] a noun phrase. The sequence of preposition and its complement is known as a *prepositional phrase*, and its role may be to act as a postmodifier in noun-phrase structure (such that the whole sequence *The elderly man in the raincoat* of [3] constitutes a complex noun phrase: 17.1*ff*). But as we have seen in Chapter 8, prepositional phrases can also function as adverbials, and the 'link' can then be between the prepositional complement and a whole clause. Compare, for example, the adverbial in [4]:

In a few minutes, we'll know the result of the blood test. [4]

Prepositions may be simple or complex (9.3), and in either case their complements are usually noun phrases; but they can also be nonfinite (*-ing*) clauses or nominal (*wh-*) clauses. For example:

{*near* / *on top of*} + the control tower

{*from* / *in terms of*} + {the financial estimates / scrutinizing the results / what you were saying / where she was sitting}

NOTE [**a**] Although also having a nominal function, *that*-clauses and infinitive clauses cannot be prepositional complements. Compare:

I was surprised {
at her angry response.
at hearing her objection.
at what she said.
to hear her objection.
that she responded so angrily.
}

[**b**] A prepositional complement is 'object territory' (6.7) and personal pronouns are therefore in the objective case:

They moved towards *me*/*us*/*him*/*her*/*them*.

After *and*, however, subjective forms are sometimes found in hypercorrect usage; *cf* 6.7 Note [b].

Deferred prepositions

9.2 Though prepositions normally precede their complements, there are circumstances in which this cannot happen:

(a) Where the subject of a passive construction corresponds to the prepositional complement in the active analogue; thus

> We have paid *for the car*.
> ~ *The car* has been paid *for*.

(b) Where the prepositional complement is thematized (18.23*ff*) in sentences with infinitive or *-ing* clauses; thus

> It is unpleasant to work *with that man*.
> ~ *That man* is unpleasant to work *with*.
> It is not worth listening *to his advice*.
> ~ *His advice* is not worth listening *to*.

In addition, there are circumstances where deferment is optional, depending chiefly on stylistic preference. Where the prepositional complement is an interrogative pronoun, deferment indeed is normal:

> *What* are you looking *at*?
> *Who* is she talking *about*?

In such cases, the close relation between the verb and the preposition (16.5*f*) makes alternative arrangement awkward and rare. Elsewhere, there can be a choice:

> *Who* did you sell your house *to*?
> *To whom* did you sell your house? ⟨formal⟩

A similar choice is more general where the prepositional complement is a relative pronoun:

> The building (*that*) you're standing *in front of* was designed by Lutyens.
> The building *in front of which* you are standing was designed by Lutyens. ⟨formal⟩

NOTE [a] With some simple prepositions (such as *through*) and most complex ones (such as *because of, in addition to*), deferment is virtually disallowed.

[b] Superficially resembling deferred prepositions are *prepositional adverbs*, identical in form with the corresponding prepositions except that, unlike them, they are never unstressed. Compare:

Until you recover, you must 'stay *in the 'house*.
Until you recover, you must 'stay *'in*.
I should have parked the car *behind the house* but I left it *in front*.

Simple and complex prepositions

9.3 The commonest prepositions are a small number of monosyllabic items such as *at, for, in, on, to, with,* typically unstressed and often with reduced vowel except when deferred. Compare:

What are you looking *at* [at]?
I'm looking *at* [ət] *this huge telephone bill.*

But in addition there are polysyllabic prepositions, some of them compounds formed historically from the monosyllabic ones (such as *inside, within*) or derived from participles (such as *during*) or adopted from other languages (such as *despite, except*). Thus although prepositions are a closed class in comparison with truly open classes like nouns, they are less literally a closed class than determiners or pronouns.

The number of prepositions has been increased partly by using still more participles (for example, *barring, concerning, granted*) but chiefly by combining prepositions with other words to form 'complex prepositions'. These are of two main types:

(a) a simple preposition preceded by a participle, adjective, adverb, or conjunction, as with *owing to, devoid of, away from, because of*;
(b) a simple preposition followed by a noun and then a further simple preposition, as with *in charge of, by means of, at variance with, in addition to, as a result of.*

NOTE [a] Some prepositions of foreign origin are not thoroughly 'acclimatized' in general use; for example, *qua, re, vis-à-vis, à propos.*

[b] Items of quasi-preposition status include *near (to)* which admits comparison ('He came and sat *nearer the front*') as well as *than* and *as* which can also be – and for some people can only be – conjunctions:

She is taller *than* I am. (*than* as conjunction)
She is taller *than* I. (*than* as conjunction with ellipsis: rather formal)
She is taller *than me*. (*than* as preposition)

[c] Some complex prepositions ending in *of* admit alternative genitive constructions:

for the sake of the family ~ for the family's sake
on behalf of my friend ~ on my friend's behalf

Prepositional meanings

9.4 Though the relationship between two linguistic units as mentioned in 9.1 may be wide-ranging in meaning, most of them are either spatial or figuratively derived from notions of physical space. Consider *in* as used in the following examples:

I like being *in this room.* [1]
She'll finish the work *in the present month.* [2]
His life is *in danger.* [3]
They told me this *in all seriousness.* [4]

The period of time in [2], the danger in [3], and the seriousness in [4] are to be understood as having the capacity to envelop in a kind of three-dimensional space analogous to the physical room in [1]. We must therefore begin by understanding the ways in which prepositions refer to some of the basic spatial dimensions, as set out in Fig 9.4. This shows three different kinds of distinction.

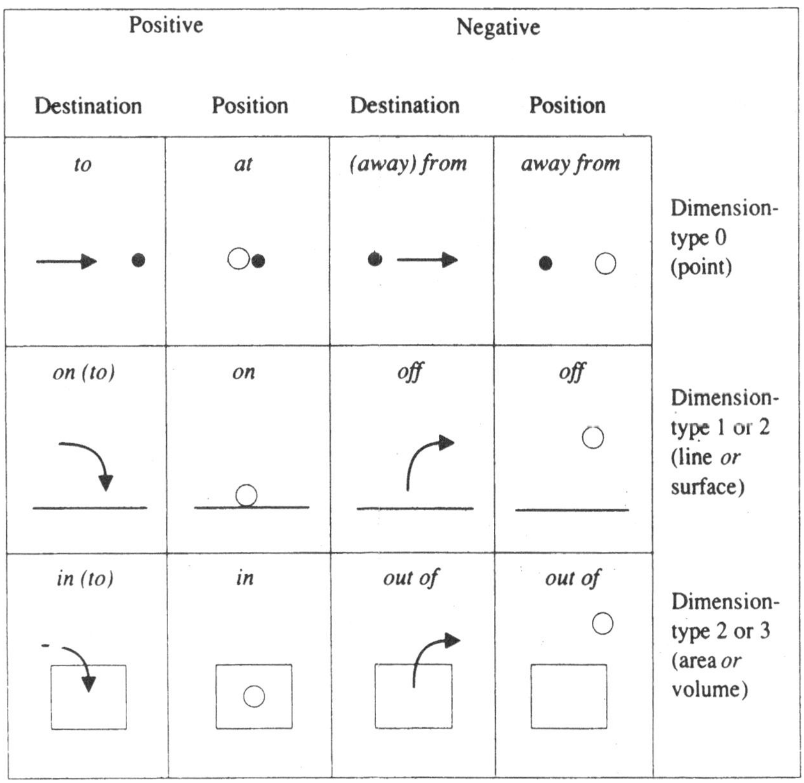

Fig 9.4

First, the prepositions are contrasted as 'positive' or 'negative' (such that *off*, for example, means 'not *on*'). Secondly, the prepositions distinguish between 'destination' (movement with respect to an intended location) and 'position' (static location). Thirdly, we have three dimension types: one which ignores dimension altogether, treating location as a point even if in reality it is a continent:

> He walked *to the lamp-post.*
> They flew *to Australia.*

The second dimension type embraces what is in real space either one-dimensional or two-dimensional:

> She put her toe *on the line.*
> They were alone *on the tennis-court.*

The third dimension similarly straddles two actual dimensions: two-dimensional or three-dimensional space:

> Some cows were grazing *in the field.*
> My coat is *in the wardrobe.*

Space

Position and direction

9.5 Between the notions of directional movement and static position there is a cause-and-effect relation which applies equally to (a) the positive prepositions and (b) the negative prepositions:

(a) Jack ran *to the corner* and then stood *at the corner.*
Put the book *on(to) the top shelf* and leave it *on the top shelf.*
She went *into her office* and stayed *in her office.*
(b) Mildred moved *from Bloomsbury* last year and enjoys living *away from the city centre.*
Take the typewriter *off the table* and leave it *off the table.*
He walked *out of the house* and stayed *out of the house* all afternoon.

Where places are regarded as points on a route or as institutions to which one is attached, dimension-type 0 is invoked:

> Does this train stop *at Lincoln*?
> Our daughter is *at Oxford* studying philosophy.

But where that same place is thought of in terms of residence, dimension-type 2/3 is appropriate:

> I've never lived either *in Lincoln* or *in Oxford.*

Analogously, if the referent is considered as a surface, dimension-type 1/2 is appropriate, while if it is considered as necessarily enclosing, then dimension-type 2/3 comes into play:

> They were rowing *on* } *Lake Windermere.*
> I was swimming *in* }

I'll lie *on the bed* for a few minutes.
There was a child asleep *in the bed.*

NOTE [a] While *to* usually implies achieving the destination, *towards* is more neutrally directional:

She drove *to Edinburgh* (and arrived at noon).
She drove *towards Edinburgh* (but that may not be her destination).

[b] Though the relationship 'X is on Y' usually involves Y being a horizontal surface below X, this is by no means necessary:

There are several people on the mountain-side.
. . . pictures . . . wall
. . . flies . . . ceiling
. . . apples . . . tree

Contiguity with a side surface is often expressed by *against* ('Who left the ladder *against the fence*?').

[c] The use of *at, in, on* is often idiomatic; thus *on earth* but *in the world*; 'She is doing well *at school*' is often preferred in BrE, while '. . . *in school*' is general in AmE. *Cf* (with different determiner constraints: 5.19) '*on* land, *at* sea, and *in* the air'.

Relative position

9.6 Rather than absolute position, many prepositions indicate the position of something relative to the position of something else:

The police station is *opposite my house.*
~My house is *opposite the police station.*

Some prepositions form antonymic pairs, as indicated in Fig 9.6. A is *above X* and B is *below X* (as X is *below A* and *above B*); C is *in front of X* and D is *behind X* (as X is *behind C* and *in front of D*).

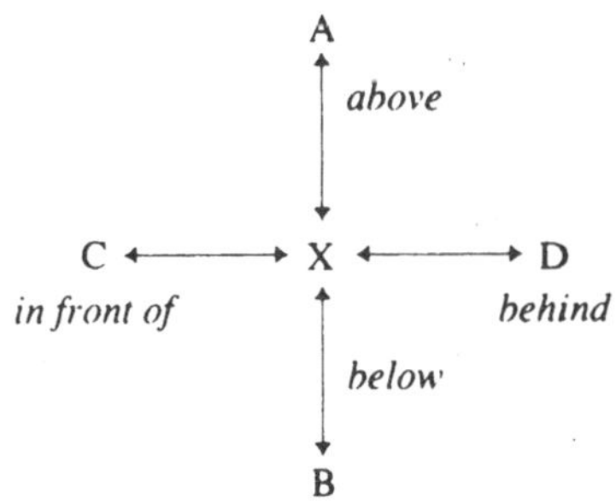

Fig 9.6

Similar to *above* and *below* are *over* and *under* respectively, though the latter tend to mean '*directly* above' and '*directly* below'. Similar to *in front of* and *behind* are *before* and *after*, though the latter tend to imply relative precedence rather than physical position. Like *under* are the less common *beneath* (somewhat formal) and *underneath*. With *on top of* we combine the sense of 'above' with abutment.

Abutment is also normally implied with *by*, *beside*, and *with*:

> She left the keys { *by* / *with* / *beside* } *her purse.*

By contrast, *close to* and *near (to)* generally exclude actual contact; these prepositions are unique in admitting comparative inflection (7.39):

> Please move this desk { *close(r) to* / *near(er) (to)* } *the wall.*

With *between*, we positionally relate two objects or groups of objects, whereas with *among* (and *amid(st)*, more formally) we are dealing with a more general plurality:

> There must be space to walk *between the chairs and the wall.*
> I left the letter *among my birthday cards.*

The converse of *between* and *among* is to some extent expressed by *around* (esp AmE, *round* is esp BrE):

> There were trees *around the house.*
> ~There was a house *among the trees.*

NOTE [a] The reciprocal relativity of *opposite (to)* and *facing* is reflected in their frequently having reciprocals (6.28 Note [a]) as their complement:

> Let's sit { *opposite (to)* / *facing* } *each other.*

[b] Especially in BrE, *about* is used like *around*:

> She put her arms *about him.*

[c] Most prepositions of relative position can also be used of relative direction and destination; for example:

> The mouse scampered *under the bookcase* and disappeared.

Passage

9.7 The notion of passage combines position and motion, disregarding destination:

> The referee complained because people were moving *behind the goalposts.*
> I love walking *through woods* in spring.

Other prepositions commonly used for passage are *by*, *over*, *under*, *across*, and *past*. It is worth noting the parallel between positional *on* and *in* on the one hand and *across* and *through* on the other:

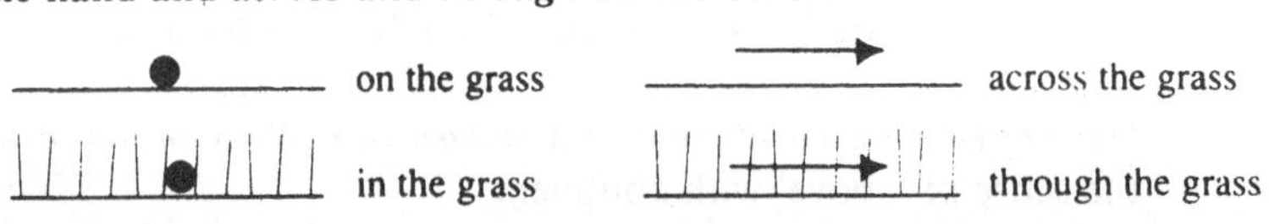

Passage and direction are frequently related to conceptual axes, especially the vertical and horizontal, as shown in Fig 9.7. With *(a)round*, on the other hand, the relation is to a real or fancied point such as a corner or a centre:

> Be careful as you drive *round corners*.
> The children were playing *around the park*.

But spatial relations are often expressed by orientation to the speaker, so that 'He lives *down the hill*' will relate not only to the vertical axis as in Fig 9.7 but will imply 'further down from where I am speaking' or 'further down from the place I am speaking about'. Similarly:

> Their house is *past the church*. (ie 'beyond the church' in relation to the orientation point)
> They have gone *across the moors*. (ie 'from here')

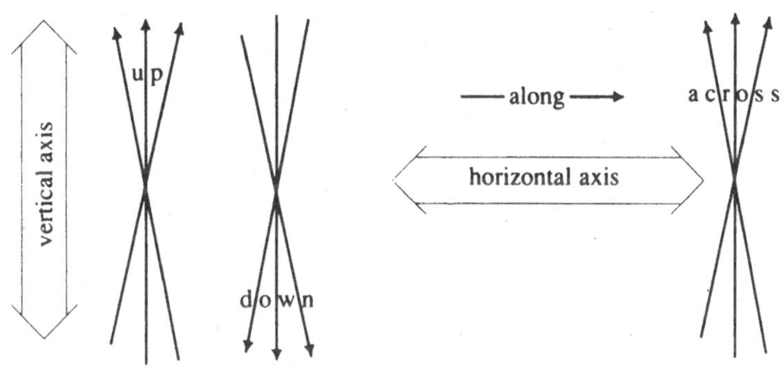

Fig. 9.7

Note that the difference between '(coming) *up the road*' and '(going) *down the road*' may have more to do with personal orientation than with relative elevation. *Cf* also:

> There's someone walking *up and down the drive*.

NOTE [a] Just as verbs like *come* and *go* strongly imply the personal orientation, so others are congruent with prepositional meaning, even to the extent of enabling the preposition to be omitted; for example *climb (up)*, *jump (over)*, *flee (from)*, *pass (by)*.
[b] Prepositions that can convey motion or direction can be used also to express the static resultative meaning of having reached the destination:

> The horse has successfully jumped *across the gap*.

[c] Especially when preceded by *all* and *right*, prepositions such as *over*, *(a)round*, and *through* express pervasive meaning:

> Crowds were cheering *(all) along the route*
> There were police *(right) round the house*.

Metaphorical extension with spatial prepositions

9.8 With many spatial prepositions, metaphor enables similar but abstract relations to be expressed. This is particularly striking with time (9.9) but a wide range of other meanings must also be noted, where the proximity to literal use can be readily perceived. For example:

in the room	:	in this book, in some difficulty
out of the bottle	:	out of danger, out of the competition
beneath the branches	:	beneath contempt
under the floorboards	:	under suspicion
up the hill	:	up the social scale
downhill	:	down market
beyond the post office	:	beyond endurance
over the mountain	:	(she is getting) over her illness when her temperature was over 40 °C
from Boston to Bangor	:	from generation to generation
between the trees	:	between ourselves
through the tunnel	:	through the ordeal

NOTE Some prepositions are used in what would seem a converse relationship:

The cow is *in calf*. (~?the calf is *in the cow's womb*)
The office is *out of envelopes*. (~?All envelopes seem to be *out of the office*).

Note also: *in/out of luck*

Time

Time position

9.9 Three prepositions, *at*, *on*, and *in*, are used in expressions answering the question 'When?' and they reflect a concept of time as analogous to space. Thus *at* is used for points of time, where time is conceived as being 'dimensionless':

The film will begin *at 7.20 p.m.*

It is not only instants that can be so considered:

What are you doing *at the weekend*?
She last saw her parents *at Christmas*.
Chaucer frequently speaks of books because *at that time* they were rare and highly valued.

Where time is regarded as a period, the usual preposition is *in*, reflecting analogy with two- or three-dimensional space:

In the evening, I listened to some Beethoven records.
Where did he live *in his childhood*?
I saw her *in March*/*in 1988*/*in the following week*.

But in expressions referring to *days*, the preposition is *on*:

We can come *on Monday* or *on any other day that you may prefer.*
The baby was born *on July the twelfth.*

So too with an interval that is specifically part of a day:

on Sunday afternoon; *on Thursday night.*

NOTE [a] Reference to *night* may disregard its 'dimension' as in:

I have to sleep *in the afternoon* because I cannot sleep *at night* very easily.

But it can also be viewed as a period, with the regular use of *in*:

We heard her coughing several times *in the night.*

[b] A phrase like *in three days* may be used to indicate a duration or a point three days hence; thus 'He'll do it *in three days*' may mean *either* 'He'll take three days to do it' (without commitment to when the three days will be) *or* 'He'll do it three days from now' (the converse of 'He did it three days ago').

Time duration

9.10 In answer to *How long?* we have above all phrases with *for*:

We stayed in a rented cottage *for the summer.*

The same meaning, with some emphasis on the duration, can be expressed with *throughout* and *all through.* By contrast, *during* indicates a stretch of time within which a more specific duration can be indicated:

During the summer, we stayed in a rented cottage *for a month.*

But with appropriate lexical support in the context, the difference between *during* and *for* (*throughout*, etc) can be neutralized:

Try to stay alert {*throughout* / *during*} *the entire ceremony.*

Duration expressions with *over* carry the implication of a period containing some divisions or 'fences'. Thus one can stay *overnight, over the weekend, over the Christmas period* but hardly *?*over the ceremony*, *?*over the evening.*

Duration can be specified by reference to the beginning and ending:

The office will be open *from Monday to Friday.*

While *from . . . to* corresponds to *for* ('The office will be open *for five days*'), *between . . . and* can be used in the more general sense of *during*:

The office will be open *between Monday and Friday.* (*ie* '*for a period* within the stretch specified').

NOTE The expression *from x to y* is chiefly BrE and although it normally means that the periods *x* and *y* are both included, there can be uncertainty. The corresponding AmE expression *(from) x through y* is inclusive.

9.11 Duration specifying only a starting point or a terminal point is expressed by phrases with *by, before, from, after, since, till, until, up to*. For example:

> She will be here *by Friday night*.
> She will not be here *before Friday night*.
> I worked *from eight o'clock (onwards)*.
> I began working (at some time) *after eight o'clock*.
> I have been working *since eight o'clock*.
>
> He did not set out {*till* / *until*} *Monday afternoon*.
>
> You can stay here *till/until/up to lunch time*.

Note the contrast in:

> We slept *until midnight*. (= we stopped sleeping then)
> We didn't sleep *until midnight*. (= we started sleeping then)

NOTE With the rather formal *pending*, the complement usually denotes a period and the preposition thus roughly corresponds to 'up to the start of and during (the period)':

> They should cease action *pending negotiations*.

But the complement can also refer to a point of time and in such cases the preposition means 'until':

> They should cease action *pending the court's decision*.

The items *prior to* and *in advance of* can replace *before* in formal style.

Cause and purpose

9.12 There is a spectrum of relations extending from cause to purpose. For the part covering cause, reason, and motive, we have prepositional phrases with items such as *because of, on account of, for, out of*:

> He lost his job *because of his laziness*.
> She was fined *for dangerous driving*.
> He misdirected the letter *out of spite*.
> They died *from exposure*.
> She can't turn the heating on *for fear of a fire outbreak*.
> The plane crashed *through some navigational error*.

But of course the notion of 'motive' shades into purpose, goal, and target, for all of which the common preposition is *for*:

> An appeal is being opened *for a new hospital*.
> They are appealing *for donations*.
> We had better set out *for home*.
> She is applying *for a better job*.

Where the complement is animate, the phrase usually means 'intended recipient':

He built a play-pen *for the little girl.*

By contrast, *to* is used with the 'actual recipient':

She presented a plaque *to the retiring supervisor.*

With *at*, the goal or target is usually viewed with hostility; contrast:

He shouted *at them.* ('loudly reproved')
He shouted *to them.* ('called')
The police rushed *at the house.* ('charged')
The police rushed *to the house.* ('hurried')

But with *aim*, *point*, and above all *smile*, the target can be viewed neutrally; contrast:

She smiled (kindly) *at the child.*
They laughed (unsympathetically) *at the idea.*

NOTE [a] The converse of goal is source, expressed usually by *from* or *out of* (but *cf* 9.14 Note [c]):

She made it *for me* ~ *from a piece of pigskin.*
X lends *to Y* ~ Y borrows *from X.*

Compare also 'He comes *from America*' (= 'He is an American') in contrast to

'He has come *from America* (= 'He was in America recently').

[b] When *as* is used in the sense 'in the role of', the phrase comes close to expressing reason:

As a subscriber, I ought to have been consulted.

From means to stimulus

9.13 Another spectrum of relations expressed by prepositions covers means, instrument, agency, and stimulus. The first two respond to the question 'How?' with *by* used for means and *with* for instrument, as in:

I go to work *by car.*
Please send this to the Delhi office *by telex.*
The burglar entered *by the back door.*
She won the match *with her fast service.*
He levered it up *with a crowbar.*

Note the corresponding negative of *with*:

He managed to open the car *without a key.*

In contrast to means and instrument, the agent is an animate which instigates or causes something. It is expressed by the preposition *by*, the complement of which frequently corresponds to the subject of a transitive verb:

> This picture was painted *by Degas*.
> ~ *Degas* painted this picture.
> I was bitten *by a neighbour's dog*.
> ~ *A neighbour's dog* bit me.

But an agent phrase need not be accompanied by a passive verb phrase:

> People thought the play was *by Webster*.

Stimulus and reaction are expressed chiefly by *at*:

> I'm surprised *at her attitude*.

In AmE this is general, but in BrE *with* is preferred if the stimulus is a person:

> They were furious *with Paul*.

Other stimulus and reaction prepositions include *about*, *in*, *of* and *to*:

> I was pleased *about the choice of date*.
> Are you interested *in quantum theory*?
> I think he's jealous *of her*.
> *To me*, her proposal is broadly acceptable.

NOTE With means of transport, *on* plus article can often be used in place of *by* plus zero:

> I often go to work *on the 8.15 train*.

The use of *on* here is shown to be means and not locative, since the latter sense would require *in* (9.5).

Accompaniment

9.14 Especially when the complement is animate, *with* conveys the meaning 'in the company of', *without* the converse:

> I hope you will come to dinner *with your husband*. (*ie* 'accompanied by')
> I hope you will come to dinner *with us*. (*ie* – usually – 'at our home')
> He is going for a walk *with his dog*.
> For once, Jill went *without her husband*.

But the complement need not be animate:

> What will you drink *with your meal*?
> I cannot concentrate *without silence*.

The accompaniment may therefore become a circumstance and the phrase connote 'manner':

He entered the room *with a worried look.*
She set off *without a care.*

NOTE [a] Manner is also expressed with *(un)like*:

He spoke *with a barrister's skill.* (Contrast: 'He spoke with a barrister')
Fred, *(un)like his brother*, is trusted by few. (Contrast: 'Fred is (un)like his brother')

[b] The sense of accompaniment can shade into or even cooccur with opposition:

She was arguing *with her brother.* (*cf* 'She and her brother were arguing')

But there is also a contrast between *with* and *against*, *for* and *against*:

I would rather have him *with me* than *against me.*

Are you $\left\{\begin{array}{l}\textit{with}\\ \textit{for}\end{array}\right\}$ the government or *against it*?

[c] Expressions of accompaniment are used also for possession, so that there is some interchange between *with(out)*, *of*, and the genitive:

The pianist has great talent. ~A pianist *with great talent*
~A pianist *of great talent*
~The pianist's great talent

Another close tie is with the notion of 'ingredients', expressed by *with* and *(out) of*:

The sauce was made *with fresh cream.*
The fence is *of wood* but the posts are *of concrete.*

Concession and other relations

9.15 Prepositions expressing *concession* include *in spite of* and its more formal synonym *despite*, the still more formal *notwithstanding*, and the somewhat informal *for all*, *with all*:

The article is being published $\left\{\begin{array}{l}\textit{in spite of}\\ \textit{for all}\end{array}\right\}$ her disapproval.

For *exception*, the chief prepositions are *except (for)*, *excepting*, *with the exception of*, *excluding*, *apart from* ⟨esp BrE⟩, *aside from* ⟨esp AmE⟩, *but*, and the rarer *save*, *bar*, and *barring*:

Except for the weather, our stay in Scotland was enjoyable.
Everyone seemed tired *but me.*

The converse of exception is *addition*, expressed by *besides*, *as well as*, *in addition to*; compare:

The orchestra was disappointing $\left\{\begin{array}{l}\textit{except for}\\ \textit{as well as}\end{array}\right\}$ the soloist.

Negative condition is expressed by *but for*, as in:

But for me, the case would have been lost. (*ie* 'If it hadn't been for me')

For the relationship *respect*, we have the prepositions *as for*, *as to*, *about*, *on the matter of*, *concerning*, *as regards*, *with regard to*, and the more formal *with reference to*, *with respect to*, and *re*.

Now, *about your application*, are you sure you would like a job of this kind?
The coat is splendid *as to the material*, but I'm less happy *as regards the cut*.

The pair *as to* and *as for* differ in that the latter tends to introduce a topic transition:

The coat is splendid but *as for the hat* I don't think it suits you.

Many expressions of respect occur in complementation of verbs and adjectives (Chapter 16):

He told her *of his problems* but was silent *on his failed marriage*.
They argued *about the children* and quarrelled *over money*.

One aspect of respect is to make explicit a *standard* by which assessment is made; for this, several prepositions are in common use:

For a teacher, he seems extraordinarily ignorant.
I'm better *at squash* than I am *as a tennis player*.
She is very clever *with her hands*.

Modification

9.16 Both prepositions and prepositional adverbs (9.2 Note [b]) can be modified in terms of *measure* and *degree* by being accompanied by intensifiers (7.33). For example:

She arrived { *shortly after ten*. / at ten or *shortly after*. }

He expected to be *well ahead of Compton* but he finished in fact *just behind*.
Please rehang the picture *about half a metre further down* (*the wall*).

Though in many cases such modification seems clearly to apply to the preposition, there are equally cases where it seems to apply to the whole prepositional phrase:

Should I stand at one side or *right in the middle?*
Many people are *against public ownership completely*.

Bibliographical note

For general and theoretical studies of prepositions, see Bennett (1975); Vestergaard (1977). Guimier (1981) provides a valuable bibliography.

On specific issues, see Buyssens (1987); Jacobsson (1977); Jaworska (1986); Leech (1969); Lindkvist (1976); Quirk (1968, Ch. 14).

10 The simple sentence

Clause structure

Clause types

10.1 A simple sentence consists of a single independent clause, which may be one of seven types. The types differ according to whether one or more clause elements (*cf* 2.3) are obligatorily present (*cf* 10.4) in addition to the S(ubject) and V(erb). The V element in a simple sentence is always a finite verb phrase (*cf* 3.19).

1. *SV* The sun (S) is shining (V).
2. *SVO* That lecture (S) bored (V) me (O).
3. *SVC* Your dinner (S) seems (V) ready (C).
4. *SVA* My office (S) is (V) in the next building (A).
5. *SVOO* I (S) must send (V) my parents (O) an anniversary card (O).
6. *SVOC* Most students (S) have found (V) her (O) reasonably helpful (C).
7. *SVOA* You (S) can put (V) the dish (O) on the table (A).

Optional adverbials can be added to sentences of any of these types:

Luckily, the sun is *already* shining. [SV]
Later, you can *perhaps* put the dish on the table. [SVOA]

Multiple class membership of verbs

10.2 A given verb can belong, in its various senses, to more than one class, and hence can enter into more than one clause type. The verb *get* is particularly versatile, being excluded only from type *SV* (and even then not universally; *cf* Note):

SVO He'll get a surprise.
SVC He's getting angry.
SVA He got through the window.
SVOO He got her a splendid present.
SVOC He got his shoes and socks wet.
SVOA He got himself into trouble.

Through the multiple class membership of verbs, ambiguities can arise:

She made a good model. – *SVO* or *SVC*
I found her an entertaining partner. – *SVOC* or *SVOO*
He is cooking his family dinner. – *SVO* or *SVOO*

The complementation of verbs receives detailed treatment in Chapter 16.

NOTE In informal (especially dialectal) AmE, *get* is used imperatively as an intransitive verb (= 'leave at once') in type *SV*: *She told him to get.*

Verb classes

10.3 There are three main verb classes, which are exemplified in 10.1:

> INTRANSITIVE VERBS are followed by no obligatory element, and occur in type *SV* (*eg*: *shine*).
> TRANSITIVE VERBS are followed by an OBJECT, and occur in types *SVO* (*eg*: *bore*), *SVOO* (*eg*: *send*), *SVOC* (*eg*: *find*), *SVOA* (*eg*: *put*).
> COPULAR VERBS are followed by a SUBJECT COMPLEMENT or an ADVERBIAL, and occur in types *SVC* (*eg*: *seem*), *SVA* (*eg*: *be*).

NOTE The term TRANSITIVE is applied to all verbs that require an object. Transitive verbs can be further classified:

> MONOTRANSITIVE VERBS occur in type *SVO*.
> DITRANSITIVE VERBS occur in type *SVOO*.
> COMPLEX-TRANSITIVE VERBS occur in types *SVOC* and *SVOA*.

Complementation

10.4 The elements O, C, and A in the patterns exemplified in 10.1*f* are obligatory elements of clause structure in that they are required for the complementation of the verb. By that we mean that if we use a particular verb in the relevant sense, the sentence is incomplete when one of these elements is omitted: *eg*: * *Your dinner seems* (type *SVC*) and * *You can put the dish* (type *SVOA*) are unacceptable. In some cases, however, an element could be considered grammatically optional:

They're eating. [SV]	*cf* They're eating lunch. [SVO]
We elected her. [SVO]	*cf* We elected her our delegate. [SVOC]
He's teaching. [SV]	*cf* He's teaching chemistry. [SVO]
	He's teaching them chemistry. [SVOO]

We regard the verbs in these sentences as having multiple class membership (*cf* 10.2), so that *eat* (for example) can be either transitive or intransitive.

Syntactic functions of clause elements

Objects and complements

10.5 There are two subcategories each of object and complement. The two types of object can cooccur:

Justin poured David some whisky. [1]

In [1] *David* is the indirect object and *some whisky* is the direct object. Whenever there are two objects (in type *SVOO*) the indirect object normally comes before the direct object. Although the indirect object is more central in being closer to the verb, in other respects it is more peripheral than the direct object: it is more likely to be optional (*Justin poured some whisky*), and it can often be paraphrased by a prepositional phrase functioning as an adverbial (*Justin poured some whisky for David*).

The two types of complement occur in different clause patterns. The subject complement is found in the *SVC* pattern:

Robert is becoming quite mature. [2]

The object complement, on the other hand, is found in the *SVOC* pattern:

Doris considers Robert quite mature. [3]

In [2] the subject complement characterizes the subject *Robert*, whereas in [3] the object complement characterizes the direct object *Robert*. In [2] and [3] the complement is an adjective phrase, but the same distinction applies where the complement is a noun phrase:

Benjamin is becoming a *conscientious student* [C_s].
His parents consider Benjamin a *conscientious student* [C_o].

Obligatory adverbials

10.6 Obligatory adverbials typically refer to space. They can be divided into those occurring in the *SVA* pattern, in which a location is attributed to the referent of the subject, and those occurring in the *SVOA* pattern, in which a location is attributed to the referent of the direct object. There is a parallel between obligatory adverbials and complements, which is demonstrated in the pairs of sentences below:

Daniel stayed *very quiet* [C_s]. [1]
Daniel stayed *in bed* [A_s]. [2]
Linda kept Daniel *very quiet* [C_o]. [3]
Linda kept Daniel *in bed* [A_o]. [4]

In [2] the adverbial is subject-related (like the subject complement in [1]), and in [4] it is object-related (like the object complement in [3]). The parallel is further evident in the verb classes, and we therefore call the verb in both [1] and [2] copular (since it is equivalent in function to the copula *be*) and call the verb in both [3] and [4] complex-transitive (*cf* 16.24*ff*).

NOTE Space adverbials include not only position (*in bed* in [2]), but also direction (*to bed*, as in *John and Linda went to bed*). Other meanings conveyed by obligatory adverbials include metaphorical extensions of space:

The next meeting will be *in March*.
We kept him *off cigarettes*.

Still others have no connection with spatial meanings:

> They treated her *kindly*.
> He is *without a job*.

Syntactic characterization of clause elements

10.7 The VERB is always realized by a verb phrase. It is normally present in all clauses, including imperative clauses (where the subject is typically absent). The verb determines what other elements (apart from the subject) may or must occur in the clause (*cf* 10.3*f*).

The SUBJECT:

(a) is typically a noun phrase (*cf* Chapters 5, 6, and 17);
(b) normally occurs before the verb in declarative clauses and after the operator in *yes–no* interrogative clauses (*cf* 11.3*ff*);
(c) determines the number and person, where relevant, of the verb (*cf* 10.19);
(d) in finite clauses requires the subjective form for pronouns that have distinctive case forms (*cf* 6.6*f*).

The OBJECT:

(a) is typically a noun phrase;
(b) normally follows the subject and verb (but *cf* 10.35*f*, 11.10, 11.20, 18.14*f*), and if both objects are present, the indirect object normally comes before the direct object (*cf* 18.26 Note [b]);
(c) may generally become the subject of the corresponding passive clause;
(d) in finite clauses requires the objective form for pronouns that have distinctive case forms.

The COMPLEMENT:

(a) is typically a noun phrase or an adjective phrase;
(b) normally follows the subject and verb if subject complement, and the direct object if object complement;
(c) relates to the subject if subject complement, or to the direct object if object complement (*cf* 10.5);
(d) does not have a corresponding passive subject;
(e) in finite clauses requires the subjective form of pronouns in formal use (especially in AmE), but otherwise the objective form.

The ADVERBIAL (*cf* Chapter 8):

(a) is normally an adverb phrase, prepositional phrase, or clause, but can also be a noun phrase;
(b) is typically capable of occurring in more than one position in the clause, though its mobility depends on the type and form of the adverbial;
(c) is optional, except for adverbials in the *SVA* and *SVOA* clause types.

NOTE [**a**] The distinction between obligatory adverbial and complement is not clear-cut for all prepositional phrases. Some prepositional phrases are semantically similar to adjective or noun phrases functioning as complement:

They were *under suspicion*.	They were *suspects*.
Norma was *in good health*.	Norma was *healthy*.

Unlike obligatory adverbials, they can be used as complementation for copular verbs other than BE, a characteristic of subject complements:

Barbarba appeared *out of breath*.
That seems *of no importance*.

We similarly find prepositional phrases functioning as object complement:

I don't consider myself *at risk*.
Charles put me *at my ease*.

Some adverbs can also function as complements:

The performance is *over*.
I am *behind* in my rent.

[**b**] Equally, the distinction between optional adverbial and subject complement is not clear-cut for adjective and noun phrases. We find instances where the adjective or noun phrase is optional, unlike clear cases of subject complement:

They married *young*.
We parted *good friends*.

Sometimes there is a close connection between the verb and the final element:

The sun shone *bright*.
The door banged *shut*.

[**c**] After some verbs, noun phrases of measure are indeterminate between direct object and adverbial:

Kathy jumped *ten feet*.
The book costs *ten dollars*.

Unlike objects, however, these do not generally permit the passive, and they allow adverbial questions (*How far did Kathy jump?*)

[**d**] MIDDLE VERBS, a small group of verbs that seem transitive in other respects, normally occur only in the active:

Fred and Anita *have* four children.
The coat doesn't *fit* me.
Five times six *equals* thirty.

[**e**] Prepositional phrases, adverbs, and also clauses that otherwise function as adverbials may sometimes function as subject:

Slowly is exactly how Jeremy speaks.
Will *after the show* be soon enough?
Because Sally wants to leave doesn't mean that we have to. ⟨informal⟩

Semantic roles of clause elements

Participants

10.8 Every clause describes a situation which involves one or more PARTICIPANTS, *ie* entities realized by noun phrases. We find two participants in [1]:

Unfortunately, *their child* broke *my window* yesterday. [1]

The sentence in [1] contains a verb describing the nature of the action, a subject denoting an agentive participant (the doer of the action), and a direct object denoting the affected participant. In addition, it contains an adverbial evaluating the situation (*unfortunately*) and an adverbial locating the situation in time (*yesterday*).

Agentive, affected, recipient, attribute

10.9 The typical semantic role of a subject in a clause that has a direct object is that of the AGENTIVE participant: that is, the animate participant that instigates or causes the happening denoted by the verb:

Margaret is mowing the grass.

The typical role of the direct object is that of the AFFECTED participant: a participant (animate or inanimate) which does not cause the happening denoted by the verb, but is directly involved in some other way:

James sold *his digital watch* yesterday.

The typical role of the indirect object is that of the RECIPIENT participant: *ie* of the animate being that is passively involved by the happening or state:

We paid *them* the money.

The typical role of a subject complement and an object complement is that of ATTRIBUTE. We can distinguish two subtypes of role for the attribute: identification and characterization:

IDENTIFICATION:

Kevin is *my brother*. Sidney is now *the Dean*.
His response to the reprimand seemed *a major reason for his dismissal*.
They named their daughter *Edna*.

CHARACTERIZATION:

Martha was *a good student*. Daniel remains *helpful*.
I consider the operation *a success*.

NOTE [a] Attributes may be 'current', normally with verbs used statively, or 'resulting' (*ie* from the event described by the verb), with verbs used dynamically (*cf* 4.2, 4.11):

CURRENT ATTRIBUTE:

He's *my brother.*	She remained *silent.*
He seems *unhappy.*	I want my food *hot.*
We felt *cold.*	They consider me *their closest friend.*

RESULTING ATTRIBUTE:

We became *restless.*	They elected him *president.*
He turned *traitor.*	The heat turned the milk *sour.*
He felt *ill.*	He drives me *mad.*

[b] If the verb is BE, identification attributes allow reversal of subject and complement:

Kevin is *my brother.* *My brother* is Kevin.

Only characterization attributes can also be realized by adjective phrases.

Subjects

Subject as external causer, instrument, and affected

10.10 The subject sometimes has the role of EXTERNAL CAUSER; that is, it expresses the unwitting (generally inanimate) cause of an event:

The avalanche destroyed several houses.
The electric shock killed him.

It may also have the role of INSTRUMENT; that is, the entity (generally inanimate) which an agent uses to perform an action or instigate a process:

A car knocked them down.
The computer has solved the problem.

With intransitive verbs, the subject also frequently has the AFFECTED role elsewhere typical of the direct object:

Jack fell down (accidentally).
The pencil was lying on the table.

The term 'affected' can also be applied to subjects of copular verbs:

The pencil was on the table.

But we can make some further distinctions according to whether the subject complement as attribute identifies or characterizes (*cf* 10.9). Thus, the subject is IDENTIFIED in [1] and CHARACTERIZED in [2]:

Kevin is my brother. [1]
Martha was a good student. [2]

NOTE There is sometimes a regular relation, in terms of clause function, between transitive verbs expressing CAUSATIVE meaning and corresponding intransitive verbs or adjectives. In the last group, *the company* and *my dog* as object are affected but as subject are agentive.

(i)	*SVO*	*SV*
	Tom is cooking the dinner.	The dinner is cooking.
	Brenda is improving her writing.	Her writing is improving.
(ii)	*SVO*	*SV*
	The frost has killed the flowers.	The flowers have died.
	Fred is waving the flag.	The flag is waving (in the breeze).
(iii)	*SVO*	*SVC*
	They have dimmed the lights.	The lights became dim.
	The sun (almost) blinded him.	He (almost) went blind.
(iv)	*SVO*	*SV*
	The sergeant paraded the company.	The company paraded.
	I am exercising my dog.	My dog is exercising.

Recipient and experiencer subjects

10.11 The subject may have a recipient role with verbs such as *have, own, possess, benefit (from)*, as is indicated by the following relation:

Mr Smith has given his son a radio. [So now his son has a radio.]

The perceptual verbs *see* and *hear* require an experiencer subject, in contrast to *look at* and *listen to*, which are agentive. The other perceptual verbs *taste, smell*, and *feel* have both an agentive meaning corresponding to *look at*, as in [1], and an experiencer meaning corresponding to *see*, as in [2]:

I want you to taste the soup. [1]
I can taste the pepper in my soup. [2]

The soup in [3] has the affected role:

The soup tastes good. [3]

Verbs indicating cognition or emotion may also require an experiencer:

I thought you were mistaken.
I liked the play.

Normally, recipient and experiencer subjects go with verbs used statively.

Positioner subject

10.12 The subject may have the role of POSITIONER with intransitive stance verbs (*cf* 4.11) such as *sit, stand, lie, live* ['dwell'], *stay, remain*, and with transitive verbs related to stance verbs such as *carry, hold, keep, wear*. The transitive verbs are causative and the direct objects that follow them have an affected role. In this positioner role the participant is in control, but the situation is not resultative in that no change is indicated in the positioner during the period in which the situation lasts:

I have lived in London most of my life.
The hijacker was holding a revolver.
They are staying at a motel.

He kept himself upright.
My friend is sitting in a chair near the door.

Locative, temporal, and eventive subjects

10.13 The subject may have the LOCATIVE role of designating the place of the state or action, or the TEMPORAL role of designating its time:

Los Angeles is foggy. ['It's foggy in Los Angeles.']
This jar contains coffee. ['There's coffee in this jar.']
Yesterday was a holiday. ['It was a holiday yesterday.']

An important role of the subject is EVENTIVE. The noun at the head of the noun phrase is commonly deverbal (*ie* derived from a verb) or a nominalization (*cf* 17.23):

The match is tomorrow.
The Norman invasion took place in 1066.
The dispute over the inheritance lasted a decade.

Prop *it* subject

10.14 There are clauses in which no participant is required. In such cases, the subject function may be assumed by the 'prop' word *it* (*cf* 6.9), which has little or no semantic content.

Prop *it* mainly occurs in clauses signifying (a) time, (b) atmospheric conditions, and (c) distance:

(a) It's ten o'clock precisely.
It's our wedding anniversary next month.
(b) Is it raining?
It's getting dark.
(c) It's not very far to York.
It's just one more stop to Toronto.

Objects

Locative, resultant, and cognate objects

10.15 The direct object may have a LOCATIVE role with such verbs as *walk*, *swim*, *pass*, *jump*, *turn*, *leave*, *reach*, *surround*, *cross*, *climb*:

Joan swam *the river*. ['Joan swam *across* the river.']
I passed *a cyclist*. ['I passed *by* a cyclist.']

A RESULTANT (or 'effected') object is an object whose referent exists only by virtue of the activity indicated by the verb:

Baird invented *television*. They are designing *a new car*.

With an agentive subject and an affected object, one may always capture part of the meaning of a clause (*eg*: *X destroyed Y*) by saying 'X did something to Y'; but this does not apply to a resultant object: *Baird invented television* does not imply 'Baird did something to television'.

Contrast the affected object in *I'm digging the ground* with the resultant object in *I'm digging a hole*.

A COGNATE object is similar to a resultant object in that it refers to an event indicated by the verb:

> Chris will sing *a song* for us. She lived *a good life*.

The noun head is semantically and often morphologically related to the verb, and its function is merely to repeat, wholly or partially, the meaning of the verb.

NOTE In one type of resultant object, the activity re-creates the referent:

> She acted *the part of Ophelia*.
> They are playing the *Egmont Overture*.

Eventive object

10.16 A frequent type of object generally takes the form of a deverbal noun preceded by a common verb of general meaning, such as *do, give, have, make, take*. This EVENTIVE object (*cf* 10.13) is semantically an extension of the verb and bears the major part of the meaning. Compare:

> They *are arguing*. [verb only]
> They *are having an argument*. [verb + eventive object]

Other examples:

> I *gave* them *some advice*.
> Sarah *is doing her homework*.
> The baby'*s having a bath*.
> We *made allowance* for his inexperience.
> I *took a shower* earlier.

The construction with the eventive object provides greater weight than the corresponding *SV* type, especially if there are no optional adverbials, and is often preferred to the *SV* construction in informal English.

Affected indirect object

10.17 The affected indirect object is the one exception to the normal role of recipient taken by the indirect object (*cf* 10.9). The affected indirect object combines with an eventive direct object (*cf* 10.16), and the most common verb is *give*:

> I gave *Helen* a nudge. ['I nudged Helen.']
> We gave *the baby* a bath. ['We bathed the baby.']
> I should give *the car* a wash. ['I should wash the car.']
> Judith paid *me* a visit. ['Judith visited me.']
> Derek owes *us* a treat. ['It's Derek's turn to treat us.']

The indirect object has the same role as the affected direct object in the paraphrases.

NOTE The object may occasionally be instrumental (*cf* 10.10):

> We employ *a computer* for our calculations.
> She is playing *the piano.*
> He nodded *his head.*

Summary

10.18 Although the semantic functions of the elements (particularly S and O_d) are quite varied, there are certain clear restrictions, such as that the object cannot be agentive; a subject (except in the passive) cannot be resultant; an indirect object normally has only two functions – those of recipient and affected. The following system of priorities generally obtains:

> If there is an agentive, external causer, or positioner, it is S; if not,
> If there is an instrument, it is S; if not,
> If there is an affected item, it is S; if not,
> If there is a temporal, locative, or eventive item, it may be S; if not,
> The prop word *it* is S.

Naturally, the role of the direct or indirect object in an active clause is assigned to the subject in passive clauses.

The semantic functions of clauses are treated in Chapter 15.

Subject–verb concord

General rule

10.19 The most important type of concord in English is concord of 3rd person number between subject and verb. A singular subject requires a singular verb:

> My daughter *watches* television after supper.

A plural subject requires a plural verb:

> My daughters *watch* television after supper.

The number of a noun phrase depends on the number of its head:

> The *change* in male attitudes *is* most obvious in industry.
> The *changes* in male attitude *are* most obvious in industry.

For coordinated noun phrases, see 10.22*ff*.

Clauses as subject (*cf* 15.1*ff*) count as singular for number concord: *How you got there doesn't concern me*; *Smoking cigarettes is dangerous to your health*. The same applies to prepositional phrases and adverbs functioning as subject: *In the evenings is best for me*; *Slowly does it!*.

Nominal relative clauses, on the other hand, resemble noun phrases in this respect (cf 15.7*f*) and may have plural as well as singular concord: *What was once a palace is now a pile of rubble*; *What ideas he has are his wife's.*

NOTE [a] It is possible to generalize the rule of concord to 'A subject which is not clearly semantically plural requires a singular verb'; that is, to treat singular as the unmarked form, to be used in neutral circumstances, where no positive indication of plurality is present. This would explain, in addition to clausal subjects, the tendency in informal speech for *is/was* to follow the pseudo-subject *there* in existential sentences (*cf* 18.30) such as *?There's hundreds of people on the waiting list* and in sentences such as *?Where's the scissors?*; *?Here's John and Mary*. As what precedes the subject here is not marked for plural, the singular verb follows by attraction.

On the other hand, the principle of proximity (*cf* 10.20) effects a change from singular to plural more often than the reverse, and this perhaps suggests that we should regard the plural as the unmarked form.

[b] Apparent exceptions to the concord rule arise with singular nouns ending with an apparent plural *-s* (*measles, billiards, mathematics*, etc, *cf* 5.43) or conversely plural nouns lacking the inflection (*cattle, people, clergy*, etc, *cf* 5.44):

> Measles *is* sometimes serious.
> Our people *are* complaining.

[c] Plural phrases (including coordinate phrases) count as singular if they are used as names, titles, quotations, etc:

> *Crime and Punishment* is perhaps the best constructed of Dostoyevsky's novels, but *The Brothers Karamazov* is undoubtedly his masterpiece.
> 'Senior citizens' means, in common parlance, people over sixty.

The titles of some works that are collections of stories, etc, may be counted as either singular or plural:

> *The Canterbury Tales* {*exists* / *exist*} in many manuscripts.

Notional concord and proximity

10.20 Two factors sometimes conflict with GRAMMATICAL CONCORD as described in 10.19. NOTIONAL CONCORD is agreement according to the idea of number rather than the presence of the grammatical marker for that idea. In BrE, for example, collective nouns such as *government* are often treated as plural (*cf* 10.21): *The government have broken all their promises.*

The principle of PROXIMITY denotes agreement of the verb with a noun or pronoun that closely precedes it in preference to agreement with the head of the noun phrase:

> ?*No one* except his own supporters agree with him.
> *One* in ten take drugs.

Attraction of number through proximity occurs mainly in unplanned discourse.

Collective nouns

10.21 In BrE grammatically singular collective nouns are treated as notionally plural if the group is considered as a collection of individuals:

The audience *were* enjoying every minute of it. [1]
England *have* won the cup. [2]

Singular and plural verbs are more or less interchangeable in the contexts of [1] and [2], but singular has to be used in sentences like *The audience was enormous*, where the group is being considered as a single undivided body.

In AmE grammatically singular collective nouns are generally treated as singular, especially when they refer to governments and sports teams.

NOTE In both BrE and AmE, plural pronouns are often used to refer to singular collective *nouns* even when the verb is singular; for example, *they* is an alternative to *it* in *The committee has not yet decided how they should react to the letter*.

Coordinated subject

Coordination with *and*

10.22 When a subject consists of two or more noun phrases (or clauses) coordinated by *and*, a distinction has to be made between coordination and coordinative apposition.

Coordination comprises cases that correspond to fuller coordinate forms. A plural verb is used even if each conjoin is singular:

Tom and Alice *are* now ready.
What I say and what I think *are* my own affair.

Conjoins expressing a mutual relationship, even though they can only indirectly be treated as reductions of clauses in this way, also take a plural verb:

Your problem and mine *are* similar. ['Your problem is similar to mine and mine is similar to yours.']
What I say and do *are* two different things. ['What I say is one thing and what I do is another thing.']

With the less common COORDINATIVE APPOSITION, no reduction is implied, since each of the units has the same reference. Hence, a singular verb is required if each noun phrase is singular:

This temple of ugliness and memorial to Victorian bad taste *was* erected in the main street of the city.

The two opening noun phrases here both refer to one entity (a statue). The following example, however, could have either a singular or plural verb, depending on the meaning:

His brother and the subsequent editor of his collected papers {*was* / *were*} with him at his deathbed.

Singular *was* is used if the brother and the editor are the same person, and plural *were* if they are two different people.

NOTE [a] A plural verb is required in asyndetic coordination (without a coordinator):

His camera, his radio, his money *were* confiscated by the customs officials.

[b] Subject noun phrases may be linked by quasi-coordinators, *ie* prepositions (such as *along with*, *rather than*, and *as well as*) that are semantically similar to coordinators. Grammatical concord requires a singular verb if the first noun phrase is singular:

The captain, as well as the other players, *was* tired.

[c] If an adverbial is present in the second noun phrase, the construction is considered parenthetic, and grammatical concord requires the verb to agree in number with the first noun phrase:

The ambassador – and perhaps his wife too – *is* likely to be present.

The same grammatical rule applies when the second phrase is negative, whether or not linked by *and*, though here the principle of notional concord reinforces the use of the singular:

The Prime Minister, (and) not the monarch, *decides* government policy.

10.23 A singular noncount noun head with coordinate premodifiers may imply two (or more) separate sentences. It may be followed legitimately by a plural verb:

American and Dutch beer *are* (both) much lighter than British beer. ['American beer is . . . and Dutch beer is . . .']

The same phenomenon occurs with nominal relative clauses:

What I say and do *are* my own affair. ['What I say is . . . and what I do is']

The singular would mean 'That which I say and do is my own affair'.

NOTE A singular verb is required when the phrases are postmodifying:

Beer from America and the Netherlands *is* much lighter than British beer. ['Beer that comes from America and the Netherlands is . . .']

Coordination with *or* and *nor*

10.24 For subject phrases or clauses that are coordinated with (*either* . . .) *or* and with *neither* . . . *nor*, grammatical concord is clear when the conjoins have the same number. In [1] the verb is singular and in [2] it is plural:

Either the Mayor or her deputy *is* bound to come. [1]
Either the strikers or the bosses *have* misunderstood the claim. [2]

When conjoins differ in number, recourse is generally made to the principle of proximity: the number of the second conjoin determines the number of the verb, as in [3] and [4]:

Either your brakes or your eyesight *is* at fault. [3]
Either your eyesight or your brakes *are* at fault. [4]

In less formal usage, phrases coordinated with *neither* . . . *nor* are treated more like *and* for concord. Thus, [5] is more natural in speech than [6]:

Neither he nor his wife *have* arrived. [5]
Neither he nor his wife *has* arrived. [6]

When *or* is used for coordinative apposition (*cf* 10.22), grammatical concord requires the verb to agree in number with the first appositive:

Gobbledygook, or the circumlocutions of bureaucratic language, *is* intentionally difficult to understand.
The circumlocutions of bureaucratic language, or gobbledygook, *are* intentionally difficult to understand.

Indefinite expressions as subject

10.25 Some indefinite pronouns and determiners have both noncount and count uses. With noncount nouns (present or implied), the verb is singular:

Some (of the cement) *is* arriving later today.
So far *no* money *has* been spent on repairs.

With plural nouns (present or implied), the verb is plural:

No people of that name *live* here.
Some (of the books) *are* being placed on the shelves today.

The pronouns *either* and *neither* generally take a singular verb:

The two guests have arrived, {and *either* / but *neither*} is welcome.

With *none*, the plural verb is more frequently used than the singular, because of notional concord, even without the effect of the proximity principle:

None (of the books) *are* being placed on the shelves today.

10.26 The proximity principle may lead to plural concord even with indefinites such as *each*, *every*, *everybody*, *anybody*, and *nobody* (or indefinite phrases such as *every one*, *any one*), which are otherwise unambivalently singular:

Nobody, not even the teachers, {*was* / ?*were*} listening.

> Every member of the vast crowd of 50,000 people {*was* / *?were*} pleased to see him.

Although these sentences with plural verbs might well be uttered in casual speech, or inadvertently written down, most people would probably regard them as ungrammatical, because they flatly contradict grammatical concord. Other, more acceptable, instances arise with expressions involving quantity (where the singular would seem pedantic):

> A (large) number of people *have* applied for the job.
> The majority *agree* with me.

NOTE The following illustrates an idiomatic anomaly: there is a discrepancy in number between the noun and the determiner *those*, as well as with the verb:

> {These / Those} {sort / kind / type} of parties are dangerous. ⟨informal⟩

Rephrasing can avoid the anomaly:

> {Those kinds of parties are / That kind of party is / Parties of that kind are} dangerous.

Concord of person

10.27 In addition to number concord, there is concord of person in the present tense:

> I *am* your friend. [1st PERSON SINGULAR CONCORD]
>
> He *is* your friend. / He *knows* you. } [3rd PERSON SINGULAR CONCORD]

In the past tense, only the verb BE has distinctions of person:

> I *was* your friend. / He *was* your friend. } [1st and 3rd PERSON SINGULAR CONCORD]
>
> You *were* my friend. [2nd PERSON]

In a coordinate subject noun phrase where the coordinator is *or* or *nor*, the last noun phrase determines the person of the verb, in accordance with the principle of proximity:

> Neither you, nor I, nor anyone else *knows* the answer. [1]
> (?)Either my wife or I *am* going. [2]

NOTE [a] Because of the awkwardness of the choice in [1] and especially [2], a speaker may avoid it by using a modal auxiliary which is invariable for person (*eg*: *Either my wife or I will be going*) or by postposing the last noun phrase (*eg*: *Either my wife is going or I am*).

[b] In relative clauses and cleft sentences, a relative pronoun subject is usually followed by a verb in agreement with its antecedent: *It is I who am to blame*, *It is Kay who is in command*, *It is they who are complaining*. But 3rd person concord prevails in informal English where the objective case pronoun *me* is used: *It's me who's to blame*. Similarly, 3rd personal singular may be used in informal English in these constructions when the pronoun *you* has singular reference: *It's you who's to blame*.

Other types of concord

Subject–complement and object–complement concord

10.28 There is usually concord of number between subject and subject complement and between direct object and object complement:

My child is an angel.	I consider my child an angel.
My children are angels.	I consider my children angels.

This type of concord arises naturally from the semantic role of the two complements (*cf* 10.9). There are, however, exceptions:

Their principal crop is potatoes.
Good manners are a rarity these days. [also ?*is*]
The younger children are a problem.
The next few bars are pure Tchaikovsky. [also ?*is*]
Dogs are good company.

Pronouns and determiner reference

10.29 The agreement between a pronoun or determiner and its antecedent is coreference rather than grammatical concord, but it is convenient to treat the phenomenon here.

A reflexive pronoun must agree with its antecedent in number, person, and gender:

He injured *himself* in both legs.
She's making a sweater for *herself*.
I wrote to them about *myself*.

Personal pronouns and possessive determiners in the 1st and 3rd persons agree with their antecedents in number. Those in the 3rd person singular also agree with their antecedents in gender:

Tom hurt *his* foot. [1]
Beatrice knows that *she* is late. [2]
The books were too heavy, so I left *them*. [3]

In [1] and [2] the pronoun may of course also refer to somebody other than the subject.

The relative pronouns *who*, *whom*, and *which* agree with their antecedent in gender, the first two being personal, and the last nonpersonal:

> Here's the hammer *which* I borrowed yesterday.
> That's the man *who(m)* I saw talking to your parents.

10.30 The pronoun *they* is commonly used as a 3rd person singular pronoun that is neutral between masculine and feminine. It is a convenient means of avoiding the dilemma of whether to use the *he* or *she* form. At one time restricted to informal usage, it is now increasingly accepted even in formal usage, especially in AmE.

Rather than use *he* in the unmarked sense or the clumsy *he or she*, many prefer to seek gender impartiality by using a plural form where possible in reference to the indefinite pronouns *everyone*, *everybody*, *someone*, *somebody*, *anyone*, *anybody*, *no one*, *nobody*:

> Everyone thinks *they* have the answer. [1]
> Has *anybody* brought *their* camera? [2]

A similar use of the plural occurs with coordinate subjects referring to both sexes, as in [3], and with a singular noun phrase subject having a personal noun of indeterminate gender as head, as in [4]:

> *Either he* or *she* is going to have to change *their* attitude. [3]
> *Every student* has to hand in *their* paper today. [4]

In formal English, the tendency has been to use *he* as the unmarked form when the gender is not determined. The formal equivalent of [1], though increasingly ignored now, is therefore:

> *Everyone* thinks *he* has the answer. [1a]

A more cumbersome alternative is the conjoining of both masculine and feminine pronouns:

> *Every student* has to hand in *his* or *her* paper today. [4a]

The indefinite pronoun *one* is followed in formal usage by the same pronoun for subsequent references:

> *One* should choose *one's* friends carefully. [5]

But AmE may also use the masculine pronoun:

> *One* should choose *his* friends carefully. [5a]

NOTE One way of circumventing the gender problem is to make the subject plural:

> *All students* have to hand in *their* paper today. [4b]

Similar methods can usually be employed for the indefinite pronouns too:

All of them think *they* have the answer. [1b]
Have *any of you* brought *your camera*? [2a]

For [3] the only alternative in formal English is to rephrase the sentence:

Either he is going to have to change *his attitude* or *she hers*. [3a]

For [5a], indefinite *one* can be replaced with indefinite *we*, *you*, or *they*, as appropriate:

We should choose *our* friends carefully. [5b]

Vocatives

10.31 A vocative is usually a noun phrase, denoting the one or more persons to whom the sentence is addressed. It is either a CALL, drawing the attention of the person or persons addressed, singling them out from others in hearing, as in [1], or an ADDRESS, expressing the speaker's relationship or attitude to the person or persons addressed, as in [2] and [3]:

JOHN, DINner's ready. [voc SVC_s] [1]
And THAT, my FRIENDS, concludes my SPEECH. [voc SVO_d] [2]
My BACK is aching, DOCTor. [SV voc] [3]

Sentences [1–3] show that a vocative may take initial, medial, or final position in the sentence; in its optionality and freedom of position, it is more like an adverbial than any other element of clause structure.

Intonationally, the vocative is set off from the rest of the clause either by constituting a separate tone unit or by forming the tail of a tone unit. The most characteristic intonations are fall–rise for an initial vocative functioning as a call, and otherwise rise; and rise for a vocative functioning as an address.

10.32 Vocatives may be:

(a) Names, perhaps with a title: *David, Mrs Johnson, Dr Turner, Ginger*.

(b) Standard appellatives, usually without modification:

(i) terms for family relationships: *mother*, *father*, *uncle*; or more familiar forms like *mom(my)* ⟨AmE⟩, *mum(my)* ⟨BrE⟩;

(ii) title of respect: *madam, sir, my Lord, your Honour*;

(iii) markers of status (sometimes with initial capital even for those not so marked here); *Mr President, Prime Minister, Father* [for priest], *professor, doctor*.

(c) General nouns, often used in more specialized senses: *brother*, *buddy* ⟨informal AmE⟩, *lady*, *ladies* and *gentlemen*; *man*, *mate* ⟨BrE⟩.

(d) The personal pronoun *you* (*You, why haven't you finished yet?*) is markedly impolite. An indefinite pronoun (as in *Get me a pen, somebody*) is abrupt.

(e) Nominal clauses (very occasionally): *Whoever said that*, (*come out here*).

(f) Items from (a), (b), (c), and (d) may be expanded by the addition of modifiers or appositive elements of various kinds:

(a) *my dear Mrs Johnson*; *young David*
(b) *my old friend*; *you filthy liar*
(c) *old man, young man*; *old chap* ⟨BrE⟩
(d) impolite: *you over there*; *you with the red hair*; informal: *you boys, you people, you chaps* ⟨esp BrE⟩, *you guys* ⟨esp AmE⟩.

Negation

Clause Negation

Clause negation through verb negation

10.33 A positive clause can be negated by inserting *not* between the operator (*cf* 3.11) and the predication:

I have finished.	I have not finished.
They are ready.	They are not ready.

If no operator is present in the positive clause, the dummy operator DO is introduced (but *cf* 3.23 Note [b]):

She works hard.	She does not work hard.
They know you.	They do not know you.

Except in formal English, the negator more usually occurs also as an enclitic (*ie* attached to the preceding word) in the contracted form *n't*:

I haven't finished   They don't know you.

NOTE There are commonly two possibilities for contraction in negative clauses in informal English: negator contraction and auxiliary contraction (*cf* 3.13*ff*):

I haven't finished.	I've not finished.
They aren't ready.	They're not ready.

Syntactic features of clause negation

10.34 Negative clauses differ syntactically from positive clauses:

(i) They can typically be followed by positive tag questions:

They aren't ready, *are* they?
[*cf*: They are ready, *aren't* they?]

(ii) They can be followed by negative tag clauses, with additive meaning:

They aren't ready, and *neither* are you.

(iii) They can be followed by negative agreement responses:

A: He doesn't know Russian. B: No, he *doesn't*.

(iv) They can be followed by nonassertive items (*cf* 10.37):

He won't notice *any* change in you, *either*.

Other kinds of clause negation

Words negative in form and meaning

10.35 We sometimes have a choice between verb negation and negation of some other element:

An honest man would *not* lie.	*No* honest man would lie.
That was *not* an accident.	That was *no* accident.
He would*n't* say a word.	He would say *not* a word.
I wo*n't* make that mistake ever again.	I will *never* make that mistake again.

The scope of negation (*cf* 10.38) is frequently different. For example, *Many people did not come to the party* implies the absence of many people, whereas *Not many people came to the party* implies the presence of few people.

In formal style, the negative element may often be moved from its usual position to initial position, in which case there is inversion of subject and operator:

Not a word would he say.
Never will I make that mistake again.

Words negative in meaning but not in form

10.36 Several words are negative in meaning but not in form. They include:

seldom, rarely
scarcely, hardly, barely
little, few (in contrast to the positive *a little* and *a few*)

They can effect clause negation, inducing the characteristic syntactic features of clause negation (*cf* 10.34):

They *scarcely* seem to care, *do they*?
I *hardly* have any friends, and *neither* do you.
A: Crime *rarely* pays. B: No, it *doesn't*.
I *seldom* get *any* sleep, *either*.
Few members have *ever* attended the annual general meeting.

When positioned initially, the adverbs normally cause subject-operator inversion (*cf* 10.35):

Little did I expect such enthusiasm.
Scarcely ever has Britain suffered so much criticism.

Verbs, adjectives, and prepositions with negative meaning may be followed by nonassertive items (*cf* 10.37):

He *denies* I *ever* told him.
We were *unaware* of *any* hostility.
I'm *against* going out *anywhere* tonight.

NOTE [a] *Only* is to some extent negative. When it focuses on a subject noun phrase, the latter is followed by nonassertive items: *Only two of us had any experience in sailing*. And when it focuses on a fronted initial element rather than the subject, it may occasionally (but need not) take subject–operator inversion: *Only on Sundays do they eat with their children*.
[b] *Rarely* may be positive when placed initially as an adjunct (*cf* 8.13), in which case it does not cause subject–operator inversion: *Rarely, crime pays well*. ['On rare occasions, crime pays well.']

Nonassertive items

10.37 Clause negation is frequently followed (not necessarily directly) by one or more nonassertive items. The following examples illustrate the range of these items, which may be determiners, pronouns, or adverbs:

ASSERTIVE	NONASSERTIVE
We've had some lunch.	We haven't had *any* lunch.
I was speaking to somebody.	I wasn't speaking to *anybody*.
They'll finish it somehow.	They won't finish it *at all*.
He sometimes visits us.	He doesn't *ever* visit us.
He's still at school.	He's not at school *any longer*.
Her mother's coming, too.	Her mother's not coming *either*.
I like her a great deal.	I don't like her *much*.

In many instances, the negative particle and the nonassertive form can combine to produce a negative form (*not ever* ~ *never*) or can be replaced by a negative form (*not anywhere* ~ *nowhere*).

NOTE [a] The primary difference between *some* and *any* (and between the *some-* and *any-* compounds) is that *some* is generally specific, though unspecified, while *any* is nonspecific. That is, *some* implies an amount or number that may be known to the speaker. This difference tends to correlate with the difference between positive and negative contexts:

I have *some money* on me. [a specific, though unspecified amount of money]
I don't have *any money* on me. [an unspecified, and also nonspecific amount of money]

[b] Nonassertive items appear in other contexts: questions (11.4*f*); conditional clauses (15.19 Note [a]); comparative clauses (15.36); putative *should*-clauses (14.14); restrictive relative clauses within generic noun phrases, which have conditional meaning (*Students who have any complaints should raise their hands*, 'If students have any complaints . . .').

[c] If a clause is negative, nonassertive items that come within the scope of negation (*cf* 10.38) are used in place of every assertive item that would have occurred in the corresponding positive clause:

> I haven't *ever* been on *any* of the big liners, *either*.
> Not many of the refugees have *anywhere* to live *yet*.

[d] Occasionally two negatives occur in the same clause: *Nobody has nothing to eat* ('Everybody has something to eat'), *None of us have never told lies* ('All of us have told lies at some time'), *I can't not obey her* ('I have to obey her'). The two negatives cancel each other out, producing positive values; but the sentence remains negative syntactically, as indicated (for example) by the normal tag question: *I can't not obey her, can I?*

[e] The multiple negatives in nonstandard English are intensifying, and do not cancel each other out. *No one never said nothing about it* is equivalent to standard English *No one ever said anything about it.*

[f] Some nonassertive expressions are used to give emotive intensification to negatives; for example, *by any means*, *a bit* (informal), *in the least*, *at all*; *We didn't like it in the least*. Negative determiners and pronouns are emphasized by *at all* and *whatever*: *You have no excuse whatever. Never* is repeated for emphasis or combined with intensifying phrases (such as *in all my life*): *I'll never, never go there again*; *I've never seen anything like it in all my life*. Other emotively coloured expressions are exemplified in *He didn't give me a thing*; *I didn't sleep a wink*; *We didn't see a soul.*

Scope of negation

10.38 A negative item may be said to govern (or determine the occurrence of) a nonassertive item only if the latter is within the SCOPE of the negative, *ie* within the stretch of language over which the negative item has a semantic influence. The scope of the negation normally extends from the negative item itself to the end of the clause. There is thus a contrast between these two sentences:

> She definitely didn't speak to him.
> ['It's definite that she didn't.']
> She didn't definitely speak to him.
> ['It's not definite that she did.']

When an adjunct is final, it may or may not lie outside the scope:

> I wasn't LÌSTENING all the TÌME.
> [*ie* I listened none of the time.]
> I wasn't listening all the TÌME.
> [*ie* I listened some of the time.]

If an assertive form is used, it must lie outside the scope:

> I didn't listen to some of the speakers.
> [*ie* I listened to some.]
> I didn't listen to any of the speakers.
> [*ie* I listened to none.]

The scope can sometimes extend into a subordinate clause: *I wouldn't like to disturb anyone*.

Focus of negation

10.39 We need to identify not only the scope, but also the FOCUS of a negation. The focus is signalled in speech by the placement of nuclear stress, which indicates that the contrast of meaning implicit in the negation is located at that spot while the rest of the clause can be understood in a positive sense. The focus can precede the negative item, and hence we must allow for discontinuous scope. Different placements of the focus distinguish the following sentences. The parts that are not within the scope are understood positively:

> I didn't take Joan to swim in the PÒOL today. – I forgot to do so.
> I didn't take JŎAN to swim in the pool today. – It was Mary.
> I didn't take Joan to SWĬM in the pool today. – Just to see it.
> I didn't take Joan to swim in the PŎOL today. – I took her to the seaside.
> I didn't take Joan to swim in the pool TODĂY. – It was last week that I did so.
> Ĭ didn't take Joan to swim in the pool today. – It was my brother who took her.

Scope must include the focus. One way of signalling the extent of the scope is by the position of the focus:

> I didn't leave HÓME because I was afraid of my FÀTHER. [1]
> [= Because I was afraid of my father, I didn't leave home.]
> I didn't leave home because I was afraid of my FĂTHER. [2]
> [= I left home, but it wasn't because I was afraid of my father.]

With the intonation given (which is the more common), [1] allots a separate tone unit to each clause, and so places the *because*-clause outside the scope of the negative. (This interpretation can also be singled out by a comma in writing.) But [2] extends a single tone unit over both, and places a contrastive fall + rise on *father*. The effect of this is to place negative focus on the *because*-clause, so that the main clause is understood positively.

Intonation may be crucial also in marking whether or not the subject is the focus of negation in noun phrases containing one of the universal items *all* or *every*:

> All the children didn't SLÈEP. ['All the children failed to sleep.']
> ĂLL the children didn't sleep. ['Not all the children slept.']

NOTE In denial sentences the clause negator may have the focus, since the rest of the clause has already been asserted or implied:

I did NÒT offer her some chocolates. ['It is not true that I offered her some chocolates.']

The same effect is achieved by focus on a negative operator:

I DÌDN'T offer her some chocolates.

or some other negative word:

I NÈVER offered her some chocolates.

Local negation

10.40 Local negation negates a word or phrase, without making the clause negative (*cf* 10.34). One common type involves the combination of *not* with a morphologically negated gradable adjective or adverb:

She's a *not unintelligent* woman. ['She's a fairly intelligent woman.']
I visit them *not infrequently*. ['I visit them rather frequently.']

The negative particle partly cancels out the negative prefix, as indicated by the paraphrases.

Other types of local negation are exemplified below:

I saw a *not too sympathetic* report about you. ['rather unsympathetic']
I saw Dave *not long ago*. ['fairly recently']
We sensed *not a little hostility* in his manner. ['quite a lot of hostility']
She was decorated *by none other than the President*. ['by the President himself']

If moved to initial position, these do not cause subject–operator inversion (*cf* 10.35):

Not long ago I saw David mowing his lawn.

Negation of modal auxiliaries

10.41 The scope of negation may or may not include the meaning of the modal auxiliaries. We therefore distinguish between AUXILIARY NEGATION and MAIN VERB NEGATION. The contrast is shown in the two following sentences with *may not*, where the paraphrases indicate the scope of negation:

AUXILIARY NEGATION

You may not smoke in here. ['You are not allowed to smoke here.']

MAIN VERB NEGATION

They may not like the party. ['It is possible that they do not like the party.']

We give examples below of the modal auxiliaries in their various senses (*cf* 4.21*ff*) according to whether the scope of negation usually includes the auxiliary or excludes it:

AUXILIARY NEGATION

may not [='permission']

> You may not go swimming. ['You are not allowed to . . .']

cannot, can't [in all senses]

> You can't be serious. ['It is not possible that . . .']
> You can't go swimming. ['You are not allowed to . . .']
> He can't ride a bicycle. ['He is not able to . . .']

need not, needn't ⟨both esp BrE⟩

> You needn't pay that fine. ['You are not obliged to . . .']
> It needn't always be my fault. ['It is not necessary that . . .']

dare not, daren't

> I daren't quarrel with them. ['I haven't got the courage to quarrel with them.']

MAIN VERB NEGATION

may not [='possibility']

> They may not bother to come if it's wet. ['It is possible that they will not bother to come . . .']

shall not, shan't ⟨all senses; esp BrE; *shan't* rare⟩

> Don't worry. You shan't lose your reward. ['I'll make sure that you don't lose your reward . . .']
> I shan't know you when you return. ['I predict that I will not know . . .']

must not, mustn't ['obligation']

> You mustn't keep us waiting. ['It is essential that you don't keep us waiting.']

ought not, oughtn't [both senses]

> You oughtn't to keep us waiting. ['obligation.']
> He oughtn't to be long. ['tentative inference.']

The distinction between auxiliary and main verb negation is neutralized for *will* in all its senses, as the paraphrases below indicate:

> Don't worry. I won't interfere. ['I don't intend to interfere'; 'I intend not to interfere.']
> He won't do what he's told. ['He refuses to do what he's told'; 'He insists on not doing what he's told.']
> They won't have arrived yet. ['It's not probable that they've arrived yet'; 'I predict that they haven't arrived yet.']

In the necessity sense, the auxiliary negation of *must* is usually achieved through *can't*; hence, the negation of *They must be telling lies* is usually

They can't be telling lies. Needn't and *don't have to* are used for auxiliary negation in both senses of *must*:

We {don't have to / needn't} pack till tomorrow.

The past tense negative auxiliaries (*mightn't, couldn't, wouldn't, shouldn't*) follow the same negative pattern as their present tense equivalents.

NOTE [a] Because of the diametric opposition of meaning between 'permission' and 'obligation', an odd-seeming equivalence exists between *may not* ['not permitted to'] and *mustn't* ['obliged not to']:

You mustn't go swimming today.
[= You may not go swimming today.]

[b] Very rarely, PREDICATION NEGATION occurs in the context of denials and permission. The scope of negation is different from that normal with the particular modal auxiliary:

They may 'not go swimming'. ['They are allowed not to go swimming.']
I can, of course, 'not obey her'. ['It's possible, of course, not to obey her.']

In such instances of main verb negation, the clause is not negated (*cf* 10.34), and it is possible to have double negation – auxiliary negation and predication negation: *I cannot*, of course, *not obey her*. (*cf* 10.37 Note [d]).

Bibliographical note

On major theoretical discussions, see Lyons (1977); Stockwell et al. (1973).

On syntactic structures and functions, see Ellegård (1978) for frequency data; Halliday (1967–68); Schopf (1988).

On semantic roles, see Fillmore (1968; 1977b); Halliday (1967–68); Longacre (1976, Ch. 2); Lyons (1977, Ch. 12); Schlesinger (1979; 1989).

On number concord, see Juul (1975).

On vocatives, see Zwicky (1974).

On negation, see Bolinger (1977, Chs. 2 and 3); Horn (1978a); Jackendoff (1969); Jespersen (1917); Klima (1964); Stockwell et al. (1973, Ch. 5); Tottie (1977, 1980).

11 Sentence types and discourse functions

Introduction

11.1 Simple sentences may be divided into four major syntactic types, whose use correlates largely with different discourse functions:

(I) DECLARATIVES are sentences in which it is normal for the subject to be present and to precede the verb:

> Pauline gave Tom a digital watch for his birthday.

On declaratives without a subject *cf* 12.16, and on declaratives where the verb precedes the subject *cf* 18.16*f*.

(II) INTERROGATIVES are sentences which are formally marked in one of two ways:

(i) yes–no interrogatives: an operator is placed in front of the subject (*cf* 11.3*ff*):

> Did Pauline give Tom a digital watch for his birthday?

(ii) *wh*-interrogatives: an interrogative *wh*-element is positioned initially (*cf* 11.9) and there is generally subject-operator inversion (*cf* 11.10):

> What did Pauline give Tom for his birthday?

(III) IMPERATIVES are sentences which normally have no overt grammatical subject, and whose verb has the base form (*cf* 11.15*f*):

> Give Tom a digital watch for his birthday.

(IV) EXCLAMATIVES are sentences which have an initial phrase introduced by *what* or *how*, usually with subject–verb order (*cf* 11.20):

> What a fine watch he received for his birthday!

Associated with these four types are four major classes of discourse functions:

(a) STATEMENTS are primarily used to convey information.

(b) QUESTIONS are primarily used to seek information on a specific point.

(c) DIRECTIVES are primarily used to instruct somebody to do something.

(d) EXCLAMATIONS are primarily used for expressing the extent to which the speaker is impressed by something.

NOTE [a] Direct association between syntactic type and discourse class is the norm, but the two do not always match. For example, a declarative question (*cf* 11.7) is syntactically a declarative but semantically a question, and a rhetorical question (*cf* 11.13) is syntactically an interrogative but semantically a statement.

[b] We can make many more refined distinctions in the use of sentences. For example, *It's going to rain any minute now* and *I'm sorry about the delay* are both statements, but the first can be used to make a prediction and the second to make an apology; *Could you please make less noise?* is a question intended as a request, whereas *Do you want another cup?* is a question that may be intended as an offer; *Make your bed at once* and *Make yourself at home* are both directives, but the first has the force of a command and the second the force of an invitation.

Questions

Major classes

11.2 Questions can be divided into three major classes according to the type of reply they expect:

1 Those that expect affirmation or negation, as in *Have you finished the book?*, are *YES–NO* QUESTIONS.
2 Those that typically expect a reply from an open range of replies, as in *What is your name?* or *How old are you?*, are *WH*-questions.
3 Those that expect as the reply one of two or more options presented in the question, as in *Would you like to go for a WÁLK or stay at HÒME?*, are ALTERNATIVE questions.

Yes–no questions

Form of *yes–no* questions

11.3 *Yes–no* questions are usually formed by placing the operator before the subject and giving the sentence a rising intonation:

The boat has LÈFT. ~ Has the boat LÉFT?

If there is no item in the verb phrase that can function as operator, DO is introduced, as with negation (*cf* 10.33):

They live in Sydney. ~ Do they live in Sydney?

Again as with negation, main verb BE functions as operator; in BrE main verb HAVE often acts as operator, but informally HAVE . . . *got* is more common:

Patrick was late. ~ Was Patrick late?

She has a cold. ~ { Does she have a cold? ⟨esp AmE⟩ / Has she (got) a cold? ⟨esp BrE⟩ }

NOTE By placing the nuclear stress on a particular part of a *yes–no* question, we are able to focus the interrogation on a particular item of information which, unlike the rest of the sentence, is assumed to be unknown (*cf* 10.39). Thus the focus falls in different places in the following otherwise identical questions:

Was he a famous actor in THÓSE days?
['I know he was once a famous actor – but was it then or later?']
Was he a FÁMOUS actor in those days?
['I know he was an actor in those days – but was he a famous one?']

Positive *yes–no* questions

11.4 Like negative statements, *yes–no* questions may contain nonassertive items such as *any* and *ever* (*cf* 10.37). The question containing such forms is generally neutral, with no bias in expectation towards a positive or negative response.

STATEMENT	QUESTION
Someone called last night.	Did *anyone* call last night?
The boat has left *already*.	Has the boat left *yet*?

But questions may be CONDUCIVE, *ie* they may indicate that the speaker is predisposed to the kind of answer he has wanted or expected. Thus, a positive question may be presented in a form which is biased towards a positive answer. It has positive orientation, for example, if it uses assertive forms rather than the usual nonassertive forms:

Did *someone* call last night? ['Is it true that someone called last night?']
Has the boat left *already*?

Negative *yes–no* questions

11.5 Negative questions are always conducive. Negative orientation is found in questions which contain a negative form of one kind or another:

Don't you believe me?	Have they never invited you home?
Hasn't he told you what to do?	Has nobody called?

Negative orientation is complicated by an element of surprise or disbelief. The implication is that the speaker had originally hoped for a positive response, but new evidence now suggests that the response will be negative. Thus, *Hasn't he told you what to do?* means 'Surely he has told you what to do, hasn't he? I would have thought that he had told you.' Here there is a combining of a positive and a negative attitude, which one may distinguish as the OLD EXPECTATION (positive) and NEW EXPECTATION (negative). Because the old expectation tends to be identified with the speaker's hope or wishes, negatively orientated questions often express disappointment or annoyance:

Can't you drive straight? ['I'd have thought you'd be able to, but apparently you can't.']
Aren't you ashamed of yourself? ['You ought to be, but it appears you're not.']
Hasn't the boat left *yet*? ['I'd hoped it would have left by now, but it seems it hasn't.']

If a negative question has assertive items, it is biased towards positive orientation:

> Didn't *someone* call last night? ['I expect that someone did.']
> Hasn't the boat left *already*? ['Surely it has.']

Such questions are similar in effect to type (i) tag questions (*cf* 11.6).

NOTE The enclitic negative particle precedes the subject, since it is attached to the operator, whereas *not* (used in less informal style) generally follows the subject:

> Did*n't* they warn you? Did they *not* warn you?

Some speakers find it acceptable for *not* to be placed (in rather formal style) in the same position as the enclitic. This construction is especially likely where the subject is lengthy:

> Does *not* everything we see testify to the power of Divine Providence?

But in printed texts *not* may merely represent (misleadingly) the printed equivalent of the attached enclitic.

Tag questions

11.6 Maximum conduciveness is expressed by a tag question appended to a statement (in the form of a declarative):

> Joan recognized you, *didn't she*? ['Surely Joan recognized you.']
> The boat hasn't left, *has it*? ['Surely the boat hasn't left.']

For the most common types of tag question, the tag question is negative if the statement is positive and vice versa. The tag question has the form of a *yes–no* question consisting of merely an operator and a subject pronoun, the choice of operator and pronoun depending on the statement. The nuclear tone of the tag occurs on the operator and is either rising or falling.

Below are the four main types of tag questions, which vary according to whether the statement is positive or negative, and whether the tag question is rising or falling:

POSITIVE STATEMENT + NEGATIVE TAG

(i) RISING TONE on tag	(iii) FALLING TONE on tag
He likes his JÒB, DÓESn't he?	He likes his JÒB, DÒESn't he?

NEGATIVE STATEMENT + POSITIVE TAG

(ii) RISING TONE on tag	(iv) FALLING TONE on tag
He doesn't like his JÒB, DÓES he?	He doesn't like his JÒB, DÒES he?

The meanings of these sentences, like their forms, involve a statement and a question; each of them, that is, asserts something, then invites the listener's response to it. Sentence (i), for example, can be rendered 'I assume he likes his job; am I right?', (ii) means the opposite: 'I assume he doesn't like his job, am I right?'. These sentences have a positive and a negative orientation respectively. A similar contrast exists between (iii) and (iv). But it is important, again, to separate two factors: an ASSUMPTION (expressed by the statement) and an EXPECTATION (expressed by the question). On this principle, we may distinguish four types, where '+' indicates a positive form of the statement or tag and '−' a negative form:

		statement	tag
(i)	Positive assumption + neutral expectation	+	− rising
(ii)	Negative assumption + neutral expectation	−	+ rising
(iii)	Positive assumption + positive expectation	+	− falling
(iv)	Negative assumption + negative expectation	−	+ falling

The tag with a rising tone invites verification, expecting the hearer to decide the truth of the proposition in the statement. The tag with the falling tone, on the other hand, invites confirmation of the statement, and has the force of an exclamation rather than a genuine question. The truth of the statement may be self-evident however, and therefore no response is expected:

I wasn't born yesterday, was I?

NOTE [a] There is a further, less common, type of tag question in which both statement and question are positive:

Your car is outsÍDE, ís it?
You've had an ÀCcident, HÁVE you?

The tag typically has a rising tone, and the statement is characteristically preceded by *oh* or *so*, indicating the speaker's arrival at a conclusion by inference, or by recalling what has already been said. The tone may sometimes be one of sarcastic suspicion:

So THÀT's your little, game, ís it?

[b] Tag questions can also be appended to imperatives and exclamatives:

Turn on the light, won't you?
Open the door, can't you?
Don't make a noise, will you?
Let's not discuss it now, shall we?
How thin she is, isn't she?
What a beautiful painting it is, isn't it?

[c] Several tag questions are invariant, *ie* they have the same form whether the statement or exclamation is positive or negative: *isn't that so?*, *don't you think?*, *right?* ⟨informal⟩, *wouldn't you say?*

Declarative questions

11.7 The declarative question has the form of a declarative, except for the final rising intonation:

You've got the TÍCKets?
They've spoken to the amBÁSSador, of course?
You realize what the RÍSKS are?
Boris will be THÉRE, I suppose?

Declarative questions are conducive (*cf* 11.4), and resemble tag questions with a rising tone in that they invite the hearer's verification. Positive questions have positive orientation and can therefore accept only assertive items (10.37):

He wants something to eat?
Somebody is with you?

Negative questions have negative orientation, and nonassertive forms may be used following the negative:

You didn't get anything to eat?
Nobody ever stays at your place?

Yes–no questions with modal auxiliaries

11.8 The formation of *yes–no* questions with modal auxiliaries is subject to certain limitations and shifts of meaning. The modals of permission (*may* ⟨esp BrE⟩, and *can*) and of obligation (*must* ⟨esp BrE⟩, and *have to*) generally involve the speaker's authority in statements and the hearer's authority in questions:

A: {May / Can} I leave now? ['Will *you* permit me . . .']

B: Yes, you {may / can}. ['*I will* permit you . . .']

A: {Must I / Do I have to} leave now? ['Are *you* telling me to . . .']

B: Yes, you {must / have to}. ['*I* am telling you to . . .']

The question form anticipates the form appropriate for the answer.

In the possibility sense, *can* or (more commonly in AmE) *could* are used rather than *may*:

A: {Can / Could} they have missed the bus?

B: Yes, they {may have. / might have.}

The past forms *might* [permission], *would* [volition], and *could* [volition] are regularly used for politeness in place of the present forms; for example, *Might I call you by your first name?*; *Would you stand at the back, please?*; *Could I see you for a moment?*

NOTE [**a**] *Shall* [volition] is used ⟨esp in BrE⟩ to involve the hearer's will in questions: *Shall I switch off the television?* As common alternatives we have *Should I?* or *Do you want me to?*

[**b**] *Need* (esp in BrE) is used as a nonassertive modal auxiliary with negative

orientation: *Need they leave now?*. Common substitutes ⟨esp in AmE⟩ are the main verb *need to* and *have to*: *Do they need/have to leave now?* On the other hand, *must* in the necessity sense has positive orientation: *Why must it always rain when we want to have a picnic?*

[c] *Dare* is occasionally used as a nonassertive modal auxiliary, especially in BrE: *Dare we complain?* Common substitutes are the main verb *dare* and ⟨esp in AmE⟩ the blend construction with DO and the bare infinitive: *Do we dare to complain?*; *Do we dare complain?*

Wh-questions

Form of *wh*-question

11.9 *Wh*-questions are formed with the aid of one of the following simple interrogative words (or *wh*-words):

who/whom/whose, what, which, when, where, how, why

Unlike *yes–no* questions, *wh*-questions generally have falling intonation. As a rule,

(i) the *wh*-element (*ie* the clause element containing the *wh*-word) comes first in the sentence,

(ii) the *wh*-word itself takes first position in the *wh*-element.

The main exception to the second principle occurs when the *wh*-word is within a prepositional complement. Here English provides a choice between two constructions, one being formal. In formal style, the preposition precedes the complement, whereas otherwise the complement comes first and the preposition is deferred to the end of the sentence:

On what did you base your prediction? ⟨formal⟩
What did you base your prediction *on*?

We may perhaps express this difference more neatly by saying that nonformal style generally requires that the *wh*-word comes first, but formal style requires that the *wh*-element as a whole comes first.

Function of *wh*-element

11.10 The following sentences exemplify the various clause functions in which the *wh*-element operates:

Who is coming to the PÀRty? [*wh*-element: S] [1]
What did you buy for your sìster? [*wh*-element: O_d] [2]
Whose beautiful anTÌQUES are these? [*wh*-element: C_s] [3]
How wide did they make the BÒOKcase? [*wh*-element: C_o] [4]
When will you be proMÒTed? [*wh*-element: A] [5]
Where shall I put the GLÀSSes? [*wh*-element: A] [6]
Why didn't you TÈLL me? [*wh*-element: A] [7]
How did you MÈND it? [*wh*-element: A] [8]
How much does he CÀRE? [*wh*-element: A] [9]
How long have you been WÀITing? [*wh*-element: A] [10]
How often do you visit New YÒRK? [*wh*-element: A] [11]

We see above that the normal statement order of elements is altered in *wh*-questions not only by the initial placing of the *wh*-element, but by the inversion of subject and operator in all cases except when the *wh*-element is subject, where the rule that the *wh*-element takes initial position is given precedence.

Subject–operator inversion is the same in its application to *wh*-questions as in its application to *yes–no* questions; if there is no operator in the equivalent statement, DO is introduced as operator in the question. The main verb BE and (occasionally, esp in BrE) HAVE act as operator: *Where is she?*, *What kind of car have they?*

NOTE [a] Adjuncts of instrument, reason, and purpose are normally questioned by the prepositional construction: *What shall I mend it with?*; *What did you do that for?* Although the latter could be replaced by *Why did you do that?*, it has no alternative with a proposed preposition: **For what did you do that?*; In this respect it is like informal questions with BE followed by a final preposition: *What was it in?*

[b] Abbreviated questions consisting of a *wh*-word and a final preposition (which in this construction regularly bears nuclear stress), *eg*: *What FÒR?*, *Where FRÒM/TÒ?*, *What WÌTH?*, *Who WÌTH/BỲ?*, are as common in informal speech as questions consisting of the *wh*-word only: *Where?*, *Why?*, *Who?* There is a common abbreviated negative question *Why NÒT?* and an informal abbreviated reason question ⟨esp in AmE⟩ *How CÒME?*

[c] Except in formal style, *who* rather than *whom* is used as object (*Who did you want?*) or complement of preposition (*Who did you give it to?*).

[d] Many speakers do not accept an indirect object as *wh*-element: ?*Who(m) did you give the present?* They use the equivalent prepositional phrase instead: *Who(m) did you give the present to?* or (in formal style) *To whom did you give the present?* Some speakers, however, find the construction acceptable if there is no ambiguity as to which object is direct and which indirect. (There is ambiguity in **Who did you show your daughter?*)

[e] There can be more than one *wh*-element:

> *Which present* did you give to *whom*?
> *Who* said *what* to *whom*?
> *Who* did you see *where*?

Alternative questions

11.11 There are two types of alternative questions. The first resembles a *yes–no* question, and the second a *wh*-question:

> Would you like CHÓcolate, vaNÍLla, or STRÀWberry (ice-cream)? [1]
> Which ice-cream would you LÌKE? CHÓcolate, vaNÍLla or STRÀWberry? [2]

The first type differs from a *yes–no* question only in intonation; instead of the final rising tone, it contains a separate nucleus for each alternative: a rise occurs on each item in the list, except the last, on which there is a fall, indicating that the list is complete. The difference of intonation between alternative and *yes–no* questions is important, in that ignoring it can lead to misunderstanding – as the contrast between these replies indicates:

alternative: A: Shall we go by BÚS or TRÀIN?
B: By BÙS.
yes–no: A: Shall we go by bus or TRÁIN?
B: No, let's take the CÀR.

The second type of alternative question is really a compound of two separate questions: a *wh*-question followed by an elliptical alternative question. Thus [2] might be taken as a reduced version of:

Which ice-cream would you LÌKE? Would you like CHÓcolate, vaNÍLla, or STRÀWberry?

NOTE [a] Any *yes–no* question can be converted into an alternative question:

ÁRE you ready or ÁREn't you ready?
ÁRE you ready or NÒT?

Since the alternative variant unnecessarily spells out the negative possibility, it introduces a petulant tone to the question.
[b] Ellipted forms are generally preferred, *ie* [4] rather than [3]:

Did ÍTaly win the World Cup or did BraŽIL win the World Cup? [3]
Did ÍTaly win the World Cup or BraZÌL? [4]

The second part can be placed within the first part:

Did ÍTaly or BraZÌL win the World Cup?
ÁRE you or ÀREn't you coming?

Minor types of questions

Exclamatory questions

11.12 The exclamatory question is interrogative in structure, but has the force of an exclamatory assertion (*cf.* 11.20). Typically it is a negative *yes–no* question with a final falling instead of rising tone:

Hasn't she GRÒWN!
Wasn't it a marvellous CÒNcert!

These invite the hearer's agreement to something on which the speaker has strong feelings. The meaning, contrary to the appearance of the literal wording, is vigorously positive.

A positive *yes–no* question, also with a falling tone, is another (but less common) way of expressing a strong positive conviction:

'Am 'I HÙNGry! 'Did 'he look anNÒYED! 'Has 'she GRÒWN!

Both operator and subject usually receive emphatic stress. In written English an exclamation mark is usual at the end of the sentence for both kinds of exclamatory questions.

Rhetorical questions

11.13 The rhetorical question is interrogative in structure, but has the force of a strong assertion. The speaker does not expect an answer.

A positive rhetorical *yes–no* question is like a strong negative assertion, while a negative question is like a strong positive one.

POSITIVE:

Is that a reason for desPÁIR? ['Surely that is not a reason . . .']

Can anyone doubt the wisdom of this action? ['Surely no one can doubt . . .']

NEGATIVE:

Isn't the answer ÓBVious? ['Surely the answer is obvious.']

Haven't you got anything better to DÓ? ['Surely you have something better to do.']

Unlike exclamatory questions, these rhetorical questions have the normal rising intonation of a *yes–no* question, and are distinguished chiefly by the range of pitch movement.

There are also rhetorical *wh*-questions. The positive question is equivalent to a statement in which the *wh*-element is replaced by a negative element:

Who KNÔWS/CÂRES? ['Nobody knows/cares' or 'I don't know/care.']

What DÎFference does it make? ['It makes no difference.']

How should Î know? ['There is no reason why I should know.']

The less common negative question is equivalent to a statement in which the *wh*-element is replaced by a positive element:

Who DÔESn't know? ['Everybody knows.']

How CÔULDn't you remember? ['You certainly should have remembered.']

Rhetorical *wh*-questions generally have a rise–fall tone, less commonly a simple falling tone.

Echo questions

11.14 Echo questions repeat part or all of what has been said. Replicatory echo questions do so as a way of having their content confirmed:

A: The Browns are emigrating. B: Émigrating?

A: He's a dermatologist. B: WHÁT is he?

A: I'll pay for it. B: You'll WHÁT?

A: Have you ever been to Valladolid?
B: Have I ever been WHÉRE?

A: She always wears a quizzical expression.
B: She always wears a WHÁT expression?

A: She sat there and ratiocinated.
B: She sat there and {WHÁT? / WHÁTed?}

Explicatory echo questions, which are always *wh*-questions, ask for clarification. They have a falling tone on the *wh*-word:

A: Take a look at this! B: Take a look at WHÀT?
A: He's missed the bus again. B: WHÒ's missed the bus?

NOTE [a] The generalized recapitulatory *wh*-question *WHÁT did you say?* is sometimes truncated to the monosyllable *WHÁT?* (impolite except among friends), just as the alternative formula *I beg your pardon?* can be reduced simply to *Pardon?* Other abbreviated requests for repetition are *Pardon me?* ⟨AmE⟩, *Excuse me?* ⟨AmE⟩, and *Sorry?* ⟨BrE⟩.
[b] *What?* on its own can also express general incredulity:

A: I paid £1,000 for that picture. B: WHÁT? You must be mad.

Directives

Directives without a subject

11.15 Directives typically take the form of an imperative sentence, which differs from a declarative sentence in that:
(i) it generally has no subject;
(ii) it generally has a verb in the base form.
Otherwise, the clause patterns of imperative sentences show the same range and ordering of elements as declaratives (*cf* 10.1); for example;

(S) V: Jump.
(S) VC: Be reasonable.
(S) VOC: Consider yourself lucky.

The imperative verb lacks tense distinction and does not allow modal auxiliaries. The progressive form is rare, and the perfect even rarer:

Be listening to this station the same time tomorrow night.

Passives with *be* occur chiefly in negative directives, where they generally have the meaning 'Don't allow yourself to be . . .':

Don't be deceived by his looks.
Don't be bullied into signing.

They are less common in positive directives: *Be guided by what I say*. What might be analysed as passives occur with *get*: *Get washed*; *Don't get dressed yet*.

Imperatives are restricted to verbs used dynamically, hence the incongruity of **Be old*. Many predications that are stative with respect to disallowing the progressive (*cf* 4.11) are available with a dynamic interpretation: *Forgive us*; *Love your enemies*; *Don't be a stranger*.

Directives with a subject

11.16 The meaning of a directive implies that the omitted subject is the 2nd person pronoun *you*. The implication can be demonstrated by the occurrence of *you* as subject of a following tag question (*Be quiet, will you?*), by the occurrence of only *yourself* or *yourselves* as the reflexive (*Behave yourself* or *Help yourselves*), and by the occurrence of only the emphatic possessive *your own* (*Use your own comb*).

There is, however, a type of directive in which the stressed subject *you* is added. *You* may be noncontrastive and admonitory:

> 'You be QÙIet!
> 'You 'mind your own BÙSiness, and 'leave this to MÈ!
> 'You 'take the BÒOK.

It frequently expresses strong irritation or (as in the last example) merely insistence. On the other hand, noncontrastive *you* may be persuasive:

> I know you can do it if you try hard enough. 'You 'show me what you can DÒ.

You may also be contrastive in the sense of singling out one person or one set of persons.

> Don't tell MÈ to be QUÍET. YÒU be quiet!

Third person subjects are also possible:

> *Somebody* open this door.
> *Parents with children* go to the front.
> *Nobody* move.

NOTE There is blurring of subject and vocative (*cf* 10.31*f*) in these commands. But whereas the subject always precedes the verb, the vocative is an element that can occur in final and medial, as well as initial, positions in the sentence. Another difference is that the vocative, when initially placed, has a separate tone unit (typically fall–rise); the subject merely receives ordinary word stress:

VOCATIVE:	MǍRY, play on MỲ side.
	Play on MỲ side, MÁRY.
SUBJECT:	'Mary play on MỲ side.

The distinctness of vocative and imperative subject is confirmed by the possibility of their cooccurrence: *JǑHN, 'you listen to MÈ!*

Vocative *you*, as opposed to imperative subject *you*, is very impolite: *YÒU, 'come HÈRE.*

Directives with *let*

11.17 First person imperatives can be formed by preposing the verb *let* followed by a notional subject in the objective case:

Let us work hard. ['We must work hard.']
Let me see now. Do I have any money on me? ['I must consider this now.']

The same applies to 3rd person subjects:

Let no one think that a teacher's life is easy. ['No one must think . . .']
Let each man decide for himself. ['Each man must decide . . .']

Except for the *let me* type, these are generally rather archaic and elevated in tone. A colloquial alternative to *let us*, however, is the common abbreviated form *let's*: *Let's have a party*.

Negative imperatives

11.18 To negate imperatives, one simply adds an initial *Don't* or *Do not*, replacing assertive by nonassertive items where necessary:

Open the door.	*Don't* open the door.
Get some wine.	*Don't* get any wine.
You open the door.	*Don't you* open the door.
Someone open the door.	*Don't anyone* open the door.

NOTE Imperatives with *let* are informally negated with *don't*:

Don't let's say anything about it. ⟨esp BrE⟩
Let's don't say anything about it. ⟨esp AmE⟩
Don't let me disturb you. ⟨esp BrE⟩
Don't let anyone fool himself he can get away with it.

Variants occur, especially with *let's*, where *not* is inserted after the pronoun: *Let's not say anything about it.*

Do with positive imperatives

11.19 A positive imperative can be made more persuasive or insistent (esp in BrE) by adding *do* (usually with a nuclear tone) before the verb:

DÒ have some more tea. DÒ let's go for a walk.

This use of *do* applies only when a subject is absent or when *let's* is present.

NOTE *Do*, like *don't* and *let's*, acts as an introductory imperative marker. When used with imperatives, *do* and *don't* are not acting as dummy operators (*cf* 3.11), and so they can be used with *be*: *Do be quiet*; *Don't be silly*. (Contrast the unacceptability of **They do be quiet*.) The same applies in the quasi-imperative construction *Why don't you be more careful?*

Exclamatives

11.20 Exclamatives as a formal category of sentence are restricted to the type of exclamatory utterance introduced by *what* or *how* (*cf* 11.12). The *wh*-word indicates an extreme position on some scale of value, and therefore can only appear at points where an expression of degree is possible: *What* as predeterminer in a noun phrase [1]; and *how* as intensifier of an adjective [2] or adverb [3], or as a degree adverbial [4]. The *wh*-element is fronted, but in contrast to *wh*-questions there is no subject–operator inversion:

What a time we've had today! [1]
How delightful her manners are! [2]
How quickly you eat! [3]
How I used to hate geography! [4]

Sometimes, one must infer from the context whether the reference is to one end of the scale or the other. For example, *What a time* in [1] could refer to a very good time or a very bad time.

NOTE **[a]** When the *wh*-element is the complement of a preposition, the preposition is normally left in final position: *What a mess we're in!*
[b] Echo exclamations do not have an exclamative structure, but it is convenient to mention them here. Like the echo question (*cf* 11.14), the echo exclamation repeats part or all of a preceding utterance. It is characterized by a rise–fall or high–fall tone:

A: I'm going to London for a holiday.
B: *To LÔNdon!* That's not my idea of a rest.
A: Have you been to Paris?
B: *Been to PÂris!* I certainly have.
A: I hear you're a linguist.
B: *I a linguist!* ⟨formal⟩
B: *Me a linguist!*

Irregular sentences

11.21 IRREGULAR sentences do not conform to the regular patterns of clause structures (*cf* 10.1) or to the variations of those structures in the major syntactic classes (*cf* 11.1). Some types are listed below.

(i) The formulaic (or 'optative') subjunctive, one use of the base form of the verb, survives in a few fossilized expressions. It is combined with subject–verb inversion (induced by the initial adverb) in, for example:

*Long **live*** the Republic! *So **help** me* God.

It is found without inversion in, for example:

God ***save*** the Queen! God ***forbid***!

A less archaic formula (with subject–verb inversion) for expressing wishes has *may* in front:

May the best man win! May you always be happy!

(ii) There are several kinds of irregular *wh*-questions, which occur mainly in conversation, for example:

How about another kiss? *What about* coming to my place?
How come you're so late? *Why* listen to him?
Why all the noise? *What* if it rains?

(iii) Several kinds of subordinate clauses are used as sentences, generally with exclamatory force:

That I should live to see such ingratitude!
To think that you might have been killed!
Well, if it isn't Susan! ['It is indeed Susan!']
If only I'd listened to my parents!

(iv) Adverbials may have the force of commands, sometimes in combination with another element:

Left, right! Everybody inside!
Hands up! On with the show!

(v) Many proverbs have an aphoristic sentence structure, in which two short constructions are balanced against each other:

The more, the merrier. First come, first served.
Waste not, want not. Out of sight, out of mind.

Block language

11.22 Block language appears (especially in writing) in such functions as labels, titles, newspaper headlines, headings, notices, and advertisements. Simple block-language messages often consist of a noun phrase in isolation:

Entrance	50 mph limit
English Department	*The New York Times*
For Sale	No dogs without leash

Newspaper headlines commonly contain block language because of pressure on space, and they are imitated on radio and television news broadcasts. They can often be analysed in terms of clause structure, but with the omission of words that may be understood from the context, such as the finite forms of the verb BE and the articles:

OIL SPILL THREAT DECREASING [SV]
PRESIDENT CALLS FOR CALM [SVA]
SHARE PRICES NOW HIGHER [SAC]

Omissions of words that can be inferred from the context occur in other types of writing:

Wish you were here. [postcard]
MANUSCRIPT RECEIVED CHANGES ACCEPTED [cable]
Refrigerate after opening [label]

NOTE [a] Notices of prohibition often take the form of a noun phrase introduced by *No*: *No entry*; *No smoking*.

[b] In informal conversation many types of phrases occur as complete utterances: *The things they get up to!*; *You and your ideas!*; *Of all the stupid things to say!*; *Taxi!*; *More coffee?*; *Your name?*; *No news*. In addition there are many formulae used for stereotyped communication situations; for example: *Good morning*; *Goodbye*; *How do you do?*; *Thanks*; *Happy Birthday*.

[c] Interjections are purely emotive words which do not enter into syntactic relations. Among the common interjections are *Ah*, *Boo*, *Oh*, *Ouch*, *Sh*, *Wow*.

Bibliographical note

On the pragmatic functions of sentences in utterances see Austin (1962); Cole and Morgan (1975); Leech (1983); Lyons (1977); Searle (1979).

On questions see Bolinger (1957); Hudson (1975); Pope (1976); Stenström (1984); Stockwell et al. (1973, Ch. 9); on tag questions, Algeo (1990); Bald (1979); Nässlin (1984); on negative questions, Kontra (1980).

On directives see Bolinger (1967c) and (1977, Chs. 8 and 9); Downes (1977); Stein (1976); Stockwell et al. (1973, Ch. 10).

12 Pro-forms and ellipsis

Motivation for abbreviation

12.1 Pro-forms and ellipsis are syntactic devices for abbreviating constructions to avoid redundancy. For example, we can avoid the repetition of *sing tonight* in [1] by the substitution of the pro-form *do so*, as in [1a], or by ellipsis (which is indicated by the symbol ▵), as in [1b]:

She might sing tonight, but I don't think she will sing tonight. [1]
She might sing tonight, but I don't think she will *do so*. [1a]
She might sing tonight, but I don't think she will ▵. [1b]

Other things being equal, language users will follow the maxim 'Reduce as much as possible'.

The preference for abbreviation is not merely a preference for economy. Abbreviation can contribute to clarity, since attention is focused on new information, as in [2]:

A: Have you spoken to Bob?
B: ▵ Not yet ▵. [2]

Recoverability

12.2 In order that constructions with pro-forms and ellipsis should be interpreted correctly, the full form must be recoverable. We list below three types of recoverability, and mention first the most important type from the grammatical point of view:

(i) TEXTUAL RECOVERABILITY: The full form is recoverable from a neighbouring part of the text.

(ii) SITUATIONAL RECOVERABILITY: The full form is recoverable from the extralinguistic situation.

(iii) STRUCTURAL RECOVERABILITY: The full form is recoverable from knowledge of grammatical structure.

The use of the pronoun *she*, for example, presupposes that the speaker and hearer know the identity of the person to whom the pronoun refers. In [1] and [2] we can identify the referent from the linguistic context. We understand *she* to refer to the same person as does *the poor girl*:

The poor girl did not complain, although *she* was badly hurt. [1]
Although *she* was badly hurt, *the poor girl* did not complain. [2]

There are two types of textual recoverability: [1] is an example of the ANAPHORIC use of the pronoun, where the ANTECEDENT (*the poor girl*) comes before the pronoun, and [2] is an example of the less common CATAPHORIC use, where the antecedent follows the pronoun.

Situational recoverability is exemplified in:

> Is *she* badly hurt? [3]

One can imagine someone saying [3] on arriving at the scene of an accident in which a girl has been struck down by a car. The identity of the person meant by *she* is then obvious from the situation.

The third type of recoverability, structural recoverability, is illustrated by the optional ellipsis of the conjunction *that* in [4]:

> He admits (*that*) he prefers his mother's cooking. [4]

Here, contextual information is irrelevant: the optionality of *that* is purely a matter of grammatical structure.

Antecedents and the replaced expressions

12.3 Pro-forms and their antecedents may be linked by COREFERENCE, a linkage of 'cross-reference' between two expressions that refer to the same thing or set of things. For example, in [1] *George* and *he* will generally be understood to refer to the same person:

> *George* was the best runner in our school, and so everyone expected that *he* would win the prize. [1]

We can also replace the pronoun *he* by *George* without changing the meaning of the sentence.

But the relation between a pro-form and its antecedent is not necessarily a relation of coreference. For example, in [2] the pronoun *one* substitutes for *a first prize*, as the grammatical and semantic equivalence of [2] with [2a] shows:

> Fiona got *a first prize* this year, and I got *one* last year. [2]
> Fiona got *a first prize* this year, and I got *a first prize* last year. [2a]

It is clear, however, that the pronoun *one* in [2] does not refer to the same prize as does its antecedent *a first prize*. Similarly, the two uses of *a first prize* are not coreferential in [2a].

The antecedent is not necessarily identical with the expression that is replaced or ellipted. For example, in [3] the pronoun *it* refers to an antecedent clause, but – as [3a] demonstrates – the clause that *it* replaces is not identical with the antecedent clause:

If you don't study for the examination, you'll regret *it*. [3]
If you don't study for the examination, you'll regret *not studying for the examination*. [3a]

When we refer to a pro-form as replacing a particular syntactic form, we mean the form for which it substitutes and not necessarily the antecedent.

Pro-forms

Pro-forms for noun phrases and their constituents

12.4 The most obvious pro-forms for noun phrases are the 3rd person pronouns and determiners:

Cindy was by far the best speaker, and so everyone expected that *she* would win the prize. [1]
Ten per cent of insomniacs sleep soundly when *they* come to a sleep clinic. [2]
The islanders pay all *their* lives on insurance policies for expensive funerals. [3]

Despite the name, almost all pronouns are pro-forms for noun phrases rather than simply for nouns.

Other items that can be pro-forms for noun phrases include in particular indefinite pronouns such as *any*, *all*, *both*, *each*, *either*, *some*, and *none*. These, however, can also be regarded as elliptical, since they can be expanded, usually with an *of*-phrase:

When the *children* entered, *each (of the children)/(child)* was given a small present.
Some *equipment* has been damaged, but *none (of the equipment)* has been lost.
Both of the *engines* had been hit, and *neither (of the engines)/(engine)* could be relied upon to bring us safely home.
Her cousins go to the same school as she did, and *all (of her cousins)/(her cousins)* want to become doctors.
This year we produced more *coal*, but we sold *less (coal)*.

The demonstratives (*cf* 6.19*f*) can be pro-forms for noun phrases and they can also be regarded as elliptical:

I read his first novel, and *that (novel)* was boring too.
The paintings of Gauguin's Tahiti period are more famous than *those (paintings)* he painted in France.

The same can be a pro-form for a noun phrase ([4]), but it can also substitute for a prepositional phrase ([5]) or an adjective phrase ([6] and

[7]) functioning as a subject or object complement:

A: Can I have *a cup of black coffee with sugar*, please?
B: Give me *the same*, please. [4]
Yesterday I felt *under the weather* and today I feel *the same*. [5]
The Denison house is *small but very comfortable*, and ours is just *the same*. [6]
I want my steak *rare* and David wants his *the same*. [7]

In all its substitute uses (*cf* 12.8 Note [b]), *the same* does not imply *identity* but *similarity* with the antecedent.

One as a pro-form

12.5 There are two pro-forms *one*: one has the plural *some*, and the other has the plural *ones*. Both are always unstressed (and are thereby distinguished from the numeral *one*), and both substitute for phrases with count nouns as heads.

(i) *One/some* is a substitute for an indefinite noun phrase:

A: Can you give me *a few nails*? I need *one*.
B: I'll get you *some* soon.

Compare:

I need {*a nail.* / *one.*} I need {*some nails.* / *some.*}

(ii) *One* and *ones* are substitutes for a NOMINAL EXPRESSION, a noun phrase head with or without one or more modifiers (not the whole noun phrase):

Have you any *knives*? I need a sharp *one*. [1]
I wish I'd bought a few *jars of honey*. Did you notice the *ones* they were selling? [2]

In [1], *one* substitutes for the noun *knife*, and in [2] *ones* substitutes for *jars of honey*. *One* as a pro-form for a nominal expression must have an overt determiner. The equivalent pro-form for noncount nouns is *some*:

Shall I pass the *butter*? Or have you got *some* already?

Pro-forms for clauses and clause constituents

Pro-form *do*

12.6 The dummy operator *do* is a pro-form for the predicate in [1], despite the structural parallelism with other operators, as in [2], that are followed by ellipsis of the predication (*cf* 12.14, 12.20 Note [a]):

Martin drives a car, and his sister does, TÒO. [1]
Martin can drive a car, and his sister can$_{\triangle}$, TÒO. [2]

In BrE many allow the possibility of adding after the auxiliary or auxiliaries an optional intransitive main verb *do* as a pro-form for the predication (*Martin can drive a car, and his sister can do, too*). This happens rarely after the operator *do*, but is more common after a modal or after the perfect auxiliary *have*:

> Bob says he is going to join the Labour Party.
> It will be interesting to see whether he DÒES (*do*). ⟨rare⟩
>
> The Americans are reducing their defence expenditure this year. I wonder if the RÙSSIANS will (*do*) TÒO.
>
> I didn't touch the television set; but PÈRCY might have (*done*).

Do so

12.7 The main verb *do* combines with *so* to form a unit *do so* that functions as a pro-form for the predicate or predication. The verb in this combination occurs in both finite and nonfinite forms, and the combination appears in infinitive and *-ing* participle clauses as well as in finite clauses. Since the *do so* construction is somewhat formal, in informal use the general preference is for the alternative ellipsis of the predication where possible (*cf* 12.20), which is indicated by the parentheses in the examples below:

> They planned to reach the top of the mountain, but nobody knows if they *did (so)*.
>
> You can take the train back to Madrid, but I shouldn't (*do so*) until tomorrow morning.
>
> As no one else has succeeded in solving the mystery, I'll attempt to (*do so*) myself.
>
> As no one else has succeeded in *doing so*, I'll attempt to solve the mystery myself.

NOTE Unlike the intransitive *do* of 12.6, the *do* in *do so* is usually stressed (but the *so* is always unstressed).

Do it, do that, do so

12.8 The transitive main verb *do* also combines with the pronouns *it* and *that* to form a unit that functions as a pro-form for the predicate or predication:

> Is Connie still trying to light the stove? She should have *DÒNE it* by NÓW.
>
> Are you trying to light the stove with a match? I wouldn't *do THǍT*.

In general, *do* in these two combinations has dynamic and agentive reference; *ie* it refers to an action that is performed or intentionally initiated by the referent of the subject. It is hence abnormal for *do it* and *do that* to substitute for predicates or predications that are stative or denote involuntary processes:

A: They think he's mad.
B: *We *do it* TÒO.
A: He owns a Cadillac.
B: *Yes, his BRÒther *does* {*that* / *THÁT*} TÒO.

With regard to *do so*, there is divided usage. Some speakers, particularly in AmE, treat the *do* in *do so* as dynamic and agentive, while others accept *do so*, at least to some extent, even when the combination is associated with stative or involuntary process predications:

(?) They think he is mad, and Ì *do so* TÒO.
(?) Peter likes work, and BÒB *does so* TÒO.
A: Bob might have heard the strange noises.
B: (?) He might WÈLL have *done so*.

NOTE [a] *Do that* gives more prominence to the object *that*, which often receives nuclear stress and is treated to some extent as new or contrastive information. The *it* of *do it*, on the other hand, is always unstressed.

[b] *Do the same*, *do likewise*, and *do similarly* are alternatives to *do that* when a comparison is involved:

I'll contribute ten dollars, if you'll *do the same*.

They refer to a similar event and not to the identical event referred to by their antecedent.

Pro-forms for adverbials

12.9 *Here* and *there* can be pro-forms for place adverbials, and *then* for time adverbials:

Between London and Oxford there is *a famous inn called the George and Dragon*. *Here* we stopped for lunch.
If you look *in the top drawer*, you'll probably find it *there*.
One morning the captain invited us to the bridge. He told us *then* about his secret orders.

There is the unmarked place pro-form, whereas *here* specifically denotes closeness to the speaker.

So and *thus* can be pro-forms for process adverbials (*cf* 8.27*f*). Both appear in formal contexts, and otherwise *(in) that way* or *like that* are used:

To the Greeks, Pan was *a herdsman, half-man, half-goat*; and he is *so*/*thus* represented in their sculpture. ⟨formal⟩

. . .; and he is represented {*(in) that way* / *like that*} in their sculpture.

It is convenient to refer here to the use of *so* and *that* as pro-forms for intensifiers of adjectives and adverbs:

> Though Bairstow designed the car to exceed *400 miles per hour*, few people believed that it would go *so/that* fast.
> I had a headache and a high temperature, but I'm not feeling *so/that* bad today.

So as pro-form for complement

12.10 *So* can substitute for an adjective phrase or a noun phrase functioning as complement:

> Brett's work is not yet *consistent in style and quality*, but will no doubt become *so*.
> If he's *a criminal*, it's his parents who have made him *so*.

After *be*, ellipsis is preferred, or (informally) the substitutes *like that* or *that way* are used:

> The plants are healthy enough now, but I wonder how long they will
> - *be (?so).*
> - *be like that.*
> - *remain so.*

After *appear* and *seem*, with initial anticipatory *it*, both *so* and its negative equivalent *not* can be pro-forms for the *that*-clause:

> Ruth is waiting to hear whether she has been promoted, and it appears *so/not*.

NOTE [**a**] *So* as pro-form for the subject complement can also be initial:

> We hoped that the event would be a success, and *so* it turned out.

So it appears and *so it seems*, with initial *so*, are common expressions of reaction to previous utterances.

[**b**] *So* is a synonym for *true*, and not a pro-form, after *be* in examples like *That is so; It may be so; I fear that this is not so.*

So and *not* as pro-forms for object *that*-clause

12.11 *So* and its negative equivalent *not* can be pro-forms for a *that*-clause functioning as direct object:

> A: Will Oxford win the next boat race?
> B: I hope
> - *so* [= that Oxford will win . . .]
> - *not* [= that Oxford will not win . . .]

This use of *not* is restricted mainly to verbs of belief or assumption, whereas the corresponding use of *so* is frequently found also in some verbs of saying such as *say* and *tell*. Verbs that commonly allow both *so* and *not* include:

believe	guess	imagine	reckon	suspect
expect	hope	presume	suppose	think

NOTE [a] With certain verbs (such as *say* and *believe*), the pro-clause *so* occasionally appears in initial position (*cf* 12.10 Note [a]). Subject–verb inversion is possible if the subject is not a pronoun:

A: Oxford will win the boat race.

B: {*So* most of the sports writers say. / *So* say most of the sports writers.}

A: Most people are backing the Oxford crew.
B: *So* I believe.

[b] With verbs taking transferred negation, the use of *not* (*eg I think not*) as a pro-form is rather formal, and is often replaced by *so* preceded by negation in the main clause:

I don't think so. I don't suppose so. I don't believe so.

[c] Unlike *so*, the pro-form *not* usually receives nuclear stress:

A: Has the news reached home yet?

B: {*I'm a*FRǍID SO. / I'm afraid NÒT.}

_So_ as pro-form for predication

12.12 Initial *so* can be pro-predication in a construction consisting of *so* followed by the subject and the operator (*So* + S + op):

You asked me to leave, and 'so I DÌD. [= indeed I DÌD] [1]
A: It's starting to snow. B: 'So it ìs!
A: You've spilled coffee on your dress. B: Oh dear, 'so I HÀVE.

So here is equivalent to the *so* in *do so* (*cf* 12.7):

You asked me to leave, and I DÌD SO. [1a]

The difference in meaning between [1] and [1a] is that [1] introduces an emphasis that might otherwise be conveyed by *indeed* or *in fact*. In replies, the construction *So* + S + op expresses surprised confirmation of what the previous speaker has asserted:

A: It's past midnight. B: [looks at watch] 'So it ìs!

Initial _so_ with subject–operator inversion

12.13 A construction superficially similar to that in 12.12 has initial *so* followed by subject–operator inversion (*So* + op + S):

YǑU asked him to leave, and 'so did ì. [= I asked him to leave, too]
The corn is ripening, and 'so are the ÀPPles.
You've spilled coffee on the table, and 'so have ì.

In this construction *so* is not a pro-form at all, but an additive adverb equivalent in meaning to *too* or *also*, and the construction is elliptical. *So* here is parallel to the negative adverbs *neither* and *nor*, which similarly take subject–operator inversion:

The corn isn't ripening, and *neither/nor* are the apples (ripening).

Ellipsis

The nature of ellipsis

12.14 Ellipsis is grammatical omission. In the strict application of the term, ellipsis requires VERBATIM RECOVERABILITY; that is, the actual word or words that are implied must be precisely recoverable. We postulate ellipsis to explain why some normally obligatory element of a grammatical sentence is missing. For example, the infinitive marker *to* occurs in [1] without the infinitive which it normally introduces:

If he works hard, I won't have to △. [1]

We therefore say that the predication *work hard* has been ellipted.

Strict ellipsis requires that when we insert the missing words we do not change the meaning of the original sentence. The subject in [2] is therefore not elliptical at all:

The poor need more help. [2]

Though *the poor* refers to people, if we add a word such as *people* we change the meaning. *The poor people* has specific reference to a particular group of poor people, whereas *the poor* has generic reference (*cf* 5.22).

A further requirement for strict ellipsis is that when we insert the missing words the sentence should remain grammatical. The comparative construction in [3] is therefore strictly elliptical, as we see from [3a]:

He always wakes up earlier than *I*. ⟨formal⟩ [3]
He always wakes up earlier than *I wake up*. [3a]

On the other hand, the construction in [4] is not strictly elliptical, because when we try to insert *wake up* the resulting sentence [4a] is ungrammatical.

He always wakes up earlier than *me*. ⟨informal⟩ [4]
*He always wakes up earlier than *me wake up*. [4a]

An analogous example involves the dummy operator *do*. The construction with the unstressed dummy operator *does* in [5] is structurally parallel to constructions with other operators, such as *can* in [6]:

SHĚ understands the problem better than HÈ does. [5]
SHĚ can understand the problem better than HÈ can. [6]

But whereas we can regard *understand the problem* as ellipted in [6], it would not be possible to do so in [5]:

> *SHĔ understands the problem better than HÈ does understand the problem.

Positional categories of ellipsis

12.15 We distinguish three categories of ellipsis according to where the ellipsis occurs within a construction. In INITIAL ellipsis, the initial elements are ellipted:

> (I) hope he's there.

In MEDIAL ellipsis medial elements are ellipted:

> Jill owns a Volvo and Fred (owns) a BMW.

And in FINAL ellipsis the final elements are ellipted:

> I know that we haven't yet set the record straight, but we will (set the record straight).

Recoverability types of ellipsis

Situational ellipsis

12.16 In SITUATIONAL ellipsis, the interpretation may depend on a knowledge of the extralinguistic context. For example, *Get it?* in one situation might be understood to mean the same as *Did you get it?* (*eg*: 'Did you get the letter?') and in another situation as *Do you get it?* (*ie*: 'Do you understand?'). In other cases, the structure will make it clear what has been omitted, *eg it* in *Looks like rain.*

Typically situational ellipsis is initial, especially taking the form of omission of subject and/or operator; *eg*: *(Do you) Want something?* In such cases, which are restricted to familiar (generally spoken) English, the ellipted words are those that normally have weak stress and low pitch.

Here are some examples of situational ellipsis, with an indication of what has been ellipted:

(a) Ellipsis in declarative sentences

> (I) Told you so.
> (You) Want a drink, do you?
> (It) Serves you right.
> (I'm) Sorry I couldn't be there.
> (It's) Good to see you.
> (I'll) See you later.
> (It's a) Pity he won't help.

(b) Ellipsis in interrogative sentences

> (Are you) In trouble?
> (Is there) Anybody in?

(Do you) Want some?
(Have you) Got any money?
(Is) Anything the matter?
(Does) Anybody need a lift?
(Has) Joan finished?
(Is the) Television not working?

NOTE **[a]** Some other cases are less productive and tend to occur with certain expressions. For example, the ellipsis of the article alone in *(The) Fact is I don't know what to do*; the ellipsis of the preposition *of* in *(Of) Course he's there*; and ellipsis that includes the initial syllable of a word in *(I am a) 'Fraid I won't* be there.
[b] In many instances of initial ellipsis, the omission may be at least partly due to subaudibility or some other process of phonological reduction.

Structural ellipsis

12.17 In STRUCTURAL ellipsis, the interpretation depends on knowledge of grammatical structure, as in the ellipsis of the conjunction *that* in [1] and the preposition *for* in [2]:

I believe (that) you are mistaken. [1]
We're staying there (for) another three weeks. ⟨informal⟩ [2]

Many examples are confined to written language. They involve the common omission of determiners, pronouns, operators, and other closed-class words in block language (*cf* 11.22) – *eg* in headlines, book titles, notices – and in such written varieties as lecture notes, diaries, and telegrams:

US heading for new slump. [*ie: The* US *is* heading for *a* new slump.]

NOTE There is no clear dividing line between structural ellipsis and some instances of situational ellipsis given in 12.16, where the structure alone would yield the interpretation.

Textual ellipsis

Categories of textual ellipsis

12.18 In TEXTUAL ellipsis, the interpretation depends on what is said or written in the linguistic context. We distinguish two kinds of ellipsis according to the relative positions of the ellipsis and its antecedent: ANAPHORIC ellipsis and CATAPHORIC ellipsis. In anaphoric ellipsis, the interpretation depends on what comes before:

I'm happy if you are (happy).

In cataphoric ellipsis, on the other hand, the ellipsis depends on what comes after:

Those who prefer (to stay indoors), can stay indoors.

It is often necessary to take account of the larger construction in which the antecedent construction and elliptical construction participate, since some categories of ellipsis are possible only in certain constructions. We therefore distinguish between GENERAL ELLIPSIS, where the functional relation between the elliptical and antecedent constructions is irrelevant, and SPECIAL ELLIPSIS, where the possibilities of omission are determined by that relation (*eg* in coordination). In this chapter we confine ourselves chiefly to general ellipsis, since special ellipsis is more appropriately handled in the chapters dealing with coordination (13.17*ff*), nonfinite and verbless clauses (14.4*ff*), and comparative clauses (15.36*ff*).

General textual ellipsis is typically final and anaphoric. We distinguish two major categories: elliptical noun phrases and antecedent clauses.

General ellipsis

Elliptical noun phrases

12.19 Except in coordination, elliptical noun phrases result from final ellipsis. This means that heads and any postmodifiers tend to be ellipted:

My own camera, like *Peter's* △, is Japanese.
He had to admit that *Sarah's drawings* were as good as *his own* △.
The first expedition to the Antarctic was quickly followed by *another two* △.
Tomorrow's meeting will have to be *our first* and *our last* △.
Although Helen is *the oldest girl in the class*, Julie is *the tallest* △.

Noun-phrase ellipsis, like clause ellipsis (*cf* 12.20*ff*), involves some degree of parallelism between the original construction and the elliptical construction.

The dominance of final ellipsis in noun phrases means that it is possible to omit postmodifiers alone:

Stan spent PÀRT *of his winnings*, and *the rest* △ he saved.
If you need any *of that firewood*, I can give you *plenty* △.

Noun phrases can occur with medial ellipsis if a postmodifier is retained while the head of the phrase is ellipted:

They claim that *Danish butter* is *the finest* △ *in the world.*
That letter was *the last* △ *I ever received from her.*

In other cases one or more modifiers, as well as the head, may be ellipted:

His recent performance of 'Macbeth' is *the best* △ *he has ever done.* [1]
That new thick plastic rope that they sell is *stronger than any other* △ *you can get.* [2]

NOTE [a] In general ellipsis an elliptical noun phrase must retain more than just the postmodifiers:

*Joan prefers *the trios of Mozart*, while I prefer △ *of Haydn*.

We can make the sentence grammatical by inserting the pro-form *those* before *of Haydn*:

Joan prefers *the trios of Mozart*, while I prefer those of *Haydn* △.

Alternatively, we can replace the final prepositional phrase by a genitive:

Joan prefers *the trios of Mozart*, while I prefer *Haydn's* △.

[b] The elliptical phrases in [1] and [2] are ambiguous, according to whether the modifiers are assumed to be ellipted. In [1] it may be *the best performance* or *the best performance of 'Macbeth'*. The ambiguity is multiple in [2], where *any other you can get* may simply be elliptical for *any other rope you can get*, or the ellipsis may include also *plastic* or *thick plastic* or *new thick plastic*. To avoid such ambiguity, one has to repeat the words of the antecedent.

Elliptical clauses

Ellipsis of the predication in finite clauses

12.20 For general ellipsis in the finite clause, as in the noun phrase, the dominant type is final. Typically, the subject and operator (and perhaps other auxiliaries) remain, and the predication is ellipted:

I'm happy if you are △. [1]
If I could have bought a ticket, I would have △. [2]
His father was at Oxford when the Prime Minister was △. [3]
Tom will be playing, but I don't think Martin will (be) △. [4]
I'll do what I can △. [5]
When Marilyn resigns from the committee, I'm sure that a number of other people will △. [6]

NOTE **[a]** If the clause in its unreduced form has no operator, the dummy operator DO is introduced:

I left school when Dennis *did*. [7]

Did, however, in [7] is a pro-form and there is strictly no ellipsis, since the insertion of the predication after *did* would result in an unacceptable sentence:

*I left school when Dennis *did leave school*. [7a]

But there are other constructions with the operator DO that are elliptical:

I don't like living in the country. *Do* you (like living in the country)? [8]
A: Does she like writing for the press?
B: Yes, she *DÒES* (like writing for the press). [9]

In [9] *does* is used as an emphatic operator in both the elliptical and the unreduced constructions.

[b] Unlike adjuncts (8.13) and subjuncts (8.32), disjuncts (8.40) and conjuncts (8.43) are not carried over to the elliptical clause. We can contrast the adjunct *sometimes* with the disjunct *wisely*:

A: Has Bob sometimes walked to work?
B: No, but his sĭster *has*. [= has sometimes walked to work]
A: Bob has wisely walked to work.
B: Well, at least he CLĂIMS he *has*. [= has walked to work]

Similarly, a final auxiliary in the elliptical clause excludes other, contrasting auxiliaries in the antecedent clause:

Not many people could have enjoyed that trip as much as your mother *has*. [= has enjoyed that trip]

Medial ellipsis

12.21 There is genuinely medial ellipsis when a contrasting adverbial occurs in final position:

There are more hungry people in the world today than there were △ in 1900.

In the next example, only the lexical verb is omitted:

I'll gladly pay for the hotel, if you will △ for the food.

Ellipsis of a clause

12.22 A more thoroughgoing reduction involves ellipsis of the whole clause or the whole clause except for an introductory word.

A *wh*-interrogative clause, whether independent or subordinate, may be reduced to the *wh*-word:

A: We're bound to win the prize some day.
B: Yes, but WHÈN △?
Somebody has hidden my notebook, but I don't know WHO/WHỲ/WHÈRE △.

There is also a reduced negative *wh*-question, but this occurs only with *why* and with *wh*-infinitive clauses:

Why NŎT? I don't KNÒW why not.
I don't want to accept, but I don't know how not (to).

A *to*-infinitive clause may be omitted if it functions as the complementation of a verb or adjective (*cf* Chapter 16). An elliptical *to*-infinitive clause may consist of just the introductory unstressed particle *to*:

You can borrow my pen, if you WÁNT to △. [1]
You will speak to who(m)ever I TÈLL you to △. [2]
Somebody ought to help. Shall I ask PÉTER to △? [3]

In the negative, *not* is placed before *to*:

She borrowed my pen, although I told her NŎT to.

To may also be ellipted, and the result is then ellipsis of the whole clause:

You can borrow my pen, if you WÁNT △. [1a]
Somebody ought to help. Shall I ask PÉter △? [3a]

NOTE* The marginal modal auxiliaries *ought to* and *used to*, the modal idiom *have got to*, and semi-auxiliaries such as *be able to, be going to, have to, be supposed to* (*cf* 3.17*f*) must retain the *to*:

We don't save as much money these days as we used to △.
I won't disturb you again unless I have to △.

Appended clauses

12.23 One type of special ellipsis is found in appended clauses. An appended clause is an elliptical clause (usually parenthetical or an afterthought) for which the whole or part of the preceding or interrupted clause constitutes the antecedent:

I caught the train – *just*. [1]
The train arrived – *on time for a change*. [2]

These presuppose that two separate assertions are being made. For example, [1] may be viewed as elliptical for [1a]:

I caught the train – I just caught the train. [1a]

In the examples that follow, only part of the initial clause (the italicized part) acts as the antecedent:

They are meant to wound, perhaps △ to kill.
He is playful, △ even mischievous.

On the related construction of appended coordination, *cf* 13.30.

Bibliographical note

On reduction generally, see Halliday and Hasan (1976).
On pro-forms and substitutes, see Crymes (1968).
On ellipsis, see Greenbaum and Meyer (1982); Gunter (1963).
For further references see the Bibliographical notes for Chapters 13 and 19.

13 Coordination

Syntetic, asyndetic, and polysyndetic coordination

13.1 We distinguish between syndetic (or linked) coordination and asyndetic (or unlinked) coordination. In syndetic coordination, the more usual form, the units are linked by a COORDINATING CONJUNCTION (or, more simply, COORDINATOR) – *and, or, but*:

Slowly and stealthily, he crept towards his victim. [1a]

In asyndetic coordination, coordinators are not present, but could be inserted:

Slowly, stealthily, he crept towards his victim. [1b]

When more than two units are linked by *and* or *or*, it is usual to insert the coordinator once only – between the last two units:

The wind roared, the lightning flashed, *and* the clouds raced across the sky. [2a]

In polysyndetic coordination, however, the coordinator is repeated between each pair of units:

The wind roared, *and* the lightning flashed, *and* the clouds raced across the sky. [2b]

Coordination and subordination

13.2 Both coordination and subordination involve the linking of units; but in coordination the units are on the same syntactic level, whereas in subordination one of the units is a constituent of a superordinate unit. For example in [1] the two clauses linked by the coordinator *but* are main clauses, each of which could be an independent sentence:

They are my neighbours, *but* I don't know them well. [1]

In [2] the subordinate *where*-clause is the direct object of the sentence:

I don't know *where they are staying*. [2]

Similar semantic relationships may be expressed through coordination and subordination, as in the concessive relationship expressed by coordination with *but* in [3a] and subordination with *although* in [3b] and [3c]:

He tried hard, *but* he failed. [3a]
Although he tried hard, he failed. [3b]
He tried hard, *although* he failed. [3c]

A third means of expressing this relationship by coordination is through a conjunct (*cf* 8.43), such as *yet*:

He tried hard, *yet* he failed. [3d]

NOTE Despite its appearance, [3d] illustrates asyndetic coordination. We can make the coordination syndetic by inserting *and*:

He tried hard, *and yet* he failed.

Coordinators

Coordinators identified

13.3 Three conjunctions are clearly coordinators: *and*, *or*, *but*. *And* and *or* are central coordinators, and *but* differs from them in certain respects. On the gradient between 'pure' coordinators and 'pure' subordinators are *for* and *so that* (in the meaning 'with the result that').

Coordinators, subordinators, and conjuncts are all LINKERS. In what follows, we examine six features that apply to the central coordinators *and* and *or* and note whether they apply also to other linkers. At this stage we restrict ourselves mainly to connections between clauses.

Syntactic features of coordinators

(a) Clause coordinators are restricted to clause-initial position

13.4 *And*, *or*, and *but* are restricted to initial position in the second clause:

John plays the guitar, *and* his sister plays the piano.
*John plays the guitar; his sister *and* plays the piano.

This is generally true of both coordinators and subordinators, but it is not true of most conjuncts

John plays the guitar; his sister, *moreover*, plays the piano.

NOTE There are three subordinators (*as*, *that*, and *though*) which are exceptional in that they can occur noninitially (*cf* 15.21 Note [a], 15.26 Note [b]):

Though he is poor, he is happy.
Poor *though* he is, he is happy.

(b) Coordinated clauses are sequentially fixed

13.5 Clauses beginning with *and*, *or*, and *but* are sequentially fixed in relation to the previous clause, and therefore cannot be transposed without producing unacceptable sentences, or at least changing the relationship between the clauses:

They are living in England, *or* they are spending a vacation there.
**Or* they are spending a vacation there, they are living in England.

This is true for coordinators and conjuncts, but not for most subordinators. Contrast the unacceptability of [1a], containing the conjunct *nevertheless*, with the acceptability of [1b], containing the subordinator *although*:

**Nevertheless* John gave it away, Mary wanted it. [1a]
Although Mary wanted it, John gave it away. [1b]

In this respect the subordinators *for* and *so that* resemble coordinators. Contrast:

**For* he was unhappy, he asked to be transferred.
Because he was unhappy, he asked to be transferred.

NOTE Related to the fixed position of the coordinate clause is the fact that when clauses are linked by the coordinators *and*, *or*, and *but* (also by *for* and *so that*), a pronoun in the first clause cannot normally ~~have~~ cataphoric (*ie* forward) reference to a noun phrase in the second clause. For example, *she* in [1a] does not corefer to *my mother*:

She felt ill, but *my mother* said nothing. [1a]

On the other hand, a pronoun can (but need not) have cataphoric reference when it occurs in an initial subordinate clause:

Although *she* felt ill, *my mother* said nothing. [1b]

(c) Coordinators are not preceded by a conjunction

13.6 The coordinators *and*, *or*, and *but* and the subordinators *for* and *so that* ('with the result that') do not allow another conjunction to precede them. Other subordinators as well as conjuncts can usually be preceded by conjunctions (*cf* 13.8):

He was unhappy about it, *and yet* he did as he was told.

(d) Coordinators can link clause constituents

13.7 *And*, *or*, and *but* may link constituents smaller than a clause, for example predicates (*cf* 13.19*ff*):

I may see you tomorrow *or* may phone late in the day.

This feature does not apply to most other linkers:

*He did not want it, *for* was obstinate.

The exceptions are the conjunct *yet* and (in informal spoken English) the conjunct *so* and the time adverb *then* ('after that'):

> They didn't like it, *yet* said nothing.
> They were tired, *so* left early.
> They went home, *then* went straight to bed.

NOTE A subordinator does not allow this feature even when its clause is linked by a coordinator:

> *She didn't say anything about it *because* he was new *and because* looked unwell. [1]

If the second *because* of [1] is omitted, there is a regular permissible case of coordination of predications:

> She didn't say anything about it *because* he was new *and* looked unwell.

(e) Coordinators can link subordinate clauses

13.8 As well as linking two main clauses, *and* and *or* can link subordinate clauses:

> He asked to be transferred, because he was unhappy and {because / although} he saw no prospect of promotion.

> I wonder *whether* you should go and see her or *whether* it is better to write to her.

Such linking is not possible for conjuncts or for the other conjunctions except *but*. *But*, however, is restricted to linking a maximum of two clauses and even so it can link only certain types of subordinate clauses.

> She said *that* John would take them by car *but (that)* they might be late.

(f) Coordinators can link more than two clauses

13.9 *And* and *or* can link more than two clauses, and the construction may then be called one of MULTIPLE COORDINATION. All but the final instance of these two conjunctions can be omitted. Thus:

> The battery may be disconnected, the connections may be loose, *or* the bulb may be faulty.

is interpreted as:

> The battery may be disconnected, *or* the connection may be loose, *or* the bulb may be faulty.

In this respect, *and* and *or* differ from subordinators and conjuncts. They differ even from *but*, since *but* semantically speaking can only link two units at the same level.

Coordination of clauses and lesser constituents

13.10 In 13.4–9 we have focused on the linkage of clauses. But an important distinguishing characteristic of coordinators is that they can also be used to link elements that are parts of clauses, *eg* in [1] linked adjectives that are functioning as subject complement and in [2] linked adjectives that are functioning as premodifier:

The weather will be *cold and cloudy*. [1]
The *warm but windy* weather will continue for several more days. [2]

In this respect, however, some linking words that are not coordinators resemble coordinators. Certain concessive subordinators and conjuncts, in particular, are capable of replacing *but* in [2] and in similar linkings of adjectives and other constituents:

Tim's *squat yet ferocious* bulldog could be heard growling on the patio.
I immediately recognized Sarah's *bold if barely legible* handwriting.
Martin was inclined to boast about his *rich though disreputable* ancestors.
The admiral walked *clumsily, yet with dignity*.

Similarly, *nor* (in its capacity as a correlative after *neither*, *cf* 13.14) can link constituents that are less than clauses:

They were *neither able nor willing* to provide the necessary capital.

In discussing the uses of the central coordinators in 13.11–13 we generally take our examples from clause coordination, but the same semantic relations apply to lesser constituents.

The uses of coordinators

The uses of *and*

13.11 *And* indicates that there is some relation between the contents of the linked clauses. The relation can generally be made explicit by the addition of an adverbial, as indicated in parentheses in the examples:

(a) The event in the second clause is chronologically SEQUENT to that in the first:

I washed the dishes *and (then)* I dried them.

(b) The event in the second clause is a CONSEQUENCE or RESULT of the event in the first:

He heard an explosion *and* he (*therefore*) phoned the police.

(c) The second clause introduces a CONTRAST:

Peter is secretive *and (in contrast)* David is open.

(d) The first clause has CONCESSIVE force:

She tried hard *and (yet)* she failed.

(e) The first clause is a CONDITION of the first:

Give me some money *and (then)* I'll do the shopping.

(f) The second clause makes a point SIMILAR to the first:

A trade agreement should be no problem, *and (similarly)* a cultural exchange could be easily arranged.

(g) The second clause is a 'pure' ADDITION to the first:

He has long hair *and (also)* he often wears jeans.

(h) The second clause adds an appended COMMENT on, or EXPLANATION of, the first:

They disliked John – *and* that's not surprising in view of his behaviour.
There's only one thing to do now – *and* that's to apologize.

NOTE The addition meaning is inclusive in *Don't argue and quarrel* (equivalent to 'Don't argue or quarrel'), whereas the conditional meaning is exclusive in *Don't drink and drive* ('If you drink, don't drive'). *Cf* 13.12.

The uses of *or*

13.12 (a) Typically, *or* is EXCLUSIVE: it excludes the possibility that the contents of both clauses are true or are to be fulfilled:

You can sleep on the couch in the lounge *or* you can go to a hotel.

Even when both alternatives are clearly possible, *or* is normally interpreted as exclusive:

You can boil yourself an egg *or (else)* you can make some sandwiches

The exclusive meaning can be strengthened by the conjuncts *else* or *alternatively*.

(b) Sometimes *or* is INCLUSIVE. We can add a third clause that makes this inclusive meaning explicitly:

You can boil an egg, (*or*) you can make some sandwiches, *or* you can do both.

And can replace *or* in its inclusive meaning.

(c) The alternative expressed by *or* may also be a restatement or a CORRECTIVE to what is said in the first conjoin:

They are enjoying themselves, *or (at least)*/*(rather)* they apPĔAR to be enjoying themselves.

(d) In addition to introducing alternatives as indicated above, *or* may imply a NEGATIVE CONDITION. Thus in:

Switch on the radio *or* we'll miss the news.

the implication can be paraphrased by the negative conditional clause:

Switch on the radio. *If you don't switch on the radio*, we'll miss the news.

The conditional use of *or* is thus the negative analogue of the conditional use of *and* (*cf* 13.11). Unlike *and*, however, *or* typically follows a negative imperative clause:

Don't be too long, *or* you'll miss the bus.

In this case, the most appropriate paraphrase with an *if*-clause is positive instead of negative:

If you are too long, you'll miss the bus.

NOTE [a] In written varieties of the language where precision is required (*eg* in official instructions), the third possibility can be explicitly included by the use of both coordinators (usually written *and/or*):

If the appliance is defective, write directly to the manufacturer *and/or* complain to your local consumer protection service.

[b] Because *and* and *or* contrast with one another in meaning, *or* following a negative is in some respects equivalent to *and*. Thus:

He doesn't have long hair *or* wear jeans. [1]

is logically equivalent to '*He doesn't have long hair* AND *He doesn't wear jeans*'. Conversely:

He doesn't (*both*) have long hair *and* wear jeans. [2]

is logically equivalent to 'EITHER *He doesn't have long hair* OR *He doesn't wear jeans (or both)*'. The reversal of meaning arises because in [1] and [2], the coordinator is within the scope of negation (*cf* 10.38).

The uses of *but*

13.13 *But* expresses a contrast.

(a) The content of the second clause is unexpected in view of the content of the first:

John is poor, *but* he is happy.

In this use, *but* can be replaced by *and yet*.

(b) The second clause expresses in positive terms what the negation in the first clause conveys:

Jane did *not* waste her time before the exam, *but* (*on the contrary*) studied hard every evening.

I am *not* objecting to his morals, *but (rather)* to his manners.

In this use, *but* can be emphasized by the conjuncts *on the contrary* or *rather*. It normally does not link two clauses, but two lesser constituents.

Correlatives

Either . . . or, both . . . and, neither . . . nor

13.14 The three pairs *either or*, *both . . . and*, and *neither . . . nor* are correlatives. The first word is an ENDORSING ITEM and the second is a coordinator.

Either . . . or emphasizes the exclusive meaning of *or* (*cf* 13.12). The linked units may be complete clauses or lesser constituents:

> *Either* the room is too small *or* the piano is too large.
> You may *either* stand up *or* sit down.
> *Either* Sylvia *or* her sister will be staying with us.

Both . . . and emphasizes the additive meaning of *and* (*cf* 13.11):

> David *both* loves Joan *and* wants to marry her.
> This new machine will *both* accelerate the copying process *and* improve the quality of reproduction.
> *Both* Mary *and* Peter washed the dishes.
> The regulations are *both* very precise *and* very detailed.

It also singles out the segregatory meaning of *and* (*cf* 13.23*f*) rather than the combinatory meaning:

> Both David and Joan got divorced. [not from each other]

Neither . . . nor is the negative counterpart of *both . . . and*. It emphasizes that the negation applies to both units:

> David *neither* loves Joan, *nor* wants to marry her.
> Mary was *neither* happy *nor* sad.
> *Neither* Peter *nor* his wife wanted the responsibility.

Unlike *either . . . or*, *both . . . and* and *neither . . . nor* cannot link complete clauses:

> **Both* Mary washed the dishes *and* Peter dried them.
> **Neither* Peter wanted the responsibility, *nor* his wife did.

NOTE [a] When *either . . . or* is within the scope of negation (*cf* 13.12 Note [b]), it is equivalent to *neither . . . nor*, so that these two sentences are similar in meaning:

> He *hasn't* met *either* her mother *or* her father.
> He has met *neither* her mother *nor* her father.

[b] According to a prescriptive tradition, the use of correlative coordinators is unacceptable when there are three or more conjoins:

?We are *both* willing, able, *and* ready to carry out the survey. [1]
?*Either* the Minister, *or* the Under-Secretary, *or* the Permanent Secretary will attend the meeting. [2]
?Tompkins has *neither* the personality, *nor* the energy, *nor* the experience to win this election. [3]

[c] Another prescriptive tradition holds that correlatives should introduce parallel units, *ie* units of equivalent function. Hence in written English [1b] is preferred to [1a], and [2b] or [2c] to [2a]:

?Evelyn is *either* stupid *or* pretends that she is. [1a]
Either Evelyn is stupid *or* she pretends that she is. [1b]
?*I admire *both* the drawings of Rembrandt *and* of Rubens. [2a]
I admire *both* the drawings of Rembrandt *and* those of Rubens. [2b]
I admire the drawings of both Rembrandt *and* Rubens. [2c]

***Nor* and *neither* as negative adverbs**

13.15 *Nor* and *neither*, followed by subject–operator inversion, can be used without being a correlative pair. They generally presuppose that a previous clause is negative either explicitly, as in [1], or implicitly, as in [2] and [3]:

He did *not* receive any assistance from the authorities, *neither* did he believe their assurance that action would soon be taken. ⟨rather formal⟩ [1]
Many people are *only* dimly aware of the ways in which the environment can be protected. *Nor* have governments made sufficient efforts to educate them. ⟨formal⟩ [2]
All the students were obviously very *miserable*. *Nor* were the teachers satisfied with the conditions at the school. ⟨formal⟩ [3]

The morphology of *nor* suggests that it is the equivalent of *or* plus *not*, but in fact both *nor* and *neither* are nearer to being the equivalent of *and* plus *not*:

All the students were obviously very miserable. *And (also)* the teachers were *not* satisfied with the conditions at the school. [3a]

NOTE [a] For many speakers, the adverbs *neither* and *nor* can be linked to a preceding clause by *and* or *but*:

They never forgave him for the insult, { (*and*) / (*but*) } { (*neither*) / (*nor*) } could he rid himself of the feelings of guilt for having spoken that way.

This possibility excludes them from the class of central coordinators (*cf* 13.6).
[b] There is a mixed construction in which *neither* and *nor* behave like additive adverbs in certain respects, but at the same time they are a correlative pair and have the segregatory meaning associated with *both . . . and* (*cf* 13.14):

Sam *neither* has long hair, *nor* does he wear jeans. [1]
Mary was *neither* happy, *nor* was she sad. [2]

Here *neither* appears medially, and *nor* appears in initial position followed by subject–operator inversion, but the units that follow *neither* and *nor* are not parallel, as one would expect them to be in a construction of coordination (*cf* 13.14) Note [c]). Some writers would therefore recast a sentence such as [1] to conform with the normal correlative structure:

Sam *neither* has long hair, *nor* wears jeans. [1a]

Not (only) . . . but

13.16 The negator *not/n't* or the combination *not/n't only* may be correlative with a following *but*:

He did*n't* come to help, *but* to hinder us. ['but rather'] [1]
They *not only* broke into his office and stole his books,
but (they) (*also*) tore up his manuscripts. [2]

Their status as correlatives is even clearer when the negative particle is moved out of its normal position to make the two units parallel:

He came *not* to help, *but* to hinder us. [1a]
Not only did they break into his office and steal his books,
but they also tore up his manuscripts. [2a]
Not Henry, *but* his wife is the owner. [3]

Where the two units are complete clauses, a more dramatic effect is achieved by positioning *not only* initially, with subject–operator inversion, as in [2a].

Simple coordination

13.17 The usual kind of coordination is SIMPLE COORDINATION, in which a single clause or clause constituent is linked to others that are parallel in meaning, in function, and (generally) in form. The coordinated units are CONJOINS, and the resulting combination is a CONJOINT.

There are two ways of analysing simple coordination of clause constituents: (1) We may examine a construction as an elliptical version of clause coordination, noting what elements are ellipted, or (2) we may examine the construction in terms of the units themselves, noting what elements are present. For example, the sentence *Sam has trimmed the hedge and mowed the lawn* can be viewed as the coordination of two clauses in which a subject (*Sam*) and an operator (*has*) have been ellipted from the second clause:

Sam has trimmed the hedge and $_{\triangle}$ mowed the lawn.

Or it can be viewed as a single clause containing two coordinated predications, which together constitute the predication of the clause:

Sam has [[trimmed the hedge] and [mowed the lawn]].

For simple coordination (though less so for other kinds of coordination), there are advantages in adopting the coordination analysis rather than the ellipsis analysis.

Types of simple coordination

Coordination of clauses

13.18 Complete independent clauses may be coordinated:

The winter had come at last, *and* snow lay thick on the ground.

Subordinate finite clauses may be coordinated, so long as they belong to the same function class:

If you pass the examination and *(if) no one else applies*, you are bound to get the job.
[COORDINATED ADVERBIAL CLAUSES]

The Minister believes *that the economy is improving* and *(that) unemployment will soon decrease*.
[COORDINATED NOMINAL *THAT*-CLAUSES]

I didn't know *who she was* or *what she wanted*.
[COORDINATED NOMINAL *WH*-CLAUSES]

Someone *who knows the area*, but *whose home is outside it*, is more likely to be a successful representative.
[COORDINATED RELATIVE CLAUSES]

Nonfinite clauses of the same type and also verbless clauses may be coordinated:

I've asked him *to come this evening* or *(to) phone us tomorrow*.
[COORDINATED *TO*-INFINITIVE CLAUSES]

Samantha is fond of *working at night* and *getting up late in the morning*.
[COORDINATED *-ING* PARTICIPLE CLAUSES]

All the villagers helped to rebuild the houses *damaged by the storm* or *washed away by the floods*.
[COORDINATED *-ED* PARTICIPLE CLAUSES]

With George ill and *(with) the children at home*, Jenny is finding life very difficult.
[COORDINATED VERBLESS CLAUSES]

Coordination of predicates and predications

13.19 Coordination of predicates (as in [1–3]) and coordination of predications (as in [4–8]) are very common:

Peter *ate the fruit* and *drank the beer.* [1]
I *send you my very best wishes*, and *look forward to our next meeting.* [2]
Margaret *is ill*, but *will soon recover.* [3]
Most people will have *read the book* or *seen the film.* [4]
They should have *washed the dishes, dried them, and put them in the cupboard.* [5]
They were *married in 1960*, but *divorced in 1970.* [6]
Are you *working* or *on holiday*? [7]
Why couldn't she *have finished work late* and *still be travelling home*? [8]

In both types of coordination the subject is shared. The most reduced form of the sentence will be preferred, and therefore the predication coordination of [4] will be preferred over the predicate coordination of [4a], where the auxiliaries *will have* are repeated:

Most people *will have read the book* or *will have seen the film.* [4a]

Coordination and the scope of adverbials

13.20 Adverbials, as more peripheral elements of the clause, often stand outside the structure of coordination. We may then say that the conjoins are within the scope of the adverbials:

Yesterday [the sun was very warm] and [the ice melted]. [1]
Unfortunately, we [missed the train] and [had to wait six hours]. [2]
The guests were [walking], [talking], and [drinking wine] *in the garden.* [3]

In [1] and [2] and in the usual reading of [3], the scope of the adverbial extends across the remainder of the sentence. The more complex example of predication coordination in [4] takes place (according to a likely interpretation) within the scope of three adverbials; one in initial, one in medial, and one in final position:

In those days they *often* used to [shoot the birds], [bring them home], [cook them], and [eat them] *on a single day.* [4]

Coordination of noun phrases and their constituents

Noun-phrase coordination

13.21 Two or more noun phrases may be conjoined to form a conjoint noun phrase; for example, the conjoint noun phrases functioning as subject in [1] and as object in [2]:

Some of the staff and all of the students have voted for these changes [1]
On this farm, they keep *cows, sheep, pigs, and a few chickens.* [2]

A conjoint noun phrase may contain general ellipsis of the kinds discussed in 12.19*ff*:

> Which do you prefer; the red *dress*, the green △, or the white△?
> That must be either John's responsibility or Bridget's △.

NOTE [a] It is considered polite to follow the order within a conjoint noun phrase of placing 2nd person pronouns first, and (more importantly) 1st person pronouns last: *Jill and I*; *you and Jill*; *you, Jill and me*.

[b] Like other conjoin types, noun phrases may have asyndetic coordination (*cf* 13.1):

> We had *no friends, no family, no material resources.*

Combinatory and segregatory coordination of noun phrases

13.22 Phrases linked by *and* may express COMBINATORY or SEGREGATORY meaning. The distinction is clearest with noun phrases. When the coordination is segregatory, we can paraphrase it by clause coordination:

> *John and Mary* know the answer. [=John knows the answer, and Mary knows the answer]

When it is combinatory we cannot do so, because the conjoins function in combination with respect to the rest of the clause:

> *John and Mary* make a pleasant couple. [≠ *John makes a pleasant couple, and Mary makes a pleasant couple]

Many conjoint noun phrases are in fact ambiguous between the two interpretations:

> *John and Mary* won a prize.

This may mean that they each won a prize or that the prize was awarded to them jointly.

Further examples of combinatory meaning:

> *John and Mary* played as partners in tennis against *Susan and Bill.*
> *Peter and Bob* separated (from each other).
> *Paula and her brother* look alike.
> *Mary and Paul* are just good friends.
> *John and Peter* have different tastes (from each other).
> *Mary and Susan* are colleagues (of each other).
> *Law and order* is a primary concern of the new administration.

NOTE The distinction between the two meanings applies to plural noun phrases in general. The combinatory meaning in *The three girls look alike* contrasts with the segregatory meaning in *The three girls have a cold*, and *They are married* is ambiguous.

Indicators of segregatory meaning

13.23 Certain markers explicitly indicate that the coordination is segregatory:

both (. . . *and*)	*neither* . . . *nor*	*respectively* ⟨formal⟩
each	*respective* ⟨formal⟩	*apiece* ⟨rather rare⟩

While *John and Mary have won a prize* is ambiguous, we are left in no doubt that two prizes were won in:

John and Mary have *each* won a prize.
John and Mary have won a prize *each*.
Both John and Mary have won a prize.
John and Mary have *both* won a prize.

Similarly, whereas *John and Mary didn't win a prize* is ambiguous, *Neither John nor Mary won a prize* is unambiguously segregatory.

The adjective *respective* premodifies a plural noun phrase to indicate segregatory interpretation. For example, *Jill and Ben visited their respective uncles* can only mean that Jill visited her uncle or uncles and that Ben visited his uncle or uncles, whereas *Jill and Ben visited their uncles* is ambiguous between the *respective* reading and the reading that they visited persons who were uncles to both. The related nouns can be in different clauses or even in different sentences:

Bob and his best friend have had some serious trouble at school lately. Their *respective* parents are going to see the principal about the complaints.

The adverb *respectively* indicates which constituents go with which in the two parallel sets of conjoint phrases:

John, Peter, *and* Robert play football, basketball, *and* baseball *respectively*.
[=John plays football, Peter plays basketball, and Robert plays baseball].
Thomas Arnold *and* his son Matthew were *respectively* the greatest educator *and* the greatest critic of the Victorian age.
[=Thomas Arnold was the greatest educator of the Victorian age, and his son Matthew was the greatest critic of the Victorian age.]

NOTE *Both*, *each*, *respective*, and *apiece* also mark segregatory meaning with plural noun phrases that are not coordinated: *My children have both won a prize*; *The boys visited their respective uncles*.

Coordination within noun phrases

Coordinated noun heads

13.24 When heads are coordinated, the usual interpretation is that the determiner, premodifier, and postmodifier apply to each of the conjoins:

his wife and child [= *his* wife and *his* child]
old men and women [= *old* men and *old* women]
some cows and pigs *from our farm* [= *some* cows *from our farm* and *some* pigs *from our farm*]
the boys and girls *staying at the hostel* [= *the* boys *staying at the hostel* and *the* girls *staying at the hostel*]

It is also possible to interpret some of these phrases as coordinated noun phrases:

old men and women [= women and old men]
some cows and pigs from our farm [= pigs from our farm and some cows]

Coordinated modifiers

13.25 Only the segregatory meaning is ordinarily possible when the coordinated modifiers denote mutually exclusive properties:

old and new *furniture* [= old *furniture* and new furniture]
workers from France and from Italy [= *workers* from France and *workers* from Italy]

Exceptions to this are colour adjectives (as in *red, white, and blue flags*), which allow the combinatory sense 'partly one colour, partly another'. On the other hand, only the combinatory meaning is possible if the head is a singular count noun:

a dishonest and lazy *student* [= a *student* who is both dishonest and lazy]
a *book* on reptiles and amphibians

The same meaning applies when the coordination is asyndetic: *a dishonest, lazy student*.

In other instances there may be ambiguity:

old and valuable books [= books that are old and valuable *or* old books and valuable books]
buses for the Houses of Parliament and for Victoria Station [either the same bus or buses go to both places or a different bus or buses go to each place]

NOTE **[a]** The coordination of determiners (*eg*: *these and those chairs*; *your and my problems*) is comparatively rare, and the synonymous construction with conjoint noun phrases (*eg*: *these chairs and those*; *your problems and mine*) is preferred.

[b] Cardinal numbers are frequently coordinated with *or* in an idiomatic approximative function: *one or two guests* ('a small number'), *five or six letters* ('approximately in the range of five and six'), *ten or twenty students* ('a number from ten to twenty').

[c] The conjoins in a conjoint noun phrase may be words (*eg*: *his wife and child*, where the two nouns share the determiner) or phrases (*eg*: *his wife and his* *child*). They may also be the intermediate units called NOMINAL EXPRESSIONS (*cf* 12.5), *eg*: *eldest child* in *his wife and eldest child*.

[d] The tags *and so on*, *and so forth*, and *et cetera* (Latin = 'and others', abbreviated in writing as *etc*) are abbreviatory devices which are added to a coordinated list, to indicate that the list has not been exhaustively given:

> He packed his clothes, his books, his papers, *etc*.

And so on and *and so forth* (and their combination *and so on and so forth*) are used in the same way, but are restricted to informal use, and tend to occur after coordinated clauses rather than coordinated phrases. A less common phrase of the same kind is *and the like*.

Coordination of other constituents

13.26 All the main variations of constructions that we have noted for clauses and noun phrases are found in the coordination of other constituents. Examples of the coordination of various constituents are given below:

(a) Verb phrases:

> Good cooking *can disguise, but cannot improve* the quality of the ingredients.

(b) Main verbs:

> Many people might have been *killed or injured* by the explosion.

(c) Auxiliaries:

> The country *can and must* recover from its present crisis.

(d) Adjective phrases:

> The journey was *long and extremely arduous*.

(e) Adjective heads:

> I'm feeling *younger and healthier* than I felt for years.

(f) Adverbs:

> She made the announcement *quietly but very confidently*.

(g) Prepositional phrases and prepositions:

> He spoke *for the first motion but against the second motion*.
> She climbed *up and over* the wall.

Part of the prepositional complement may be ellipted in the first conjoin or a subsequent conjoin:

> He spoke *for the first* $\triangle$ *but against the second motion*. ⟨formal⟩
> He spoke *for the first motion but against the second* $\triangle$.

(h) Coordination of subordinators and other clause-introducing words:

> I am prepared to meet them *when and where* they like.
> I am determined to find out *who or what* caused this uproar.

The general principle governing coordination is that the conjoins must belong to the same category in form, function, and meaning. There may, however, be differences in form:

The enemy attacked *quickly* and *with great force*.
You can wash them *manually* or *by using a machine*.
They can call *this week* or *whenever you wish*.
Dennis was *carefree* and *in good health*.

NOTE The order of conjoined words can be influenced by a tendency for the shorter item to come first. This is particularly noticeable in BINOMIALS, *ie* relatively fixed conjoint phrases having two members; *eg*: *big and ugly*, *cup and saucer*. One principle at work here appears to be a principle of rhythmic regularity: *eg* the dactylic rhythm of *'ladies and 'gentlemen*, and the trochaic rhythm of *'men and 'women*, are preferable to the less balanced rhythm of *'gentlemen and 'ladies* and *'women and 'men*. It has also been argued that semantic factors play a role; *eg* that other things being equal, the first position is given to the semantically salient or culturally dominant member, as in *father and son*, *gold and silver*, *great and small*, *this and that*. Phonological constraints have also been suggested: that low vowels come after high ones; that back vowels come after front ones, etc. Whatever the constraints may be, they lead to stereotyped coordinations where the conjoins are in an irreversible order or virtually so; *eg*: *odds and ends*, *bread and butter*, *law and order*, *by hook or by crook*, *through thick and thin*; *knife, fork, and spoon*.

Complex coordination

13.27 COMPLEX COORDINATION is coordination in which the conjoins are combinations of units rather than single units. Such coordination usually requires – and then reinforces – a strong parallelism between the conjoins and for this reason it tends to be associated with a premeditated, written style of English, rather than with informal conversation.

In the first type, each conjoin consists of contiguous elements and the conjoins are combined in final position in the clause. For example:

(a) Indirect object + direct object

We gave *William a book on stamps and Mary a book on painting*.

(b) Object + object complement

Jack painted *the kitchen white and the bathroom blue*.

(c) Object + adverbial

You should serve *the coffee in a mug and the lemonade in a glass*.

The parallelism is weaker when one conjoin contains one or more adverbials that the other conjoin lacks:

He wears *smart clothes and sometimes a yachting cap at weekends.*

Such examples are more likely to occur in informal speech.

13.28 In the second type of complex coordination, the conjoins are not in final position:

Gregory Peck *always* WÁS | *and always* WÌLL *be* | her favourite Hollywood STÀR | [1]
Richard admires, but Margaret despises, the ballyhoo of modern advertising. [2]

The second conjoin is separated by intonation in speech (as in [1]) and by punctuation in writing (as in [2]).

As in the first type of complex coordination, the parallelism is weaker when one conjoin contains one or more adverbials that the other conjoin lacks:

He is, or at least he was, a major composer of modern classical music. [3]
In these days, few people *learn, or indeed see any point in learning*, the languages of Homer and Virgil.
She *thought about, but never revisited*, the haunts of her childhood.

Similar structures are also found with subordination:

Richard admires, *though Margaret despises*, the ballyhoo of modern advertising. [2a]
He is – *even if people don't think he is* – a major composer of modern classical music.
She reads, *though not speaks*, several Oriental languages.

NOTE Because of its medial position and its separation by intonation or punctuation, the second conjoin seems parenthetic.

Gapping

13.29 GAPPING is a type of complex coordination in which a second or subsequent conjoin contains a medial ellipsis, so that the elements in these conjoins are not contiguous. For example:

(a) Subject + object

One girl has written a poem, and *the other* △ *a short story.*

(b) Subject + adverbial

Smith completed the course in thirty-five minutes, and *Johnson* △ *in thirty-seven.*

(c) Subject + complement

Jane has looked more healthy, and *Maurice* ^ *more relaxed*, since their vacation.

NOTE Coordination with gapping is more difficult to understand than coordination without gapping, and therefore nongapped interpretations are more likely to be intended where both are possible. For example, the reading of [1] as [1a] is more likely than as [1b]:

Barbara gave Sue a magnolia and Ada a camellia. [1]
[= Barbara gave Sue a magnolia and Barbara gave Ada a camellia] [1a]
[= Barbara gave Sue a magnolia and Ada gave Sue a camellia] [1b]

Appended coordination

13.30 APPENDED COORDINATION, which is characteristic of informal speech, occurs when an elliptical clause (involving one element or contiguous elements) is appended to a previous clause (*cf* appended clauses, 12.23):

John writes extremely well – and SÀLly, TÒO.
My mother plays badminton, and sometimes even tennis.
He got a bike for his birthday, and a book and a pen.
His left hook could fell the champion, and indeed any other boxer in his class.

NOTE **[a]** With *or* and *but*, appended coordination is also likely to occur in careful speech and writing:

I am not sure whether JǍNE wrote the letter, or SÀLly
PĚTer plays football, but not JÒHN.

[b] The second conjoin may be interpolated as a parenthesis, in which case the structure is a type of complex coordination (*cf* 13.28):

John – and Sally, too – writes extremely well.
She can, and probably will, beat the world record.

Pseudo-coordination

13.31 There are several types of PSEUDO-COORDINATION, mostly found in informal speech:

(a) The coordination of two verbs that has an idiomatic function similar to that of a catenative construction (*cf* 3.18 Note):

I'll *try and come* tomorrow. [= try to come]
They've *gone and upset* her again.
They *sat and talked* about the old times. [= sat talking]

(b) The coordination of two adjectives of which the first functions as an intensifier of the second:

This room is *nice and warm*. [= comfortably warm]
His speech was *nice and short*.
It was *lovely and cool* in there.

Some speakers ⟨esp in AmE⟩ use *good* in the same way:

The road is *good and long*.

even where the adjectival form following *and* is used as an adverb:

I hit him *good and hard*.
She drove *good and fast*.

(c) The coordination of identical comparative forms of adjectives, adverbs, and determiners (usually just two conjoins) that expresses a continuing increase in degree:

She felt *more and more* angry. [= increasingly angry]
The car went *slower and slower*.

(d) The coordination of two or more identical forms of verbs and adverbs that expresses continuation or repetition:

He *talked and talked and talked*. [= talked for a very long time]
They *knocked and knocked*. [= knocked repeatedly]
She talked *on and on and on*. [= continuously]

(e) The coordination of two identical nouns to indicate different kinds:

There are *teachers and teachers*. [roughly: 'good and bad teachers']
You can find *doctors and doctors*. [roughly: 'good and bad doctors']

(f) The coordination of three or more identical nouns to indicate a large number or quantity:

We saw *dogs and dogs and dogs* all over the place.
There was nothing but *rain, rain, rain* from one week to the next.

Quasi-coordination

13.32 Most of the QUASI-COORDINATORS are related to comparative forms: *as well as, as much as, rather than, more than*. They sometimes resemble coordinators in that they link a variety of constituents:

She *publishes as well as prints* her own books.
The speech was addressed *to the employers as much as to the strikers.*
He is to be *pitied rather than disliked.*

They may also have a prepositional or subordinating role in that the unit that they introduce is an adverbial and can be placed in initial or final position:

As well as printing the books, he publishes them.
I'm going to forget the whole affair, *rather than cause trouble.*

These quasi-coordinators are not fully coordinative, since in subject position they normally do not cause plural concord if the first noun phrase is singular:

John, *as much as his brothers,* was responsible for the loss.

In this they resemble prepositions such as *with, in addition to* and *after* more than coordinators like *and*; compare:

John, *with his brothers,* was responsible for the loss.

Bibliographical note

General studies of coordination include: Dik (1968); Dougherty (1970–71); Schachter (1977); Stockwell et al. (1973, Ch. 6).

On coordination in relation to subordination and other kinds of connectivity, see Greenbaum (1969, 1988); Halliday and Hasan (1976); Talmy (1978).

On coordination in relation to ellipsis/reduction, see Greenbaum and Meyer (1982); Harries–Delisle (1978); Hudson (1976); Meyer (1979); Sanders (1977).

On coordination of noun phrases, see Hudson (1970).

14 The complex sentence

Subordinate and superordinate clauses

14.1 A COMPLEX sentence is like a simple sentence in that it consists of only one MAIN clause, but unlike a simple sentence it has one or more SUBORDINATE clauses functioning as an element of the sentence. For example, [1] is a simple sentence in that the sentence consists of one main clause without any subordinate clauses:

I reject her conclusions. [1]

On the other hand, [2] is a complex sentence because the main clause contains a subordinate clause functioning as an adverbial:

Although I admire her reasoning, I reject her conclusions. [2]

The subject (*I*), verb (*reject*), and direct object (*her conclusions*) are identical in the main clauses (or sentences) in [1] and [2]. The subordinate clause has its own subject (*I*), verb (*admire*), and direct object (*her reasoning*). The main clause is SUPERORDINATE to the subordinate clause that it contains.

In [3] we have a more complicated example:

He predicted that he would discover the tiny particle
when he conducted his next experiment. [3]

The sentence is a complex sentence consisting of one main clause. The main clause is superordinate to the subordinate *that*-clause (which is a direct object) that continues to the end of the sentence. The *that*-clause is in turn superordinate to the subordinate *when*-clause (which is an adverbial) that extends from *when* to the end of the sentence. The hierarchy of superordination and subordination is displayed in Fig. 14.1.

For certain purposes it is useful to distinguish between a subordinate clause and the MATRIX clause. The matrix clause is the superordinate clause minus its subordinate clause. For example, in [4] the matrix clause is *I'll lend you some money*:

I'll lend you some money if you don't have any money on you. [4]

NOTE Some grammarians use *main clause* in the sense that we give to *matrix clause*.

Fig 14.1

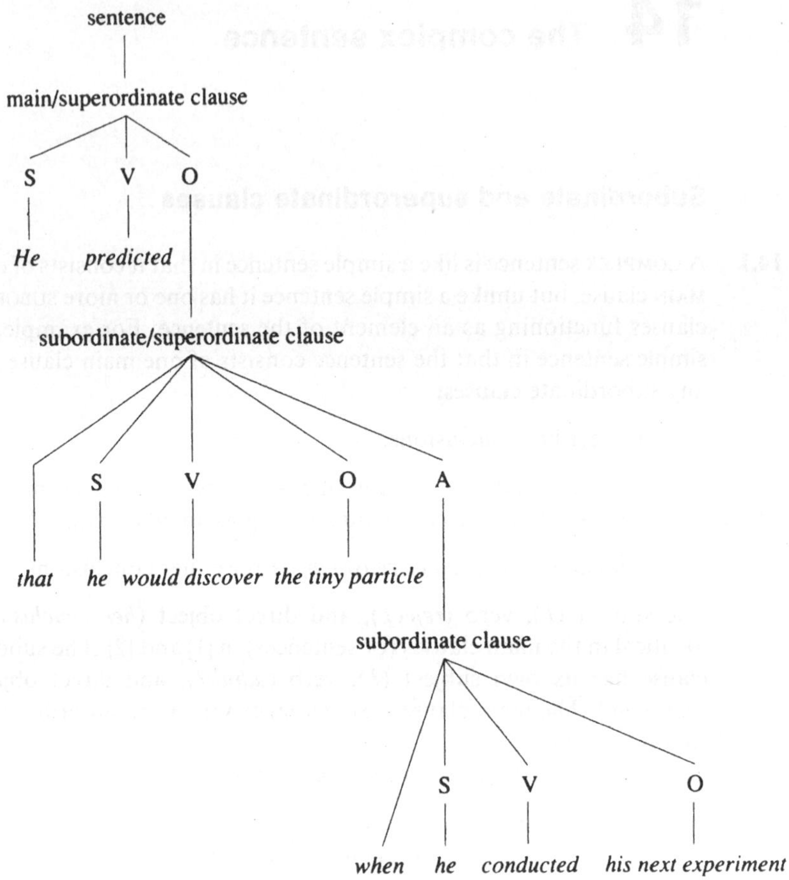

Fig 14.1 Superordinate and subordinate clauses

Subordination and coordination

14.2 The device of subordination enables us to construct a multiple hierarchy of clauses, one within the other, sometimes resulting in extremely involved sentences. Further complexity and structural variability are provided by the interrelation of subordination and coordination. Each main clause in a compound sentence may include one or more subordinate clauses, each of which may in turn include subordinate clauses. For example, [1] displays a compound sentence in which two main clauses are coordinated:

> I think *that your new position demands sensitive judgments*
> and I would hope *that you will mature as the years go by.* [1]

Each main clause has a subordinate *that*-clause as direct object. The *that*-clause in the second main clause is superordinate to an *as*-clause, which functions as adverbial in the *that*-clause.

On the other hand, the complex sentence in [2] contains two subordinate clauses that are coordinated and as a unit function as direct object of the sentence:

> I have heard *that you are a car mechanic and that your brother is a plumber.* [2]

NOTE A subordinate clause may function as a constituent of a phrase, for example as a relative clause acting as a postmodifier in a noun phrase:

> The school *which my children attend* is within walking distance.

The noun phrase is complex, but we do not consider that the sentence is therefore a complex sentence, since the subordinate clause does not function as a constituent of the sentence.

Finite, nonfinite, and verbless clauses

14.3 We recognize three main structural classes of clauses:

FINITE CLAUSE: a clause whose verb element is finite (such as *takes, took, can work, has worked, is writing, was written*; *cf* 3.3, 3.19); *eg*:

> I can't go out with you *because I am studying this evening.*

NONFINITE CLAUSE: a clause whose verb element is nonfinite (such as *to work, having worked, taken*; *cf* 3.3, 3.20).; *eg*:

> *Knowing my temper*, I didn't reply.

VERBLESS CLAUSE: a clause that does not have a verb element, *eg*:

> *Although always helpful*, he was not much liked.

We recognize nonfinite and verbless structures as clauses because we can analyse their internal structure into the same functional elements that we distinguish in finite clauses. Consider, for example, the analysis of the nonfinite clause in:

> *Knowing* [V] *my temper* [O_d], I didn't reply.

The analysis depends on the analogy with the corresponding finite clause:

> *I* [S] *know* [V] *my temper* [O_d].

Similarly, the verbless clause *although always helpful* in:

> *Although* [conj] *always* [A] *helpful* [C_s], he was not much liked.

is analysed as in the corresponding finite clause:

> *Although* [conj] *he* [S] *was* [V] *always* [A] *helpful* [C_s], he was not much liked.

NOTE One structural type of clause may be embedded within another:

> *Too nervous to reply after other speakers had praised her devotion to duty,* Margaret indicated that she would speak later.

The italicized subordinate clause is a verbless clause that contains a subordinate nonfinite clause (beginning *to reply*) that in turn contains a subordinate finite clause (beginning *after other speakers*).

Nonfinite clauses

14.4 The classes of nonfinite verb phrase serve to distinguish four structural subclasses of nonfinite verb clauses:

(i) TO-INFINITIVE
Without subject: The best thing would be *to tell everybody*.
With subject: The best thing would be *for you to tell everybody*.

(ii) BARE INFINITIVE
Without subject: All I did was *hit him on the head*.
With subject: *Rather than you do the job*, I'd prefer to finish it myself.

(iii) -ING PARTICIPLE
Without subject: *Leaving the room*, he tripped over the mat.
With subject: *Her aunt having left the room*, I asked Ann for some personal help.

(iv) -ED PARTICIPLE
Without subject: *Covered with confusion*, they apologized abjectly.
With subject: *The discussion completed*, the chairman adjourned the meeting for half an hour.

Subclasses (i) and (iii) are used most frequently, especially (iii) without subject; subclass (ii) is relatively rare.

NOTE In negative nonfinite clauses, the negative particle is generally positioned before the verb or the *to* of the infinitive:

> It's his fault for *not* doing anything about it.
> The wisest policy is (for us) *not* to interfere.

On the split infinitive, *cf* 8.11 Note.

14.5 Because nonfinite clauses lack tense markers and modal auxiliaries and frequently lack a subject and a subordinating conjunction, they are valuable as a means of syntactic compression. Certain kinds of nonfinite clause are particularly favoured in written prose, where the writer has the leisure to revise for compactness. We recover meanings associated with tense, aspect, and mood from the sentential context. We can also normally see a correspondence with a finite clause that has a form of the verb *be* and a pronoun subject with the same reference as a noun or pronoun in the same sentence. For the sentences in [1–4], one might make the insertions shown in parentheses:

When (she was) *questioned*, she denied being a member of the group. [1]
(Since/Because/As they were) *considered works of art*, they were admitted into the country without customs duties. [2]
(If it is) *kept in the refrigerator*, the drug should remain effective for at least three months. [3]
(Since/After he was) *allowed unusual privileges*, the prisoner seemed to enjoy his captivity. [4]

On the other hand, [5] shows how the advantage of compactness must be balanced against the danger of ambiguity; for the absence of a subject leaves doubt as to which nearby nominal element is notionally the subject:

We met you (*when you?/we? were*) leaving the room. [5]

With infinitive clauses, a corresponding finite clause also enables one to identify an understood subject:

I expected *to go.* ~ I expected that *I would go.*
I expected *him to go.* ~ I expected that *he would go.*

When no referential link with a nominal can be discovered in the linguistic context, an indefinite subject may be inferred, or else the 'I' of the speaker:

To be an administrator is to have the worst job in the world. ['For a person to be . . .]
It's hard work *to be a student.* [indefinite subject, eg: *anyone*]
It's hard work, *to be honest.* [*I* as subject]

NOTE Auxiliary *have* is sometimes used in *to*-infinitive clauses (*to have happened*) and *-ing* participle clauses (*having happened*) to indicate anteriority in time.

Verbless clauses

14.6 With verbless clauses it is usually possible to postulate a missing form of the verb *be* and to recover the subject, when omitted, from the context:

Whether right or wrong, he always comes off worst in argument. ['whether *he is* right or wrong']
One should avoid taking a trip abroad in August *where possible.* ['where *it is* possible']

When a clause has a subject, only the verb has to be recovered:

Seventy-three people have been drowned in the area, *many of them children*. ['many of them being children']
There he stood, *a tray in each hand*. ['having a tray in each hand']

The subject is often introduced by *with* or *without* (*cf* 14.8 Note [b]):

With the children at school, we can't take our vacations when we want to.
Without you at my side, I am not willing to answer questions.

Since it is usually possible to interpret the clause as having an omitted form of the verb *be*, the verbless clause is limited to the two clause-types *SVC* and *SVA*, with or without a subordinator (*sub*):

I do not wish to describe his assertions, *some of them highly offensive*. [S (V) C]
Though somewhat edgy, she said she would stay a little longer. sub [S (V) C]
Mavis sat in the front seat, *her hands in her lap*. [S (V) A]
While at college, he was a prominent member of the dramatic society. sub [(S V) A]

Formal indicators of subordination

14.7 Subordination is generally marked by a signal in the subordinate clause. The signal may be of various kinds: a subordinating conjunction, a *wh*-element, the item *that*, subject–operator inversion in declarative clauses, or (negatively) the absence of a finite verb.

NOTE More than one subordination signal may cooccur in the same subordinate clause. For example, a nonfinite or verbless clause may be introduced by a subordinating conjunction.

Subordinators

14.8 SUBORDINATORS (or, more fully, SUBORDINATING CONJUNCTIONS) are the most important formal device of subordination, particularly for finite clauses. Like prepositions, which they resemble in having a relating function, subordinators forming the core of the class consist of a single word, but there is a large range of multi-word subordinators which function, to varying degrees, like a single conjunction. In addition, there is a small class of correlative subordinators, which combine two markers of subordination, one being a subordinator.

Single-word subordinators

after, *although*, *as*, *because*, *before*, *directly* ⟨informal, esp BrE⟩, *for*, *if*, *immediately* ⟨informal, esp BrE⟩, *lest* ⟨esp AmE⟩, *like*

⟨informal, esp AmE⟩, *once, since, that, though, till, unless, until, when, whenever, where, whereas, whereupon, wherever, while, whilst* ⟨esp BrE⟩

Multi-word subordinators

ending with *that*:

but that, in that, in order that, insofar that ⟨informal, rare⟩, *in the event that, save that* ⟨literary⟩, *such that*

ending with optional *that*:

(a) participle form:

assuming, considering, excepting, given, granted,
granting, provided, providing, seeing, supposing } (*that*)

(b) others:

except, for all,
now, so } (*that*)

ending with *as*:

according as, as far as, as long as, as soon as, forasmuch as ⟨formal⟩, *inasmuch as* ⟨formal⟩, *insofar as, insomuch as* ⟨formal⟩

Others:

as if, as though, in case

Correlative subordinators

as ... *so*

as
so
such } ... *as*

so
such } ... *that*

less
more (/*-er*) } ... *than*

no sooner than ... *than, when* ⟨informal⟩

barely
hardly
scarcely } ... *when, than,* ⟨informal⟩

the ... *the*

whether
if } ... *or*

NOTE [a] There are also optional conjuncts that endorse the meaning of a subordinator that introduces the preceding clause:

although
even if
(even) though
while
} . . . *yet, nevertheless,* etc

if
once
since [reason]
unless
} . . . *then*

because
seeing (that)
} . . . *therefore*

[b] Nonfinite clauses (except bare infinitive clauses) and verbless clauses may have the subordinators *with* and *without*, which are required to introduce the subject:

Without you to consult, I would be completely lost.
With the mortgage paid, they could afford to go abroad for their vacation.
Don't walk around *with your shirt hanging out*.
With you as my friend, I don't need enemies.

Occasionally *without* is used with *-ing* clauses when there is no subject:

Without mentioning any names, someone has been gossiping to the boss about you.

Compare also *What with (paying) my mortgage and my taxes, I have no money to spare for luxuries.*
[c] Bare infinitive clauses are limited to the two synonymous subordinators *rather than* and *sooner than*:

He paid the fine *rather than appeal to a higher court.*

As a subordinator with infinitive clauses, *for* is restricted to clauses with their own subject and indeed is often obligatory (*cf* 15.9):

It would be an absurd idea *for them to move to another house at this stage of their careers.*

Marginal subordinators

14.9 There are also three types of borderline cases of multi-word subordinators: (1) habitual combinations of a subordinator with a preceding or following adverb (*eg*: *even if, if only*); (2) temporal noun phrases (*eg*: *the moment (that), every time (that)*), but the following clause is better analysed as a restrictive relative clause; (3) prepositional phrases ending in *the fact that* (*eg*: *because of the fact that, in spite of the fact that*), but the subordinate clause is better analysed as in apposition to the preceding noun phrase.

Other indicators of subordination

14.10 We now turn to other indicators of subordination apart from subordinators.

(i) *Wh*-elements are initial markers of subordination in subordinate interrogative clauses (*cf* 15.4*f*) and subordinate exclamative clauses (*cf* 15.6), in *wh*-relative clauses (*cf* 15.7*f*, 15.33, 17.5*ff*), and in conditional–concessive clauses (15.22*f*).

(ii) The relative pronoun *that*, which can often replace *wh*-pronouns, is a subordination marker in restrictive relative clauses (*cf* 17.8*f*).

(iii) Subject–operator inversion is a marker of subordination in certain clauses, particularly in conditional clauses (*cf* 15.19 Note [c]). It is typical of a literary and elevated style. The operators that permit the inversion are *had*, *were*, *should*, and (less commonly) *could* and *might*:

Were she here, she would support the motion.

Inversion of a different kind – the fronting of the whole or part of the predication – may occur with the subordinators *as*, *though* and *that* in concessive and reason clauses (*cf* 15.21 Note [a], 15.26 Note [b]).

Eloquent though she was, she could not persuade them.

(iv) The absence of a finite verb is itself an indicator of subordination, since nonfinite and verbless clauses are generally subordinate (but *cf* 11.21).

NOTE There are three types of subordinate clauses that have no clear indicator of subordination within them:

(a) Nominal *that*-clauses allow the omission of *that* in certain contexts (*cf* 15.3), but they may be said to be recognizable as subordinate through the potentiality for the insertion of *that*:

I suppose *(that) I can use your phone*.

(b) Zero relative clauses (*cf* 17.8*f*) have no overt marker of subordination, but they are generally structurally deficient:

I can't find the note *you sent me*.

You sent me in this example lacks a direct object, since *me* is intended as the indirect object (= 'to me').

(c) Some comment clauses (*cf* 15.32) have no overt marker of subordination, but they – like zero relative clauses – generally lack an obligatory complementation of the verb:

I have no alternative, *I suppose*.

The verb phrase in subordinate clauses

The present tense in adverbial and nominal clauses

14.11 The simple present is commonly used in preference to the auxiliary *will* or *shall* in certain types of adverbial clauses to express future meaning:

When she *arrives*, the band will play the National Anthem.
Even if tomorrow's match *is* cancelled, Lancashire will still be at the top of the league.
While I *am* away, the children will look after the house.
Whether or not they *win* this battle, they won't win the war.
Whatever they *say*, I won't pay.
Next time I'll do as he *says*.
The harder you *exercise*, the better you'll feel.

The subordinators chiefly involved belong to the temporal, conditional, and conditional–concessive categories.

Nominal *that*- and *wh*-clauses tend to contain the simple present when the matrix clause (as well as the subordinate clause) refers to the future; but when the matrix clause refers to the present, *will* is likely to be used in the subordinate clause. Contrast:

In a few minutes I'll ask him what he *wants* tomorrow.
The question is what he *will want* tomorrow.

However, there are exceptional verb constructions like *hope*, *bet*, *see (to it)*, *take care*, *be careful*, and (both in the imperative) *suppose* and *assume*, after which the simple present is often or (for *take care* and *be careful*) regularly used:

I hope that the parcel *comes* in time. [also *will come*]
Suppose he *loses* his way. [also *will lose*]
Take care that she *doesn't* fall.

NOTE *Will* and *won't* occur in adverbial clauses, particularly in *if*-clauses, in certain uses:

(i) Where the modals have a volitional meaning:

If you'*ll help* us, we can finish early. ['are willing to']
If you *won't help* us, all our plans will be ruined. ['refuse to']

(ii) Where the modals express timeless and habitual prediction:

If drugs *will cure* him, this drug should do the job.
If sugar *will dissolve* in a hot liquid, this chemical will do so too.

(iii) Where the modals express the present predictability of the occurrence or nonoccurrence of a future event:

If you *won't arrive* before six, I can't meet you. ['If you won't be arriving before six'] [1]

If the game *won't be finished* until ten, I'll spend the night at your place. ['If the game is not going to be finished until ten'] [2]

The matrix clause conveys the consequence of the present predictability. In [1] and [2] the consequence is a present decision on a future action.

The hypothetical past and hypothetical past perfect

14.12 The verbs in hypothetical conditional clauses are backshifted (*cf* 14.18), the past tense form being used for present and future time reference and the past perfect form for past time reference. When these forms have such hypothetical implications we term them HYPOTHETICAL PAST and HYPOTHETICAL PAST PERFECT. The general rule for verbs in both clauses of hypothetical conditions may be expressed as in Table 14.12.

***Table* 14.12: Verbs in hypothetical conditions**

	CONDITIONAL CLAUSE	MATRIX CLAUSE
Present and future reference	HYPOTHETICAL PAST	PAST MODAL
Past reference	HYPOTHETICAL PAST PERFECT	PAST PERFECT MODAL

The modal most commonly used in the matrix clause is *would*. It is used to express the hypothetical implication, without necessarily any other modal implications:

If she {*tried* / *were to try*} harder next time, she *would pass* the examination.
[future reference: 'but I expect she won't try harder']
If they *were* alive, they *would be* moving around.
[present reference: 'but I assume they are not alive']
If they *had invited* him to the conference, he *would have attended.*
[past reference: 'but they didn't invite him']

As the bracketed implications indicate, the hypothetical meaning is more absolute in the past, and amounts to an implied rejection of the condition; whereas with present and future reference the meaning may be merely one of negative expectation or assumption, the positive not being ruled out completely.

Hypothetical past or past perfect are obligatory in certain other constructions that have hypothetical meaning:

It's time you *were* in bed.
I wish this bus *went* to the university.
If only I *had listened* to my parents!

They are optional with other constructions that also have hypothetical meaning, where the simple present is an alternative:

He acts as if he *knew* you.
It's not as though we *were* poor.
Suppose we *told* her the truth.
Imagine your child *played* truant.
I'd rather we *had* dinner now.

Generally a negative inference can be drawn, which is more strongly negative with the hypothetical past perfect. Thus *If only I had listened to my parents* implies 'I did not listen to my parents', and *He acts as if he knew you* implies the expectation 'He doesn't know you'. In *I'd rather we had dinner now*, the hypothetical past may express tentative politeness rather than hypothetical meaning.

NOTE When modal auxiliaries are used in hypothetical conditional clauses they combine with past and past perfect:

If you *could* type, you would save a lot of money.
If she *would have* agreed, I would have married her.

In the matrix clause they replace *would*, since two modal auxiliaries cannot cooccur:

If we had enough money, we *could* buy a computer.
If he had apologized, you *should have* done so too.

The present and past subjunctive

14.13 The present subjunctive (*cf* 3.23*f*) is used in *that*-clauses (especially in AmE), even if the matrix verb is past, after verbs, adjectives, or nouns that express a necessity, plan, or intention for the future:

Congress has voted that the present law *be* maintained. [1]

We insisted that $\left\{\begin{matrix}\text{he}\\ \text{they}\end{matrix}\right\}$ *leave* at once. [2]

They expressed the wish that $\left\{\begin{matrix}\text{she}\\ \text{I}\end{matrix}\right\}$ *accept* the award. [3]

It is essential that a meeting *be* convened this week. [4]

In BrE, putative *should* (*cf* 14.14) with infinitive is more common. In both AmE and (especially) BrE, indicative forms are also often used in this construction; for example, *left* in [2] and *is* in [4].

The past (or *were*-) subjunctive (*cf* 3.23*f*) is used in formal style in hypothetical conditional clauses and in other constructions with hypothetical meaning exemplified in 14.12:

> I wish she *were* married.
> If only I *were* not so nervous.
> If she *were* here, she would speak on my behalf.
> The stuffed dog barked as if it *were* a real one.
> Suppose he *were* lost.
> I'd rather I *were* in bed.

In nonformal styles, the hypothetical past (*cf* 14.12) replaces subjunctive *were*. In all the above examples, the hypothetical past would be *was*.

NOTE [a] The present subjunctive is used very occasionally, and generally in formal style, in open conditional clauses (*cf* 15.19) and in concessive clauses (*cf* 15.21):

> Whether she *be* right or wrong, she will have my unswerving support.

More usually, the simple present indicative is used.

Clauses of concession and purpose may also very occasionally in formal style contain a present subjunctive (especially in AmE) to express putative meaning (*cf* 14.14):

> Though he *be* the President himself, he shall hear us. ['Though he *is* . . .']

Contrast the use of the past subjunctive for hypothetical meaning in *Though he were the President himself, he should hear us*, where the implication is that he is not the President.

The more usual verb forms for the putative meaning in *though*-clauses are the simple present indicative or putative *should* followed by the infinitive. Clauses of purpose require modal auxiliaries, and therefore only the *should*-construction is a possible alternative.

[b] In nonformal styles, the hypothetical past *was* replaces subjunctive *were* (*eg*: *I wish she was not married*). The present indicative is a possible alternative after *as if* and *as though* when the reference is to present time (*eg*: *The stuffed dog barks as if it is a real one*) and after imperatives *suppose* and *imagine*.

Putative *should*

14.14 The modal auxiliary *should* is used extensively (esp in BrE) in *that*-clauses to convey the notion of a 'putative' situation, which is recognized as possibly existing or coming into existence. Contrast:

> I'm surprised that he *should feel* lonely. [1]
> I'm surprised that he *feels* lonely. [2]

While [1] questions the loneliness, [2] accepts it as true. Here, as often, the difference is mainly one of nuance, since the factual bias of the matrix clause overrides the doubt otherwise implicit in the *should*-construction. On the other hand, the nonfactuality is clearer in these examples:

> It worries me that their only child *should travel* alone. [3]
> It's unthinkable that they *should* ever *deny* my requests. [4]

I prefer that she *should drive*. [5]
I'm anxious that I *shouldn't be* in the way. [6]
They've arranged that I *should absent* myself for part of the committee meeting. [7]
I can understand their eagerness that you *should be* the main speaker. [8]

The expressions in the matrix clause may convey an emotional reaction (for example, surprise or worry), as in [1–4], or the notions of necessity, plan, or intention for the future, as in [5–8]. For [5–8], the present subjunctive is preferred in AmE (*cf* 14.13).

The perfect with temporal *since*-clauses

14.15 A temporal *since*-clause generally requires the present perfect in the matrix clause when the whole construction refers to a stretch of time up to (and potentially including) the present:

I *have lost* ten pounds since I started swimming. [1]
Since leaving home, Larry *has written* to his parents just once. [2]

In informal AmE, and increasingly in informal BrE, nonperfect forms are commonly used in the matrix clauses; for example, *lost* instead of *have lost* in [1], and *wrote* instead of *have written* in [2].

When the whole construction refers to a stretch of time up to (and potentially including) the present, the verb in the *since*-clause may be the simple past or the present perfect. The simple past is used when the *since*-clause refers to a point of time marking the beginning of the situation:

She has been talking since she *was* one year old.
Since I *saw* her last, she has dyed her hair.
Derek hasn't stopped talking since he *arrived*.

The present perfect is used in both clauses when the *since*-clause refers to a period of time lasting to the present:

Max has been tense since he's *been taking* drugs.
Since I *have been* here, I haven't left my seat.
Since I'*ve known* Caroline, she has been interested in athletics.
I've had a dog ever since I'*ve owned* a house.
I've gone to concerts ever since I'*ve lived* in Edinburgh.

When the whole period is set in past time, the past perfect or the simple past is used in both clauses:

Since the country (*had*) *achieved* independence, it (had) revised its constitution twice.

Since he {*had known* / *knew*} her, she {had been / was} a journalist.

The perfect with other temporal clauses

14.16 When an *after*-clause or a *when*-clause refers to a sequence of two past events, the verb in the temporal clause may be in the past perfect, though it is more commonly in the simple past:

We ate our meal $\left\{\begin{array}{l}\text{after}\\ \text{when}\end{array}\right\}$ we $\left\{\begin{array}{l}\text{returned}\\ \text{had returned}\end{array}\right\}$ from the game.

All four forms of these sentences are acceptable, and mean roughly the same. The only difference is that *when* and the simple past (probably the most popular choice) suggests that the one event follows immediately on the other in sequence. There may, however, be a contrast when the subordinator is *when* if the predication in the *when*-clause is durative:

They walked out when I $\left\{\begin{array}{l}\textit{gave}\\ \textit{had given}\end{array}\right\}$ the lecture.

The variant with the simple past would normally mean 'as soon as I started giving the lecture' or 'during the time I was giving the lecture', whereas that with the past perfect means 'after the lecture was over'.

The present perfect is common in temporal and conditional clauses when the clauses refer to a sequence of future events:

When they'*ve scored* their next goal, we'll go home.
As soon as I'*ve retired*, I'll buy a cottage in the country.
After they *have left*, we can smoke.
If I'*ve written* the paper before Monday, I'll call you.

In each case, the simple present is an alternative.

NOTE These four sentences seem to be equivalent in meaning:

I *saw* him before he *saw* me. [1]
I *had seen* him before he *saw* me. [2]
I *saw* him before he *had seen* me. [3]
I *had seen* him before he *had seen* me. [4]

Sentence [3] appears to be paradoxical in that the second in the succession of events is marked with the past perfect. One explanation is that the *before*-clause in [3], and perhaps also in [4], is nonfactual; *ie* 'He did not get a chance to see me'. But it is also possible that the meaning of the subordinator *before* has influenced the use of the past perfect as one of the choices of verb forms, or possibly there is an analogy with the use of the past perfect in an *after*-clause.

Direct and indirect speech

14.17 DIRECT SPEECH purports to give the exact words that someone utters or has uttered in speech or writing. INDIRECT SPEECH, on the other hand, conveys a report of what has been said or written, but does so in the words of a subsequent reporter. Contrast the direct speech in [1] with two possible versions in indirect speech as given in [1a] and [1b]:

> David said to me after the meeting, 'In my opinion, the arguments in favour of radical changes in the curriculum are not convincing.' [1]
>
> David said to me after the meeting that in his opinion the arguments in favour of radical changes in the curriculum were not convincing. [1a]
>
> David told me after the meeting that he remained opposed to any major changes in the curriculum. [1b]

The report may be a representation of mental activity, which by its nature is unspoken. Thus [2] and [2a] contain direct speech and indirect speech respectively:

> 'Should I tell them now,' I thought to myself, 'or should I wait until they're in a better mood?' [2]
>
> He asked himself whether he should tell them then or wait until they were in a better mood. [2a]

Direct speech is usually signalled by being enclosed in quotation marks, as in [1] and [2]. The reporting clause may occur before, within, or after the direct speech.

When the reporting clause is positioned medially or finally, subject–verb inversion may occur if the verb is in the simple present or simple past:

> 'I wonder,' { *John said* / *he said* / *said John* }, 'whether I can borrow your bicycle'. [3]
>
> 'The radio is too loud,' { *Elizabeth complained.* / *she complained.* / *complained Elizabeth.* } [4]

Inversion is most common when the verb is *said*, the subject is not a pronoun, and the reporting clause is medial. It is unusual and archaic or dialectal, however, when the subject of the reporting clause is a pronoun, even when the verb is *said* (*eg*: *said he*).

NOTE The structural relationship between the reporting clause and direct speech is problematic. In [1] the direct speech seems to be a direct object, but in the other examples above of direct speech – [2], [3], and [4] – the reporting clause seems subordinate. The direct speech may comprise what would be represented in writing as a number of sentences.

Backshift in indirect speech

14.18 Several changes are usually made in converting direct speech to indirect speech. If the time of reporting is expressed as later than the time of the utterance, there is generally a change of verb forms. The change is termed BACKSHIFT, and the resulting relationship of verb forms in the reporting and reported clauses is known as the SEQUENCE OF TENSES. Below we assume an exact correspondence for the reporting of direct and indirect speech in illustrating the changes.

	DIRECT SPEECH	BACKSHIFTED IN INDIRECT SPEECH
(i)	present	past
(ii)	past	past or past perfect
(iii)	present perfect	past perfect
(iv)	past perfect	past perfect

Thus, if the present references in the direct speech become past references in the indirect speech, there is a corresponding shift of verb forms into the past, or if necessary into the past perfect. The verbs in the indirect speech are thereby related to the time of the reporting. Examples of each part of the rule are:

'I *am being paid* by the hour,' she said.
~ She said she *was being paid* by the hour.
'The exhibition finished last week,' explained Ann.
~ Ann explained that the exhibition {*finished* / *had finished*} the preceding week.
'I've *been waiting* over an hour for you,' she told him.
~ She told him that she *had been waiting* over an hour for him.
'I *had studied* French for four years at school before I abandoned the subject,' I said.
~ I said that I *had studied* French for four years at school before I abandoned the subject.

Backshift is optional when the time-reference of the original utterance is valid at the time of the reporting:

Their teacher had told them that the earth *moves* around the sun.
Sam told me last night that he *is* now an American citizen.
They thought that prison conditions *have* improved.
I didn't know that our meeting *is* next Tuesday.
She said that they *are* being discriminated against.
The waiter told me that lunch *is* now being served.

NOTE The reporting verb may be in the present tense for communications in recent past time:

Joan *tells* me that she'*s* going to the airport in an hour's time.
She *says* she *was* too busy to join us last night.

The present tense is also used for reports attributed to famous works or authors which have present validity:

The Bible says that adultery is a sin.
Chaucer somewhere writes that love is blind.

Verbs of cognition may also be used in the reporting clause in the present tense:

I *know* they *don't* care.
Sylvia *thinks* Paul *went* to Lancaster last night.

Other changes in indirect speech

14.19 The reference to persons in indirect speech must be appropriate to the situation at the time of reporting. There may therefore be changes in pronouns or nouns, as illustrated below:

'*I*'ll behave *myself*,' he promised.
~He promised that *he*'d behave *himself*.
'*You* know my family,' she said.
~She told *him* [or *Tom*, for example] that *he* knew *her* family.

Other changes may be necessary to adjust the references to time or place. For example, *yesterday* to *last Monday*, *now* to *then*, *here* to *there* or *at college*.

Indirect statements, questions, exclamations, directives

14.20 All the main discourse types may be converted into indirect speech.

INDIRECT STATEMENT:	subordinate *that*-clause
INDIRECT QUESTION:	subordinate *wh*-clause or *if*-clause
INDIRECT EXCLAMATION:	subordinate *wh*-clause
INDIRECT DIRECTIVE:	subordinate *that*-clause or *to*-infinitive clause (without subject)

Our examples have so far been of indirect statements. Here are examples of the last three categories:

'Are you ready yet?' asked Joan. [*YES–NO* QUESTION]
~Joan asked (me) *whether I was ready yet*.
'When will the plane leave?' I wondered. [*WH*-QUESTION]
~I wondered *when the plane would leave*.
'Are you satisfied or not?' I asked her. [ALTERNATIVE QUESTION]
~I asked her *whether or not she was satisfied*.
'What a brave boy you are!' Margaret told him. [EXCLAMATION]
~Margaret told him *what a brave boy he was*.
'Tidy up the room at once,' I said to Tom. [DIRECTIVE]

~I insisted *that Tom* { *tidy* ⟨esp AmE⟩ / *should tidy* ⟨esp BrE⟩ } *up the room* at once.

~I told Tom *to tidy up the room*.

All the types of changes outlined in 14.18*f* apply to questions and exclamations as well as statements. With directives, there is no tense backshift in the verb forms exemplified above: mandative subjunctive, putative *should*, *to*-infinitive.

The modal auxiliaries in indirect speech

14.21 If there is a change in time-reference, a modal auxiliary is backshifted from present tense forms to past tense forms even if these do not normally indicate past time in direct speech:

> 'You *may* be able to answer this question,' he told her.
> ~He told her that she *might* be able to answer that question.
> 'I *won't* pay another penny,' I said.
> ~I said that I *wouldn't* pay another penny.

If a modal auxiliary in the direct speech is already in the past tense form, then the same form remains in the indirect speech:

> 'You *shouldn't* smoke in the bedroom,' he told them.
> ~He told them that they *shouldn't* smoke in the bedroom.

Several modal auxiliaries or marginal modals have only one form: *must*, *ought to*, *need*, and *had better*. That form remains in indirect speech:

> 'You *must be* hungry,' he said.
> ~He said that they *must be* hungry.
> 'You *had better* not say anything about this,' he warned me.
> ~He warned me that I *had better* not say anything about that.

In its obligational sense, however, the past of *must* may be replaced by *had to* in indirect speech:

> 'You *must* be in by ten tonight,' his parents told him.
> ~His parents told him that he {*must* / *had to*} be in by ten that night.

Free indirect speech and free direct speech

14.22 FREE INDIRECT SPEECH is used extensively to report speech or (particularly in fiction) the stream of thought. It is basically a form of indirect speech, but (a) the reporting clause is omitted (except when retained as a parenthetical clause, as in direct speech), and (b) the potentialities of direct-speech sentence structure are retained (for example, direct questions and exclamations, vocatives, tag questions, and interjections). It is therefore only the backshift of the verb, together with equivalent shifts in personal pronouns, demonstratives, and time and place references, that signals the fact that the words are being reported, rather than being in direct speech. The italicized verbs below are backshifted to the past tense:

> So that *was* their plan, *was* it? He well *knew* their tricks, and *would show* them a thing or two before he *was finished*. Thank goodness he *had* been alerted, and that there *were* still a few honest people in the world!

FREE DIRECT SPEECH is also used in fiction writing to represent a person's stream of thought. It is basically a form of direct speech, but it is merged with the narration without any overt indication by a reporting clause of a switch to speech. It is distinguished from the past time-reference of the narration by its use of unshifted forms. In the following example the free direct speech is italicized:

> I sat on the grass staring at the passers-by. Everybody seemed in a hurry. *Why didn't I stay at home?*

Transferred negation

14.23 TRANSFERRED NEGATION, particularly common in informal style, is the transfer of the negative from a subordinate clause, where semantically it belongs, to the matrix clause. *I don't think it's a good idea* is an example of transferred negation, since it can be understood as virtually synonymous with *I think it isn't a good idea*.

The matrix verbs that allow transferred negation convey notions of opinion (*eg*: *believe*, *expect*, *imagine*, *suppose*, *think*) or perception (*eg*: *appear*, *seem*, *feel as if*, *look as if*, *sound as if*). Here are some examples:

> I don't believe I've met you before. ['I believe I haven't met you before']
> She didn't imagine that we would say anything. ['She imagined that we wouldn't say anything']
> He didn't expect to win. ['He expected not to win']
> It doesn't seem that we can get our money back. ['It seems that we can't get our money back']
> The baby doesn't appear to be awake. ['The baby appears not to be awake']
> It doesn't look as if it's going to rain. ['It looks as if it isn't going to rain']

NOTE When the subject of the main clause is *I*, the tag question corresponds with the subordinate clause:

> I don't imagine he CÀRES, DÒES he? [I imagine he doesn't CÀRE, DÒES he?]

Bibliographical note

On the terminology for sentence and clause, see Greenbaum (1988).

On the complex sentence and subordination in general see Nakajima (1982); Smaby (1974).

On nonfinite and verbless clauses beginning with a subordinator, see Bäcklund (1984).

On the overlap of conjunction and preposition, see Jacobsson (1977); Matthews (1981, esp pp. 174–81).

On the choice of verb in subordinate clauses, including backshift in indirect speech, see Palmer (1979, 1988), both *passim*.

On transferred negation, see Cattell (1973); Horn (1978b).

15 Syntactic and semantic functions of subordinate clauses

Syntactic functions of subordinate clauses

15.1 Subordinate clauses may function as subject, object, complement, or adverbial in a superordinate clause:

Subject: *That we need a larger computer* has become obvious.
Direct object: He doesn't know *whether to send a gift.*
Indirect object: You can tell *whoever is waiting* that I'll be back in ten minutes.
Subject complement: One likely result of the postponement is *that the cost of constructing the college will be very much higher.*
Object complement: I know her *to be reliable.*
Adverbial: *When you see them,* give them my best wishes.

In addition, subordinate clauses may function within these elements, *eg*:

Postmodifier in noun phrase: (Few of the immigrants retained) the customs *that they had brought with them.*
Prepositional complement: (It depends) on *what we decide.*
Adjectival complementation: (We are) happy *to see you.*

NOTE There are constraints on the functioning of clauses as indirect objects or as object complements. Among the finite clauses, only nominal relative clauses (*cf* 15.7*f*) function as indirect object or as object complement.

Functional classes of subordinate clauses

15.2 On the basis of their potential functions, we distinguish four major categories of subordinate clauses: NOMINAL, ADVERBIAL, RELATIVE, and COMPARATIVE.

Like noun phrases NOMINAL CLAUSES (*cf* 15.3*ff*) may function as subject, object, complement, appositive, and prepositional complement. But the occurrence of nominal clauses is more limited than that of noun phrases, because semantically the clauses are normally abstract; *ie* they refer to such abstractions as events, facts, and ideas. The one exception is the nominal relative clause, which may refer to persons and things and may in fact be alternatively analysed as a noun phrase (*cf* 15.7). Since indirect objects normally refer to persons, we can see why only the nominal relative clause can function as indirect object. Nominal clauses involved in the complementation of verbs and adjectives are discussed in detail in Chapter 16.

ADVERBIAL CLAUSES (*cf* 15.13*ff*) function mainly as adjuncts (8.13) or disjuncts (8.40). In those functions they are like adverb phrases, but in their potentiality for greater explicitness, they are more often like prepositional phrases:

We left *after the speeches ended.*
We left *after the end of the speeches.*

RELATIVE CLAUSES generally function as restrictive or nonrestrictive modifiers of noun phrases and are therefore functionally parallel to attributive adjectives. Compare:

a man *who is lonely* ~ *a lonely man*

But they are positioned like postmodifying prepositional phrases:

tourists *who come from Italy* ~ tourists *from Italy*

These relative clauses are discussed in Chapter 17. Two types of relative clauses, however, are treated in this chapter: nominal relative clauses (15.7*f*) and sentential relative clauses (15.33)

COMPARATIVE CLAUSES (*cf* 15.36*ff*) resemble adjectives and adverbs in their modifying functions:

She has *more* patience *than you have.*
He's not *as* clever a man *as I thought.*
I love you *more* deeply *than I can say.*

Semantically, the comparative clauses together with their correlative element (*eg*: *more*, *as*, *-er*) are equivalent to degree adverbs.

NOTE Unlike noun phrases, nominal clauses may also function as adjective complementation without a preposition (*cf* 16.39):

I'm not sure *that I can remember the exact details.*

Nominal clauses

That-clauses

15.3 Nominal *that*-clauses may function as:

Subject: *That the invading troops have been withdrawn* has not affected our government's trade sanctions.
Direct object: I noticed *that he spoke English with an Australian accent.*
Subject complement: My assumption is *that interest rates will soon fall.*
Appositive: Your criticism, *that no account has been taken of psychological factors*, is fully justified.
Adjectival complementation: We are glad *that you are able to join us on our wedding anniversary.*

They may not, however, function as object complement or as prepositional complement.

The subject *that*-clause is usually extraposed (*cf* 18.23):

> It has not affected our government's trade sanctions *that the invading troops have been withdrawn.*

When the *that*-clause is direct object, complement, or extraposed, the conjunction *that* is frequently omitted except in formal use, leaving a zero *that*-clause:

> It's a pity *you don't know Russian.*

But *that* cannot be omitted in a subject clause or in a nonrestrictive appositive clause (*cf* 17.13 Note), since without the subordinate marker the clause would be initially misinterpreted as a main clause:

> * *You don't know Russian* is a pity.
> *Your criticism, *no account has been taken of psychological factors*, is fully justified.

NOTE The zero *that*-clause is particularly common when the clause is brief and uncomplicated. Retention of *that* is necessary under certain conditions other than when the clause is an unextraposed subject or a nonrestrictive appositive clause:

(i) To clarify whether an adverbial belongs to the matrix or the *that*-clause:

> They told us once again *that the situation was serious.*
> They told us *that once again the situation was serious.*

(ii) To prevent a coordinated *that*-clause from being misinterpreted as a coordinated main clause:

> I realize that I'm in charge and *that everybody accepts my leadership.*
> I realize that I'm in charge, and everybody accepts my leadership.

(iii) When the object *that*-clause is fronted (as with an initial subject clause):

> *That she ever said such a thing* I simply don't believe.

(iv) When a clause or long phrase intervenes between the verb and the *that*-clause:

> We decided, in view of his special circumstances, *that we would admit him for a probationary period.*

Wh-interrogative clauses

15.4 Subordinate *wh*-interrogative clauses occur in the whole range of functions available to the nominal *that*-clause and in addition may function as prepositional complement:

> Subject: *How the book will sell* depends on the reviewers.
> Direct object: I can't imagine *what they want with your address.*

Subject complement: The problem is *who will water my plants when I am away*.
Appositive: Your original question, *why he did not report it to the police earlier*, has not yet been answered.
Adjectival complementation: I'm not sure *which she prefers*.
Prepositional complement: They did not consult us on *whose names should be put forward*.

These subordinate clauses resemble *wh*-questions semantically in that they leave a gap of unknown information, represented by the *wh*-element. Contrast the known information expressed in the *that*-clause with the unknown information in the *wh*-clause:

I know *(that) Caroline* will be there.
~Do you know *who* will be there?
I'm sure *(that) Ted* has paid.
~I'm not sure *who* has paid.

There are also grammatical similarities to independent *wh*-questions in that the *wh*-element is placed first. If it is a prepositional phrase, we have the same choices as for the *wh*-element in *wh*-questions (*cf* 11.9):

I asked them *on what* they based their predictions. ⟨formal⟩
I asked them *what* they based their predictions *on*.

An infinitive *wh*-clause (with an obligational sense) can be formed with all *wh*-words, though instances with *why* are rare:

I don't know *what to say*. ['. . . what I should say.']
You must explain to them *how to start the motor*. ['. . . how one/they should start the motor.']
I never know *who to speak to*. ['. . . who one/I should speak to.']
I'm wondering *where to put my coat*. ['. . . where I should put my coat.']

NOTE [a] Although the subordinate clause usually does not have subject–operator inversion, such inversion may occur, particularly when the clause functions as complement and the superordinate verb is a form of the verb *be*, or when it functions as appositive:

The problem is *who can we get to replace her*.
Your original question, *why did he not report it to the police earlier*, has not yet been answered.

In literary style, subject–verb inversion occasionally occurs when the *wh*-element is the subject complement or an obligatory adverbial, particularly if the subject is lengthy:

She told us *how strong was her motivation to engage in research*.
It took me some time to discover *in which village stood the memorial to our fallen comrades*.

In addition, subject–operator inversion is common in Irish English and in some nonstandard dialects:

> Whenever I see her, she wants to know *when will I be visiting her mother.*

[b] Prepositions are optionally omitted before *wh*-clauses:

> We have solved the problem (*of*) *who was at fault.*

Yes–no and alternative interrogative clauses

15.5 Subordinate *yes–no* interrogative clauses (*cf* 11.3*ff*) and subordinate alternative interrogative clauses (*cf* 11.11) occur in the whole range of functions available to subordinate *wh*-interrogative clauses, and may include infinitive clauses. The *yes–no* clause is introduced by the subordinators *whether* or *if*:

> Do you know *whether*/*if the banks are open?*

The alternative clauses are formed with the correlatives *whether . . . or* or *if . . . or*. The subordinator is repeated only if the second unit is a full clause:

> I can't find out {*whether* / *if*} *the flight has been deLÁYED or*
> {*whether* / *if*} *it has been CÁNcelled.*
>
> They didn't say *whether it will RÁIN or be SÙNny.*
> I asked them *if they wanted MÉAT or FÌSH.*
> I don't care *if they JÓIN us or NÒT.*

Repetition is possible for some speakers with *to*-infinitive clauses:

> He didn't tell us *whether to wait for him or* (*whether*) *to go on without him.*

But the subordinator is not repeated if the second clause is abbreviated by the omission of the infinitival *to*:

> He didn't tell us *whether to wait for him or go on without him.*

NOTE *If* is more restricted syntactically than *whether*. For example, it cannot introduce a subject clause:

> {*Whether she likes the present* / **If she likes the present*} is not clear to me.

It cannot introduce a *to*-infinitive clause:

> I don't know *whether to see my doctor today.*
> *I don't know *if to see my doctor today.*

And it cannot be followed directly by *or not*:

He didn't say *whether or not he'll be staying here.*
*He didn't say *if or not he'll be staying here.*

But *or not* can be postposed:

He didn't say *if he'll be staying here or not.*

Exclamative clauses

15.6 Subordinate exclamative clauses generally function as extraposed subject, direct object, or prepositional complement:

Extraposed subject: It's incredible *how fast she can run.* ['It's incredible that she can run so fast.']
Direct object: I remember *what a good time I had at your party.* ['I remember that I had such a good time at your party.']
Prepositional complement: I read an account of *what an impression you had made.* ('I read an account that you had made an excellent (*or* a terrible) impression.']

As in independent exclamative clauses (*cf* 11.20), the exclamative element is formed with *what* as predeterminer in a noun phrase and *how* as intensifier of an adjective, adverb, or clause; the exclamative element is positioned initially regardless of its normal position in a declarative clause.

NOTE A subordinate clause may be ambiguous between exclamatory and interrogative interpretations:

You can't imagine *what difficulties I have with my children.*

Exclamatory interpretation: You can't imagine the great difficulties I have with my children.
Interrogative interpretation: You can't imagine the kinds of difficulty I have with my children.

I told her *how late she was.*

Exclamatory interpretation: I told her she was very late.
Interrogative interpretation: I told her the extent to which she was late.

Nominal relative clauses

15.7 Nominal relative clauses resemble *wh*-interrogative clauses in that they are also introduced by a *wh*-element. In some respects they are more like noun phrases, since they can refer to concrete entities as well as abstract entities. They can be analysed as noun phrases modified by relative clauses, except that the *wh*-element is merged with its antecedent:

Whoever did that should admit it frankly. [1]
['The person who did that . . .']
I took *what they offered me.* [2]

['. . . the thing(s) that they offered me.']

I took *what books she gave me.* [3]

['. . . the books that she gave me.']

Macy's is *where I buy my clothes.* [4]

['. . . the place where I buy my clothes.']

Like noun phrases, they may display number concord with the verb of the sentence. Contrast, for example:

Whatever book you see is yours to take.

Whatever books I have in the house are borrowed from the public library.

The *wh*-element may be a pronoun, such as *whoever* in [1] and *what* in [2]; a determiner, such as *what* in [3]; or an adverb, such as *where* in [4].

Nominal relative clauses have the same range of functions as noun phrases.

Subject: *What I want* is a cup of hot cocoa.

Direct object: You should see *whoever deals with complaints.*

Indirect object: He gave *whoever asked for it* a copy of his latest paper.

Subject complement: April is *when the lilacs bloom.*

Object complement: You can call me *what(ever) you like.*

Appositive: I'll pay you the whole debt: *What I originally borrowed and what I owe you in interest.*

Prepositional complement: You should vote for *which(ever) candidate you think best.*

Like noun phrases, nominal relative clauses require prepositions in adjective complementation:

He's aware of *what I write.*

To-infinitive clauses may be nominal relative clauses, but they seem to be restricted to the functions of subject complement and prepositional complement:

Subject complement: That's *where to go for your next vacation.*

['. . . the place to go . . .']

Prepositional complement: The book is on *how to use a computer.*

['. . . the way to use . . .']

15.8 The *wh*-element may express either a SPECIFIC meaning (where the *-ever* suffix is disallowed) or a NONSPECIFIC meaning (generally indicated by the presence of the *-ever* suffix):

SPECIFIC

I took what was on the kitchen table. ['. . . that which was on the kitchen table.'] [1]

May is *when she takes her last examination.* ['. . . the time when she takes her last examination.'] [2]

NONSPECIFIC

Whoever breaks this law deserves a fine. ['Anyone who breaks this law . . .'] [3]
I'll send *whatever is necessary.* ['. . . anything that is necessary.'] [4]

NOTE A subordinate clause may be ambiguous between a nominal relative interpretation and an interrogative interpretation:

They asked me *what I knew.*

Relative interpretation: They asked me things that I knew.
Interrogative interpretation: They asked me, 'What do you know?'

What she wrote was a mystery.

Relative interpretation: She wrote a mystery story.
Interrogative interpretation: I don't know what she wrote.

To-infinitive clauses

15.9 Nominal *to*-infinitive clauses may function as:

Subject: *To be neutral in this conflict* is out of thr question.
Direct object: He likes *to relax.*
Subject complement: The best excuse is *to say that you have an examination tomorrow morning.*
Appositive: Your ambition, *to become a farmer*, requires the energy and perseverance that you so obviously have.
Adjectival complementation: I'm very eager *to meet her.*

Extraposition is usual with subject clauses (*cf* 18.23):

It is out of the question *to be neutral in this conflict.*

The presence of a subject in a *to*-infinitive clause normally requires the presence of a preceding *for*. When the subject is a pronoun that distinguishes subjective and objective cases, it is in the objective case:

For your country to be neutral in this conflict is out of the question.
~It is out of the question *for your country to be neutral in this conflict.*
For us to take part in the discussion would be a conflict of interest.
~It would be a conflict of interest *for us to take part in the discussion.*
I'm very eager *for them to meet her.*

When the clause is a direct object, however, *for* is generally absent before the subject:

He likes *everyone to relax.*

The nominal *to*-infinitive often indicates that its proposition is a possibility or a proposal rather than something fulfilled, and it is then closest semantically to a *that*-clause with putative *should* (*cf* 14.14):

It's natural *for them to be together.*
It's natural *that they should be together.*

Other types of nominal *to*-infinitive clauses are treated elsewhere: *wh*-interrogative clauses (15.4), *yes–no* and alternative interrogative clauses (15.5), and nominal relative clauses (15.7*f*).

NOTE Certain verbs of wanting and their antonyms allow an optional *for* in the object clause in AmE:

He didn't like *me to be alone at night.*
He didn't like *for me to be alone at night.* ⟨AmE⟩.

-ing clauses

15.10 Nominal *-ing* clauses may function as:

Subject: *Watching television* keeps them out of mischief.
Direct object: He enjoys *playing practical jokes.*
Subject complement: Her first job had been *selling computers.*
Appositive: His current research, *investigating attitudes to racial stereotypes*, takes up most of his time.
Adjectival complementation: They are busy *preparing a barbecue.*

If the *-ing* clause has a subject, the subject may be in the genitive case or it may be in the objective case (for those pronouns having an objective case) or common case (for all other heads of noun phrases):

GENITIVE: I object to *his/Jeremy's* receiving an invitation.
OBJECTIVE: I objected to *him/Jeremy* receiving an invitation.

There is a traditional prescription in favour of the genitive: it is preferred if the subject is a pronoun, the noun phrase has personal reference, and the style is formal. The genitive is also preferred if the subject is initial in the sentence.

My forgetting her name was embarrassing.

On the other hand, the common case is preferred where the subject is a nonpersonal noun phrase and not a pronoun and the style is not formal:

I don't know about *the weather* being so awful in this area.

The genitive is avoided when the noun phrase is lengthy and requires a group genitive (*cf* 17.26):

Do you remember *the students and teachers protesting against the new rule?*

A nominal *-ing* clause may refer to a fact or an action:

Fact: *Your driving a car to New York in your condition* disturbs me greatly.
Action: *Your driving a car to New York* took longer than I expected.

NOTE [a] The *-ing* participle in a nominal *-ing* clause is commonly called a 'gerund'.
[b] Extraposition is less common with the *-ing* participle and often seems like an informal afterthought (*cf* 18.23):

It was tough *answering all the questions.*

Bare infinitive clauses

15.11 The most common functions of the nominal bare infinitive clause are as subject or subject complement in a pseudo-cleft sentence (or a variant of it, *cf* 18.20), where the other subordinate clause has the substitute verb DO:

What the plan does is *(to) ensure a fair pension for all.*
Turn off the tap was all I did.

The *to* of the infinitive is optional when the clause is subject complement.

NOTE A bare infinitive clause may function as object complement with a relatively few superordinate verbs (*cf* 16.28):

They made her *pay for the damage.*

It may follow prepositions of exception (*cf* 9.15):

She did everything but *make her bed.*

Verbless clauses

15.12 The nominal verbless clause is a more debatable category than the other nominal clauses.

A friend in need is a friend indeed. [proverb] [1]
Wall-to-wall carpets in every room is their dream. [2]
Are *bicycles* wise *in heavy traffic?* [3]

These may be paraphrased:

To be a friend in need is *to be a friend indeed.* [1a]
Having wall-to-wall carpets in every room is their dream. [2a]
Is *it* wise *to have bicycles in heavy traffic?* [3a]

The paraphrases suggest a clausal analysis. Note also the apparent semantic anomaly of *bicycles are wise* (implying *wise bicycles*), and the singular verb in [2].

Adverbial clauses

15.13 In Chapter 8 we distinguish four broad categories of syntactic functions for adverbials: adjuncts, subjuncts, disjuncts, and conjuncts. Adverbial clauses, however, function mainly as adjuncts and disjuncts.

In this chapter we focus on the semantic functions of adverbial clauses. Semantic analysis of adverbial clauses is complicated by the fact that many subordinators introduce clauses with different meanings: for example a *since*-clause may be temporal or clausal. Furthermore, some clauses combine meanings; in such cases, we treat the clauses under sections that deal with what appears to be their primary meaning.

Clauses of time

15.14 Finite adverbial clauses of time are introduced by such subordinators as *after*, *as*, *once*, *since*, *until*, *when*, *while*:

> Buy your ticket *as soon as you reach the station*.
> My family, *once they saw the mood I was in*, left me completely alone.
> Drop by *whenever you get the chance*.
> We came in *just as it started to rain*.
> Wait *until you're called*.

The *-ing* clauses are introduced by *once*, *till*, *until*, *when*, *whenever*, *while*, and ⟨esp BrE⟩ *whilst*. The *-ed* and verbless clauses are introduced by *as soon as*, *once*, *till*, *until*, *when*, *whenever*, *while*, and ⟨esp BrE⟩ *whilst*:

> *Once having made a promise*, you should keep it.
> The dog stayed at the entrance *until told to come in*.
> Complete your work *as soon as possible*.

To-infinitive clauses without a subordinator or a subject may have temporal function, expressing the outcome of the situation:

> I rushed to the door, *only to discover that it was locked and barred*.
> I awoke one morning *to find the house in an uproar*.

With durative verbs in the matrix clause, the construction expresses duration of time together with outcome:

> She lived *to be 100*. ['She reached 100 years of age.']
> You'll live *to regret it*. ['You'll eventually regret it.']

15.15 An adverbial clause of time relates the time of the situation in its clause to the time of the situation in the matrix clause. Depending in large part on the subordinator, the time of the matrix clause may be previous to that of the adverbial clause (*eg until*), simultaneous with it (*eg while*), or subsequent to it (*eg after*). The time relationship may also convey duration (*eg as long as*), recurrence (*eg whenever*), and relative proximity (*eg just after*).

NOTE [**a**] The matrix clause with an *until*-clause must be durative, the duration lasting to the time indicated by the *until*-clause. A negative clause is always durative, even though the corresponding positive clause is not durative, since the absence of the event extends throughout the indicated period:

> I didn't start my meal *until Adam arrived.*
> *I started my meal *until Adam arrived.*

[**b**] When the matrix clause is imperative, the sentence with a *before*-clause may imply a conditional relationship as well as time:

> Go *before I call the police.* ['Go! If you don't go, I'll call the police.']

[**c**] Nonassertive items (*cf* 10.37) can appear in *before*-clauses, perhaps because *before*-clauses, like conditional clauses (*cf* 15.18*ff*), inherently relate to matters unfulfilled in respect of the matrix clause:

> I spoke to them *before I ever heard any gossip about them.*
> ['At the time I spoke to them I had not heard any gossip about them']

[**d**] The sequential meaning of *after*, *when* and *whenever* may induce an implication of cause:

> He felt better *after he had a short nap.*
> I hit him back *when he hit me.*
> My heart leaps *whenever I see you.*

[**e**] *When* may imply concession as well as time:

> They were gossiping, *when they should have been working.*
> ['. . . whereas they should have been working.']
> She cleans the house by herself, *when she could easily have asked her children to help her.*

[**f**] The meaning of several subordinators that primarily express time, place, or condition may be neutralized in certain contexts to convey a more abstract notion of recurrent or habitual contingency: *when*, *whenever*, *once*; *where*, *wherever*; *if*. The subordinators may then be paraphrased by such prepositional phrases as 'in cases when' or 'in circumstances where':

> *When(ever)*
> *Where(ver)*
> *If*
> *Once*
> { *there's smoke*, there's fire.
> *children are involved*, divorces are particularly unpleasant.
> *known*, such facts have been reported. }

Clauses of place

15.16 Adverbial clauses of place are introduced mainly by *where* or *wherever*. *Where* is specific and *wherever* nonspecific. The clause may indicate position [1] or direction [2]:

> *Where the fire had been*, we saw nothing but blackened ruins. [1]
> They went *wherever they could find work.*
> ['to any place where'] [2]

Several temporal subordinators may have primarily a place meaning in descriptions of scenes, when the scenes are described dynamically in terms of movement from one place to another:

Take the right fork *when the road splits into two.*
The river continues winding *until it reaches a large lake.*
The building becomes narrower *as it rises higher.*
The road stops *just after it goes under a bridge.*
Once the mountains rise above the snow line, vegetation is sparse.

NOTE [a] *Where*-clauses may combine the meanings of place and contrast:

Where I saw only wilderness, they saw abundant signs of life.

[b] The archaic forms *whence* ['from where'] and *whither* ['to where'] are occasionally found, particularly in religious language.

Clauses of condition, concession, and contrast

15.17 There is considerable overlap in adverbial clauses that express condition, concession, and contrast (*cf* 15.15 Note [f]).

The overlap between the three roles is highlighted by the overlapping use of subordinators: for example, *if* introduces all three types of clauses and *whereas* both contrast and concessive clauses. Furthermore, *even if* expresses both the contingent dependence of one situation upon another and the unexpected nature of this dependence:

Even if they offered to pay, I wouldn't accept any money from them.

All three types of clauses tend to assume initial position in the superordinate clause.

Conditional clauses

15.18 In general, conditional clauses convey a DIRECT CONDITION in that the situation in the matrix clause is directly contingent on the situation in the conditional clause. For example, in uttering [1] the speaker intends the hearer to understand that the truth of the prediction 'she'll scream' depends on the fulfilment of the condition of 'your putting the baby down':

If you put the baby down, she'll scream. [1]

The most common subordinators for conditional clauses are *if* and *unless,* which are also used with nonfinite and verbless clauses. Other conditional subordinators are restricted to finite clauses (but *cf* Note [b] below); for example: *given (that)* ⟨formal⟩, *on condition (that), provided (that), providing (that), supposing (that).* Here are other examples of conditional clauses:

Unless the strike has been called off, there will be no trains tomorrow.
He doesn't mind inconveniencing others *just so he's comfortable.* ⟨informal⟩

You may leave the apartment at any time, *provided that you give a month's notice or pay an additional month's rent.*
In case you want me, I'll be in my office till lunchtime.
Given that $x = y$, then $n(x+a) = n(y+a)$ must also be true. ⟨in formal argumentation⟩
Assuming that the movie starts at eight, shouldn't we be leaving now?
Unless otherwise instructed, you should leave by the back exit.
Marion wants me to type the letter *if possible*.
If not, I can discuss the matter with you now.

NOTE [**a**] Some conditional clauses express an INDIRECT CONDITION, in that the condition is not related to the situation in the matrix clause. Here are some examples:

His style is florid, *if that's the right word.* [1]
If you remember your history lessons, the war was started by the other side. [2]
If you're going my way, I need a lift. [3]
She's far too considerate, *if I may say so.* [4]

In uttering [4], the speaker does not intend the truth of the assertion 'She's far too considerate' to be dependent on obtaining permission from the hearer. Rather, the condition is dependent on the implicit speech act of the utterance: 'I'm telling you, if I may, that she's far too considerate.' In conventional politeness, the speaker is making the utterance of the assertion dependent on obtaining permission from the hearer, though the fulfilment of that condition is conventionally taken for granted.
[**b**] Nonfinite and verbless clauses with *with* or *without* as subordinator may express a conditional relationship:

Without me to supplement your income, you wouldn't be able to manage.
With them on our side, we are secure.

Open and hypothetical condition

15.19 A direct condition may be either an OPEN CONDITION or a HYPOTHETICAL CONDITION. Open conditions are neutral: they leave unresolved the question of the fulfilment or nonfulfilment of the condition, and hence also the truth of the proposition expressed by the matrix clause:

If Colin is in London, he is undoubtedly staying at the Hilton.

The sentence leaves unresolved whether Colin is in London, and hence it leaves unresolved whether he is staying at the Hilton.

A hypothetical condition, on the other hand, conveys the speaker's belief that the condition will not be fulfilled (for future conditions), is not fulfilled (for present conditions), or was not fulfilled (for past conditions) and hence the probable or certain falsity of the proposition expressed by the matrix clause:

If he changed his opinions, he'd be a more likeable person. [1]
They would be here with us *if they had the time.* [2]
If you had listened to me, you wouldn't have made so many mistakes. [3]

The conditional clauses in these sentences convey the following implications:

He very probably won't change his opinions. [1a]
They presumably don't have the time. [2a]
You certainly didn't listen to me. [3a]

For the verb forms in hypothetical conditions, see 14.12*f*.

NOTE **[a]** Conditional clauses are like questions in that they are generally either neutral in their expectations of an answer or biased towards a negative response, and they therefore tend to admit nonassertive items (*cf* 10.37):

If you *ever* touch me again, I'll scream.
She's taking a stick with her in case she has *any* trouble on the way.

[b] Two ways of expressing future hypothetical conditions are occasionally used in formal contexts. They have overtones of tentativeness:

(i) *was to* or *were to* followed by the infinitive (*cf* subjunctive *were*, 14.13):

If it {*was* / *were*} *to* rain, the ropes would snap. They're far too tight.

(ii) *should* followed by the infinitive (*cf* putative *should*, 14.14):

If a serious crisis *should* arise, the public would have to be informed of its full implications.

[c] Conditional clauses may have subject–operator inversion without a subordinator if the operator is *were*, *should*, and (especially) *had*:

Had I known, I would have written before. ['If I had known, . . .']
Were she in charge, she would do things differently.
Should you change your mind, no one would blame you.
Should she be interested, I'll phone her. [with present subjunctive *be*; *cf* 14.13 Note [a]]

[d] Infinitive clauses sometimes combine condition with other contingency relations such as purpose or reason:

You must be STRÒNG to lift that weight. ['. . . in order to lift that weight'; '. . . because you were able to lift that weight', '. . . if you were able to lift that weight']
You'd be a fool *not to take the scholarship*. ['if you didn't . . .']

[e] *If only* is an intensified equivalent of *if*, typically used in hypothetical clauses to express a wish:

If only you would help me next week, I would not be so nervous.

[f] *Given (that)* and *assuming (that)* are used for open conditions which the speaker assumes were, are, or will be fulfilled, and from which a proposition is deduced. A clause introduced by *granted (that)* is also used as a premise for a deduction, but usually implies a previous statement on which the premise is based. *If* may be used in the same way: *If you were there (and you say you were), you must*

have seen her. *Given (that)* and *granted (that)* tend to be used in formal written style, particularly in argumentation.
[g] *As long as* and *so long as* are less formal than the semantically similar but formal *provided (that)* and *providing (that)*. *Just so (that)* tends to appear in informal conversation. They all mean 'if and only if'.
[h] *Unless* introduces a negative condition; the *unless*-clause is usually roughly similar to a negative *if*-clause. With *unless* there is a greater focus on the condition as an exception ('only if . . . not'). There are therefore contexts in which the *unless*-clause cannot occur:

> I'll feel much happier { *if he doesn't come with us.* / **unless he comes with us.* }

> { *If you hadn't studied hard,* / **Unless you had studied hard,* } you'd have failed the exam.

Rhetorical conditional clauses

15.20 Rhetorical conditional clauses give the appearance of expressing an open condition, but (like rhetorical questions, *cf* 11.13) they actually make a strong assertion. There are two types:

(a) If the proposition in the matrix clause is patently absurd, the proposition in the conditional clause is shown to be false:

> *If they're Irish*, I'm the Pope. ['Since I'm obviously not the Pope, they're certainly not Irish.']
> *If you believe that*, you'll believe anything. ['You certainly can't believe that.']

(b) If the proposition in the conditional clause (which contains measure expressions) is patently true, the proposition in the matrix clause is shown to be true. The *if*-clause is positioned finally:

> He's ninety *if he's a day*. ['If you'll agree that he's at least a day old, perhaps you'll take my word that he's ninety.']
> The package weighed ten pounds *if it weighed an ounce*. ['The package certainly weighed ten pounds.']

Concessive clauses

15.21 Concessive clauses are introduced chiefly by *although* or its more informal variant *though*. Other subordinators include *while*, *whereas* ⟨formal⟩, and *even if*:

> *Although he had just joined*, he was treated exactly like all the others.
> No goals were scored, *though it was an exciting game*.
> *While I don't want to make a fuss*, I feel I must protest at your interference.
> *Whereas the amendment is enthusiastically supported by a large majority in the Senate*, its fate is doubtful in the House.

Except for *whereas*, these subordinators may introduce *-ing*, *-ed*, and verbless clauses, *eg*: *Though well over eighty, she can walk faster than I can.*

Concessive clauses indicate that the situation in the matrix clause is contrary to what one might expect in view of the situation in the concessive clause. It is often possible to view each situation as unexpected in the light of the other and therefore to choose which should be made subordinate:

> No goals were scored, *although it was an exciting game.*
> It was an exciting game, *although no goals were scored.*

NOTE [a] In a rather formal style, the predication in the concessive clause may be fronted if the subordinator is *though* and must be if it is *as*:

> *Fail though I did,* I would not abandon my goal.
> *Naked as I was,* I braved the storm. ['Even though I was naked, . . .']

That is also used concessively with obligatory fronting of a subject complement, normally a noun phrase:

> *Fool that he was,* he managed to evade his pursuers.
> *Poor that they were,* they gave money to charity. ⟨BrE⟩

Cf 15.26 Note [b] for a similar fronting with reason clauses.

[b] *Even if* combines the concessive force of *even* with the conditional force of *if*:

> *Even if you dislike ancient monuments,* Warwick Castle is worth a visit.

The *even if* clause leaves open whether or not 'you dislike ancient monuments' is true, whereas an *even though* clause would presuppose that it was true.

If itself may be used concessively, synonymous either with *even if* or with *even though*:

> It's possible, *if difficult.* ['. . ., even if it may be difficult.']
> Her salary was good, *if not* up to her expectations. ['. . ., even though it was not up to her expectations.']

Alternative conditional–concessive clauses

15.22 The correlative sequence *whether . . . or (whether)* combines the conditional meaning of *if* with the disjunctive meaning of *either . . . or*. If the second unit is a full finite clause, *whether* may be repeated:

> *Whether Martin pays for the broken vase or (whether) he replaces it with a new vase,* I'm not inviting HÌM again.
> He's getting married, *whether or not he finds a job.*
> *Whether trained or not,* Marilyn is doing an excellent job.
> *Whether right or wrong,* your son needs all the support you can give him.

The concessive meaning comes from the implication that it is unexpected for the same situation to apply under two contrasting conditions.

NOTE [a] *It doesn't matter whether* and the more informal *No matter whether* can also introduce alternative conditional–concessive clauses and universal conditional–concessive clauses (*cf* 15.23):

> *It doesn't matter* } *whether you want to or not*, you will
> *No matter* } have to face the publicity.

[**b**] The correlative sequence *with . . . without* is used concessively with verbless clauses:

> *With a bank loan or without it,* } we'll buy the house.
> *With or without a bank loan,* }

There may be further reductions:

> *Bank loan or no bank loan,* } we'll buy the house.
> *Bank loan or no,* }

Universal conditional–concessive clauses

15.23 The universal conditional–concessive clause indicates a free choice from any number of conditions. It is introduced by the *wh*-words that combine with *-ever*:

> *Whatever I say to them*, I can't keep them quiet. [1]
> Stand perfectly still, *wherever you are*.
> *However much advice you give him*, he does exactly what he wants.
> Don't let them in, *whoever they are*.

The concessive implication in [1] comes through the inference that I can't keep them quiet even if I choose to say something to them from any possible choices.

NOTE The verb *be* can be omitted from a universal clause if the subject of an *SVC* clause is an abstract noun phrase:

> *Whatever your problems (are/may be)*, they can't be worse than mine.
> *However great the pitfalls (are/may be)*, we must do our best to succeed

Clauses of contrast

15.24 Clauses of contrast are introduced by several of the subordinators that introduce concessive clauses (*cf* 15.21): *whereas*, *while*, and ⟨esp BrE⟩ *whilst*. Indeed, there is often a mixture of contrast and concession. The contrastive meaning may be emphasized by correlative antithetic conjuncts such as *in contrast* and *by contrast* when the contrastive clause is initial:

> Mr Larson teaches physics, *while Mr Corby teaches chemistry*.
> I ignore them, *whereas my husband is always worried about what they think of us*.

Clauses of exception

15.25 Clauses of exception are introduced by *but that* ⟨formal⟩, *except* ⟨informal⟩, *except that*, *only* ⟨informal⟩, and less frequently *excepting (that)*, *save* ⟨rare and formal⟩, and *save that* ⟨formal⟩:

I would pay you now, *except that I don't have any money on me.*
No memorial remains for the brave who fell on that battlefield, *save that they will leave their image for ever in the hearts and minds of their grateful countrymen.* ⟨formal⟩
Nothing would satisfy the child *but that I place her on my lap.* ⟨formal⟩
I would've asked you, *only my mother told me not to.* ⟨informal⟩

Clauses introduced by *but that* and *only* must follow the matrix clause.

NOTE The subordinator *but* without *that* is used in infinitive clauses, where it is more common than *but that* in finite clauses:

Nothing would satisfy the child *but for me to place her on my lap.*

Reason clauses

15.26 In general, reason clauses convey a direct relationship with the matrix clause. The relationship may be that of cause and effect (the perception of an inherent objective connection, as in [1]), reason and consequence (the speaker's inference of a connection, as in [2]), motivation and result (the intention of an animate being that has a subsequent result, as in [3]), or circumstance and consequence (a combination of reason with a condition that is assumed to be filled or about to be filled, as in [4]):

He's thin *because he hasn't eaten enough.* [1]
She watered the flowers *because they were dry.* [2]
You'll help me *because you're my friend.* [3]
Since the weather has improved, the game will be held as planned. [4]

Reason clauses are most commonly introduced by the subordinators *because* and *since*. Other subordinators include *as*, *for* ⟨somewhat formal⟩, and (with circumstantial clauses) *seeing (that)*:

I lent him the money *because he needed it.*
As Jane was the eldest, she looked after the others.
Since we live near the sea, we often go sailing.
Much has been written about psychic phenomena, *for they pose fascinating problems that have yet to be resolved.*
Seeing that it is about to rain, we had better leave now.

A *for*-clause must be in final position.

NOTE [a] Reason clauses may express an INDIRECT REASON. The reason is not related to the situation in the matrix clause but is a motivation for the implicit speech act of the utterance:

As you're in charge, where are the files on the new project? ['As you're in charge, I'm asking you . . .?']

> Vanessa is your favourite aunt, *because your parents told me so*. ['Since your parents told me so, I can say that Vanessa is your favourite aunt.']
> *As long as you're here*, why don't we discuss our plans?
> *Since you seem to know them*, why don't you introduce me to them?

[b] When *as* is a circumstantial subordinator, the predication may optionally be fronted:

> *Writing hurriedly as she was*, she didn't notice the spelling errors.
> *Tired as they were*, they stayed up for the late news.

That may be a circumstantial subordinator, when the subject complement is obligatorily fronted:

> *Clumsy idiot that he was*, Michael completely ruined the dinner.

Cf 15.21 Note [a] for a similar fronting with concessive clauses.

Purpose clauses

15.27 Purpose clauses are usually infinitival, and may be introduced by *in order to* ⟨formal⟩ and *so as to*:

> Students should take notes *(so as) to make revision easier*.
> The committee agreed to adjourn *(in order) to reconsider the matter when fuller information became available*.
> They left the door open *(in order) for me to hear the baby*.

Finite clauses of purpose are introduced by *so that* or (less commonly and more informally) by *so*, and (more formally) by *in order that*:

> The school closes earlier *so (that) the children can get home before dark*.
> The jury and the witnesses were removed from the court *in order that they might not hear the arguments of the lawyers on the prosecution's motion for an adjournment*.

These finite clauses, which are putative (*cf* 15.28), require a modal auxiliary.

NOTE Negative purpose is expressed in the infinitive clauses by *so as not to* and *in order not to*, and in finite clauses by *in order that . . . not*; *for fear (that)*, *in case* ⟨BrE⟩, or *lest* ⟨archaic and very formal⟩ convey an implied negative purpose:

> Turn the volume down *so as not to wake the baby*.
> They left early *for fear (that) they would meet him*.
> They evacuated the building *in case the wall collapsed*. ⟨BrE⟩

Result clauses

15.28 Result clauses are introduced by the subordinators *so that* and *so*:

> We paid him immediately, *so (that) he left contented*.
> I took no notice of him, *so (that) he flew into a rage*.

The same subordinators are used for purpose clauses but, because they are putative rather than factual, purpose clauses require a modal auxiliary:

> We paid him immediately, *so (that) he would leave contented.*

NOTE The subordinator *so* is indistinguishable from the conjunct *so* in asyndetic coordination, but if *and* is inserted *so* is unambiguously the conjunct:

> We paid him immediately, *and so* he left contented.

Clauses of similarity and comparison

15.29 For both similarity clauses and comparison clauses, there is a semantic blend with manner if the verb is dynamic.

Clauses of similarity are introduced by *as* and ⟨esp informal AmE⟩ *like*. These subordinators are commonly premodified by *just* and *exactly*:

> Please do *(exactly) as I said.* [1]
> It was *(just) like I imagined it would be* ⟨esp informal AmE⟩ [2]

Clauses of comparison are introduced by *as if*, *as though*, and ⟨esp informal AmE⟩ *like*:

> She looks *as if she's getting better.* [3]

If the comparison is hypothetical (implying lack of reality), a subjunctive or hypothetical past may be used as an alternative (*cf* 14.12*f*):

> She treated me as *though* { *I was* / *I were* / *I had been* } *a stranger.*

The subordinators *as*, *as if*, and *as though* can introduce nonfinite and verbless clauses:

> Fill in the application form *as instructed.*
> You should discuss the company with him *as though unaware that you were being considered for a job.*

As if and *as though* may also introduce *to*-infinitive clauses:

> She winked at me *as if to say that I shouldn't say anything.*

NOTE [a] If the *as*-clause is placed initially, correlative *so* introduces the matrix clause in formal literary style:

> *(Just) as a moth is attracted by a light, so* he was fascinated by her.

The clause then expresses an analogy.

[b] There are prescriptive objections to the use of *like* as a subordinator. It is more acceptable when it expresses pure similarity, as in [2], since that is the meaning expressed by the preposition *like*, than when it expresses manner or comparison. Hence *like* would be less acceptable if it replaced *as* in [1] or [3].

Clauses of proportion

15.30 Proportional clauses involve a kind of comparison. They express a proportionality or equivalence of tendency or degree between two situations. They may be introduced by *as*, with or without correlative *so* ⟨formal⟩, or by the fronted correlative *the* . . . *the* followed by comparative forms:

> *As he grew disheartened, (so)* his work deteriorated.
> *As the lane got narrower, (so)* the overhanging branches made it more difficult for us to keep sight of our quarry.
> *The more* she thought about it, *the less* she liked it.

Noncorrelative *the* is also used in the same sense:

> She liked it less, *the more* she thought about it.

Clauses of preference

15.31 Clauses of preference are usually nonfinite. They may be introduced by the subordinators *rather than* and *sooner than*, with the bare infinitive as the verb of the clause:

> *Rather than go there by air*, I'd take the slowest train. ['I'd prefer to take the slowest train.']
> They'll fight to the finish *sooner than surrender*. ['They prefer to fight to the finish.']

The same subordinators may introduce finite clauses:

> *Rather than (that) she should miss her train*, I'll get the car over.

Comment clauses

15.32 Comment clauses are parenthetical disjuncts. They may occur initially, finally, or medially, and thus generally have a separate tone unit:

> KÌNGston, | *as you probably* KNÓW, | is the capital of JaMÀica |

We distinguish the following types:

(i) like the matrix of a main clause:

> There were no other applicants, *I believe*, for that job.

(ii) an adverbial finite clause (introduced by *as*):

> I'm working the night shift, *as you know*.

(iii) a nominal relative clause:

> *What was more upsetting*, we lost all our luggage.

(iv) *to*-infinitive clause as style disjunct:

> I'm not sure what to do, *to be honest*.

(v) *-ing* clause as style disjunct:

I doubt, *speaking as a layman*, whether television is the right medium for that story.

(vi) *-ed* clause as style disjunct:

Stated bluntly, he had no chance of winning.

In each category, there are idiomatic or cliché expressions: *you see*, *as I say*, *what's more to the point*, *to be fair*, *generally speaking*, *put bluntly*. Similarly, in each category there is at least some freedom to coin new expressions.

Comment clauses, many of which are characteristic of spoken English, are generally marked prosodically by increased speed and lowered prominence.

NOTE Type (i) comment clauses, which are the most important, generally contain a transitive verb or an adjective which elsewhere requires a nominal *that*-clause as complementation. We can therefore see a correspondence between sentences containing such clauses and sentences containing indirect statements:

There were no other applicants, *I believe*, for that job.
I believe that there were no other applicants for that job.

Since the *that* of an object *that*-clause is normally deletable, only the intonation (reflected by comma separation in writing) distinguishes an initial comment clause from an initial matrix clause:

You KNÓW, ‖I think you're WRÒNG| } [*You know* is a comment clause]
You know, I |think you're WRÒNG| . }

You |know (that) I think you're WRONG| . [*You know* is a matrix clause]

Sentential relative clauses

15.33 Closely related to comment clauses of type (ii) (*as you know*) and type (iii) (*what's more surprising*) are SENTENTIAL RELATIVE CLAUSES. Unlike adnominal relative clauses, which have a noun phrase as antecedent, the sentential relative clause refers back to the predicate or predication of a clause ([1] and [2]), or to a whole clause or sentence, ([3] and [4]), or even to a series of sentences ([5]):

They say he *plays truant, which he doesn't*. [1]
He *walks for an hour each morning, which would bore me*. [2]
Things then improved, *which surprises me*. [3]
Colin married my sister and I married his brother, *which makes Colin and me double in-laws*. [4]

– *which is how the kangaroo came to have a pouch.* [said at the end of a story] [5]

Sentential relative clauses parallel nonrestrictive postmodifying clauses in noun phrases (*cf* 17.11) in that they are separated by intonation or punctuation from their antecedent. They are commonly introduced by the relative pronoun *which*, but *which* may also be a relative determiner of abstract nouns, as in [6] and [7]:

The plane may be several hours late, *in which case there's no point in our waiting.* [6]
They were under water for several hours, *from which experience they emerged unharmed.* [7]

The subject of nonfinite and verbless clauses

15.34 Nonfinite and verbless adverbial clauses that have an overt subject but are not introduced by a subordinator are ABSOLUTE clauses, so termed because they are not explicitly bound to the matrix clause syntactically. Absolute clauses may be *-ing*, *-ed*, or verbless clauses:

No further discussion arising, the meeting was brought to a close.
Lunch finished, the guests retired to the lounge.
Christmas then only days away, the family was pent up with excitement.

Apart from a few stereotyped phrases (*eg*: *present company excepted*, *weather permitting*, *God willing*), absolute clauses are formal and infrequent.

When a subject is not present in a nonfinite or verbless clause, the normal ATTACHMENT RULE for identifying the subject is that it is assumed to be identical in reference to the subject of the superordinate clause:

The oranges, *when (they are) ripe*, are picked and sorted mechanically.

The attachment rule is commonly given for participle clauses, but it applies equally to infinitive and verbless clauses:

Persuaded by our optimism, he gladly contributed time and money to the scheme. ['Since he was persuaded . . .']
Driving home after work, I accidentally went through a red light. ['While I was driving home after work . . .']
Confident of the justice of their cause, they agreed to put their case before an arbitration panel. ['Since they were confident . . .']
To climb the rock face, we had to take various precautions. ['So that we could climb . . .']

Sometimes the attachment rule is violated:

> ?*Driving to Chicago that night*, a sudden thought struck me. ['I was driving']

The violation is considered to be an error. Such unattached (or dangling) clauses are totally unacceptable if the sentence provides no means for identifying the implied subject:

> **Reading the evening paper*, a dog started barking.

NOTE The attachment rule does not apply, or at least is relaxed, in certain cases:

(a) The clause is a style disjunct, and the *I* of the speaker is the implied subject:

> *Putting it mildly*, you have caused us some inconvenience.

(b) The implied subject is the whole of the matrix clause:

> I'll help you *if necessary*. ['. . . if it is necessary.']

(c) If the implied subject is an indefinite pronoun or prop *it* (*cf* 10.14), the construction is considered less objectionable:

> *When dining in the restaurant*, a jacket and tie are required. ['When one dines . . .']
> *Being Christmas*, the government offices were closed. ['Since it was . . .']

Supplementive clauses

15.35 Adverbial participle and verbless clauses without a subordinator are SUPPLEMENTIVE CLAUSES: they do not signal specific logical relationships, but such relationships are generally clear from the context (*cf* also 7.14). The formal inexplicitness of supplementive clauses allows considerable flexibility in what we may wish them to convey. According to context, we may wish to imply temporal, conditional, causal, concessive, or circumstantial relationships. In short, the supplementive clause implies an accompanying circumstance to the situation described in the matrix clause. For the reader or hearer, the actual nature of the accompanying circumstance has to be inferred from the context:

> *Reaching the river*, we pitched camp for the night. ['When we reached the river, . . .']
> Julia, *being a nun*, spent much of her time in prayer and meditation. ['. . ., since she was a nun, . . .']
> *Aware of the dangers to American citizens during the crisis*, she still insisted on staying with the others.
> The sentence is ambiguous, *taken out of context*. ['if/when it is . . .']
> *Using a sharp axe*, Gilbert fought his way into the building. ['By using a sharp axe . . .']
> Marilyn crawled through the narrow tunnel, *hands in front*.
> We spoke *face to face*.

They stood silently, *their eyes fixed on the horizon.*
Elizabeth dived in *head first.*
They strolled through the park *with their arms intertwined.*

Comparative clauses

15.36 In a comparative construction, a proposition expressed in the matrix clause is compared with a proposition expressed in the subordinate clause. Words that are repeated in both clauses may be omitted in the subordinate clause (*cf* 15.38):

Jane is as healthy *as her sister (is).* [1]
Jane is healthier *than her sister (is).* [2]

The comparison is with respect to some STANDARD OF COMPARISON: health in [1] and [2]. The clause element that specifies the standard is the COMPARATIVE ELEMENT (henceforth 'comp-element'): as *healthy* in [1] and *healthier* in [2]. The BASIS OF COMPARISON (which may be implied from the context rather than overtly expressed) is Jane's sister in [1] and [2].

Broadly conceived, comparison includes comparisons of EQUIVALENCE (as in [1]) and NONEQUIVALENCE (as in [2]), and comparisons of SUFFICIENCY and EXCESS (as in [3] and [4]):

Don is *sensitive enough to understand your feelings.* [3]
Marilyn was *too polite to say anything about my clothes.* [4]

More narrowly, comparison covers the types exemplified in [1] and [2] or even just those comparisons – like [2] and [5] – that require a *than*-clause:

Jane is { *more healthy* / *healthier* / *less healthy* } *than her sister is.* [5]

Comparisons of equivalence, nonequivalence, and excess (*cf* 15.41) are nonassertive, as can be seen from the use in them of nonassertive forms:

She works { as hard as / harder than } she *ever* did.

He eats vegetables { as much as / more than } *any* other food.

We use *more* and the inflectional variant in *-er*, the typical comparative items, to exemplify comparative instructions in the sections that follow.

NOTE The standard of comparison involves a scale without commitment to absolute values. Hence, [1] and [2] do not presuppose that Jane's sister is healthy.

Clause functions of the comp-element

15.37 The comp-element of a comparative construction can be any of the clause elements, apart from the verb:

subject:

More people use this brand than (use) any other window-cleaning fluid.

direct object:

She knows *more history* than most people (know).

indirect object:

That toy has given *more children* happiness than any other (toy) (has).

subject complement:

Lionel is *more relaxed* than he used to be.

object complement:

She thinks her children *more obedient* than (they were) last year.

adverbial:

You've been working *much harder* than I (have).

The comp-element may also be a prepositional complement:

She's applied for *more jobs* than Joyce (has (applied for)).

The same range is available for the comp-element in comparisons of equivalence; for example:

As many people use this brand *as (use)* any other window-cleaning fluid.

NOTE **[a]** There is a type of nonclausal comparison in which *more . . . than*, *less . . . than*, and *as . . . as* are followed by an explicit standard of comparison:

I weigh more than 200 pounds.
It goes faster than 100 miles per hour.
The strike was nothing less than a national catastrophe.
Our factory consumes as much as 500 tons of solid fuel per week.

Another nonclausal comparison is exemplified by:

I was more angry than frightened.
I was angry more than frightened. } ['It is more true to say that I was . . .']

The inflectional form is not possible:

*I was angrier than frightened.

[b] When *more* precedes an adjective in a noun phrase, there may be ambiguity. For example, *more expensive clothes* is ambiguous in:

Morton has more expensive clothes than I have.

In one interpretation *more* modifies *expensive* ('clothes that are more expensive'); in the other interpretation *more* is the determiner for the noun phrase ('a greater quantity of expensive clothes').

[c] The modifying sequences *more of a* . . . and *less of a* . . . occur with gradable singular noun heads:

He's more of a fool than I thought (he was).
It was less of a success than I imagined (it would be).

Cf the *how*-question, *How much of a fool is he?* ['To what extent is he (in your view) a fool?']

There are parallel constructions with *as much of a* . . . *as* and *as little of a* . . . *as*:

It was as much/little of a success as I imagined (it would be).

[d] When the contrast involves two points on the same scale, one higher than the other, the part following *than* cannot be expanded into a clause. *Than* is then functioning as a preposition in a nonclausal comparison:

It's hotter *than* just warm. (*cf* It's hotter than 90°.)
She's wiser *than* merely clever.
We drove farther *than* (beyond) Chicago.
They fought harder *than* that.

Another type of nonclausal comparison is expressed by *more than*:

I am *more than* happy to hear that.
She behaved *more than* fairly to him

Semantically, *more than* expresses a higher degree, but it also conveys a comment on the inadequacy of what is said in the linguistic unit it modifies.

[e] Some people prefer to use *so* . . . *as* instead of *as* . . . *as* when the matrix clause is negative:

He's not *so naughty as* he was.

Ellipsis in comparative clauses

15.38 Ellipsis of a part of the comparative clause is likely to occur when that part is a repetition of something in the matrix clause. Since it is normal for the two clauses to be closely parallel both in structure and content, ellipsis is the rule rather than the exception in comparative constructions. Here is a set of examples of optional ellipsis and optional substitutions by pronouns and by pro-predicate or pro-predication:

James and Susan often go to plays but

(i) James enjoys the theatre more than Susan enjoys the theatre.
(ii) James enjoys the theatre more than Susan enjoys it.
(iii) James enjoys the theatre more than Susan does.
(iv) James enjoys the theatre more than Susan.
(v) James enjoys the theatre more.

Ellipsis of the object generally cannot take place unless the main verb too is ellipted, as in (iii) and (iv), where there is a choice between the retention of an operator and its omission:

*James knows more about the theatre than Susan *knows*.

The comp-element is the hinge between the matrix clause and the comparative clause. Since the comp-element specifies the standard of comparison, the same standard cannot be specified again in the comparative clause:

*Jane is healthier than her sister is healthy.
*James enjoys the theatre more than Susan much enjoys the theatre.

The standards of comparison in the two clauses may, however, be different.

Mary is cleverer than Jane is pretty.

Ambiguity through ellipsis

15.39 When normal ellipsis is taken to its fullest extent, ambiguity can arise as to whether a remaining noun phrase is subject or object:

He loves his dog more than his children.

The above example could mean either [1] '. . . than his children love his dog' or [2] 'than he loves his children'. If *his children* is replaced by a pronoun, formal English makes the distinction:

He loves his dog more than *they*. [1]
He loves his dog more than *them*. [2]

In other styles, however, the objective case *them* is used for both [1] and [2]. Since both forms can be criticized (on account of stiffness on the one hand, and 'bad grammar' on the other), and since in any event we cannot be sure that the objective case in [2] represents choice in formal style and is therefore unambiguous, it is better to expand the clause (*than they do*; *than he does them*) where there is danger of ambiguity.

Partial contrasts

15.40 If the two clauses in a comparison differed solely in the comp-element (**I hear it more clearly than I hear it*), the comparison would of course be nonsensical; therefore, a contrast of at least one variable is required between the two clauses. The contrast may affect only tense or the addition of a modal auxiliary. In such cases it is normal to omit the rest of the comparative clause after the auxiliary:

I hear it more clearly than I *did*. ['than I used to hear it']
I get up later than I *should*. ['than I should get up']

If the contrast lies only in tense, it may be expressed in the comparative clause solely by an adverbial:

She'll enjoy it more than (she enjoyed it) last year.

This provides the basis for the total ellipsis of the subordinate clause in examples like:

You are slimmer (than you were).
You're looking better (than you were (looking)).

NOTE [a] There are two other contexts in which the comparative clause is omitted. One is where there is anaphoric reference to an implied or actual preceding clause or sentence:

I caught the bus from town: but Harry came home *even later*. [*ie* 'later than I came home']

The other is where the reference is to the extralinguistic situation:

You should have come home *earlier*. [*ie* 'earlier than you did']

[b] The partial contrast may be in a superordinate clause in the matrix clause or the comparative clause:

She thinks she's fatter than she (really) is.
He's a greater painter than *people suppose* (he is).
She enjoyed it more than *I expected* (her to (enjoy it)).

Enough and *too*

15.41 There are comparative constructions that express the contrasting notions of sufficiency and excess, chiefly with *enough* and *too* followed by a *to*-infinitive clause. Paraphrase pairs may be constructed with antonymous items:

{They're rich enough to own a car.
{They're not too poor to own a car.

{The book is simple enough to understand.
{The book is not too difficult to understand.

If the context allows, the infinitive clause may be omitted.

The negative force of *too* is shown in the use of nonassertive forms. Contrast:

She's old *enough* to do *some* work.
She's *too* old to do *any* work.

The infinitive clause may contain an overt subject:

It moves too quickly *for most people to see (it)*.
He was old enough *for us to talk to (him) seriously*.

As these examples indicate, a direct object or the object of a prepositional verb may be omitted if it substitutes for the superordinate subject.

When there is no subject in the infinitive clause, it is identified with the superordinate subject or with an indefinite subject:

She writes quickly enough *to finish the paper on time.* ['for her to finish the paper on time']
He was old enough *to talk to him seriously.* ['for others to talk to him seriously']

And there may be ambiguity as to which identification to make:

She was too *young to date.* ['. . . to date others' or 'for others to date her']

When neither subject nor object is expressed in the infinitive clause, ambiguity is possible with verbs that may be used transitively:

$$\text{She is friendly enough} \left\{ \begin{matrix} \text{(for others)} \\ \text{(for her)} \end{matrix} \right\} \text{to help} \left\{ \begin{matrix} \text{(her).} \\ \text{(others).} \end{matrix} \right\}$$

NOTE *Enough of a* . . . and *too much of a* . . . may be constructed with gradable nouns (*cf* 15.37 Note [c]):

$$\text{He's} \left\{ \begin{matrix} \text{enough} \\ \text{too much} \end{matrix} \right\} \text{of a coward to do that.}$$

Cf also: *He was fool enough to go out without a coat.*

So . . . (that) and *such . . . (that)*

15.42 The correlatives *so . . . (that)* and *such . . . (that)* introduce constructions that combine the notion of sufficiency or excess with that of result. *So* is an adverb premodifying an adjective or adverb, and *such* is a predeterminer. Paraphrase pairs may be obtained between these constructions when the *that*-clause is negative and constructions with *too* and an infinitive clause:

It's *so* good a movie *that* we mustn't miss it.
~It's *too* good a movie *to* miss.
It was *such* a pleasant day *that* I didn't want to go to school.
~It was *too* pleasant a day *to* go to school.

There may be also similar paraphrases with constructions with *enough* when the *that*-clause is positive:

It flies *so* fast *that* it can beat the speed record.
~It flies fast *enough to* beat the speed record.
I had *such* a bad headache *that* I needed two aspirins.
~I had a bad *enough* headache *to* need two aspirins.

When *so* is used alone with a verb and *such* is used with a noun that is not premodified, they express a high degree and the construction conveys the notion of result:

I *so* enjoyed it *that* I'm determined to go again. ['I so much enjoyed it . . .']

There was *such* a crowd *that we* couldn't see a thing. ['There was such a large crowd . . .']

NOTE [a] The subordinator *that* may be omitted from the *that*-clause. An informal variant substitutes intensifier *that* for *so* and omits the subordinator *that*:

I was '*that* tired I couldn't keep my eyes open.

[b] The somewhat formal construction *so/such . . . as* with the infinitive is sometimes used in place of *so/such* with a *that*-clause:

His temper was *so* violent *as* to make even his closest companions fear him.
The brilliance of her satires was *such as* to make even her victims laugh.

Bibliographical note

On nominal clauses in general, see Huddleston (1971, Chs. 4 and 5); Stockwell et al. (1973, Ch. 8); Vendler (1968). On *that*-clauses in particular, see Hooper (1975).

On adverbial clauses of time in general, see Edgren (1971).

On adverbial clauses of concession, see Aarts (1988); Altenberg (1986).

On clauses of reason, see Altenberg (1984).

On comment clauses, see Lakoff, G. (1974).

On nonfinite and verbless adverbial clauses introduced by a subordinator, see Bäcklund (1984).

On adverbial *-ing* clauses, see Greenbaum (1973).

On comparative clauses, see especially Huddleston (1971, Ch. 6).

16 Complementation of verbs and adjectives

Introduction

16.1 In this chapter we examine the COMPLEMENTATION of verbs and adjectives, *ie* the grammatical patterns that follow a verb or adjective and complete the specification of a meaning relationship which that word implies. We begin with multi-word verbs.

Multi-word verbs

16.2 The two main categories of multi-word verbs consist of a lexical verb plus a PARTICLE, a neutral designation for the overlapping categories of adverb and preposition that are used in such combinations (*cf* 16.3*ff*). In PHRASAL VERBS the particle is an adverb (*eg*: *drink up*, *find out*) and in PREPOSITIONAL VERBS it is a preposition (*eg*: *dispose of*, *cope with*). In addition, there are PHRASAL–PREPOSITIONAL VERBS with verbs with two particles, an adverb followed by a preposition (*eg*: *put up with*, *cf* 16.9), and types of multi-verbs that do not consist of lexical verbs followed simply by particles (*eg*: *cut short*, *put paid to*), *cf* 16.10.

There is not a sharp boundary between multi-word verbs and free combinations, where the parts have distinct meanings. Rather, there is a gradience ranging from idiomatic and syntactically cohesive combinations to combinations that are loosely connected.

Intransitive phrasal verbs

16.3 One common type of multi-word verb is the intransitive phrasal verb consisting of a verb plus an adverb particle, as exemplified in:

The plane has just *touched down*.
He is *playing around*.
I hope you'll *get by*.
How are you *getting on*?
The plane has now *taken off*.
Did he *catch on*?
The prisoner finally *broke down*.
She *turned up* unexpectedly.
When will they *give in*?

The tank *blew up*.
One of my papers has *gone astray*.
The two girls have *fallen out*. [= 'quarrelled']

In phrasal verbs like *give in* ['surrender'] or *blow up* ['explode'], we cannot predict the meaning of the idiomatic combination from the meaning of verb and particle in isolation. But in free combinations (*eg*: *walk past*) we can do so. Furthermore, the semantic separability of the two parts is shown by possible substitutions: for *walk* in *walk past*, for example, we can substitute *run*, *trot*, *swim*, *fly*, etc; and for *past* we can substitute *by*, *in*, *through*, *over*, etc. In other cases the adverb in a free combination has an intensifying force (*eg*: *chatter away*) or an aspectual force (*eg*: *drink up*).

There are also syntactic signs of cohesion. Normally the particle of a phrasal verb cannot be separated from the lexical verb (**She turned right up*), but this separation is possible in free combinations (*Go straight on*). Similarly, the adverb can be fronted in free combinations (*Out came the sun*; *Up you come*), but not in phrasal verbs (**Up blew the tank*; **Out he passed* ['fainted']).

Transitive phrasal verbs

16.4 Many phrasal verbs may take a direct object, and are therefore transitive:

We will *set up* a new unit.
Shall I *put away* the dishes?
Find out if they are coming.
She's *bringing up* two children.
Someone *turned on* the light.
They have *called off* the strike.
He can't *live down* his past.
I can't *make out* what he means.
We *pushed home* our advantage.
She *looked up* her friends.
I've *handed in* my resignation.
They may have *blown up* the bridge.

Some combinations, such as *give in* and *blow up*, can be either intransitive or transitive. In some cases, *eg give in*, there is a substantial difference in meaning, whereas in others, *eg blow up*, there is not.

As with free combinations of the same pattern, the particle can generally either precede or follow the direct object:

They *turned on* the light. ~ They *turned* the light *on*.

But when the object is a personal pronoun, the particle must usually follow the object:

*They *turned on* it. ~ They *turned* it *on*.

The particle tends to precede the object if the object is long, or if it is intended that the object should receive end-focus (*cf* 18.2, 18.5).

Like intransitive phrasal verbs, transitive phrasal verbs are distinguished semantically from free combinations of verb and adverb. Contrast the phrasal verb *take in* in *She took in her parents* ['deceived'] with the free combination in *She took in the box* ['brought inside'], where the two parts preserve their separate meanings.

If the transitive phrasal verb is fully idiomatic, the particle cannot normally be separated from the lexical verb by anything except the object, not even by an intensifier such as *right*. Hence, *bring up* is a free combination in *She brought the girls right up* ['led them up' (the stairs, etc)], since the phrasal verb *bring up* ['rear'] does not allow the interruption.

NOTE **[a]** Some transitive phrasal verbs do not easily allow the particle to come after the object, unless the object is a pronoun; *eg*: ?*They had given hope up*; ?*They laid their arms down*. Conversely, some do not easily allow it to come before the object; for example, only final position is possible in the idiomatic hyperbolic expressions *I was crying my eyes out*; *I was sobbing my heart out*.

[b] Some phrasal verbs are semi-idiomatic and allow a limited number of substitutions, *eg* for *Let's turn on the light*:

Let's { turn / switch / put } it { on. / out. / off. / down. / up. }

Similarly, it is possible to insert an intensifier of the particle for at least some of these phrasal verbs (*eg*: *They turned the music right up*).

Type I prepositional verbs

16.5 A type I prepositional verb consists of a lexical verb followed by a preposition with which it is semantically and/or syntactically associated:

Look at these pictures.
I don't *care for* Jane's parties.
We must *go into* the problem.
Can you *cope with* the work?
I *approve of* their action.
His eyes *lighted upon* the jewel.

The noun phrase following the preposition is a PREPOSITIONAL OBJECT, a term that suggests an analogy with the term *direct object*. Compare the 'transitive' relationship of *look at* and *these pictures* in *Look at these pictures* with that of *examine* and *these pictures* in *Examine these pictures*. Similarly, the passive is frequently possible for prepositional verbs, as in:

The picture *was looked at* by many people.

On the other hand, we can easily insert an adverbial between the lexical verb and the preposition:

> Many people *looked* disdainfully *at* the picture.

By contrast, insertion between verb and direct object is usually avoided unless the direct object is long:

> ?*Many people *examined* disdainfully the picture.

We can also isolate the whole prepositional phrase from the verb in other ways, *eg*:

> *On whom* did he call? *On his mother.*
> He called on his mother and *on his sister.*
> He called on his mother more often than *on his sister.*

There are therefore two complementary analyses of a sentence like *She looked after* ['tended'] *her son*:

ANALYSIS 1:	S	V	A	
	She	*looked*	*after*	*her son*
ANALYSIS 2:	S	V		O

(Analysis 1: S = *She*, V = *looked*, A = *after her son*; Analysis 2: S = *She*, V = *looked after*, O = *her son*.)

The distinction between prepositional verbs and free combinations

16.6 One criterion for distinguishing prepositional verbs (*eg*: *We called on the dean*) from free combinations of verb plus preposition (*eg*: *We called after lunch*) is the possibility of making the prepositional object the subject of a corresponding passive clause. In this PREPOSITIONAL PASSIVE the preposition is STRANDED in its post-verbal position. Contrast:

> The dean *was called on.* *Lunch *was called after.*

Here are some examples of the prepositional passive:

> Though something very different from ordinary forest management *is called for*, the trees in the parks do need the forester's skilled consideration.
> This matter will have to *be dealt with* immediately.
> Other possibilities *are talked of* by many of our colleagues.
> If a woman with a university degree rejects a career for marriage, her education is not to *be thought of* as thrown away unless we count the family arena of no importance.

A second criterion is that *wh*-questions eliciting the prepositional object are formed with the pronouns *who(m)* and *what* (as with direct objects) rather than with adverbial questions:

> John called on *her*. ~ *Who(m)* did John call on?
> John looked for *it*. ~ *What* did John look for?

Contrast the free combinations in:

John called from *the office*. ~ *Where* did John call from?
John called after *lunch*. ~ *When* did John call?

NOTE [a] The passive is acceptable in some instances where the preposition introduces a prepositional phrase of place and is not in idiomatic combination with the verb. For example:

They must have *played on* this field last week.
~ This field must have *been played on* last week.
Visitors are not to *sit on* these Louis XV chairs.
~ These Louis XV chairs are not to *be sat on*.
Primitive men once *lived in* these caves.
~ These caves *were* once *lived in* by primitive men.

The passive is possible in these instances because the prepositional complement is being treated as an affected participant in the clause (*cf* 10.9*f*).
[b] Some combinations allow both types of *wh*-questions: *She died of pneumonia* could be an answer either to *How did she die?* or (more usually) *What did she die of?*

The distinction between prepositional verbs and phrasal verbs

16.7 Type I prepositional verbs resemble transitive phrasal verbs superficially, but the differences are both syntactic and phonological. The contrast is exemplified for the prepositional verb *call on* ('visit') and the phrasal verb *call up* ('summon').

(a) The particle of a prepositional verb must precede the prepositional object (unless the particle is stranded), but the particle of a phrasal verb can generally precede or follow the direct object:

She *called on* her friends.	She *called up* her friends.
~ *She *called* her friends *on*.	~ She *called* her friends *up*.

(b) When the object is a personal pronoun, the pronoun follows the particle of a prepositional verb but precedes the particle of a phrasal verb:

She *called on* them.	She *called* them *up*.
~ *She *called* them *on*.	~ *She *called up* them.

(c) An adverb (functioning as adjunct) can often be inserted between verb and particle in prepositional verbs, but not in phrasal verbs:

She *called* angrily *on* her friends.
~ *She *called* angrily *up* her friends.

(d) The particle of a phrasal verb cannot precede a relative pronoun or *wh*-interrogative:

the friends *on* whom she *called*
~ *On* which friends did she *call*?

*the friends *up* whom she *called*.
  ~ * *Up* which friends did she *call*?

(e) The particle of a phrasal verb is normally stressed, and in final position normally bears the nuclear tone, whereas the particle of a prepositional verb is normally unstressed and has the 'tail' of the nuclear tone that falls on the lexical verb:

Which friends did she CÀLL on?
  ~ Which friends did she call ÙP?

Type II prepositional verbs

16.8 Type II prepositional verbs are ditransitive verbs. They are followed by two noun phrases, normally separated by the preposition: the second noun phrase is the prepositional object:

He *deprived* the peasants *of* their land.
They *plied* the young man *with* food.
Please *confine* your remarks *to* the matter under discussion.
This clothing will *protect* you *from* the worst weather.
Jenny *thanked* us *for* the present.
May I *remind* you *of* our agreement?
They have *provided* the child *with* a good education.

The direct object becomes the subject in the corresponding passive clause:

The gang *robbed* her *of* her necklace.
  ~ She was *robbed of* her necklace (by the gang).

NOTE There are two minor subtypes in which the direct object is part of the idiomatic combination:

(1) The first is exemplified by *make a mess of*, *make allowance for*, *take care of*, *pay attention to*, *take advantage of*. It allows a second less acceptable passive in which the prepositional object becomes subject:

A (terrible) *mess* has been *made of* the house.
  ~ (?) The house has been *made* a (terrible) *mess of*.

(2) The second is exemplified by *catch sight of*, *keep pace with*, *give way to*, *lose touch with*, *cross swords with*, *keep tabs on*, *give rise to*. Only the prepositional object can become the passive subject, though it is considered somewhat clumsy:

The lifeboat was suddenly *caught sight of*.

Phrasal–prepositional verbs

16.9 PHRASAL–PREPOSITIONAL VERBS have in addition to the lexical verb, both an adverb and a preposition as particles. Type I phrasal–prepositional verbs have only a prepositional object:

We are all *looking forward to* your party on Saturday.
He had to *put up with* a lot of teasing at school.

Why don't you *look in on* Mrs Johnson on your way back?
He thinks he can *get away with* everything.

The prepositional passive is possible, though liable to sound cumbersome. These examples, however, are normal and acceptable:

These tantrums could not be *put up with* any longer. ['tolerated']
The death penalty has been recently *done away with.* ['abolished']
Such problems must be squarely *faced up to.* ['confronted']
They were *looked down on* by their neighbours. ['despised']

Type II phrasal–prepositional verbs are ditransitive verbs (*cf* 16.32). They require two objects, the second of which is the prepositional object:

Don't *take* it *out on* me! ['vent your anger']
The manager *fobbed* me *off with* a lame excuse. <esp BrE>
We *put* our success *down to* hard work. ['attribute to']
I'*ll let* you *in on* a secret.

Only the active direct object can be made passive subject with these:

Our success can be *put down to* hard work.

For both types, the *wh*-question eliciting the prepositional object is formed with the pronouns *who(m)* and *what* (*cf* 16.6):

She looked in on *Mrs Johnson* on our way back.
~*(Who(m))* did she look in on?
They put their success down to *hard work.*
~*What* did they put their success down to?

Other multi-word verb constructions

16.10 In addition to the types of multi-word verbs discussed in 16.3–9, some other idiomatic verb constructions may be noted:

(a) VERB–ADJECTIVE COMBINATIONS

These are similar to phrasal verbs. Compare:

Meg *put* the cloth *straight.*   Meg *put* the cat *out.*

The constructions may be copular, *eg*: *break even, plead guilty, lie low.* Or they may be complex-transitive with a direct object following the verb (or the adjective if the object is long) *eg*: *cut* (their trip) *short, work* (the nail) *loose, rub* (herself) *dry* (*cf* 16.25 Note [c]). Sometimes the idiom allows additional elements, such as a modifier of the adjective (*cut as short as possible*), an infinitive (*play hard to get*), or a preposition (*ride roughshod over*).

(b) VERB–VERB COMBINATIONS

In these idiomatic constructions the second verb is nonfinite, and may be either an infinitive:

make do with, make (N) *do, let* (N) *go, let* (N) *be*

or a participle, with or without a following preposition:

> *put paid to*, *get rid of*, *have done with*, *leave* N *standing*, *send* N *packing*, *knock* N *flying*, *get going*

(c) VERBS WITH TWO PREPOSITIONS
These are a further variant on prepositional verbs:

> It *developed from* a small club *into* a mass organization in three years.

Similarly: *struggle with* N *for* N, *compete with* N *for* N, *apply to* N *for* N, *talk to* N *about* N. Normally either one or both prepositional phrases can be omitted.

Verb complementation

Intransitive verbs

16.11 Where no complementation occurs, the verb has an INTRANSITIVE use. Some verbs are always intransitive:

> John has *arrived*. Your views do not *matter*.

Others can also be transitive with the same meaning and without a change in the subject–verb relationship:

> He *smokes* (a pipe). She is *reading* (a book).

In some cases the intransitive verb acquires a more specific meaning: *eg*: *John drinks* (*heavily*) ['drinks alcohol'].

Other intransitive verbs can also be transitive, but the semantic connection between subject and verb is different:

> The car *stopped*. She *stopped* the car.

NOTE Intransitive verbs include intransitive phrasal verbs, *eg*: *fall out* ['quarrel'], *cf* 16.3.

Copular verbs

Subject complement

16.12 A verb has COPULAR complementation when it is followed by a subject complement or a predication adjunct (*cf* 8.14) and when this element cannot be dropped without changing the meaning of the verb. Such verbs are COPULAR (or linking) VERBS, the most common of which is the copula *be*.

Copular verbs fall into two main classes, according to whether the subject complement has the role of current attribute or resulting attribute (*cf* 10.9):

CURRENT: The girl *seemed* very restless.
RESULTING: The girl *became* very restless.

The most common copular verbs are listed below. Those that are used only with adjective phrases are followed by '[A]':

CURRENT copulas: *appear, be, feel, look, seem, smell* [A], *sound, taste* [A]
RESULTING copulas: *become, get* [A], *go* [A], *grow* [A], *prove, turn*

See also 10.7 Note [a].

NOTE [a] After certain copulas (*appear, feel, look, seem, sound*), both AmE and BrE prefer an infinitive construction with *to be* rather than simply a noun phrase:

It appears the only solution. It appears *to be* the only solution.

There is also a tendency with such copulas, especially in informal AmE, to prefer a construction in which the verb is followed by *like*: *It seems like the only solution.*
[b] Some copulas are severely restricted as to the words that may occur in their complement. The restriction may be to certain adjectives or to a semantic set of words. Here are some examples, with typical adjective complements: *loom (large), fall (silent), plead (innocent), rest (assured), run (wild), spring (open)*. See also 10.7 Note [b].

Complementation by adverbials

16.13 The principal copula that allows an adverbial as complementation is *be*. The adverbials are mainly space adjuncts (*eg*: *The kitchen is downstairs*) but time adjuncts are common with an eventive subject (*eg*: *The party will be at nine*) and other types of adjunct are possible too (*eg*: *She is in good health*). Two other copula verbs that occur with space adjuncts (or adjuncts metaphorically related to these) are *get* (*eg*: *How did you get here?*) and *keep* (*eg*: *They kept out of trouble*).

With intransitive verbs such as *live, come, go, lie, remain, stand,* and *stay*, the adverbial is not always clearly obligatory. But the positional or directional meaning of these verbs is completed by the adverbials:

My aunt lives *in Toronto.*
They are staying *nearby.*
Come *over here.*

NOTE [a] The verbs *seem, appear, look, sound, feel, smell,* and *taste* may be complemented by an adverbial clause beginning *as if* or *as though*: *It seems as if the weather is improving.*
[b] *Behave* is complemented by a manner adverbial (*He behaved badly*) and *last* and *take* by a duration adverbial (*The course lasted (for) three months*).

Monotransitive verbs

16.14 Monotransitive verbs require a direct object, which may be a noun phrase, a finite clause, or a nonfinite clause. We include in this category, for our present purposes, type I prepositional verbs such as *look at* (*cf* 16.5) and type I phrasal–prepositional verbs such as *put up with* (*cf* 16.9).

Noun phrase as direct object

16.15 Direct objects are typically noun phrases that may become the subject of a corresponding passive clause:

> Everybody understood *the problem*.
> ~ *The problem* was understood (by everyone).

Some common examples of the numerous monotransitive verbs that may be used in the passive: *believe, bring, call, close, do, enjoy, feel, find, get, hear, help, keep, know, lose, love, make, need, receive, remember, see, take, use, win.*

A few stative monotransitive verbs (some in particular senses) normally do not allow the passive. These MIDDLE VERBS include *have, fit, suit, resemble, equal, mean ('Oculist' means 'eye doctor'), contain, hold (The hall holds over three hundred people), comprise, lack.*

> They have a large house. ≁ *A large house is had (by them).

NOTE There are also monotransitive phrasal verbs, *eg*: *bring about, put off* (*cf* 16.4). These take a direct object and can be used in the passive.

Noun phrase as prepositional object

16.16 The prepositional object of type I prepositional verbs (*cf* 16.5) and type I phrasal–prepositional verbs (*cf* 16.9) resembles the direct object in accepting the passive (though often with some awkwardness in style) and in being elicited by a pronoun in questions:

> The management paid for *his air fares*.
> ~ *His air fares* were paid for by the management.
> ~ *What* did the management pay for?
> Your sister has checked up on me.
> ~ *I* have been checked up on by your sister.
> ~ *Who(m)* has your sister checked up on?

NOTE Another indication of the closeness of a prepositional object to a direct object is that when a prepositional verb is followed by a *that*-clause or a *to*-infinitive clause, the preposition disappears and the prepositional object merges with the direct object of the monotransitive pattern:

> They *agreed* { *on* the meeting. / *(that)* they would meet. / to meet each other. }

Yet the preposition that is omitted before a *that*-clause can reappear in the corresponding passive: *That they should meet was agreed (on)*. This is so even in extraposition (*cf* 18.23), where the preposition immediately follows the passive verb phrase:

> It was *agreed* (*on*) that they should meet.

Complementation by a finite clause

That-clause as object

16.17 The conjunction *that* in *that*-clauses functioning as object is optional, as in *I hope (that) he arrives soon*; but when the clause is made the passive subject, the conjunction is obligatory (*cf* 15.3). The normal passive analogue has *it* and extraposition, *that* being again to some extent optional:

> Everybody hoped (that) she would sing.
> ~That she would sing was hoped by everybody. <stilted>
> ~It was hoped by everybody (that) she would sing.

We distinguish four categories of verbs that are complemented by *that*-clauses: FACTUAL, SUASIVE, EMOTIVE, and HYPOTHESIS. Most verbs belong to the first two categories. The four categories are distinguished semantically, but also by the types of verbs that appear in the *that*-clauses.

Factual verbs

16.18 FACTUAL verbs are followed by a *that*-clause with an indicative verb:

> They *agreed* that she *was* misled.

There are two subtypes of factual verbs. PUBLIC verbs consist of speech act verbs introducing indirect statements; PRIVATE verbs express intellectual states and intellectual acts that are not observable.

Examples of public factual verbs: *admit, agree, announce, argue, bet, claim, complain, confess, declare, deny, explain, guarantee, insist, mention, object, predict, promise, reply, report, say, state, suggest, swear, warn, write.*

Examples of private factual verbs: *believe, consider, decide, doubt, expect, fear, feel, forget, guess, hear, hope, know, notice, presume, realize, recognize, remember, see, suppose, think, understand.*

Suasive verbs

16.19 SUASIVE verbs are followed by a *that*-clause either with putative *should* (preferred in BrE) or with the subjunctive (*cf* 14.13*f*). A third possibility, a *that*-clause with an indicative verb, occurs, though more commonly in BrE:

> People are demanding that he { *should leave* / *leave* / *leaves* <esp BrE> } the company.

A common alternative to the *that*-clause for some suasive verbs is an infinitive clause:

> They intended { the news *to be* suppressed. / that the news *(should) be* suppressed. <more formal> }

Examples of suasive verbs: *agree, ask, command, decide, demand, insist, intend, move, order, prefer, propose, recommend, request, suggest, urge.*

Emotive and hypothesis verbs

16.20 EMOTIVE verbs are followed by a *that*-clause with either the indicative or putative *should*:

> I regret that she / It surprises me that he { *worries* about it. / *should worry* about it. }

This group of verbs includes *annoy, concern, marvel, rejoice, regret, surprise, wonder, worry.*

HYPOTHESIS verbs comprise *wish, suppose* (in the imperative), and the modal idiom *would rather* or its contraction *'d rather*. They are followed by a *that*-clause with the hypothetical past or the *were*-subjunctive.

> I wish (that) she { *taught* us. / *were* here. }

Complementation by an extraposed subject *that*-clause

16.21 The *that*-clause in examples like *It seems (that) you are mistaken* is an extraposed subject, not an object of the verb. It resembles other *that*-clauses in previous sections in that the conjunction is optional and the clause is obligatory. The verb in the *that*-clause is indicative:

> It appears (that) you have lost your temper.

Common verbs in this pattern include *seem, appear*, and *happen*, and the phrasal verbs *come about* ['happen'] and *turn out* ['transpire'].

***Wh*-clause as object**

16.22 Many of the factual verbs which can take a *that*-clause as object can also take a *wh*-interrogative clause (*cf* 15.4).

> I don't *know* if we can get there in time.
> Have you *heard* whether she's coming with us?
> I *doubt* whether the flight has been booked.

The use of the *wh*-interrogative clause (which generally implies lack of knowledge on the part of the speaker) is particularly common where the superordinate clause is interrogative or negative. But verbs that themselves express uncertainty, such as *ask* and *doubt*, occur without this nonassertive constraint.

Examples of verbs taking the *wh*-interrogative clause: *ask, care, decide, depend, doubt, explain, forget, hear, know, mind, notice, prove, realize, remember, say, see, tell, think, wonder.*

NOTE The list includes prepositional verbs where the preposition is optionally omitted before a *wh*-clause:

I *inquired (about)* whether the tickets were ready.
I haven't *decided (on)* which flight I will take.

Nonfinite clauses as direct object

16.23 We distinguish five types of nonfinite clauses that function as direct object in monotransitive complementation:

(1) *wh*-infinitive clause:

The Curies discovered *how to isolate radioactive elements.*

(2) subjectless infinitive clause:

Ruth prefers *to go by bus.*

(3) subjectless *-ing* participle clause:

They like *talking about their work.*

(4) *to*-infinitive clause with subject:

Charles wants *you to stand for election.*

(5) *-ing* participle clause with subject (*cf* 15.10):

I hate *them/their gossiping about our colleagues.*

When the nonfinite clause has no subject – as in (1), (2), and (3) – its implied subject is usually identical with that of the superordinate clause.

The status of these clauses as direct object is confirmed when they are replaced by a coreferential pronoun *it* or *that*; for the example sentence in (1): *The Curies discovered that.* Another indication of their status is that they can be made the focus of a pseudo-cleft sentence (*cf* 18.20): *What Ruth prefers is to go by bus.* The passive is usually not admissible (but *cf*: *How to isolate radioactive elements was discovered by the Curies*).

Many monotransitive verbs take more than one type of nonfinite complementation. Common verbs are listed below for the five types:

(1) *decide, discuss, explain, forget, know, learn, remember, say, see, tell, think.*

(2) *ask, dislike, forget, hate, help, hope, learn, like, love, need, offer, prefer, promise, refuse, remember, try, want, wish.*

(3) and (5) *(can't) bear, dislike, enjoy, forget, hate, (can't) help, like, love, (not) mind, miss, need, prefer, remember, (can't) stand, start, stop.*

(4) *(can't) bear, dislike, hate, like, love, prefer, want, wish.*

Where both infinitive clauses – (2) and (4) – and participle clauses – (3) and (5) – are admitted, several factors influence the choice. The infinitive is biased towards potentiality and is therefore favoured in hypothetical and nonfactual contexts (*Would you like to see my stamp collection?*), whereas the participle is favoured in factual contexts (*Brian loathed living in the country*). For the three retrospective verbs *forget, remember,* and *regret* this potentiality/performance distinction is extended into the past:

I remembered *to fill out* the form. ['I remembered that I was to fill out the form and then did so.']
I remembered *filling out* the form. ['I remembered that I had filled out the form.']

NOTE [a] Monotransitive prepositional verbs are found in all five types. The preposition is optionally omitted in (1) and obligatorily omitted in (2), *cf.* 9.1:

(1) I couldn't *decide (on)* which bicycle to buy.
(2) She *decided* to buy a bicycle.
(3) She *decided on* buying a bicycle.
(4) We *longed for* the lesson to end.
(5) Don't *count on* their helping you.

Phrasal verbs and phrasal–prepositional verbs are found with types (3) and (5):

(3) She {*took up* / *got around to*} driving a bicycle.

(5) I {*put off* / *look forward to*} their seeing us.

[b] For the verbs *deserve*, *need*, and *require* in type (3), the implied object of the participle is identical with the subject of the superordinate clause: *Your shoes need mending* (*cf Your shoes need to be mended*).

Complex–transitive verbs

16.24 In COMPLEX–TRANSITIVE complementation, the two elements following the complex-transitive verb have a subject–predicate relationship:

She considered *her mother a sensible woman.* [1]
She considered *her mother to be a sensible woman.* [2]

The relationship between the elements *her mother* and *a sensible woman* in [1] and [2] is equivalent to the same elements in the subordinate finite clause in [3]:

She considered *that her mother was a sensible woman.* [3]

Yet the passive suggests that the two elements in [1] and [2] are not a single constituent, since the first element – as direct object – is separated from the second element and becomes the passive subject:

Her mother was considered (by her) *(to be) a sensible woman.*

Direct object and object complement

16.25 In the clausal pattern *SVOC* (*cf* 10.1), the object complement is an adjective phrase or a noun phrase. The attribute role of the object complement may be CURRENT, as in [1] and [2], or RESULTING, as in [3] and [4] (*cf* 10.9 Note [a]):

The secretary left all the letters *unopened*. [1]
I have often wished myself *a millionaire*. [2]
The long walk made us all *hungry*. [3]
The committee has elected you *its chairman*. [4]

The direct object can be made the passive subject:

All the letters were left unopened (by the secretary). [1a]

Many verbs admit both adjective phrases and noun phrases as object complements. The most common verbs for this construction are listed below. Those used only with adjective phrases are followed by '[A]', and those used only with noun phrases are followed by '[N]':

appoint [N], *believe*, *call*, *choose* [N], *consider*, *declare*, *elect* [N], *find*, *get* [A], *like* [A], *make*, *name* [N], *prefer* [A], *think*, *want* [A].

NOTE [a] For some verbs, the object complement is optional; *eg*: *elect* in *The committee has elected you* (its chairman).

[b] Prepositional verbs, mainly with the preposition *as*, take a prepositional object complement; *eg*: *They described her as a genius*; *He took me for a fool*. Sometimes the preposition is optional; *eg*: *They elected me (as) their leader*. Common examples of these prepositional verbs follow, with those taking an optional preposition listed first: *choose (as)*, *consider (as)*, *elect (as)* [N], *make (into)* [N]; *accept as*, *define as*, *intend as* [N], *mistake for*, *regard as*, *see as*, *take as/for*, *treat as*, *use as*.

[c] The *SVOC* pattern includes a number of verb–adjective collocations; for example: *boil (an egg) hard*, buy [N] *cheap*, *freeze* [N] *hard*, *paint* [N] *red/blue* . . ., *knock (someone) senseless*. The adjectives *open*, *loose*, *free*, and *clean* are particularly common: *push* [N] *open*, *shake* [N] *loose*, *set* [N] *free*, *wipe* [N] *clean*.

[d] The object is generally postposed by extraposition if it is a *that*-clause, and an anticipatory *it* then precedes the object complement:

I think *it* very odd *that nobody is in*.

The collocations *make sure* and *make certain* are followed by an object *that*-clause without anticipatory *it*:

Please *make sure* that you enclose your birth certificate.

Direct object and adjunct

16.26 In the *SVOA* pattern (*cf* 10.1), the complex–transitive verb is complemented by a direct object followed by a predication adjunct. The adjuncts are characteristically prepositional phrases of direction or metaphorical extensions of the notion of direction:

I slipped the key *into the lock*.
Take your hands *out of your pockets*.
May I see you *to your seat*? ['escort you . . .']
They talked me *into it*. ['persuaded me . . .']
He stood my argument *on its head*.

Space position adjuncts also occur in this construction:

> Always keep your eyes *on the road* when driving.
> The attackers caught us *off our guard.*

The passive of this construction is exemplified for this last sentence:

> We were caught off our guard (by the attackers).

Adjuncts of other semantic types are less common, but they include a manner adjunct with *treat* (*Her parents treated her badly*).

Direct object and *to*-infinitive clause

16.27 Some of the verbs taking a direct object and *to*-infinitive clause in complex-transitive complementation correspond to the factual verbs that take a *that*-clause with an indicative verb (*cf* 16.18):

> The police reported the traffic to be heavy. 〈formal〉
> = The police reported that the traffic was heavy.
> John believed the stranger to be a policeman. 〈formal〉
> = John believed that the stranger was a policeman.

In such cases, the infinitive clause normally contains a verb used statively, especially *be*. The finite clause is preferred in normal usage, but the infinitive clause provides a convenient passive form:

> The traffic was reported to be heavy.

Common factual verbs: *believe, consider, expect, feel, find, know, suppose.*

Nonfactual verbs include verbs of intention, causation, modality, and purpose:

> They intended Maria to sing an aria.
> The meeting elected her to be the next treasurer.
> My contract allows me to take one month's leave.
> Our teachers encouraged us to think for ourselves.

Common nonfactual verbs. *allow, appoint, cause, compel, condemn, dare, get, help, intend, mean, permit, require.*

NOTE [**a**] Some verbs in this construction occur only in the passive: *rumour, say, see.*

> The field marshal was said to be planning a new strategy.

Others occur chiefly in the passive: *repute, think.* The verb *get* is not found in the passive.

[**b**] Examples of multi-word verbs in this pattern are the prepositional verbs *count on, depend on, rely on*; the phrasal verb *make out*; and the phrasal–prepositional verb *keep on at.*

Direct object and bare infinitive clause

16.28 Two small groups of verbs take this pattern of complex–transitive complementation: three causative verbs (*have, let, make*) and some perceptual verbs of seeing and hearing (*feel, hear, notice, observe, overhear, see, watch*). In addition, *help* and ⟨esp BrE⟩ *know* may occur with the bare infinitive or the *to*-infinitive.

> They *had* me *repeat the message.*
> You shouldn't *let* your family *interfere with our plans.*
> We must *make* the public *take notice of us.*
> Did you *notice* anyone *leave the house*?
> The crowd *saw* Gray *score two goals.*
> Sarah *helped* us (to) *edit the script.*
> I have *known* John (to) *give better speeches than that.* ⟨esp BrE⟩

The passive normally requires a *to*-infinitive:

> John must be made to take notice of us.

NOTE Certain verbs in this pattern do not occur in the passive: *feel, have, let, watch*. There is an apparent passive in *let fall* and *let go (They were let go/fall)*, but these are fixed expressions. Only *let* has a passive of the infinitive clause (*They let themselves be led away*). Corresponding passives of the infinitive clause with verbs of perception require a copula, usually *being (The crowd watched two goals being scored)*, *cf* 16.29; *see* also admits a passive construction formed with the *-ed* participle without *be* (*The crowd saw two goals scored, cf* 16.30), which is the only passive if the verb is *have (They had the message repeated)*.

Direct object and *-ing* participle clause

16.29 Three small groups of verbs take this type of complex–transitive complementation: perceptual verbs, many of which also occur with the bare infinitive, *cf* 16.28 (*feel, hear, notice, observe, overhear, perceive, see, smell, spot, spy, watch*), verbs of encounter (*catch, discover, find, leave*), and the two causative verbs *get* and *have*. See also 4.35.

This complementation pattern differs from the monotransitive pattern (5) in 16.23 in that the noun phrase following the superordinate verb cannot take the genitive case (*cf* 15.10):

> I saw *him* lying on the beach. *I saw *his* lying on the beach.

The passive with this pattern is regular:

> We could *hear* the rain *splashing on the roof.*
> ~The rain could *be heard splashing on the roof.*
> A teacher *caught* them *smoking in the playground.*
> ~They *were caught smoking in the playground* (by a teacher).

Direct object and *-ed* participle clause

16.30 Three small groups of verbs occur with this type of complex–transitive complementation: perceptual verbs (*see, hear, feel, watch*), volitional verbs (*like, need, want*), and the two causative verbs *get* and *have*:

Someone must have *seen* the car *stolen*.
I *want* this watch *repaired immediately*.
She *had* the car *cleaned*.

For some verbs there are corresponding constructions with an infinitive copular verb, generally *be*: *I want this watch to be repaired immediately*.
Since the participle clause is passive, the superordinate clause is not normally in the passive: ?*The car must have been seen stolen*.

Ditransitive verbs

Noun phrases as both indirect and direct object

16.31 Ditransitive complementation in its basic form involves two object noun phrases: an indirect object, which is normally animate and positioned first, and a direct object, which is normally inanimate:

He *gave* the girl a doll
S V O_i O_d

Most ditransitive verbs can also be monotransitive. The indirect object can often be omitted: *She may give (us) a large donation*. With a few verbs (*eg*: *ask*, *pay*, *teach*, *tell*, *show*) either object can be omitted:

He taught us physics.
~He taught us.
~He taught physics.

Some ditransitive verbs have two passive analogues, which we distinguish as 'first' and 'second':

The girl was given a doll. [FIRST PASSIVE]
A doll was given the girl. [SECOND PASSIVE]

Of these two, the first passive, in which the indirect object becomes subject, is the more common. The prepositional paraphrase is more usual, as an alternative, than the second passive: *A doll was given to the girl*. We list ditransitive verbs in 16.32 together with their prepositional paraphrases.

Object and prepositional object

16.32 There are numerous ditransitive verbs that take a prepositional object as the second object (*cf* 16.8):

We *addressed* our remarks *to* the children. [1]
We *reminded* him *of* the agreement. [2]

Ditransitive verbs with prepositional objects normally have only the first passive:

Our remarks were addressed to the children. [1a]
He was reminded of the agreement. [2a]

Here are examples of ditransitive prepositional verbs:

accuse of	introduce to
advise about	persuade of
charge with	prevent from
compare with	protect from
congratulate on	punish for
deprive of	sentence to
explain to	suspect of
inform of	thank for
interest in	treat to

Some verbs allow more than one preposition. The different possibilities provide a means of achieving different end-focus (*cf* 18.5):

Sidney provided Justin with *a Danish apple pastry*.
~Sidney provided a Danish apple pastry for *Justin*.

Most ditransitive verbs that take two noun phrases as objects can also be paraphrased with a prepositional object equivalent to the indirect object:

Robert read *me* a chapter.
~Robert read a chapter *to me*.
I gave *Justin* some of my shirts.
~I gave some of my shirts *to Justin*.

We list some common ditransitive verbs that allow both possibilities. Those in list (1) take the preposition *to* and those in list (2) take the preposition *for*:

(1) *bring, deny, give, hand, lend, offer, owe, promise, read, send, show, teach, throw*
(2) *find, make, order, save, spare*

NOTE [a] A few ditransitive prepositional verbs (*eg*: *pay, serve, tell*) take one of two prepositions. In one the prepositional object is equivalent to the indirect object, in the other to the direct object:

Doris told David her version of the events.
~Doris told her version of the events *to David*.
~Doris told David *about her version of the events*.

A few other verbs (*eg*: *envy, excuse, forgive*) have a prepositional object (introduced by *for*) that is equivalent to the direct object:

Matthew envied me my video-recorder.
~Matthew envied me *for my video-recorder*.

[b] *Ask* takes the preposition *of* to introduce a prepositional object that is equivalent to the indirect object:

Robert asked Benjamin a favour.
~Robert asked a favour *of Benjamin*.

[c] A few ditransitive verbs do not have prepositional paraphrases: *allow*, *charge*, *fine*, *refuse*.
[d] See 16.8 Note for idiomatic combinations with prepositional verbs such as *make a mess of* and 16.9 for ditransitive phrasal–prepositional verbs.

Indirect object and *that*-clause object

16.33 Some ditransitive verbs take as direct object a *that*-clause:

Natalie convinced Derek (that) she was right. [1]

Only the first passive is acceptable:

Derek was convinced (by Natalie) (that) she was right. [1a]

With some verbs, including *convince*, the indirect object cannot be omitted.

If the *that*-clause introduces an indirect statement, it contains an indicative verb:

Ava told Jack that dinner *was* ready.

If it introduces an indirect directive (*cf* 14.20), there are several options (*cf* 16.19): the verb may be indicative or subjunctive, and often contains putative *should* or another modal auxiliary:

A dozen students petitioned the college chef that he

provides provide should provide might provide	} them with vegetarian meals. ⟨formal⟩

The indirect directive construction is rare and formal in comparison with the equivalent infinitive construction (*cf* 16.36): *A dozen students petitioned the college chef to provide them with vegetarian meals.*

We list common verbs that take an indirect object and (a) a *that*-clause object as indirect statement: *advise*, *bet*, *convince*, *inform*, *persuade*, *promise*, *remind*, *show*, *teach*, *tell*, *warn*, *write*; (b) a *that*-clause as indirect directive: *ask*, *beg*, *command*, *instruct*, *order*, *persuade*, *tell*.

Prepositional object and *that*-clause object

16.34 Some ditransitive prepositional verbs take a prepositional object and a *that*-clause:

Estelle mentioned (to me) that her daughter was getting married.
Philip recommended (to me) that I buy Harrods malt whisky.

As shown by the parentheses, the prepositional phrase is optional. Some of the ditransitive verbs listed in 16.33 can be optionally followed by a preposition:

Jonathan wrote (to) me that he was going to a summer camp this year.

Unlike the verbs in 16.33, ditransitive prepositional verbs allow the *that*-clause to become subject of a corresponding passive clause, more acceptably with extraposition:

That David was innocent has been proved by Jonathan.
~It has been proved (by Jonathan) that David was innocent.

We list examples where (a) the *that*-clause is an indirect statement, and (b) it is an indirect directive: (a) *admit*, *announce*, *complain*, *confess*, *explain*, *mention*, *point out*, *prove*, *remark*, *report*, *say*, *write (to)*; (b) *ask (of)*, *propose*, *recommend*, *suggest*.

Indirect object and *wh*-clause object

16.35 The second object may be a finite *wh*-clause:

Martin asked me what time the meeting would end.
Wendy didn't tell me whether she had phoned earlier.

Besides *ask* and *tell*, the verbs used in this construction are those listed in group (a) in 16.33. A preposition, usually optional, may precede the *wh*-clause:

Would you *remind* me (*about*) how we start the engine?

Some of the verbs also take a *wh*-infinitive clause as second object:

She advised us what to wear for the party.

Prepositional verbs also appear in this pattern:

Could you please *suggest to* me which museums to visit?

Indirect object and *to*-infinitive clause object

16.36 This pattern is used with verbs that introduce indirect directives. Only the indirect object can be made subject of the corresponding passive construction:

I persuaded Mark to see a doctor. [1]
Mark was persuaded to see a doctor. [1a]

The subject of the superordinate clause (*I* in [1]) refers to the speaker of a speech act, and the indirect object refers to the addressee (*Mark* in [1]). The implied subject of the infinitive clause is generally identified with the indirect object ('I persuaded Mark that he should see a doctor').

Here is a list of common verbs used in this pattern: *advise*, *ask*, *beg*, *command*, *entreat*, *forbid*, *implore*, *instruct*, *invite*, *order*, *persuade*, *remind*, *request*, *recommend*, *teach*, *tell*, *urge*.

NOTE [**a**] With some superordinate verbs, the infinitive clause may be replaced in rather formal style by a *that*-clause containing a modal or a subjunctive:

I persuaded Mark that he should see a doctor. [1b]

[**b**] The verb *promise* is exceptional in that the implied subject of the infinitive clause is the superordinate subject: *I promised Howard to take two shirts for his father* ('I promised Howard that I would take two shirts for his father').

Infinitival complementation: monotransitive, ditransitive, complex-transitive

16.37 We can now distinguish three superficially identical structures that conform to the pattern N, V N_2 *to* V N_3, where N is a noun phrase and V is a verb phrase. The three structures display three types of complementation of the first verb phrase: monotransitive (*cf* 16.23), ditransitive (*cf* 16.36), and complex-transitive (*cf* 16.27).

MONOTRANSITIVE

O

The governors like all parents to visit the school. [1]

N_2 N_3

DITRANSITIVE

Oi O_d

I persuaded Justin to write an essay. [2]

N_2 N_3

COMPLEX-TRANSITIVE

O C_o

They expected Robert to win the race. [3]

N_2 N_3

In monotransitive complementation, N_2 is within the infinitive clause and functions as its subject. Accordingly, we find the following features associated with this type of complementation:

(a) The infinitive clause, including N_2, can be replaced by a pronoun:

> The governors like *all parents to visit the school*, and the teachers like *that* too.

(b) When preceded by *for*, the infinitive clause, including N_2, can easily be made the focus of a pseudo-cleft construction:

> What the governors like is *for all parents to visit the school.*

(c) The object of the infinitive clause can be made into its subject if the clause is turned into the passive:

The governors like *the school to be visited by all parents.*

(d) In a reduced construction, infinitival *to* is obligatorily retained:

The governors like them *to.*

The governors like them and *We like them to* are not synonymous.

(e) Existential *there* can function as subject of the infinitive clause:

We like *there to be a full attendance.*

In ditransitive complementation, none of the features (a)–(e) apply, since N_2 functions as indirect object within the superordinate clause and is not a constituent of the infinitive clause:

*I persuaded *that.* [2a]
*What I persuaded was *for Justin to write an essay.* [2b]
*I persuaded *the essay to be written by Justin.* [2c]

The infinitive direct object clause can be omitted:

I persuaded Justin. [2d]

On the other hand, the indirect object can be made passive subject of the superordinate clause:

Justin was persuaded to write an essay. [2e]

Contrast, the unacceptability of:

**All parents* were liked to visit the school.

A complex-transitive verb such as *expect* in *They expected Robert to win the prize* displays the same features as a monotransitive verb such as *like*, except that (like ditransitive *persuade*) N_2 is an object and can become the passive subject of the superordinate clause:

Robert *was expected* to win the prize. [3a]

With *expect*, though not with all complex-transitive verbs, there are two other possible passive constructions (the first applicable also to monotransitive complementation):

They expected the prize *to be won* by Robert. [3b]
The prize *was expected to be won* by Robert. [3c]

In [3c] there are passives in both the superordinate clause and the infinitive clause.

Adjective complementation

Adjective complementation by a prepositional phrase

16.38 Like prepositional verbs, adjectives often form a lexical unit with a following preposition. The lexical bond is strongest with adjectives for which, in a given sense, the complementation is obligatory; for example, *averse to*, *bent on*, *conscious of*, *fond of*.

Below we give some examples of adjectives listed according to the prepositions that accompany them. They include participial adjectives (*cf* 7.5). It is often possible for an adjective to take a choice of prepositions, as in *angry about*, *angry at*, and *angry with*.

ABOUT:	*happy annoyed, reasonable, worried*
AT:	*alarmed, clever, good, hopeless*
FOR:	*grateful, sorry*
FROM:	*different, distant, distinct, free*
OF:	*afraid, fond, full, tired*
ON/UPON:	*dependent, keen, based, set*
TO:	*close, due, grateful, similar, opposed*
WITH:	*bored, friendly, happy, pleased*

Adjective complementation by a finite clause

16.39 Like *that*-clauses following a verb (*cf* 16.17*ff*), *that*-clauses following an adjective may have an indicative verb, a subjunctive verb, or putative *should* (*cf* 14.13*f*). Three types are distinguished:

(a) The indicative is used with adjectives expressing degrees of certainty or confidence (*eg*: *aware*, *certain*, *confident*, *sure*):

We were *confident* that Karen *was* still alive.

(b) The subjunctive or putative *should* is used with adjectives expressing volition (*eg*: *anxious*, *eager*, *willing*):

I am *anxious* that he {*be* / *should be* / *?is*} permitted to resign.

(c) The indicative or putative *should* is used with emotive adjectives (*eg*: *angry*, *annoyed*, *glad*, *pleased*, *surprised*). The indicative is chosen when the *that*-clause is intended to refer to an event as an established fact. The following pairs illustrate the choices:

I am sorry {(that) you *have* to leave so early. / (that) you *should have* been (so) inconvenienced.}

I am surprised {(that) you *didn't call* the doctor before. / (that) anyone of your intelligence *should swallow* a lie like that.}

In a superficially similar construction, the *that*-clause is an extraposed subject. Three types of adjectives and the corresponding verb choices are again distinguished, matching those given above:

(a) It is *true* that she *is* a vegetarian.

(b) It is *essential* that the ban $\left\{\begin{matrix}\textit{(should) be}\\ \textit{is}\end{matrix}\right\}$ lifted tomorrow.

(c) It is *strange* that she $\left\{\begin{matrix}\textit{is}\\ \textit{should be}\end{matrix}\right\}$ so late.

We list common examples of each type:

(a) *certain, clear, likely, obvious, plain, possible, true, unlikely*

(b) *essential, important, impossible, necessary*

(c) *curious, disappointing, fortunate, odd, sad, surprising, unfortunate*

NOTE Some adjectives take a *wh*-clause (normally with an indicative verb) as complementation. One type has an experiencer as subject and may be followed by an optional preposition:

I was *doubtful* (as to) whether I should stay.
He is *careful* (about) what he does with his money.

Other examples: *careful (about), fussy (about), unclear (about), uncertain (of), unsure (of).*

In the second type the *wh*-clause is an extraposed subject:

It was *unclear* what they would do.
It was not *obvious* how far the modernization would go.

Adjective complementation by a *to*-infinitive clause

16.40 We distinguish seven kinds of construction in which an adjective is followed by a *to*-infinitive clause. They are exemplified in the following sentences, which are superficially alike:

(i) Bob is *splendid* to wait.
(ii) Bob is *slow* to react.
(iii) Bob is *sorry* to hear it.
(iv) Bob is *hesitant* to agree with you.
(v) Bob is *hard* to convince.
(vi) The food is *ready* to eat.
(vii) It is *important* to be accurate.

In types (i–iv) the subject of the main clause (*Bob*) is also the subject of the infinitive clause. We can therefore always have a direct object in the infinitive clause if its verb is transitive. For example, if we replace intransitive *wait* by transitive *build* in (i), we can have: *Bob is splendid to build this house.*

For types (v–vii), on the other hand, the subject of the infinitive is unspecified, although the context often makes clear which subject is intended. In these types it is possible to insert a subject preceded by *for*: *eg* in type (vi): *The food is ready (for the children) to eat.*

Type (i) has an analogue in a construction involving extraposition (*cf*

18.23): *It is splendid of Bob to wait.* This type also permits a head noun between the adjective and the infinitive: *Bob must be a splendid craftsman to have built this house.* Adjectives in this type are evaluative of human behaviour. They include *careful, careless, crazy, foolish, mad, nice, silly, wise, wrong.*

In type (ii), the sentence corresponds to one in which the adjective becomes an adverb, while the infinitive becomes the finite verb:

Bob is *slow* to react. Bob reacts *slowly*.

In another analogue, the adjective is followed by *in* and an *-ing* participle: *Bob is slow in reacting.* Other adjectives in this small group are *quick* and *prompt.*

In type (iii), the head of the adjective phrase is an emotive adjective (commonly a participial adjective), and the infinitive clause expresses causation:

I'm *sorry* to have kept you waiting. ['I'm *sorry* because I have kept you waiting']
I was *excited* to be there. ['To be there *excited* me']

Other adjectives in this type include *afraid, ashamed, disappointed, glad, happy, interested, relieved, surprised, worried.*

In type (iv), the head of the adjective phrase expresses volition or a modal meaning such as ability or possibility. Adjectives in this type include *able, anxious, certain, eager, inclined, keen, likely, ready, reluctant, sure, unable, willing.* Some of the most common adjectives in this type tend to link with the preceding copula *be* to form a semi-auxiliary verb (*cf* 3.18): *be able to, be willing to, be sure to.*

In type (v), the subject of the sentence is identified with the unexpressed object of the infinitive clause, which must therefore have a transitive verb; hence we could not have **Bob is hard to arrive.* There is an analogous construction in which the adjective is complement to an infinitive clause acting as subject or extraposed subject (*cf* 18.23):

To convince Bob is hard. *It is hard to convince Bob.*

Unless there is ellipsis, we cannot omit the infinitive clause, and so a sentence like *The bread was hard to bake* in no way implies *The bread was hard.* Like types (vi) and (vii), type (v) permits *for* + subject to be inserted at the beginning of the infinitive clause: *Those darts are awkward (for a beginner) to use.* Other adjectives in this group include *difficult, easy, impossible, nice* ⟨informal⟩, *pleasant.*

In type (vi) too the subject of the main clause is identified with the object of the infinitive clause. But unlike type (v), type (vi) has no analogous construction with an infinitive clause subject:

The food is ready (for you) to eat.
*To eat the food is ready.

We can generally omit the infinitive clause (*The food is ready*), and we can substitute a passive infinitive clause without change of meaning (*The food is ready to be eaten*). Other adjectives in this type include *available*, *free*, *soft*.

In type (vii) the infinitive clause is an extraposed subject:

To spray the trees every year is *essential*.
It is *essential* (for you) to spray the trees every year.

Adjectives in this type express volition, modality, or emotion (*cf* 16.39). They include *fortunate*, *important*, *possible*, *surprising*, *wrong*.

NOTE [a] Some adjectives belong to types (iv) and (vi) (*eg*: *available*, *fit*, *free*, *ready*), so that a sentence like *The lamb is ready to eat* is ambiguous: either equivalent to *The lamb is ready to be eaten* (type vi) or *The lamb is ready to eat something* (type iv).
[b] In both type (v) and type (vi), the infinitive clause can end with a stranded preposition: *He is difficult to talk to*: *The paper is too flimsy to write on*.

Adjective complementation by an *-ing* participle clause

16.41 An adjective may take an *-ing* participle clause as its complementation. In some cases, a preposition optionally intervenes:

I'm *busy (with)* getting the house redecorated.
We're *fortunate (in)* having Aunt Mary as a baby-sitter.

In other cases the preposition is obligatory:

We are *used to* not having a car.
I'm *hopeless at* keeping the garden tidy.
She's not *capable of* looking after herself.

Bibliographical note

On phrasal verbs and other types of multi-word verbs, see Aarts (1989); Akimoto (1983); Bolinger (1971); Dixon (1982b); Fraser (1976); Lipka (1972); Makkai (1972); Sroka (1972).

On general aspects of verb classification and complementation, see Allerton (1982); Andersson (1985); Chomsky (1965, Ch. 2); Fillmore (1968, 1977a, 1977b); Halliday (1967–68); Lyons (1977, Ch. 12).

On verb complementation by finite clauses (especially by *that*-clauses), see Behre (1955); Kiparsky and Kiparsky (1970).

On verb complementation by nonfinite construction, see Van Ek (1966); Freed (1979); Mair (1990).

17 The noun phrase

17.1 In discussing nouns, determiners, and pronouns in Chapters 5 and 6, we were of course dealing with the fundamentals of noun-phrase structure. But we have deferred until this point in the book our consideration of the noun phrase itself so that other constituents common in noun-phrase structure (such as adjectives, adverbs, and clauses) had themselves been individually explored. In other words, just as we have seen in Chapter 14 that the *sentence* may be indefinitely complex, so may the *noun phrase*. This must be so, since sentences themselves can be reshaped so as to come within noun-phrase structure. For example, the following simple and complex sentences [1a–1e] can be re-expressed as one simple sentence [2] with a very complex noun phrase as subject:

That girl is Angela Hunt. [1a]
That girl is tall. [1b]
That girl was standing in the corner. [1c]
You waved to that girl when you entered. [1d]
That girl became angry because you waved to her. [1e]
That tall girl standing in the corner who became angry because you waved to her when you entered is Angela Hunt. [2]

Moreover, working back from [2], we could unhesitatingly reconstruct any of the sentences [1a–1e] and in fact we could not understand the noun-phrase subject of [2] unless we recognized its component parts as they are set out in [1].

Yet [2] has introduced many changes. We have suppressed all or part of the verbs in [1b] and [1c] (different in tense and aspect); we have put the complement *tall* of [1b] before the noun *girl*; we have replaced *that girl* of [1e] by *who*.

The purpose of the present chapter is to state the conditions governing such changes.

17.2 In describing complex noun phrases, we distinguish three components:

(a) *The head*, around which the other components cluster and which dictates concord and other kinds of congruence with the rest of the sentence outside the noun phrase. Thus, we can have [1], [2], and [3]:

That tall girl *standing in the corner* . . . is . . . [1]
Those tall girls *standing in the corner* . . . are . . . [2]
He addressed *that* girl *standing in the corner*. [3]

(b) *The premodification*, which comprises all the items placed before the head – notably, determiners, adjectives, and nouns. Thus:

That tall girl
Some very expensive office furniture

(c) *The postmodification*, comprising all the items placed after the head – notably, prepositional phrases, nonfinite clauses, and relative clauses:

The chair *by the wall*
All the boys *playing in the garden*
A car *which she bought recently*

We shall also be concerned in this chapter with *apposition*, a construction typically presenting noun phrases of identical reference, as in:

My dentist, Susan Williams, is heavily overworked. (my dentist *is* Susan Williams)
The authorities are worried by *the problem of vandalism*. (the problem *is* vandalism)

Restrictive and nonrestrictive

17.3 Modification can be restrictive or nonrestrictive. That is, the head can be viewed as a member of a class which can be linguistically identified only through the modification that has been supplied (*restrictive*). Or the head can be viewed as unique or as a member of a class that has been independently identified (for example, in a preceding sentence); any modification given to such a head is additional information which is not essential for identifying the head, and we call it *nonrestrictive*.

In example [2] of 17.1, the girl is only identifiable as Angela Hunt provided we understand that it is the particular girl who is *tall*, who was *standing in the corner*, and who *became angry*. Such modification is restrictive. By contrast, consider the following:

Come and meet my famous mother.

Here, the modification *famous* is understood as nonrestrictive. Again:

Angela Hunt, who is (over there) in the corner, wants to meet you.

This sentence has a nonrestrictive relative clause since Angela Hunt's identity is independent of whether or not she is in the corner, though the information on her present location may be useful enough. In these examples, the modification is *inherently* nonrestrictive, since the heads in question – being treated as unique – will not normally admit restriction. But any head can be nonrestrictively modified:

The tall girl, who is a chemist, is Angela Hunt.

Here the only information offered to identify the girl as Angela Hunt is the allusion to her tallness; the mention of her work as a chemist is not offered as an aid to identification but for additional interest.

Modification at its 'most restrictive' tends to come after the head: that is, our decision to use an item as a premodifier (such as *silly* in *The silly boy got lost*) often reflects our wish that it be taken for granted and not be interpreted as a specific identifier. Secondly, restrictive modification tends to be given more prosodic emphasis than the head; nonrestrictive modification, on the other hand, tends to be unstressed in pre-head position, while in post-head position, its 'parenthetic' relation is endorsed by being given a separate tone unit (2.15), or – in writing – by being enclosed by commas.

Temporary and permanent

17.4 There is a second dichotomy that has some affinities with the distinction between restrictive and nonrestrictive but rather more with the contrast of nonprogressive and progressive in predication (4.7*ff*), and generic or specific reference in determiners (5.11*ff*, 5.22*ff*). Modification in noun-phrase structure may also be seen as permanent or temporary, such that items placed in premodification position are given the linguistic status of permanent or at any rate characteristic features. Although this does not mean that postmodification position is committed to either temporariness or permanence, those adjectives which cannot premodify have a notably temporary reference. Thus *The man is ready* would be understood as having reference only to a specific time, and this corresponds to the nonoccurrence of **The ready man*. On this basis, we see that *timid* and *afraid* are contrasted in part according as the first is seen as permanent, the second as temporary:

A man who is timid ~ A timid man
A man who is afraid ~ *An afraid man

Just as some modifiers are too much identified with temporary status to appear in pre-head position, so there can be modification constrained to pre-head position because it indicates permanent status. Compare *original* in *the original version* and *Her work is quite original*; in the latter, it would permit adverbial indication of time span (*now*, *always*, . . .), as well as use in premodification.

Postmodification

Explicitness

17.5 As we saw in 17.1, premodification is in general to be interpreted (and most frequently can only be interpreted) in terms of postmodification and its greater explicitness. It will therefore be best to begin our detailed study of noun-phrase structure with the forms of postmodification.

Explicitness in postmodification varies considerably, however. It is greater in the finite relative clause

The taxi which is waiting outside

than in the non-finite clause

The taxi waiting outside

from which the explicit tense (*is*?/*was*?) has disappeared, though this in turn is more explicit than

The taxi outside

from which the verb indicating a specific action has also disappeared. We are able (and usually must be able) to infer such facts as tense from the sentential context much as we infer the subject of nonfinite adverbial clauses (15.34):

The taxi waiting outside {*now* is / *last night* was} for me.

Have you noticed the taxi outside?

Part of the relative clause's explicitness lies in the specifying power of the relative pronoun. It is capable (a) of showing agreement with the head, and (b) of indicating its status as an element in the relative clause structure.

Agreement is on the basis of a two-term 'gender' system, personal and non-personal (5.45*ff*):

Joan, who . . .	London, which . . .
The boy/people who . . .	The fox/animals which . . .
The human being who . . .	The human body which . . .
The fairy who . . .	The unicorn which . . .

It will be seen from these examples that 'personality' is ascribed basically to human beings but extends to creatures in the supernatural world (angels, elves, etc) which are thought of as having human characteristics such as speech. It does not extend to the body or character, in part or whole, of a human being, living or dead, when this is considered as separate from the entire person. Pet animals can be regarded as 'personal' (at least by their owners):

Rover, *who* was barking, frightened the children.

On the other hand, human babies can be regarded (though rarely perhaps by their parents) as not having developed personality:

> This is the baby *which* needs inoculation.

Though ships may take the personal pronoun *she* (5.46 Note [c]), the relative pronoun is regularly nonpersonal:

> Is *she* the ship *which* is due to leave for Panama tomorrow?

It is noteworthy that collective nouns (5.46) are usually treated as personal when they have plural concord, nonpersonal when they have singular:

$$\text{The} \left\{ \begin{matrix} \text{committee} \\ \text{group} \end{matrix} \right\} \left\{ \begin{matrix} \textit{who were} \\ \textit{which was} \end{matrix} \right\} \text{responsible for this decision . . .}$$

Case in the relative pronoun

17.6 Case is used to indicate the status of the relative pronoun in its clause. There are two situations to consider. First, if the pronoun is in a genitive relation to a noun head, the pronoun can have the form *whose*:

The woman *whose* daughter you met is Mrs Brown. [1]
(The woman is Mrs Brown; you met *her* daughter)
The house *whose* roof was damaged has now been repaired. [2]
(The house has now been repaired, *its* roof was damaged)

In examples like [2] where the antecedent head is nonpersonal, there is some tendency to avoid the use of *whose* (by using, for example, *the roof of which*), presumably because many regard it as the genitive only of the personal *who*.

Secondly, with a personal antecedent, the relative pronoun can show the distinction between *who* and *whom*, depending on its role as subject of the relative clause or as object or as prepositional complement:

The girl who spoke to him [3]
The girl to whom he spoke [4]
The girl who(m) he spoke to [5]
The girl who(m) he met [6]

It will be noticed that when the governing preposition precedes its complement (*cf* 9.2) as in the rather formal [4], the choice of *whom* is obligatory. When it does not, as in the more informal [5], or when the relative pronoun is the object, as in [6], there is some choice between *who* or *whom*, the latter being preferred in formal written English and by some speakers, the former being widely current informally.

Relative pronoun and adverbial

17.7 The relative pronoun can be replaced by special adjunct forms for place, time, and cause:

That is the place *where* he was born. [1]
That is the period *when* he lived here. [2]
That is the reason *why* he spoke. [3]

There are considerable and complicated restrictions on these adjunct forms, however. Many speakers find their use along with the corresponding antecedent somewhat tautologous – especially [3] – and would prefer the *wh*-clause without antecedent:

That is *where* he was born. [1a]
That is *when* he lived here. [2a]
That is *why* he spoke. [3a]

If *how* is used, such clauses cannot in any case have an antecedent noun:

That is *how* he spoke. [4]

Moreover, there are restrictions on the antecedent nouns that can occur in [1–3]. With [3], *reason* is virtually alone, and with [1] and [2], it is also the most general and abstract nouns of place and time that seem to be preferred. Thus while

The office *where* he works . . . The day *when* he was born . . .

are acceptable to most users of English, others would prefer a prepositional phrase in each case:

The office {at which . . . (formal) / which . . . at}

The day {on which . . . (formal) / which . . . on}

or one of the less explicit forms that we shall now be considering (*The office he works at, The day he was born*).

Restrictive relative clauses

Choice of relative pronoun

17.8 Though most of the examples in 17.5*ff* have been of restrictive clauses, it is in the nonrestrictive relative clauses that the most explicit forms of relative pronoun are typically used. In restrictive clauses, frequent use is made of a general pronoun *that* which is independent of the personal or nonpersonal character of the antecedent and also of the function of the pronoun in the relative clause:

The boy *that* is playing the piano . . . (or *who*) [1]
The table *that* stands in the corner . . . (or *which*) [2]
The boy *that* we met . . . (or *who(m)*) [3]
The table *that* we admire . . . (or *which*) [4]
The boy *that* the dog barked at . . . (or *at whom*) [5]
The table *that* the boy crawled under . . . (or *under which*) [6]

Provided the relative pronoun is not the subject of the relative clause, as in [1] and [2], a further option exists in relative clause structure of having no relative pronoun at all: the clause with 'zero' (∅) relative pronoun. The examples [3–6] could take this form:

> The boy we met . . . (who(m), that)
> The table we admire . . . (which, that)
> The boy the dog barked at . . . (at whom, who(m)/that . . . at)
> The table the boy crawled under . . . (under which, which/that . . . under)

Some choice exists in placing a preposition which has a *wh*-pronoun as its complement (17.6); there is no such choice with *that* and zero, where the preposition must be postposed.

The choices are summarized in the diagram:

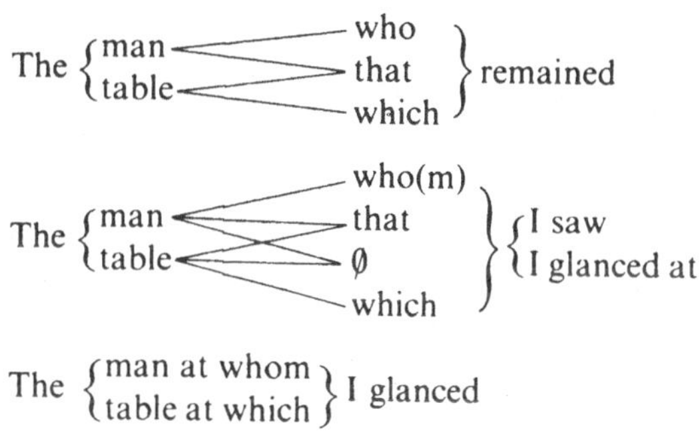

NOTE Choices are not only connected with relative formality. Some prepositions cannot be postposed (**the meeting that I slept during*). *Who* is often preferred to *that* when it is subject and when the antecedent is personal (*people who visit me*); but *that* is preferred to *who(m)* when it is object, in part perhaps to avoid the *who/whom* choice (*people that I visit*). When the verb in the relative clause is *be*, the complement pronoun must be *that* or zero (*John is not the man he was*). This example illustrates one of the most favoured uses of zero: *ie* when the pronoun is object or complement, the subject is pronominal, and the relative clause is short. When the antecedent is long and complex, *wh*-pronouns are preferred:

> I have interests outside my daily professional work which give me great pleasure.

17.9 Just as *that* and zero are available when the relative pronoun is dominated by a preposition, so they can be used when the relative pronoun is part of a place, time, or cause adjunct. With place adjuncts, the preposition must usually be expressed:

> This is the garden (that) he sunbathes in.
> This is the university (that) she works at.

With the time adjuncts, however, omission of the preposition is usual whether the pronoun is *that* or zero:

This is the time (that) she normally arrives (at).
Monday was the day (that) he left (on).

But when (less frequently and more formally) the pronoun is *which*, the preposition must be expressed in these instances and it would be usual to make it precede the pronoun (*cf* 17.7):

This is the time *at which* she normally arrives.
Monday was the day *on which* he left.

With cause and manner adjuncts, the usual pronoun is *that* or zero, and there is no preposition:

This is the reason (that) she came.
This is the way (that) he did it.

NOTE With manner adjuncts, it would not be abnormal to find *which* with a preposition in a more formal style:

This is the way *in which* he did it.

Quantified heads

17.10 Beside the noun phrase *the girls that he knew*, we may have one in which the head is made quantitatively indefinite with the predeterminer *such*, the relative pronoun *that* being replaced by *as*:

Such girls *as* he knew were at the party.

Compare: *As many girls as he knew* . . . A further connection with comparative sentences (*cf* 15.36) can be seen in:

{*More* / *Fewer*} girls *than* he knew were at the party.

Nonrestrictive relative clauses

17.11 The loose nonrestrictive relationship is often semantically indistinguishable from coordination (with or without conjunction) or adverbial subordination, as we indicate by paraphrases in the examples below. The repertoire of pronouns is limited to the *wh*-items:

Then he met Barbara, {*who* invited him to a party. / *and she* invited him to a party.}

Here is Ronald Walker {, *who(m)* I mentioned the other day. / ; I mentioned *him* the other day.}

He got lost on Snowdon, {*which* was enveloped in fog. / *when it* was enveloped in fog.}

He got lost on Snowdon, {*which* he was exploring. / *while* he was exploring *it*.}

NOTE As a determiner, *which* appears in nonrestrictive clauses that are introduced by adjuncts, but this is largely in formal style:

> He emigrated in 1840, *at which time* there was much hardship and unrest.

Cf also *for which purpose, in which city, for which reason, by which device.*

Sentential relative clauses

17.12 One type of nonrestrictive clause has as its antecedent not a noun phrase but a whole clause or sentence or even sequence of sentences. As with the clauses in 17.11, the relationship frequently resembles coordination, but these clauses are also very much like disjuncts (*cf* 8.42, 15.33). For example:

> He admires Mrs Hewitt, which {surprises me. / I find strange.}

Cf 'and this surprises me'; 'to my surprise'.

Quite often, *which* is used in these clauses as a determiner of factive nouns which represent the antecedent clause or sentence:

> The train may have been held up, *in which case* we are wasting our time.

Appositive clauses

17.13 The appositive clause resembles the relative clause in being capable of introduction by *that*, and in distinguishing between restrictive and nonrestrictive. It differs in that the particle *that* is not an element in the clause structure (subject, object, etc) as it must be in a relative clause. It differs also in that the head of the noun phrase must be an abstract noun such as *fact, proposition, reply, remark, answer*, and the like. For example.

> The belief *that no one is infallible* is well-founded.
> I agree with the old saying *that absence makes the heart grow fonder.*

As with apposition generally (*cf* 17.27), we can link the apposed units with *be* (where the copula typically has nuclear prominence):

> The belief *is* that no one is infallible. (. . . Is . . .)
> The old saying *is* that absence makes the heart grow fonder.

Or we may replace deverbal nouns like *belief* by the corresponding verb plus object clause: *He believes that no one is infallible.*

It will be noticed that these restrictive examples have the definite article before the head noun: this is normal but by no means invariable (except with a few nouns referring to certainty, especially *fact*):

> A message *that he would be late* arrived by special delivery.

Plural heads are also rare with appositive postmodification and are regarded as unacceptable, for example, with *belief, fact, possibility.*

NOTE Nonrestrictive appositive clauses can less easily resemble relative clauses since irrespective of nonrestrictiveness they still involve the particle *that*, in sharp contrast with nonrestrictive relative clauses:

> This fact, that *that* is obligatory, should be easy to remember.

Postmodification by nonfinite clauses

-ing participle clauses

17.14 Postmodification of the noun phrase is possible with all three of the nonfinite clause types (14.4), and the correspondence between restrictive relative and nonfinite clauses will be illustrated. For example:

> The man who
> - will { write / be writing }
> - writes
> - is writing
> - wrote
> - was writing
>
> the obituaries is my friend.

> The man *writing the obituaries* is my friend.

The latter will be interpreted, according to the context, as equivalent to one or other of the former more explicit versions. So too:

> A tile *falling from a roof* shattered into fragments at his feet. ('which *fell* from a roof')
> At the station you will see a lady *carrying a large umbrella.* ('who *will be carrying* a large umbrella')
> The student *writing on the board* when you came in . . . ('who *was writing . . .*')

But not all *-ing* forms in nonfinite postmodifiers correspond to progressive forms in relative clauses. Stative verbs, which cannot have the progressive in the finite verb phrase, can appear in participial form:

> He is talking to a girl *resembling Joan.* ('who *resembles* Joan' not '*who is resembling Joan')
> It was a mixture *consisting of oil and vinegar.* ('that *consisted . . .*')

In all instances, the antecedent head corresponds to the implicit subject of the nonfinite verb clause; there is no nonfinite postmodifier, therefore, corresponding directly to the relative clause in:

> The obituary *that the man is writing* will be published tomorrow.

Instead, we must have recourse to the passive: *being written by the man* (17.15).

-ed participle clauses

17.15 Consider now the different versions of the following:

The only car that { will be repaired / is (being) repaired / was (being) repaired } by that mechanic is mine.

The only car *(being) repaired by that mechanic* is mine.

Again, the latter will be interpreted, according to the context, as equivalent to one of the former. Thus:

The only car	repaired	by that mechanic	next week . . .
	being repaired		now . . .
	repaired		on Tuesdays . . .
	repaired		before he left . . .

Another example:

Any coins *found on this site* must be handed to the police.
('that are found . . .' or, more precisely, 'that may be found . . .')

The antecedent head is identical with the implicit subject of the *-ed* postmodifying clause as it is with the *-ing* construction, but in this case the participle concerned is as firmly linked with the passive voice as that in the *-ing* construction is linked with the active. Hence, with intransitive verbs, there is no *-ed* postmodifier corresponding exactly to a relative clause:

The train *which has arrived at platform one* is from York.
*The train *arrived at platform one* is from York.

Infinitive clauses

17.16 The nonfinite clause in

The next train *to arrive* was from York.

could, in a suitable context, have precisely the same meaning as the relative clause *which arrived*. But the subject of an infinitive clause need not be the antecedent. It may be separately introduced by the *for*-device (15.9) or it may be entirely covert:

The man *for John to consult* is Wilson.
The man *to consult* is Wilson.

The latter nonfinite clause could be understood, according to context, as '(The man) that *you/he*, etc, should consult' or 'that *everyone* should consult'. Still more elliptically, the infinitive clause may omit also an entire adjunct phrase, as in:

The time (*for you*) *to arrive* is 8 p.m.
A good place (*for her*) *to stay* is the White Hart.

Here a fairly common alternative is to introduce the relative pronoun and retain the infinitive clause:

> . . . time *at which to arrive* . . . } (*the subject obligatorily absent*)
> . . . place *at which to stay* . . . }

Compare *the way in which to do it* beside *the way to do it*.

Finally it should be noted that voice and mood are variable, the latter covertly:

> The time *to arrive* (= at which you should arrive)
> The case *to be investigated* (= that will *or* is to be investigated)
> The money *to buy* food (= with which you (*or* they *etc*) may buy)
> The procedure *to be followed* (= which must *or* should *or* will be followed)

Nonrestrictive postmodification

17.17 Postmodification with nonfinite clauses can also be nonrestrictive:

> The apple tree, *swaying gently in the breeze*, had a good crop of fruit. ('which was swaying . . .')
> The substance, *discovered almost by accident*, has revolutionized medicine. ('which was discovered . . .')
> This scholar, *to be seen daily in the British Museum*, has devoted his life to the history of science. ('who can be seen . . .')

These clauses can be moved to initial position without change of meaning, but in that case they can no longer be expanded into finite relative clauses. Indeed, they have an implicit semantic range beyond that of a relative clause (*cf* 15.35). Thus the nonfinite clause in this example:

> The woman, *wearing such dark glasses*, obviously could not see clearly.

could be a reduction of a relative clause 'who was wearing . . .' or of a causal clause 'because she was wearing . . .' or of a temporal clause such as 'whenever she wore . . .'.

NOTE *Cf* the semantic versatility noted in finite nonrestrictive relative clauses, 17.11.

Appositive postmodification

17.18 Appositive postmodification is fairly common by means of infinitive clauses. A restrictive example:

> The appeal *to join the movement* was well received.

This would correspond to the finite *that people should join the movement*. A corresponding nonrestrictive example:

> This last appeal, *to come and visit him*, was never delivered.

There are cases of nonfinite postmodification where no corresponding finite apposition exists:

> Any attempt *to leave early* is against regulations.
> (*. . . that one should leave early . . .)
> He lost the ability *to use his hands*.

In all these examples, the construction obliges us to infer the (often indefinite) subject of the infinitive clause from the context. But a subject may be explicitly introduced by a prepositional device:

> The appeal *for Winifred* to join . . .
> Any attempt *by Harold* to leave . . .

Postmodification by prepositional phrases

Relation to more explicit modifiers

17.19 A prepositional phrase is by far the commonest type of postmodification in English: it is three or four times more frequent than either finite or nonfinite clausal postmodification. The full range of prepositions is involved:

The road *to Lincoln*	Two years *before the war*
A tree *by a stream*	A man *from the electricity board*
The house *beyond the church*	This book *on grammar*

including the complex prepositions (9.3):

> Action *in case of fire* Passengers *on board the ship*

and including those having participial form:

> A delay *pending further inquiry*

Among the prepositions less commonly used in postmodification we should mention *like* in the sense 'resembling': 'The man *like John* is over there'. But it is common and fully acceptable in the sense 'such as':

> A man *like John* would never do that.

It is natural to relate such prepositional postmodifications to sentences or relative clauses with *be* ('the man in the corner' ~ 'the man (*who*) *is* in the corner'), though in some instances more seems to be ellipted than the verb *be*. For example, we presumably need to regard

> The university *as a political forum*

as related to a somewhat fuller predication:

The university is $\left\{\begin{matrix}\text{acting}\\ \text{regarded}\end{matrix}\right\}$ as a political forum.

Again, although there is no problem with

The present *for her birthday* cost a great deal. (The present is for her birthday)

we cannot interpret so straightforwardly

The *person for the job* is Anita (= the *right person* for the job . . .)

So too, it is not through *be* sentences that we must understand

The man *with a red beard*   The guest *with a funny hat*

but rather through *have* sentences ('The man *has* a red beard'): *cf* 9.14 Note [c].

The *of*-genitive

17.20 It is with *have* sentences that we must find the most obvious resemblance when we turn to the commonest prepositional postmodification of all, the *of*-phrase:

A man of courage ~ The man has courage

But, as we saw in 5.50, many relationships find expression through the *of*-genitive, and one that deserves brief consideration here is the appositive relation (17.27) which in fact resembles a *be* sentence:

The pleasure of your company ~ Your company is a pleasure

Where the postmodification has an *-ing* clause, the subject may have to be inferred from the context or it may be identified with a premodifier or the head:

The hope of winning a prize (= X hoped that X would win a prize)
John's hope of winning a prize (= *John* hoped that *he* would . . .)

But a separate subject may be introduced:

John's hope of *Mary('s)* winning a prize (= John hoped that *Mary* would . . .)

On *Mary* versus *Mary's* here, see 15.10. Where the postmodification has a deverbal noun, a specified 'subject' must, of course, be genitive:

Bill's hope of *Sarah's* arrival (= Bill hoped that *Sarah* would arrive)

Restrictive and nonrestrictive

17.21 Prepositional phrases may thus be nonappositive or appositive, and in either function, they can be restrictive or nonrestrictive:

This book on grammar	(nonappositive, restrictive)
This book, on grammar,	(nonappositive, nonrestrictive)
The issue of student grants	(appositive, restrictive)
The issue, of student grants,	(appositive, nonrestrictive)

But we must mention some limitations. The last example is rare and rather awkward: nonrestrictive appositives would more usually be without a preposition, as in

> The issue, student grants,

It would thus have the primary form described in 17.27. On the other hand, if the ambiguous noun phrase

> The issue(,) of student grants(,)

had its nonappositive meaning (objective *of*: 'someone issued student grants'), nonrestrictive function would be rare and unnatural, plainly suggesting an awkward afterthought.

Position and varied relationship

17.22 As with nonfinite postmodifiers when nonrestrictive, so with prepositional phrases, the nonrestrictive function merges with adverbial expressions; compare [1] and [2]:

> The children {behind the fence / on the bus} jeered at the soldiers. [1]

which means 'Those children who were . . .'

> The children, {behind the fence / on the bus}, jeered at the soldiers. [2]

which means 'The children, who (by the way) were . . .' or, on the other hand, 'The children, now that they were (safely . . .)'. It is rather this latter implication that becomes uppermost if the prepositional phrase is moved into initial position:

> {Behind the fence, / On the bus,} the children jeered at the soldiers.

Again, the prepositional phrase in the following is poised between interpretation as nonrestrictive postmodifier and as adverbial:

> Money, in aid of the refugees, was collected from students and staff.

In the former interpretation, the money collected was in aid of the refugees, whereas in the latter, *the act* of collecting money was in aid of the refugees, since in this case the adverbial modifies the whole predication just as it would in initial position:

> In aid of the refugees, money was collected . . .

Nominalization

17.23 We should not, however, exaggerate the difference between the prepositional phrase as adverbial and the prepositional phrase as postmodifier. The second of these should rather be regarded as a special instance of the first, depending for its interpretation on our ability to relate it to a sentence in which it is adjunct. In the following, for instance,

(a) A quarrel broke out *in the morning over pay*.

both the prepositional phrases are introduced as adjuncts. If we wish to refer again to the quarrel, these adjuncts may now become postmodifiers:

(b) The quarrel *in the morning* ruined their friendship.
(c) The quarrel *over pay* was the reason for his resignation.

The relation of postmodifier to adjunct may be even clearer if, instead of (a), (b), and (c), we take a sentence in which *quarrel* occurs as a verb:

(d) They quarrelled in the morning over pay.

We can now see that there is a one-for-one correspondence between the verb *quarrelled* in (d) and the head of the subject noun phrase *quarrel* in (a), (b), and (c); likewise between the adjuncts in (d) and the postmodifiers in (b) and (c). It is when we have such a correspondence between clause elements and noun-phrase constituents that we speak of such a noun phrase as a nominalization. Further examples:

She refused to answer.	~ *Her refusal to answer*
He writes well.	~ (He is) *a good writer*
The reviewer severely criticized the book.	~ *The reviewer's severe criticism of the book*

NOTE In relation to (d), we might also have in place of (b) and (c) respectively '*Their quarrelling in the morning* ruined . . .', '*Their quarrelling over pay* was . . .'. On such *-ing* clauses, see 15.10; but we recognize a gradience from concrete count nouns in *-ing*, through what is traditionally called 'gerund', to the purely participial form in a finite verb phrase:

Some paintings of Brown's (*ie* some paintings that Brown owns) [1]
Brown's paintings of his daughter (*ie* paintings owned by Brown, depicting his daughter but painted by someone else) [2]
Brown's paintings of his daughter (*ie* they depict his daughter and were painted by him) [3]
The painting of Brown is as skilful as that of Gainsborough. (*ie* Brown's (a) technique of painting *or* (b) action of painting) [4]
Brown's deft painting of his daughter is a delight to watch. (*ie* It is a delight to watch while Brown deftly paints his daughter) [5]
Brown's deftly painting his daughter is a delight to watch. (= [4b] and [5] in meaning) [6]
I dislike Brown's painting his daughter. (*ie* I dislike *either* (a) the fact *or* (b) the way Brown does it) [7]

I dislike Brown painting his daughter. (= [7a]) [8]
I watched Brown painting his daughter. (*ie*: *either* I watched Brown as he painted *or* I watched the process of Brown('s) painting his daughter) [9]
Brown deftly painting his daughter is a delight to watch. (= [4b] and [5]) [10]
Painting his daughter, Brown noticed that his hand was shaking. [*ie* while he was painting) [11]
Brown painting his daughter that day, I decided to go for a walk. (*ie* because Brown was painting) [12]
The man painting the girl is Brown. (*ie* who is painting) [13]
The silently painting man is Brown. (*ie* who is silently painting) [14]
Brown is painting his daughter. [15]

Minor types of postmodification

17.24 We come now to some relatively minor types of postmodification. These are by (a) adverb phrases; (b) postposed adjectives (*cf* 7.8); and (c) postposed 'mode' qualifiers. For example:

(a) *The road back* was dense with traffic.
(b) *Something strange* happened last night.
(c) *Lobster Newburg* is difficult to prepare.

In (a) we recognize some such phrases as '*The road* which leads *back* (to London)', from which all but the subject and an important adjunct have been dropped. Similarly '*The way* (which leads) *in* (to the auditorium)', '*The people* (who are sitting) *just behind*'.

In (b), we have in fact two subtypes. The first has been illustrated. The indefinite pronouns such as *anybody*, *someone* can be followed but not preceded by adjective modification. The pronouns concerned are the *any-*, *some-*, *no-* series (6.21*ff*) plus one or two others (*cf*: *what else*, *who next*, etc). But we are not free to postpose with indefinites all modifying items that can be preposed with ordinary noun heads:

A party official is waiting. *but not* **Somebody party* is waiting.

Even adjectives need generally to be 'permanent' and hence eligible equally for attributive and predicative use (17.4); thus:

Somebody timid *rather than* *Somebody afraid

The other subtype in (b) consists chiefly of the sprinkling of noun-plus-adjective phrases (modelled on French) like *blood royal*, *heir apparent*. These are of little importance in themselves, being infrequently used (though our ability to form names like *Hotel Majestic* suggests that they are more than mere fossils) and it is likely that the native speaker feels them to be very similar to compound nouns. Nevertheless, beside this subtype, there is a similar but much more general phenomenon. When a head is nonrestrictively modified by a coordinated string of adjectives, it is common to postpose them:

A man, timid and hesitant, approached the official.

though the potential mobility of the string allows it to be detached from the noun phrase altogether (*cf* 17.17). Even a restrictively modifying adjective can be postposed if it is itself modified (by an adverb capable of being an adjunct, not by the intensifier *very*: *cf* 7.9):

A man notoriously timid is unfit for this task. (*cf*: **A man very timid*)

But this is particularly common where the modification is of a 'temporary' nature (17.4). Thus beside *The finest available car*, we have *The finest car (currently) available*.

With (c), we again encounter a French model: *Lobster Newburg*. Though virtually confined to cuisine, it is moderately productive within these limits, perhaps especially in AmE. In BrE one finds *veal paprika* and many others, but there is some resistance to this type of postposition with other than French lexical items, as in *pâté maison, sole bonne femme*.

Though technically a prepositional phrase phenomenon, expressions involving *à la* clearly belong here. It appears in culinary formations like *chicken à la king*, and also (informally or facetiously) to designate style:

Another play à la Beckett has appeared, though I forget who wrote it.

Multiple modification

17.25 (a) A head may have more than one postmodification. Thus

The girl in the corner *and* The girl talking to Peter

can be brought together as

The girl in the corner (and) talking to Peter

Without conjunction, there would usually be a hierarchy:

{[The girl (in the corner)] talking to Peter}

(b) A modification may be applicable to more than one head. Thus

The girl in the corner *and* The boy in the corner

can be brought together by multiple-head rules which permit the determiner to apply to both heads (*cf* 13.25):

The girl and boy in the corner

By bringing (a) and (b) together, we can produce complexes such as:

The girl and boy in the corner (and) talking to Peter

(c) The head of a modifying phrase may itself be modified; thus

The girl in the corner *and* The corner nearest the door

may be brought together as

The girl in the corner nearest the door

By bringing (a), (b), and (c) together, we can form

The girl and boy in the corner nearest the door talking to Peter

But fastidious users of English would prefer to end with a relative clause here ('. . . who are talking to Peter'), no doubt in response to an instinct that prompts the introduction of explicitness at a point which is relatively distant from the head.

Ambiguity and constraints on multiple modification

17.26 Frequently, careful ordering of constituents in a noun phrase is essential to communicate all (and only) one's intention. To take an obvious example, the following pair differ in meaning and are not mere stylistic variants:

The man in black talking to the girl
The man talking to the girl in black

One of the chief reasons for preferring the *of*-phrase to the *-s* genitive is to avoid discontinuity (with unwanted humour); thus:

The ears of the man in the deckchair

and not

*The man's ears in the deckchair

On the other hand, the *group genitive* construction enables us to postpose the *'s* inflection and avoid sequential *of*-phrases:

The man in the deckchair's ears

Cf also *a teacher of music's qualifications, the principal of the college's appointment, a week or so's rest, an hour and a half's discussion.*

A special type of multiple modification that requires careful ordering occurs when the modifying clause becomes itself embedded in a clause. Consider the following series:

Jane will write a poem for you.
Tom hopes (that) Jane will write a poem for you.
I will read the poem (*which*) Tom hopes (that) *Jane will write for you.*

In this last sentence, the relative pronoun (*which*) is object in the italicized relative clause. When, however, a relative pronoun is subject, the conjunction *that* must be omitted:

A poem will be written for you.
Tom hopes (that) a poem will be written for you.

I will read the poem *(which) Tom* {*hopes will* / **hopes that will*} *be written for you*

NOTE Even with simpler examples and the most careful ordering, we may find clarity and acceptable grammar difficult to attain in multiple modification. Beginning with

He liked the smiles of delight on all the faces.

a noun phrase based on this sentence and having *smiles* as its head may be ambiguous in one ordering:

The smiles of delight on all the faces that he liked

(was it *the smiles* or *the faces* that he liked?), and grammatically awkward in another.

Apposition

17.27 Two or more noun phrases are in apposition when they have identity of reference. The appositives may be juxtaposed as in [1] or separated as in [2], without formal expression of their relationship; or the apposition may be indicated by a conjunction as in [3] and [4] or by forms such as *that is* and *namely* as in [5]. Particularly in [4] and [5], we see that apposition often involves explanatory paraphrase.

A professional singer, someone trained in Paris, had been engaged for the concert. [1]
His birthday present lay on the table, *a book on ethics, the work of his professor*. [2]
My husband, and *(my) co-author* is dissatisfied with the last chapter. [3]
Linguistics or *the study of language* attracts many students. [4]
The outcome, that is *her re-election*, was a complete surprise. [5]

As we have already seen in earlier sections, apposition can also be expressed by *that*-clauses (17.13), by nonfinite clauses (17.18), and by prepositional phrases (17.20*f*).

In all the examples [1–5] above, the apposition has been nonrestrictive, but the relation can also be restrictive (*cf* 17.3). Compare:

He was examined by James Kelly, a doctor. [nonrestrictive]
He was examined by James Kelly the doctor. [restrictive]

Cf also *my friend Anna, the year 2000, the verb 'know'*. Titles and designations can be regarded as a special form of restrictive apposition: *Doctor James Kelly, Lake Michigan*.

NOTE [a] Appositives need not be noun phrases; compare:

She is *bigger* than her brother, *heavier*, that is.
Sixthly and *lastly*, I reject the claim on ethical grounds.
He *angered*, nay *infuriated*, his audience.

[b] References to words, books, etc, are often expressed in appositive form: 'the word *geese*', 'the good ship *Venus*', 'the play *Romeo and Juliet*'. This explains why, when the generic item is absent, concord is singular: '*geese* is irregular'. 'Has *Romeo and Juliet* ever been filmed?'

Premodification

Types of premodifying item

17.28 Holding constant a lexical frame (*his . . . cottage*) and nonrestrictive function, we have the following range of premodifying items:

(a) ADJECTIVE

I visited *his delightful cottage*. (His cottage is delightful)

(b) PARTICIPLE

I visited *his crumbling cottage*. (His cottage is crumbling)
I visited *his completed cottage*. (His cottage has been completed)

(c) *-S* GENITIVE

I visited *his fisherman's cottage*. (*Cf* The cottage belonged to a fisherman)

It should be noticed that if we had used a more normal genitive example (*his uncle's cottage*) we would have changed the relationship of *his*.

(d) NOUN

I visited *his country cottage*. (His cottage is in the country)

(e) ADVERBIAL

I visited *his far-away cottage*. (His cottage is far away)

(f) SENTENCE

(?) I visited *his pop-down-for-the-weekend cottage*. (*Cf* His cottage is one that he can pop down to for the weekend)

This last type is largely playful and informal. Somewhat more generally used are noun phrases which can be interpreted either as having a sentence as premodifier or as being object (usually of *know*) in an embedded noun clause:

> He asked *I don't know* HÒW *many people*.

Premodification by adjectives

17.29 A premodifying adjective, especially when it is the first item after the determiner, can itself be premodified in the same way as it can in predicative position (7.32):

> His *really quite unbelievably* delightful cottage

Some intensifiers tend, however, to be avoided with premodifying adjectives. Thus the predicative phrase in *His cottage which is so beautiful* would seem a little affected in premodification: *His so beautiful cottage*. With indefinite determiners, *so* would be replaced by *such* (*cf* 7.35):

> A cottage which is so beautiful ~ Such a beautiful cottage

Or else *so* plus adjective would be placed before the determiner: *So beautiful a cottage*.

There is resistance also to transferring clause negation to a structure of premodification, and this is possible only in limited circumstances (usually *not* plus intensifier or negative affix):

$$\text{The dinner was not} \begin{cases} \text{very pleasant.} \\ \text{unpleasant.} \end{cases}$$

$$\sim \text{The not} \begin{Bmatrix} \text{very pleasant} \\ \text{unpleasant} \end{Bmatrix} \text{dinner.}$$

NOTE On adjectives that cannot be used in premodification, see 7.22. By contrast, there are premodifying adjectives that cannot be related to clauses with a corresponding predicative usage: *cf* 7.17*ff*.

Premodification by participles

-ing participles

17.30 Everything here depends on the potentiality of the participle to indicate a permanent or characteristic feature. To a lesser extent, gradability (especially as indicated through intensification by *very*) is involved. Consider:

> She has a very interesting mind.

Here *interesting* is fully adjectival (7.5*f*) despite the direct relation to the verb *interest*:

Her mind *interests* me very much.

But an item can be a premodifier and yet disallow *very*:

A roaring bull (*very roaring)

And the converse can be true:

The man was very {reassuring. / shocked. / surprised.} ?He was a {reassuring / shocked / surprised} man.

This last example will illustrate the crucial significance of the 'permanence' characteristic; such participles can freely premodify nouns such as *look*, *smile*:

He greeted me with a very {reassuring / shocked / surprised} expression.

The man himself cannot have shock or surprise attributed permanently to him, but a particular look can of course be permanently associated with such a value. So too we may speak of *a smiling face* rather than of *a smiling person*. It is thus necessary to realize that we are not here concerned with particular participles so much as with their contextual meaning. *A wandering minstrel* is one habitually given to wandering, but if we saw a man wandering down the street, we could not ask:

*Who is the wandering man?

Again, someone who told good stories could be *a (very) entertaining person*, but one could not say this of someone who happened, at the moment of speaking, to be entertaining some friends with a good story

17.31 The indefinite article favours the habitual or permanent, the definite article the specific or temporary (*cf* 17.4). Thus

?The approaching train is from Liverpool.

is strange (especially in BrE) but not

He was frightened by an approaching train.

where we are concerned perhaps with what is characteristic in 'approaching trains'. Similarly, ?*The barking dog is my neighbour's*, compared with the quite normal *I was wakened by a barking dog*. On the other hand, after an indefinite head has been postmodified by an *-ing* clause, the *-ing* participle can premodify the same head plus definite article:

A proposal offending many members . . . → The offending proposal . . .

In addition, the definite article may be used generically (5.24) and hence evoke the same generality and permanence as the indefinite:

The beginning student should be given every encouragement.

-ed participles

17.32 Much of what has been said of *-ing* participles applies to *-ed* participles also, but there are additional complications. In the first place, an *-ed* participle can be active or passive, but as with postmodification (17.15) the active is rarely used in premodification. Contrast

The immigrant who has arrived *with* *The arrived immigrant

The vanished treasure ('The treasure which has vanished') and *A retired teacher* are exceptional, but exceptions are somewhat more general when an active participle is adverbially modified:

The newly-arrived immigrant
Our recently-departed friend

Within the passive, we must distinguish the statal from the actional or true passive (3.25); a statal example:

Some complicated machinery ~ The machinery is complicated. (*The machinery was complicated by the designer)

Here belong also *born* and some uses of *hidden, married, troubled, darkened*, etc, but in premodification they must either have 'permanent' reference or be adverbially modified: *a married man, a newly-born child, a carefully-hidden spy*. The last example illustrates a noteworthy general contrast between *-ing* and *-ed* participles. Beside the similarity in postmodification between the following:

A spy, carefully hidden in the bushes, } kept watch on the house.
A spy, carefully hiding in the bushes, }

the latter unlike the former resists premodification:

*A carefully-hiding spy . . .

17.33 Most *-ed* participles are of the agential type and naturally only a few will easily admit the permanent reference that will permit premodifying use. We may contrast:

The wanted man was last seen in Cambridge. (The man goes on being wanted by the police)
*The found purse was returned to its owner. (The purse was found at a particular moment)

But *a lost purse* is grammatical, because although a purse is no longer regarded as 'found' after it has been retrieved, a purse will be regarded as 'lost' throughout the period of its disappearance. So too: *the defeated army, a broken vase, a damaged car, its relieved owner*. But not: **a sold car*, **the mentioned article*, **a built house*, **a described robber*.

But there are exceptions which suggest that the semantic and aspectual factors are more complicated than here described. For example, although a sum of money can go on being needed, one does not normally say **the needed money*. Modified by adverbs, of course, the starred examples become acceptable: *a recently(-)sold car*, etc.

Finally, some items in *-ed* are not participles at all but are directly formed from nouns:

the vaulted roof, a fluted pillar, a wooded hillside

But constraints occur (perhaps dictated merely by semantic redundancy), such that there is no **a powered engine*, **a haired child*, **a legged man*, though we have *a diesel-powered engine*, *a red-haired child*, *a long-legged man*.

Premodification by genitives

17.34 A noun phrase like *a fisherman's cottage* is ambiguous: the cottage belongs to a fisherman or belonged to a fisherman (or resembles the cottage of a fisherman). As distinct from *a delightful cottage* or *a completed cottage*, the determiner need not refer forward to the head: more usually, it refers only to the genitive. If the latter, then any intermediate modifiers between the determiner and the genitive must also refer only to the genitive. Thus

These French women's clothing

where *these* must predetermine the plural *women's* and the phrase must mean 'the clothing of these French women' and not 'the French clothing of these women' which would require the order *These women's French clothing*. If the former ('the clothing of...'), then an intermediate modifier will be interpreted as referring to the head. Thus

This French women's clothing

would mean 'this French clothing belonging to (or designed for) women'. Ambiguous instances are, however, common: *an old man's bicycle* (contrast: *a man's old bicycle*) could mean 'the bicycle belonging to an old man' or 'an old bicycle designed for a man' (or – in principle – even 'a bicycle designed for an old man').

NOTE On genitive modification in general, see 5.49*ff*; on the group genitive, see 17.26.

Premodification by nouns

17.35 Noun premodifiers are often so closely associated with the head as to be regarded as compounded with it. In many cases, they appear to be in a reduced-explicitness relation with prepositional postmodifiers:

The question of partition ~ The par'tition question
The door of the cupboard ~ The cupboard 'door
A village in Sussex ~ A Sussex 'village

But not all noun premodifiers have prepositional-phrase analogues:

Bernard Miles was both actor and producer ~ The actor-pro'ducer

Attention must be drawn to two important features in premodification by nouns:

(1) Plural nouns usually become singular, even those that otherwise have no singular form (*cf* 5.44):

The leg of the trousers ~ The 'trouser leg

But while singularization is normal it is by no means universal (*cf*: *the arms race*), especially with noun premodification that is not hardening into a fixed phrase or compound: *The committee on promotions* ~ *The pro'motions committee.*

(2) According to the relationship between the two nouns, the accent will fall on the premodifier or the head; for example, *An iron 'rod* but *A 'war story*. The conditions under which the latter stress pattern is adopted are by no means wholly clear but they are also connected with the conventionalizing of a sequence in the direction of compounding.

A notable constraint against making postmodifying phrases into premodifying nouns is the relative impermanence of the modification in question. Thus while *The table in the corner* will readily yield *The corner table*, we cannot do the same with

The girl in the corner (spoke to me) ~ **The corner girl* . . .

We must insist again that this is not a property of the lexical item (in this instance, *corner*) but of the semantic relation; *cf* 17.4.

Multiple premodification

With single head

17.36 The three types of multiple modification specified in 17.25 apply to premodification also. More than one premodifier may be related to a single head, with no grammatical limit on the number:

His brilliant book ~ His last book ~ His (. . .) book.
~ His last brilliant (. . .) book

This is, however, misleading in giving the impression that the multiple modifiers constitute an unordered and coordinate string. It usually follows a recursive process:

His book → His brilliant book → His [last (brilliant book)]

We would here mean that, of several brilliant books, we are speaking only of his last one; by contrast

His book → His last book → His [brilliant (last book)]

indicates that his last book was brilliant without commitment to whether any of his others were. In some instances, however, we do indeed have multiple modifications in which no priority among modifiers need be assumed; to these we may give separate prosodic emphasis or introduce commas in writing:

His LÁST BRÍLLIANT BÒOK ('his last and brilliant book')

Or we may formally coordinate them. Thus there would be little difference between

Her forceful, lucid remarks *and* Her lucid (and) forceful remarks.

When coordinated modifiers relate to properties that are normally thought to conflict, the coordinator will probably not be *and*:

His handsome but scarred face His scarred but handsome face

With multiple head

17.37 Modification may apply to more than one head (*cf* 13.25):

The new table }
The new chairs } ~ The new table and chairs

The multiple head thus produced can now be subject to recursive or coordinate modification:

The new table and chairs → { The beautiful new table and chairs
The new (but) ugly table and chairs }

If we coordinated *learned papers* and *books* as in *(He wrote) learned papers and books*, we would suggest that *learned* applies to both *papers* and *books*. If it should not, we can either reorder (*books and learned papers*) or introduce separate determiners (*some learned papers and some books*).

With modified modifier

17.38 We have already seen two types of modification with modified modifier:

His *really quite unbelievably delightful* cottage (17.29)
These French women's clothing (17.34)

In a third type, the noun premodifier can be itself premodified by either adjective or a noun and, if the latter, this can in turn be similarly premodified:

The office furniture → { The *small office* furniture
The *tax office* furniture }

→ The *property tax* office furniture
→ The *house property* tax office furniture

It should be noted, however, that if we were to introduce an adjective in this last noun phrase, already clumsy and improbable, (i) it would have to come immediately after the determiner, and (ii) it would normally be interpreted as relating directly to the head *furniture* rather than to *house*, the only other possibility:

The {pleasant [⟨(house property) tax⟩ office] furniture}

This is not to say, however, that obscurity cannot exist or that noun premodifiers can modify only the next following noun. Consider *A new giant size cardboard detergent carton*, where *size* does not premodify *detergent* but where the linear structure is rather:

A ⟨new {(giant size) [cardboard (detergent carton)]}⟩

Other complexities in premodification

17.39 A friendship between a boy and girl becomes *A boy and girl friendship*. A committee dealing with appointments and promotions can readily be described as *The appointments and promotions committee*, while one whose business is the allocation of finance can be *The allocation of finance committee*.

A noun phrase in which there is noun premodification can be given the denominal affix which puts it into the 'consisting of' class of adjectives (7.26) while retaining the noun premodifier; hence, from *party politics* we have *(a) party political (broadcast)*.

Similarly, a noun phrase having a denominal adjective may itself take a denominal affix to become a premodifier in a noun phrase. For example, beside *cerebral palsy* (= 'palsy' of the cerebrum), we have *cerebral palsied children* which has the structure (*cf* 17.33):

{[(cerebral palsy)ed] children}   *and not*   *[cerebral (palsied children)]

NOTE Coordination gives rise to numerous difficulties in premodification. Beside the relatively explicit *children with impaired speech*, we have the premodified form *speech-impaired children*. But, since speech and hearing are so often jointly impaired, we are involved in the need to have a corresponding premodification, *speech(-) and hearing(-) impaired children*, clear enough in spoken English but possibly requiring a clumsy double hyphenation to make it clear in writing.

Relative sequence of premodifiers

Denominal and nominal

17.40 The item that must come next before the head is the type of denominal adjective often meaning 'consisting of', 'involving', or 'relating to', and this can be preceded by a wide range of premodifying items:

the {extravagant / pleasant / only / London} *social* life   a {serious / city / mere / United States} *political* problem

Next closest to the head is the noun premodifier, already exemplified with *London*, *city*, and *United States* in the foregoing examples. When two nouns premodify, one which corresponds to the head as object to verb will follow one relating to material or agency:

$$\text{a} \left\{\begin{matrix} \textit{detergent} \\ \textit{cardboard} \end{matrix}\right\} \left\{\begin{matrix} \text{container} \\ \text{carton} \end{matrix}\right. \sim \text{ a } \textit{cardboard detergent} \left\{\begin{matrix} \text{container} \\ \text{carton} \end{matrix}\right.$$

$$\text{my} \left\{\begin{matrix} \text{ciga'rette} \\ \text{'gas} \end{matrix}\right\} \text{lighter} \sim \text{ my } \textit{,gas ciga'rette} \text{ lighter}$$

not *my cigarette gas lighter

Classes of adjectives

17.41 Next before a noun modifier, the most important class of items is the adjective of provenance of style:

a *Russian* trade delegation *Gothic* church architecture

and preceding this type is the participle:

a *carved* Gothic doorway some *interlocking* Chinese designs

Preceding the participle, we have adjectives of colour:

a *black* dividing line a *green* carved idol

These are preceded by adjectives of age, together with the premodifiers and postmodifiers that these and other freely gradable adjectives may have:

an *old* blue dress a *really very elderly* trained nurse
a *very young* physics student a *large enough* lecture room

Next comes the large class that we may call 'general', except that between 'general' and colour (and usually all other modifiers to the right) comes the diminutive unstressed use of *little*. Thus, not **an old little blue ornament*, but:

$$\text{a} \left\{\begin{matrix} \text{gracious} \\ \text{typical} \\ \text{beautiful} \\ \text{peculiar} \\ \text{handsome} \\ \text{hideous} \\ \text{splendid} \end{matrix}\right\} \text{little} \left\{\begin{matrix} \text{old blue ornament} \\ \text{old carved Gothic doorway} \end{matrix}\right.$$

See Fig 17.41 which illustrates the relative positions of items in premodification.

NOTE There are many qualifications to the foregoing. The 'general' adjectives, for example, are not placed randomly but comprise several subclasses. We would prefer *a small round table* to ?*a round small table*; *several thick even slices* to *several even thick slices*; *a fierce shaggy dog* to *a shaggy fierce dog*; *a tall angry man* to *an angry tall man*; *a brief hostile glance* to *a hostile brief glance*. Evaluative or subjective adjectives frequently precede those that are relatively objective or measurable; size often precedes shape; within size, height often precedes girth. 'General' adjectives are themselves preceded by semantically weak items like *nice*, by non-predicable items like *mere*, by quantifiers, numerals, determiners, and associated closed-system items (5.3*ff*).

Determiners	*general*	*age*	*colour*	*participle*	*provenance*	*noun*	*denominal*	*head*
the	hectic						social	life
the	extravagant					London	social	life
a				crumbling		church		tower
a			grey	crumbling	Gothic	church		tower
some	intricate	old		interlocking	Chinese			designs
a	small		green	carved		jade		idol
his	heavy	new					moral	responsibilities

Fig 17.41 Examples of premodification sequence

Discontinuous modification

17.42 It is not uncommon for a noun phrase to be interrupted by other items of clause structure. Note for instance the time adjunct between the head and postmodifier in the following:

> You'll meet *a man* tomorrow *carrying a heavy parcel.*

There are more striking examples:

> I had *a nice glass of beer* but in *an ugly glass.*

This is not as contradictory as it may seem, since it is only in the second noun phrase that *glass* is premodified by an adjective; in the first, it is better to regard *glass of beer* as a complex unit modified as a whole but with *glass* being less a concrete noun than a unit of measure. So too with *a weak cup of tea*, and phrases of the form *kind/sort of N* which take premodifiers plainly related to *N* rather than *sort*, both in semantics and in concord:

> A *big awkward* sort of *carton*
> ?*These big awkward* kind of *cartons*

17.43 Discontinuous modification more aptly applies to examples like the following (*cf* 7.9):

Comparable facilities *to ours*
Different production figures *from those given earlier*

The prepositional phrases here do not directly relate to the head (as they do in *roads to London*, *people from the village*) but to the premodifying adjective: 'facilities *comparable to ours*', 'figures *different from those*'. Compare also *The tall man that I saw* with *The first man that I saw* (= 'The man that I saw first'); 'An *attractive* scheme *financially*' (= 'A scheme which is *financially attractive*'); *cf* 7.32.

Most discontinuities, however, are brought about by interpolating a parenthesis or the finite verb of the sentence (where the noun phrase is subject) between the head and the postmodifier; and the usual motive is to correct a structural imbalance (*cf* 18.27*f*) as in '*The story* is told *that he was once a boxer*', or to achieve a more immediate clarity as in:

The woman is by the DÒOR, who sold me the TÍCKets and told me the play doesn't begin till THRÉE.

Bibliographical note

On postmodification, see Bresnan and Grimshaw (1978); de Haan (1987); Downing (1978); Elsness (1982); Olofsson (1981); Schachter (1973); Sears (1972); Young (1980).

On premodification, see Bache (1978); Bolinger (1967a); Johansson (1980); Levi (1978).

On the relation between modifiers and heads, see Seppänen (1978).

On the genitive and *of*-construction, see Dahl (1971), Jahr Sørheim (1980); Lyons (1986); Wieser (1986).

On nominalization, see Chomsky (1972); Colen (1984); Kjellmer (1980); Vendler (1968).

On apposition, see Austin (1980); Meyer (1987).

18 Theme, focus, and information processing

Introduction

18.1 In the processing and receiving of information, whether written or spoken, lexical choice and grammatical organization have an important role. Consider these examples:

Will the new law help old people? [1]
The road will ultimately be repaired. [2]
I'll visit them occasionally. [3]
The honeymoon couple returned to Edinburgh in bright sunshine today. [4]

In the following variants, the truth value is fundamentally unchanged, but the presentation is very different:

In your view, will the new law give old people the help they need? [1a]
It will be some time before the road is repaired. [2a]
I don't think I can do more than pay them an occasional visit. [3a]
It was bright sunny weather that welcomed the honeymoon couple back to Edinburgh today. [4a]

It is not merely that the variants are more verbose. In each case, an introduction has been provided which puts the utterance in a communicative context, as in [1a] and [3a], or which highlights an aspect of the utterance that is communicatively effective, as in [2a] and the journalistic [4a]. Moreover, care has been taken in [1a], [3a], and [4a] to make the ending an appropriate climax. Before we consider other modes of information processing, we must look closely at the vital role of intonation and other aspects of prosody.

Information and communicative dynamism

18.2 COMMUNICATIVE DYNAMISM refers to the variation in communicative value as between different parts of an utterance. Consider the following as the answer to the question 'When shall we know what Mary is going to do?' The subject, verb, and adjunct in:

She will de | cide 'next WÈEK |

are uttered with sequentially increasing prominence, with the S conveying least information, the V rather more, and the A conveying most, namely, the information sought by the *wh*-element of the question 'When (shall we know what Mary is going to do)?' A TONE UNIT (2.15) is a stretch of speech containing one intonation nucleus, and since each such nucleus serves to highlight a piece of information, it follows that a tone unit is coextensive with an INFORMATION UNIT.

But although an information unit highlights one item, this does not mean that the rest of the unit is devoid of information. As in the present example, the 'communicative dynamism' can range from very low (corresponding to weak stress, as with the subject *she*), through medium (corresponding to nonnuclear stress, as with the verb phrase, *will decide*), to very strong stress (corresponding to intonation nucleus, as with the adverbial, *next week*). And, again as in this example, it is common – though by no means necessary – for the range of such communicative dynamism to increase from low to high in accordance with the linear progression of the information unit. To put it another (and better) way, it is common to process the information in a message so as to achieve a linear presentation from low to high information value. We shall refer to this as the principle of END-FOCUS.

Tone units and grammar

18.3 Every sentence has at least one tone/information unit, and it is usual for such a unit to be coextensive with a grammatical unit. Sometimes this is the sentence itself, as in the example we have been considering:

She will de | cide 'next WEEK |

But far more commonly, the tone unit corresponds to a grammatical unit within a sentence. This may be:

(a) An initially placed optional adjunct (*cf* 8.15), other than closed-class items:

| After my ILLness | I | went to FRÀNCE |

Contrast:

| Then I went to FRÀNCE |

(b) An initially or finally placed disjunct or conjunct (*cf* 8.40, 43), especially when realized by a polysyllabic item:

More | ŏver | the | chairman may not be WÌLLing |
It was dis | GRÀCEful || FRÁNKly |

(c) An initially placed vocative:

| DÒCtor | I'm | very ÀNXious |

Contrast:

I'm | very ÀNXious 'Doctor |

(d) The subject, if this element is realized by a clause or a long noun phrase, especially one with postmodification (*cf* 17.5*ff*):

| What we WÁNT | is | plenty of RÀIN |
The | tall 'lady by the DÓOR || spoke to JÒHN |

Contrast:

| John 'spoke to the 'tall 'lady by the DÒOR |

(e) A fronted object or complement (*cf* 18.14*f*):

Her | WRÌTing | I | find uninTÈLligible |

(f) The coordinated clauses in a compound sentence, especially when the clauses have different subjects:

She | WON the RÁCE | and he was de | LÌGHTed |
They | WÁLKED | they | SWÁM | they | played GÒLF |

Contrast coordinated predicates and predications (*cf* 13.19):

He | went out and 'slammed the DÒOR |
I have | seen them and 'offered my HÈLP |

Given and new information

18.4 When we construct a message, it is a courtesy to the receiver, as well as a convenience for ourselves, to provide the point of the message with enough context for this point to be both clearly identified and unambiguously understood, as well as being placed in a normal linguistic framework. To return to the question at the beginning of 18.2:

When shall we know what Mary is going to do?

The answer might have been:

We'll know *next week*.

Here the unitalicized portion replicates material from the question; so far as the receiver is concerned, it is entirely GIVEN. But as well as providing assurance that the answer is indeed attending to the question, it serves as a convenient introduction to the actual point of the message, the NEW information conveyed by *next week*. Of course, in this instance, the message would have been adequately comprehensible if it had been confined to the new information alone:

Next week.

But in 18.2, the answer we considered was:

She will decide *next week*.

The italicized portion again presents the main point of the message and the entirely new information, but the introduction is less obviously and directly 'given'. Nonetheless, it serves as the necessary background, and by contrast with the 'new' information, it is relatively 'given'. The subject *she* and the futurity expressed by *will* are indeed entirely given, and in replacing *we* and *know* by *she* and *decide* (with consequently increased communicative dynamism; *cf* 18.3), we oblige the receiver to infer that if, as we might expect, we learn of her decision when it is made, the new information – in the context of this specific given information – constitutes an adequate answer to the question.

Theme and focus

18.5 There is commonly a one-to-one relation between 'given' in contrast to 'new' information on the one hand, and 'theme' in contrast to 'focus' on the other. THEME is the name we give to the initial part of any structure when we consider it from an informational point of view. When it occurs in its expected or 'unmarked' form (but *cf* 18.13), its direct relation to given information can be seen informally as announcing that the starting point of the message is established and agreed. In this sense, the definite article is thematic in relation to a noun phrase such as *the lecturer* in announcing that the identity has been established; but, comparably, in the noun phrase *the lecturer's name*, it is the genitive premodifier *the lecturer's* that is thematic. More usually, however, we apply the term 'theme' to the first element of a clause, such as the subject in *The lecturer's name wasn't announced*. Consider now these three examples as 'messages' in isolation:

> The *lecturer*
> The lecturer's *name*
> The lecturer's name *wasn't announced.*

We should note a significant prosodic similarity between the unitalicized theme and the remainder of each structure. The theme's relative lack of stress mimes its status as 'given' and therefore in no need of emphasis. By contrast, the italicized portions are given greater prosodic prominence and it would be on these that the intonation nucleus would be placed if they were uttered as messages:

> (Who led the discussion?) The | LÈCTurer |
> (What did she want to know?) The | lecturer's NÀME |
> (Didn't she know who was lecturing?) The | lecturer's 'name wasn't anNÒUNCED |

In other words, the new information in each case is the 'focus' of the message, and just as we saw in 18.4 that it seemed natural to place the new information after providing a context of given information, so we can regard focus (identified prosodically) as most naturally and normally occurring at the end of the information unit.

NOTE [**a**] Since the new information often needs to be stated more fully than the given (that is, with a longer, 'heavier' structure), it is not unexpected that an organization principle which may be called END-WEIGHT comes into operation along with the principle of end-focus. The principle of end-weight can be seen operating in the following examples:

She visited him that very day.
She visited her best friend that very day.
She visited that very day an elderly and much beloved friend.

In this last example, even had the speaker/writer preferred to put the focus on the time adjunct and to locate it in the unmarked final position, the weight of the object noun phrase makes it preferable to have the adjunct at *iE* (*cf* 8.11). An even better position might have been *I*: '*That very day*, she visited . . .'

[**b**] In contrast to 'given' and 'new', which are *contextually* established and to that extent 'extralinguistic', 'theme' and 'focus' are linguistically defined, in terms of position and prosody respectively. With 'theme' there is an attractive alternative contrast, 'rheme', and the latter term (favoured by some linguists) will be used from time to time, especially in its adjectival form, 'rhematic', since it provides a convenient way of referring to degrees of communicative dynamism. Some linguists use the distinction 'topic'/'comment' for our 'theme'/'focus' or 'theme'/'rheme' (and sometimes for our 'given'/'new'). Others speak of given information as 'old', 'shared', or 'presupposed' information.

The relation between focus and new information

18.6 New information can be anything from a syllable to a whole clause. If the nucleus falls on the last stressed syllable of the clause (according to the unmarked end-focus principle), what is 'new' could, for example, be the entire clause, or the last element (*eg* complement) of the clause, or the predication of the clause. In the following sentence, we mark the extent of the new information for three possible uses of the same sentence:

Whole clause is 'new':

NEW (spanning: We're going to the RÀces)

(What's on today?) We're going to the RÀces. [1]

Predication is 'new':

NEW (spanning: going to the RÀces)

(What are we doing today?) We're going to the RÀces. [2]

Final adverbial is 'new':

NEW (spanning: to the RÀces)

(Where are we going today?) We're going to the RÀces. [3]

The sentence as heard (and the same would of course apply to writing, *cf* 18.1) is neutral as to the three possible stretches of new information indicated by our marking, since the focus is at the same point in each case. Only the parenthesized questions (more broadly put, our knowledge of the context) provide the clue as to how much of the information is assumed as 'given' and how much is thus new.

When the nucleus occurs on a syllable earlier than that predicted by the principle of end-focus, however, no such openness of interpretation is possible:

(Have you decided whether you're going to the races?)

NEW

Yes, we ÀRE going to the races. [4]

This is an instance of 'marked' focus, to which we turn in 18.7.

NOTE **[a]** In conversation, where the sentences [2–4] were replies to the corresponding questions, it would be common of course for ellipsis (*cf* 12.16) to permit more or less only the *new* information to be uttered; *cf* 18.10. For example, in place of [2], [3], [4], we could have:

Going to the RÀces [2a]
To the RÀces [3a]
We ÀRE [4a]

[b] The contrast in the following is worth remarking:

Among those present were the Mayor and { MÌS(IZ) Martin [5]
mis(IZ) MÀRtin [6] }

In [6] the Mayor is accompanied by a woman having a different surname from his; in [5] the woman – his wife or daughter, perhaps – has the same surname as the Mayor and the speaker implies that the hearer knows already what this is.

[c] In examples like the following (especially with respect to items of personal wear), the final phrase is normally treated as given, being added only for informal clarification:

She's buying a SCÀRF for herself.

Contrast:

She's buying her mother a birthday present but she's also buying a SCÁRF for hersÈLF.

Marked focus

18.7 The principle of end-focus entails that we can confidently predict that a reader will interpret *blue* as the focal item in the written sentence:

I am painting my living room blue.

In other words, we are confident that it would be read aloud as:

I am | painting my 'living room BLÙE | [1]

The sentence has an increasing degree of communicative dynamism from *painting* to *blue*. But as we have just seen in 18.6, *all* of the information in this sentence may be new, and when we reflect upon the sentence, we must realize that in fact no part is necessarily more obvious or predictable than another. This means that it is perfectly possible to make the sentence informationally appropriate with the intonation nucleus (and hence the information focus) elsewhere:

I am | painting my LÌVing room 'blue | [2]
I am | painting MỲ 'living room 'blue | [3]
I am | PÀINting my 'living room 'blue | [4]
I | ÀM 'painting my 'living room 'blue | [5]
| Ì am 'painting my 'living room 'blue | [6]

It is when we move the focus from its predictable position as in [1] to another position as in [2–6] that we speak of MARKED FOCUS.

The condition for marked focus arises when special emphasis is required. Frequently such emphasis is needed for the purposes of contrast or correction. Thus it would be easy to imagine [2] as following someone else's remark:

I am | painting my 'bathroom BLÙE |

or question:

| Are you 'painting your 'kitchen BLÚE |

Equally, [3] might follow on from:

| John is 'painting his 'living room BLÙE |

Again, [4] might follow on from:

I've | changed my 'mind about PǍPering |

So too, [5] might be a response to:

| Weren't you in'tending to 'paint your 'living room BLÚE |

And [6] might follow on from:

| So 'John is 'painting your 'living room BLÙE |

But contrast, in the sense of replacing one presumed item by another, is not the only occasion for the special emphasis of marked focus. More generally, it is a matter of adjusting the focus according to what is presupposed in a particular context.

NOTE [a] Since in reading we assign end-focus unless the context makes it unambiguously clear that the focus should be elsewhere, other devices than prosody are usefully invoked where end-focus would produce a misreading. For example, the cleft-sentence structure; *cf* 18.18*ff*. But for some instances of marked focus, as in [3], [4], and [5], considerable reworking is required. Thus in place of [3], we might have a written version:

The living room I am painting blue is { my own. / mine. } [3]

[b] Examples [3], [5], and [6] above illustrate the fact that, although focus is normally expected to fall on an open-class lexical item, exceptions can readily be made where a closed-class item requires special emphasis for contrastive or other purposes (*cf* 18.11). Even the articles may be thus focused:

Are you | talking about THÉ 'Mrs 'Reagan | (or only someone else of the same name)?
A: Did you | see the po'liceman conCÉRNED |
B: Well I | saw Ǎ po'liceman | [pronounced /eɪ/]

Compare also:

| YÒU should worry | [= This shouldn't worry YǑU |]
| NÒW what does she want |

The feeling of exasperation is expressed with the marked focus and fronted adverbial more strongly than in the otherwise equivalent:

| What does she want NÒW |

18.8 In certain circumstances, it is quite normal to have the focus on a noun phrase as subject of a clause, in violation of the end-focus principle. This is frequently because, with the subject concerned, the predicate is relatively predictable and thus has lower communicative dynamism. It is significant that the phenomenon in question is especially associated with intransitives, where (if English structure permitted it freely) we might expect the element order *VS*; *cf* 18.16. Compare:

The | TÈLephone's 'ringing |
The | SÙN is 'shining |
The | KÈTtle's 'boiling |
A | VÌsitor called |
| Has your SǏster 'come 'home |

Predictability is easy to see with the first two examples, but it is arguable analogously that, in a domestic context, the most obvious thing to announce about kettles is that they are boiling; a visitor cannot visit without 'calling' at one's house; and what more predictable for a caller, interested in a person, than to ask whether she is at home?

But there are other factors that may lead us to identify by focus a subject and named individual (*John*, *The President*) or else an entity or activity that has great generality or whose existence is well known (*A visitor*, *The kettle*). Second, the predicate denotes typically a very general or commonly associated activity (especially one that presents a starkly positive/negative choice), such as the act of appearing/disappearing; or it denotes demise or other misfortune, again of a general nature. Some examples:

The | PRÈSident has 'died |	*contrast*:	| Someone has DÌED |
My | CÒAT is 'torn |	*contrast*:	My | coat is FÀWN |
The | BÀby's 'crying |	*contrast*:	The | baby's SMÌLing |

Emphasis may be given to an initial noun phrase (or indeed to any nonfinal item) by interposing a parenthesis with its own tone unit:

> | This in SHÒRT | is | why I reFÙSED |

The device is comparably valuable in writing, where this conjunct would be separately punctuated and thus allow *This* to have more weight than it otherwise would:

> This, in short, is why I refused.

NOTE Although we have associated this phenomenon with noun phrases as *subject*, it arises more broadly with noun phrases in construction with succeeding verb phrases:

> | Joan has a PLÀNE to 'catch |
> We have | various PRÒBlems to 'solve |

By contrast, where it is less congruent with or less predictably associated with the noun phrase, it is the verb phrase that might be focused:

> . . . texts to compÙTerize |

Similarly, within a noun phrase, if the head is more general and carries less semantic weight and specificity than the premodifier, it is the latter that may sometimes be focused:

> She's a | BRÌLliant 'person |
> (*contrast*: She's a | brilliant DÒCtor |)

Again, where the noun-phrase object is of general reference, focus may be moved forward on to the head of the verb phrase:

> You should | always 'try to HÈLP a 'guy |
> (*contrast*: You should | always 'try to 'help a poLÌCEman |)

Compare also noun phrases of mere expletive or evaluative force:

> I've been CHÈATed by the dirty scoundrel.

18.9 The instances of marked focus in 18.8 involved putting the focus earlier than where it would occur in unmarked focus. But there are two further types, (a) and (b), to be considered:

(a) First, the focus can be moved to a point subsequent or immediately prior to its expected position. This is sometimes because the unmarked focus is misleading, as it might be in:

> | Who's the NÒvel by |

If there were any danger that the hearer might take *novel* as emphatic (for example in contrast to the *review*), the question would be put with marked focus upon the preposition:

| Who's the 'novel BỲ |

Consider an exchange like the following:

A: So what did you SÀY?
B: There was nothing TÒ say.

It may seem vacuous to highlight the mere infinitive marker. But on the one hand, *say* is given and would thus be an inappropriate bearer of a nucleus; on the other hand, there is a positive reason for placing the nucleus on the only part of this verb phrase which represents the modality. Some further examples of marked focus:

So we | bought THÌS 'house | (*instead of that one*)
| Hand your 'ticket ÌN | (*you're not allowed to keep it*)

(b) Secondly, we can have contrastive focus at precisely the point of unmarked focus. In speech, such marked focus may be realized with additional stress or wider range of nucleus (*cf* 2.15). In writing, the comparable effect can often be conveyed only by expansion or a rather elaborate paraphrase, but sometimes typographical devices are invoked, especially italics. In S H Perelman's *Last Laugh* (1981), we find the following piece of dialogue:

'Was that how you became a rustler?'
'A rustler?' I repeated. 'Not a rustler, Miss Cronjager – *a wrestler.*'

The word that requires marked contrastive focus for corrective purposes comes at the point where unmarked focus would occur. Perelman presumably expects the italics to represent greater prominence than on the original nucleus:

Was | that how you became a RÚstler |
A | RÚstler | . . . | Not a RŬstler | . . . a " | WRÈstler |

NOTE Where marked focus is required on a preposition, it is sometimes possible to achieve the required meaning with end-focus by using a paraphrase. Thus beside:

. . . apart from his LÀziness |

we may have

. . . aPÀRT from his 'laziness |

or:

. . . his 'laziness aPÀRT |

With the adverbial particle in phrasal verbs, the same result is achieved merely by movement:

He's | bringing 'in the CÀses | He's | bringing the 'cases ÌN |

This helps to explain why such particles are in final position when the object is a personal pronoun (*cf* 16.4) or is a noun phrase of very general meaning:

She's | bringing it/the matter ÙP |
(*cf* *She's | bringing 'up the MÀTter |)

18.10 Just as marked focus frequently involves putting emphasis on an unexpected part of a phrase, so also it may involve unexpected emphasis on part of a word or name. Normally we put the main stress on a person's family name and not the first name:

Dylan THOMas

But marked focus may reverse this, sometimes in making a correction:

(By the poet Thomas, I meant)
DỲLan 'Thomas – | not ÉDward 'Thomas

Conversely, compound nouns with normal first-element stress can switch to second-element stress with marked focus:

I | just 'wanted a 'couple of PÌCture hooks | and he | started 'showing me some 'picture BÒOKS |

So also, in order to make a contrast, two words can be equally given unusual accentuation:

They fought for DĚMocracy but they've ended up with ÀUTocracy.
She suddenly changed the subject from ĚMigration to ÌMmigration.

Focus on the operator

18.11 One type of marked focus that deserves separate treatment is focusing on the operator, which often has the particular function of signalling contrast between positive and negative meaning:

(A: Why haven't you had a bath?) B: I | HÀVE had a 'bath |
(A: Look for your shoes.) B: I | ÀM looking for them |
She | PRŎMised | so she | MÙST 'take him 'with her |

When the operator is positive, the meaning is 'Yes in contrast to No'; when the operator is negative, the meaning is contrastive in the opposite direction:

So you | HÀVEn't lost it | ['You thought you had']

When the finite verb phrase is in the simple present or past tense, and so would not otherwise have an auxiliary verb to function as operator, the 'dummy' operator *do* is introduced to bear the nuclear stress (*cf* 3.11):

So you | DÌD go to the 'concert this 'evening | [*ie* 'I thought you might, but . . .']

But I |DÒ think you're a 'good 'cook| [*ie* '. . . even if you imagine I don't']

With a rise or fall-rise as intonation nucleus, focus on auxiliaries indicating past or future often draws contrastive attention to the tense or aspect rather than to the positive/negative polarity:

He |owns – or DǏD own |– a |Rolls-RÒYCE |
We've |sold ÒUT |but we |WǏLL be 'getting 'more |

Similarly, the nucleus on auxiliaries such as *may*, *ought to*, and *could* often signals a contrast between the supposed real state of affairs, and a state of affairs thought desirable or likely:

The o|pinion 'polls MǍY be 'right| [*ie* 'but I suspect they're not']

NOTE In courtesy enquiries about health and wellbeing, where there are in effect no information-bearing lexical items, focus on the operator carries no special emphasis:

How |ÀRE you 'these 'days |
Well, how |ÀRE you 'now, 'Mr 'Brown |

If normally unstressed operators receive stress (especially nuclear stress), the effect is often to add exclamatory emphasis to the whole sentence:

That WǏLL be nice!   You DÒ look tired!

Divided focus

18.12 It sometimes happens that we want to put nuclear focus upon two items in an information unit. An intonation pattern particularly associated with this in BrE is the fall-plus-rise contour (*cf* 2.15). Compare the following:

He's |fairly CLÈver | [1]
He's |FÀIRly CLÉver | [2]

The implications differ in two ways. Semantically, [1] implies a positive estimate, though cautiously worded, while [2] is relatively grudging and disparaging, calling in question the estimate of cleverness. Informationally, [1] is compatible with answering a general inquiry about the person ('What do you think of Alec?'), while [2] implies that the question of his cleverness has already been raised ('Alec is clever, isn't he?'). Where such DIVIDED FOCUS is realized by fall-plus-rise, therefore, the item carrying the rise is made subsidiary to the other focused item, accepts that it represents information that is to some extent 'given', but (compatible with the rise) calls its status in question.

Compare:

|William WÒRDSworth is my 'favourite PÓET |

This may be in reply to the question 'Who is your favourite poet?' or to a contrary statement 'I understand that John Keats is your favourite poet'.

But frequently the second focus conveys little more than courtesy; thus it is used with final vocatives and formulaic subjuncts (8.34):

| What's the TÌME, JÓHN | At|TÈNtion, PLÉASE |

NOTE In contrast to the fall-plus-rise, the rise-plus-fall contour is used to mark a divided focus where the first of the two focused items is made subsidiary to the second. We can thus contrast the two types of divided focus:

I | went to FRÀNCE in 'nineteen ÉIGHTY | [3]
I | went to FRÁNCE in 'nineteen ÈIGHTY | [4]

[3] suggests a context in which there is discussion of what I had done in 1980, this part therefore being relatively given; [4] suggests one in which the discussion concerns when I went to France, the rise again coinciding with the relatively given, but this time preceding the relatively new instead of following it.

Marked theme

18.13 The two communicatively significant parts of an information unit, the theme and the focus, are typically as distinct as they can be: one is the point of initiation, and the other the point of completion. The theme of an information unit, coming first, is more often 'given' information than any other part of it. Yet the two can coincide; for instance, when, as marked focus, the nucleus falls on the subject of a statement:

(Who gave you that magazine?) | BÌLL gave it to me | [1]

This is the extreme form of MARKED THEME, and we can compare [2] which has an unmarked theme (*he*) with minimum prosodic prominence:

He | gave me a magazÌNE | [2]

Clearly, theme and focus must coincide in one-word utterances, whether these are questions, responses, or military commands. For example:

| CÓFFee | | THÀNKS |

Even so, many such short units have an initial portion that can be used as thematic preparation. A striking instance of this is found in the military order, 'Attention!' The word is typically uttered with considerable drawl on the first two syllables, and (ignoring the fact that the word ordinarily has stress on the second syllable) with the final syllable given word stress and the climactic nuclear focus:

at|ten—TION |

The theme carries considerable prosodic weight when it is an item that is not (like subject or conjunction, for example) normally at initial position in a clause (*cf* 8.11). Consider the following exchange:

A: Are you |going to in'vite JÓHN |
B: Oh |John I've al'ready invÌTed |

In B's response, *John* is a marked theme, and the term will be used for any such fronted item, whether or not it carries (as such items commonly do) a marked focus (*cf* further 18.14).

The value of marked theme in information processing can be seen in comparing the following, where [3–5] have *SVC* order but [6] has *CSV*:

|John is LÀZY| (but I think he will help me) [3]
Al|though 'John is LǍZY | (I think he will help me) [4]
Al|though 'John is LÁZY | . . . [5]
|Lazy though John ís | . . . [6]

In [3], *lazy* is new information; there is no assumption on the speaker's part that the listener knows. In [4], the fall–rise on *lazy* also implies that the information is new; the rise part of the complex nucleus is conditioned by the dependent status of the clause of which this is the focus. In [5], however, the simple rise on *lazy* is compatible both with the dependence of the clause concerned and the implication that the hearer already shares the speaker's view of John. In [6], making *lazy* a marked theme again implies the givenness of the information and additionally enables the speaker to focus upon the operator (*cf* 18.11) with consequent emphasis on its positive polarity (*cf* 3.11). A further example: 'Serious as has become the food shortage, worse news is to follow'; this embodies inversion of subject and verb (*cf* 18.16).

NOTE Common short adverbials in initial position are often given some thematic marking:

|Then he LÈFT |

Longer and semantically weightier adverbials at *I* will be more heavily marked themes or they may actually carry a nucleus:

|Suddenly he LÈFT | |SǓDdenly |he |LÈFT |

Note that marked theme can be used to draw attention to contrasting pairs, and this often involves separate tone units:

|VĚRdi |is |splendid in his WǍY |but |MŎzart's operas |I re|gard as 'pure perFÈCTion |

Fronting

18.14 Fronting is the term we apply to the achievement of marked theme by moving into initial position an item which is otherwise unusual there. The reason for fronting may be to echo thematically what has been contextually given:

(You should take up swimming for relaxation)
| RelaxÀtion you 'call it |

Alternatively, the item fronted may be the one contextually most demanded:

| WILson his NÁME is |
An | utter FÒOL she 'made me 'feel |

Fronting is very common both in speech and in conventional written material, often serving the function of so arranging clause order that end-focus falls on the most important part of the message as well as providing direct linkage with what has preceded:

That much the jury had thoroughly appreciated.
Most of these problems a computer could take in its stride.
To this list may be added ten further items of importance.

The determiners *that*, *this*, and *these* in the above examples suggest that the marked theme in such cases most often expresses given information. It is common to find *-ing* participle predications fronted in similar information-processing circumstances:

Sitting at her desk in deep concentration was my sister Flora. She looked as though she had spent a sleepless night.

(*Cf* subject–verb and subject–operator inversion, 18.16*f*.)

NOTE [a] A fronted item, like a fronted *wh*-element (*cf* 11.9*f*), is sometimes an element from a subordinate clause:

Everything – or nearly everything – that the Labour movement exists to stop the Tories from doing Labour will be asked to support the Cabinet in doing.

The whole of the italicized part of this example is the object of a nonfinite clause, itself a prepositional object within an infinitive clause within the main clause.
[b] Exceptionally, a part rather than the whole of a clause element may be fronted. In the following case, a prepositional phrase equivalent to a postmodifier of the subject complement (but *cf* 17.22) acts as theme: '*Of all the early examples of science fiction*, the fantastic stories of Jules Verne are the most remarkable.'

18.15 A more striking type of fronting is found in the heightened language of rather mannered rhetoric, including the strenuous colourfulness of journalistic writing. It is frequently employed to point a parallelism between two parts of a clause or between two related but contrasting pairs of neighbouring clauses. The fronted parts may be prosodically marked as marked theme or marked focus, the latter typically with divided focus (*cf* 18.12), and they may be grammatically any of a wide range of units:

His face not many {admired, / were enamoured of,} while *his character*

still fewer could praise. [O]
Traitor he has become and *traitor* we shall call him. [C]
She might agree under pressure: *willingly* she never would. [A]
They have promised to finish the work, and *finish it* they will. [Predication]

With predications and predication adjuncts in front position, we often find subject–verb inversion (*cf* 18.16) if the subject is other than a personal pronoun:

Into the stifling smoke we plunged. [A S V]
Into the stifling smoke plunged the desperate mother. [A V S]

NOTE In examples like the following, common in journalism, the fronting of the predication seems largely determined by the desire to give end-focus to the subject, at the same time using (as is normal) the early part of the sentence to 'set the scene':

Addressing the demonstration was a quite elderly woman.
Shot by nationalist guerrillas were two entirely innocent tourists.

Even the cleft sentence, itself a grammatical focus device (*cf* 18.18*f*) can be subject to fronting:

They hoped that Herbert Frost would be elected and *Frost* indeed it was that topped the poll.

Subject–verb inversion

18.16 The clause patterns *SVC* and *SVA* (*cf* 10.1) have their obligatory third element in large measure because the V is commonly of itself so lacking in communicative dynamism:

SVC: Her oval face was especially remarkable. [1]
SVC: The sound of the bell grew faint. [2]
SVA: His beloved body lies in a distant grave. [3]

In consequence, where information processing makes it desirable to front the third element concerned, the result would tend to be bathetic or misleading if normal SV order were preserved. In consequence, fronting naturally carries with it the inversion that puts S in final position, and indeed it is to achieve end-focus on the S that the fronting is generally undertaken:

CVS: Especially remarkable was her oval face. [1a]
CVS: Faint grew the sound of the bell. [2a]
AVS: In a distant grave lies his beloved body. [3a]

These particular examples have a rather mannered tone (poetic in the case of [2a] and [3a]), but the phenomenon is common enough in ordinary informal speech:

Here's the milkman.
And there at last was the book I'd been looking for.
Down came the rain.

In the instances with *here/there + be*, indeed, it is not simply a matter of stylistic choice: there is a clear difference of meaning from the alternatives with SVA order. Although we must distinguish these from existential *there* (*cf* 18.31), there is in fact a close similarity. In contrast to AVS, the SVA order invites us not merely to put the nuclear focus upon the A but to see these adjuncts as referring to specific places. Compare:

{Here's the milkman – he's come at last.
{The milkman is here – at the door: shall I get two pints?

{There's the book I want – I've been looking for it all week.
{The book is there – by the typewriter.

NOTE Subject–verb inversion (as distinct from subject–operator inversion; *cf* 18.17) with fronted object chiefly represents direct speech (including speech that is 'thought') and usually the subject is not a personal pronoun:

'Please go away,' said one child. 'And don't come back,' pleaded another.

This is something of a literary convention, and in ordinary speech, VS would usually be replaced by SV (*cf* 14.17). More important are CVS, AVS, where the C or A make comparative reference to something that has preceded:

His answer was a disgrace and *equally regrettable* was his departure immediately afterwards.

Subject–operator inversion

18.17 In addition to the inversion in questions, there are four common circumstances in which the operator precedes the subject.

(a) First, we have elliptical clauses with initial *so* or the corresponding negatives *neither* or *nor* (*cf* 12.13):

John saw the accident and so did Mary.
[*cf* . . . and Mary did (so), too]
John didn't see the accident and {neither / ?nor} did Mary.
[*cf* . . : and Mary didn't, either]
She was angry and so was I.
He won't go and neither should you.

But inversion is less common with certain modal auxiliaries (notably *may*, *might*, *ought*), and alternative substitute expressions with normal order are preferred:

She might be ill and he might (be) too.

(b) Secondly, we have S–op inversion where a phrase of negative form or meaning is fronted (*cf* 10.35*f*):

Least of all is it in our interest to open negotiations now.
At no time must this door be left unlocked.
He refused to apologize. Nor would he offer any explanation.
Scarcely had he started speaking when heckling broke out.
(*cf* He had scarcely started speaking when heckling broke out.)

(c) Thirdly, we have S–op inversion in comparative clauses when the S is not a personal pronoun:

Oil costs less than would atomic energy. (*cf* Oil costs less than it did).
She looks forward, as does her secretary, to the completion of the building.

(d) Finally, S–op inversion occurs in subordinate clauses of condition and concession (*cf* 15.19 Note [c]), especially in rather formal usage:

Were we to withdraw our support, they would be justifiably indignant.
Should you change your plans, please let me know.
Even had she left a will, it is unlikely that the college would have benefited.

NOTE If an initial negative item is the vehicle for only a local negation (*cf* 10.40), no S–op inversion is possible. Thus, with the sentence adjunct (*cf* 8.15) in:

Not without reason, Charles had flown into a rage.
= 'He had flown into a rage and it was not without reason'

Contrast, with predication adjunct (*cf* 8.14):

Not without reason had Charles flown into a rage.
= 'He hadn't flown into a rage without reason'

Cleft sentences

18.18 In 18.14, we looked at examples of where heightened prominence was achieved with no other grammatical change involved beyond fronting. For example:

His callousness I shall ignore. [1]

We now turn to devices for giving prominence by more elaborate grammatical means, involving the division of the sentence into two clauses, each with its own verb:

It is *his callousness* that I shall ignore. [2]
What I shall ignore is *his callousness*. [3]
The thing I shall ignore is *his callousness*. [4]
His callousness is something I shall ignore. [5]

By reason of the division, these constructions have been called 'cleft sentences', though we shall distinguish the CLEFT SENTENCE proper, as in [2], from the PSEUDO-CLEFT sentence represented most typically by [3].

With the subject pronoun *it* as an empty theme, followed by the verb *be*, the cleft sentence readily achieves focus on the final item; in effect, end-focus within an *SVC* clause:

It is his CÀLlousness.

For this reason, while very common in spoken English, the construction is particularly convenient in writing, since it provides unerring guidance to the reader in silently assigning appropriate prosody. But the cleft sentence does not of itself indicate what the appropriate prosody is. Essentially, the cleft sentence indicates divided focus (*cf* 18.12), and which of the two focused items is dominant (*ie* new) will depend on the context:

A: You should | criticize his CÀLlousness |
B: | No, it is his CĂLlousness that I shall ig|NÒRE |
[*callousness* given, *ignore* new]
A: You should ig|nore his disHÒNesty |
B: | No, it is his CÀLlousness that I shall igNÓRE |
[*callousness* new, *ignore* given]

NOTE [a] Subject pronouns other than *it* sometimes occur:

(No,) *that* was the DÒCTor I was speaking to.
Those are my FÈET you're treading on.
He was a real GÈNius that invented this.

In each of these, we could find divided focus (*cf* 18.12), with a rising tone on *speaking*, *treading*, and *this*.

[b] We need to remember that, especially in writing, an example like the following is ambiguous between a cleft sentence and an *SVC* where C is a postmodified noun phrase:

It is the dog that scared me.

In the relative-clause version, the S could be replaced by another pronoun (such as *this*) and *that* could be replaced by *which*. In cleft sentences, such alternatives are not generally acceptable.

18.19 The flexibility of the cleft-sentence device can be seen in the ease with which different parts can be highlighted. Consider the sentence:

John wore a white suit at the dance last night.

From this, four cleft sentences can be derived. In the following, we shall assume that the aim in each case is to make the second focus subsidiary as relatively 'given':

S as focus:

It was | JÒHN {who / that} wore a 'white 'suit at the DÁNCE 'last 'night |

O_d as focus:

It was a | white SÙIT (that) 'John 'wore at the DÁNCE 'last 'night |

A_{time} as focus:

It was | last NÌGHT (that) 'John 'wore a 'white 'suit at the DÁNCE |

$A_{position}$ as focus:

It was at the | DÀNCE that 'John 'wore a 'white SÚIT 'last 'night |
It was the | DÀNCE (that) 'John 'wore a 'white SÚIT at 'last 'night | ⟨informal⟩

Two other clause elements can marginally act as the initial focus of a cleft sentence:

(a) informally O_i (otherwise replaced by a prepositional phrase):

It was *me* he gave the book *to*.
It was *to me* that he gave the book.

(b) C_o as focus: It's *dark green* that we've painted the kitchen.

There are severe restrictions (except informally in Irish English) on the use of C_s in this function, especially with the verb *be* and especially C_s realized by an adjective phrase:

?It's *very tall* you are.

But, without these restrictions, C_s can be generally acceptable:

It was *a doctor* that he eventually became.

NOTE [a] If the initial focal item is a personal pronoun, it may informally be in the objective case even though it is in fact a subject (of the *that*-clause) and the usage is hence widely condemned:

It was ?her that gave the signal.

[b] Though the verb form in the first clause of a cleft sentence is usually simple present or past, forms with modals are perfectly possible.

It *may be* his father that you're thinking of.
It *would have been* at that time that she went to live near Mannheim.

Where the verb of the second clause is present, that of the first will be present:

It is novels that Miss Williams enjoys reading.

Where the second verb is past, the first can be past:

It was novels that Miss Williams enjoyed as a pastime.

But the first verb may be in the present where the persons concerned are still living or the objects concerned still familiar in the participants' experience:

It is these very novels that Miss Williams enjoyed reading as a pastime.

[c] The cleft-sentence structure can be used in questions, exclamations, and subordinate clauses; we have italicized the first focal item:

Was it *for this* that we suffered and toiled?
What a glorious bonfire it was you made!

Pseudo-cleft sentences

18.20 The pseudo-cleft sentence is another device whereby, like the cleft sentence proper, the construction can make explicit the division between given and new parts of the communication. It is essentially an *SVC* sentence with a nominal relative clause as subject or complement (*cf* 15.7*f*). It thus differs from the ordinary cleft sentence in being completely accountable in terms of the categories of main clause and subordinate clause discussed in Chapter 14. The following are virtually synonymous:

It's a good rest that you need most.
A good rest is what you need most.

The pseudo-cleft sentence occurs more typically, however, with the *wh*-clause as subject, since it can thus present a climax in the complement:

What you need most is a good rest.

Unlike the cleft sentence, it rather freely permits marked focus to fall on the predication:

What he's done is *(to) spoil the whole thing.*

Here we would expect an anticipatory (rising) focus on the *do* item, the main focus coming at normal end-focus position. Thus: '. . . DÓNE . . . THÌNG'. When the verb in the *wh*-clause has progressive aspect, the complement matches it with an *-ing* clause:

What *I'm doing* is *teaching him Japanese.*

But in some respects, the pseudo-cleft sentence is more limited than the cleft sentence proper. It is indeed only with *what*-clauses that we can make a direct comparison (or choice) between the two constructions. Clauses with *where* and *when* are sometimes acceptable, but mainly when the *wh*-clause is subject complement:

Here is *where the accident took place.*
(In) Autumn is *when the countryside is most beautiful.*

Clauses introduced by *who, whose, why,* and *how* do not easily enter into the pseudo-cleft sentence construction at all, and to compensate for these restrictions, there are numerous 'paraphrases' of the pseudo-cleft construction involving noun phrases of general reference in place of the *wh*-item:

The person who spoke to you must have been the manager.
Somebody whose writing I admire is Jill.
The way you should go is via Cheltenham.

The reason we decided to return was {that / because ⟨informal⟩} he was ill.

NOTE The cleft and pseudo-cleft types can cooccur. For example:

> What it was you asked for was a ticket to *Brighton*. Did you mean *Birmingham*?

Cf also the following (common informally) from Ivy Compton-Burnett: 'What seems to me is, that we ought to be . . . careful' (*Men and Wives*).

Postponement

18.21 One important communicative difference between the two types of cleft construction is that while the cleft sentence with *it* is often used to put the main focus near the *front* of the sentence, the pseudo-cleft is chiefly used to postpone the focus to *end* position. In this respect it is often in competition with the passive. In [1], focus is placed on the noun phrase *the manufacturers* by means of the passive, and in [2] by means of a pseudo-cleft 'paraphrase':

> The device was tested by the manufacturers. [1]
> The people who tested the device were the manufacturers. [2]

It should be noted that [2] presupposes that the hearer knows that testing has taken place; with [1] this is not so.

Given the importance of end-focus (*cf* 18.2), it is not surprising that English has numerous resources to ensure the distribution of information according to our wishes. There are, for example, lexical and grammatical devices which reverse the order of roles:

> {An uncle, three cousins, and two brothers *benefited from* the will.
> {The will *benefited* an uncle, three cousins, and two brothers.

> {An unidentified blue liquid *was in* the bottle.
> {The bottle *contained* an unidentified blue liquid.

> {A red sports car was *behind* the bus.
> {The bus was *in front of* a red sports car.

NOTE A special case of converseness is the relation of reciprocity expressed by certain terms such as *similar to*, *different from*, *near (to)*, *far from*, *opposite*, *married to*, where reversing the order of the participants preserves the essential meaning without any other change in the construction:

> My house is *opposite* the hotel. = The hotel is *opposite* my house.

A more complex relation of converseness is illustrated by:

> The dealer *sold* the car *to* my friend.
> My friend *bought* the car *from* the dealer.

Compare also *rent to*/*rent from*, *lend (to)*/*borrow from*, *give (to)*/*receive from*.

Voice and postponement

18.22 With transitive clauses, the passive voice provides a convenient way of postponing the agentive subject by turning it into the agent in a passive construction (*cf* 3.25). We thus reverse the active order of the agentive and affected elements (*cf* 10.9) where the agentive requires end-focus:

> A: Who makes these table mats?

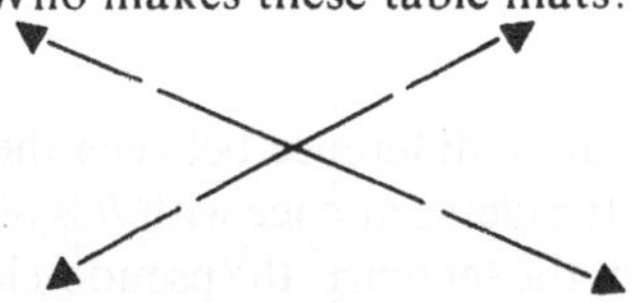

> B: They are made by my sister-in-law.

A preference for end-focus (in this instance, coinciding with end-weight) can even override an aversion to passive constructions that are in themselves rather awkward (*cf* 16.8 Note):

> The regulations *were taken advantage of* by all the tramps and down-and-outs in the country.

A finite clause as subject is also readily avoided by switching from the active to the passive voice:

> {*That he was prepared to go to such lengths* astonished me.
> {I was astonished *that he was prepared to go to such lengths*.

While the V element cannot be focused in the cleft-sentence construction, such focus can be achieved with a transitive verb by the use of the passive, provided that the agent can be ignored as given. Compare:

> But our | scientists 'finally SÒLVED 'all 'these 'problems |
> But | all 'these 'problems were 'finally SÒLVED |

The passive can also ensure a smooth crescendo of communicative dynamism with ditransitive verbs by making the indirect object thematic. Compare:

> They a|warded Marion the PRÌZE |
> Marion was a|warded the PRÌZE |

NOTE The passive of *have* is rarely used, but when it occurs, the verb has an agentive meaning usually absent from the active:

I wanted to buy sherry but there was none to be had.

Extraposition of a clausal subject

18.23 Postponement which involves the replacement of the postponed element by a substitute form is termed EXTRAPOSITION. It operates almost exclusively on subordinate nominal clauses. The most important type of extraposition is that of a subject realized by a finite or nonfinite clause. The subject is moved to the end of the sentence, and the normal subject position is filled by the anticipatory pronoun *it*. The resulting sentence thus contains two subjects, which we may identify as the POSTPONED SUBJECT (the one which is notionally the subject of the sentence) and the ANTICIPATORY SUBJECT (*it*). Thus in place of [1] we have [2]:

To hear him say that surprised me. [1]
It surprised me *to hear him say that.* [2]

The pattern of [2] is in fact far more usual than that of [1] (*cf* Note [a]). Examples in terms of the major clause types (10.1):

Type *SVC*:	It is a pleasure *to teach her.*
Type *SVA*:	It was on the news *that income tax is to be lowered.*
Type *SV*:	It doesn't matter *what you do.*
Type *SVO*:	It surprised me *to hear him say that.*
Type *SVOC*:	It makes her happy *to see others enjoying themselves.*
Type SV_{pass}:	It is said *that she wanted to go into politics.*
Type $SV_{pass}C$:	It was considered impossible *for anyone to escape.*

NOTE [**a**] For certain constructions which have all the appearance of clausal extraposition (*It seems/appears/happened/chanced*/etc), the corresponding nonextraposed version does not occur. For example, there is no sentence **That everything is fine seems* to correspond with *It seems that everything is fine*, nor do we find **That she wanted to go into politics is said.* In such cases, we may say that the extraposition is obligatory. With *be*, this type of extraposition is used for expressions of possibility and (especially) for reflective questions:

It may be that she no longer trusts you.
Could it be that you left the keys in your office?

Other characteristics of the verbs entering into this category are presented in 18.25.
[**b**] Unlike finite clauses, *-ing* clauses occur very naturally in ordinary subject position:

Teaching her to drive turned out to be quite enjoyable.

Extraposed *-ing* clauses are uncommon outside informal speech, and they often seem to be untidy afterthoughts:

It turned out to be quite enjoyable(,) *teaching her to drive.*

Extraposition of a clausal object

18.24 When the object is an *-ing* clause in *SVOC* and *SVOA* clause types, it can undergo extraposition; when it is a *to*-infinitive clause or a *that*-clause, it must do so:

SVOC
- You must find *it* exciting *working here*.
- *Cf*: You must find *working here* exciting.
  - *Working here* is exciting.
- I made *it* my objective *to settle the matter*.
- *Cf* *I made *to settle the matter* my prime objective.
  - *To settle the matter* was my prime objective.
- *But*: I made *settling the matter* my prime objective.
  - *I made *it* my prime objective *settling the matter*.

SVOA
- I owe *it* to you *that the jury acquitted me*.
- *Cf*: *I owe *that the jury acquitted me* to you.
- *Contrast*: I owe *my acquittal* to you.
  - [with corresponding nominalization]
- Something put *it* into his head *that she was a spy*.
- *Cf*: *Something put *that she was a spy* into his head.
  - Something put *the idea of her being a spy* into his head.

The construction type *She's a pleasure to teach*

18.25 In a sentence of type *SVC* where the extraposed clause of 18.23 has an object or prepositional complement, the noun phrase concerned can sometimes be fronted to become the theme in place of *it*. For example:

To teach Elizabeth is a pleasure.
~It is a pleasure *to teach Elizabeth*. (*cf* 18.23)
~*Elizabeth* is a pleasure to teach.

Compare also:

It's impossible to deal with *Bill*.
~*Bill* is impossible to deal with.
It's easy/difficult to beat *them*.
~*They*'re easy/difficult to beat.
It's fun (for us) to be with *Margaret*.
~*Margaret* is fun (for us) to be with.

There is a similar construction with *be sure*, *be certain*, *seem*, *appear*, *be said*, *be known*, etc, except that in these cases the corresponding construction with anticipatory *it* requires a *that*-clause, and it is the *subject* of the extraposed clause that is fronted:

It's certain that *we*'ll forget the address.
~*We*'re certain to forget the address.
It seems that *you*'ve made a mistake.

~ *You* seem to have made a mistake.
It is known that *he*'s a coward.
~ *He*'s known to be a coward.

NOTE A combination of the movement explained in 18.23*ff* permits a valuable range of sentence forms for adjusting the development of communicative dynamism and the assignment of end-focus as desired. Thus along with the canonical *SVC* sentence:

To pour cream out of this jug is difficult.

we have three further possibilities. First, with ordinary *it* extraposition:

It is difficult to pour cream out of this jug.

The two other possibilities are:

This | jug is DÌFficult to pour CRÉAM out of |
| Cream is DÌFficult to pour out of this JÚG |

The former implies difficulties with the jug (perhaps its spout is too narrow); the latter implies difficulties with cream (perhaps it is too thick).

Postponement of object in *SVOC* and *SVOA* clauses

18.26 When the object is a long and complex phrase, final placement for end-focus or end-weight is possible in *SVOC* and *SVOA* clause types. This does not involve an *it*-substitution.

(a) Shift from SVO_dC_o order to SVC_oO_d order:

They pronounced guilty *every one of the accused.*
He had called an idiot *the man on whose judgment he now had to rely.*

(b) Shift from SVO_dA to $SVAO_d$:

I confessed to him *all my worse defects.*
We heard from his own lips *the story of how he had been stranded for days without food.*
She dragged (right) in(side) *the two heavy boxes of chemicals.*

NOTE **[a]** The fact that we are disturbing the normal order in such clauses is indicated by a tendency to adopt a different intonation pattern. Thus the movement forward of the C or A is usually accompanied by the assignment to it of a marked (subsidiary) focus (*cf* 18.12); compare:

She | pulled to 'one SÍDE the 'heavy CÙRtain |
She | pulled the 'heavy 'curtain to 'one SÌDE |

[b] In ditransitive complementation (*cf* 16.31*ff*), the indirect object precedes the direct object:

She | gave {her 'brother / him} a sìGnet 'ring | [1]

Thus whether or not the O_i is pronominalized, the implication is that it carries less communicative dynamism (is relatively 'given') as compared with the O_d. Where the converse is true, the O_i is replaced by a prepositional phrase and placed after O_d:

She | gave a 'signet ring to her BRÒTHer | [2]

But there is a third possibility; the prepositional paraphrase of the O_i can itself precede the O_d:

She | gave to her BRÒTHer a SIGnet 'ring | [3]

The O_d in [3] has the same rhematic force as in [1] but the O_i has been replaced by a form that raises its communicative dynamism above that of the O_i in [1] though still below that of the paraphrase in [2].

Discontinuous noun phrases

18.27 Sometimes to achieve end-focus or end-weight, only part of an element is postponed. The most commonly affected part is the postmodification of a noun phrase (*cf* 17.42*f*), and the units most readily postponed are nominal (in this case appositive) clauses.

A rumour circulated widely *that he was secretly engaged to the President's daughter*. (*Cf*: '*A rumour that he was secretly engaged to the President's daughter* circulated widely.')

However, other postmodifying clauses, and even phrases, can be so postponed:

The time had come *to decorate the house for Christmas.*
That loaf was stale *that you sold me.*
A steering committee had been formed, *consisting of Messrs Ogawa, Schultz, and Robinson.*

Discontinuity often results, too, from the postponement of postmodifying phrases of exception (*cf* 9.15):

All of us were frightened *except the captain.*

The discontinuous noun phrase can be a complement or object:

What business is it *of yours*? (*Cf* 'It is no business of yours')
We heard *the story* from his own lips *of how he was stranded for days without food.*
I met *a man* this morning *cárrying an ìnjured child.*

But we may speak analogously of internal discontinuities: that is, where there is movement of parts of a noun phrase to achieve end-focus, without the intervention of material not forming part of the noun phrase as a whole. In the nominalizations of [1] below, we see how the parts in quotation marks corresponding to the original clause elements can be moved to affect the internal communicative dynamism:

Lovell discovered the new star in 1960. SVOA [1]
Lovell's discovery of the new star in 1960 . . . 'SVOA' [2]

The discovery by Lovell in 1960 of the new star . . . 'VSAO' [3]
The discovery of the new star in 1960 by Lovell . . . 'VOAS' [4]
(?)Lovell's 1960 new star discovery . . . 'SAOV' [5]

NOTE [a] In apposition, the emphatic reflexive pronoun (*himself*, etc) may vary in position:

The driver himsÈLF told me.
~The driver told me himsÈLF.
Did you yoursÉLF paint the portrait?
~Did you paint the portrait yoursÉLF?

As the emphatic reflexive pronoun frequently bears nuclear stress, the postponement is necessary if the sentence is to have end-focus. Such postponement is possible, however, only if the noun phrase in apposition with the pronoun is the subject:

I showed Ian the letter *myself*.
*I showed *Ian* the letter *himself*.
(But *cf*: 'I showed *Ian himself* the letter')

[b] With some other cases of pronominal apposition, we may prefer to postpone the second element to a position immediately following the operator rather than to the end of the sentence. This is especially true with *all*, *both*, *each* (*cf* 6.24). For example:

The advisers had *all* been carefully selected.

Other discontinuities

18.28 Some degree of discontinuity is the rule rather than the exception in sentences containing comparative clauses, though where the comp-element (*cf* 15.36*f*) is a degree adverbial, examples without discontinuity are fairly easy to find. Compare the following:

He has worked for the handicapped *more than any other politician (has)*. [1]
He has worked *more* for the handicapped *than any other politician (has)*. [1a]
She is earning *higher* wages *than (are) average*. [2]
She is earning *higher-than-average* wages. [2a]

Beside a norm with minimum discontinuity as in [3], however, the correlative item can be moved to final position as in [3a] if this is informationally desirable.

He is *more* skilled *than his brother (is)* in matters of fiNÀNCE. [3]
He is | more 'skilled in 'matters of FÍNance ‖ than his | BRÒTHer (is) ‖ [3a]

Some adjectives that take complementation (*cf* 7.9, 16.38*ff*) can simultaneously function as premodifiers. Compare:

(a) This result is { *different from yours.* / *similar to hers.* }

(b) This is a { *different* result *from yours.* / *similar* result *to hers.* }

In cases like (b), discontinuity is felt to be quite normal. So also:

> She works in the *opposite* room *to this.*
> It is a *timid* dog *with strangers.*

NOTE [a] Similarity with prepositional phrases postmodifying a head can produce ambiguity, as in:

> They made an embarrassing protest to the authorities.

In such instances, revision is essential to make it clear which of the two possible meanings is intended:

> They made a protest that was embarrassing to the authorities. [1]
> [*ie* 'Their protest embarrassed the authorities']
> They made a protest to the authorities that was embarrassing. [2]
> [*ie* 'They protested to the authorities in a way that was (generally) embarrassing']

[b] Within adjective complementation and prepositional phrases, discontinuity is possible, especially by the insertion of degree adverbials:

> They were *fond* to some extent *of Brecht's early work.*
> It was *different* in many respects *from what she had expected.*
> He worked hard, *without* for the most part *any reward.*

The commonest prepositional phrase discontinuities are of the type:

> *Which group* shall we put him *in*?

Note also the interruption of a verb phrase by the insertion of adverbials at *M*; *cf* 8.11. In writing, it is often convenient to use an adverbial along with the emphatic operator where prosodic prominence would have sufficed in speech:

> They *did* indeed *find* a solution. ~ They | FÒUND a solution |

Structural compensation

18.29 From the structure of most clauses, we develop the expectation that the V element will be at a transition point between a thematic low communicative dynamism and a focal high:

> | Jill will de'cide next WÈEK |
> The | boy 'broke the WÌNdow |
> My | friend be'came ÀNgry |

This has the effect of making the simplest realization of the *SV* clause type sound oddly incomplete:

> | Mary SÀNG | My | friend CÒOKED |

It is more usual to find such sentences augmented by an adjunct (*cf* 8.13*ff*):

Mary sang for hours. My friend cooked enthusiastically.

Alternatively, we make intransitive verbs bipartite, an auxiliary serving as a transition between theme and focus:

| Mary was SÌNGing | My | friend would CÒOK |

Such rephrasing is obviously context-dependent; it is not often, for example, that a verb phrase might equally well be progressive or nonprogressive. Other means have therefore had to be devised for 'stretching' the predicate into a multi-word structure. One of the most generally serviceable (though it tends to be rather informal in tone) is to replace the intransitive verb by a transitive one of very general meaning, and give it as eventive object a nominalization of the intransitive item (*cf* 10.16, 17.23). The general verbs *do*, *make*, *give*, *have*, *take* are widely used in this construction:

{My friend cooked.
{My friend did the cooking.

{He ate.
{He had a meal.

{She replied (briefly).
{She made a (brief) reply.

{They strolled.
{They took a stroll.

{Mary shrieked.
{Mary gave a shriek.

So also *solve* ~ *find a solution*; *agree* ~ *reach* (or *come to*) *an agreement*; *apply* ~ *submit an application*; *suggest* ~ *offer* (or *make*) *a suggestion*; *permit* ~ *grant* (or *give*) *permission*; *attend* ~ *pay attention*, etc.

Existential sentences

18.30 We have seen in 18.4 that a sentence usually begins with reference to 'given' information and proceeds to provide 'new' information. But there are many occasions when we must make statements whose content does not fall neatly into these two categories:

A | car is 'blocking my WÀY | [1]
| Many 'students are in fi'nancial TRÒUBle | [2]
| Quite a 'few 'species of 'animals are in 'danger of EXTÌNCtion | [3]

These sentences may oblige the recipient to interpret a theme as entirely new and unconnected with anything previously introduced. In such circumstances, it is convenient to have devices for providing some kind of dummy theme which will enable the originator to indicate the 'new' status of a whole clause, including its subject. Thus in place of [1], [2], and [3], we might have:

There is } { a car blocking } my WÀY [1a]
I have } { a CAR blocking }

There are } { many STÚdents in financial TRÒUBle [2a]
We have } { quite a 'few 'species of ÁNimals in
One finds } { danger of exTÌNCTtion [3a]

In serving to bring the existence of an entire proposition to the attention of the hearer, the resultant constructions are known as 'existential sentences', by far the commonest being the type introduced by unstressed *there*, accompanied by the simple present or past of *be*.

NOTE [a] Many other constructions than those illustrated above are invoked to serve the same purpose; for example, *it* with the proposition as extraposed subject (*cf* 18.23):

It is a fact that } many students are in financial trouble.
It has to be said that }

Alternatively again, the proposition can be made a clausal object:

One finds that }
We must recognize that } many students are in financial trouble.
I have to say that }

[b] Block language (*cf* 11.22) often consists of verbless sentences that can be regarded as existential:

DANGER!
MEN AT WORK OVERHEAD

Note that there are two types of negative directives and slogans:

No way out = 'There *is* . . .'
No discrimination = 'There *must be* . . .'

Existential *there*

Correspondence with basic clause patterns

18.31 There is a regular correspondence between existential sentences with *there* + *be* and clauses of equivalent meaning as specified in terms of the basic clause patterns (*cf* 10.1), provided that the clause concerned has

an indefinite subject (but *cf* Note [c]); and
a form of the verb *be* in its verb phrase.

Allowing for these two requirements, we may relate basic clauses to existential forms such that [2] corresponds to [1]:

subject (+auxiliaries) + *be* + predication [1]
there (+auxiliaries) + *be* + subject + predication [2]

The subject of the original clause may be called the 'notional' subject of the *there*-sentence, so as to distinguish it from *there* itself, which for most purposes is the 'grammatical' subject (*cf* 18.32). Examples of the seven clause types with the existential correspondences are given below:

Type *SVC*

Something must be wrong.
~There must be something wrong.

Type *SVA*

Was anyone in the vicinity?
~Was there anyone in the vicinity?

Type *SV*

No one was waiting.
~There was no one waiting.

Type *SVO*

Plenty of people are getting promotion.
~There are plenty of people getting promotion.

Type *SVOC*

Two bulldozers have been knocking the place flat.
~There have been two bulldozers knocking the place flat.

Type *SVOA*

A girl is putting the kettle on.
~There's a girl putting the kettle on.

Type *SVOO*

Something is causing my friend distress.
~There's something causing my friend distress.

Passive versions of the correspondences are also to be noted:

Type SV_{pass}

A whole box was stolen.
~There was a whole box stolen.

Type $SV_{pass}C$

No children will be left hungry.
~There'll be no children left hungry.

NOTE [a] The notional subject can be postponed (*cf* 18.21) if it is required to have focal prominence:

There was in the vicinity a helpful doctor.

[b] Especially in informal usage, there is an existential sentence with an *-ed* clause following the noun phrase:

There's a book gone from my desk.

[c] Existential sentences need not have an indefinite noun phrase as 'notional subject'. In B's reply below, a definite noun phrase conveys new information, providing a specific (and hence definite) instance of something contextually given:

A: Have we any loose cash in the house?
B: Well, there's the money in the box over there.

The status of existential *there* as subject

18.32 The *there* of existential sentences differs from *there* as an introductory adverb in lacking stress, in carrying none of the locative meaning of the place adjunct *there*, and in behaving in most ways like the subject of the clause, doubtless reflecting the structural dislocation from the basic clause types:

(i) It follows the operator in *yes–no* and tag questions:

Is there any more soup?
There haven't been any phone calls, *have there*?

(ii) It can act as subject in infinitive and *-ing* clauses:

I don't want *there to be any misunderstandings*.
He was disappointed at *there being so little to do*.
There having been trouble over this in the past, I want to treat the matter cautiously.

NOTE [a] The absence of locative meaning is indicated by the acceptability of existential sentences where *here* cooccurs with introductory *there*:

There's a screwdriver here.

By contrast, adjunct *there* with inversion (*cf* 18.16), as in 'There's the girl', would be contradictory with an added *here*:

*There's the screwdriver here! (*But cf* | "THÈRE's the SCRÉWdriver | – | Right "HÈRE |)

[b] Especially informally, *there* is treated like a singular subject where the 'notional' subject is plural:

There's some letters here for you to read.

[c] Apart from sentences related to basic clause types in the manner described in 18.31, we have to consider various other types of sentence introduced by existential *there*. Among them is the 'bare' existential (sometimes called 'ontological') sentence, which simply postulates the existence of some entity or entities:

There was a moment's silence.
Is there any other business? [as spoken from the chair at the end of a meeting]

Such sentences are perhaps to be explained as cases in which the final element is omitted as understood:

There was a moment's silence (in the room).

Existential sentences with relative clauses

18.33 An additional type of existential sentence consists of *there* + *be* + noun phrase + relative clause, and resembles the cleft sentence (*cf* 18.18, example [2]) in its rhetorical motivation. Such sentences can be related to sentences of orthodox clause types without the two restrictions mentioned in 18.31; the verb need not be a form of *be*, and although there must be an indefinite element, it need not be the subject:

Two students would like to see you.
~There are two students (that/who) would like to see you.

It is interesting that the relative pronoun can be omitted (especially in informal usage) even when it is subject of the relative clause. This is something not permissible according to the normal rule for relative clause formation (*cf* 17.8) and is a sign of the special status within the main clause of the annex clause here, as in cleft sentences.

As with cleft sentences, too, we can have different tenses in the two parts of the sentence. Compare:

Some planets were discovered by the ancients.
There are some planets that were discovered by the ancients.

The existential-with-relative construction is particularly common as a means of emphasizing a negative (*cf* Notes below):

I can do nothing about it.
~There's nothing I can do about it.

NOTE [a] We can negate either part or both parts; compare:

There was a student who didn't pass the exam.	[= one failed]
There wasn't a student who passed the exam.	[= all failed]
There wasn't a student who didn't pass the exam.	[= all passed]

[b] A further common existential sentence pattern, *there* + *be* + noun phrase + *to* + infinitive clause, is problematic to the extent that it cannot be directly related to the basic clause types of 10.1:

There was no one for us to talk to.
There's (always) plenty of housework to do.

[c] Note also the rather restricted use of *-ing* clauses (*cf* 15.10), as in:

There's no telling what Janet will do next.

Existential sentences with verbs other than *be*

18.34 The 'presentative' role of the existential sentence seems especially clear in a rather less common, more literary type in which *there* is followed by a verb other than *be*. For example:

> There rose in his imagination grand visions of a world empire.
> There exist a number of similar medieval crosses in various parts of the country.
> There may come a time when the Western Nations will be less fortunate.
> Not long after this, there occurred quite a sudden shift in public taste.

This construction, which may be related to other sentence forms by the simple correspondence S + V ~ *there* + V + S (where S is usually indefinite), is equivalent in effect and style to subject–verb inversion after an initial adverbial (*cf* 18.16, 18.35). Grammatically, *there* is a subject (*cf* 18.32) with operator inversion when the statement pattern is turned into a question, *eg*: *Will there come a time . . .? Did there occur a shift in public taste?*

The present construction requires that the verb be intransitive and of fairly general presentative meaning: verbs of motion (*arrive*, *enter*, *pass*, *come*, etc), of inception (*emerge*, *spring up*, etc), and of stance (*live*, *remain*, *stand*, *lie*, etc); but *cf* 18.35. The normal basic sentence pattern concerned is *SVA*:

> A shift occurred in public taste.
> ~ There occurred a shift in public taste.

Existential sentences with initial space adjuncts

18.35 Let us look now at an example that pairs a verb of stance with the usual existential verb *be*:

> In the garden there {was / stood} a sundial. [1]

Since the place adverbial, *In the garden*, provides in itself the condition enabling us to position the subject after the verb (*cf* 18.16), there is no grammatical requirement for *there* to be present:

> In the garden {was / stood} a sundial. [2]

It should be noted that the range of verb-phrase forms with this type of ordering is considerably wider than was specified in 18.34. Nor need the S be indefinite. Compare:

> Into the back of his stationary car *had collided* a massive goods vehicle. [3]

In the garden lay {*Joan* / *his father* / *the old lady*} (fast asleep). [4]

Indeed, the variant with *there* as in [1] is much less likely in [3] or [4] than in [2], and this seems to correlate with the less 'presentative' verb phrase in [3] and the definiteness of the noun phrase in [4]. We might summarize the difference between [1] and [2] by saying that the latter, without *there*, is motivated by the wish to achieve end-focus, while the *there*-construction as in [1] has the more general 'presentative' function; *cf* 18.34.

The *have*-existential device

18.36 There is a type of existential sentence in which the thematic position is not occupied by a mere 'dummy' element but by a noun-phrase subject preceding the verb *have* (or, esp in BrE, *have got*). Compare:

Two buttons are missing on my jacket. [1]
~ There are two buttons missing on my jacket. [2]
~ My jacket has two buttons missing. [3]
~ I have two buttons missing on my jacket. [4]

We are concerned here with the last two of these examples, and we can see that the thematic noun phrase can vary sharply in its relation to the rest of the sentence. Indeed, beyond saying that it has considerable involvement in the existential proposition, we cannot specify what that involvement will be. Thus in

The porter has a taxi ready (for you). [5]

there is a strong implication that the subject has an *agentive* role, whereas in

You have a taxi ready. [6]

it is just as strongly implied that it has a *recipient* role. Calling it 'affected' seems perhaps to state the involvement with a degree of generality that satisfactorily accounts for most cases. Compare:

{A valuable watch was stolen (from/belonging to my friend). [7]
{*My friend* had a valuable watch stolen. [8]

{There are several oak trees in the(ir) garden. [9]
{*They* have several oak trees in the(ir) garden. [10]

{A brother of mine works in Chicago. [11]
{I have a brother working in Chicago. [12]

Turning from the role to the identity of the thematic element, we see from the examples throughout this section that it is often provided (if optionally) in the corresponding nonexistential sentence: *jacket* in [1] in relation to [3], *my* in [1] in relation to [4], *you* in [5] in relation to [6], *my friend* in [7] in relation to [8], *their* in [9] in relation to [10], and *mine* in [11] in relation to [12].

NOTE [a] In *have*-existentials, the 'notional' subject (*ie* the subject of the corresponding basic clause type) can freely be definite:

> *John's* friend is helping him.
> John has *his* friend helping him.

By contrast: 'There is a *friend* helping him' but *'There is *John's friend* helping him'.

[b] Corresponding to *there*-sentences of the same character (*cf* 18.33), the following illustrate *have*-sentences containing relative and nonfinite clauses:

> {There's something (that) I've been meaning to tell you.
> {I've something (that) I've been meaning to tell you.

> {There is a guest staying with her.
> {She has a guest staying with her.

[c] Existential clauses can also be nonfinite or verbless; for example:

> There soon being a taxi available, }
> (His) Soon having a taxi available, } Dr Lowe caught his train.
> With a taxi soon available, }

Emotive emphasis

18.37 Apart from the emphasis given by information focusing, the language provides means of giving a unit purely emotive emphasis. They include exclamations (*cf* 11.20), the persuasive *do* in imperatives (*cf* 11.19), interjections (*cf* 11.22 Note [c]), expletives and intensifiers (*cf* 7.18, 7.32*ff*, 8.35*ff*), including the general clause emphasizers such as *actually*, *really*, and *indeed*. Here we mention two particularly common strategies.

(a) Emphatic operators

Consider the difference between pairs like the following:

> {I'm | SÒRRY | }
> {I | ÀM 'sorry | } [1]

> {You | look PÀLE this 'morning | }
> {You | DÒ 'look 'palè this 'morning | } [2]

> {| Mary will be PLÈASED | }
> {| Mary WÌLL be 'pleased | } [3]

> {I | TÒLD you | }
> {I | did TĚLL you | } [4]

The second utterance in each case resembles prosodically the operator-stressed items discussed in 18.11. But as we see with [4], the operators, though emphasized, need not carry the nuclear force. More importantly, they are not necessarily contrastive. It is not that any one has implied that I am not sorry [1] or that Mary won't be pleased [3]. Rather, the speaker (in a style that is sometimes felt to be rather gushing and extravagant) is conveying a personal concern or (as in [4]) even reproach or petulance. It is in this last connection that the *will/would* of 'insistence' (*cf* 4.27) is regularly stressed:

> He | WÒULD go and make a 'MÉSS of it |

(b) Noncorrelative *so* and *such*

In familiar speech of a rather extravagant style, the determiner *such* and the adverb *so* are stressed so as to give exclamatory force to a statement, question, or directive. In this usage, there is no accompanying correlative clause or phrase (*cf* 15.42):

> She was | wearing 'such a lovely DRÈSS |
> I'm | so afraid they'll get LÒST |

In consequence, *so* and *such* become equivalent to *how* and *what* in exclamations (*cf* 11.20):

> They were so cross! ~ How cross they were!

Reinforcement

18.38 Reinforcement is a feature of colloquial style whereby some item is repeated for purposes of emphasis, focus, or thematic arrangement. Its simplest form is merely the reiteration (with heavy stressing) of a word or phrase:

> It's *far*, *far* too expensive.
> I agree with *every word* you've said – *every single word*.

In very loose and informal speech, a reinforcing or recapitulatory pronoun is sometimes inserted within a clause where it stands 'proxy' for an initial noun phrase:

> *This man I was telling you about* – well, *he* used to live next door to me.
> *The book I lent you* – have you read *it* yet?

These two examples show a complete noun phrase being disjoined from the grammar of the sentence, its role (as subject and object respectively) grammatically performed by subsequent pronouns. But in being thus fronted, as marked themes (*cf* 18.13), the disjoined noun phrases clearly set out the 'point of departure' for the utterance as a whole. This is a device that may be a convenience alike to hearer (in receiving an early statement of a complex item) and speaker (in not having to incorporate such an item in the grammatical organization of his utterance).

In contrast to such fronting of items, an amplificatory phrase may be informally added after the completion of a clause structure which contains a coreferential pronoun:

> *They're* all the same, *these politicians*.
> I wouldn't trust *him* for a moment, *your brother-in-law*.

Such utterances are usually spoken with divided focus (*cf* 18.12), with a rise on the 'tag' confirming its relatively 'given' status:

> They're | all the ŜAME, these poliTÍcians |

The tag can be inserted parenthetically, and need not be final:

> He's got a good future, your brother, if he perseveres.

NOTE [a] An even more informal type of tag comprises a subject and operator:

> That was a lark, *that was*!
> He likes a drink now and then, *Jim does*.
> She's a good player, *Ann (is)*.

In some dialects of English (especially Northern BrE), the operator may precede the subject:

> She's a good player, *is Ann*.

[b] Postposed nonfinite clauses, of the kind discussed in 18.24, sometimes closely resemble amplificatory tags; contrast:

> It was tough getting the job finished on time.
> [| tough . . . . . . TÌME |]
> It was tough, getting beaten in the last match.
> [| TÒUGH | / . . . . . . MÁTCH |]

[c] Expletives (in the broadest sense) provide a common mode of amplification in extremely informal speech, serving as a rhetorical transition between theme and an emotionally coloured focus:

> I | told them to 'darned 'well LÌsten |

Expletives can also amplify the theme in *wh*-questions: 'How *on earth* did you lose it?'

Bibliographical note

On information processing in relation to given and new, see Allerton (1980); Chafe (1976); Dahl (1974); Halliday (1967–68); Kuno (1976b); Li (1976); Taglicht (1984).

On functional sentence perspective, see Daneš (1974); Firbas (1986); Kuno (1972).

On communicative dynamism, see Firbas (1979).

On existential constructions, see Breivik (1983); Erdmann (1976); Jenkins (1975); Lakoff (1987); Milsark (1979).

On inversion, see Jacobsson (1986); Penhallurick (1984).

On extraposition and other aspects of ordering, see Enkvist (1987); Erdmann (1981); Hartvigson and Jakobsen (1974); Rudanko (1982).

On grammar and style in relation to prosodic features, see André (1974); Bald (1979); Bolinger (1972b); Brazil (1985); Chafe (1976); Crystal (1969, 1980); Enkvist (1980); Faber (1987); Halliday (1967).

Other relevant studies include: Biber (1988); Bolinger (1977); Burton-Roberts (1986a, b); Lakoff (1987); Lyons (1977); Mathesius (1975); Schmerling (1976).

19 From sentence to text

General

19.1 We apply the term 'text' to a stretch of language which makes coherent sense in the context of its use. It may be spoken or written; it may be as long as a book or as short as a cry for help. Linguistic form is important but is not of itself sufficient to give a stretch of language the status of a text. For example, a road-sign reading

Dangerous Corner

is an adequate text though comprising only a short noun phrase. It is understood as an existential statement (18.30), paraphraseable as something like 'There is a dangerous corner near by', with such block language features (11.22) as zero article that are expected in notices of this kind. By contrast, a sign at the roadside with the same grammatical structure but reading

Critical Remark

is not an adequate text, because although we recognize the structure and understand the words, the phrase can communicate nothing to us as we drive by, and is thus meaningless.

In earlier chapters, as is normal in grammars, we have exemplified our statements by way of printed sentences which have made an implicit double demand on readers. First, we have assumed that the examples would be read as if they were *heard*, mentally given by each reader appropriate features of stress and intonation. Second, we have assumed that readers would imagine for each example an appropriate context in which it could have a plausible textual role.

19.2 In the present chapter, we take the formation of phrases, clauses, and sentences for granted, and we look at the way they are deployed in the formation of texts. This is of course far from being a matter of grammar alone. It is primarily by the choice of vocabulary that language connects us with the world beyond language, as we saw in comparing the examples 'Dangerous Corner' and 'Critical Remark' in 19.1. Moreover, lexical choice is used constantly to shape the internal cohesion of texts. Note the use of the hypernymically related *family*, *children*, *parents* and *fruit*, *apple*, *Granny Smiths* in the following:

> I like my family to eat lots of fruit, and Granny Smiths are especially popular because this apple has a juicy crispness much enjoyed by the children and their parents alike.

Nonetheless, since this book is devoted to grammar, we must exclude all aspects of text construction other than grammatical features and their concomitant prosody and punctuation.

Parts of a text may cohere without formal linkage (*asyndetic* connection):

I'm in a state of shock. Jack's mother has just died.

Alternatively, conjunctions or other formal features may make the connection explicit:

Jack's mother has just died *and (so)* I'm in a state of shock.

Frequently the rheme of a clause (18.4*f*) is represented in what follows by a thematic pro-form; an example of such *thematic* connection:

I've just read *your new book*. *It*'s very interesting.

But pro-forms can also be used to show *rhematic* connection:

I've just read *your new book*. Have you seen *mine*?

Place and time relators

19.3 Textual structure requires firm orientation in respect to place and time. Consider the following example:

Years ago, I lived for a time in the Far East, where my father worked at a naval base. I've been back there once to look at our old home but that was after the base had closed.

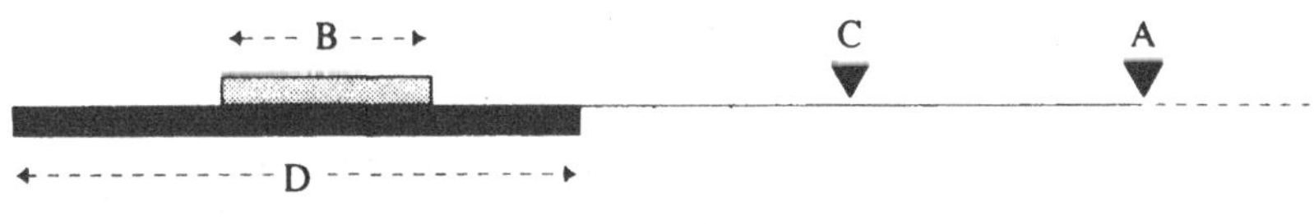

Fig 19.3

In relation to the implicit *here* and *now* of the speaker and hearer, the text refers to one other location in space and two other 'locations' in time. Taking A in Fig 19.3 as 'here and now', we are impelled to imagine a remote place where for some long unspecified span in the past (D), there had existed a naval base. Within that period, for a shorter but also unspecified span B, the speaker had lived there. Between A and the end of D, a time C is mentioned and narratively represented as without duration. It is noteworthy that the temporal and locational relations are clear though no dates or precise places are given: the 'Far East' is *far* only from (say) Britain and is *east* only in relation to somewhere that lies to the west of it; the time is 'long ago' only in relation to 'now' – it was itself 'now' when the speaker lived in the Far East.

Place relators

19.4 Certain spatial relations are firmly linked to grammatical expressions which are heavily exploited in textual structure. Thus an opening question or statement will normally involve reference to location in space (as well as in time):

Where are you going tonight? [1]
It's ages since I was *over there*. [2]
On Tuesday evening, I was *at the front door* talking to a caller. Suddenly we heard a crash and two cars collided *just opposite*. We hurried *across* to see if we could help. One driver was scrambling *out*, bleeding profusely, and my visitor helped him *over* to the pavement. Then *along* came some people, running *up the street*. I dashed *back in* and phoned for help. When I went *out* again, the other driver was trying to move her car *down the road* a little and *in to the side*. [3]

In all three examples, spatial reference is essential, as well as orientation to the participants' *here* (*cf* 19.3): *where* in [1] entails a *here* from which to set out; *over there* in [2] entails 'in contrast to here'. But let us look more closely at the part played by spatial reference in [3], both in respect to orientation and to the structure of the narrative.

Even totally out of context, the institutionalized phrase *at the front door* would be understood as referring to the main entrance of someone's home, whether this was a house or a small apartment. Likewise, *just opposite* is at once understood as *just opposite* to where the speaker and his visitor were standing. A road is implied by the car crash and in this context *across* means 'across the intervening space (of footpath and street)'. The *back in* signifies a return across this intervening space and *into* the speaker's home. The two instances of *out* are of sharply different reference: the first refers implicitly to emergence from the car, the second to re-emergence from the speaker's home (thus correlating with the earlier *back in*). The contrasting phrases *up* (*the street*) and *down* (*the road*) are interesting in making spatial reference not necessarily in terms of relative elevation (though this is not excluded). The immediate contrast is in terms of orientation again: *up* indicating an approach towards the speaker (and his home), *down* indicating the converse (*cf* 9.7). The cluster of spatial references provides a continuous set of coordinates in relation to a base (the speaker's home, though this is merely a pragmatic implication) as well as a coherent account of the movements involved in the narrative.

NOTE In a text where it was known that a physical slope was involved, *up/down* (*the street*) would be used with respect to this absolute and objective physical feature, and it would outweigh personal orientation. The latter could then be expressed by alternative means: 'She *went (away)* up the street'; 'They *came* down the street'. Contrast also: 'They hurried *up* Fifth Avenue' (*ie* away from 'downtown' Manhattan); 'They sauntered *down* Fifth Avenue' (*ie* towards downtown Manhattan); 'They walked *along* Fifth Avenue' (neutral as to direction).

Ellipses and pro-forms

19.5 Where place relators operate in text structure, ellipsis is often involved (*cf* 12.19):

> He examined the car. The *front* was slightly damaged. [1]
>
> The building was heavily guarded by police. The windows {on the *top storey* / at the *top*} were covered with boards. [2]

The ellipted items in [1] and [2] are *of the car* and *of the building* respectively. Often the ellipted items are not in the previous context, but are understood from the situational context (either accompanying the communication or established by the communication):

> The traffic lights eventually changed. She walked *across* quickly. [3]

Across here implies *the road* or some similar noun phrase (*cf* 9.7, 19.4).

A few place adverbs do not involve ellipsis: *here*, *there*, *elsewhere*, the relative *where*, and (in formal contexts) *hence*, *thence*, *hither*, and *thither*. They are pro forms:

> The school laboratory reeked of ammonia. *Here*, during the first week of the term, an unusual experiment had been conducted. [4]
>
> All my friends have been to Paris at least once. I am going *there* next summer for the first time. [5]

Here in [4] is a substitute for *in the school laboratory* and *there* in [5] for *to Paris*.

NOTE In sentences like *Stand there* and *Here it is*, the pro-forms may refer directly to the situational contexts without any linguistic mention of location, but with orientation to the speaker:

> I'm glad to welcome you *here*, especially since at the last meeting I could not be *there*.

19.6 Place relators often comprise two components. Most commonly these are a dimension or direction indicator plus a location indicator (*cf* 9.4). The latter is usually an open-class noun (or proper noun), but its locational use is often institutionalized, making the whole expression quasi-grammatical. Examples:

at the window	in town
on the ceiling	off work
in the air	on board
at the seaside	on the way

Another common type of pairing is a distance indicator plus a dimension indicator; for example:

(not) far / further / farther	+	in / out / off / away / from	nearer	+	in / to + noun phrase
			higher(er)	+	up
			low(er)	+	down
			close	+	by / to + noun phrase

The partially antonymous *home* and *abroad*, *ashore* and *on board* are exceptional in combining the dimension and location factors:

After being *out* for a couple of hours, I'm now {going / staying} *home* for the evening. [reference to personal residence]. [1]

After {living / being / going} *abroad*, I like to {come / be} *home* (= 'my own country') for a year or so. [2]

NOTE Locational connections in relation to coherence are not merely a necessary feature of individual texts. It is customary in newspapers to group the otherwise separate news-item texts on a regional basis. So too in radio broadcasts, a place relator may serve to give some kind of coherence to otherwise unrelated stories. For example:

> They are worried that another strike could break out in the United States similar to the one that affected Canada's economy so seriously two years ago.
>
> IN CÁNada news is coming in of a plane accident near Toronto. The aircraft, a privately owned four-seater . . .

The textual justification for IN is that a main focus on *Canada* would be misleading since *Canada* is in some sense already 'given'.

Time relators

19.7 Like space, time has its lexically specific and labelled 'areas' and 'locations'. Along with open-class nouns, some of them – like places – are treated as proper nouns: *century*, *decade*, *year*, *1989*, *January*, *week*, *day*, *Thursday*, *evening*, etc. Again like units of space, these nouns have an institutionalized and hence quasi-grammatical use. In addition to being elements in clause structure, they lend themselves to the connections and transitions of textual structure:

I've been working on this problem *all year* and I must find a solution *before January* when I'm due to go abroad *for a month or so*. [1]

Nouns of more general meaning are still more firmly harnessed for grammatical use:

I've been working *a long time*. [2]
I'm going abroad *for a while*. [3]
She hasn't visited me *for ages*. [4]

In addition, therefore, to closed-class items like *afterwards*, we take account here of numerous open-class words which, though with clear lexical meaning, are largely used in the constant process of keeping track of the many and complex references that are necessary for coherent text. Since time passes irrespective of location (which need not change), temporal cues to periods, and to references *before*, *after*, *within*, and *during* these periods, are more inherently essential than locational cues.

Once a time reference has been established, certain temporal adjectives and adverbs may order subsequent information in relation to the time reference.

Temporal ordering

19.8 (i) Temporal ordering *previous* to a given time reference:

ADJECTIVES

earlier, *former*, *preceding*, *previous*, *prior*

For example:

He handed in a good essay. His *previous* essays (*ie* 'those done *earlier*') were all poor.

ADVERBIALS

already, *as yet*, *before*, *beforehand*, *earlier*, *first*, *formerly*, *hitherto* (formal), *previously*, *so far*, *yet*; and phrases with pro-forms: *before that*, *before this*, *before now*, *before then*, *by now*, *by then*, *until now*, *until then*, *up to now*, *up to then*

For example:

I shall explain to you what happened. But *first* I must give you a cup of tea.

First is to be interpreted here as 'before I explain to you what happened'.

19.9 (ii) Temporal ordering *simultaneous* with a given time reference:

ADJECTIVES

coexisting ⟨formal⟩, *coinciding* ⟨formal⟩, *concurrent* ⟨formal⟩, *contemporary*, *contemporaneous* ⟨formal⟩, *simultaneous*

For example:

> The death of the President was reported this afternoon on Cairo radio. A *simultaneous* announcement was broadcast from Baghdad.

Here *simultaneous* means 'simultaneous with the report of the death of the President on Cairo radio'.

ADVERBIALS

> *at this point*, *concurrently* ⟨formal⟩, *contemporaneously* ⟨formal⟩, *here*, *in the interim* ⟨formal⟩, *meantime*, *meanwhile*, *in the meantime*, *in the meanwhile*, *now*, *presently*, *simultaneously*, *then*, *throughout*, and the relative *when*

For example:

> Several of the conspirators have been arrested but their leader is as yet unknown. *Meanwhile* the police are continuing their investigation into the political sympathies of the group.

Here *meanwhile* means 'from the time of the arrests up to the present'.

NOTE [**a**] The use of *presently* for time relationship (ii), with the meaning 'now', 'at present', is very common in AmE. In BrE, *presently* is more commonly synonymous with *soon*.

[**b**] An example of *here* as time indicator:

> I've now been lecturing for over an hour. I'll stop *here* since you all look tired.

19.10 (iii) Temporal ordering *subsequent* to a given time reference:

ADJECTIVES

> *ensuing* ⟨formal⟩, *following*, *later*, *next*, *subsequent* ⟨formal⟩, *succeeding* ⟨formal⟩, *supervening* ⟨formal⟩

For example:

> I left him at 10 p.m. and he was almost asleep. But at some *later* hour he must have lit a cigarette.

Here *later* might mean 11 p.m. but equally 4 a.m., a time otherwise called 'the *early* hours of the morning'.

ADVERBIALS

> *after*, *afterwards*, *(all) at once*, *finally*, *immediately*, *last*, *later*, *next*, *since*, *subsequently* ⟨formal⟩, *suddenly*, *then*; and the phrases *after that*, *after this*, *on the morrow* ['the day after']

For example:

> The manager went to a board meeting this morning. He was *then* due to catch a train to London.

NOTE The ordinals constitute a temporal series of adjectives *first*, *second*, *third* . . . with *next* as a substitute for any of the middle terms when moving up the series, and *final* or *last* as a substitute for the term marking the end of the series. There is a corresponding series of conjuncts with *first* (also *at first* and, less commonly, *firstly*) as the beginning of the set; *secondly*, etc; *next*, *then*, *later*, *afterwards*, as interchangeable middle terms; and *finally*, *lastly*, or *eventually* as markers of the end of the set (*cf* general ordinals, 5.10).

Tense, aspect, and narrative structure

19.11 As a further indication of the importance of time in language, all finite clauses (and many nonfinite ones) carry a discrete indication of tense and aspect. Although the contrasts involved are severely limited in comparison with adverbial distinctions, they contribute to the textual cohesion and progression. Compare the different implications in the second part of what follows:

> She told me all about the operation on her hip.
> It seemed to have been a success. [1]
> It seems to have been a success. [2]

In [1], in accordance with our expectations with respect to sequence of tenses and backshift (*cf* 14.18), the past ties the second part to the first, and thus, like this, derives its authority from the woman concerned: 'It seemed *to her* . . .'; that is, '*She* was of the opinion that the operation had been successful'. The possibility of repudiation is therefore open: 'Unfortunately, this is not so'. In [2], by contrast, the present disjoins the second part and may imply an orientation to the 'I' narrator: 'It seems *to me* . . .', '*I* am of the opinion . . .'

Alternation of past and present in this way is a regular mode of switching reference from the 'then' of the narrative reference to the 'now' of both the narrator and the hearer or reader (some items like parenthetic *you see* being confined to this 'now'):

> As a child, I lived in Singapore. It'*s* very hot there, you *know*, and I never owned an overcoat. I *remember* being puzzled at picture books showing European children wrapped up in heavy coats and scarves. I *believe* I thought it all as exotic as children here *think* about spacemen's clothing, you *see*. [3]

Consider the instances of past tense in this text: *lived*, *owned*, *thought*. Not merely are these verbs morphologically identical: the text actually represents the past as being referentially identical. All the verbs refer back to a stretch of time during which these things were true. *Cf* Fig 19.11.

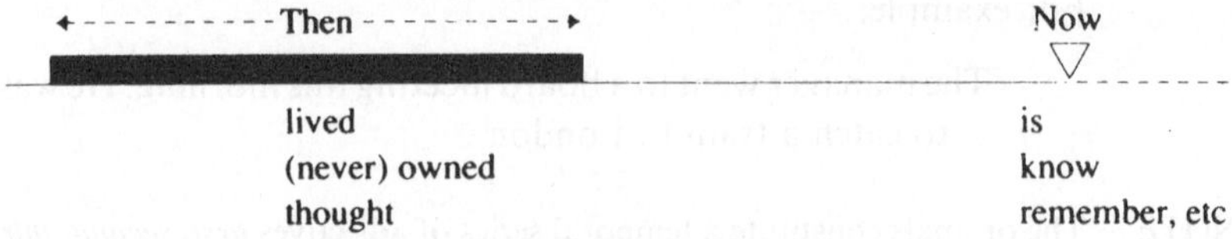

Fig 19.11

19.12 But past tenses need refer neither to the same time nor to stretches of time. With verbs which connote discrete actions, a narrative string of past tenses will be interpreted as referring to a sequence of events iconically represented by the sequence of verbs. Consider for example:

> Do you want to hear about my adventures last Thursday? I *got up* at six, *had* some coffee, *kissed* my wife goodbye, and *set off* for Rome. I *took* a taxi and then the underground, *arrived* at Heathrow, *started* to check in my case, *patted* my pocket and *found* – no ticket, no passport. *Picked up* my case, *caught* the underground, *got* another taxi, *arrived* at my front door, *rushed in*, and of course *gave* my poor wife the shock of her life. [1]

This calls for a very different diagram, as shown in Fig 19.12.

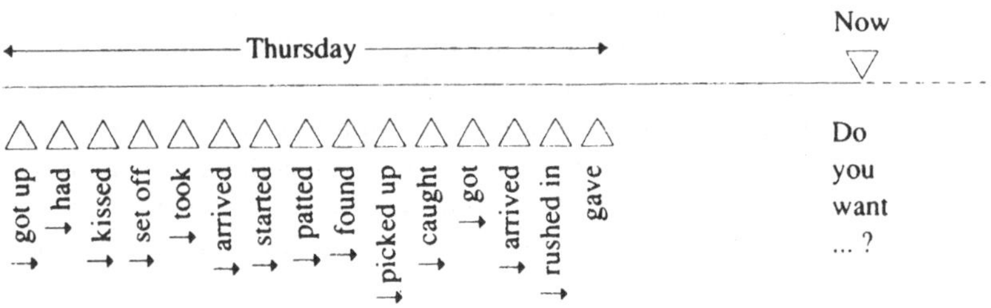

Fig 19.12

NOTE [**a**] While a sequence of past tenses implies sequential events if the lexical meaning of the verb makes this plausible as in [2], a sequence of past verbs with progressive aspect (*cf* 4.10) can imply simultaneity, as in [3]:

> René raged with anger. Janet went out for the evening. [2]
> René was raging with anger. Janet was going out for the evening. [3]

[**b**] Use of the past perfect (*cf* 4.9) can enable us to reverse the order of sentences in a text. Note the way in which 'Time One' [T_1] precedes T_2 in [4], where T_2 precedes T_1 in [5]:

> There was a sudden violent noise outside [T_1]. John telephoned the police [T_2]. [4]

John telephoned the police [T2]. There had been a sudden violent noise outside [T1]. [5]

Note also the use of present perfect with simple present, as illustrated in the latter part of 19.2.

Tense complexity in narrative

19.13 More usually, however, texts comprise much greater time-reference complexity than the examples in 19.11*f* show. They will have a mixture of state verbs and discrete-action verbs; the narrative will weave backwards and forwards, with a mixture of tenses and aspects, of finite and nonfinite clauses, enabling the narrator to depart from the linear sequence of historical order so as both to vary the presentation and to achieve different (*eg* dramatic) effects:

I was reading Chaucer's *Troilus* the other night, and it suddenly occurred to me to wonder what Chaucer {expects / expected} us to make of the fact that Criseyde {has / had} been widowed, whereas Troilus {has / had} never even been in love. Surely this is significant, yet I had never thought of it before. [1]

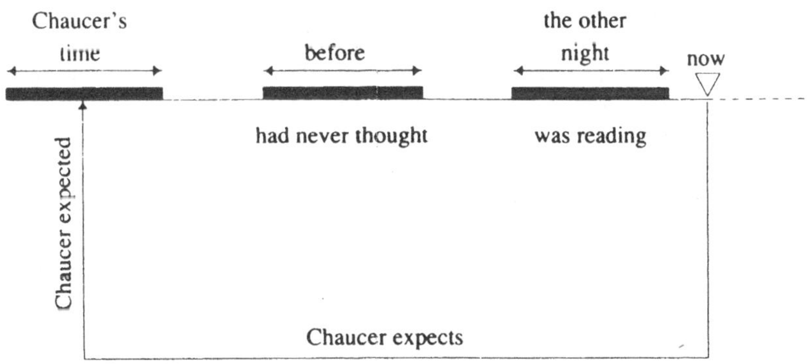

Fig 19.13a

Here we have the additional complication of a narrative about a narrative within a narrative (see Fig 19.13a). The account of the narrator's reading and reflection is itself of some complexity: within a period in the past, a durative activity (*reading*) is represented as being interrupted by a sudden thought. But the thought had significance not merely at the time of thinking it nor merely during the rest of the reading period; it is represented as being permanently significant. The appeal to the hearer ('Surely . . .') does not connote that *is* refers only to the *now* of the speaker and hearer; there is no room for some such adverbial as *at present* :

*Surely this is *at present* significant.

The narrator is here using the present tense of timeless reference (*cf* 4.3). It is the potentiality for such a use of the present that made us give the two possibilities, 'Chaucer expects' and 'Chaucer expected'. The latter takes the historical view: a comment on the poet as he wrote in the fourteenth century. The former treats the Chaucer canon as timeless, permanently existing.

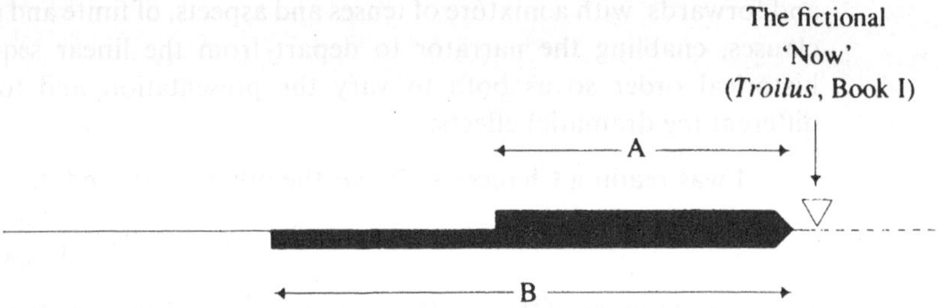

Fig 19.13b

An analogous choice exists in referring to the fictional narrative of Chaucer's poem. In Fig 19.13b, 'A' represents the (unknown) period during which Criseyde has been a widow before the poem begins; 'B' represents the longer period (in effect, Troilus's whole life) during which Troilus has never been in love. It will be noticed that in this commentary we have adopted the 'timeless' view of the fiction ('When the poem *begins*, Criseyde *has been* a widow for some time'). In the original example [1], the past variant was also given, implying a retelling of the story ('When Troilus first *saw* Criseyde, she *had been* a widow for some time').

NOTE Narrative introductions like 'They tell me that . . .' 'I hear/gather/understand that . . .' impose no constraints upon the tenses to follow.

Special uses of present and past

19.14 We have seen that the present tense can cooccur in textual structure with two distinct types of time references: ordinary 'state present' and universal 'state present' ('timeless'; *cf* 4.3):

I *think* she had undergone an operation before I met her. [1]
Troilus *is* totally fancy-free until he *sees* Criseyde. [2]

A third type of present, 'habitual' (*cf* 4.3), is common in ordinary narrative, and it can readily cooccur with past tenses:

I had forgotten that they *dine* very early and I arrived at an awkward moment for both them and me. [3]

But there is a further use of the present tense: the so-called 'historic present' (*cf* 4.4). As well as occurring in rather mannered and formal prose of an old-fashioned tone, it is common in colloquial spoken narrative, especially at points of particular excitement. The time reference is unequivocally past. For example:

> It was on the Merritt Parkway just south of New Haven. I was driving along, half asleep, my mind miles away, and suddenly there was a screeching of brakes and I catch sight of a car that had been overtaking me apparently. Well, he doesn't. He pulls in behind me instead, and it's then that I notice a police car parked on the side. [4]

NOTE **[a]** In nonstandard speech, the reporting verb in narrative is often in the historic present:

> 'Where did you put my coat?' he says. 'I never touched it,' I says. [5]

[b] As well as being able to use the present tense to refer to the past, we can conversely use the past to refer to a narrator's 'now', exploiting that form of backshift that is referred to as free direct and indirect speech (*cf* 14.22). Textual cohesion and congruity of reference are maintained by careful consistency of tense and aspect usage, present replaced by past, past by past perfect, even in the prolonged absence of reminders to the hearer/reader in the form of reporting verbs ('He reflected . . .', 'She said . . .'). For example:

> He was suddenly afraid. What on earth was he to do now? How could he have been so silly as not to tell Sheila he'd forgotten his keys? [6]

Determiners, pro-forms, and ellipsis

19.15 Let us consider the following independent sentences:

> An argument over unilateral disarmament broke out between them. [1]
>
> An argument over unilateral disarmament finally put an end to their friendship. [2]

If we wished to make these sentences into a textual whole, there would be numerous possibilities, even keeping the first part unchanged:

> . . . between them. {The / This / That} argument finally put an end to their friendship. [3]
>
> . . . between them. {The / This / That} {dispute / controversy} finally put . . . [4]
>
> . . . between them. {The / This / That} {issue / matter / affair} finally put . . . [5]
>
> . . . between them – an argument that finally put . . . [6]
>
> . . . between them, which finally put . . . [7]

... between them, and $\left\{\begin{matrix}\text{this}\\ \text{that}\end{matrix}\right\}$ finally put ... [8]

... between them, and it finally put ... [9]
... between them and finally put an end to their friendship. [10]

All these versions have two things in common. They abbreviate the second part and they connect it with the first part.

In some ways the most straightforward is [6], where a simple and direct shortening of the first subject phrase is used appositively; *cf* 17.27. There is something similar in [3], where reduction retains the original head-word of the noun-phrase *argument*, but here the coreference with the preceding subject is indicated not by apposition but by the anaphoric determiners *the*, *this*, or *that*; *cf* 5.3*f*. In [4] and [5] coreference is again carried by deixis, but in [4] the original noun phrase is not merely abbreviated but its head-word is replaced by a semantic paraphrase. In [5], on the other hand, the head-word is replaced by a quasi-pronominal noun of very general meaning. In [8], anaphoric deixis again points to the coreference, as in [4] and [5], but this time with the head-word replaced by zero; the demonstrative *this* or *that* is used pronominally; *cf* 6.19*f*. In [9], the vaguest possible pronoun (*it*) is used, while in [7] a relative pronoun replaces the earlier noun-phrase subject (*cf* 17.11). Finally, in [10], there is total omission of the second subject (*cf* 13.19).

All eight of [3–10] provide satisfactory coherence of the two parts. It is perhaps closest in [10], but only at the cost of muting the separate significance of the second part – in contrast to [3] and [4], for example, which insist on our considering the *beginning* of the argument, on the one hand, as well as its *result* on the other hand.

Discourse reference: clausal

19.16 Common signals for sentence or clause reference include:

anaphoric and cataphoric: *here*, *it*, *this*
anaphoric only: *that*, *the foregoing* ⟨formal⟩
cataphoric only: *as follows*, *the following*, *thus* ⟨formal⟩

Anaphoric examples:

Many years ago their wives quarrelled over some trivial matter, now long forgotten. But one word led to another and the quarrel developed into a permanent rupture between them. *That* is why the two men never visit each other's houses. [1]

Some students never improve. They get no advice and therefore they keep repeating the same mistakes. *It* is a terrible shame. [2]

Students want to be shown connections between facts instead of spending their time memorizing dates and formulas. Reflecting *this*, the university is moving away from large survey courses and breaking down academic fences in order to show subjects relating to one another. [3]

Cataphoric examples:

> *This* should interest you, if you're still keen on boxing. The world heavyweight championship is going to be held in Chicago next June, so you should be able to watch it live. [4]
>
> *Here* is the news. A diplomat was kidnapped last night in London . . . [radio announcement] [5]
>
> *It* never should have happened. He went out and left the baby unattended. [6]
>
> My arguments are *as follows* . . . [7]

In some instances, we can replace the reference signal by a corresponding *that*-clause. For example, *that* in [1] could be said to refer to a *that*-clause which corresponds to the immediately preceding clause:

> . . . That the quarrel developed into a permanent rupture between them is why the two men . . . [1a]

In [2], on the other hand, *it* could be said to stand for the whole of the two preceding sentences. In [5], *here* could refer forward to a following discourse of indeterminate length, and this is usual with cataphoric signals.

NOTE [a] *Above* and *below* are used for discourse reference to refer to (written) units of varying length, but not necessarily to immediately neighbouring parts of the discourse:

> . . . the arguments given *below* [perhaps referring to several sentences]
> . . . the question mentioned *above*

The above but not **the below* can be used as a noun phrase:

> *The above* illustrates what we mean by . . .

[b] The nonrestrictive relative clause, with a previous clause or sentence as the antecedent of introductory *which* (*cf* 17.12), is sometimes made into a separate orthographic sentence. *Which* is then an anaphoric signal equivalent to *(and) that*:

> *She's borrowed a history book. Which* suggests her teacher is having some influence on her.

[c] In some (especially disapproving or ironic) contexts, *that* can be used cataphorically:

> *THÀT'S* what I like to SÉE: a chap who enjoys his work.

Otherwise, *that* is used anaphorically.

[d] In informal spoken English, *what* can have cataphoric reference when it is the direct object of *know* in a question, or *guess* in a directive, or *tell* in a statement:

> (Do you) Know WHAT? }
> Guess WHÀT. } He won't pay up.

> (I'll) Tell you WHÀT: I've forgotten the keys!

[e] In legal English *the said*, *the (a)forementioned*, and *the aforesaid* are used for anaphoric reference, the last two both as a premodifier ('the aforementioned provisions') and as a noun phrase. In the latter function, they would normally refer to a previous noun phrase with personal reference.

Formulaic utterance

19.17 While deictic reference and ellipted matter must, from a grammatical viewpoint, be recoverable (*cf* 12.2), discourse permits a good deal of vagueness. This is especially common in informal conversation, not least in the semi-formulaic responses to expressions of thanks, apology, inquiry, and the like. Consider how difficult it would be to specify the precise references or the exact ellipses in the following responses:

A: Thank you very much.
B: Not at all. / Not a bit. / Don't mention it. / You're WELcome. ⟨esp AmE⟩ [1]

A: I'm terribly sorry.
B: Not at all. / Not a bit. / It's nothing. [2]

A: I wonder if you'd mind coming and taking some dictation?
B: { Of course. / Surely. ⟨esp AmE⟩ / ÒḰ / { RÌGHT Ó / WÌLL DÓ } ⟨esp BrE⟩ } ⟨informal⟩ }, Mrs Stewart. [3]

A: Would you mind my asking if you've ever taken drugs, Mr Hoover?
B: Absolutely NÒT. [4]

A: You wouldn't know a fortune-teller around here, I suppose?
B: { TRỲ me. [5]
Try MÈ. } [6]

In [5] the implication is that B knows one ('Try asking if I know one'); in [6], B is saying that he himself can tell fortunes. In [4], only the context could clarify whether B is saying that he 'absolutely (does) not (mind)', or that it is 'absolutely not' true that he has taken drugs. In [3], the formulaic response *Will do*! is a conventional way of saying 'I *will do* as you request', and B has interpreted (correctly, of course) A's polite inquiry as a request. In [1] and [2], the reference of *it*, in *Don't mention it*, *It's nothing*, is doubtless anaphoric in some way. But in the first line of [7], *it* is cataphoric if almost equally vague in its reference; the initial imperative by B is little more than an informal attention-requesting signal, a more severe form of which includes a cataphoric *here*:

A: By the way, Cynthia. It's awful of me, I know. But would you be able to look after my dog while I'm away next week?
B: (Now look) (Here), this is the third time you've left me with your dog. [7]

Within sentence sequences that are strictly alike from a grammatical point of view, a discourse pronoun can have sharply different reference:

She hoped he would not mention her unfortunate marriage.
{It / This / That} would be very {CÒURTeous of him. [8] / CÒURTeous of him in a WÁY, of course. [8a]}

In [8], the reference is to the predication including the negative ('His not mentioning the marriage would be courteous'). In [8a], the reference excludes the negative ('His mentioning the marriage would be courteous'). It is only the pragmatic implications of the hedging adverbial *in a way* and the concessive *of course* that leads us to this interpretation.

NOTE An interesting use of cataphoric *it* in textual structure is in the cleft sentence device (*cf* 18.18*ff*):

It was at 9.15 this morning that the government proclaimed a state of emergency. [9]
It was on their way from the airport that Gillian dropped the bombshell. In carefully casual tones, she asked him if he would agree to a divorce. [10]

In [9], it is unlikely that the narrator wishes to highlight the time adjunct: rather, the textual device is pointing to the climax at the end of the sentence. In [10], the same applies, but with a double cataphora: *the bombshell* which ends the first sentence is climactically explained in the sentence that follows.

Discourse reference: noun phrases

19.18 Certain determiners are used to signal that a noun phrase is referentially equivalent to a previous noun phrase (*cf* 5.4*f*):

the this–these that–those

Such noun phrases may be discourse abstractions, and the heads may either be identical as in [1] or nominalizations (17.23) that add lexical variation as in [2]:

She set up a hypothesis that chemotherapy destroyed the will to live as well as the unwanted cells. *This hypothesis* attracted the attention of . . . [1]
Deconstructionism holds that knowledge about literature is

strictly unattainable . . . *This doctrine* is puzzling in several respects. [2]

It is not always certain, however, when such a reference is to a previous noun phrase or is a nominalization of a wider, clausally expressed proposition. The text from which [2] is quoted is a case in point. As presented in the abbreviated form of [2], *doctrine* seems to refer back unambiguously to *deconstructionism* and be a lexical variant of it. But in the original, there are several lines where we have indicated the curtailment, and these include the following:

We must therefore abandon the old-fashioned quest to discover what a given author was trying to communicate. [2a]

The reference of *this doctrine* must therefore include, not merely the specific abstract *deconstructionism*, but the speculated consequence which the author went on to state. A fuller version might therefore read:

This doctrine *of deconstructionism and the need to abandon the old-fashioned quest* . . . is puzzling in several respects. [2b]

When *such* is used, the intention is often to indicate disapproval (which may be sympathetic):

We visited the Browns yesterday and heard their complaints about the condition of the house they live in. I never heard such a sorry tale. [3]
. . . such a rigmarole. [3a]
. . . of such wretchedness. [3b]

In [3] and [3a], the reference is primarily to the *complaints*, [3a] lexically indicating impatience rather than sympathy; in [3b] the reference is rather to the *condition*, with an implication of the speaker's sympathy.

NOTE Use of *the former* and *the latter* is largely confined to (rather formal) noun-phrase reference:

They were full of resentment because no one came to visit them and also because their roof was leaking. I helped them over *the latter* [*ie* about the roof] and promised to let some friends know about *the former* [*ie* the complaint about neglect].

For broader reference, both phrases might be expanded to include a noun head:

I helped them over *the latter issue* and promised to let some friends know about *the former problem*.

19.19 *So* and *that* can have anaphoric reference when they are intensifiers premodifying an adjective (*that* so used is informal and often criticized):

There were two thousand people in the theatre. I didn't

expect it to be {*so* / *that*} full. [1]

I had a terrible headache yesterday and had to take some aspirins. I'm not feeling {*so* / *that*} bad today. [2]

We took them to a circus, and then to a zoo, and gave them lots of ice-cream and chocolate. They haven't had {*so* / *that*} good a time for years. [3]

Such is used more commonly than *so* or *that* when (as in [3]) the adjective accompanies a noun phrase, but *such* is followed by normal noun-phrase order:

... They haven't had *such a good time* for years. [3a]

Note the different implications when *this*, *that*, and *so* are used as intensifiers; *this* has present orientation, *that* past orientation (both being informal), while *so* is neutral both temporarily and stylistically. Compare:

Did you expect {*this* / *that* / *so*} many people?

Personal pronouns

19.20 As explained in 6.10, *we* has several possible noun-phrase references. In discourse, we are concerned chiefly with the 'inclusive' *we* (as in the present sentence), and with the 'exclusive' *we* as in:

Will you stay here while *we* go for a policeman? [1]

In formal writing, and frequently indeed in the present book, *we* 'inclusive' and *we* 'exclusive' can cooccur. The former accompanies verbs implying shared knowledge (*understand*, *see*, *appreciate*, etc), the latter verbs of communication (*say*, *state*, *write*, etc). It would be possible to use both in the same sentence, though this would usually be avoided:

We see now why *we* expressed reservations earlier. [2]

In [2], the second *we* is exclusive, the first inclusive or even (as often) indefinite and roughly equivalent to a more formal *one* or *the reader*.

The indefinite use of *you* and the *you* of direct 2nd person address (*cf* 6.12) can also cooccur. In [3], the first *you* is indefinite, the second makes direct address:

In fourteenth-century England, *you* had a very poor chance of being taught to read, *you* see. [3]

Unlike the two uses of *we*, however, *you* is rather rare in formal writing and the indefinite use is virtually excluded. The same applies to the indefinite use of *they*; in formal styles, *they* in [4] would refer only to the council authorities, where informally it is more plausible with indefinite reference:

> I intend to ask the council authorities why *they* are digging up the road again. [4]

In place of the informal indefinite *you*, there is *one*, but it can be used only sparingly without making a piece of writing (or even more so a spoken utterance) sound intolerably pompous. This is perhaps especially constraining in BrE, which lacks in general the facility (now in any case frowned on for social reasons) of replacing *one* by *he* in second and subsequent use:

> *One* cannot control *one's* temper easily if *one* is discussing a matter over which *one* has feelings of guilt or great personal involvement. ⟨esp BrE⟩ [5]

NOTE In [5], we could have in AmE: *One* . . . *his* . . . *he* . . . *he* . . . Other indefinite pronouns such as *anyone*, *everybody* can be followed by *he* in both AmE and BrE, but this is vulnerable to the objection of seeming to have a male orientation, while the use of *they* to refer back to these indefinites is open to the objection of seeming ungrammatical in the switch from singular to plural. It is therefore largely confined to spoken (esp informal) usage.

Comparison

19.21 Signals of comparison and contrast play a frequent part in providing textual coherence. Most can be regarded as involving ellipsis (*cf* 12.14*ff*).

The most obvious comparison signal is found in adjectives and adverbs, whether in the inflected forms or in the periphrastic forms with *more*, *most*, *as*, *less*, *least* (*cf* 7.39). If the basis of comparison (*cf* 15.36) is not made explicit in the clause, it must be inferred from the previous context:

> John took four hours to reach London. Bill, on the other hand, was driving *more slowly*. [1]
>
> Mary used to listen to records most of the time. Sally was a *more serious* student. [2]
>
> There were ten boys in the group. Bob was by far the *best*. [3]
>
> Barbara dances beautifully. Jack dances *no less well*. [4]
>
> Gwen always hands in a well-constructed and intelligent paper. I'm afraid Joan doesn't expend *as* much effort and time on her papers. [5]

We can demonstrate the anaphoric reference by supplying the basis of comparison:

> . . . more slowly *than John (drove)*. [1a]
>
> . . . a more serious student *than Mary (was)*. [2a]
>
> . . . the best *(of the ten boys) (in the group)*. [3a]
>
> . . . no less well *than Barbara (dances)*. [4a]

. . . as much effort and time on her papers *as Gwen (expends on her papers)*. [5a]

So too with expressions of similarity or difference; these may involve the use of equative and antithetic conjuncts (*cf* 8.44). For example:

Mrs White was the victim of a confidence trick. Bill was cheated {*very differently.* / *in the same way.*} [6]

Tom gets ten dollars a week for pocket money. Bob receives a *similar* amount. [7]

Mrs Hayakawa complained that the roof leaked and the windows fitted badly, so that the place was freezing cold. Her husband complained *likewise*. [8]

Jim behaved himself at the party. However, the *other* boy had to be sent home. [9]

Fred didn't like the car. He asked to see a *different* one. [10]

We can display the basis of similarity or difference:

{. . . very differently *from the way in which Mrs White was (cheated).* / . . . in the same way *as Mrs White (was (cheated)).*} [6a]

. . . an amount similar *to what Tom receives.* [7a]

. . . complained *about the same things as Mrs Hayakawa (complained about).* [8a]

. . . the boy other *than Jim* . . . [9a]

. . . see one different *from the car he didn't like.* [10a]

NOTE Expressions involving *respective(ly)*, *mutual(ly)*, *converse(ly)*, *opposite* (*-ly* is rare), etc, effect considerable neatness and economy in discourse:

Brahms and Verdi wrote orchestral and operatic music, *respectively*.

The chairman and the guest speaker expressed their *mutual* admiration.

Mary told Harry that she never wanted to see him again. He *reciprocated*, but with even greater bitterness.

I thought that Oregon had a greater rainfall than British Columbia, but Caroline says *the opposite*.

The textual role of adverbials

19.22 In 19.17 we saw in example [8a] the communicative impact of the inserted adverbials *in a way* and *of course*. While the basic functions of adverbials are set out in Chapter 8, we need here to emphasize their dual role in textual structure: interpreting the text to the hearer/reader (*eg* in encouraging a particular attitude), and expressing the relevant connection between one part of a text and another. The former is achieved primarily by subjuncts and disjuncts (*cf* 8.32*ff*, 8.40*ff*), the latter by conjuncts (*cf* 8.43*f*). Consider the following:

My dog is fourteen {months / years} old and ▲ he is very frisky. [1]

Given the appropriate general knowledge, the choice of *months* or *years* will determine the aptness of adverbials that might be added at the insertion sign: *of course* or *naturally* on the one hand; *yet, still, surprisingly enough* on the other. A further example.

My next-door neighbour {is an entomologist. / is a travelling salesman. / works for an oil company.}

▲ He knows more about treating mosquito bites than anyone I've ever met. [2]

The second sentence of [2] might be preceded by *Not surprisingly*, but this would seem appropriate only if we knew what an entomologist was, or if we connected travelling salesmen or oil executives with experience of mosquito-ridden areas. Preceding the second sentence with *All the same* or *Nonetheless* would obviously have very different implications.

But the postulated insertions in [1] and [2] would serve not only to nudge the hearer in the direction of adopting a particular attitude or to let the hearer know something of the speaker's attitude: they would also indicate the nature of the connection between the two parts of each text. Without the adverbials, each text is presented as offering two pieces of information; in this spirit, the second parts might have read respectively:

. . . and he sleeps in the kitchen. [1a]
. . . He got married last week to a former girlfriend of mine. [2a]

In other words, the connection is thematic only, in the sense of 19.2. With the adverbials inserted, the second part of each text is shown to be (as the original versions might chance to be *interpreted* as being) specifically related to the preceding rheme, either as a natural consequence or as a surprising paradox.

NOTE Since *of course* can hint at incongruity (concession: 'admittedly') instead of expressing congruity, [1] might still be a well-formed text as:

My dog is fourteen years old and of course he is very frisky (still) (, though I think he's beginning to show his age). [1b]

This use of *of course* commonly expresses superficial agreement with what has preceded, while at the same time hinting at a more fundamental disagreement. For example:

The treasurer is of course absolutely right to draw attention to the error in my presentation. On the other hand, I wonder whether he is not using this lapse of mine to prevent discussion of the serious issue involved. [3]

Other adverbials that can convey such implications include *admittedly*, *certainly*, *doubtless*, *undeniably*, *undoubtedly*. Of these, *doubtless* is particularly barbed.

19.23 Responses in dialogue often begin with an adverbial which indicates the direction of transition between what has just been said and what is about to be said. On transitional conjuncts, *cf* 8.44. For example:

A: That man speaks extremely good English.

B: { [1] Well, / [2] Yet } he comes from a village in Mongolia.

In one sense, the content of B's response is identical whether it begins as [1] or [2]. It presents an additional fact about the man, and without the adverbial, B's response would have only a thematic link with A's statement. With either of the adverbials inserted, however, B is making a significant comment not merely on the man but on the propensity of villagers in Mongolia to speak good English. If he begins with *Well*, he implies that it is an established fact (*Well, of course!*) that Mongolian villages provide excellent bases for learning English. If he begins with *Yet*, he implies that the man's good command of English was *despite* his Mongolian upbringing.

NOTE [a] The use of *well* is itself context-dependent, however. It would be perfectly plausible to use *well* in [1] as a very different transition (*Well, now!*) so as to connote 'Well, I'll tell you something surprising: he actually comes from a village in Mongolia'. Such an antithetic–concessive transition (*cf* 8.44) is implicit in the frequent note of reservation struck by the use of *well*. Consider a converse exchange of remarks on the same subject:

A: That man is from Mongolia.

B: { [1a] Well, / [2a] Yet } he speaks extremely good English.

Here, both [1a] and [2a] would connote 'Despite that . . .'. There is in fact no one-word adverbial to express the relationship of the original [1] at [1a]; we would have to resort to a fully clausal expression, as in:

{ So that explains why / Now I understand why } he speaks . . .

[b] Elliptical responses (*cf* 19.17) often contain an obligatory connective; for example (where in [4] intonation enables us to dispense with the use of an adverbial):

A: { Have a good weekend! / How nice to see you again! }

B: { You *TÒO!* [3]
ÀND YÓU! } [4]

Adverbials as structural indicators

19.24 Basic relational structures depend rather heavily on adverbial pointers, especially when any great degree of complexity is involved.

(a) *General to particular*: Any of the following would usefully assist the relationship at the insert mark in [1]:

for example thus even indeed

Many of the audience became openly hostile. ▲ My uncle wrote a letter to the management next day. [1]

(b) *Progression*: According as the progression is locational, temporal, or logical, adverbials both help to indicate the direction and mark the successive stages. For example:

First, boil the rice in well-salted water; drain it *immediately*. *Next*, warm the lightly buttered base of a small pie-dish. You may *now* put the rice in the dish. *Then* add the cheese, tomato, and onion. The pie is *at last* ready to be put in the oven. [2]

(c) *Compatibility*: It is frequently important to mark the match or mismatch between two parts of a text. Consider the presence or absence of (for example) *so too* in [3]:

The ordinary saw is not easy to use. ▲ A plane demands years of careful practice. [3]

Similarly, a contrastive conjunct (*cf* 8.44) such as *on the other hand* in the variant [3a]:

The ordinary saw is not easy to use. ▲ A hammer is something that any novice can handle. [3a]

19.25 Different discourse strategies will likewise call for different adverbial indicators. A 'step' technique is simplest, following as it does a progressive relation as in [2], 19.24. With a 'chain' mode, however, it is particularly helpful to point to the existence and direction of transitions in the structure. Thus (using adverbial linkage more densely than is usual or desirable):

Hamlet poignantly represents the indecisions that plague us all. *Admittedly*, indecision is not the worst of our ills. *Indeed*, in some ways decisiveness can be more damaging. *At any rate*, many people have come to grief that way . . . [1]

In a text of 'stack'-like structure, the 'layers' may call for enumeration (*first*, *at the outset*, *fundamentally*: *secondly*, *next*, . . .; *still more importantly* . . .), but it is especially desirable to draw the hearer's attention to what is to be regarded as the most crucial point: *thus*, *all in all*, *finally*, *last but by no means least* (though this alliterative conjunct is too hackneyed for a resounding climax), *in conclusion*, and many others.

A 'balance' strategy, like the chain, requires adverbial pointers both to assist the sense of rhetorical balance and to ensure that the author's presuppositions match those of the audience. Consider the following:

> I am always thrilled at the prospect of having a mid-winter break in Switzerland. ▲ The weather is often quite warm . . . [2]

It might not be at all clear whether the second sentence of [2] contributed to the pleasure (vision of deckchairs) or was a counterbalancing unwelcome aspect (poor weather for skiing); in other words, we have left inadequate indication of *compatibility*. For the balance strategy, we need to insert at the marked place some such indicator as *granted*, *admittedly*, *true*, *of course*, *even so*, etc. Most frequently, the balanced movement is indicated by the items *on the one hand*, *on the other (hand)*, but there is usually a goal resembling that of the 'stack' and so demanding a final summative such as *all in all* (*cf* 8.44).

Coordination and subordination

19.26 In 19.2 we pointed out that two utterances gave the impression of being textually related, even when juxtaposed without any formal indicator of connection. Asyndetic relation of this kind, moreover, raises the expectation that the second utterance followed the first as an iconic representation of being sequential in time or consequential in reasoning – and often both, as in:

> He ate too much for dinner. He was ill the next day. [1]

A simple coordination (*cf* 13.17) of the two not only links them more firmly (since more formally); it can also enable us to show that a third utterance in the sequence is less closely linked to the second than the second is to the first; and, further, that the first and second form a sub-unity which as a whole has a relation to the third:

> He ate too much for dinner and he was ill the next day. He decided to be less greedy in future. [2]

But since a result or conclusion seems in some sense more important than the factors leading to the result or conclusion, it is natural to seek a linguistic emblem of this hierarchical relation by subordinating one part to the other instead of coordinating the one with the other:

> Because he ate too much for dinner, he was ill the next day. [3]

In [3], we have not merely made the first part of [1] the explicit reason for the second (*Because*), we have grammatically expressed the connection by making a totally new unit where the second part is the main clause of a complex sentence in which the original first part is reduced to the role of adjunct (*cf* 8.13).

19.27 English has four monosyllabic connective items which semantically belong together as constituting a symmetry of two related subsystems:

and: what precedes is congruent
but: what precedes is incongruent (*cf* 13.13)
so: what follows is a consequence
for: what follows is a reason (*ie* what precedes is a consequence)

For example:

The rain has stopped, *and* she's gone for a walk. [1]
The rain hasn't stopped, *but* she's gone for a walk. [2]
The rain has stopped, *so* she's gone for a walk. [3]
She's gone for a walk, *for* the rain has stopped. [4]

This last is rather unnatural since the conjoins are so short. In any case, the symmetry is imperfect in several respects. In [1], [2], and [4], we have conjunctions (*cf*: **and but*, **and for*); in [3], we have a conjunct (*cf: and so*). Moreover, *and* and *but* are distributionally distinct, *and* demanding in some respects greater structural similarity between the coordinated parts. Compare:

?*The rain has stopped *and* let's go for a walk. [5]
The rain hasn't stopped *but* let's go for a walk. [6]

In this respect, although we normally think of *and* and *but* as closely related converses, the converse of *but* is in fact *so*:

The rain has stopped (and) *so* let's go for a walk.

Most significantly (from the viewpoint of text cohesion), the symmetry is imperfect in that *for* is a much less frequently used connective than the other three: textual structure is resistant to stating a consequence in advance of the condition. In the event of this order being desirable, it is more usual to make the condition structurally subordinate to (rather than coordinate with) the consequence:

She's gone for a walk, { because / since } the rain has stopped. / the rain having (at last) stopped. [7]

Even so, the prior condition would often be stated first:

Since the rain has stopped, she's gone for a walk. [8]

Pairs and triads

19.28 One of the ways in which coordination is exploited in textual structure is to assist the desire for parallelism and balance. For example:

These terrorists have destroyed their credibility. They resisted arrest and then they gave themselves up. They went on a hunger strike and then they started taking food. Some of them claim that they are all nationalists and some of them claim that they are all opposed to nationalism. [1]

We note that the last three sentences in [1], each with clauses coordinated by *and*, form a triad, a rhetorical pattern that seems to be widely attractive. Coordination achieves the seemingly impossible task of giving three units equal status and yet of making the third climactic; for example:

She cleaned the room, (she) made a birthday cake, and (she) finished preparing a lecture. [2]

But the climax of the third part may express a point which is strongly counter-consequential and concessive:

She works ten hours a day in the clinic, she spends ages helping him with his thesis, and he calls her lazy! [3]

The balanced units, whether in pairs or threes, may of course be coordinated *subordinate* clauses:

Because you're tired, because you're lonely, and because you're depressed, I want to insist on your coming to stay with us for a week or so. [4]

Subordinate coordination, however, is especially associated with alternatives rather than accretions. For this reason, pairing is very common since this gives the convenient impression of a total or very general polarization:

He doesn't know whether his wife is unhappy because the baby died or whether she's just no longer in love with him. [5]

When you're lonely or when you're unhappy for other reasons, listening to music can be a great consolation. [6]

Questions too can be linked to form a satisfyingly coherent sequence:

Did he jump or was he pushed? [7]

Will they arrive on time, will they listen carefully, and will they enjoy our performance? [8]

NOTE [**a**] Of course, in ordinary unambitious writing and in familiar speech, coordination is used without striving for the balanced effects on which we have been concentrating in this section. But the momentum and implications of sequence, the relative cohesion of explicit coordination, and the contrasting entailments of the chief coordinating conjunctions are inherent in even the least self-conscious discourse.

[**b**] Informal conversation is characterized by an overtly uncompleted pairing, especially through unfinished *but*-coordinations. These often occur where one speaker is effectively inviting another participant to speak. It can give a pleasantly apologetic and self-effacing tone:

A: My wife's not been feeling too well. She's seen the doctor, though, and he's told her it's nothing serious. But (er) [trails off into silence]
B: I'm sorry to hear about this. [9]

A's speech might equally have ended: 'But I don't know . . .' or 'But don't let's talk about our little problems' or 'But how's the book going?' These all have in common: '*But*: let's change the subject.'
[c] Only *and*, *or*, and asyndeton can be used to form triads.

Contrasting coordination and subordination

19.29 In several of the examples provided in 19.28, coordination has been used along with subordination. This is in fact textually representative. Although from the viewpoint of grammar these two types of clause relation are thought of as alternatives, and although coordination is a far more frequently occurring form of cohesive device, it is normal to find both types in any text of a few lines (or a few seconds) in extent. It is particularly rare to find a text with subordination but without coordination.

It is the flexible use of both devices that endows a text with variety of expression on the one hand, and with a well-ordered presentation of information on the other. The combination also enables one to achieve a high degree of complexity within a single, unified whole. For example:

Although I know it's a bit late to call, seeing your light still on and needing to get your advice if you'd be willing to help me, I parked the car as soon as I could find a place and ventured to come straight up without ringing the bell because, believe me, I didn't want to add waking your baby to the other inconveniences I'm causing you. [1]

Taking nonfinite as well as finite clauses into account, there are nearly twenty clauses in this example, which, without any pretensions to elegance, is grammatically well formed as well as being textually coherent. And while it is often thought that a single sentence of such complexity belongs only to the most formal styles of written English, the example [1] is in fact only slightly edited from the transcribed form of an actual spoken utterance in informal conversation. Again, it is sometimes put as a generalization that nonfinite clauses are characteristic of formal texts, finite clauses of less formal ones. There is some truth in this so far as *-ing* adverbial clauses are concerned, especially those with subject, and especially passive clauses with subject:

The rain having (at last) stopped, she's gone for a walk. [2]
The play now having been reviewed, no one can ignore it. [3]
Having now seen the play myself, I agree that it is rather weak. [4]

Contrast:

Since the rain has stopped, she's gone for a walk. [2a]
Now that the play has been reviewed, no one can ignore it. [3a]

Now that I have seen the play myself, I agree that it is rather weak. [4a]

But it is not true for nominal *-ing* clauses:

Finding you at home is a great surprise. [5]
He didn't mind *waiting for them in the rain*. [6]

In fact [5] and [6] are decidedly less formal than:

That I (should) find you at home is a great surprise. [5a]
He didn't mind *that he waited [was waiting, had to wait] for them in the rain*. [6a]

NOTE With *to*-infinitive clauses, the finite verb correspondences (to the extent that they exist) are almost always more formal in tone. For example:

To close the doors, just press the green button. [7]
In order that you may close the doors, merely press the green button. [7a]

Again, there are verbless clauses that can occur in the most natural and informal usage:

When in doubt, you should consult a doctor.
Though decidedly scared, I kept my voice steady.
He hadn't much money, *if any*.

Prosody and punctuation

19.30 Consider the written sequence:

I smiled at the supervisor and she greeted me. [1]

It would be possible to utter this with two markedly different prosodic realizations, reflecting different interpretations and different bases of linkage:

. . . and she GRÈETed me [1a]
. . . and SHĔ greeted MÈ [1b]

In [1a], there is lexical contrast between the two parts; a verbal greeting is indicated: something actually heard in contrast to the silent smile in the first part of the text. In [1b], *greeted* is merely a lexical variant of *smiled*: the smile was a greeting and there was some kind of greeting in response. This is prosodically indicated by *greeted* having no intonational prominence; it is 'given' informationally (*cf* 18.4), whereas in [1a] *greeted* is contrastive and 'new', as is indicated by the intonational nucleus. In [1b] what is new is neither the participants nor the verbal action but only the reciprocation; the roles are reversed and hence the subject and object pronouns are intonationally highlighted. But the endings of both [1a] and

[1b] are equally dependent in their different ways on the preceding parts to which they are linked.

While there is a direct relation between speech and writing, as also (broadly) between prosodic features of speech and the punctuation devices of writing, the former must be given precedence in each case. In fact, as we see from [1] above, it is impossible to understand a written text until we assign to it a prosody – silently or aloud.

Since such prosodic features as stress, rhythm, and intonation have to do with information processing (*cf* 2.13*ff*, 18.3*ff*), it follows that prosody is a vitally important factor in textual coherence.

The independence of prosody

19.31 The central place of prosodic features is emphasized throughout this book, and in the present chapter they are best illustrated along with the grammatical features they accompany. But we should note that prosodic variables are to some extent quite independent of the particular words used – and indeed no actual words need be used.

It is a characteristic of even the most one-sided conversation that the speaker expects a response, though this may be realized only prosodically, without institutional 'words':

A: So I told him that it was none of his business and that I would do as I pleased.
B: |M̀| [1]
A: After all, it's not as if I still owed him money.
B: |Ḿ| [2]
A: I repaid him that money I borrowed – well, nearly all of it, so I'm no longer under any obligation to him.
B: |M̌| [3]

In [1], B is assuring A with his falling tone (*cf* 2.15) that he follows (and perhaps agrees with) what A is saying. In [2], however, the rising tone indicates surprise or a question or some form of challenge; it is apparently enough to divert A from his thread of discourse to tell B about the loan repayment. In [3], B's fall–rise indicates understanding, but with only qualified assent, and A's next utterance might well go further into the morality of the position as he sees it. All three of B's contributions are textually important and in some circumstances their absence would bring the discourse to a halt: A would be puzzled, or he might be offended, at B's silence. On the telephone, he would have interrupted himself to ask 'Are you still there?' or 'Can you hear me all right?'

19.32 Irrespective of response-dependence (and in radio discourse, no response is usually possible), a speaker prosodically empathizes with the hearer in numerous ways. Pauses are helpfully introduced after completing a significant information unit; this indicates the end of what may be called a prosodic 'paragraph', and such a termination will be marked by being given a specially long curve to an intonation nucleus (usually a fall). Or a pause may be introduced immediately before a lexical item which the speaker feels may be unfamiliar or which he wishes to be heard clearly:

> The library has hundreds of extremely valuable books including several [pause] incuNÀBula. [1]

By contrast he may tactfully increase the tempo over parts of his discourse that he expects will be particularly familiar or which he modestly wishes to be treated as rather unimportant. As with B in [3] of 19.31, a speaker will use a fall–rise to hint at reservation and uncertainty, so that a contrast would be heard with the all-embracing summative conjunct (*cf* 8.44) in:

> On the WHÓLE my childhood was a happy one. [2]
> On the WHǑLE my childhood was a happy one. [3]

In [2] we have a confident statement, in [3] it is hedged with some doubt. A rising tone will especially be heard, however, to indicate clearly that something is to follow: a main clause, a further item in a list, and the like. It will also be used in direct appeals for the listener's cooperation and understanding, in such cases the rise being rather narrow in range and each appeal having lower prominence than the surrounding text. For example:

> I had no idea where she had gone, you SÉE – and I could hardly wait there all night, Ḿ [4]

One final general point may be made. We saw in 19.31 that prosodic features could be used without actual words. In a similar way, prosody enables us to dispense with words that would be necessary for clarity in a written version of the same text. The two following utterances are obviously very different:

> And so it's just possible that she's ill. [5]
> And so she may be actually ill. [6]

A single string of fewer words could convey the difference by assigning different prosody:

> And so she MǍY be ill [5a]
> And so she may be ÌLL [6a]

Punctuation

The paragraph

19.33 Although in this book we repeatedly emphasize the primacy of speech over writing, and of prosody over punctuation, we have to recognize that many types of text take shape first on paper and have their normal realization in graphic form. Punctuation thus has a greater interest for the study of texts than for linguistics as a whole, where it can be generally looked upon as a rather inadequate substitute for the range of phonologically realized prosodic features at our disposal.

In considering the grammatical system of English, we think in terms of such units as sentence, clause, and phrase. From a textual viewpoint, however, such distinctions are not particularly relevant: the difference between sentence and clause, for example. What is more significant is that there are textual units that cannot be recognized at all in grammar, and only the smallest of them can be recognized prosodically as units. Written texts may be in volumes, parts, chapters, sections: and few are so short as not to comprise more than one paragraph (itself a unit only uncertainly matched in prosodic terms).

A paragraph has on the one hand a relatively strong sense of internal coherence, and on the other a relatively loose linkage with the textual material before and after it. Consider the following fragment of text:

> . . . and that was how I came to have some weeks observing the behaviour of their eight-year-old son. He broke eggs on the carpet. He twisted his kitten's tail till it mewed in anguish. He put garbage in his parents' bed and burned holes in his sister's clothes. (i) He was extraordinarily [*adjective*]. (ii) His parents intended to send him to a special school . . .

According to the adjective we supply at the bracketed segment, either (i) or (ii) could be a fitting place to begin a new paragraph.

If the adjective is *wicked*, *naughty*, *ill-behaved*, we might well start a new paragraph at (ii). The preceding part would have had a stack-like structure and the sentence 'He was extraordinarily ill-behaved' would fittingly round it off with a rather self-evident conclusion.

If, on the other hand, the adjective is *intelligent*, *gifted*, *musical*, or some other item not suggested by the account of his behaviour, then (i) would be a fitting – one might say essential – point at which to begin a new paragraph. This would reveal a totally different aspect of the boy, and the text might go on to describe the special school at which his intelligence or other positive gifts could be suitably developed.

The sentence

19.34 In an analogous way, the decision to divide a paragraph into orthographic sentences depends on how the writer wishes these smaller sections of the text to be seen in relation to each other: intimately linked as though naturally indissociable (no punctuation); closely associated but separate (comma or semicolon, according to degree); relatively separate (pointed as independent sentences). Compare the different implications of the following:

I saw Miriam and Walter. [1]
I saw Miriam, and Walter. [2]
I saw Miriam – and Walter! [3]
I saw Miriam. And Walter. [4]

In [1], the normal and expected form, it seems to be suggested that Miriam and Walter are a couple who regularly appear together. This is not so in [2–4], where the punctuation may carry various implications according to the larger context. In [2], the two persons are being listed; in [3], the sight of Walter in addition to Miriam is given special and dramatic significance; in [4], Walter seems to be mentioned as an afterthought. But the suggested motivations for [3] and [4] might be expressed by either of the punctuation forms according to the taste of the writer or his belief in their communicative impact on the reader. Since punctuation is subject to fairly rigorous convention, many writers hesitate to show individuality, originality, or rhetorical effects by this means. Instead they will select grammatical constructions and carefully selected lexical items which they hope may achieve effects that in speech would be without difficulty indicated by prosodic features. Punctuation choices are made (along with grammatical and lexical ones) in the hope of providing the reader with the cues necessary for assigning the prosody that the writer would himself have used in uttering the text aloud.

But as readers we have an obligation too. In listening to a spoken text, we automatically respond to the prosodic features that help to mould its structure. When we read, we have to create those prosodic features from the visual print. Stumbling as we read is a common experience: the further context then tells us of an earlier misinterpretation and we have to go back and reread a portion of the text, redistributing our imagined internal stresses and nuclei. Sometimes the fault is in the ineptness of the writer, but often it lies in our lack of sympathetic alertness to the textual structure in front of us.

The part played by questions

19.35 There is a sense in which it is true to say 'I can't tell you anything till you've asked me something'. In other words, what we choose to talk about depends crucially on what we think our hearer does not know but wants to know. Even conversations in which a participant keenly wishes to talk and inform (rather than listen and be informed) will frequently begin with a question. For example, as a conversation-initial gambit:

Have you heard about Mr Malloy? [1]

The questioner will be alert to the reply in two quite separate respects: whether his companion has heard about Mr Malloy, and whether he seems to *want* to hear. Only if the questioner is satisfied on both counts, will he launch forth – and even so, without prompting by questions in the course of his account ('What was the weather like?' 'When did you hear this?' 'Why didn't Rita Malloy . . .?'), the speaker would soon falter, fearing that he has lost his companion's interest or not knowing which aspects of the narrative to develop and which to ignore.

In the absence of questions from a companion, a speaker may insert them for himself and in written materials, the author has no option. The motive is partly information processing (*cf* 19.40*f*), that is, providing a focus closely similar to that attained by the pseudo-cleft (*cf* 18.20). Compare:

What was he doing? He was trying to change a fuse. [2]
What was he doing but trying to change a fuse. [2a]
What he was doing was trying to change a fuse. [2b]

But in part the inserted question is to enliven and dramatize a narrative by supplying a query which the speaker thinks must be in his companion's mind – or which he thinks ought to be:

And that son of hers continues to be a big worry. And how do I know? She was in tears the other day – with a photo of him in her hand. She didn't think I saw the photo but I did. [3]

NOTE [a] A question in discourse is often directed less to the hearer than to the speaker, though in seeming to reflect the speaker's self-questioning as to how he should proceed, it equally directs the hearer's mind both to this point and to the tentativeness and spontaneity with which it is being made. For example:

The horses seemed strangely disturbed as we groomed them that morning. *How shall I put it?* It was as though they were aware that Mary and I had quarrelled. [4]

[b] Questions in dialogue may be uttered merely to elicit matter that was imperfectly heard or understood:

WHÁT's that! } ⟨informal⟩
SÓRRy? }
I beg your PÁRdon?

Questions as directives

19.36 Questions, direct and indirect, have an important role in discourse as polite equivalents of requests. On entering someone's room, a visitor will begin with such a question even if he is a fairly close friend:

Is this an awkward moment to see you about something?
Am I disturbing you?
Got a second? ⟨informal⟩
I wonder if I could talk to you for a minute.

These opening gambits would preface discourse itself. But question forms may equally preface physical action by the speaker or seek it from the hearer:

Would you mind if I closed the window?
Would you excuse me a moment? I must find a telephone.
Do you think you could lock the door when you leave?
Why don't you come and have dinner with me tonight?

Unlike questions seeking information, these can be coordinated (especially in AmE) with statements and combine a request with an expression of intention:

Why don't I go on ahead and you (can) come when you're ready?
Why don't you get a taxi and I'll be out in a minute?

In the conventional language of formal meetings, procedure is often couched in elaborately interrogative structures, each widely recognized as a formula disguising a statement:

But may we not ask ourselves whether this is an appropriate time to raise taxes? [='I am opposed to raising taxes now']
I wonder if we might now turn to the next item. [='The present discussion is closed']
Am I alone in thinking the motion is out of order?

Rhetorical questions

19.37 The rhetorical question has in common with the formulaic questions discussed in 19.36 the fact that the answer is a foregone conclusion:

She said she had been too ill to come to work that day, and certainly she sounded pretty groggy on the phone. Anyway, who was I to argue? [='I wasn't in a position to doubt her word'] [1]
The prisoners were grumbling about their cold cells and poor food. Who could blame them? [='No one could blame them'] [2]

As we see from these examples, the rhetorical question is by no means confined to the highly wrought prose of formal speeches of persuasion that we may think of in connection with 'rhetoric'. Indeed, the tag question so common in the most informal speech is strictly similar to the rhetorical question in its communicative effect, since it essentially seeks confirmation of what the speaker has explicitly assumed (by the preceding declarative) to be agreed truth:

It's a glorious day, *isn't it*? [3]
Joan Sutherland was the best coloratura singer of her generation, *wasn't she*? [4]

Compare:

When have we had a better coloratura singer than Joan Sutherland? [4a]

NOTE Such a use of tags occurs in very informal speech (especially BrE and chiefly nonstandard) where the hearer cannot possibly be expected to know the answer or to take it for granted, but where the speaker seeks by such use of the question form to imply that the answer ought to be self-evident. These tags have a falling tone on the operator:

> Well, I couldn't hear the phone, could I? It's in the next room and the door was shut. Besides, I was fast asleep, wasn't I? But I can't expect you to think of things from my angle, can I? [5]

Participant involvement

19.38 Whether this is made explicit or not, every text is addressed *by* someone ('I') *to* someone else ('you'). In many cases, the relation of both participants is quite explicit:

> *I* tell *you* it's true! [1]

But equally both can be merely implicit:

> Good luck! [= '*I* wish *you* good luck'] [2]

In very formal communications, where the precise identity of the addressee is unknown and where the originator is making the communication on behalf of an organization, the participants may be referred to in the 3rd person:

> *The management* regret(s) any inconvenience to *clients* during repair work to the premises. [3]

In a similar tone and often for similiar reasons, mention of one or both of the participants is avoided altogether:

> *The management* regrets any inconvenience during repair work to the premises. [3a]
> Any inconvenience to *clients* is regretted during . . . [3b]
> Any inconvenience is regretted during . . . [3c]

In some texts, both participants are referred to simultaneously by means of the inclusive *we* (*cf* 6.10, 19.20):

> So now *we* know why there was no traffic coming towards *us* on this road. Well, since the road is obviously blocked, *we'll* have to turn back and find a side road somewhere. [4]

In much discourse, neither the addressee nor the authority for information seems necessary:

> Julian is going to Detroit next week. In fact, if he likes it and finds a job, he may decide to stay there. His wife, of course, comes from that part of Michigan. [5]

We notice, however, that in the use of the adverbial *of course* the speaker/writer is appealing to the addressee's shared knowledge. Nor would it be unusual in such a text for the author to make explicit his relation to the information conveyed:

> Julian, *I gather*, is going to Detroit next week. In fact, if he likes it and finds a job, *he tells me* he may decide . . . [5a]

Even in a signed letter, some amplification of identity may be necessary if the writer feels it necessary to specify his role:

> As a Camden resident and also as a qualified accountant, I write to inform you of an error in the recently published expenditure figures of your Council . . . [6]

On the telephone, identification of both speaker and addressee usually prefaces discourse:

> Hello. Is that Peter? Marjorie here. What? Oh sorry! – Marjorie Wong, your wife's assistant. Is Valerie there? [7]
>
> Hello. Am I speaking to the Controller? This is the Works Department. We are having to cut off your electricity supply for an hour or so . . . [8]

NOTE The addressee may equally need to have his role specified in the particular context: *you* may be friend, wife, mother, doctor, neighbour, according to who is in communication and on what occasion:

> I wonder if I can ask you – as a friend rather than as my doctor – if you think I ought to give up smoking. I know that you discourage your children – but is this as a mother or as a doctor or because you know it affects your husband's breathing? [9]

Speaker/hearer contact

19.39 But in addition to establishing identity of participants and to indicating authority for content, textual structure tends to be punctuated by periodic references to both participants. The hearer is addressed by name, not for clarity but out of courtesy and friendliness. The speaker may repeatedly refer to himself, often successfully giving thereby an impression of courtesy and modesty rather than of egocentricity:

> I'd like you to know . . . I think . . . I hear . . . I seem to remember . . . it occurs to me . . . I mean . . . [1]

A communication from a body or organization may self-refer similarly:

> Your union officials suggest . . . we acknowledge . . . we claim . . . we hope . . . [2]

Direct allusions and appeals to the addressee are especially characteristic of speech, informally with interspersed comment clauses, *you see*, *you know*, *get it?*, *do you follow me?*, *yes?*, *right?*; more formally, *as you well know, as you may know, if I make myself clear (to you), if you will pardon the allusion.*

Addressee involvement obviously serves two related functions, often distinguished by intonation. On the one hand, the speaker wants assurance that the addressee is following the communication in all its detail and allusion; in this spirit, the involvement is essentially interrogative (*cf* 19.35) and the inserted items have a rising nucleus:

I'm writing my own software, you SÉE. [3]

On the other hand, the inserts may be assurances to the addressee that he is not being underestimated and that it is highly probable that he knows the facts already. In this case, they have a falling nucleus or are uttered with low prominence carrying no nucleus at all:

| she has reMÀRried you know | [4]

Individuals differ in the extent to which they intersperse terms of address in discourse. In letters, they are used almost solely in the initial salutation: *Dear Mrs Robinson, Dear Fred*; but between intimates, items like *darling* commonly accompany sentences throughout, as they would do in the corresponding speech. Letters to strangers can freely begin *Dear Sir* (less freely *Dear Madam*), and in formal style they may end *I remain, Sir, Yours faithfully*. A general letter may begin *Gentlemen* (rather than ?*Dear Gentlemen*), or *Dear Sirs*, or *Ladies and Gentlemen*.

In speech, it is normal to address a group as *Ladies and Gentlemen*; a group of men as *Gentlemen* (or, in military and analogous usage, as *Men*, though this would hardly be text-initial). At a formally constituted meeting, it is equally normal for individuals to be addressed as *Sir*, to or from the chair, less comfortably as *Madam*. But in chance encounters with strangers, severe constraints are felt over terms of address, especially in BrE. A request such as *I wonder if you could direct me to Pitt Street?* would in AmE (and especially in Southern AmE), be accompanied very widely by *Sir* or *Ma'am*, irrespective of the speaker's sex or an adult addressee's age. In BrE, *Sir* would be rather rare, and would be used chiefly by younger men addressing older men; it would almost never be used by women. *Madam*, though the only fully acceptable form of address to a woman, is felt to be inappropriate in most informal circumstances (though it is used in addressing customers, clients, etc). In general, women can use neither *Sir* nor *Madam* except where the speaker is in a recognizably serving role, though women students will occasionally address a male teacher as *Sir*.

NOTE [a] A younger woman is sometimes addressed by men as *Miss*, but this is widely regarded as nonstandard or felt to be demeaning to the person addressed. In nonstandard use, *Lady*, *Mister*, and *Missus* occur freely in men's speech; and *lady* also has an ironic use which is not uneducated but informal (and addressed to a woman who is *not* a stranger):

Oh, *you* can't use that argument, lady.

Man is also used to acquaintances (esp in AmE), but more familiarly than the foregoing use of *lady*.

[b] Just as a speaker involves the addressee with insertions like *right?*, *you know*, so the addressee reassures the speaker with similar short comments: *Oh I see*, *Yes I know*, *Right*.

[c] The inserts for involvement and authority sometimes occur with prosodic prominence. There is, for example, a triumphant or retributive *you see*, as in the following (uttered with a wide range of pitch, in contrast to that normal in comment clauses):

So I was RÌGHT | you "SÉE |

Compare also:

She has reMÀRried {I think / I THĬNK}

Here, the first variant is little more than a conventional reluctance to seem dogmatic, but the second is meant to express serious reservations about the truth of what has preceded. Note also:

He tries, but YÒU KNÓW, there are real problems. [='I scarcely need to remind you']

Information processing

19.40 It is appropriate to treat this aspect of grammatical organization last, since, being more centrally significant than any other, information processing has already to no small degree been seen as the motivation behind other specific features of grammar discussed elsewhere. It is paramount in the use of coordination and subordination (*cf* 19.26*ff*), and it was specifically mentioned in the treatment of questions (*cf* 19.35). Consider a sequence like the following:

Our economic troubles continue to resist solution. We have tried subsidizing our weaker industries. We have experimented with import controls. We have on occasion resorted to the drastic device of devaluation. To no avail. *How then are we to proceed?* The answer lies in higher productivity and better products. [1]

The italicized question is pivotal in this text. It contains the conjunct *then* with anaphoric reference: the remedies already tried, which have been of 'no avail', are put behind us. The question both points forward (and this is lexically matched by 'The answer' which follows) and prepares us for a climactic alternative strategy. A similar anticipation of the information focus would have been:

. . . To no avail. *The way forward* is to seek higher . . . [1a]

The essence of such anticipation is to indicate in general terms what is to follow (we are going to 'proceed', there is a 'way forward') and hence both to prepare the hearer/reader and to arouse his interest. Note the comparable function of the italicized *where*-clause in the next example:

> Robert Adam was in many respects typical of British architects of the eighteenth century. Like Inigo Jones and Lord Burlington, he drew eagerly on the inspiration both of the Renaissance and of Antiquity. He shared the enthusiasm of his contemporaries for collecting classical marbles. He was far from being alone in undertaking venturesome travel in the Mediterranean and in gazing with wonder at vase fragments and at sundrenched monuments. He was quintessentially a member of the Neo-classical movement. *Where he stands apart* is in his refusal to regard Antiquity as inviolable. It was an inspiration for new work, not a model for imitation. [2]

The major part of the paragraph is illustrative of the claim that Adam was typical of his time. The writer has one piece of counter-evidence, and he could have expressed this by the mere use of adversative *but*:

> . . . a member of the Neo-classical movement. But he refused to regard . . . [2a]

This would have made the point for an alert reader, though the exceptional feature would have been expressed rather tamely. The fact that we had come to an exception could have been more insistently expressed for the less alert reader by a further alternative:

> . . . a member of the Neo-classical movement. But there is one respect in which he stands apart: he refused to regard . . . [2b]

The writer, might, however, have arrived at a compromise between [2b] and [2], as follows:

> . . . a member of the Neo-classical movement. But he stands apart in his refusal to regard . . . [2c]

NOTE Informationally, [2c] is a subtle improvement over [2b] in seeming to assume (by the nominalization, *his refusal*) a significant item of shared knowledge. The writer credits his reader with being aware that Adam had this degree of creative independence. In fact, the original version [2] shows the writer going one better than this. He not merely achieves the objective of warning the reader that we have come to one respect in which Adam 'stands apart'; use of the pseudo-cleft (18.20) enables him also to imply that the reader was well-informed enough to know that there was such a standing apart (as well as that Adam did not 'regard Antiquity as inviolable'), and that in consequence we have now simply arrived at the point of restating it. In presenting what may well be new information as though it were given (*cf* 18.4), the writer treats his reader with flattering respect as well as enabling himself to make the main point with great force and economy.

19.41 The highlighting of the main information is associated with intonation nucleus, but in writing we have to plan carefully if we are to guide our reader so as to assign the focus in the way we intend.

Imagine an argument conducted by correspondence, where Mrs A has written to say that she denies any responsibility for a certain problem. After a week or so, she gets a reply from Mr B:

> Let me set out the case as I see it and try to show you that the problem has something to do with you. [1]

Mrs A will probably read the last phrase as having the normal end-focus (18.5):

> . . . the | problem has something to do with YÒU | [1a]

But Mr B's words are in fact a paraphrase of a remark in Mrs A's own letter: they are 'given' information; all that is new is the positive (assertion) in place of Mrs A's original negative (denial). Thus B has meant it to be read as:

> . . . the | problem HÀS something to do with you | [1b]

The required shift away from the normal (but here unwanted) end-focus could have been achieved in the first place by some such device as emphatic *do* or an inserted subjunct (or both), thus drawing attention to the new polarity:

> . . . the problem does (indeed) have something to do with you. [2]

which Mrs A would promptly have read with the required prosody:

> . . . the | problem {does inDÈED / DÒES} have something to do with you. | [2a]

Information and sequence

19.42 Much of what we have been saying in this book about the processing of information concerns sequence. The order of presentation is clearly vital, whether we are concerned with premodifying adjectives, a group of noun phrases, a pair of independent clauses, a sequence comprising a matrix clause and a subordinate clause, or of course the elements within a single clause. We have choices such as:

> {an intricate and arduous task [1a]
> {an arduous and intricate task [1b]
>
> {the cold night and the difficult journey [2a]
> {the difficult journey and the cold night [2b]
>
> {They cheered and they sang. [3a]
> {They sang and they cheered. [3b]
>
> {I saw the broken window when I arrived home. [4a]
> {When I arrived home, I saw the broken window. [4b]

Our memories of past crises were being added to our uncertainties for the future. [5a]
To our uncertainties for the future were being added our memories of past crises. [5b]

More is involved here than sequence, of course. As well as deciding on a pair (or longer set) of units, we have to decide on the actual choice of lexical items. Are they to be near-synonyms or are they to be in sharp contrast? In either case, should they prosodically resemble each other (*eg* by alliterating, having the same number of syllables, the same stress pattern: *eg*: *arduous* and *intricate*), or should they differ in these respects (*eg*: *tough* and *intricate*)? Formal similarity often conveys a sense both of euphony and of a harmony between substance and meaning; formal dissimilarity, on the other hand, can convey a sense of richness and variety. Considerations of euphony enter also into the question of sequencing, but for the most part, both in the selection of items and in their placement, we are concerned with 'the right words in the right place'.

Whatever is placed first will seem relatively introductory and 'scene-setting'. Clearly, *preparing* our hearer or reader for what is to follow is of the greatest importance if the following part is to have the proper impact. The converse of this is that whatever is placed last will be expected to be relatively consequential, of greater importance, and possibly climactic. So in choosing between [1a] and [1b], our decision may depend on whether we wish to convey that the task was arduous *because* it was intricate; intricate and *above all* arduous; arduous in *being* intricate; arduous and *furthermore* intricate. In choosing between [3a] and [3b], we may wish to imply one or other chronological sequence: that they did one thing before the other. But if the two actions are but different aspects of the same celebratory behaviour, we have decisions to make on similar principles to those concerning us in [1a] and [1b], [2a] and [2b]. With [4a] and [4b], however, the order will probably be contextually determined: one or other, the arrival or the seeing, will be relatively 'given' (that is, the hearer/reader will already have been told or been led to expect that the subject went home or that a window had been broken), and whichever is in consequence the relatively 'new' item will be placed in final position if a feeble anticlimactic 'tail' is to be avoided. So again with [5a] and [5b]: the former will be preferred if the preceding part of the text has been dealing with 'past crises' and the intention is to go on to some discussion of the future; if the converse holds, [5b] will be selected.

NOTE Some matters of sequence are determined by courtesy, convention, or idiom. In formal circumstances, women are named in address before men, and the speaker is mentioned last:

Ladies and gentlemen! It gives me great pleasure . . .
Harry and I were dismayed.

In 3rd person mention, however, sequence can freely depend upon the speaker's decision:

Joan and Peter } will be coming..
Peter and Joan }

I saw lots of { boys and girls.
{ girls and boys.

On the other hand, we have a conventional mention of males first in *(the) men and women, he and she, Mr and Mrs (Jones)*. Numerous other sequences are idiomatically fixed (as in *give and take, pots and pans, knife and fork, (Do you take) milk and sugar?)* Doubtless these have become fixed historically in response to the operation of prosodic or semantic pressures, but there are also principles like 'Short before long' and 'General setting before specific object'. *Cf* on binomials, 13.26 Note.

Bibliographical note

For general treatments and theoretical discussion of discourse and textual structure, see Beaugrande and Dressler (1981); Brown and Yule (1983); Cole and Morgan (1975); D'Angelo (1975); Dijk (1977, 1987); Grice (1975); Halliday (1978); Halliday and Hasan (1976); Hoey (1983); Nash (1980); Quirk (1986); Stubbs (1983); Winter (1982); Winterowd (1975).

On specific aspects of discourse, see Altenberg (1986); Biber (1986, 1988); Bublitz (1980, 1988); Crystal (1980); Edmondson (1981); Fleischmann (1985); Motsch (1987); Norrick (1987); Schenkein (1978); Svartvik (1980); Wierzbicka (1986).

Other relevant studies include: Brazil (1985); Chafe (1976); Condon (1986); Firbas (1979); Hawkins (1978); Kempson (1977); Li (1976); Mann and Thompson (1986); Quirk and Stein (1990); Schiffrin (1981); Sinclair (1980); Stenström (1984); Yee (1975).

Bibliography

Aarts, B. (1988) 'Concessive Clauses in Written Present-Day British English', *J of English Linguistics* **21**, 39–58

Aarts, B. (1989) 'Verb-Preposition Constructions and Small Clauses', *J of Linguistics* **25**, 277–290

Aarts, J. and J. P. Calbert (1979) *Metaphor and Non-Metaphor: The Semantics of Adjective-Noun Combinations*, Tübingen: Niemeyer

Adamczewski, H. (1978) *BE+ING dans la grammaire de l'anglais contemporain*, Lille: Atelier Reproduction des Thèses

Aijmer, K. (1972) *Some Aspects of Psychological Predicates in English*, Stockholm Studies in English 24, Stockholm: Almqvist and Wiksell

Akimoto, M. (1983) *Idiomaticity*, Tokyo: Shinozaki Shorin

Alexander, D. and P. H. Matthews (1964) 'Adjectives before *That*-Clauses in English', Linguistic Research Project, Indiana University

Algeo, J. (1973) *On Defining the Proper Name*, Gainesville: University of Florida Press

Algeo, J. (1990) 'It's a Myth, innit?' in *The State of the Language*, edd C. Ricks and L. Michaels, 443–450, Berkeley: University of California Press

Allen, R. L. (1966) *The Verb System of Present-Day American English*, The Hague: Mouton.

Allerton, D. J. (1979) *Essentials of Grammatical Theory*, London: Routledge

Allerton, D. J. (1980) 'Grammatical Subject as a Psycholinguistic Category', *Transactions of the Philological Society*, 62–80

Allerton, D. J. (1982) *Valency and the English Verb*, New York: Academic Press

Allerton, D. J. (1987) 'The Linguistics and Sociolinguistic Status of Proper Names', *J of Pragmatics* **11**, 61–92

Altenberg, B. (1984) 'Causal Linking in Spoken and Written English', *Studia Linguistica* **38**, 20–69

Altenberg, B. (1986) 'Contrastive Linking in Spoken and Written English', in *English in Speech and Writing: A Symposium*, edd G. Tottie and I. Bäcklund, 13–40, Uppsala: Almqvist and Wiksell

Anderson, J. (1977) *On Case Grammar*, New York: Humanities Press

Anderson, S. R. (1976) 'Pro-Sentential Forms and Their Implications for English Sentence Structure', in McCawley (1976), 165–200

Andersson, E. (1985) *On Verb Complementation in Written English*, Lund Studies in English 71, Lund: Gleerup/Liber.

André, E. (1974) *Studies in the Correspondence between English Intonation and the Noun Phrase in English Grammar*, Liège: Université

Attal, J. P. (1987) *Grammaire et usage de l'anglais*, Paris: Ducolot

Austin, F. (1980) ' "A cresent-shaped jewel of an island", Appositive Nouns in Phrases Separated by *of*', *English Studies* **61**, 357–366

Austin, J. L. (1962) *How to Do Things with Words*, Oxford: University Press

Auwera, J. Van der (1980) (ed) *The Semantics of Determiners*, London: Croom Helm

Bache, C. (1978) *The Order of Premodifying Adjectives in Present-Day English*, Odense: University Press

Bache, C. (1982) 'Aspect and Aktionsart: Towards a Semantic Distinction', *J of Linguistics* **18**, 57–72

Bäcklund, I. (1984) *Conjunction-Headed Abbreviated Clauses in English*, Studia Anglistica Upsaliensia 50, Stockholm: Almqvist and Wiksell

Bäcklund, U. (1970) *The Collocation of Adverbs of Degree in English*, Uppsala English and American Theses 1

Bailey, C.-J. N. and R. W. Shuy (1973) (edd) *New Ways of Analyzing Variation in English*, Washington, DC: Georgetown University Press

Bailey, R. W. and M. Görlach (1982) (edd) *English as a World Language*, Ann Arbor: University of Michigan Press

Bald, W. D. (1979) 'English Tag-Questions and Intonation', in *Anglistentag 1979*, ed K. Schuhmann, 263–291, Berlin: Technische Universität

Bald, W. D. (1980) 'Some Functions of *yes* and *no* in Conversation', in Greenbaum, Leech, and Svartvik (1980), 178–191.

Baron, N. S. (1971) 'On Defining "Cognate Object" ', *Glossa* **5**, 71–98

Bartsch, R. (1976) *The Grammar of Adverbials. A Study in the Semantics and Syntax of Adverbial Constructions*, Amsterdam: North-Holland

Beaugrande, R. de (1983) *Text Production*, Norwood: Ablex

Beaugrande, R. de and W. Dressler (1981) *Introduction to Text Linguistics*, London: Longman

Behre, F. (1955) *Meditative-Polemic* SHOULD *in Modern English* THAT*-Clauses*, Gothenburg Studies in English 4, Göteborg: Acta Universitatis Gothoburgensis

Behre, F. (1973) *Get, Come and Go. Some Aspects of Situational Grammar*, Gothenburg Studies in English 28, Göteborg: Acta Universitatis Gothoburgensis

Bennett, D. C. (1975) *Spatial and Temporal Uses of English Prepositions. An Essay in Stratificational Semantics*, London: Longman

Bennett, P. A. (1980) 'English Passives: A Study in Syntactic Change and Relational Grammar', *Lingua* **51**, 101–114

Biber, D. (1986) 'Spoken and Written Textual Dimensions in English', *Language* **62**, 384–414

Biber, D. (1988) *Variation across Speech and Writing*, Cambridge: University Press

Bolinger, D. (1957) *Interrogative Structures of American English*, Birmingham, Ala.: University of Alabama Press

Bolinger, D. (1967a) 'Adjectives in English: Attribution and Predication', *Lingua* **18**, 1–34

Bolinger, D. (1967b) 'Adjective Comparison: A Semantic Scale,' *J of English Linguistics* **1**, 2–10

Bolinger, D. (1967c) 'The Imperative in English', *To Honor Roman Jakobson* I, 335–363, The Hague: Mouton

Bolinger, D. (1971) *The Phrasal Verb in English*, Cambridge, Mass.: Harvard University Press

Bolinger, D. (1972a) *Degree Words*, The Hague: Mouton

Bolinger, D. (1972b) (ed) *Intonation*, Harmondsworth: Penguin

Bolinger, D. (1977) *Meaning and Form*, London: Longman

Bolinger, D. (1979) 'Pronouns in Discourse', *Syntax and Semantics* 12, 289–309

Bolinger, D. (1980) *Language – The Loaded Weapon: The Use and Abuse of Language Today*, London: Longman

Brazil, D. C. (1985) *The Communicative Value of Intonation*, ELR Monograph, University of Birmingham

Breivik, L. E. (1983) *Existential* There: *A Synchronic and Diachronic Study*, Studia Anglistica Norvegica 2, Bergen: Department of English

Bresnan, J. (1973) 'Syntax of the Comparative Clause Construction', *Linguistic Inquiry* **4**, 275–343

Bresnan, J. and J. Grimshaw (1978) 'The Syntax of Free Relatives in English', *Linguistic Inquiry* **9**, 331–391

Brown, G. (1977) *Listening to Spoken English*, London: Longman

Brown, G., K. L. Durrie, and J. Kenworthy (1980) *Questions of Intonation*, London: Croom Helm

Brown, G. and G. Yule (1983) *Discourse Analysis*, Cambridge: Cambridge University Press

Bublitz, W. (1980) 'Höflichkeit im Englischen', *Linguistik und Didaktik* **41**, 56–70

Bublitz, W. (1988) *Supportive Fellow-Speakers and Cooperative Conversations*, Amsterdam: Benjamins

Burton-Roberts, N. C. (1977) 'Generic Sentences and Analyticity', *Studies in Language* **1**, 155—196

Burton-Roberts, N. C. (1986a) 'Thematic Predicates and the Pragmatics of Non-descriptive Definition', *J of Linguistics* **22**, 41–66

Burton-Roberts, N. C. (1986b) 'Implications of the Pragmatics of Non-descriptive Definition', *J of Linguistics* **22**, 311–329

Buysschaert, J. (1982) *Criteria for the Classification of English Adverbials*, Brussels: Koninklijke Academie

Buyssens, E. (1979) 'The Active Voice with Passive Meaning in Modern English', *English Studies* **60**, 745–761

Buyssens, E. (1987) 'The Preposition *for* with an Infinitive Clause', *English Studies* **68**, 336–347

Carden, G. (1973) *English Quantifiers*, Tokyo: Taishukan

Cattell, R. (1973) 'Negative Transportation and Tag Questions', *Language* **49**, 612–639

Chafe, W. (1976) 'Givenness, Contrastiveness, Definiteness, Subjects, Topics, and Point of View', in Li (1976), 25–55

Chomsky, N. (1972) 'Remarks on Nominalization', *Studies on Semantics in Generative Grammar*, 11–61, The Hague: Mouton

Coates, J. (1983) *The Semantics of the Modal Auxiliaries*, London: Croom Helm

Cole, P. and J. L. Morgan (1975) (edd) *Syntax and Semantics* 3; *Speech Acts*, New York: Academic Press

Cole, P. and J.M. Sadock (1977) (edd) *Syntax and Semantics* 8: *An Introduction to Grammatical Relations*, New York: Academic Press

Colen, A. (1984) *A Syntactic and Semantic Study of English Predicative Nominals*, Brussels: Koninklijke Academie

Comrie, B. (1976) *Aspect*, Cambridge: University Press

Comrie, B. (1981) *Language Universals and Lan-*

guage Typology, Oxford: Blackwell

Condon, S. L. (1986) 'The Discourse Functions of OK', *Semiotica* **60**, 73–101

Cooper, C. R. and S. Greenbaum (1986) *Studying Writing: Linguistic Approaches*, Beverly Hills: Sage

Couper-Kuhlen, E. (1979) *The Prepositional Passive in English*, Tübingen; Niemeyer

Cowie, A. P. and R. Mackin (1975) *Oxford Dictionary of Current Idiomatic English 1: Verbs with Prepositions and Particles*, Oxford: University Press

Cruse, D. A. (1973) 'Some Thoughts on Agentivity', *J of Linguistics* **9**, 11–23

Cruttenden, A. (1981) 'Falls and Rises: Meanings and Universals', *J of Linguistics* **17**, 77–91

Crymes, R. (1968) *Some Systems of Substitution Correlations in Modern American English*, The Hague: Mouton

Crystal, D. (1966) 'Specification and English Tenses', *J of Linguistics* **2**, 1–34

Crystal, D. (1969) *Prosodic Systems and Intonation in English*, Cambridge: University Press

Crystal, D. (1980) 'Neglected Grammatical Factors in Conversational English', in Greenbaum, Leech, and Svartvik (1980), 153–166

Dahl, L. (1971) 'The *s*-Genitive with Non-Personal Nouns in Modern English Journalistic Style', *Neuphilologische Mitteilungen* **72**, 140–172

Dahl, Ö. (1974) *Topic and Comment: Contextual Boundness and Focus*, Hamburg: Buske

Daneš, F. (1974) *Papers on Functional Sentence Perspective*, The Hague: Mouton

D'Angelo, F. (1975) *A Conceptual Theory of Rhetoric*, Cambridge, Mass.: Winthrop

Daniels, H. A. (1983) *Famous Last Words: The American Language Crisis Reconsidered*, Carbondale and Edwardsville: Southern Illinois University Press

Davidson, A. (1980) 'Peculiar Passives', *Language* **56**, 42–66

Declerck, R. (1979) 'Tense and Modality in English *Before*-Clauses', *English Studies* **60**, 720-744

Declerck, R. (1986) 'The Manifold Interpretations of Generic Sentences', *Lingua* **68**, 149–188

Dietrich, T. G. and D. J. Napoli (1982) 'Comparative *rather*', *J of Linguistics* **18**, 137–165

Dijk, T. A. van (1977) *Text and Context*, London: Longman

Dijk, T. A. van (1985) *Handbook of Discourse Analysis*, Orlando: Academic Press

Dik, S. C. (1968) *Coordination: Its Implications for the Theory of General Linguistics*, Amsterdam: North-Holland

Dik, S. C. (1978) *Functional Grammar*, Amsterdam: North-Holland

Dixon, R. M. W. (1982a) *Where Have All the Adjectives Gone? and Other Essays in Semantics and Syntax*, Berlin: Mouton

Dixon, R. M. W. (1982b) 'The Grammar of English Phrasal Verbs', *Australian J of Linguistics* **2**, 1–42

Dougherty, R. C. (1970–71) 'A Grammar of Coordinate Conjoined Structures', I, *Language* **46**, 850–898; II, **47**, 298–339

Downes, W. (1977) 'The Imperative and Pragmatics', *J of Linguistics* **13**, 77–97

Downing, B. T. (1978) 'Some Universals of Relative Clause Structure', in Greenberg, Ferguson, and Moravcsik (1978), 375–418

Dudman, V. H. (1984) 'Conditional Interpretations of *if*-Sentences', *Australian J of Linguistics* **4**, 143–204

Edgren, E. (1971) *Temporal Clauses in English*, Uppsala: Almqvist and Wiksell

Edmondson, W. (1981) *Spoken Discourse*, London: Longman

Ek, J.A. van (1966) *Four Complementary Structures of Predication in Contemporary English*, Groningen: Wolters

Ellegård, A. (1978) *The Syntactic Structure of English Texts: A Computer-based Study of Four Kinds of Text in the Brown University Corpus*, Gothenburg Studies in English 43, Göteborg: Acta Universitatis Gothoburgensis

Elsness, J. (1982) '*That v.* Zero Connective in English Nominal Clauses', *ICAME News* 6, ed S. Johansson, 1–45, Bergen: Norwegian Computing Centre for the Humanities

Emons, R. (1974) *Valenzen englischer Prädikatsverben*, Tübingen: Niemeyer

Enkvist, N.E. (1980) 'Marked Focus: Functions and Constraints', in Greenbaum, Leech, and Svartvik (1980), 134–152

Enkvist, N.E. (1987) 'A Parametric View of Word-Order', in E. Sozer (ed) *Text Connexity, Text Coherence*, Hamburg: Buske, 320–336

Erdmann, P. (1976) *THERE-sentences in English*, Munich: Tuduv

Erdmann, P. (1981) 'Preposed *Ing*-Forms in English', *Folia Linguistica* **15**, 363–386

Faber, D. (1987) 'The Accentuation of Intransitive Sentences in English', *J of Linguistics* **23**, 341–358

Ferguson, C. A. and S. B. Heath (1981) (edd) *Language in the USA*, Cambridge: University Press

Fillmore, C. (1968) 'The Case for Case', in *Universals in Linguistic Theory*, edd E. Bach and R. T. Harms, 1-90, New York: Holt, Rinehart, and Winston

Fillmore, C. (1977a) 'Topics in Lexical Semantics', in *Current Issues in Linguistic Theory*, ed R. W. Cole, 76-138, Bloomington, Ind.

Fillmore, C. (1977b) 'The Case for Case Reopened', in *Syntax and Semantics* 8: *Grammatical Relations*, edd P. Cole and J. Sadock, 59-82, New York: Academic Press

Fillmore, C. and D. T. Langendoen (1971) (edd) *Studies in Linguistic Semantics*, New York: Holt, Rinehart and Winston

Firbas, J. (1979) 'A Functional View of "Ordo Naturalis"', *Brno Studies in English* **13**, 29-59

Firbas, J. (1986) 'On the Dynamics of Written Communication in the Light of the Theory of Functional Sentence Perspective', in Cooper and Greenbaum (1986), 40-71

Fishman, J. A., R. L. Cooper, and A. W. Conrad (1977) (edd) *The Spread of English: The Sociology of English as an Additional Language*, Rowley, Mass.: Newbury House

Fjelkestam-Nilsson, B. (1983) *ALSO and TOO: A Corpus-Based Study of their Frequency and Use in Modern English*, Stockholm Studies in English 58, Stockholm: Almqvist and Wiksell

Fleischmann, S. (1985) 'Discourse Function of Tense-Aspect Oppositions in Narrative', *Linguistics* **23**, 851-882

Fraser, B. (1976) *The Verb-Particle Combination in English*, New York: Academic Press

Freed, A. (1979) *The Semantics of English Aspectual Complementation*, Dordrecht: Reidel

Givon, T. (1979) *Understanding Grammar*, New York: Academic Press

Givon, T. (1984) *Syntax: A Functional-Typological Introduction*, Vol I, Amsterdam: Benjamins

Gleitman, L.R. (1965) 'Coordinating Conjunctions in English', *Language* **41**, 260-293

Gnutzmann, C., R. Ilson, and J. Webster (1973) 'Comparative Constructions in Contemporary English', *English Studies* **54**, 417-438

Granger, S. (1983) *The* Be + Past Participle *Construction in Spoken English with Special Emphasis on the Passive*, Amsterdam: North-Holland

Greenbaum, S. (1969) *Studies in English Adverbial Usage*, London: Longman

Greenbaum, S. (1970) *Verb-Intensifier Collocations in English: An Experimental Approach*, The Hague: Mouton

Greenbaum, S. (1973) 'Adverbial *-ing* Participle Constructions in English', *Anglia* **91**, 1-10

Greenbaum, S. (1974) 'Problems in the Negation of Modals', *Moderna Språk* **68**, 244-255

Greenbaum, S. (1977) (ed) *Acceptability in Language*, The Hague: Mouton

Greenbaum, S. (1985) (ed) *The English Language Today*, Oxford: Pergamon Press

Greenbaum, S. (1988) *Good English and the Grammarian*, London: Longman

Greenbaum, S., G. Leech, and J. Svartvik (1980) (edd) *Studies in English Linguistics for Randolph Quirk*, London: Longman

Greenbaum, S. and C. F. Meyer (1982), 'Ellipsis and Coordination: Norms and Preferences', *Language and Communication* **2**, 137-149

Greenberg, J. H., C. Ferguson, and E. Moravcsik (1978) (edd) *Universals of Human Language*, Stanford: University Press

Grice, H. P. (1975) 'Logic and Conversation', in Cole and Morgan (1975), 41—58

Guimier, C. (1981) *Prepositions: An Analytical Bibliography*, Amsterdam Studies in the Theory and History of Linguistic Science 5, Amsterdam: Benjamins

Guimier, C. (1988) *Syntaxe de l'adverbe anglais*, Lille: Presses Universitaires

Gunter, R. (1963) 'Elliptical Sentences in American English', *Lingua* **12**, 137-150

Haan, P. de (1987) 'Relative Clauses in Indefinite Noun Phrases', *English Studies* **68**, 171-190

Haegeman, L. (1983) *The Semantics of* Will *in Present-Day British English: A Unified Account*, Brussels: Koninklijke Academie

Haegeman, L. (1984) 'Pragmatic Conditionals in English', *Folia Linguistica* **18**, 485-502

Haiman, J. (1980) 'The Iconicity of Grammar', *Language* **56**, 515-540

Halliday, M. A. K. (1967) *Intonation and Grammar in British English*, The Hague: Mouton

Halliday, M. A. K. (1967-68) 'Notes on Transitivity and Theme in English', *J of Linguistics* **3**, 37-81, 199-244; **4**, 179-215

Halliday, M. A. K. (1978) *Language as Social Semiotic*, London: Arnold

Halliday, M. A. K. (1985) *An Introduction to Functional Grammar*, London: Arnold

Halliday, M. A. K. and R. Hasan (1976) *Cohesion in English*, London: Longman

Harries-Delisle, H. (1978) 'Coordination Reduction', in Greenberg, Ferguson, and Moravcsik (1978), 515-584

Hartvigson, H. H. (1969) *On the Intonation and Position of the So-called Sentence Modifiers in Present-day English*, Odense: University Press

Hartvigson, H. H. and L. K. Jakobsen (1974) *Inversion in Present-Day English*, Odense: University Press

Hawkins, J. A. (1978) *Definiteness and Indefiniteness*, London: Croom Helm

Helke, M. (1979) *The Grammar of English Reflexives*, New York: Garland

Heny, F.W. (1973) 'Sentence and Predicate Modifiers in English', in Kimball (1973), 217–245

Herbst, T. (1983) *Untersuchungen zur Valenz englischer Adjective und ihrer Nominalisierungen*, Tübingen: Narr

Hermerén, L. (1978) *On Modality in English*, Lund Studies in English 53, Lund: Gleerup/Liber

Hewson, J. (1972) *Article and Noun in English*, The Hague: Mouton.

Hirtle, W. H. (1982) *Number and Inner Space, A Study of Grammatical Number in English*, Québec: Presses de l'Université Laval

Hoey, M. P. (1983) *On the Surface of Discourse*, London: Allen and Unwin

Hofland, K. and S. Johansson (1982) *Word Frequencies in British and American English*, London: Longman

Hooper, J. B. (1975) 'On Assertive Predicates', in *Syntax and Semantics* 4, ed J.P. Kimball, 91–124, New York: Seminar Press

Horn, L.R. (1978a) 'Some Aspects of Negation', in Greenberg, Ferguson, and Moravcsik (1978), 127–210

Horn, L. R. (1978b) 'Remarks on Neg-Raising', in P. Cole (ed), *Syntax and Semantics* 9: *Pragmatics*, 129–220, New York: Academic Press

Huang, S. F. (1975) *A Study of Adverbs*, The Hague: Mouton

Huddleston, D. (1971) *The Sentence in Written English: A Syntactic Study Based on an Analysis of Scientific Texts*. Cambridge: University Press

Huddleston, R. D. (1976) 'Some Theoretical Issues in the Description of the English Verb', *Lingua* **40**, 331–383

Huddleston, R. D. (1980) 'Criteria for Auxiliaries and Modals', in Greenbaum, Leech, and Svartvik (1980), 65–78

Huddleston, R. D. (1984) *Introduction to the Grammar of English*, Cambridge: University Press

Hudson, R A. (1970) 'On Clauses Containing Conjoined and Plural Noun Phrases in English', *Lingua* **24**, 205–253

Hudson, R. A. (1975) 'The Meaning of Questions', *Language* **51**, 1–31

Hudson, R. A. (1976) 'Conjunction Reduction, Gapping, and Right-Node Raising', *Language* **52**, 555–561

Hughes, A. and P. Trudgill (1979) *English Accents and Dialects: An Introduction to Social and Regional Varieties of British English*, Baltimore: University Park Press

Hurford, J. R. (1975) *The Linguistic Theory of Numerals*, Cambridge: University Press

Ikegami, Y. (1973) 'A Set of Basic Patterns for the Semantic Structure of the Verb', *Linguistics* 117, 15–58

Jackendoff, R. (1968) 'Quantifiers in English', *Foundations of Language* **4**, 422–442

Jackendoff, R. (1969) 'An Interpretive Theory of Negation', *Foundations of Language* **5**, 218–241

Jackendoff, R. (1975) 'Morphological and Semantic Regularities in the Lexicon', *Language* **51**, 639–671

Jacobson, S. (1964) *Adverbial Positions in English*, Stockholm: Studentbok

Jacobson, S. (1975) *Factors Influencing the Placement of English Adverbs in Relation to Auxiliaries. A Study in Variation*, Stockholm: Almqvist and Wiksell

Jacobson, S. (1978) *On the Use, Meaning, and Syntax of English Preverbal Adverbs*, Stockholm: Almqvist and Wiksell

Jacobson, S. (1980) 'Some English Verbs and the Contrast Incompletion/Completion', in Greenbaum, Leech, and Svartvik (1980), 50–60

Jacobson, S. (1981) *Preverbal Adverbs and Auxiliaries*, Stockholm: Almqvist and Wiksell

Jacobsson, B. (1968) 'Simple Personal Pronouns and Compound Pronouns in *-Self/-Selves*', *Moderna Språk* **62**, 24–37

Jacobsson, B. (1975) 'How Dead is the English Subjunctive?', *Moderna Språk* **69**, 218–231

Jacobsson, B. (1977) 'Adverbs, Prepositions, and Conjunctions in English: A Study in Gradience', *Studia Linguistica* **31**, 38–64

Jacobsson, B. (1986) 'Another Look at Negatively Conditioned Subject–Operator Inversion in English,' *Studia Linguistica* **40**, 161–185

Jahr Sørheim, M.C. (1980) *The s-Genitive in Present-Day English*, University of Oslo, Department of English

Jaworska, E. (1986) 'Prepositional Phrases as Subjects and Objects', *J of Linguistics* **22**, 355–374

Jenkins, L. (1975) *The English Existential*, Tübingen: Niemeyer

Jespersen, O. (1909–49) *A Modern English Grammar on Historical Principles* I–VII, Copenhagen: Munksgaard

Jespersen, O. (1917) *Negation in English and Other Languages*, Copenhagen: reprinted in *Selected Writings of Otto Jespersen*, London: Allen and Unwin

Johannesson, N. L. (1976) *The English Modal Auxilaries: A Stratificational Account*, Stockholm Studies in English 36, Stockholm: Almqvist and Wiksell

Johansson, S. (1979) 'American and British English Grammar: An Elicitation Experiment', *English Studies* **60**, 195–215

Johansson, S. (1980) *Plural Attributive Nouns in Present-Day English*, Lund Studies in English 59, Lund: Gleerup/Liber

Joos, M. (1962) *The Five Clocks*, The Hague: Mouton

Joos, M. (1964) *The English Verb*, Madison: University of Wisconsin Press

Juul, A. (1975) *On Concord of Number in Modern English*, Copenhagen: Nova

Kachru, B. B. (1982) (ed) *The Other Tongue: English Across Cultures*, Urbana, Ill.: University of Illinois Press

Kachru, B. B. (1988) 'The Spread of English and Sacred Linguistic Cows', in Lowenberg (1988), 207–228

Kaluza, H. (1981) *The Use of Articles in Contemporary English*, Heidelberg: Groos

Kempson, R. M. (1977) *Semantic Theory*, Cambridge: University Press

Kempson, R. M. and R. Quirk (1971) 'Controlled Activation of Latent Contrast', *Language* **47**, 548–572

Kimball, J. P. (1973) (ed) *Syntax and Semantics* 2, New York: Seminar Press

Kiparsky, P. and C. Kiparsky (1970) 'Fact', in *Progress in Linguistics*, edd M. Bierwisch and K. E. Heidolph, 143–173, The Hague: Mouton

Kjellmer, G. (1980) ' "There is no hiding you in the house": On the Modal Use of the English Gerund', *English Studies* **61**, 47–60

Kjellmer, G. (1982) '*Each Other* and *One Another*: On the Use of the English Reciprocal Pronouns', *English Studies* **63**, 231–254

Kjellmer, G. (1984) 'Why *great: greatly* but not *big: *bigly*? On the Formation of English Adverbs in *-ly*', *Studia Linguistica* **38**, 1–19

Klima, E. S. (1964) 'Negation in English', in *The Structure of Language: Readings in the Philosophy of Language*, edd J. A. Fodor and J. J. Katz, 246–323, Englewood Cliffs, NJ: Prentice-Hall

König, E. and P. Lutzeier (1973) 'Bedeutung und Verwendung der Progessivform im heutigen Englisch', *Lingua* **32**, 277–308

Kontra, M. (1980) 'On English Negative Interrogatives', in *The Seventh LACUS Forum 1980*, edd J. E. Copeland and P. W. Davis, 412–431, Columbia, SC: Hornbeam Press

Koutsoudas, A. (1971) 'Gapping, Conjunction Reduction, and Coordinate Deletion', *Foundations of Language* **7**, 337–386

Kramsky, J. (1972) *The Article and the Concept of Indefiniteness in Language*, The Hague: Mouton

Kruisinga, E. (1931–32) *A Handbook of Present-Day English*, Groningen: Noordhoff

Kuno, S. (1972) 'Functional Sentence Perspective', *Linguistic Inquiry* **3**, 269–320

Kuno, S. (1976a) 'Gapping: a Functional Analysis', *Linguistic Inquiry* **8**, 300–318

Kuno, S. (1976b) 'Subject, Theme, and the Speaker's Empathy – A Reexamination of Relativization Phenomena', in Li (1976), 417–444

Labov, W. (1972) *Sociolinguistic Patterns*, Philadelphia: University of Pennsylvania Press

Lakoff, G. (1974) 'Syntactic Amalgams', *Papers from the Tenth Regional Meeting of the Chicago Linguistic Society*, 321–344, University of Chicago

Lakoff, G. (1975) 'Hedges: A Study in Meaning Criteria and the Logic of Fuzzy Concepts', in *Contemporary Research in Philosophical Logic and Linguistic Semantics*, edd D. Hockney et al., 211–271, Dordrecht: Reidel

Lakoff, G. (1977) 'Linguistic Gestalts', *Papers from the Thirteenth Regional Meeting of the Chicago Linguistic Society*, 236–281, University of Chicago

Lakoff, G. (1987) *Women, Fire, and Dangerous Things*, Chicago: University of Chicago Press

Lakoff, R. (1971) 'If's, And's, and But's about Conjunction', in Fillmore and Langendoen (1971), 114–149

Langacker, R. W. (1978) 'The Form and Meaning of the English Auxiliary', *Language* **54**, 853–882

Langacker, R. W. (1987) 'Nouns and Verbs', *Language* **63**, 53–94

Larson, R. K. (1985) 'Bare-NP Adverbs', *Linguistic Inquiry* **16**, 595–621

Lee, D. (1987) 'The Semantics of *just*', *J of Pragmatics* **11**, 377–398

Leech, G. (1969) *Towards a Semantic Description of English*, London: Longman

Leech, G. (1981) *Semantics*, 2nd edn, Harmondsworth: Penguin

Leech, G. (1983) *Principles of Pragmatics*, London: Longman

Leech, G. (1987) *Meaning and the English Verb*, 2nd edn, London: Longman

Leech, G. and J. Coates (1980) 'Semantic Indeterminacy and the Modals', in Greenbaum,

Leech, and Svartvik (1980), 79–90

Lehmann, W. (1978) 'The Great Underlying Ground-Plans', in *Syntactic Typology*, ed W. Lehmann, 3–56, Austin, Tex.: University of Texas Press

Lehrer, A. (1986) 'English Classifier Constructions', *Lingua* **68**, 109–148

Levi, J. (1978) *The Syntax and Semantics of Complex Nominals*, New York: Academic Press

Li, C. N. (1975) (ed) *Word Order and Word Order Change*, Austin, Tex.: Texas University Press

Li, C. N. (1976) (ed) *Subject and Topic*, New York: Academic Press

Lindkvist, K.-G. (1976) *A Comprehensive Study of Conceptions of Locality in which English Prepositions Occur*, Stockholm Studies in English 35, Stockholm: Almqvist and Wiksell

Lipka, L. (1972) *Semantic Structure and Word-Formation*, Munich: Fink

Ljung, M. (1980) *Reflections on the English Progressive*, Gothenburg Studies in English 46, Göteburg: Acta Universitatis Gothoburgensis

Longacre, R. E. (1976) *An Anatomy of Speech Notions*, Lisser: de Ridder

Lowenberg, P. H. (1988) (ed) *Language Spread and Language Policy*, Washington, DC: Georgetown University Press

Luelsdorff, P. A. and N. R. Norrick (1979) 'On *if* and *whether* Complementation', *Linguistische Berichte* **62**, 25–47

Lyons, C. (1986) 'The Syntax of English Genitive Constructions', *J of Linguistics* **22**, 123–143

Lyons, J. (1977) *Semantics*, Cambridge: University Press

McCoard, R. W. (1978) *The English Perfect*, Amsterdam: North-Holland

McDavid, R. I., Jr (1963) (ed) *The American Language by H.L. Mencken*, New York: Knopf

Mair, C. (1990) *Infinitival Complement Clauses in English*, Cambridge: University Press

Makkai, A. (1972) *Idiom Structure in English*, The Hague: Mouton

Mann, W. C. and S. A. Thompson (1986) 'Relational Propositions in Discourse', *Discourse Processes* **9**, 57–90

Mathesius, V. (1975) *A Functional Analysis of Present-Day English on a General Linguistic Basis*, ed J. Vachek, Prague: Academia

Matthews, P. H. (1974) *Morphology*, Cambridge: University Press

Matthews, P. H. (1981) *Syntax*, Cambridge: University Press

Meier, H.H. (1975) 'The Placing of English Idioms in Lexis and Grammar', *English Studies* **56**, 231–244

Meyer, C. F. (1979) 'The Greater Acceptability of Certain English Elliptical Coordinations', *Studia Linguistica* **33**, 130–137

Meyer, C. F. (1987) 'Apposition in English,' *J of English Linguistics* **20**, 101–121

Milsark, G. L. (1979) *Existential Sentences in English*, New York: Garland

Mittwoch, A. (1980) 'The Grammar of Duration', *Studies in Language* **4**, 201–227

Motsch, W. (1987) 'Zur Illokutionsstruktur von Feststellungstexten', *Z. f. Phon. Sprachw. u. Kom.* **40**, 45–67

Mourelatos, A. P. D. (1978) 'Events, Processes, States', *Linguistics and Philosophy* **2**, 5–34

Nash, W. (1980) *Designs in Prose*, London: Longman

Nässlin, S. (1984) *The English Tag Question: A Study of Sentences Containing Tags of the Type isn't it?, is it?* Stockholm: Almqvist and Wiksell

Ney, J. (1981) *Semantic Structures for the Syntax of Complements and Auxiliaries in English*, The Hague: Mouton

Nilsen, D. L. F. (1972) *English Adverbials*, The Hague: Mouton

Norrick, N. R. (1987) 'Functions of Repetition in Conversation', *Text* **7**, 245–264

Olofsson, A. (1981) *Relative Junctions in Written American English*, Gothenburg Studies in English 50, Göteborg: Acta Universitatis Gothoburgensis

Palmer, F. R. (1979) *Modality and the English Modals*, London: Longman

Palmer, F. R. (1988) *The English Verb*, 2nd edn, London: Longman

Penhallurick, J. (1984) 'Full-Verb Inversion in English', *Australian J of Linguistics* **4**, 33–56

Pennanen, E. V. (1982) 'Remarks on Syntagma and Word-Formation', *Folia Linguistica* **16**, 241–261

Perlmutter, D. M. (1970) *On the Article in English*, The Hague: Mouton

Peters, F. J. J. (1980) 'Phrasing Rules for Complex Number Sequences in English', *Studia Linguistica* **34**, 124–134

Pope, E.N. (1976) *Questions and Answers in English*, The Hague: Mouton

Postal, P. (1971) 'On the Surface Verb "Remind" ', in Fillmore and Langendoen (1971), 181–272

Poutsma, H. (1926–29) *A Grammar of Late Modern English*, Groningen: Noordhoff

Pullum, G. and D. Wilson (1977) 'Autonomous Syntax and the Analysis of Auxiliaries', *Language* **53**, 741–788

Quirk, R. (1968) *Essays on the English Language* -

Medieval and Modern, London: Longman
Quirk, R. (1970) 'Aspect and Variant Inflexion in English Verbs', *Language* **46**, 300–311
Quirk, R. (1972) *The English Language and Images of Matter*, Oxford: University Press
Quirk, R. (1978) 'Grammatical and Pragmatic Aspects of Countability', *Die Neueren Sprachen* **78**, 317–325
Quirk, R. (1982) *Style and Communication in the English Language*, London: Arnold
Quirk, R. (1986) *Words at Work: Lectures on Textual Structure*, London: Longman
Quirk, R. (1988) 'The Question of Standards in the International Use of English', in Lowenberg (1988), 229–241
Quirk, R. (1989) 'Language Varieties and Standard Language', *JALT J* **11**, 14–25
Quirk, R. and G. Stein (1990) *English in Use*, London: Longman
Quirk, R., S. Greenbaum, G. Leech, and J. Svartvik (1985) *A Comprehensive Grammar of the English Language*, London: Longman
Radford, A. (1988) *Transformational Grammar*, Cambridge: University Press
Rivara, R. (1975) 'How many Comparatives are There?', *Linguistics* **163**, 35–51
Robbins, B. L. (1968) *The Definite Article in English Tranformations*, The Hague: Mouton
Ross, J.R. (1973) 'A Fake NP Squish', in Bailey and Shuy (1973), 96–140
Rudanko, J. (1982) 'Towards a Description of Negatively Conditioned Subject Operator Inversion in English', *English Studies* **63**, 348–359
Rusiecki, J. (1985) *Adjectives and Comparison in English: A Semantic Study*, London: Longman
Saha, P.K. (1987) 'Strategies of Reflexivization in American English', *American Speech* **62**, 211–234
Sahlin, E. (1979) *'Some' and 'Any' in Spoken and Written English*, Studia Anglistica Upsaliensia 38, Stockholm: Almqvist and Wiksell
Sanders, G.A. (1977) 'A Functional Typology of Elliptical Coordinations', in *Current Themes in Linguistics*, ed F. Eckman, 241–270, Washington, DC: Hemisphere
Schachter, P. (1973) 'Focus and Relativization', *Language* **49**, 19–46
Schachter, P. (1977) 'Constraints on Coordination', *Language* **53**, 86–103
Scheffer, J. (1975) *The Progressive in English*, Amsterdam: North-Holland
Schenkein, J. (1978) (ed) *Studies in the Organization of Conversational Interaction*, New York: Academic Press
Schiffrin, D. (1981) 'Tense Variation in Narrative', *Language* **57**, 45–62
Schiffrin, D. (1985) 'Conversational Coherence; the Role of *Well*', *Language* **61**, 640–667
Schlesinger, I. M. (1979) 'Cognitive Structures and Semantic Deep Structures; the Case of the Instrumental', *J of Linguistics* **15**, 307–324
Schlesinger, I. M. (1989) 'Instruments as Agents: On the Nature of Semantic Relations', *J of Linguistics* **25**, 189–210
Schmerling, S.F. (1976) *Aspects of English Sentence Stress*, Austin, Tex.: University of Texas Press
Schopf, A. (1984) *Das Verzeitungssystem des Englischen und seine Textfunktion*, Tübingen: Niemeyer
Schopf, A. (1987) (ed) *Essays on Tensing in English*, vol. I: *Reference Time, Tense, and Adverbs*. Tübingen: Niemeyer
Schopf, A. (1988) 'The Ditransitive Clause Reconsidered', in *Essays on the English Language and Applied Linguistics*, edd J. Klegrap and D. Nehls, 110–130, Heidelberg: Julius Groos
Schopf, A. (1989) (ed) *Essays on Tensing in English*, vol 2: *Time, Text, and Modality*, Tübingen: Niemeyer
Schreiber, P. A. (1972) 'Style Disjuncts and the Performative Analysis', *Linguistic Inquiry* **3**, 321–347
Searle, J. R. (1979) *Expression and Meaning: Studies in the Theory of Speech Acts*, Cambridge: University Press
Sears, D.A. (1972) 'The Noun Adjuncts of Modern English', *Linguistics* **72**, 31–60
Seppänen, A. (1974) *Proper Names in English: A Study in Semantics and Syntax*. Publications of the Department of English Philology 1, University of Tampere
Seppänen, A. (1978) 'Some Notes on the Construction "Adjective + *A* + Noun" ', *English Studies* **59**, 523–537
Seppänen, A. (1980) 'Possessive Pronouns in English', *Studia Linguistica* **34**, 7–22
Sinclair, J. McH. (1980) 'Discourse in Relation to Language Structure and Semiotics', in Greenbaum, Leech, and Svartvik (1980), 110–124
Smaby, R. M. (1974) 'Subordinate Clauses and Assymetry in English', *J of Linguistics* **10**, 235–269
Sørensen, H. S. (1958) *Word-Classes in Modern English*, Copenhagen: Gad
Sørensen, H. S. (1959) 'The Function of the Definite Article in Modern English', *English Studies* **40**, 401–420

Sørensen, K. (1979) 'Preposition + X + Complement', *English Studies* **60**, 42–48

Sørensen, K. (1985) 'The Distributive Plural and its Limits', *English Studies* **66**, 338–350

Sroka, K.A. (1972) *The Syntax of English Phrasal Verbs*, The Hague: Mouton

Stein, G. (1976) 'The Imperative in English', *Anglo-American Forum* **5**, 83–105

Stein, G. (1979) *Studies in the Function of the Passive*, Tübingen: Narr

Stenström, A.-B. (1984) *Questions and Responses in English Conversation*, Malmö: Gleerup/Liber

Stevenson, R. J. and M. Vitkovitch (1986) 'The Comprehension of Anaphoric Relations', *Language and Speech* **29**, 335–360

Stockwell, R. P., P. Schachter, and B. Hall Partee (1973) *The Major Syntactic Structures of English*, New York: Holt, Rinehart and Winston

Stubbs, M. (1983) *Discourse Analysis*, Chicago: Chicago University Press

Svartvik, J. (1966) *On Voice in the English Verb*, The Hague: Mouton

Svartvik, J. (1980) '*Well* in Conversation', in Greenbaum, Leech, and Svartvik (1980), 167–177

Taglicht, J. (1984) *Message and Emphasis: On Focus and Scope in English*, London: Longman

Takami, K. (1985) 'Definite NP Anaphora and Adverbial Clauses', *Linguistic Analysis* **15**, 269–303

Talmy, L. (1978) 'Relations between Subordination and Coordination', in Greenberg et al. (1978), 487–513

Tedeschi, P. and A. Zaenen (1981) (edd) *Syntax and Semantics* 14: *Tense and Aspect*, New York: Academic Press

Thavenius, C. (1983) *Referential Pronouns in English Conversation*, Lund: Gleerup

Tottie, G. (1977) *Fuzzy Negation in English and Swedish*, Stockholm Studies in English 39, Stockholm: Almqvist and Wiksell

Tottie, G. (1980) 'Affixal and Non-Affixal Negation in English Two Systems in (Almost) Complementary Distribution', *Studia Linguistica* **34**, 101–123

Ungerer, F. (1988) *Syntax der englischen Adverbialen*, Tübingen: Niemeyer

Vachek, J., see Mathesius (1975)

Valdman, A. (1977) (ed) *Pidgin and Creole Linguistics*, Bloomington, Ind.: Indiana University Press

Vendler, Z. (1957) 'Verbs and Time', *Philosophical Review* **56**, 143—160

Vendler, Z. (1968) *Adjectives and Nominalizations*, The Hague: Mouton

Vestergaard, T. (1977) *Prepositional Phrases and Prepositional Verbs*, The Hague: Mouton

Vorlat, E. (1979) (ed) *Analytical Bibliography of Writings on Modern English Morphology and Syntax* 5, Leuven; University Press Editions, Nauwelaerts

Warren, B. (1984) *Classifying Adjectives*, Gothenburg Studies in English 56, Göteborg: Acta Universitatis Gothoburgensis

Wekker, H. (1976) *The Expression of Future Time in Contemporary British English*, Amsterdam: North-Holland

Wierzbicka, A. (1982) 'Why can you *have a drink* when you can't **have an eat*?', *Language* **58**, 753–799

Wierzbicka, A. (1986) 'A Semantic Metalanguage for the Description and Comparison of Illocutionary Meanings', *J of Pragmatics* **10**, 67–107

Wieser, E. (1986) 'On the Splitting in English of the *of*-genitive', *English Studies* **67**, 57–71

Winter, E.O. (1982) *Towards a Contextual Grammar of English*, London: Allen and Unwin

Winterowd, W. Ross (1975) *Contemporary Rhetoric*, New York: Harcourt Brace Jovanovich

Yee, C. T. S. (1975) 'Sequence Signals in Technical English', *RELC J* **6**, 63–101

Young, D. (1980) *The Structure of English Clauses*, London: Hutchinson

Zwicky, A. M. (1974) 'Hey, Whatsyourname', *Papers from the Tenth Regional Meeting of the Chicago Linguistic Society*, 787–801, University of Chicago

Zwicky, A. M. and G. K. Pullum (1983) 'Cliticization vs. Inflection: English *n't*', *Language* **59**, 502–513

Index

References are to section numbers and section notes ('n').
Cross-reference is indicated by an arrow.